UNITED NATIONS CONFERENCE ON TRADE AND DEVELOPMENT
Geneva

UNCTAD VIII

Analytical report by the UNCTAD secretariat to the Conference

UNITED NATIONS
New York, 1992

NOTE

Symbols of United Nations documents are composed of capital letters combined with figures. Mention of such a symbol indicates a reference to a United Nations document.

*

* *

The designations employed and the presentation of the material in this publication do not imply the expression of any opinion whatsoever on the part of the Secretariat of the United Nations concerning the legal status of any country, territory, city or area, or of its authorities, or concerning the delimitation of its frontiers or boundaries.

*

* *

Material in this publication may be freely quoted or reprinted, but acknowledgement is requested, together with a reference to the document number. A copy of the publication containing the quotation or reprint should be sent to the UNCTAD secretariat.

TD/358

UNITED NATIONS PUBLICATION

Sales No. E.92.II.D.3

ISBN 92-1-112319-4

CONTENTS

| | Paragraphs | Page |

CONTENTS (continued)

CONTENTS (continued)

Chapter I

RESOURCES FOR DEVELOPMENT

A. DOMESTIC RESOURCE MOBILIZATION IN DEVELOPING COUNTRIES

1. Financial policies

1.   The acute external financial difficulties faced by developing countries in the 1980s have heightened the importance of mobilizing domestic resources on a larger scale and allocating and utilizing them to maximum effect. This is needed not only to manage debt and the balance of payments, but also to sustain development over the longer term.

2.   In countries which have recently suffered a significant drop in living standards, improved overall savings performance must be sought largely as a consequence of economic revival, rather than as a means to initiate it (though, as explained below, tighter fiscal discipline is in a number of cases a necessity). There is considerably more room to improve the way savings are allocated and utilized, by reforming policy regarding the financial sector and the public sector. Progress in these areas can help in reviving and sustaining growth (and, hence, in raising the overall propensity to save over time), provided that the benefits are not offset by increased debt service payments or reduced inflows of external finance. Indeed, reduced debt service and/or increased inflow of funds could themselves serve to increase domestic savings by lessening the foreign exchange constraint which in many developing countries depresses activity below levels warranted by the productive capacity of the economy.

3.   The share of domestic savings in national income depends in part on social, cultural and demographic factors not amenable to influence by economic policy. However, there are also a number of other influences - such as the level of national income, its distribution among various classes and groups, and between public and private sectors, and incentives to save - which can be altered by policy choices.

4.   But it is on the way that savings are allocated and used that interest rates and other financial policies have a pronounced effect. For savings to flow to areas where the social rate of return on investment is highest, entrepreneurs must have the incentive to undertake the investment and be able to command the necessary finance. Financial policies assume great importance here, for by influencing the behaviour of savers and financial intermediaries, they affect the forms in which savings are held and transferred, and hence the terms and availability of finance to different sectors and activities.

(a) Macroeconomic instability and mobilization of resources

5.   One of the most important impediments to resource mobilization in developing countries is macroeconomic instability and unpredictability. High and volatile inflation, with unexpected changes in wages and exchange and interest rates, shortens the planning horizon of savers and in-

vestors, and encourages hedging and speculation rather than investment in productive capacity. As long as inflation remains high and out of control, attempts to change the key relative prices through currency devaluations and interest rate increases can be unproductive. Real interest rates often become highly negative when inflation is strong, but simply pushing up interest rates to match the inflation rate can make matters worse: by reducing income and increasing price instability it can reduce savings and further distort resource allocation. The remedy is therefore not to escalate nominal interest rates, but to reduce inflation, as much as possible by other measures.

6.   Uncertain rules of the game and a lack of continuity and long-term perspective in policy-making are equally harmful. Abrupt and unpredictable changes in policies towards trade, finance, public sector prices, subsidies, taxes, etc. complicate business calculations and decision-making, and encourage rent-seeking and speculative behaviour aimed at capturing windfall gains. Social and political consensus, and a secure, confident, skilled and autonomous bureaucracy, are important for continuity and confidence in policy-making. Democracy is normally a necessary (though not sufficient) condition for social and political consensus.

7.   It should be emphasized that macroeconomic mismanagement and policy discontinuity are by no means the only or even the main sources of instability. Developing countries are extremely susceptible to changes in the external economic environment, which is itself unstable. External shocks such as commodity-price or interest-rate swings are often highly disruptive, and the difficulties of adjusting to such shocks without adequate external finance is often at the origin of discontinuity in policy-making.

(b) Interest rates and the size of savings

8.   Interest rate policies are extremely important, but what constitutes an appropriate interest rate policy is in any particular situation not self-evident. For reasons already cited, a particular level of real interest rate will have different consequences for the size and allocation of resources depending on the degree of price instability present. Moreover, the impact of changes in interest rates on both debtors and creditors must be considered. A higher interest rate adds to the capacity of rentiers to save, but subtracts from the capacity of entrepreneurs to borrow and invest.

9.   Before the 1980s, policy-makers in many developing countries tended to concentrate almost exclusively on the cost aspect of interest rates even when inflation was high, giving rise to excessively negative real interest rates. By contrast, in the 1980s exclusive emphasis has been placed on the return to creditors, leading to excessively high real interest rates; these have often reached double digits. Moreover, many Governments have taxed financial incomes very lightly while allowing interest payments by corporations to be deducted from taxable income. This has shifted the interest burden onto the public sector, which has had to cut productive investment as well as social spending, and worsened income distribution.

10.   High interest rates are often thought to raise savings rates. But it is questionable whether interest rates have a systematic, strong and predictable influence on household savings behaviour. There are no compelling theoretical reasons to expect household savings to rise in response to higher real interest rates. Moreover, the empirical evidence (especially for countries that raised interest rates as part of an adjustment programme) consistently rejects the contention that interest rates systematically influence household savings. To be sure, in many cases interest rates were raised in an unstable macroeconomic environment, and at a time when incomes were falling. But this only shows that household savings are much more strongly influenced by factors other than interest rates. Indeed, in periods of falling per capita incomes and high inflation, households have been known to take advantage of interest rate increases to avoid cutting their consumption.

11.   Since changes in interest rates alter the distribution of income between debtors and creditors, higher interest rates can lower aggregate savings if debtors have a higher propensity to save than creditors. Corporations and the public sector are normally net borrowers and debtors, and the household sector a net lender and creditor. In many countries the corporate sector saves a greater proportion of its income than the household sector, and undistributed corporate savings constitute an important source of business investment. Thus, high interest rates may not only discourage corporate investment, but also reduce aggregate private savings by transferring income from high to low savers. This distribution effect is particularly important in developing countries where the

equity base of corporations is generally weak, leverage is high, debt maturities are short, and the corporate sector borrows heavily not only for investment, but also for working capital needs, which explains why in many countries the aggregate private saving rate and the aggregate saving rate have been insensitive to interest rates. Similarly, if the interest-bearing domestic debt of the public sector is large, high interest rates can cause large fiscal deficits. In designing interest rate policies, therefore, due attention needs also to be given to the degree of corporate indebtedness, the contribution of corporate savings in private investment, the state of fiscal balances and the size of public debt.

(c) Interest rates and financial savings

12.   When interest rates are deregulated and rise to market-determined levels, savings are expected to be shifted to bank deposits. One source of such shifts is funds invested in unregulated, informal financial markets. Another is unproductive assets held as hedges against inflation, including commodity stocks and real estate as well as international assets such as gold and foreign exchange.

13.   However, informal markets in developing countries do not always result from financial regulation. In many poor countries, particularly in sub-Saharan Africa and Asia, they exist side by side with formal institutions, rendering functions which the latter fail to render. They often date back to colonial times, when formal financial institutions concentrated on financing the export sector. The informal financial sector provides credit to small and medium-sized businesses and farmers lacking access to formal institutions because of their physical remoteness or because formal financial institutions find them too risky. Since deposits in the informal sector give the small and medium-sized enterprises some access to credit, they are often reluctant to shift their savings to banks. In cases where funds are so shifted, the cost and availability of finance to small producers, farmers and traders deteriorates. Informal financial institutions are not the best solution to the problem of financing small-scale business since they are usually unable to extend long-term credit, but the criticism that "curb markets" finance risky projects in return for high-risk premiums is no more than a description of the specific financial service that they provide. Policies that shift funds from the informal to the formal sector should be accompanied by measures that considerably improve the access of small and medium-size enterprises to formal financial institutions.

14.   There can be little doubt that a reduction in unproductive commodity holdings represents a gain. However, there is very little evidence to show that such commodity holdings are a response to negative real interest rates on financial assets.[1] First, since commodity holdings entail substantial storage and transaction costs, i.e. their own real rate of return is typically negative, real interest rates on financial assets must become even more negative for commodities to provide a more attractive outlet for wealth.[2] Second, under inflationary conditions prices of different commodities usually increase at different rates, something which reduces the demand for commodities as a store of value.

15.   Besides, there are other assets, such as gold and foreign currency, that are equally good hedges against inflation, but more liquid and less costly to hold. Any shift away from such international assets into domestic financial assets raises both the availability of savings for investment and the import capacity of the economy. However, it is not easy to reduce gold holdings through interest rate policies where gold has traditionally been considered as a safe store of value. Foreign

---

1   It is true that in many low-income countries, particularly in sub-Saharan Africa, commodity stocks constitute an important part of total wealth of self-employed, small agricultural producers. However, this phenomenon is not linked to the level of interest rates, but to the nature of the production process and the fact that household activities are not entirely separated from enterprise. Indeed, in the rural sector of such economies, not only savings but also incomes are realized in kind, and stocks of grains held are used for consumption and inputs between two harvests: this stored produce is simply the necessary input of a production process. Such phonemena can only disappear in the process of monetization and rural development, rather than in response to interest rate policies.

2   Under severe shortage, commodities are usually stocked in order to provide for consumption in the near future despite depreciation and storage costs. However, these stocks are not held because the interest rate is low compared to the rate of inflation. Indeed, such shortages usually appear when inflation is suppressed through price controls. Under such conditions raising higher interest rates on, for instance, bank deposits, cannot reduce commodity holdings. By contrast if the shortage is eliminated by allowing prices to rise, such commodity holdings are likely to fall.

currency holdings, by contrast, can be reduced by raising interest rates. However, many Governments have found it necessary to legalize such holdings, typically in the form of foreign exchange accounts in domestic banks. Where this has been the case, the overall effect has often been to increase rather than to reduce "dollarization" (see section (g) below).

16.   Land and real estate are other inflation hedges. However, while it is true that individuals can hold their savings in the form of land, society as a whole cannot. Consequently, reduced demand for land will simply lower its price (or the rate of its increase) and redistribute wealth, not release savings. The same is true for houses already built. However, an increase in interest rates can lower investment in new housing by households, raise their surplus and increase their bank deposits. But investment in housing is not necessarily unproductive.

17.   It is important to bear in mind that an increase in the size of the financial sector relative to GDP or investment (i.e. "financial deepening") does not always indicate an increase in savings or a shift from other forms of holding wealth. It can also be an effect of the deterioration of corporate and public finance, and the accumulation of short-term debt by these sectors rather than new investment. This can happen when a rise in interest rates redistributes income from the corporate and public sectors (i.e. debtors) to rentiers. The debtor sectors then need to borrow more in order to finance the same level of output and investment, thereby raising the stock of financial assets and liabilities relative to the latter. The experience of a number of countries shows that this can even happen in the context of a fall in savings and investment.

18.   The role of interest rates in mobilizing domestic resources thus depends on the macroeconomic and institutional environment. Consequently, generalizations regarding interest rate policies made without due attention to underlying circumstances are not very helpful. Fixed rules on real interest rates are no more useful and sensible than those on money supply growth in the conduct of monetary policy (something abandoned by central banks in many industrial countries after the experience in the early 1980s).

(d)   Efficiency and regulation

19.   Increased concentration of savings in financial institutions, banks in particular, will be beneficial only if these perform their role as financial intermediaries efficiently. The concepts of cost efficiency and allocative efficiency are relevant in this context. *Cost-efficiency* is about the cost of financial intermediation, and may be measured by the spread between lending and deposit rates, allowing for the effects of such factors as financial taxes and required reserves. *Allocative efficiency* refers to the degree to which financial resources are allocated among different sectors and activities according to the social rate of return or, more broadly, according to longer-term development objectives. It is when private and social rates of return on investment projects coincide (i.e. when external economies or dis-economies of projects are negligible) that the proportion of non-performing loans in financial institutions can serve as an indicator of allocative inefficiency. If the social rates of return on investment projects exceed the private rates (which is often the case in developing countries) an accumulation of non-performing loans may overstate the extent of allocative inefficiency resulting from project choice.

20.   The size of the spreads and the share of non-performing loans are often interrelated. Increases in non-performing loans tend to widen the spread because banks often pass the cost of such loans onto borrowers. This can push even sound borrowers to the brink of collapse, thereby increasing the share of non-performing loans in bank portfolios.

21.   In a large number of developing countries, an important portion of bank assets is non-performing. The majority of both private and public banks are technically insolvent and operate with very large intermediation margins between deposit and credit rates. Almost all episodes of financial liberalization involving deregulation of interest rates and greater autonomy for banks in the allocation of credit have been followed by a rise in the proportion of non-performing loans and an increase in the spread between lending and deposit rates.

22.   One reason is that financial liberalization has often been carried out in adverse macroeconomic conditions: external shocks, declines in external resources, increased macroeconomic instability and reduced growth, and monetary restriction had together weakened considerably the

balance sheets of the corporate sector and financial institutions. But an even more important reason has been the serious structural weaknesses present in the financial sector in developing countries. Often, ownership of banks is highly concentrated and large non-financial corporations are typically able to exert strong influence over banks; moreover, prudential regulations on banks are generally weak, and many governments are too ready to engage in financial rescue operations, thereby encouraging moral hazard. Financial liberalization therefore often leads to excessive risk taking, and a concentration of credits in large enterprises at the expense of medium and small-scale enterprises. Both cost and allocative efficiency in the banking sector suffer as a result. Experience has shown that increasing the role of the price mechanism in the allocation of resources can result in considerable waste of resources in the absence of appropriate market institutions and supervisory mechanisms. Almost all attempts of financial liberalization in developing countries have ended in a financial crash primarily because this condition was not met; often the liberalization was introduced in agreement with international financial institutions as a way out of economic stagnation and instability.

23. In the few successful cases of financial liberalization, a gradual and cautious approach was followed. Liberalization came after stability and economic and institutional development had been attained: it came out of strength rather than as a response to weakness. Structural trade deficits and the foreign exchange shortage had been eliminated through a successful process of industrialization, import substitution and export growth; the savings ratio had been raised considerably through a fast and sustained growth of per capita incomes; monetary and fiscal discipline had been maintained and price stability attained on a durable basis; and structural weaknesses in corporate finance and financial institutions had been reduced in order to prevent financial instability and fragility. Even though interest rates were deregulated and directed credits phased out, a number of means (e.g. "window guidance", "moral suasion", etc) continued to be used to prevent interest rates from rising, to avoid financial instability and to channel credit to targetted industries.

(e) Options for financial reform

24. It is believed that development of capital markets in developing countries can help solve some of the structural problems of the financial system. In particular, equity and bond issues can reduce the vulnerability of firms to sharp changes in the cost and availability of bank credit and provide them with more predictable longer-term finance, while secondary markets in securities provide savers with the liquidity they seek. Furthermore, capital markets introduce competition with financial intermediaries, thereby helping reduce inefficiency in the allocation of resources.

25. It is often argued that tight credit policies are necessary for the development of such markets because cheap credit encourages firms to rely excessively on bank credit and avoid issuing equity. However, a more important impediment to the development of equity markets in developing countries is related to the nature of ownership of corporations. Firms are often owned by families who do not wish to dilute their control. Besides, owners are often unwilling to disclose the information and accept the supervision entailed by going public. Moreover, firms that are large enough to do so prefer bank to equity financing because they can obtain preferential treatment from banks due to their interlocking ownership. On the other hand in some countries many large firms are multinational companies with little debt in domestic markets and little interest in broadening their equity base in the host country. Consequently, high interest rates on bank credit are generally not a sufficient inducement for large firms to go public. A mix of restrictions and incentives may be needed, including for instance limits on debt-equity ratios and tax exemptions and priority in government contracts for publicly-quoted joint stock companies.

26. Participants in secondary markets tend to be motivated by considerations of short-term capital gain. Consequently, asset valuations tend to be extremely unstable, and provide little guidance for return on investment in productive capacity. These markets also tend to amplify disturbances in the rest of the economy. The problem of inefficiency and instability in capital markets can be especially serious in developing countries since the general macroeconomic environment tends to be more volatile. In some of the newly emerging capital markets prices have been extremely volatile and subject to very large swings. Activity has concentrated in secondary transactions, and new issues have been rather small. Often, irregularities such as insider trading and fraud are widespread and the administrative capacity to undertake effective supervision weak.

For these reasons, steps to strengthen the institutional and regulatory framework must accompany the introduction of tax and other incentives aimed at developing capital markets.

27.   The main question, however, is how much to expect from policies to develop capital markets. A close inspection of how modern industrialization has been financed raises questions on the relevance for developing countries of the "Anglo-American" system of finance primarily based on direct security issues rather than bank debt. In Japan and the Republic of Korea, for instance, the corporate sectors have, for most of their history, relied on bank credits to meet their borrowing needs and operated with very high leverage; only recently have they started to reduce leverage through capital market funding. Corporate finance in Germany has also traditionally relied on bank credits not only for financing but also for funding investment, and the involvement of banks in industry has been important both in ensuring financial discipline and in reducing financing costs. Low-cost finance has given enterprises in these three countries an additional competitive advantage in world markets. In all of them, particularly the two late-comers to industrialization, financial policies have been an integral part of industrial policy. In those two countries the Government has exercised considerable control over the cost and allocation of finance to different industries; such controls are much easier to operate in a bank-based financial system than in a system based on capital markets.

28.   Although capital markets provide long-term financing, they tend to value the enterprise on the basis of its short-term financial performance. By contrast bank-based financing of investment along German and Japanese lines has the great advantage of permitting the enterprise to take a long view on the basis of a reliable and predictable supply of finance. This is a particularly important consideration for developing countries, where most of the benefits of investment are realized over the long term via a learning process.

29.   But at least two conditions must be met for a controlled bank-based system to work well. First, monetary stability is essential, since a bank-based system integrates finance with the monetary system. Second, finance must be effectively dovetailed with industrial policy so as to ensure that support is reciprocated by performance; otherwise close links between banks and industry will result in favourable treatment being given to inefficient, stagnant firms and not to efficient and dynamic ones. Most developing countries may be well advised to concentrate their energies in this direction, rather than pin their hope on developing capital markets. More industrialized developing countries may be able to combine the advantages of capital markets and bank finance by means of investment banks. These could be publicly owned or alternatively private (or mixed) enterprises. In either case, they could serve as an instrument simultaneously to assure long-term funds to priority sectors while imposing discipline on borrowers. The banks' lending levels could be supplemented by borrowing from the capital markets. Besides lending, the investment banks could help smaller corporations to gain access to domestic bond and equity markets, and improve their terms of access.

(f) Industrialization and internal financial liberalization

30.   While it is necessary to strengthen the role and structure of markets, it is no less important to strike the right balance between market forces and intervention in the allocation of resources. Economic development requires diversification in production and exports, both to reduce the risks of dependence for foreign earnings on a small number of commodities and markets, and to develop the economy into an integrally articulated unit that grows on the basis of its own impetus. Diversification and industrialization often necessitate the assignment of priorities to different sectors and activities, and the provision of various kinds of support, incentive and protection. Almost all modern examples of industrialization have been accompanied by a considerable degree of government intervention as regards cost and availability of finance in the pursuit of selective industrial policies (a practice still present in successful industrial countries).

31.   All developing countries have implemented selective financial policies such as directed credit allocations and differential financial taxes and subsidies for different types of credit. The financial problems in the 1970s and 1980s were in some countries the outcome of inappropriate and inefficient use of such intervention. But it is no less true that the countries which have successfully diversified and increased their exports made extensive use of those very policies. The experiences of these countries show that government intervention in the financial sector is necessary not just

to steer credit in the right direction, but to underwrite production during the learning process, something much more complex than is usually implied by the term "infant industry protection". Subsidized credit can mean the difference between establishing new industries or not, rather than simply the difference between financing more or less lucrative projects.

32. Financial intermediaries are naturally wary of financing new industries because of the difficulties of calculating the risks involved. But the need to direct credit allocation arises not only from the presence of risk, but also because the social rate of return on projects often exceeds the private rate of return. Moreover, the benefits of socio-economic objectives such as the reduction of dependence on certain imports, improvement in income distribution, reduction of poverty cannot be expressed in numerical magnitudes. The benefits from investment projects that advance these objectives accrue to the economy as a whole, and even their strictly economic advantages may be dispersed across entire regions or the whole country. It is therefore natural that the costs of such projects should not always be borne entirely by the investing units; their finance often needs to be subsidized.

33. There have been significant differences in success in directing credit and differentiating interest rates between, for example, some East and South-East Asian countries on the one hand and Latin American countries on the other. The differences have been partly due to the selection of correct priorities, i.e. skill in "picking the winners". But perhaps an even more important factor has been the extent to which governments have been able and willing to make the provision of support and protection conditional upon the performance of the beneficiaries. In the successful cases, governments saw to it that the support and protection provided by them was used for the purposes intended, rather than as pure rent (see section 2 (b) below). In many countries the prime need is to follow such a course rather than abandon government intervention altogether.

(g) Industrialization and external liberalization

34. Another significant influence on industrialization is the degree of financial openness, i.e. the ease with which residents can acquire and hold foreign exchange assets and liabilities at home or abroad and non-residents can operate in national financial markets. Although the degree of financial openness depends partly on structural factors - such as a high rate of earnings from tourism and workers' remittances, and physical proximity to hard currency areas - countries' own policies play the most important role. These include policies regarding restrictions on foreign exchange transactions with non-residents, and on holdings of foreign exchange assets and liabilities in domestic financial institutions.

35. During the last decade there has been a general easing of restrictions on the access of residents to foreign loans, and on the access of non-residents to domestic capital markets. Moreover, many governments have encouraged residents to hold foreign currency deposits at home banks. This has greatly accelerated the substitution of foreign for domestic currency, and in many countries foreign exchange deposits have come to exceed domestic currency deposits.

36. External financial liberalization is sometimes seen as a method of making capital less scarce and lowering domestic interest rates. However, external resources can be obtained without liberalizing external finance, through official channels. Moreover, unrestricted foreign borrowing can be dangerous, as has been amply demonstrated by the experience of some Latin American countries, where free access to capital markets abroad triggered a massive build-up of private external debt, resulting eventually in widespread bankruptcies and financial crisis.

37. Most developing countries exhibit more monetary and financial instability and economic and political uncertainty than developed countries. Moreover, because of structural deficiencies in their financial institutions and markets, investment in domestic financial assets is riskier than in developed countries. Consequently, when free competition for funds is permitted, domestic currency assets have to offer considerably higher interest rates than those denominated in major convertible currencies. Moreover, since savers tend to diversify their portfolios to some extent, regardless of the interest rate offered, there will always be a tendency for part of savings to be placed in safer currencies and countries. Offering still higher interest rates on domestic currency assets will not prevent this diversification; on the contrary, it may be taken as signalling trouble ahead and therefore accelerate currency substitution and capital flight. Foreign investors are often

hyper-sensitive to signs of political and economic instability, and a sudden repatriation of savings can aggravate or create instability.

38.   Financial openness reduces the degree of policy autonomy, that is, the effectiveness of national policy instruments in attaining policy goals. Ability by the public to switch from domestic to foreign currencies makes monetary policy more difficult, and reduces the ability to delink domestic from international interest rates. Currency substitution and capital flight cannot be entirely prevented by restrictions if the economy is suffering from acute macroeconomic disequilibrium and uncertainty as a result of policy shortcomings and/or external shocks. But deregulation can accelerate it considerably. Differences in the extent of capital flight among the countries experiencing similar macroeconomic and payments conditions were often the result of differences in capital controls and the administrative effectiveness with which restrictions were implemented.

39.   Economic development requires a certain degree of financial insulation, even when stability has been secured and growth is under way. Quite apart from the problems of control over the money supply, the exchange rate and the balance of payments, the inability of a developing country to delink domestic interest rates itself drastically reduces the government's ability to integrate its financial policies with its industrialization policy in order to help domestic enterprises overcome their productivity disadvantage in international markets. If enterprises in developing countries have to pay higher real interest rates than their competitors in the developed world, even greater reliance has to be placed on currency devaluations and cuts in real wages, with adverse consequences for macroeconomic stability, labour productivity and social peace. It is not therefore surprising that most of the successful late industrializers in Asia have resisted international pressures for financial opening.

(h) Conclusions

40.   The principal role of financial policies in the mobilization of resources in developing countries is to ensure that resources are allocated at the lowest possible cost for investment in areas with a high social rate of return without exerting adverse influences on the size of such resources. While it is not possible to generalize about how financial policies need to be conducted in different countries, a number of factors need to be taken into account:

- Macroeconomic stability needs to be attained, since instability leads to uncertainty, raises interest rates and shortens time horizons. Macroeconomic stability requires, *inter alia*, increased monetary control, and greater financial discipline in public and private sectors. On the other hand, monetary policy should not be overburdened when price stability is disrupted by external shocks; the required adjustment should be secured through a judicious combination of fiscal, monetary, and prices and incomes policies, based on a broad social consensus. It is particularly important to bear in mind that financial liberalization is not a remedy for stagnation and instability;
- Close attention needs to be paid to the organization of the financial system and of corporate finance since this impinges directly on industrialization, development and stability. Experience shows that no single type of financial system is suitable everywhere and at all times. For most developing countries, a system of bank-based finance combining investment banking with deposit taking appears to be more appropriate than one based on capital markets. It is more susceptible to control - an important consideration since intervention in the allocation of credit is often needed to achieve development objectives. Moreover, close relations between lenders and corporations can result in greater predictability in the availability of funds and lower the cost of finance for firms, allowing them to take a long view in designing their business strategies.

41.   However, a combination of intervention and bank-based finance can easily degenerate unless adequate precautions are taken:

- The authorities must ensure that all controls, regulations and subsidies serve the intended purposes, monitor their policies constantly, and revise them as necessary;
- Credit controls should not be used as a vehicle for facilitating financing of unproductive government expenditure. The discrepancy between tax treatment of interest incomes and payments should be eliminated by taxing the former like any other income category, thereby

ensuring equity and preventing public revenue loss.

- Closer relationships between banks and corporations can lead to waste and instability if corporations are allowed to control banks;
- Effective prudential regulations and strong bank supervision are essential to prevent excessive risk taking and speculation by the banking system, and all the more so when interest rates and lending are deregulated and deposit insurance or enhanced lender-of-last-resort facilities are provided.
- Increased cost efficiency and reduced profit margins of financial intermediaries help reduce lending rates significantly. If this cannot be attained through increased competition, ceilings on lending rates may be needed.

42.   Despite the limitations of the Anglo-Saxon model of financing, capital markets can render useful functions, particularly at later stages of development, and can function alongside banks in providing funds for investment. But capital markets do not emerge spontaneously, and tax and other incentives to broaden the equity base of the corporate sector, as well as restrictions on corporate borrowing, may be needed.

- The promotion of capital markets should be accompanied by measures to prevent secondary market activity from becoming an additional source of financial instability, including regulations to prevent fraud and other irregularities as well as mechanisms to prevent excessive speculation. A tax on capital market transactions can help to deter short-term speculative moves into and out of equities.
- It is also possible to combine the advantages of bank and capital market finance. One way is to introduce investment banks between capital markets and non-financial corporations, and allow them to raise funds in the capital markets. Another is to combine bank control over corporations, as in Germany, with equity holding by institutional investors such as provident and pension funds, as in Japan.

43.   Particular care needs to be given to the design of external financial reforms, since mistakes in this area tend to be very costly and difficult to reverse:

- A complete isolation of the financial system in a developing country from the rest of world is neither feasible nor desirable if only because successful export performance requires close interaction of banks at home with international markets in order to provide trade-related credits and facilitate international payments. But, despite the difficulties involved, it is usually possible to separate trade-related financial transactions from capital transactions through restrictions on the size and maturity of banks' foreign exchange assets and liabilities.
- Allowing domestic firms (whether private or public) uncontrolled access to international capital markets has proved damaging in many instances; short-term speculative capital flows have proved extremely troublesome even for industrial countries. Most developing countries need to exercise a considerable degree of control over external capital flows and the pace of accumulation of external debt. But that in itself will not stem capital flight if economic and political stability is absent. Foreign currency accounts can lead to dollarization, and are poor substitutes for sound policies.

2. Public sector savings and investment

(a) The fiscal crisis

(i) External shocks, trade adjustment and fiscal balances

44.   In many developing countries fiscal imbalances have been building up since the early 1980s, in large part owing to external shocks. The rise in international interest rates raised the interest bill of the public sector, especially where the government had borrowed heavily abroad. The slowdown in economic activity and collapse of commodity prices caused a fall in export earnings

and reduced government revenues, especially where the export sector was an important source of revenues.

45. The cutback in external commercial lending widened the financing gap and increased the need for fiscal adjustment. In many cases the decline in net external financial flows to the public sector was as much as 4 per cent of GDP or 20 per cent of total government expenditure. Moreover, many governments took on private sectors' external liabilities (either directly or through providing guarantees *ex post facto*), which raised the debt burden of the public sector by 15-20 per cent. Many countries responded to the large swings in external transfers by cutting import volumes; some also succeeded in raising export earnings. Generating trade surpluses (or reducing trade deficits) itself generally required restrictive fiscal measures and cuts in public sector imports. However, to the extent that the trade surpluses were generated by private enterprises, a transfer of funds to the public sector was needed to allow the latter to service its debt.

46. The domestic transfer problem was made more acute by the difficulties of achieving balance of payments adjustment and fiscal adjustment simultaneously. Reduced import levels and cuts in import taxes designed to stimulate exports caused significant shortfalls in government revenue, particularly where import taxes had been high. Many countries also reduced or completely eliminated taxation of exports, thereby adding to the revenue losses from the declines in world commodity prices.

47. Currency depreciations affected public finances by increasing the domestic currency equivalent of government revenue from trade, raising the cost of public sector imports and increasing the cost of debt servicing. The rise in real government revenues brought about by currency depreciation was in most cases insufficient to compensate for the revenue losses from import taxes. Currency depreciations raised the cost of public sector investment which generally has a high import content in developing countries. State economic enterprises which import capital and intermediate goods from abroad but sell their products mainly or exclusively on the domestic market incurred losses when they could not offset higher import costs by increasing their prices. More important, currency depreciations raised the domestic currency value of interest payments on external debt, especially in countries with sharp devaluations.

48. The overall impact of currency depreciation on the fiscal balance depended on two factors: the size of new net external borrowing of the public sector compared to its interest payments abroad, and the size of government revenues from exports compared to foreign debt-service obligations. Where net external borrowing exceeded interest payments (that is, net external transfers to the public sector were positive) devaluation improved the fiscal position. But this was the case in only a number of low-income countries; in most other indebted countries governments had to mobilize additional resources in order to finance the increased domestic currency cost of their net transfer abroad. In only a very few indebted countries did the government's revenues from exports match its external obligations.

49. Thus, while the swings in external resource availability to the public sector required an increase in government revenues, public sector revenues fell considerably because of trade policy reforms, imports cuts and commodity price declines. It was therefore extremely difficult for governments to maintain, let alone to raise, the level of public sector savings available for domestic use.

(ii) Fiscal responses

50. Fiscal responses involved mainly spending cuts rather than revenue increases. With the exception of few countries, total tax revenues declined or, at best, remained constant as a percentage of GDP, in large part because of economic slowdown. Faster inflation reduced real tax receipts due to collection lags and the tax deductibility of higher corporate interest payments. Revenues rose in a few cases, but this was largely due to increased prices of goods and services provided by the public sector rather than increases in tax revenues. Another source of revenue was the sale of public assets.

51. On the spending side, there were substantial increases in interest payments in almost all countries with external debt problems. Primary (non-interest) expenditure was reduced by more than 5 per cent of GDP. Substantial cuts were made in current expenditures, including public

administration, social spending and transfers. However, the burden fell primarily on capital spending, which fell by more than 50 per cent in a number of countries.

52.   In many countries deregulation of interest rates together with restrictive monetary policies caused domestic interest rates to rise substantially. This, together with the shifting of financing of deficits from central banks to markets, caused the interest bill and domestic debt of the government to swell. In many highly-indebted countries interest payments on domestic and external debt amounted to most of the increase in the public sector's borrowing requirement.

53.   Fiscal austerity has been accompanied by a shortening of the time horizons of policy-makers. In many cases, governments have cut spending without paying due attention to the long-term consequences for growth and development. Cuts in real wages and salaries have led to loss of skilled personnel from the public sector and further weakened the public sector's administrative and management capabilities. Reduction of spending on the maintenance of infrastructure and machinery and equipment has lowered the productivity of public physical assets and the quality of public services, while cuts in social spending and investment in health and education have lowered the quality of human resources.

(b) Public sector reform

54.   An economically and institutionally strengthened public sector is essential for restoring growth in developing countries. In many countries public finances are in an untenable state and the public sector revenue and spending need to be raised considerably. However, it is essential that this be done in the context of fiscal reforms. The principal objective of reform should be to improve economic performance. This is not necessarily the same thing as reducing budget deficits, although circumstances in some countries call for such reduction. For instance, efficiency may be lowered when the government increases its income by using the monopoly power of state enterprises to raise prices of public sector goods and services. Similarly, a deficit may not be a problem if the government is able at the same time to keep its income and expenditure under control, ensure that taxes and spending decisions are growth-oriented, and finance the deficits in a non-inflationary way. The focus should be on the effects of government expenditures and revenues, not simply the size of fiscal deficits or the public sector.

55.   Efficiency in policy-making requires (a) defining economic and social objectives explicitly; (b) assigning appropriate policy instruments to these objectives; and (c) constantly monitoring the outcomes vis-à-vis policy inputs.

56.   There is substantial scope for improvement in developing countries on all these fronts. First, there is often lack of clarity regarding the objectives pursued by policy actions, and policy-makers are not always aware of trade-offs among various policy objectives such as equity, poverty alleviation, productivity, growth, etc. Thus, policy actions do not always reflect explicit, calculated, and deliberate choices based on an awareness of alternative costs and opportunities.

57.   Secondly, policy instruments can be used better. A given policy objective may be attained by means of a number of different instruments, but one configuration of objectives and instruments may be superior to the others. For instance, poverty may be alleviated by food subsidies, provision of employment in state enterprises, tax exemptions and so on, each having different effects on productivity and growth. Again governments may be able to raise budget revenues equally through a number of different tax schemes, each having a different impact on incentives and resource allocation in the private economy, and income distribution and poverty. A correct assignment of instruments will not only increase the probability of attaining their objectives, but will also reduce their possible adverse effects on other objectives of economic policy.

58.   Finally and most important, it is necessary to monitor continuously the performance of policy instruments in attaining their objectives, and to revise policies accordingly. Typically, an assessment is needed of the fiscal incentives given to the private sector for exports, investment and employment so that reciprocity be established between incentives and performance. The effects of various categories of government spending should also be carefully monitored. The attainment of such objectives as poverty alleviation, better health and education should be measured not by how much has been spent in these areas, but by their outcomes on basic needs, life expectancy,

infant mortality and literacy. In other words, governments need to assure an adequate social rate of return on their own current and capital spending, as well as on the resources they use to provide incentives to the private sector.

59.   Reallocation of existing budgetary resources among various categories of spending along these lines could bring important gains in efficiency. The most important aim should be to arrest any deterioration of physical and human infrastructure. Priority should be given to the rehabilitation and maintenance of infrastructure and productive capacity already installed, rather than to capacity-enlarging investment. Where the most important constraint on production and growth at present is foreign exchange availability, special attention needs to be given to areas that facilitate export expansion such as communication and transport. More would also need to be spent on poverty-alleviation programmes. This helps not only improve the human condition, but also growth: poverty is a hindrance to productivity.

60.   In many areas it may be extremely difficult to make further cuts in spending without impairing the management capacity of the public sector and worsening still further the provision of public goods and services. One area where expenditure cuts may well be both possible and highly desirable is military spending; this would also bring the additional benefit of releasing scarce foreign exchange resources since arms equipment is usually imported. It may also be useful to undertake a detailed survey of subsidies with a view to assessing their role and performance, and eliminating the non-performing ones. Finally, there may be some scope to rationalize spending on public administration without lowering quality. This may involve not only reducing employment, but also raising wages and salaries and linking them to an incentive scheme.

61.   However, the key to a successful fiscal reform is greater equity and efficiency in taxation. In developing countries the tax system has serious defects in its revenue, equity and incentive aspects, and the crisis in the 1980s has further aggravated these deficiencies. Many governments have been unable to place any significant part of the burden of adjustment on capital or the highly skilled without provoking capital flight and brain drain. Indeed, they have been strongly urged to place greater emphasis on private savings, and to give incentives for flight capital to return. Consequently, taxes on financial incomes, profits and capital gains have remained remarkably low, barely exceeding 3 per cent of GDP. In many debtor countries the government has paid out more in subsidies to private corporations than it has received from them in taxes.

62.   In general the tax system has been used extensively in developing countries in order to pursue an industrialization strategy. However, special tax rates and exemptions have in many cases continued even after they ceased to be useful, at the cost of reduced tax revenues, distortions in incentives and over-complexity in tax administration. Attempts in the 1980s to increase budget revenues through *ad hoc* modifications to the tax system have introduced further distortions and worsened distribution of wealth and income; they have also encouraged the underground economy, and the emergence of an ethic of tax evasion.

63.   There may therefore be substantial scope for improving the equity and efficiency of taxation, and for raising revenues by rationalizing and simplifying the taxation system. Exemptions need to be reviewed with a view to eliminating those that do not help improve resource allocation and growth, but distort income distribution and lower tax revenues. Neither equity nor efficiency is served when financial incomes and capital gains are taxed at much lower rates than wages and salaries. Advance tax payments may need to be introduced to prevent inflation from eroding the purchasing power of tax revenues - something that would both raise real tax revenues and bring greater equity because it is usually non-wage incomes that benefit from collection lags. Even more important, tax administration may need to be strenghtened considerably; such efforts to increase the ability of the government to collect can have a very high pay-off.

64.   There are significant obstacles in undertaking such fiscal reforms. It is often politically difficult to reduce current spending even though equity and efficiency considerations would justify such a course; this is one reason why many governments tend first and foremost to cut investment spending. The political difficulties in the case of taxing incomes may be even greater; this helps explain why governments often prefer to have recourse to more anonymous taxes such as inflation or indirect taxes. Since reform of taxation and spending alters income distribution among various classes and groups, a social consensus is needed both as regards the need for fiscal reforms and the distribution of their burdens and benefits. This often calls for dialogue among the various actors involved such as political parties, trade unions, and industrial, commercial and financial groups, and for a Government with the credibility to act as arbiter.

(c) State economic enterprises

65.   While impaired performance has also been a characteristic of a large number of private firms in developing countries in the 1980s, state economic enterprises (SEEs) have been in especially acute distress.   Their capacity utilization has fallen sharply and their productivity has ceased to grow.   SEEs were particularly vulnerable to the sharp swings in international interest rates, net foreign lending and commodity prices, as well as to the effects of balance-of-payments adjustment policies.   But in many countries SEEs were suffering from mismanagement, and this was laid bare in the 1980s by the external shocks and financial stringency.

66.   SEEs have mostly been established in areas where capital costs were so large that no private investor was able or willing to bear them; or where the entrepreneurial initiative required by diversification and growth was not forthcoming; or where there were political reasons for keeping state control over strategic industries or natural resources.   Most SEEs have been operating in non-tradeable goods and services sectors, and have had relatively high capital intensity, import dependence and debt.   Thus, sharp swings in interest and exchange rates had considerable effects on this viability, particularly since they were unable to adapt through new investment and restructuring.   Other SEEs working in tradeable goods sectors, such as commodity marketing boards or mining companies, have also been hard hit by falling commodity prices, and by governments' unwillingness to pass these declines on to producers.

67.   The extent of the weakening of SEEs is not evident from their financial performance since they were obliged by the need for overall fiscal adjustment to improve their balance sheets.   Deficits of SEEs and transfers from the central government fell in the 1980s, in some cases considerably, as capital spending by SEEs was cut, and as indirect subsidies were reduced or eliminated.

68.   There is now a clear need to reform SEEs.   The appropriate measures range from liquidation to rehabilitation with many alternative variants in between.   The choice should be based on a careful assessment of the role and performance of each individual SEE.   The performance of public enterprises is often judged purely on the basis of the extent of their deficits.   However, it must be borne in mind that a deficit in the sense of an excess of investment over savings cannot be considered, *per se*, as an indicator of bad performance as long as investment yields an adequate return.

69.   Secondly, when a SEE is in deficit on its current account, this may not always indicate management inefficiency.   It may, rather, be due to the objectives assigned by the government, for instance objectives related to income distribution and industrial and agricultural development, the need to provide certain basic goods and services to the population and intermediate inputs and investment goods to industry and agriculture at low prices, and job creation.   Under such circumstances the relevant question is whether SEEs are the most appropriate means of pursuing such developmental objectives.   If it is found that there are better means of attaining such objectives (e.g. taxation, budgetary subsidies, etc.) then they can be run on a purely commercial basis and still be kept under state ownership for fiscal or other reasons.   In such cases it is essential to assign the task to other policy instruments; otherwise, eliminating the financial deficits of the SEE would simply mean forgoing these objectives.   If, on the other hand, it is found that SEEs are the appropriate institution, it would be necessary to define their objectives clearly, and to separate the effects of the objectives on the financial performance of SEEs from those due to microeconomic inefficiency.

70.   Absence of rewards and penalties, and of incentives and sanctions, can cause considerable inefficiency in SEEs.   Ability to draw on the budget or the central bank to meet losses and deficits impairs financial discipline, while a system of pay unrelated to financial performance can hinder management creativity and productive growth.   Moreover, efficiency can be seriously damaged by an absence of competition due to a natural monopoly position, as well as political influences on employment and other decisions.

71.   Privatization of SEEs has increasingly been emphasized in recent years as a way out of these problems.   While it has a role to play, it needs to be based on a careful assessment of the problems and the options.

72.   A comparison of the performance of public and private enterprises in general is not always

helpful since their areas of activity and objectives often differ widely. Besides, the evidence is mixed.[3] It is also notable that there tends to be a close correlation between the performance of public and private enterprises in different countries; where large and leading private enterprises are well managed, major public enterprises tend to be relatively well managed as well. This is because when the government is able and willing to make its support to the private sector conditional upon good performance by the latter, it will also be able and willing to discipline its own enterprises.

73.   In reforming SEEs it is useful to review the underlying reasons and circumstances that had originally given rise to public ownership, and the extent to which such reasons and circumstances continue to be valid. Cases where SEEs were created because of lack of private capital and know-how, or the nationalization of foreign-owned corporations, or rescue operations, or to establish a revenue base for the government should be approached differently from those where SEEs were created in order to serve certain collective goals. It is also important to recognize that reasons for public ownership are likely to change in the course of development. While the role of public enterprises at an early stage of development may lie in promoting basic industry, this may no longer be necessary at a more advanced stage of development. But in such a stage, SEEs may be required in new industries of strategic importance for the course of development, where initial cost and risks are too high for private initiative to assume, and in areas where developing countries begin to compete with powerful multinational firms. Also the role of SEEs as earners of public revenue is likely to change over time as the possibilities for taxation generally improve with the state of development.

74.   Better management alone, whether brought about by change of ownership or otherwise, is often not enough to improve the functioning of the firms. Improved performance typically requires an injection of new investment in order to update technology and reverse the deterioration of the existing capacity, and to allow the firm to adapt to changes in key relative prices and in policies regarding protection. Striving for quick increases in profitability and financial surpluses without investing and acquiring new techology can seriously undermine the longer-term performance, whether the firm is private or public.

75.   The effects of sales of government assets on aggregate and private investment also need to be taken into account. These effects depend on how the private sector finances its purchases and how the government uses the proceeds.[4]

76.   In a number of countries there has been an increased sale of public sector assets to non-residents in recent years. A number of points need to be made in this context.

- Such sales increase total domestic investment spending if they stimulate an additional capital inflow, but not if they are financed by external resources that would in any case be forthcoming;
- It also has to be taken into account that when non-residents buy a SEE, future profit remittances necessitate generation of foreign exchange;
- Even when the privatization is undertaken through debt-equity swaps, the net foreign exchange effect may not be positive unless substantial discounts are obtained on the debt converted;
- The question how to reform SEEs should be dealt with separately from the question how to generate non-debt-creating flows from abroad. The latter can be done by selling private as well as public enterprises to non-residents, encouraging foreign direct investment, and allowing non-residents to make portfolio investment in domestic capital markets. The reform of SEEs should aim at improving management and efficiency.

---

[3] Certain SEEs are found to have much better performance than private enterprises in terms of capacity utilization and productivity growth. Moreover, there is evidence that management of SEEs in developing countries often tends to pay more attention to training and the introduction of new techniques of production, accountancy and product control, sharing their advances in these areas with the private sector without sharing the costs. However, it is also true that the SEEs in a large number of developing countries suffer from serious problems of management and efficiency.

[4] If the government uses the proceeds from selling assets to increase debt-servicing abroad, both output and investment will be reduced. If, on the other hand, the government uses the proceeds for investment, private investment will fall and aggregate investment will remain unchanged if output is constrained by foreign exchange shortage, but agrregate investment will be higher when the binding constraint on output is effective demand. If, finally, the government uses the proceeds to reduce budget deficits, privatization will not affect output and investment. In other words, privatization will raise output and growth only if the proceeds are used for investment *and* the foreign exchange constraint is not binding; and it cannot help both debtors and creditors at the same time, except inasmuch as it increases efficiency over time.

77.   Finally, it must be borne in mind that many of the mechanisms that discipline management are either absent or ineffective in many of these countries. There is little threat of takeover because stock markets are underdeveloped and the equity base is narrow. On the other hand, as noted above, due to interlocking ownership with banks, creditors do not participate actively in monitoring the performance of the firm in order to ensure managerial efficiency. This, combined with the readiness of governments to rescue troubled firms, has often meant that the financial disciplines on large private firms are as soft as those on SEEs.

78.   It may still be expected that privatization may cause a reduction of costs, primarily by reducing employment and unionization. Nevertheless, it is no guarantee of efficiency in the allocation of resources in the economy - i.e. achieving production levels and input combinations that are socially optimum - because privatized firms may have monopoly power and therefore be under no compulsion to reduce costs, preferring instead to lower production and charge higher prices. Efficiency depends more on the extent of the competition prevailing than the nature of the ownership. Where competition is imperfect, privatization needs to be accompanied by an effective regulatory framework. Thus, it does not lessen the need for strengthening the management capacity of the public sector, including its resistance to corruption.

79.   Given the financial stringency prevailing in developing countries, the dominant concern in many privatization programmes has been to obtain cash rather than to increase efficiency. In some cases even efficient and profitable enterprises have been put up for sale, and governments have provided a variety of incentives to attract buyers, including low prices, subsidized credits, and profit guarantees, and even avoided establishing an anti-monopolistic regulatory framework. It is important, however, not to lose sight of the main issue, namely how best to deal with the SEEs in order to improve their performance and contribution to development.

3. External financial environment

80.   The external financial environment of developing countries in the 1980s has been marked by severe problems, including a collapse of financial flows, high world interest rates, depressed commodity prices and malfunction of the international monetary and financial system. While most debtor countries have made large sacrifices in growth and development in order to adjust their trade balances, the external resource situation has as yet failed to register sustained improvement, and the instability in international financial and currency markets has continued unchecked.

(a) Financial flows to developing countries

81.   As stressed in more detail in the following part on debt and external resources, the financial transfer system in the 1980s was characterized by a decline in external financial flows to developing countries, the collapse of commercial bank lending, and the occurrence of negative net financial transfers in numerous countries. Towards the end of the decade, official financial flows assumed a preponderant role, with the IMF and the World Bank becoming the lynchpin of the development finance system.

82.   These changes in the level and composition of financial flows were associated with the unfolding of the debt crisis. Despite the significant improvement in economic performance made by a small number of middle-income debtor countries which have benefitted from debt reduction programmes, the debt crisis is far from being resolved for most heavily indebted countries. The international debt strategies implemented so far have revealed various shortcomings and the debt problem will need to be more vigorously tackled by bolder measures leading to a much higher degree of debt relief.

(b) International monetary and financial system

83.　The unfavourable external financial environment for development was associated with increased instability in the international monetary and financial system as a whole. Interest rates in the main financial centres have been much more variable in the 1980s, and nominal and real rates have been pushed to extraordinary heights. Swings in equity prices have registered an intensity unprecedented in the post war period. The principal exchange rates have gyrated more in the past decade, and have deviated for substantial periods from levels warranted by differences in productivity and thrift; instability has thus been latent even when it has not actually occurred. Following recent events in the Persian Gulf, world financial markets have again exhibited significant turbulance and over-reaction, including sharp swings in exchange rates, and caused increased uncertainty about future interest rates.

84.　Financial and exchange rate instability have their sources largely in the behaviour of private finance in increasingly integrated and deregulated international markets coupled with the orientation of monetary policies in the major developed market economies. Economic policy in these countries has included a substantial degree of liberalization and deregulation of financial markets and commercial banking. Attempts by governments to retain and attract financial activity to their countries has led to competitive deregulation and reduction of taxes in the financial sector, which has substantially increased the mobility of funds.

85.　Deregulation has also encompassed interest rates and the range of activities permitted for different types of financial institutions. This has reduced considerably the degree of segmentation of markets and widened the potential for funds to move across institutions, markets and borders. Holders of liquid funds have increasingly regarded interest-bearing money-market instruments denominated in different currencies as potential substitutes for each other so that national money markets have become more closely integrated. Another aspect of the globalization of finance which has occurred during the 1980s has been the closer integration of bond and equity markets.

86.　It has been largely because of financial integration, liberalization and deregulation that international financial activity has expanded much more rapidly than world output, trade and direct investment. However, this does not appear to have improved the international allocation of savings. Most international financial transactions have been portfolio decisions, largely by rentiers, rather than business decisions by entrepreneurs. Similarly, most currency transactions have been generated by trade in the stock of financial assets rather than by flows of saving. Consequently, foreign exchange markets have been dominated by speculative forces which have frequently acted not as a stabilizing mechanism but as a source of turbulence.

87.　Another major reason for the increased instability has been that in the 1980s monetary policy became far less concerned with stabilizing interest rates and much more concerned with controlling monetary growth. Governments have also become extremely reluctant to use fiscal policy to manage the level of demand, and even more so to control prices and incomes in order to combat inflation, leaving monetary policy as the only tool for macroeconomic management. Monetary policy has been further overloaded by the need to take account of the exchange rate. Moreover, notwithstanding repeated attempts at policy coordination, governments have in practice failed to pay due regard to the impact of their own policy approaches and actions on the rest of the world, causing major inconsistencies among the policy stances of countries and resulting in vast trade imbalances and sharp swings in exchange rates. These, together with uncertainty in financial and currency markets has also increased the preference of wealth-holders for liquid over long-term assets and thus put upward pressure on interest rates.

88.　Developing countries have been affected by international financial instability mainly in four ways:

- Exchange rate instability has rendered the international trading environment more uncertain and trade more risky and costly. Currency misalignment has also fuelled protectionist pressures.
- Large and unexpected changes in the exchange rates of the major reserve currencies has also affected the cost of servicing the external debt, which depends in part on how far the currency composition of debtors matches that of foreign exchange receipts.
- High international interest rates have been an important factor in the debt crisis of the 1980s. They have also raised domestic interest rates in developing countries, depressed domestic in-

vestment and output growth, and worsened income distribution.
- There have been sudden swings in private financial flows to developing countries and capital flight, which were encouraged by financial liberalization and rising international interest rates.

89. A number of policy changes are required in order to render the international monetary system more stable and to reduce uncertainty in financial and currency markets to more tolerable levels. The exchange rate system would become more stable if governments of the major currency countries committed themselves to defending a publicly announced pattern of exchange rates. Such a pattern should be internationally agreed and be compatible with high levels of activity and employment. This could be achieved by establishing a system of adjustable pegs between the US dollar, the yen and the ECU, not unlike the Exchange Rate Mechanism of the European Monetary System.

90. It would also be useful to establish regulations for international and cross-country capital flows in order to prevent turbulence in financial and currency markets caused by speculative forces. The cost of speculation should be increased through, for instance, taxes on financial transactions. Moreover, prudential regulation needs to be tightened in order to match adequately the greater risk-taking generated by financial liberalization.

91. Finally, there is a need for a strengthened system of international policy co-ordination and multilateral surveillance, including targets for demand growth and current-account imbalances. The burden of adjusting policy when outcomes differ from those targets should be shared between deficit and surplus countries in such a way as to avoid a bias towards deflation and high interest rates. This is an especially important consideration for developing countries which are affected not only by the direct demand effects resulting from the overall stance of macroeconomic policies in the major OECD countries but also by the effect on international interest rates resulting from the mix of monetary and fiscal policies. Conduct of policies in the major economies should therefore be subject to multilateral surveillance. In this context, the role of the International Monetary Fund should be revised and its contribution to the process of international policy co-ordination be strengthened with a view to taking more adequate account of the interests of developing countries and how they are affected by economic interdependence.

92. External financial flows to developing countries have risen since 1987 but are still considerably lower than in the early 1980s. When deflated by the unit value of imports, total long-term financial flows to low and middle-income countries in 1988-1990 were lower by almost one quarter compared to 1980-1982. Official development finance stagnated until 1987 and it has risen by more than 20 per cent since then. Foreign direct investment has also risen in recent years, but lending from private sources both in the form of export credits and long-term loans has stagnated in recent years after collapsing to very low levels, despite the overall buoyancy of international capital markets. Access of developing countries to international bank credit remains extremely restricted and in 1989 net medium and long-term bank lending to countries with debt-servicing difficulties was less than one tenth of its 1980-1982 level. The persistence of high real interest rates on external debt and depressed world market prices for many primary commodities exported by debtor developing countries have further aggravated their external financial situation. Arrears on both commercial and official debt have continued to increase for many major borrowers as well as a number of low-income countries since 1987.

93. During the 1980s numerous developing countries have suffered a contraction of net financial transfers from abroad, and many have experienced an outward net financial transfer every year since 1983; these transfers were mainly to commercial banks but also to some official sources. The resource loss in debt-troubled countries through the swing in net financial transfers since the early 1980s has amounted, on average, to about 4.5 per cent of GDP. About one half of these countries turned from being net recipients to being net providers of financial resources. Most of the others continued to be net recipients but at much lower levels than before. During the 1980s the net transfer on account of credit was negative in more than 40 developing countries, as was the overall transfer of resources in more than 30 countries. Since the beginning of the debt crisis, indebted developing countries have in general had to transfer between 2 and 3 per cent of their GDP abroad; in some instances 6 per cent or more.

94. These resource losses have required a substantial adjustment of trade balances. In most cases export volumes have been raised considerably, but the scale of adjustment required has made it impossible to avoid drastic import cuts; the widespread co-existence of increased export volumes and reduced import volumes of the 1980s was unprecedented. In many countries the adjustment

to the large swings in the availability of external financial resources has been made more difficult by the depressed state of many primary commodity prices. The resulting deterioration in the terms of trade has raised the real cost of servicing external debt. While the debtor developing countries as a whole have experienced falling terms of trade since the mid-1980s, sub-Saharan Africa and the heavily-indebted countries have been particularly hard hit. The burden of adjustment has in many countries been the prime reason for stagnation and macroeconomic disorder.

95. As adjustment has in most cases been at the expense of growth, the external debt situation of developing countries remains serious. There have recently been improvements in some debt indicators, but in countries where the ratios of debt or debt service to exports fell this was largely on account of a substantial rise in these countries' export volumes after 1986. In a large number of debtor developing countries, ratios of debt to exports are still above those of 1982, and in sub-Saharan African they continue to rise. Moreover, improvements in this ratio in 1989/1990 were not accompanied by improvements in ratios of interest payments to exports, in large part because of a rise in international interest rates.

96. The failure of the international debt strategy practised until 1988 to eliminate over-indebtedness and to contribute to a revival of growth and development has led to a new approach in dealing with the debt problem of developing countries following the Brady initiative in April 1989. This approach undoubtedly constitutes important progress compared to the earlier debt strategy as it makes debt relief a central element of the new strengthened strategy. However, a solution to the debt problem of the developing countries and revival of growth and development in these countries requires a much larger scale of debt or debt-service reduction than possible on the basis of the resources available under the Brady proposal. The maximum of debt and debt-service reduction from commercial banks currently possible is only half of what has been calculated as necessary to enable debtor countries to combine a resumption of growth with a fulfilment of their remaining debt-service obligations.

B. DEBT AND EXTERNAL RESOURCES

97. On present trends, developing countries will face continued difficulties in attracting enough external finance to complement their own efforts to revive development in the 1990s. The context in which developing countries' mobilization of external resources will take place is made more complex by problems inherited from the 1980s and new pressures on international finance. The debt problems of developing countries, which hampered their development during the last decade, will continue to be a major impediment to their economic recovery. Moreover, developing country capital requirements will further increase as a result of the Gulf crisis and of environmental concerns. In addition to developing countries' needs, the international financial system will have to respond to new demands in support of the economic and social restructuring in Eastern European countries and their progressive integration into the world economy.

1. Towards a durable solution to the debt crisis

98. With the Toronto agreement on official bilateral debt of low-income countries and the Brady initiative on commercial bank debt, the international debt strategy has evolved considerably since UNCTAD VII. It now recognizes that solutions to the debt problem should include debt and debt service reduction as a central element. However, the scope of debt relief resulting from the agreements reached so far under these initiatives has been rather limited.

99. Despite the significant progress made by a small number of middle-income debtor countries (most notably Chile, Mexico and to a lesser extent Venezuela) in stabilizing their economies and in regaining access to spontaneous capital flows, the debt crisis is far from being resolved for most heavily indebted countries. These countries are facing enormous difficulties in stabilizing and re-structuring their economies, and their debt indicators, which have improved somewhat over the

past few years for the middle-income debtors, remain at unmanageable levels (see table I-3). This was reflected by the accelerating pace of debt reschedulings and the accumulation of arrears. Debt problems continue to exert downward pressure on public and private investment and, hence, on output growth of heavily indebted countries. Over the period 1983-1990, the 76 countries with recent debt-servicing difficulties experienced an average real GDP growth of 1.4 per cent, well below population growth, while domestic investment fell by 7 percentage points in relation to GDP, as compared to the average prevailing during the period 1975-1982.[5]

(a) Commercial bank debt

100.   A notable event on the private debt front during the past few years was the implementation of the strengthened debt strategy following the Brady initiative launched in early 1989. Since that date, seven debtor countries (Costa Rica, Mexico, Morocco, Nigeria, Philippines, Uruguay and Venezuela) have concluded agreements with their creditor banks under this initiative, after difficult and protracted negotiations.[6] These initiatives offer creditor banks various options of debt and debt service reduction and new money lending.

101.   The resulting amount of debt and debt service reduction falls considerably short of what is required. For some countries, the agreements are more akin to conventional reschedulings than debt reductions (especially in the cases of Morocco and the Philippines); or other countries debt reduction operations are counterbalanced by debt-increasing ones (for example as a result of credit enhancements in the form of the collateralization or guaranteeing of interest payments or repayment of principal).[7] Savings on interest payments resulting from these agreements have also been relatively minor.[8]

102.   Another purpose of the present strategy is to increase net financial transfers to debtor countries, by stimulating new lending by banks and the reversal of capital flight. The extent and strength of creditor banks' interest in providing new money is, however, questionable. A number of impediments to new lending exist, including the low perceived credit-worthiness of most debtor developing countries, owing in large part to a lack of sustained improvement in their external financial positions, as well as competitive pressures in the banking industry and new regulatory requirements, for instance as regards provisioning requirements for new lending and strengthening capital positions.[9] The experience of the Brady deals implemented so far shows how difficult it is to obtain lending.[10]

---

5   IMF, *World Economic Outlook,* May 1991, pp.67 and 70.

6   For a detailed analysis of these agreements, see UNCTAD, Trade and Development Report, 1990, pp. 25-29, and Trade and Development Report, 1991, pp.43-49.

7   In the case of Mexico, $7 billion was written off in exchange for bonds, but the debt also increased by about $7 billion ($5.7 billion from official creditors and $1.4 billion in new money). In the case of the Philippines, the country borrowed $560 million to write off old debt and issued $700 million of new money bonds, reaching a total close to the $1.3 billion retired through the agreements. In the case of Venezuela, recourse has been made to large scale financing from multilateral resources and there has been more fresh money from banks.

8   For example, in the case of Mexico, net average annual savings on interest payments were roughly equivalent to only 10 per cent of Mexico's total interest bill in 1988. Mexico will increase its cash flow by about 2 per cent of GDP, that is, about half that country's target. In the case of the Philippines, the net impact of the agreement on interest obligations was initially nil. In the case of Costa Rica, where interest arrears have also been included in the agreement, it was found that the interest obligations that this country had finally to pay after the agreement were roughly equivalent to what it had actually paid before, while accumulating interest arrears.

9   New capital adequacy requirements were set by the 1988 Basle agreement on capital adequacy. See Trade and Development Report, 1989 annex 2. Provisioning requirements on new loans by banks to heavily indebted developing countries are discussed in IMF, "International Monetary Fund, International Capital Markets Developments and Prospects", (Washington, D.C., May 1991), pp. 70-71.

10   In the Mexican deal, banks representing 47 per cent of the debt in the deal chose to convert their claims into reduced interest bonds at par; banks representing 41 per cent of the debt chose the discount bond conversion option. Banks choosing to lend new money account for the remaining 12 per cent, which is about half the figure that had been expected. In the Philippine deal (which offered to banks two options: a new money scheme and a buy-back operation), the amount of new money raised fell far short of the target set by the Government while more tenders for buy-backs were received than could be accommodated. A number of creditor banks chose not to participate. In the Costa Rican agreement, no attempt was made to obtain new money. For more details on these deals, see *World Economic Survey 1990, op.cit.,* pp. 88-93, and UNCTAD, *Trade and Development Report,* 1990, pp.27 and 28.

103.   Some other features of the agreements implemented to date have given rise to concern. For one, the agreements have rendered the remaining debt more difficult to restructure. A large proportion of bank loans have been transformed into bonds and those have been perceived as exit instruments since they generally exempt the holders from future restructuring and new money calls. Furthermore, additional multilateral debt (which in principle is not possible to restructure) has been incurred. Second, the agreements contain recapture clauses for creditors in the event of a significant rise either in the price of petroleum (in the case of Mexico and Venezuela), or in GDP growth (in the case of Costa Rica), but no analogous clauses in favour of debtor countries in the event of a significant deterioration in their economic situation. Such an asymmetry would be justifiable only if debt and debt service were reduced by a sufficiently wide margin to reduce vulnerability to external shocks.

104.   The implementation of the Brady initiative has suffered from the absence of internationally set targets for the medium-term cash flow and debt profile of the country whose debt problem is being addressed. As a result, there has been a tendency for the extent of debt and debt service reduction to be shaped by the balance of negotiating strength rather than by objective needs. In this regard, the multilateral financial institutions could play a useful role by providing authoritative estimates of the country's debt reduction and cash flow needs.

105.   In the Costa Rican agreement, the decision of IMF and the World Bank to provide financial support to the country's adjustment programme despite its arrears greatly helped persuade banks to sign the agreement. Such an attitude towards financing assurances by multilateral financial institutions (MFIs), if more systematically applied, could be a powerful instrument in increasing the scope for debt and debt service reduction. However, recent decisions by MFIs suggest that such a course may not be followed.

106.   Providing creditors with additional incentives to engage in debt and debt service reduction on a larger scale and to accept steeper discounts in such operations would also be useful. A wide variety of proposals in this vein has been put forward in recent years, for instance to establish an international debt facility. Further recourse to financial support from MFIs should be approached with great caution: unless additional funds are put at their disposal, such support could reduce lending for new investment, which is the key to successful adjustment. However, national laws and regulations in creditor countries could be directed more effectively towards achieving adequate levels of debt and debt service reduction.[11]

(b) Official bilateral debt

107.   During the past decade, debt owed to official bilateral creditors trebled. At $318 billion by 1990, it accounted for about one-third of the total stock of developing countries' debt, as compared to one-fourth in 1980. The growing importance of official bilateral debt is attributable to a large extent to workouts of existing debt, such as the taking over by official guarantors of debts to private lenders, the capitalization of interest in debt reschedulings, the accumulation of interest arrears, and bilateral borrowing in the context of the Brady initiative. However, the expansion of bilateral debt would have been somewhat higher if debtor countries (mostly low-income) had not benefited from forgiveness of ODA debt to DAC countries amounting to about $11 billion during 1978-1990, in accordance with Trade and Development Board resolution 165 (S-IX).

---

11 One recent suggestion (made with European countries in mind) is that creditors should qualify for tax deductions on their loan-loss provisions only to the extent that they participate in debt reduction packages. Another (made with the United States in mind) is that creditors who fail to participate in debt reduction packages sanctioned by IMF and the World Bank should be required to make special provisions on their loans and should not be eligible to tax relief on losses.

12 Creditors initially offered the Toronto terms to sub-Saharan African countries included in the World Bank's Special Programme of Assistance (SPA), most of them least developed countries; 18 of these African countries have so far benefited from this initiative. In 1990, this treatment was extended to countries outside sub-Saharan Africa (Bolivia and Guyana).

13 For the 17 African countries benefiting from the Toronto terms in 1989 and 1990, the additional cash flow savings totaled roughly $100 million on an annual basis, about 1.5 per cent of scheduled debt service. For a more detailed discussion of the Toronto agreement and its implementation see UNCTAD, Trade and Development Report, 1989, box 7, and UNCTAD, "Debt and managing adjustment: attracting non-debt-creating financial flows and new lending" (TD/B/C.3/234), paras. 15-21.

108.   Since the onset of the debt crisis, the frequency of Paris Club meetings (where debt owed to OECD Governments is usually rescheduled) has increased steadily: 21 agreements a year were signed on average in 1989-1990, against 16 in the previous six years. The amounts consolidated grew from an annual average of $5 billion in 1984-1985 to $17 billion in 1989-1990. The majority of rescheduling countries came repeatedly to the Paris Club. This acceleration in official debt re-scheduling is a symptom of both the protracted nature of the problems of many debtor countries and the short-term approach of the Paris Club, whereby the consolidation period (the period in which debt service payments to be rescheduled fall due) has been - until recently - typically 12-18 months. Moreover, debt service due on previously rescheduled debt accounted for an increased share of the consolidated amount, reflecting the inadequacy of the terms of the original reschedu-ling agreements. In addition, there were several new rescheduling countries - 12 since 1988, a figure which far exceeds that of debtors which have graduated from the Paris Club in recent years. For most rescheduling countries, debt relief from the Paris Club has become the largest source of exceptional external financing.

109.   Paris Club practices have substantially improved in recent years, most notably following the Toronto agreement of June 1988 which provided official creditors with a range of options re-garding the official bilateral debt owed by low-income countries:[12] partial forgiveness of debt ser-vice; longer repayment periods; and concessional interest rates. The Toronto agreement marked a major advance in the debt strategy, in that for the first time creditor Governments recognized the need for concessional relief with regard to non-concessional official debt.

110.   Application of the Toronto terms has revealed a number of shortcomings. The scale of relief they give rise to is extremely limited. The combined grant element of the three options is 20 per cent, one-third of the average grant element in new official loan commitments recently ex-tended to severely indebted low-income countries.[13]

111.   Another reason for the limited scope of the measures is that only debt service payments falling due during short consolidation periods benefited from the new terms, with the result that repeated reschedulings, which are time-consuming, remained necessary. Moreover, creditors have financed the cost of debt relief by transferring funds from their aid budgets, thus reducing the additionality resulting from the Toronto measures.

112.   Growing recognition of the inadequacy of the Toronto terms led some creditor countries to put forward bold proposals giving further impetus to the principle of debt reduction for low-income countries. At the Second United Nations Conference on the Least Developed Countries in September 1990, the Netherlands called for the cancellation of all official bilateral debt owed by the least developed and other low-income countries facing severe debt problems. Shortly thereafter, at the meeting of Commonwealth Finance Ministers held in Trinidad, the United Kingdom proposed that Paris Club creditors should cancel two-thirds of the stock of debt owed by eligible countries in a single operation, with the remaining debt rescheduled over 25 years (in-cluding 5 years of grace) and interest payments capitalized for the first 5 years. The proposal also suggests a flexible repayment schedule linked to the debtor country's export capacity. Eligibility for this scheme, known as the Trinidad terms, would be the same as for the Toronto terms.

113.   The London summit of the Group of 7 agreed that there was a need for additional debt relief measures for the poorest countries "going well beyond the relief already granted under Toronto terms". There are, however, a number of issues that need to be settled:

• The scale of debt reduction. Implementation of the British proposal would go far towards reconciling debt-service obligations of many of the potential beneficiaries with their capacity to pay. For several beneficiaries, however, debt burdens would still remain too high.[14] Official creditors - both within and outside the Paris Club - could treat the two-thirds debt reduction as a benchmark and take additional measures for them, such as a higher percentage of debt reduction (up to 100 per cent, as advocated by the Dutch proposal) and increased ODA flows. For some countries, concessional refinancing of multilateral debt service and commercial bank debt reduction would also be required.

• The modalities of debt reduction and related policy conditionality. Debt reduction is most effective if it is implemented in a single operation, thus removing once and for all the investment disincentives associated with the debt overhang and the uncertainties generated

---

[14] For a detailed analysis of the Trinidad terms, see TDR 1991, Box 4, pp.54-55.

by repeated rescheduling. If instead a policy of "tranching" is adopted, creditors' commitment to an overall amount of debt reduction should be made explicit from the start and the lion's share of total forgiveness given "upfront".

- Eligibility criteria. The intended beneficiaries appear to be those currently eligible for Toronto terms (i.e. debt-distressed IDA-only countries undertaking IMF adjustment programmes). Eligibility criteria should be widened to include all heavily indebted countries that are IDA recipients, even if they borrow from IBRD. Consideration should also be given to avoiding moral hazard by attending to the needs of those countries that have managed to meet their debt-service obligations, but only barely and at a high cost.

114. The official debt burden also poses a serious problem to a number of middle-income countries and has recently received increased attention from creditor countries. Following bilateral initiatives by France and the United States[15] and the recommendations of the Houston Summit in July 1990, the Paris Club began to apply a more favourable treatment to lower middle-income countries with high levels of official debt (Houston terms). These terms involve primarily larger maturities and grace periods and not debt reduction (apart from a limited amount of voluntary debt swaps).[16] Important advances involving significant debt reduction have been made in the treatment of the official bilateral debt of Poland and Egypt. In April-May 1991, official creditors agreed to reduce by 50 per cent the entire stock of eligible (i.e. pre-cutoff date) Paris Club debt owed by these two countries.[17]

115. These deals - which creditors have described as exceptional - constitute a major step forward in the international debt strategy by introducing the concept of official debt reduction for middle-income countries and by applying the reduction to the entire stock of debt. Furthermore, the size of debt forgiveness - about $24 billion for the two deals combined - is extraordinarily large. It is equivalent to over twice the aggregate amount of ODA debt cancellations granted by OECD countries during the past 13 years. It is to be hoped that the debt reduction needs of other middle-income countries whose burden of official bilateral debt is excessively onerous will not be ignored.

(c) Multilateral debt

116. For many developing countries, especially for the low-income category, multilateral debt represents an important share of their total debt. The increasingly large service on this debt has contributed to the sharp decline in net financial transfers from multilateral financial institutions (MFIs) and a number of debtor countries have accumulated sizeable arrears with the MFIs. The Bretton Woods institutions, in particular, have become part of the debt problem.

---

15 In June 1990, President Mitterrand announced measures to lower interest rates on non-concessional loans by France to four middle-income countries of sub-Saharan Africa (Cameroon, Congo, Côte d'Ivoire, and Gabon). At the same time, President Bush launched a programme aimed at reducing the official debt obligations of Latin American countries to the United States, within the framework of the "Enterprise for the Americas" initiative dealing with the region's trade, investment and debt. The debt reduction programme of the United States envisages a substantial cancellation of concessional loans and the payment of interest in local currency which may be used to support environmental projects. Furthermore, a portion of non-concessional official loans (such as export credits) would be sold in the market in order to facilitate the conversion of debt into equity and debt-for-nature swaps.

16 Under the Houston terms, official development assistance (ODA) loans are rescheduled with a 20-year maturity, including up to 10 years of grace and export credits and official loans other than ODA are rescheduled with a 15-year maturity and up to 8 years of grace. In conventional reschedulings, the maturity and grace period are normally 10 and 5 years, respectively. The Houston terms also include, as a major innovation, the possibility for creditor governments to sell or swap ODA loans as well as a limited amount of non-concessional credits (usually 10 per cent of the outstanding claims or $10 million, whichever is higher) through debt for nature, debt for aid, debt for equity, or other local currency debt conversions. To date, Congo, El Salvador, Honduras, Morocco and Nigeria have benefited from this initiative.

17 The debt reduction will be effected through a menu of options, including principal reduction, interest reduction, and partial interest capitalization on concessional terms. In addition, creditor countries agreed to a voluntary debt swap facility, which could include up to an additional 10 per cent of outstanding claims. For Poland, the debt reduction will occur in two stages: 30 per cent "upfront" and 20 per cent after three years. For Egypt, the reduction will take place in three stages: 15 per cent "upfront", 15 per cent after 18 months, and 20 per cent after three years. In both cases, the implementation of the stages following the "upfront" reduction is conditional upon successful completion of an IMF arrangement.

117.   The MFIs have taken some measures to alleviate the burden of multilateral debt service and thus help avoid arrears. In 1988, the World Bank decided to put aside 10 per cent of repayments to IDA to help IDA-eligible countries pay their interest on debt owed to the International Bank for Reconstruction and Development (IBRD), which was contracted at market rates. A number of donor countries provided additional resources for this purpose. IMF introduced the Structural Adjustment Facility (SAF) and the Enhanced Structural Adjustment Facility (ESAF) to provide balance-of-payments assistance on concessional terms to low-income countries.

118.   However, it has been necessary to take further measures to deal with the problem of already existing arrears to the Fund. Under the "intensified, collaborative approach", additional resources from developed members were mobilized through support groups to help those debtor developing countries in arrears to the Fund that were willing to adopt corrective measures. The success of the scheme was limited, as only two countries (Guyana and Honduras) cleared their arrears with IMF under this approach. In 1990, IMF adopted the "rights" approach, under which a member with massive and protracted arrears could earn "rights" - based on sustained performance during the period of a multiyear "rights accumulation" programme monitored by IMF - towards future financing up to the equivalent of arrears outstanding at the outset of the programme. The "rights" approach constitutes a major advance in dealing with multilateral debt problems, as under it multilateral arrears, which in principle cannot be rescheduled, may be indirectly rescheduled. However, the implementation of this scheme, which also requires medium-term financing from a support group, has proved to be extremely cumbersome and time-consuming. To date Zambia and Peru alone have benefited from the new approach. Among the problems encountered have been the absence of a scheme dealing with arrears to the World Bank, and the financial burden arising from originally scheduled debt-servicing obligations to the Fund falling due during the programme period (including interest payments on frozen arrears).

119.   The issue of arrears with MFIs is one aspect of the global debt problem that should continue to be tackled in a co-operative spirit and through a growth-oriented approach. The priorities in this respect are a substantial increase in net transfers from multilateral financial institutions, enhanced effectiveness of the "rights" approach, including more expeditious resource mobilization by support groups, and urgent implementation of the measures recommended by the Second United Nations Conference on the Least Developed Countries. These measures could include the strengthening and widening of existing mechanisms, such as interest rate subsidies or refinancing schemes funded by reflows or special trust funds.[18] In particular, the World Bank's interest subsidy scheme would need additional resources to cover not only all interest owed by eligible countries but also the concessional refinancing of IBRD principal payments. Furthermore, the African Development Bank could consider establishing a similar interest subsidy programme.

2. The external financing of development

(a) Recent trends

120.   The 1980s witnessed far-reaching changes in the volume and structure of financial flows to developing countries as well as in the policies of official and private creditors.[19] Following sharp declines from 1982 to 1987 and despite some recovery since then, in 1990 net external flows to developing countries were, in real terms, about 40 per cent below the level reached in 1981 (see table I-1). This fall was accompanied by persistently high interest payments, thus resulting in the contraction of net financial transfers and the emergence of negative net transfers in many debtor countries, especially in the heavily indebted middle-income countries. As shown in table I-2, capital-importing developing countries as a whole have experienced negative net transfers on an

---

18 See the Paris Declaration and Programme of Action of the Second United Nations Conference on the Least Developed Countries (A/Conf.147/Misc.9), paras. 42-45.

19 For a detailed analysis of external financing of development in the 1980s and the 1990s, see UNCTAD, The external financing of development, (TD/B/C.3/235), 16 February 1990.

unprecedented scale, averaging approximately $20 billion annually over the period 1983-90.[20] While part of this amount is attributable to the recent surplus economies of Asia (Hong Kong, Republic of Korea, Singapore and Taiwan, Province of China), the bulk of it was accounted for by countries that could not afford to transfer resources abroad because of their relatively low level of income. This widespread phenomenon represents a clear reversal of the past relationship between external finance and growth in which positive net transfers allowed investment to exceed the levels which would have been permitted by the volume of domestic savings alone.

121. The resource losses caused by the shift in levels of net transfers have required a substantial adjustment of trade balances. Export volumes have been raised considerably, especially in middle-income countries, but the scale and pace of adjustment required has made it impossible to avoid drastic import cuts. In many heavily indebted countries, the adjustment to the large swings in net transfers has been made more difficult by the depressed state of primary commodity prices. The resulting deterioration in the terms of trade has raised the real cost of servicing external debt.

122. Another fundamental change in development finance was the sharp fall in private flows, and the concomitant rise in the share of official flows. By 1990, these accounted for slightly over one half of total flows, as compared to one-third in 1981. However, the absolute level of official finance has been virtually stagnant in real terms over the decade.

123. The precipitous fall in commercial bank lending in response to the debt crisis was the single most important factor accounting for the overall contraction of financial flows to developing countries and the large negative net transfers. Since 1982, bank creditors received a net transfer from developing countries averaging $26 billion annually, the bulk of which came from Latin America. In 1989 and 1990 net bank lending recovered somewhat, mostly as a result of increased loans to Asian countries, concerted lending under the Brady plan and some spontaneous loans to a few heavily indebted countries. Net flows of export credits also contracted sharply during the 1980s. After a number of consecutive years of negative flows, export credits recovered to a positive level in 1989-1990 largely reflecting increases in short-term credits. Following a sharp fall in the mid-1980s, foreign direct investment (FDI) registered a strong increase since 1987, although below expectations in the case of many heavily indebted countries.

124. Official development assistance (ODA) has remained the backbone of development finance, accounting for approximately 40 per cent of total net flows in 1990. It has therefore, been a matter of concern that concessional flows virtually stagnated in real terms during the 1980s. The bulk of ODA (roughly 90 per cent during recent years) is provided by DAC member countries. Flows from these countries during the period 1982-1990 rose at an annual rate of about 3 per cent in real terms, an increase which roughly matched their GNP growth and which was barely sufficient to offset the decline in aid from OPEC and Eastern European countries. Thus, DAC countries' aid effort - measured by the ODA/GNP ratio - has not improved over the past decade, remaining virtually constant at a level of 0.33 per cent.

125. The direct contribution of the Bretton Woods institutions in meeting the financial needs of developing countries has been disappointing. Net transfers from IMF to developing countries have become largely negative, averaging over $5 billion annually during the period 1985-1990. At the same time, net transfers from the World Bank (IBRD and IDA) have continuously declined from a level of $4.4 billion in 1985 to $0.4 billion in 1990, while net transfers from IBRD alone turned negative by 1987 and reached - $4 billion in 1990. Financial transfers from multilateral financial institutions have, thus, sharply declined along with those from private sources, rather than acting as a cushion to the adverse impact of the latter.

126. The global trends described above had an uneven impact on the various regions. The swing in net transfers and the corresponding external adjustment have been particularly pronounced in

---

[20] Net financial transfer is defined as the difference between net capital inflows and net factor income payments, such as interest payments and profit remittances. It is the same size, but with opposite sign, as the balance of trade in goods and non-factor services. This concept of net financial transfer differs from the concept used by OECD. First, the OECD's net financial transfers pertain to flows provided by foreign donors and creditors and their servicing. Thus, transactions on assets held abroad by developing countries are not taken into account. Secondly, OECD includes in net transfers some items related to development co-operation that do not appear in the balance of payments of recipient countries. The largest of such item is technical assistance. Finally, OECD's concept is based on the convention to treat IMF lending as a monetary or reserve-related phenomenon and exclude it from statistics on development financing and debt. For a detailed account of different concepts of net financial transfers, See United Nations, *World Economic Survey 1990*, box IV.1, pp 79-81.

Latin America. During 1982-1990, the region experienced negative net transfers, equivalent to $25 billion a year, against positive transfers averaging $12 billion a year during 1973-1981. In sub-Saharan Africa, despite strenuous efforts and special donors' initiatives to mobilize additional resources in view of the region's economic plight, net resource flows have stagnated in real terms since 1985, at levels well below the peak reached in 1982. Aggregate net transfers remained positive, albeit reduced. In Asia, the financial picture has become increasingly complex and varied. The newly industrializing economies have transferred resources abroad, as a result of their growing economic maturity associated with a strong trade and savings performance. A number of countries in South-East Asia spontaneously reduced their reliance on external finance, as a consequence of enhanced export capacity and prudent borrowing policy. By contrast, India and China became large recipients of external finance, particularly private flows, for most of the decade.

127.   The global changes in the level and composition of financial flows were inextricably linked to the unfolding of the debt crisis. Since 1982, a close interaction emerged between the availability of external finance and the debt-servicing difficulties experienced by developing countries - particularly those heavily dependent on private flows. An initial decline in net financial flows exacerbated debt-servicing problems which, in turn, discouraged new inflows. The debt crisis had adverse consequences also for official development finance. Countries that were forced to build up arrears to the multilateral financing institutions because of their acute debt problems were barred from borrowing from these institutions. A number of donors applied the same policy to countries that had accumulated arrears on their bilateral debt. More important, deteriorating economic conditions in many highly indebted middle-income countries (HICs) and delays in policy-based loan negotiations negatively affected the volume of non-concessional multilateral flows. However, the adverse impact of the debt crisis on financial flows was somewhat attenuated by the efforts made by the World Bank and the IMF to raise additional funds, particularly for debt-distressed sub-Saharan African countries.

128.   Capital flight was an additional factor that adversely affected external resource availability in the 1980s. Although capital flight appears to have declined significantly over the past few years, it is a manifestation of financial disorder and again intimately linked to the debt-servicing difficulties experienced by developing countries. Capital flight is thus unlikely to be reversed in a significant fashion until a durable solution to the debt crisis is found.

129.   The debt crisis explains two other important features that characterized development finance during the 1980s: debt rescheduling and adjustment lending. The pervasiveness of the debt problem was such that debt rescheduling, once an isolated, one-off mechanism designed to overcome a temporary liquidity problem, became an entrenched key feature of the international financial system. During the period 1987-1990, debt rescheduling provided, on average, cash flow relief of $36 billion a year - slightly exceeding debt-service payments by all developing countries with recent debt-servicing difficulties.

130.   At the same time, adjustment lending expanded considerably, with a growing volume of external assistance, including debt rescheduling, becoming conditional on the macro-economic performance and structural reforms in recipient countries. In the evolution of adjustment lending and the associated policy dialogue, a number of fundamental questions have arisen concerning the scope of this dialogue and the necessary conditions for securing its success. Through the process of adjustment lending and its linkage to debt reschedulings, the IMF and the World Bank became the linchpin of the development finance system, and non-project financial assistance played an increasingly important role in both multilateral and bilateral activities.

131.   There is a broad agreement that thorough adjustment and reforms in many developing countries are necessary in order to restore growth and engage in a sustainable development process, notably by fostering a vigorous and competitive export sector. However, progress achieved in adjustment and restoration of growth has been mixed. For many countries that have implemented structural adjustment programmes, reductions of inflation and external deficits have been achieved at the expense of setbacks in investment and growth. Adjustment programmes have also produced a negative social impact in several countries, as a result of economic recession and cuts in Government social expenditure. Different views have been expressed on the types of policies and means through which structural changes can be brought about and on the pace of their implementation. It has also been pointed out that particular attention needs to be paid to the specific economic and social environment facing each country and to the interaction of measures aiming

at longer-term reform and short-term macro-economic balances.[21]

132.   The linkage between the World Bank's adjustment loans and IMF facilities has given rise to a significant expansion in informal cross-conditionality, especially in low-income countries where both institutions use the same policy variables in their programmes. This practice has led to concerns regarding possible concerted pressure on the borrowing country and the emergence of a kind of "cartelization" among lenders. Fears have also been expressed over the risk of progressive extension of Fund control over Bank lending, which could cause undue delays in financial support.

(b)   Financing requirements in the 1990s

133.   During the 1990s, the system of international financial co-operation will confront a number of key challenges. One of the priorities is to support efforts to restore growth and macro-economic stability in developing countries afflicted by the debt overhang. This objective would require both policy reform and increased domestic resource mobilization in debt-distressed countries as well as a return to positive net financial transfers. For the next several years, these countries are not likely to be in a position to finance the increased investment necessary to resume sustained growth out of their domestic savings alone. Growth-oriented adjustment will thus require a much higher level of external financing. At the same time, the external capital needs of the developing countries that were able to avoid the debt crisis should not be neglected. In addition, special efforts are required to redress the backsliding that occurred in the 1980s in key areas such as food security, poverty reduction, human resource development and infrastructure, and to provide adequate external financing for environmental conservation measures. International financial co-operation has recently been faced with a new set of important tasks: to respond to the financing needs of the countries most seriously affected by the Gulf crisis; and to help finance the external capital requirements of the reforming countries in Eastern Europe in a way which will be compatible with strengthened financial support to developing countries.

(i)   Repercussions of the recent Gulf crisis

134.   The Gulf conflict has had both global and specific economic repercussions on developing countries. The crisis, particularly the period of high oil prices, has adversely affected world growth, and thus growth in the developing countries. The impact of physical destruction in Iraq and Kuwait will be felt for generations. The reconstruction needs of the Gulf countries will require a concerted effort of all the countries in the region within the framework of economic co-operation fostering trade and other economic interlinkages, including multinational projects in such sectors as transport, water, energy and the environment. This approach has received strong political impetus from the London summit in July 1991. Sources of financing are or should be available within the area, both where national savings are traditionally in excess of domestic requirements and from the progressive reduction of military expenditure flowing from lower tensions. In addition, external bilateral and multilateral finance would be indispensable.

135.   A large number of developing countries outside the Gulf area have also been hurt by the recent conflict, and some of them severely, through the combined effects of higher oil-import costs, reduced worker remittances and tourism receipts, costs arising from the resettlement of repatriated workers, and lost export markets. The aggregate size of these shocks on affected countries has been estimated at $22 billion for 1990 and 1991.[22] The adverse impact of the Gulf crisis would certainly be felt by many of these countries for many years to come. To be sure, the affected countries themselves will have to reinforce domestic measures to adjust to these costs. The international community has promptly responded to these requirements, but additional external resources need to be mobilized, so that the costs of all affected countries are adequately compensated

---

21   See conclusions of the informal group of competent personalities convened by the Secretary-General of UNCTAD in September 1989 in the context of the Trade and Development Board review of interdependence (TD B L.864). For further analysis of adjustment programmes, see the Secretary-General's report to UNCTAD VIII (chapter I, section 11A) and section A (Domestic resources mobilization in developing countries) of this chapter.

22   See World Bank, *Financial Flows to Developing Countries*, March 1991, pp.20 and 21.

over the medium run.[23] These resources should be lodged in a multilateral framework and based on strictly economic criteria.

(ii) The impact of reforms in Eastern Europe

136. Economic and social restructuring in Eastern European countries and the Soviet Union, and their progressive integration into the world economy will require new inflows of financial resources in convertible currencies on an unprecedented scale. The size and timing of the financial needs will naturally depend on the scope, sequencing and tempo of the reforms, as well as on domestic efforts aimed at maintaining high savings propensity in the face of strong pressures to increase consumption. These historic events have raised two important issues for the international community: how to integrate Eastern European countries into the international financial system with no or minimum stress on the system; and how to meet their large and growing capital needs without diverting resources from developing countries.

137. The first issue is related to the more general question of the adequacy of global savings. Much concern has recently been expressed that developed countries will not prove sufficiently thrifty to meet the new demands for financing from Eastern Europe, the Middle East and elsewhere without adding to pressures on interest rates and to the financial difficulties of indebted developing countries. The fear that global savings will necessarily become increasingly scarce appears, however, to be unfounded. For one thing, there is ample scope to reduce military spending, the rationale of which is being rapidly eroded by the end of the Cold War. For another, the cost of investment goods has been falling sharply thanks to rapid technical progress. Moreover, household savings behaviour has not in reality been worsening, despite some appearances to the contrary.

138. Besides, when, as is frequently the case, the level of overall demand is insufficient to allow the world's productive potential to be fully utilized, investment can be stepped up without Governments and households having first to cut their consumption, since the investment itself will create the required savings by generating additional income. It is therefore more pertinent to focus on the factors presently constraining investment and pushing up interest rates, in particular the organization of the financial system and its impact on the cost and supply of finance.

139. Both financial institutions and Governments now face the challenge of overcoming structural weaknesses in the international financial system. In the meantime, however, stresses and strains are likely to prevent the world's production potential from being fully utilized for some time. Until it is, the constraint on financing development will not be the supply of real resources but the institutional capacity to generate finance. One way of tackling the problem is to renew SDR allocations and "link" them to development finance. Japan has recently proposed a new SDR allocation of $20 billion over 10 years, with developed countries contributing this allocation to the IMF for on-lending to developing countries. This proposal deserves serious consideration.[24]

140. Turning to the second issue, the impact of Eastern European reforms on financial flows to developing countries is likely to differ considerably depending on the nature of these flows, basically on whether they are official or private. In the case of private flows, such as commercial bank loans and foreign direct investment, supply-side considerations play a minor role, as both banks and foreign investors have generally easy access to international capital markets to fund their operations. In any event, the commercial banks have recently shown reticence to increase their exposure in many countries in the region, because of their debt servicing problems and other difficulties encountered in transforming their economies. Similarly, flows of foreign direct investment - while having increased dramatically - are, and will remain for quite some time, comparatively small, despite the great potential offered by these countries.

141. Under these circumstances, it is likely that official lenders, both bilateral and multilateral,

---

23 The Gulf Crisis Financial Co-ordinating Committee has made aid pledges equivalent to about $16 billion to help developing countries which are most affected by the crisis through the end of 1991. (Three quarters of this amount has already been allocated to three countries). Some additional finance is expected from the World Bank and the IMF.

24 For a broader analysis of the adequacy of global savings, see TDR 1991, pp 87-99.

25 See Declaration of Ministers of the "Group of 24 for Economic Assistance to Poland and Hungary", 13 December 1989.

would have to play a major role in ensuring that adequate external financing is available in the short and medium-term. OECD Governments have already formulated a significant response to the financial requirements of reforming countries. From mid-1989 to mid-1991, financial commitments made by OECD countries and multilateral institutions to Eastern European countries (excluding USSR) amounted to $31 billion. Of this amount, about $8 billion was in the form of grants, in addition to the $16.5 billion in official bilateral debt reduction accorded to Poland by the Paris Club.

142.   In the case of official flows, supply constraints are paramount, especially with regard to bilateral ODA, which depends on annual budgetary allocations. Unsurprisingly, considerable discussion - in both developed and developing countries - has focused on the extent to which concessional bilateral assistance to reforming countries might divert resources from traditional aid recipients, which already face stagnant ODA and much reduced private flows. Concern over this issue has led to repeated reassurances by DAC member countries that the support to Eastern Europe will not diminish their determination to give high priority to their development co-operation with the third world. At the same time, "some Ministers foresee the possibility of also having recourse, within such assistance programmes, to official development aid funds while safe-guarding flows to traditional recipients of official development aid".[25]

143.   Nevertheless, there have already been some derogations, albeit modest, from the principle of additionality.[26] It is widely recognized that, at least in the short run, there is a risk of diversion of funds from development aid budgets, especially in donor countries where the budgetary situation is particularly tight. Every effort should be made to avoid a situation where additional concessional funds to Eastern Europe come at the expense of existing levels of ODA or its "growth" portion. True additionality could be ensured by careful monitoring and co-ordination at the multilateral level. Estimates should be made of additional flows required so as to arrive at an assessment of potential shortfalls. However, once the critical initial phase of reforms is completed, bilateral aid from OECD countries is likely to be increasingly in the form of technical assistance rather than financial support, while most external flows going to Eastern Europe are expected to be non-concessional, as in the case of developing countries at similar income levels. Nevertheless, there is a risk that the transition period and the need for substantial concessional support from the OECD countries may be more prolonged than currently anticipated.

144.   With regard to multilateral flows, the issue that arises is whether a massive lending programme for Eastern Europe could be accommodated within the existing lending limits of multilateral institutions without "crowding out" planned financial assistance to developing country members. In the near term, the World Bank has some leeway to expand total lending with existing resources. But the need for a general capital increase might soon arise in order to meet the much expanded financial requirements of a larger membership, especially when the USSR becomes a full member. Under that scenario, however, most of the OECD contributions to the capital increase of the Bank will be in the form of callable capital, that is guarantees, rather than cash. These guarantees will allow the Bank to increase its borrowing from international capital markets where, in contrast to foreign aid, supply constraints are much less important. In the case of the IMF, these considerations call for a quick ratification of the quota increase under the ninth general review and an early start to the tenth review.

145.   One of the most immediate repercussions of the changes in Eastern European countries has been on the official development assistance provided by them to developing countries. At present, this aid has been drastically reduced or abandoned. Moreover, the substantial economic assistance provided in the form of large implicit trade subsidies has virtually disappeared. A number of developing countries are suffering from these developments. As the Committee for Development Planning has recently recommended, the international community should urgently consider special programmes of assistance for developing countries experiencing severe adjustment problems as a result of the reforms in Eastern Europe.[27]

---

26 See United Nations, Report of the Committee on Development Planning on its twenty-seventh session (E 1991 32 dated 13 June 1991), paras 89-90.

27 See Committee for Development Planning, *op.cit.* para 16.

28 See UNDP, *Human Development Report 1991*, p.81.

(iii)   The adequacy of official development finance

146.   Given the increasing demand pressures on international financial co-operation, fundamental questions arise regarding the adequacy of the supply of official development finance. Official flows will have to remain the principal component of development finance in the 1990s since a substantial return of private capital to developing countries is unlikely, especially in view of the expected behaviour of commercial banks. But prospects for official finance are poor, especially for ODA. Aid is not a large claimant on budgetary resources of DAC countries. In recent years, it has accounted for about 1.3 per cent of central government expenditures in these countries, and half of that amount in the United States. Nevertheless, ODA from DAC countries is expected to grow at best by 2 per cent in real terms over the next few years, given the poor outlook for the aid budget of the United States (which has fallen to 0.15 per cent of GNP) and despite the substantial increase in aid volume expected to come from Japan and France. Thus, on present indications the overall ODA/GNP ratio for DAC countries is likely to remain at 0.33 per cent, less than half the internationally agreed target of 0.7 per cent. The outlook for aid from non-DAC donors, notably Eastern European countries and OPEC (which in 1989 still accounted for slightly over 10 per cent of global ODA) is even bleaker, in the light of recent events.

147.   Prospects for multilateral concessional assistance are also unfavourable. The ninth IDA replenishment implies no increase in real terms over the resources of IDA-8. But the unabated debt crisis, commodity price declines and the urgent need for further structural adjustment have considerably raised recipients' requirements. At the same time, stagnant IDA resources have to accommodate the needs of several newly eligible low-income countries from sub-Saharan Africa, such as Nigeria, and a number of lower-middle income countries from Latin America and Asia, which have suffered from steep declines in per capita incomes. Strenuous, urgent efforts are required in order to avoid a situation where concessional support for new recipients is made at the expense of low-income countries already heavily dependent on IDA resources.

148.   There are, however, a number of positive aspects to the generally sombre ODA picture. The Lomé IV agreement provides for a substantial increase in resources over Lomé III. It is also encouraging to note that at the Second United Nations Conference on the Least Developed Countries, donors committed themselves to a significant and substantial increase in resource flows to LDCs and adopted alternative undertakings to this end, which include moving more rapidly towards to 0.15 per cent target and also incorporate the new target of 0.20 per cent of GNP as ODA to LDCs. Furthermore, under the recent extension of the Special Programme of Assistance for low-income countries of sub-Saharan Africa, bilateral donors have pledged up to $8 billion in co-financing, a substantial increase over previous commitments.

149.   A clearly positive dimension of changes in Eastern Europe is the end of the Cold War. This should result in a "peace dividend" - a reduction in arms expenditures resulting from the relaxation of East-West tensions - which could be used, at least in part, for development. ODA from OECD countries is equivalent to only 5 per cent of their military expenditures. If such expenditures could be reduced by 2-4 per cent a year during the 1990s, this would generate savings of $200 billion a year by 1995. An earmarking for aid of 25 per cent of these savings would result in a doubling of DAC aid to close to 0.7 per cent of donors' GNP.[28]

150.   Assessing the future adequacy of non-concessional multilateral resources has become a difficult task, because of their increasing complementarity with private flows and debt reduction operations. The main issue here is the extent to which lending from the multilateral financial institutions (MFIs) to the highly indebted middle income countries (HICs) can safely increase in the absence of further considerable reduction in debt owed to commercial banks and bilateral creditors, without jeopardizing MFIs' ability to provide adequate financing to other borrowers and their own creditworthiness.

151.   With the implementation of the Brady plan, the Bretton Woods institutions are playing an increasingly important role in the strengthened debt strategy. In this context, concerns have been raised as to the uneven burden-sharing between the official sector and the commercial banks. It may be argued, however, that massive bank lending in the 1970s was a historical aberration, and what is currently taking place is not only a transfer of risks from the private to the official sector but, more important, a transfer of tasks. The capital markets' reluctance to lend to the HICs may also be viewed as a temporary market failure, which strengthens the case for a greater role for official flows until creditworthiness is restored. The multilateral institutions have a special commitment to assist developing countries in restoring growth and financial viability, a commitment that

private lenders do not have. The challenge is how to strike the right balance between the increased exposure of the official creditors and the losses incurred by private creditors. Such a balance should contribute to both a major improvement in the HICs' creditworthiness and the preservation of the MFIs' credit-standing.

152. A related issue is how the IMF can play a significant role in reducing - rather than increasing - negative net transfers in developing countries generally. The crucial question is whether the IMF should be withdrawing resources from borrowing countries before the process of external adjustment with growth has been completed. While the revolving nature of the Fund's resources should be respected, the period over which such resources ought to revolve should depend on the wider nature of the persistent, structural imbalances facing member countries.

153. If the volume of net financial transfers from official sources is not adequate, the existing pattern of exceptional finance is likely to persist. Heavily indebted countries would first be forced to accumulate arrears in order to finance their current account deficits and later seek to reschedule such arrears, thus postponing for several additional years the restoration of orderly debtor-creditor relations.

(iv) Aid effectiveness

154. The shortage of aid funds has focused attention on the need for enhancing aid effectiveness and channelling an increased share of aid flows towards such priority tasks as human development and poverty reduction.

155. Factors affecting aid effectiveness originate from both recipient and donor sides. On the recipient side, shortcomings in providing a stable policy environment which would encourage long-term investment and increase its efficiency have reduced effectiveness in the use of aid. A number of countries have also failed to ensure good governance entailing an efficient public service, a reliable legal framework to enforce contracts and an administration that is accountable to its public.

156. On the donor side, the factors impairing aid effectiveness have included shortcomings in the co-ordination process, the tying of aid, and the importance given in some cases to objectives other than the genuine promotion of long-term development. Moreover, in several instances aid provided in the form of technical assistance - which represents one quarter of total ODA granted by DAC member countries - did not contribute adequately to capacity-building or institutional development of recipient countries.

157. An effort has been made in co-ordinating aid from bilateral and multilateral donors through the mechanisms of consultative groups and round-table meetings. However, problems in this area remain, which weaken the aid-coordination process and call for corrective measures.[29] First, there is a need for the co-ordination process to be based on better-formulated development strategies over a longer period. Secondly, the role of recipient countries in the process should be strengthened. Thirdly, the development assistance programme and practices of donor agencies should be effectively directed to building the institutional and managerial capacities of recipient countries. Fourthly, the follow-up and joint monitoring system should be enhanced.

158. There is also a need for an integrated approach to debt relief and aid efforts. This calls for closer co-ordination between the Paris Club and donors' groups. This has become more urgent because since the adoption of the Toronto terms the Paris Club has been empowered to extend concessional assistance. Several proposals have been made to merge the fragmented and cumbersome activities of the Paris Club and consultative groups or round-tables for low-income countries, so that the need for debt relief and new flows can be assessed in a holistic fashion. These proposals deserve serious consideration.[30]

---

[29] See Devandra Raj Panday and Maurice Williams, "Aid Co-ordination and aid-effectiveness: least developed countries 1981-1989" - study prepared for the Second United Nations on the Least Developed Countries (UNCLDC II/4, 8 March 1990).

[30] See UNCTAD "Review of the implementation of the guidelines contained in Board resolution 222 (XXI)", (TD/B/1167), 12 February 1988, paras 70-71, C. Lancaster, *African Economic Reforms: The External Dimension*, Institute for International Economics, Washington, D.C., 1991; and "Abidjan Declaration on Debt Relief Recovery and Democracy in Africa", by Parliamentarians from Africa and Northern countries, 9 July 1991.

159.   Attention has also been increasingly paid to reforms in aid policies in order to effectively support strategies for poverty reduction.[31] Such strategies would encompass measures to expand income-earning opportunities for the poor, to enhance human resource development (notably by increasing the allocation of funds to social sectors such as education, health, nutrition), and to provide safety nets for the vulnerable groups in the population. Implementation of these measures would accordingly require changes in the sectoral composition and country allocation of aid, increased financing of local and recurrent expenditures, and untying of aid.

160.   Donors are increasingly emphasizing the need for participatory development in developing countries, including broad-based economic growth and equity, protection of human rights and improvement of governmental effectiveness.[32] This new emphasis has raised fears over the possible adverse effects of "political conditionality". However, the developing countries themselves recognize that good governance is essential for economic and social progress for all countries. At the Second United Nations Conference on the Least Developed Countries, it was unanimously agreed that "all countries should broaden popular participation in the development process. Respect of human rights .... along with democratization and observance of the rule of law, is a part of the process of development".[33] At the same time, consensus was achieved on the respective roles of recipient countries and the international community in meeting these goals: "Each particular country may therefore freely determine its own ways of advancing towards this established objective. It also entails a realization that any progress in this direction should be encouraged and supported by the international community, through development co-operation efforts among development partners".[34]

3.   Promotion of non-debt-creating flows

(a)   Recent developments

161.   Since the onset of the debt crisis, developing countries have made considerable efforts to improve the policy environment for foreign direct investment (FDI) and other forms of equity and quasi-equity finance. These actions included the liberalization of guidelines on FDI, introduction of privatisation programmes, debt-equity swaps and other debt reduction arrangements. Their objectives have been to expand rapidly the role of FDI as a means of redressing the imbalance between debt-creating and non-debt-creating flows, and to compensate in part for the sharp decline in commercial bank lending. These efforts reflect a growing feeling that FDI has strategic advantages in its ability to combine project finance, technology and markets, and they have received substantial support from a number of developed countries and the multilateral financial institutions.

162.   The result has been a marked improvement in the investment climate in developing countries and a recovery in the volume of net FDI flows. In real terms, net FDI flows to developing countries in 1990 represented a three-fold increase from the trough registered in 1985 (see table I-2). However, these flows were only about 10 per cent above their 1981 level. In addition, FDI flows to developing countries were highly concentrated in a few destinations in Asia and Latin America. Brazil, China, Malaysia and Mexico received about half of these flows over the last 10 years. As a result, most severely indebted (both low- and middle-income) countries were still not benefiting from the sustained rebound in net inflows. In 1989, net FDI flows to these countries were still about 20 per cent below their 1981 level. Furthermore, the share of developing countries

---

31 See World Bank, *World Development Report, 1990* and UNDP, *Human Development Report, 1991.*

32 See, for example, "Development co-operation in the 1990s: policy statement by DAC Aid Ministers and Heads of Aid Agencies", OECD press release of 5 December 1989 and communiqué of Ministerial Council of OECD, 5 June 1991.

33 Programme of Action for the Least Developed Countries for the 1990s, para 64.

34 *Ibid.*

in world FDI inflows fell from more than one-quarter in 1981 to less than one-fifth in 1990.

163.   Several factors were responsible for this trend. Foremost among such factors is the debt crisis. On the one hand, in debt-distressed countries, the debt overhang and the accompanying macro-economic disorder contributed to a climate that was not conducive to FDI. Reduced profitability of existing foreign investments not only acted as a disincentive for further investment but also decreased the funds available for that purpose[35] The debt crisis has continued to stifle FDI flows by feeding the general perception of high risks, diminished profitability and poor prospects for growth. Depressed commodity prices during much of the 1980s and overcapacity in a number of important industrial sectors such as textiles, steel and petrochemicals also contributed to this trend in FDI. Technological advances relating to new materials, and the reduction of energy and raw materials consumption have also had adverse consequences on FDI in commodity-exporting developing countries. Meanwhile, cross-border investment opportunities within OECD countries have been expanding, as a result of improved economic performance, financial deregulation and intensified business competition fostered, among other things, by the prospects of a unified EEC market after 1992.

164.   The debt crisis has also stimulated the search for new financial instruments which provide more balanced risk-sharing between lenders and borrowers[36], enhance portfolio diversification, and strengthen a pro-cyclical pattern of profit remittances and external service payments. Relevant mechanisms include debt-equity conversions, portfolio investment projects and asset-based lending.

165.   One way of reducing external debt and at the same time expanding FDI is through the conversion of debt into equity.[37] Since the introduction of the debt-equity swap programme in Chile in 1985, all major debtor developing countries have resorted to some form of debt conversion. The recent expansion of privatization programmes, mainly in Latin America, and debt-reduction agreements with commercial banks under the Brady plan have led to a resurgence in debt-equity schemes.

166.   Debt-equity swaps could contribute to a reduction in the stock of debt and the flow of scheduled debt service payments. Swaps could on balance be beneficial to the debtor country if profit remittances and capital repatriation are of roughly the same order of magnitude as reductions in debt service payments and are of a pro-cyclical nature. In addition, such schemes help to encourage the return of flight capital, provide support for privatization programmes and promote FDI. Potential negative effects include the adverse impact on budgetary and monetary controls, "round-tripping" of capital,[38] subsidization of foreign investors (through the benefit of debt discount), the diversion of planned investment, and increase in foreign ownership and control of domestic enterprises. There is, however, increasing evidence that debt-equity swaps encourage additionality, i.e. new investment that would not have taken place in the absence of these schemes.[39]

167.   The emerging equity markets have attracted considerable attention in recent years. The few

35 Measured in 1985 dollars, average annual reinvestment dropped from US$ 2.3 billion in 1976-1982 to US$ 1.5 billion in 1983-1989, a decline of 32 per cent, for 7 Latin American countries namely: Argentina, Brazil, Colombia, Costa Rica, Ecuador, Mexico and Peru. See, Institute of International Finance, Inc., *Fostering Foreign Direct Investment in Latin America*, Washington D.C., 1990.

36 Risk-sharing refers to the extent to which the contractual obligation is linked explicitly to some aspect of the borrower's economic situation and thus shifts risks in the domestic economy to the world economy. See, Donald R. Lessard, "Beyond the Debt Crisis: Alternative Forms of Financing Growth", in *Dealing with the Debt Crisis*, edited by Ishrat Husain and Ishac Diwan, World Bank, Washington, D.C., 1989.

37 The annual value of these swaps rose rapidly from about US$ 0.5 billion in 1985 to about US$ 6 billion in 1988. However, it fell to below US$ 5 billion in 1989 as several major debtor countries, including Argentina, Brazil, Mexico, and the Philippines either suspended or significantly slowed these operations in response to the adverse impact of the schemes on monetary expansion, "round-tripping" of capital, etc. Estimates for 1990 indicate a substantial upturn in the volume of debt-equity swaps. See, *World Bank, Financial Flows to Developing Countries*, December 1990.

38 For a description of "round-tripping" see UNCTAD, Trade and Development Report 1988, box 6: "The scope for debt-equity swaps".

39 Empirical studies conducted by IFC and the Institute of International Finance, Inc. have concluded that debt-equity swap programmes enhance additionality. See, J. Bergsman and W. Edisis, *Debt-Equity Swaps and Foreign Direct Investment in Latin America*, IFC Discussion Paper Number 2, Washington D.C. 1988; and Institute of International Finance, Inc., *op.cit.*

40 See, WIDER, *Foreign Portfolio Investment in Emerging Equity Markets*, Helsinki, 1990. See also World Bank, *Emerging Stock Markets Factbook, 1991*.

well-established capital markets in developing countries, mainly centered in Asia and Latin America, are regarded as having a large untapped potential for growth.[40] This is demonstrated by the fact that though 30 developing countries with emerging equity markets accounted for about 11 per cent of world GNP in 1988, they represented only 4 per cent of global equity market capitalization. Also, shares appear, on average, to be undervalued in terms of price/earnings ratios and yields relative to similar ratios on major markets. Though developing countries shares are often considered high-risk, they also tend to produce high returns. Country-specific funds and equity markets in some developing countries, such as Thailand, the Republic of Korea, Malaysia, Chile, Mexico, and Brazil have recently experienced rapid expansion[41] Emerging equity markets are likely to play an increasingly important role in fostering economic development in the 1990s.

168.   In their efforts to achieve a realignment of risks, rewards and responsibilities, new innovative project and trade financing techniques have began to flourish. Asset-based arrangements, such as the build-own-operate (BOO) and build-operate-transfer (BOT) schemes and leasing, have enabled both foreign investors and recipient developing countries to maintain a viable partnership. BOO/BOT schemes, for example, facilitate the development of limited-recourse funding arrangements in which returns are related to the performance of the project. Such arrangements have the benefits of assuring the foreign lender about the security of debt service, guaranteeing the availability of foreign technical and managerial know-how, and linking the interests of both the foreign and domestic partners in the profitability of the project. Similarly, leasing arrangements have enabled developing countries to acquire the services of capital assets, which would normally require large capital outlays, without ceding control over the entire project. Asset-based arrangements enable the foreign investor to establish and maintain a profitable presence in difficult markets, avoiding or limiting both commercial and political risks associated with equity. However, the successful implementation of such mechanisms requires that host countries possess a reasonably well established industrial base and a local capacity for the mobilization of necessary equity counterpart.

169.   Among the "new" financial instruments that are better tailored to borrowers' capacities to pay are the commodity bonds, a quasi-equity instrument whose returns (either interest or redemption value or both) vary with the price of the underlying commodity. From a developing country's perspective, the objective of issuing commodity bonds would be to raise external resources by exploiting its commodity export base and, at the same time, to hedge the risk of commodity price fluctuations, which is, in most cases, outside its control. Debt-servicing difficulties experienced by heavily-indebted developing countries since the early 1980s were partly caused by the coincidence of the rise in international interest rates and the decline in the prices of developing countries' export commodities. In the recent past, a considerable number of commodity bonds have been issued in the United States and European markets, but only a few developing countries (such as Mexico and the Philippines) have so far issued such bonds.

(b)   Policies to encourage FDI and other non-debt-creating flows

170.   Developing countries must continue to improve their policy environment for FDI, portfolio investment and other non-debt-creating flows. This can be done by reassessing the remaining barriers to FDI, especially those in sectors with substantial export potential. Regional initiatives could also be strengthened. However, in the absence of a durable solution to the debt crisis, investment flows to a wider number of developing countries will continue to be stifled.

171.   Though equity markets in developing countries have experienced rapid growth in recent years, they are still far from realizing their full potential. The small number of emerging equity markets of interest to foreign investors hampers portfolio diversification. The number of relatively

---

41   The IFC estimated that during the five-year period that ended December 1988, market capitalization (i.e. the market value of shares) for a group of 30 "emerging markets" rose by nearly 500 per cent to US$ 378 billion, and value traded increased by a factor of 16 in US dollar terms. The number of companies listed also increased by 63 per cent to almost 11,000. See IFC, *Emerging Stock Markets Factbook, 1989.*

42   With an initial U.S. Government contribution of US$ 500 million, the fund is intended to provide a source of additional support for advancing specific market-oriented investment reforms. The initiative also provides for the sale of a portion of outstanding Eximbank loans and Commodity Credit Corporation assets in order to facilitate debt-for-equity and debt-for-nature conversions.

advanced developing countries where such markets could successfully operate are few. One way of overcoming this limitation is through the establishment of multi-country, subregional and regional investment funds and cross listing of stocks on national stock exchanges. Improving the supply of stock over the longer-run through privatisation and by encouraging the public listing of privately held firms, and a strengthened regulatory framework in developing countries would enhance their attractiveness to both domestic and foreign investors.

172.   The potential use and benefits of commodity bonds should be fully explored for both heavily indebted developing countries and for those countries that have escaped the debt crisis. Commodity bonds could be used in debt renegotiations, where commercial banks or official bilateral creditors could be offered such bonds in exchange for their loans. Commodity bonds could also be used in project financing and as a vehicle for long-term trade financing linked to long-term purchases by private importers and official entities in developing countries. Also, the potential offered by new asset-based arrangements such as BOO/BOT schemes and leasing is promising and deserves further study.

173.   These efforts will need to be complemented by adequate and timely action by FDI-exporting countries and multilateral financial institutions. Despite recent trends towards the liberalization of capital outflows, institutional investors in the OECD countries are still faced with strict limits on the placement of their assets abroad. However, Japan's recycling programme and the United States "Enterprise for the Americas" initiative have added new dimensions to official bilateral support for FDI flows to developing countries. In the case of Japan, recycling relies extensively on "hybrid" flows, that is, joint financing arranged by the Government in collaboration with the private sector, the bulk of which has been centered on Asian developing countries. The investment component of the Enterprise for the Americas initiative is based on the Enterprise for the Americas Investment Fund to be established within the Inter-American Development Bank (IDB).[42]Comprehensive regional arrangements encompassing trade, investment and debt reduction backed by adequate financing and enhanced hybrid financing programmes are steps in the right direction which deserve consideration by other FDI-exporting countries.

174.   Fiscal and regulatory policies in home countries regarding capital outflows also need to be reexamined. In particular, home countries' tax regimes and economic adjustment policies should not discourage FDI flows to developing countries.

175.   Recent efforts within the Paris Club to facilitate debt conversions of official bilateral debt into equity should be strengthened and extended to all rescheduling countries, while taking care to minimize any negative side effects and to ensure additionality.

176.   At the multilateral level, the World Bank Group has substantially broadened its role as a catalyst for increasingly large and complex financial packages. The International Finance Corporation (IFC) has been particularly active in the setting-up of investment funds and in the mobilization of foreign investment. The recent increase in its capital would enable IFC to greatly expand that role.[43]The Multilateral Investment Guarantee Agency (MIGA), whose primary objective is to promote the flow of foreign investment to developing countries by issuing guarantees against non-commercial risks, has had a promising start.[44] However, major host countries such as Argentina, Brazil, India, Mexico and Venezuela have not yet joined MIGA. Governments could also act to strengthen the role of MIGA by increasing its capacity to provide guarantees for investment projects[45]

177.   Investment promotion efforts also need to be intensified. For a large number of developing countries, investment promotion activities often lack credibility and seldom impress potential investors. Closer cooperation at the regional level and a stronger sponsorship role by the World Bank Group, UNIDO and the regional development banks would help to overcome some of these difficulties.

178.   Finally, the interrelationships between FDI and trade, finance, technology and services re-

---

43 Agreement was reached in June 1991 to increase the IFC capital by $1 billion to be paid in over 5 years.

44 In fiscal year 1990, MIGA issued its first four guarantees covering a maximum contingent liability of US$ 132.3 million, for projects in Chile, Hungary and Indonesia. Total direct investments were estimated at over US$ 1 billion. Registered applications for investment guarantees represented investors from 12 countries, including all the major industrial countries, considering investment projects in 36 member countries. See MIGA, *Annual Report 1990*, Washington, D.C. 1990.

45 MIGA is endowed with an insurance capacity of only SDR 1 billion.

quire closer examination. FDI has become a primary vehicle for the globalization of finance, production and trade. It has been a major factor in the expansion and diversification of manufactured exports, the development of the services sector, financial and technological innovation and the transfer of technology to developing countries. The importance of these interrelationships has been recognized in the Uruguay Round of multilateral trade negotiations. Their complexity and the role of FDI as an engine of growth and development have become crucial issues of the 1990s. In this regard, the proposal by the United Nations Centre on Transnational Corporations for the organization of a global conference on foreign direct investment and development deserves urgent consideration.[46]

4. The environment and development finance

179.   The primary responsibility for protecting the environment in developing countries no doubt rests with developing countries themselves. However, the effective implementation of environmentally sound policies and measures in developing countries must be supported by new and additional resources from the industrialized countries. It is widely recognized that industrialized countries are the main source of global environmental degradation and the best placed to provide the financial and technological means to deal with it. The fair sharing of environmental risks, costs and benefits must be central to international co-operation in this domain. Equity concerns must emphasize not just past responsibilities but future needs and capabilities as well. Developing countries must be given adequate financial and technological assistance to increase their contribution to the protection of the global and domestic environment, including through the enhancement of their development efforts.

180.   To be sure, a good deal of work remains to be done to establish definitive estimates of the financial needs of developing countries in this domain. As the UNCED secretariat has pointed out, the evidence already indicates that the amounts required will be far beyond current levels of funding and will require an in-depth re-examination of existing sources and methods, as well as consideration of new and innovative approaches.[47]

181.   It is also important to ensure that new resource flows for global environmental protection are put on a more automatic and stable footing, and must be clearly additional to current ODA flows and development commitments. There is a danger, however, that resources would be diverted from national developmental priorities to global environmental ones. Mechanisms for the verification of additionality should be established.

182.   Thus far, notable progress has been achieved with the agreements to provide funding for the Interim Multilateral Fund (established under the Montreal Protocol on Substances that Deplete the Ozone Layer) to assist developing countries signatories of the Protocol, and the Global Environment Facility (GEF). The GEF, a three-year $1.5 billion pilot programme, was established in November 1990 to provide grants or concessional loans to developing countries in four main areas, namely limiting emissions of greenhouse gases, protecting international waters, preserving biological diversity, and protecting the earth's ozone layer.[48] Several countries have pledged contributions to these funding mechanisms from sources additional to that of their traditional development assistance.

183.   Possible new environmental conventions on climate change and bio-diversity will pose again the question of long-term financial and technological requirements and the need for appropriate mechanisms to ensure their provision on a reliable basis over time. Reliance on voluntary funding

---

[46] Proposal contained in UNCTC report to the Seventeenth Session of the Commission on Transnational Corporations, April 1991. See, *The Triad in Foreign Direct Investment*, (E C.10 1991) New York, 1991.

[47] See United Nations, *Progress Report on Financial Resources (Preparatory Committee for the United Nations Conference on Environment and Development, Second Session), A CONF.151 PC 18, January 1991.*

[48] Projects planned for implementation in 1991 were expected to cost $272 million. The fund is administered by a tripartite arrangement between the World Bank, UNEP and UNDP.

[49] A substantial amount of work has already been done on this subject. See, for example, Michael Grubb, The Greenhouse Effect: Negotiating Targets, Royal Institute of International Affairs, London, 1989; and Leiv Lunde, The North/South Dimension in Global Greenhouse Politics, Fridtjof Nansen Institute (Norway), 1990.

arrangements may prove to be inadequate. Every effort must be made to encourage developing countries to accede to international environmental conventions by meeting the full incremental costs of accession. Developing countries must also be assured that their environmental needs will be met without the imposition of new forms of conditionality or the distortion of their developmental priorities.

184.   There are possibilities for the imposition of taxes and user fees on environmentally-damaging activities and products. One way of ensuring long-term stability of resource transfers to developing countries for the alleviation of poverty and the protection of the environment could be the development of new market-based trade-related mechanisms. There is now growing awareness that a global scheme for tradable carbon emission entitlements, properly designed, could form the basis of a CO&lf2. reduction agreement that would reward efforts at limiting emissions while satisfying the fundamental concerns of energy efficiency, equity and the development needs of developing countries.[49] Some initial investigations have shown that tradable permits are among the most cost-effective means of limiting emissions of greenhouse gases that cause global warming.[50] Their introduction could also be combined with more traditional methods such as taxes and quotas. However, further research is needed *inter alia* to harness experiences involving the use of tradable permits and other such schemes, to deepen knowledge concerning methodologies for the initial allocation of entitlements, the structure and functioning of the market for tradable permits and the likely volume of resource flows that would arise under alternative scenarios.

185.   As an interim measure, a system of "rights" could be considered for developing countries that implement environmental programmes which benefit third countries. These "rights" would be used to facilitate the acquisition of environmentally benign technologies and to support other environmental programmes.

186.   Debt-for-nature conversions could also make an important contribution to the protection of the environment. These schemes have been introduced in an increasing number of developing countries, most notably in Bolivia, Costa Rica, Ecuador, Madagascar, Mexico and the Philippines. The United States Enterprise for the Americas initiative provides for the application of substantial local currency interest payments on rescheduled debt to be used for environmental protection and conservation of forests, wildlife and natural systems. Debt-for-nature swaps have also been incorporated into the rescheduling terms of the Paris Club, originally as part of the Houston terms. They were later included in the debt reduction packages for Poland and Egypt, and in the agreement with Senegal under the Toronto terms. The Polish Government has recently proposed to Paris Club creditors the establishment of a $3.1 billion debt-for-environment fund. Brazil's efforts to develop a pilot programme for the conservation of its rainforests have also received encouraging support from the 1991 Group of 7 summit meeting in London.[51] Developing countries should be assisted in designing domestic and multicountry environmental swap programmes, while taking steps to minimize adverse monetary and inflationary impacts.

187.   Above all, the preparatory process for the United Nations Conference on Environment and Development (UNCED) in Rio de Janeiro in June 1992 has enabled the international community to better co-ordinate and channel the rapid multiplication of efforts. UNCED's Programme of Action, the so-called "Agenda 21", and its related financial requirements would undoubtedly constitute the pillars of multilateral co-operation for the period ahead. Bold initiatives would have to be agreed to meet unprecedented environmental, financial and technological demands.

5. Other aspects of financing and payments in trade among developing countries

188.   Among the noteworthy manifestations of the international financing squeeze affecting de-

---

50 See, for example, Joshua Epstein and Raj Gupta, *Controlling The Greenhouse Effect: Five Global Regimes Compared*, The Brookings Institution, Washington, D.C. 1990..

51 Brazil is reportedly considering a $1.5 billion debt-for-nature swap for the conservation of Brazilian rainforests. See *Financial Times*, July 12, 1991. See also the Group of 7, London Economic Summit communiqué, *Economic Declaration: Building World Partnership*, 17 July 1991.

veloping countries' financing and payments are recent disruptions of the functioning of their national subregional export credit agencies as well as certain regional credits and payment arrangements. The strains which followed the debt crisis in 1982 forced developing countries to revise development plans, postpone investment projects and compress imports from all sources. At the same time, regional and subregional development projects in all sectors were given lowest priority, even where the foreign-exchange component of the project costs were either negligible or non-existent. Exports for projects to other developing countries were redirected towards the North with a view to securing foreign-exchange earnings to service external debt, even in cases where foreign-exchange earnings were marginal. As regards imports from other developing countries, they were equally reduced either because of overall compression of domestic absorption or in order to save on the use of scarce foreign exchange even within subregional integration groupings which have had multilateral clearing arrangements. Consequently, finance for intra-trade, both from domestic and subregional sources, fell sharply, particularly for the commercially indebted Latin American countries and Africa.

189.   However, the scale of the problem differs for different exporters. In particular, traders in non-traditional exports face the most acute manifestations of this problem. In traditional exports, such as commodities, the typical developing country exporter usually needs post-shipment financing. Traditionally, banks, whether national or international, have extended short-term credits (bridging loans) against letters of credit, trade documents, warehouse certificates, etc., for 90-180 days. Since most such exports have gone to developed countries, banks have often known the importer or his bank and could easily locate credit information about them. Naturally, more complications arise if the importer is from a developing country, as such importers and their banks are not always known to the exporter and his bank. Nonetheless, until the eruption of the debt crisis in 1981 and the severe access problems of developing countries which have arisen in its aftermath, access to finance for traditional exporters had been limited mostly by cost. In recent years, however, even in the case of traditional exports like grain, the needed credit period has increased to six months to one year.

190.   The situation in other branches of trade - i.e. in non-traditional exports - is quite different. The typical exporter in such a trade usually requires pre-shipment finance in foreign exchange as well as post-shipment finance. He is not, therefore, always in possession of the necessary trade documentation against which credits can be extended. Moreover, such an exporter needs medium-to long-term credits running up to five years. When he is exporting to another developing country, his counter party, the importer, is usually unknown to his bank or to his national export-credit institution. The exporter himself might also be new or be exporting to a new market with unknown marketing and performance risks. Hence, such an exporter presents altogether a different type of risk from that of the traditional exporter. He needs different types of financing at different stages of the production-exporting process.

191.   In most developing countries, the financial structure is not well enough developed to accomodate non-traditional exporters. Often, the trade financing infrastructure is plagued with gaps, and when institutions do extend such credits, they are heavily tied to collateral and limited to low percentages of the values of the trade involved. Moreover, the resources that developing countries can divert to export-financing, especially foreign exchange resources, are limited and plainly inadequate for the task. This is one of the manifestations of under-development and it will not, in the short run, meet with an easy solution.

192.   International banks, which have in the past financed traditional exports, show little interest in extending medium- to long-term export credits, and much less interest in granting pre-shipment credits. When they do so, it is for a customer they know and deal with or for a very large and creditworthy trader. Moreover, in typical cases they also assess the credit risk in terms of the country risk, and this is especially the case in intra-developing-country trade.

193.   This problem has to be solved by developing countries if their efforts to liberalize their trade and increase their exports are to succeed. However, since in the short run they cannot generate an adequate increase in their savings, nor allocate more to export financing at the expense of other uses, nor significantly increase their foreign-exchange earnings, the solution must come through international co-operation. Such co-operation can take place either regionally or interregionally and with the help of their developed-country partners. It goes without saying that everybody benefits from trade expansion and that world trade grows with increased intra-developing-country trade. While it is possible to effect such co-operation at the national level, interregional co-operation promises more benefits, savings, cost advantages and possible additionalities.

194.   The above demonstrates the various shortcomings, problems and gaps in the infrastructure of developing-country trade-financing. The factual evidence shows that, in terms of institutions, only 16 developing countries have specialized trade-finance institutions. In most cases, it is the central banks and/or commercial banks that handle trade financing. Not only are both of these institutional types non-specialized in the matter, but both approach trade finance as subsidiary to other objectives or as second-best to other assets, as the case may be. The coverage of credit available for trade-financing is limited; it ranges between 0.5 per cent and 20.6 per cent of exports to other developing countries with volume in most cases clustering around 10-16 per cent of the transaction.[52] Such volumes place developing-country exporters at a dinstinct disadvantage with regard to finance availability. Furthermore, the reach of the credit is usually limited to direct exporters. It is attached to heavy collateral and the great bulk of it is for short terms (up to 180 days). While short-term credit might be suitable for traditional exporters, it is entirely inappropriate for the needs of non-traditional exporters. And when the importer in such a trade is from another developing country, the availability of such credit finance is altogether uncertain.

195.   The difficulties of commercial trade-financing are relieved neither by government intervention in the vast majority of countries nor by international banks, which are shown to privilege established customers or traders with collateral banking business. This means, in effect, that big firms or old customers or importers in their home countries may expect relief, but not small traders, or traders to new markets, or traders with other developing countries. Moreover, all international banks superimpose country risk on credit risk in their creditworthyness evaluation so that a trade contract financeable for a developed-country exporter might not be so for a developing-country exporter.

196.   The question therefore arises whether developing countries can individually resolve these problems. If it is accepted that all developing countries have a problem of savings shortages (relative to their investment requirements) then any increased allocation of savings to export financing must be at the expense of either domestic private investment or public expenditure, or must come from surplus in the basic payments balance. This might be possible in a handful of newly industrialized countries, but it is certainly not possible in those developing countries now reeling under heavy indebtedness or in the less advanced ones with limited access to external finance or in those with lagging economic performance.

197.   Hence, international co-operation is imperative in this area. The first level of such co-operation is regional/subregional. Regional and subregional banks, like any multilateral funding facility, offer several advantages. They can pool risks and spread non-national trade risks over several countries. They provide a context for international co-operation. They are, if properly managed, capable of getting as good access to financial markets as the most creditworthy countries. Lastly, they are in a position to standardize trade papers and procedures. But this co-operation has produced insignificant results.

198.   For one thing, the scope of the underlying intraregional or subregional trade might not offer the best trade complementarity. After all, regional affinities are geographic, cultural and historical rather than economic in nature. It is evident that trade complementarity is usually greater interregionally than in a smaller context. The evidence also shows that interregional trade has been the most resistant to shocks and the most dynamic component of intra-developing-country trade. Furthermore, any of the merits and arguments in favour of regional/subregional co-operation such as risk-pooling and spreading, scale economies, specialization, market niches, access to external resources and so on are likely to be greater on an interregional scale. Thirdly, the developed countries have not, on the evidence, flocked to the regional/subregional institutions of developing countries. Fourthly, most of the regional/subregional facilities that now exist will have to alter their charters and established modes of practice, not just augment their resources, to answer developing-country needs in non-traditional South-South trade. The existing regional/subregional facilities are predominantly involved in North-South trade, and the three that extend non-traditional export-financing cover countries with specific, extra-economic characteristics. Finally, except for BLADEX, these facilities have not been able to secure additionality via access to secondary financing from international markets.

199.   To deal with this problem, the approach proposed consists in determining first whether the existing financial structure shows major problems which call not only for national action but also

---

52 See UNCTAD, "Trade Financing in Developing Countries" TD/B/1300, June 1991, and Suppl. 1 and 2.

for international co-operation. If so, then the merits, benefits and possible advantages of an interregional facility are to be examined.

200.   Consequently, developing countries may profitably do two things: explore the possibility of establishing a trade finance mechanism, and simultaneously undertake a series of national measures to improve their existing national schemes.

Annex table I-1

NET FINANCIAL FLOWS TO DEVELOPING COUNTRIES, 1981 AND 1983-1990

(billions of dollars, at current prices)

	1981	1983	1984	1985	1986	1987	1988	1989	1990	Percentage of total 1981	Percentage of total 1990
Official flows	44.7	40.7	46.2	46.5	53.8	60.3	63.1	62.9	75.9	33.6	54.2
Official development assistance	36.0	32.5	33.4	34.9	41.8	46.8	48.8	50.1	59.5	27.1	42.5
Bilateral	28.1	24.9	25.8	26.7	32.9	36.9	37.7	37.9	46.3	21.1	33.1
Multilateral	7.9	7.6	7.6	8.2	8.9	9.9	11.1	11.6	13.2	6.0	9.4
Non-concessional official flows	8.7	8.2	12.8	11.6	12.0	13.5	14.3	12.8	16.4	6.5	11.7
Bilateral	3.1	1.1	4.6	3.9	4.2	6.8	7.8	5.6	6.0	2.3	4.3
Multilateral	5.6	7.1	8.2	7.7	7.8	6.7	6.5	7.2	10.4	4.2	7.4
Total export credits	17.1	4.4	6.2	4.4	0.1	-2.1	-1.8	9.9	5.0	12.9	3.6
Private flows	69.2	43.3	26.7	25.1	27.1	30.2	33.6	40.4	54.6	52.0	39.0
Direct investment	16.9	9.4	11.1	6.3	11.1	20.4	24.7	29.6	31.1	12.7	22.2
of which: Offshore centres	4.1	3.7	3.8	3.7	6.2	12.6	11.4	8.0	..	3.1	..
International bank lending	49.9	33.9	16.8	14.0	11.0	8.8	7.9	9.8	18.7	37.5	13.3
of which: Short-term	22.0	-25.0	-6.0	12.0	-4.0	5.0	4.0	8.0	9.0	16.9	6.4
Total bond lending	0.8	-0.1	-1.5	3.5	1.0	-1.6	-4.3	-2.7	-0.2	0.6	-0.1
Other private	1.6	0.1	0.3	1.3	4.0	2.6	5.3	3.7	5.0	1.2	3.6
Grants by non-governmental organisations	2.0	2.3	2.6	2.9	3.3	3.5	4.2	4.0	4.5	1.5	3.2
Total net resource flows	133.0	90.7	81.7	78.9	84.3	91.9	99.1	116.6	140.0	100.0	100.0
Total net resource flows at 1989 prices and exchange rates	196.8	138.2	127.9	122.4	103.7	97.5	97.8	116.6	125.1		
Memo items:											
IMF flows:											
IMF purchases and loan disbursements	7.1	12.2	6.2	4.1	4.6	4.8	3.9	5.6	5.7		
IMF repurchases, loan repayments and charges	..	3.3	4.9	6.6	10.0	12.6	10.8	10.0	10.8		
IMF net transfers	..	8.9	1.3	-2.5	-5.4	-7.8	-6.9	-4.4	-5.1		
Flows from the World Bank Group:											
Gross disbursements	7.2	9.7	10.8	11.0	13.2	14.9	15.7	14.2	16.4		
Net disbursements	5.9	7.6	8.4	8.0	8.7	8.6	7.5	7.1	8.0		
Net transfers	4.0	5.0	5.3	4.4	3.6	2.4	0.5	0.6	0.4		

Source: OECD, IMF and World Bank.

Annex table I-2

NET TRANSFER OF RESOURCES
OF THE CAPITAL-IMPORTING DEVELOPING COUNTRIES, 1980-1990

(Billions of dollars)

	1980	1982	1984	1986	1987	1988	1989	1990
Net transfer through: [a]								
Private sources	13.0	5.5	-19.2	-23.4	-27.6	-27.0	-25.7	-26.5
of which:								
Medium and long-term credit	11.3	3.8	-21.8	-27.2	-31.7	-31.8	-29.1	-29.8
Private grants	1.7	1.7	2.6	3.8	4.1	4.8	3.4	3.3
Short-term credit, domestic outflows [b]	5.0	-27.5	-13.7	0.5	-2.3	-10.4	-3.4	1.2
Official flows	28.8	32.3	25.2	12.2	9.5	10.5	11.7	22.6
of which:								
Grants	11.2	9.2	10.8	11.2	12.6	12.8	13.4	17.8
Credit [c]	17.6	13.1	14.4	1.0	-3.1	-2.3	-1.7	4.8
Direct investment	-4.9	-2.7	-2.4	-1.2	1.3	5.9	4.9	4.5
Total transfer (financial basis)	41.9	7.6	-10.2	-11.9	-19.1	-21.0	-12.6	1.7
Use of official reserves [d]	-14.7	19.2	-18.8	8.3	-14.1	-10.6	-14.6	-23.4
Total transfer (expenditure basis)	27.2	26.8	-29.0	-3.6	-33.2	-31.6	-27.1	-27.1

Source: Department of International Economic and Social Affairs of the United Nations Secretariat, based on data of the International Monetary Fund, OECD and the World Bank.

a A negative sign indicates an outward transfer of resources.

b Short-term credit and domestic outflows have been calculated as a residual including short-term trade financing, capital flight, arrears on interest due and other flows captured in balance-of-payments data as "errors and omissions" and presumed to be financial flows.

c Including IMF credit.

d A negative sign indicates addition to reserves.

Annex table I-3

DEBT INDICATORS OF DEVELOPING COUNTRIES, 1980-1990

(Percentages)

	1980	1982	1986	1988	1989	1990
Debt/GDP:						
Highly-indebted countries *a*	32.8	41.0	44.9	40.4	39.2	37.2
Sub-Saharan Africa *b*	38.6	51.3	66.7	69.3	73.1	75.7
Debt/exports:						
Highly-indebted countries *a*	168.2	266.6	344.9	295.5	266.7	244.3
Sub-Saharan Africa *b*	147.5	213.8	303.8	338.2	341.0	359.3
Interest payments/exports:						
Heavily-indebted countries *a*	16.0	31.1	27.9	24.8	18.9	21.3
Sub-Saharan Africa *b*	7.4	9.7	10.2	10.0	10.1	12.0

Source: IMF, *World Economic Outlook*, various issues.

   a Including Argentina, Bolivia, Brazil, Chile, Colombia, Côte d'Ivoire, Ecuador, Mexico, Morocco, Nigeria, Peru, Philippines, Uruguay, Venezuela, Yugoslavia.

   b Excluding Nigeria and South Africa.

Chapter II

THE CHANGING INTERNATIONAL TRADING ENVIRONMENT

INTRODUCTION

201. International economic exchanges have undergone far-reaching changes over the last decade: growing evidence now suggests that these changes are fundamentally altering the composition of traded goods and services as well as modes and loci of their production.[53] The changes in composition reflect a greater share of services and knowledge-intensity in final output, increased diversification in sourcing of technologies and supplies and the tailoring of production cycles to specific market demand for goods and services. These changes revolve around the phenomenon now widely referred to as globalization of production, investment and trade.[54]

202. The process of financial deregulation in the 1980s and the emergence of global financial markets was a major factor in furthering the globalization of production as was the role played by new technologies - particularly as they converged around computer, communication, control and design technologies. These developments now render it possible for the transnational enterprises and service firms to install world-wide information and commercial networks through which management can link together production, marketing and distribution facilities around the world.

203. These transformations in the nature and pattern of international transactions have been primarily the result of actions taken by private corporations in response to changing production possibilities and consumption patterns. However, they have been accompanied by, and also partially driven by, changes in governments' strategies towards international transactions.

204. For most of the period since 1945, developed countries have been in the forefront of efforts to liberalize international trade, with considerable success achieved for most manufactured goods. During the 1980s, however, some of these countries seemed to have relinquished their role in this area and to have become selective in their trade policies. Selectivity was in some instances country-based - resulting, for example, in various forms of quantitative restraints and tiered preferences - and in other cases was product-based, often in the form of non-tariff barriers. The overall approach has frequently been referred to as managed trade.

205. Another fundamental change in the trading environment in the 1980s was the continuing formal evolution of regional trading groups in Europe and North America. These arrangements embrace some of the newer dimensions of international transactions, such as services, intellectual property, and foreign direct investment. Inasmuch as they involve at least an implicit bias against non-participants, the development of regional blocs, together with some actions of the developed countries in trade and related areas, have tended to strengthen tendencies towards segmentation of trade relations, in contrast with the technological and other forces leading to a globalization of the world economy.

206. Developing countries, on the other hand, have been making increasing efforts to integrate themselves into the world economy and have become the standard-bearers for trade liberalization. Their international transactions are comparatively more transparent and non-discriminatory. For

---

[53] Geza Feketekuty "Changes in the World Economy and Implications for the World Trading System" *IMF Survey*, 15 July 1991. Mr. Feketekuty, Senior Policy Adviser, USTR, has stated that "We are going through a revolution in the organisation of production and trade that is of a magnitude similar to the industrial revolution in the 18th Century..."

[54] For a comprehensive discussion of the issues relating to globalization see, "Informal encounter on international governance: Trade in a globalizing economy", UNCTAD report, forthcoming. Also see, S. Ostry "Governments and corporations in a shrinking world", New York Council for Foreign Relations Press, 1990.

instance, developing countries imports are less likely to be "relational exchanges", e.g."intra-firm trade", a form of trade which has a growing share in developed countries trade. A majority of the recent trade policy reforms were undertaken unilaterally by developing countries and usually on a most-favoured-nation basis. Many of the developing countries also reduced controls on other forms of international transactions, particularly foreign direct investment. In addition to such actions by individual countries, several of the economic groupings of developing countries also reduced tariff and other barriers.

207.   One conclusion that emerges from the review that follows is that trade performance among regions and groups is undergoing marked shifts, and among the developing countries a small group is succeeding in integrating investments, technology and trade with the emerging global modes of production. Their success has placed them on the threshold of deep economic transformation. For most developing countries, which remain at the margin of the globalization process, the major challenge is to find ways and means of joining the mainstream of trade and growth dynamics. At its eighth session, the Conference can make an important contribution by agreeing on the role that the international community should play towards this end. A first step in this direction is to ensure a balanced outcome of the Uruguay Round, in which the concerns of all contracting parties are addressed.

A. TRENDS IN WORLD TRADE, 1980-1990

208.   The 1980s witnessed the emergence of a more integrated global economy driven by rapid technological progress. The performance of world trade improved as the decade unfolded. After economic recession and stagnating trade in the early 1980s, growth of world output and exports gained new momentum towards the middle of the decade. The volume of world exports increased on average at an annual rate of 6.5 per cent in 1985-1990, compared to a low rate of 2.3 per cent recorded in 1980-1985. By the end of the decade, the pace of export expansion decelerated again, together with a slowdown in the growth of world output (see table II-1). Trade in manufactures, in particular capital goods, was the driving force behind the growth in world merchandise trade in the 1980s. Exports of many primary commodities were constrained by slow growth in world demand, and supply-side problems prevented a number of developing countries, in particular in Africa, from deriving the maximum benefit from temporary improvements in market conditions.

209.   The developed market-economy countries continued to occupy the dominant place in world trade, with a share in the value of world exports of about 70 per cent in 1990. Their share in world manufactured exports was even more substantial, accounting in the same year for nearly 80 per cent, but it had been larger at the beginning of the decade. The decline mirrored the growing importance in world trade of some major exporters of manufactures among the developing countries, particularly in the region of South and South-East Asia, which became a dynamic growth centre in world trade.

210.   The developing countries as a group recorded a slight decline in the volume of exports in 1980-1985, followed by strong expansion at an average annual rate of 9 per cent in 1985-1990, nearly double the growth rate achieved by the developed market-economy countries over the same period. However, this seemingly encouraging evolution masked less favourable developments.

211.   Above all, differences in the export performances of developing regions remained profound. The fast pace in export expansion in the second half of the 1980s was essentially the result of the dynamic export performance of a greater number of developing economies in South and South-East Asia. On average, export growth was modest in Latin America and sluggish in Africa (see table II-1). This uneven performance was due partly to the commodity composition of exports of the different regions: primary commodities with slowly expanding demand and fluctuating prices predominate in the exports of most African and many Latin American countries, while a greater number of Asian economies derive a large proportion of their export earnings from manufactures in high demand in the world markets. It also reflected long-standing differences in trade strategies. Furthermore, the debt crisis and the instability it engendered prevented many countries, particularly in Latin America and Africa, from expanding and diversifying their export supply capabilities.

Table II-1

CHANGES IN TRADE VOLUMES AND PURCHASING POWER OF EXPORTS, BY ECONOMIC GROUPING AND REGION, 1980-1990

(Percentage change per annum)

Economic grouping and region	Period	Exports	Total merchandise Purchasing power of exports	Manufactures [a] Imports	Exports	Imports [b]
WORLD	1980-1985	2.3	..	2.3	3.0	3.0
	1985-1990	6.5	..	6.5	7.0	7.0
By economic grouping:						
Developed market-economy countries	1980-1985	3.3	3.4	3.2	4.0	6.0
	1985-1990	5.4	8.0	7.0	6.2	7.5
Developing countries	1980-1985	-1.2	-2.1	0.4	10.0	-1.0
	1985-1990	9.0	4.5	6.0	13.0	7.5
Least developed countries	1980-1985	1.9	1.6	1.7	-3.5	-1.4
	1985-1990	1.2	-3.4	0.0	11.6	-4.3
By economic region:						
Africa	1980-1985	-5.3	-5.1	-2.5	3.9	-5.7
	1985-1990	2.5	-5.8	-4.4	14.5	-3.3
North Africa	1980-1985	-6.2	-5.3	-9.6	7.6	-2.6
	1985-1990	5.0	-3.9	-6.4	21.3	-2.8
Sub-Saharan Africa	1980-1985	-4.4	-2.0	-6.0	0.1	-9.2
	1985-1990	0.3	-6.4	-1.0	7.5	-3.9
Latin America	1980-1985	5.6	5.2	-6.0	12.0	-6.9
	1985-1990	4.3	0.0	2.0	7.1	4.7
West Asia	1980-1985	-12.3	-11.6	-0.6	-0.6	-0.8
	1985-1990	9.0	0.4	-3.8	-0.6	-5.2
South and South-East Asia	1980-1985	7.4	6.7	5.5	11.3	4.1
	1985-1990	13.0	12.7	12.5	13.3	13.0
East Asia [c]	1980-1985	9.2	5.2	6.6	10.6	8.8
	1985-1990	14.2	14.8	15.7	15.0	16.0
ASEAN [d]	1980-1985	3.3	0.4	0.6	15.5	-0.5
	1985-1990	12.6	8.6	10.5	21.6	16.5
China	1980-1985	11.0	10.0	21.5	11.5	20.0
	1985-1990	12.4	7.8	2.7	21.0	-0.5
USSR	1980-1985	1.5	..	5.8	..	..
	1985-1990	0.5	..	0.0	..	..
Countries in Eastern Europe [e]	1980-1985	5.1	..	1.1	..	..
	1985-1990	-1.7	..	2.2	..	..
Memorandum:						
WORLD OUTPUT	1980-1985	2.4				
	1985-1990	3.3				

Source: UNCTAD secretariat, based on data from official international sources. Data for 1990 are estimates.
   a Defined as SITC 5 to 8 less 68.
   b Imports of developing countries are estimates partly based on exports of developed market-economy countries.
   c Hong Kong, Republic of Korea, Singapore, Taiwan Province of China.
   d Indonesia, Malaysia, Philippines, Thailand.
   e Bulgaria, Czechoslovakia, former German Democratic Repuglic, Hungary, Poland and Romania.

212. The evolution of the purchasing power of exports (i.e. changes in the volume of exports adjusted for changes in the terms of trade) was distinctly less favourable for the developing coun-

tries than for the developed market economies. In 1985-1990, the purchasing power of exports from developing countries increased at an annual average rate of 4.5 per cent, while the developed market-economy countries recorded nearly double this growth rate over the same period. South and South-East Asia was, in fact, the only developing region which could improve the purchasing power of its exports in the second half of the 1980s (see table II-1).

213.   The importance of such improvements for a country's capacity to import is self-evident. Not surprisingly, South and South-East Asia was also the only developing region with a dynamic import performance in the 1980s, in particular in the second half of the decade. Imports into Latin America which had declined in 1980-1985 under the devastating impact of the debt crisis recovered somewhat in the second half of the 1980s, while imports into Africa and West Asia continued to decline in 1985-1990 (see table II-1). The adverse impact of import constraints on further progress in the development process became apparent in many developing countries.

214.   The export performance of developing countries in manufactured products provides further insights into competitive positions of the developing economies in international trade. As a group, they increased their share in the value of world exports of manufactures from less than 10 per cent in 1980 to more than 15 per cent at the end of the decade. Hence, progress was undoubtedly made, but the global picture is again somewhat misleading. It does reveal a number of less satisfactory developments.

215.   The bulk of exports of manufactures from developing countries continued to come from a small number of these economies. The same group of some 15 developing economies[55] accounted for slightly more than 80 per cent of the value of manufactured exports of all developing countries both at the beginning and at the end of the 1980s. The growing share in world exports of manufactures reflected, therefore, the progress of only a few developing countries towards greater participation of their industrial supply capability in the international division of labour.

216.   Furthermore, only this small group of major exporters of manufactures made significant progress in upgrading the product composition of their exports. These developing countries progressed fairly systematically, moving from exports of simple manufactures, especially of textiles and clothing, into engineering goods, including mid-tech electrical and electronic goods, and, to some extent into capital-intensive and skill-sophisticated products. The majority of the developing countries, on the other hand, continued to rely heavily on exports of natural-resource-based manufactures as well as on unskilled-labour-intensive manufactured products. These countries made hardly any progress with diversifying and upgrading the product patterns of their exports. The same five products groups (textiles, clothing, chemicals, non-metallic mineral manufactures and basic forms of iron and steel) accounted for about two thirds of the exports of manufactures from these developing economies to developed market-economy countries both in 1980 and at the end of the decade.

217.   Moreover, differences among developing regions in their export supply capabilities for manufactured products did not narrow over the past decade; rather they became more pronounced. Their export performance in developed market-economy countries was revealing in this regard. Among the developing regions, only South and South-East Asia gained significant importance for the developed market-economy countries as a source of imports of manufactured products. At the end of the 1980s, some 11 per cent of the value of manufactured imports by developed market economies were supplied by developing countries in South and South-East Asia, compared to about 7 per cent in 1980. By contrast, the value of manufactured products from Latin America accounted for barely 3 per cent of the imports of manufactures by the developed economies at the end of the decade, only marginally more than in 1980. And only half a per cent of the value of manufactured imports into developed market-economy countries was supplied by Africa at the end of the 1980s. The same share had already been recorded at the beginning of the decade.

218.   An important contribution to the dynamic export performance of South and South-East Asia in manufactured products came from four developing countries and territories which have become a major factor in world trade: the Republic of Korea, Taiwan Province of China, Singapore and Hong Kong. Furthermore, rapidly growing manufactured exports from some other developing countries in South-East Asia such as Indonesia, Malaysia and Thailand added a new dimension to the economic dynamism of the region in the second half of the 1980s. In the same

---

55 Taiwan Province of China, Republic of Korea, Singapore, Hong Kong, Mexico, Brazil, Yugoslavia, Malaysia, India, Thailand, Indonesia, Philippines, Pakistan, Argentina and Morocco.

vein, the volume of imports into South- and South-East Asia of manufactured products increased strongly in 1985-1990, testifying to the dynamic development process under way in a number of countries in the region (see table II-1).

219.   The growth in the volume of manufactured exports from Latin America was on average less rapid in 1985-1990 than during the first half of the decade, despite increases in export values which, however, reflected largely significant price rises.   The creation of trade surpluses by restrictive economic policies chiefly in order to meet interest payments on foreign debt proved to be no basis for lasting export growth.   Rather, industrial sectors in many Latin American countries had been weakened by the sharp drop of investment in manufacturing capacity in the first half of the 1980s, with the effect that self-sustained export growth became difficult.   Recovery of investment in the second half of the 1980s was slow and uneven between countries, but import constraints eased somewhat and imports of manufactures, including key capital goods, started to grow again after the dramatic fall in 1980-1985 (see table II-1).

220.   The bulk of Latin America's manufactured exports continued to come from only a few countries, especially Mexico and Brazil.   In 1990, the two countries supplied three quarters of the value of manufactured products which the developed countries purchased on the Latin American continent.   In the same year, supplies of machinery and transport equipment from Latin America to the United States came nearly exclusively from these two countries.   Modernization of production and access to the newest technology are important requirements if more countries in Latin America are to improve their competitiveness and expand their shares in world manufacturing exports.

221.   The growth in the volume of manufactured exports from both North Africa and sub-Saharan Africa accelerated significantly in 1985-1990, but export values remained small.   Few African countries have export supply capabilities for manufactured products.   Furthermore, product concentration, which is a salient feature of the structure of manufactured exports from Africa, continued to be pronounced, with clothing and textiles representing the most important group of manufactured export items.   In 1990, three countries (Mauritius, Morocco and Tunisia) accounted for over 90 per cent of the value of clothing items sold by producers in Africa in the markets of developed economies.   In the same year over 70 per cent of the value of textiles purchased by developed economies in Africa originated in just four countries (Côte d'Ivoire, Egypt, Morocco and Tunisia).   The volume of Africa's imports of manufactures continued to decline in 1985-1990, with potentially adverse impacts on the rehabilitation of machinery and equipment and investment in new capacity (see table II-1).   Stagnation in Africa in the process of industrialization and the growth of productive capacity and productivity is by no means a past phenomenon.   Moreover, Africa's poor infrastructure as well as high transport costs to major overseas markets remain formidable obstacles to a more rapid expansion of exports.

222.   The performance of the trade sector of the least developed countries was disappointing in the 1980s, with near stagnation in the volume of both exports and imports.   Furthermore, the purchasing power of exports recorded no improvement in 1980-1985 and declined in the second half of the decade.   The fall in purchasing power, the persistent claim of foreign debt service on export earnings and, in many cases, the implementation of deflationary adjustment policies resulted in import compression, particularly of manufactured goods in the second half of the 1980s. Shortages in crucial imports and low levels of capacity utilization were, in turn, major consequences of import compression.   Manufactured exports recorded strong volume growth in 1985-1990, but the export base of the least developed countries remained dependent on agricultural commodities and raw materials (see table II-1).

223.   China recorded rapidly rising exports in the 1980s, particularly of manufactures (see table II-1).   The volume of total exports grew in 1980-1990 at an annual average rate of 11-12 per cent, with the share of manufactured exports rising from 50 per cent in 1980 to over 70 per cent at the end of the decade.   The product concentration in China's exports was, however, high, with clothing and textiles accounting for more than two fifths of the country's manufactured exports to developed market economies.   Changes in the product composition of exports towards products with higher skill and technology contents were emerging, but they will need time to become more pronounced.

224.   The significance of the countries in Eastern Europe and the Soviet Union as suppliers to world markets remained small in the 1980s.   The share of these countries in the value of world exports only accounted for 6.5 per cent at the end of the decade, less than in 1980.   Furthermore,

the largest part of their trade was carried out among themselves. Their exports to third markets amounted to slightly more than 3 per cent of world exports in 1989. The volume growth of their exports slowed down considerably in 1985-1990, reflecting in particular economic disruption in the wake of fundamental systemic changes which commenced at the end of the decade (see table II-2).

225. The international competitiveness of the countries in Central and Eastern Europe and the USSR deteriorated considerably in the 1980s. Thus, their shares in imports by developed market-economy countries declined or stagnated in practically all production sectors, particularly in manufacturing.[56] The countries in Central and Eastern Europe and the USSR are poorly represented where exporting developing economies have their particular strength. Moreover, they are practically absent with more skill- and technology-intensive manufactures in developed-country markets.

226. The slowdown in the growth of world trade, which commenced in 1989, continued in 1990 and 1991. The considerable deceleration in output growth in some major industrialized countries, especially in the United States, was the principal cause for the signs of fatigue in world trade, besides the deep recession in Central and Eastern Europe and the Soviet Union. The volume growth of exports from both the developed market-economy countries and the developing countries decelerated in 1990-1991 in line with the trend in world trade, while the volume of exports from the countries in Central and Eastern Europe and the USSR declined dramatically over this period, as systemic changes gained further momentum and the trade and payments system of the Council of Mutual Economic Assistance (CMEA) fell into disarray (see table II-2). Some of them, especially Hungary and Poland, succeeded in expanding their deliveries to Western markets, benefiting in particular from easier access to the markets of the EEC. By contrast, the export performance of the Soviet Union in East-West trade worsened dramatically.

227. The major events of the recent past - the Gulf crisis, systemic change in Central and Eastern Europe, and German unification - all have implications for world trade and for trade of developing countries. While the overall impact of the Gulf crisis on the growth of world trade has not been dramatic, adverse effects on individual developing countries have in many cases been severe. The steep increase in oil prices resulted temporarily in a deterioration of the terms of trade for oil-importing developing countries, reducing their real income. Furthermore, those developing countries for which Kuwait and Iraq were important markets suffered tangible losses in their merchandise exports. And a number of developing countries lost worker remittances on a large scale and were, in addition, burdened with significant cost for the repatriation of their nationals. For at least 40 developing economies, the total cost inflicted upon them by the Gulf crisis has been estimated to exceed 1 per cent of their GNP in 1990 alone - an impact "akin to a widespread natural disaster".[57]

228. As regards the developments in Central and Eastern Europe and the Soviet Union, the breakdown of the trade and payments system of the CMEA and the concomitant switch to world-pricing and convertible currency settlement had severe impacts on a number of developing countries, primarily those which were members (Cuba, Mongolia, Viet Nam), but also some other developing economies which had maintained close economic ties with Central and Eastern Europe and the Soviet Union. The former CMEA members especially, but also countries such as Afghanistan, Angola, Cambodia, Ethiopia and Mozambique, had enjoyed preferential terms in their trade with the European CMEA members and received development assistance on a significant scale from these countries.

229. In central Europe, German unification was the dominant event. As unification injected substantial, purchasing power into the former German Democratic Republic, the enormous pent-up demand of the population led to a boom in consumption. The reorientation in German trade flows was dramatic. Imports started to soar, while export growth declined sharply. The export gains of developing countries were unevenly distributed. Exporters of raw materials and food products (excluding mineral fuels) barely benefited, while manufactured products from developing economies performed well. However, it was the member countries of the EEC which reaped the largest gains. Thus, imports of manufactures from Community countries by Germany increased in 1990 by $26 billion, equal to the value of German imports of manufactures from all developing countries in the same year.

---

56 See also A. Inotai, "Competition between the European CMEA and rapidly industrializing countries in the OECD market for manufactured good", *Empirca-Austrian Economic Papers*, vol.1 (1988).

57 See "The impact of the Gulf crisis on developing countries", Briefing paper, Overseas Development Institute, London, March 1991.

Table II-2

CHANGES IN TRADE VOLUMES, 1988-1992

(Percentage change per annum)

	1988	1989	1990	1991 [a]	1992 [b]
WORLD EXPORTS	8.5	7.0	4.3	3.0	6.0
Developed market-economy countries:					
Exports	8.3	7.5	5.1	3.0	6.0
Imports	8.3	7.7	5.3	3.0	6.0
Developing countries					
Exports	11.3	7.2	5.0	4.5	7.0
Imports	14.7	7.0	7.7	7.2	8.5
China					
Exports	14.4	8.0	13.0	3.0	10.0
Imports	16.9	6.5	-9.0	10.0	10.5
Countries in Central and Eastern Europe [c]					
Exports	3.7	-2.1	-9.8	-11.0	1.5
Imports	3.0	0.6	0.0	-1.5	1.5
USSR					
Exports	4.8	-0.3	-13.0	-20.0	-8.0
Imports	9.5	9.3	0.0	-20.0	-5.0
Memoramdum:					
WORLD OUTPUT	4.5	3.3	2.4	1.2	2.9

Source: UNCTAD secretariat, based on data from official international sources.
 a Preliminary.
 b Forecasts.
 c Bulgaria, Czechoslovakia, former German Democratic Republic until 1990, Hungary, Poland and Romania.

230. The boom of consumer goods imports is unlikely to continue unabated. Demand for investment goods, on the other hand, will increase significantly once investment comes on stream. The main beneficiaries can be expected to be producers in the western part of Germany and other western European countries. Export gains of the few developing countries which have competitive supply capabilities are likely to be marginal.

231. The trade performance of the developing countries will remain linked to the fortunes of world trade. In the short term, the developing economies are expected to experience a somewhat faster pace of export expansion with the upswing in the world economy. Prospects that growth of world output and trade will rebound in 1992 are seemingly good (see table II-2).

B. DEVELOPMENTS IN THE INTERNATIONAL TRADING SYSTEM SINCE UNCTAD VII

1. Overview

232.   The 1980s witnessed a steady decline in multilateral trading disciplines. The implications of this trend for the health of the world economy have been the subject of extensive analysis.[58] Although one of the objectives of the launching in 1986 of the Uruguay Round of multilateral trade negotiations under the auspices of the General Agreement on Tariffs and Trade (GATT) was to arrest the erosion of the multilateral system and trade disciplines, the process has been undermined by a combination of protectionist and restrictive trade policies. Since the seventh session of the Conference there has been for example a drift away from multilateral reciprocity and unconditional MFN treatment and an increasing emphasis on bilateral and regional approaches to trade problems, seeking solutions outside the multilateral mechanism. There has also been an intensification of unilateralism in the trade policies and trade legislation of some major trading countries as well as an increased threat of retaliatory action; trade-balancing arguments to press for bilateral reciprocity have been increasingly used; attempts have been made under the auspices of GATT to amend the multilateral rules on anti-dumping and countervailing measures to provide greater flexibility in their application, with the possible result of facilitating the use of such measures as a tool for trade harassment; efforts have been presented to decelerate the proliferation of VERs or VIEs (voluntary import expansions)[59] by evolving new forms of managed trade;[60] the respect of standstill and rollback commitments has been irregular or absent; and the preferential liberalization measures in favour of developing countries are being withdrawn unilaterally. Paradoxically, these developments are taking place at a time when most developing countries have become GATT contracting parties, and some developing countries, China and countries in Central and Eastern Europe have entered into accession negotiations or indicated their considerable interest in future accession,[61] - in short, when it appears as if the long-awaited universalization of GATT membership has moved closer to reality.

(a) Bilateral and plurilateral approaches

233.   The movement to bilateral approaches appears to be accelerating both in the form of bilateral pressures with the implied threat of retaliatory action, as well as of bilateral free trade liberalization agreements. Such arrangements are being pursued essentially in two contexts: (a) the free trade agreements covering goods, services and investment between the United States and certain trading partners, and (b) the consolidation of the European Economic Community, towards completion of the Single Market in 1992 and its possible enlargement covering EFTA countries and association agreements with several Central and East European countries (for a fuller dis-

---

58 See UNCTAD, TD/328/Rev.1. See also "Trade policies for a better future: proposals for action", (GATT, 1985).

59 The concept of VIEs where the importing countries are asked to increase imports of specific items from particular countries by given amounts is the counterpart of the familiar concept of VERs (voluntary export restrictions) where exports by these countries are restrained thus. For details of the concept and terminology of VIEs, see Jagdish Bhagwati, "VERs, Quid Pro Quo DFI and VIEs: Political-Economic-Theoretic Analyses", *International Economic Journal*.

60 For example, the United States-Japan Semiconductor Arrangement and the recent efforts towards an international agreement on steel. On July 25, 1989 President Bush announced a Steel Trade Liberalization programme which extended the steel voluntary restraint arrangements programme until March 31, 1992. Such programme also called for negotiating an international consensus on effectively disciplining government aid and intervention in steel sector by eliminating subsidies and market access barriers with a view to having a multilateral agreement on trade in steel by March 1992.

61 Since UNCTAD VII eight developing countries and territories have acceded to GATT as Contracting Parties, five other developing countries as well as Bulgaria and China, are in the process of negotiations. Poland has applied for renegotiation of its Protocol of Accession and the USSR has been granted GATT observer status.

cussion see section C.5). In addition, in Latin America liberalization under the various structural adjustment programmes has provided a catalyst for overcoming the protectionist forces which had frustrated earlier efforts to facilitate freer trade among countries of that region.

234. In the 1980s, while the United States continued to pursue its trade interests through multilateral negotiations in the Uruguay Round, it has also supplemented these negotiations with bilateral initiatives.[62] Bilateral mechanisms range from product-specific approaches such as "reciprocity" talks (e.g. the market-opening, sector-specific (MOSS) talks with Japan) to comprehensive free trade agreements with Canada and Israel,[63] and planned negotiations with Mexico and Canada on North American Free Trade Agreement (NAFTA)[64] and with other developing countries in Latin America (the "Enterprise for the Americas") and elsewhere.

235. The implications of these arrangements are important for two reasons: first, they influence the pattern of growth of international trade and specialization and pose a variety of policy choices for non-participants in arrangements. Often they are required to seek selective preferential arrangements in order to minimize the potential costs to their economies. Clearly, the larger the volume of trade covered under such arrangements, the greater will be the pressures on non-participants to seek special arrangements which are often derogations from multilateral disciplines. Secondly, regional and subregional groupings have a discriminatory effect inasmuch as they grant preferential market access to partners in the arrangements. The creation of trade groupings and similar arrangements - either bilaterally or in a plurilateral context - increase the potential for trade disputes, raise trade tensions, and generate concern about the future of the multilateral trading system. Countries with small weight in international trade are likely to experience greater losses from the discriminatory effects of selective trading arrangements.

(b) Unilateralism

236. Another major recent development which has affected the international trading system has been the enactment of the United States Omnibus Trade and Competitiveness Act of 1988. The Act touches on a wide range of trade issues but the most problematic provisions which have focussed the attention of the international trading community in recent years was the inclusion of the so-called "Super" and "Special" Section 301.[65] Throughout the first decade after its entry into force, Section 301 of the United States Trade Act of 1974 was used sparingly. However, the amendments to this provision contained in the Trade and Tariffs Act 1984, and particularly those in the 1988 Act, have converted Section 301 into a major tool of the United States trade policy. It provides for trade retaliation against trading partners for actions that are unilaterally determined as "unreasonable", "unjustified" or "discriminatory", not only in the areas of goods, and not only where the United States trade rights are affected, but also in areas where no specific obligations exist - such as services, investment, and intellectual property rights. The so-called Section 301, as amended by the 1988 Act, has enlarged the Administration's scope for taking retaliatory action,

---

62 The United States approach was a rather large deviation from its traditional abstention from the use of GATT Article XXIV, signalling that regionalism, or plurilateralism (as distinct from unconditional MFN for multilateral trade) was now acceptable to it. For details, see Jagdish N. Bhagwati, "U.S. Trade Policy at Crossroads", *World Economy*, December 1989.

63 See Peter Clark and Peter Burn, Canada-United States Free Trade Agreement and its Impact on Developing Countries, UNCTAD/ITP/42, pp. 261-316, and Peter Burn, Professional Services and the Uruguay Round: Lessons from the Canada-United States Free Trade Agreement, UNCTAD/ITP/26, pp. 365-406.

64 As an important development towards such process, a joint communique was issued by the governments of Canada, Mexico and the United States on 5 February 1991, with a view to negotiating a three-way free-trade agreement. The negotiations began in June 1991.

65 Note that the terms Super 301 and Special 301 are not actually used in the law, but rather have been adopted as the common names identifying these new statutory mechanisms. They are more formally cited as Sections 1302 and 1303 of the Omnibus Trade and Competitiveness Act of 1988, which respectively (and retroactively) create new Sections 310 and 182 of the Trade Act of 1974. The principal difference between "Regular Section 301" of the Trade Act of 1974 and "Super 301" is that under "Regular Section 301", the USTR deals with one trade barrier at a time, while under "Super 301", the USTR could investigate an entire array of barriers of a particular foreign country in the same investigation. "Super 301" also had a time limit of two years and expired on 31 December 1990. "Special 301" has no time limit and deals only with barriers to trade caused by the inadequate protection of intellectual property rights. For example, on 26 April 1991, in its 1991 "Special 301" review, the United States Administration has identified China, India and Thailand as priority foreign countries and placed Brazil, European Community and Australia on the priority watch list. It has also placed 23 trade partners on the watch list.

and reduced discretion with respect to such action through shorter time limits for action. It also expanded the definition of unfair trade practices, and included a new "Super 301" provision[66] to negotiate changes in trade practices that restrict United States access across the board. These devices have been actively resorted to in the pursuance of objectives at the bilateral, regional and multilateral levels, whether for opening individual markets abroad in areas of trade policy not addressed elsewhere, such as protection of international property rights and access to markets in specific sectors, or in coming to grips with broader problems of chronic trade imbalance. A common threat has been the suspension of the benefits of the generalized system of preferences (GSP).[67]

237.   Section 301 has also influenced the conduct of the Uruguay Round of multilateral trade negotiations. One of the considerations of developing countries in seeking to separate negotiations on services from those on the traditional areas in the Uruguay Round was to avoid the legitimization of retaliation on goods in order to obtain concessions on services (as in the Trade and Tariff Act of 1984). The retaliatory provisions are being used not simply (as originally intended) to withdraw equivalent concessions with respect to a country which has been found to violate its GATT obligations so as to nullify the rights of the United States, but as a means of exerting pressure on countries to modify policies where no international obligations exist, and to influence the negotiating positions of weaker countries in the Uruguay Round. The seriousness of such a situation was demonstrated by the use of this Section to retaliate against Brazilian intellectual property rights legislation.[68] In this context, punitive trade measures, designed to convince developing countries to abandon certain positions, have been threatened and in some cases applied, despite the standstill and rollback commitments. Some developing countries have been placed on the "priority" list for Section 301 action and then appear to have been removed when their positions become more conciliatory. This approach has been most frequently applied with respect to the property rights issues mentioned above, particularly TRIPs. On the other hand, the United States has been reluctant to use Section 301 against trading partners with a credible retaliatory capacity such as the EEC. In fact, an important objective of most countries in the final phase of the Uruguay Round is to ensure that this new United States legislation does not receive multilateral legitimization through the Uruguay Round and also that the ability of the United States to invoke these provisions is circumscribed rather than enhanced through these negotiations. For instance, the EEC has stated that it will take actions "aimed at ensuring that United States shortcomings in the application of international trade law are corrected"[69]

238.   The implications of an approach whereby negotiations take place under threat of retaliation rather than under exchanges of offers are obvious. Developing countries which find themselves in particularly vulnerable situations may find it difficult to pursue long-term goals when faced with the imminent threat of serious trade or other economic difficulties. On the other hand, concessions extracted under such threats will have little legitimacy in the view of the weaker partners who will consider themselves morally justified in reneging on such agreements when future circumstances permit. Needless to say, this is hardly the "more durable" international trading system foreseen in the Final Act of UNCTAD VII as a desired result of the Uruguay Round.

---

[66] See VanGrasstek Communications, "Trade-Related Intellectual Property Rights: United States Trade Policy, Developing Countries and the Uruguay Round", Uruguay Round - Further Papers on Selected Issues, UNCTAD/ITP/42, pp.105-6.

[67] See UNCTAD/MTN/INT/CB/1/Add.20, 29 and 31. See also Jagdish Bhagwati, "The International Trading System", speech given at the Symposium for the 25th Anniversary of UNCTAD, Geneva, 18-19 September 1989.

[68] On June 10, 1987, the Pharmaceutical Manufacturers Association (PMA) of the United States filed a complaint with the USTR under Section 301 of the U.S. Trade Act of 1974 after U.S./Brazilian bilateral consultation failed to result in a commitment from Brazil to provide patent protection for U.S. pharmaceutical products. The PMA complaint focused on Brazilian regulations which, although recognizing patent rights in general, expressly deny protection for products and processes of pharmaceutical industry and for some other specialty chemicals.In view of the PMA, the Brazilian regulations could encourage infringers to copy, manufacture, and market pharmaceutical industry invented by its members. On October 20, 1988, the U.S. Government levied $39 million in trade sanctions against Brazil-100-percent tariffs on imports of nonbenzenoid drugs, consumer electronics, and some paper products. On December 20, 1988, Brazil brought this matter to the GATT Council and requested for a dispute settlement panel. It was the view of the Brazilian government that its patent policy was consistent with international rules and therefore the U.S. sanctions were illegal. On February 21, 1989, a GATT dispute settlement panel on this issue was set up. On May 26, 1989, Brazil was designated by the USTR on a "priority watch list" under the "Special 301" provision of the 1988 Trade Act. However, in June 1990 the USTR lifted these tariff sanctions, in response to the new Brazilian Government's commitment to protecting foreign intellectual property rights. For details see USITC publications 2095, 2208 and 2317 on pp. 4-54/55, pp. 133-35, and pp. 122-25 respectively.

[69] Commission of the European Communities, Directorate-General I, External Relations, 1989 EC Report on US Barriers to Trade, Burssels, 1 May 1989.

(c) The Uruguay Round of multilateral trade negotiations

239.   The scope of the Uruguay Round of multilateral trade negotiations - the eighth Round undertaken under the aegis of GATT - extends beyond the traditional issues dealt with in previous multilateral trade negotiations. Unlike the earlier negotiations, which dealt primarily with the reduction of barriers to trade in goods at the border, the present Round addresses several new such issues as the movement of capital in the form of foreign investment, the development of new technologies, and the trade and production of services (see section C.1 below). In other words, the Uruguay Round attempts to cover not only cross border movement in products but also in services and in factors of production such as labour, capital and technology. Its outcome therefore is bound to have a significant impact on the patterns of trade, competition, production investments and domestic regulations in the course of this decade. A satisfactory outcome of the Uruguay Round is thus crucial for the health of the world economy.

240.   The Final Act of UNCTAD VII recognized a number of objectives for the Uruguay Round, particularly the need for a balanced outcome and to develop a more open trading system promoting growth and development. Other objectives, in this context, included: (a) the improvement in the access to markets, especially for the products of export interest to developing countries, (b) the liberalization of trade in the textiles and clothing sector, and its eventual integration into GATT, (c) the removal of discriminatory restraints on exports, particularly on those from developing countries, (d) the need to bring more discipline and predictability to agricultural trade, (e) the need to keep in view the special problems of the least-developed, landlocked and island developing countries and (f) ensuring that the observance of multilaterally agreed commitments with respect to trade in goods should not be made conditional on receiving concessions in other areas.

241.   One of the major objectives of the Uruguay Round is "to bring about further liberalization and expansion of world trade to the benefit of all countries, especially less-developed contracting parties, ..." In order to achieve that objective, it was agreed that the principle of differential and more favourable treatment and "non-reciprocity" as embodied in Part IV and other relevant provisions and decisions of the GATT should apply to the negotiations. However, the extent to which results in relation to differential and more favourable treatment were embodied in the proposals submitted at Brussels is very limited.[70]

242.   The objectives of providing special treatment for developing countries was clearly recognized in the Punta del Este Declaration. Since the launching of the Uruguay Round, this commitment has been questioned by some developed countries[71] However, the failure to conclude the Uruguay Round within the agreed time frame has raised further questions about the appropriateness of seeking uniform rules for all sectors, regardless of differences in levels of development while preserving a wide range of exceptions, derogations and waivers on a large share of trade, such as agriculture, and textiles and clothing. Therefore, the acceptance by all parties of tighter disciplines over their resort to trade policy measures on a mutual and equitable basis, taking into account the importance of flexibility as well as levels of development, should be a major objective of the Uruguay Round.

243.   It is obvious that the strengthening of the trading system requires that participants accept higher levels of disciplines over their trade policy measures. Such acceptance of tighter disciplines should take place on a mutual and equitable basis, taking into account the importance of the flexible application of trade-policy measures, particularly as a response to balance-of-payments problems, as component of coherent development strategies, and the impact of the disciplines on

---

[70] GATT, MTN.TNC/W/35 Rev.1, 3 December 1990 - "Draft Final Act Embodying the Results of the Uruguay Round of Multilateral Trade Negotiations" contains 391 pages and has four Annexes. Annex I contains all the agreements on trade in goods (including tariff concessions, the amended GATT Articles, the revised Tokyo Round Codes and new agreements). Annex II is the General Agreement on Trade in Services. Annex III is the Agreement on TRIPs (some developed countries prefer to incorporate TRIPs agreements in Annex I). Annex IV contains the "Basic Elements of an Organizational Agreement".

[71] For example, one of the United States Trade negotiating objectives, as drawn from the Omnibus Trade and Competitiveness Act of 1988, is to greatly integrate developing countries in to the GATT system. It clearly states in Section 1101 (b) (4) of the Act, regarding developing countries, that the principal negotiating objectives of the United States are: (A) to ensure that developing countries promote economic development by assuming the fullest possible mesure of responsibility for achieving and maintaning an open international trading system by providing reciprocal benefits and assuming equivalent obligations with respect to their import and export practices; and (B) to establish procedures for reducing nonreciprocal trade benefit for the more advanced developing countries.

countries at a lower level of development. The acceptance of stronger disciplines would lead to a legal structure for the implementation of the results of the Uruguay Round, which would preclude the resort to unilateral trade action outside the framework of the GATT and the possibilities of cross-sectoral retaliation between trade in goods and measures relating to services and intellectual property protection.

(d) Central and Eastern European countries and the trading system

244.   Although several countries in Central and Eastern Europe have been contracting parties to GATT for several decades, the existing multilateral rules and disciplines are still not fully applied to them in trade relations. The legislations of most developed market-economy countries provide for special trade-policy measures, such as discriminatory QRs, or selective safeguards and special anti-dumping rules, against the exports of Central and Eastern European countries in order to offset situations of market disruption caused by low-priced exports (though usually there was no clear evidence of massive exports, especially low-cost exports). Some of these measures also appear in some multilateral instruments such as the Protocols of Accession of some countries in Central and Eastern Europe to the GATT, in bilateral trade agreements and in the GATT Subsidies Code.

245.   Recent years have witnessed an improvement in the East-West trading environment. All the major trading nations have expressed support for the integration of the countries of Central and Eastern Europe into the multilateral trading system, and have recognized that improved market access for Central and Eastern European countries is an essential requisite, as these countries implement both internal market reforms and trade policies in line with multilateral rules.[72] Concrete trade policy actions have been carried out by some major trading countries in favour of countries in Central and Eastern Europe in 1989-91, which has substantially reduced the discriminatory element in East-West trade relations. In particular, most of discriminatory QRs were eliminated by the EEC and some countries in Central and Eastern Europe were granted the GSP treatment by the EEC, the United States, and some other developed market-economy countries.

246.   The rapid economic and political evolution in the countries of Central and Eastern Europe, and the concomittant shifts in the East-West relations have created the necessary conditions for their fuller integration into the international trading system. Efforts to achieve such integration would need to address the political, economic and legal/institutional basis on which trade evolved during the post-war period and determine the relevance of such arrangements in the present context.

2. Momentum towards trade liberalization

247.   Since UNCTAD VII the objective of a continued momentum towards trade liberalization on a multilateral basis, particularly in those sectors where existing multilateral disciplines have not been effectively applied, has been pursued within the context of the Uruguay Round. Developing countries have accorded top priority to seek substantial concessions with respect to tariffs and non-tariff measures in order to promote trade liberalization and to expand the opportunities for their exports into world markets.

---

72 See "London Economic Summit Declaration", *Financial Times*, 18 July 1991, p.4.

BOX II-1

PARTICIPATION OF DEVELOPING COUNTRIES IN THE URUGUAY ROUND

Unlike the previous rounds of multilateral trade negotiations, developing countries' participation in the Uruguay Round is impressive in both quantitative and qualitative terms. More than 80 developing countries and territories are taking part in these negotiations. Their active and constructive contribution to the negotiating process has been widely acknowledged. More than 30 developing countries have been undergoing unilateral trade liberalization programmes, thus contributing in advance to the attainment of the Round's objectives. In fact, it has been recognized that many developing countries are now in a process of genuine trade policy "revolutions" as part of their economic reform packages.

Despite differing nuances and emphases placed by developing countries on individual subjects and issues in the Uruguay Round, as well as the emergence of issue-based coalitions among like-minded developing and developed countries, such as the Cairns Group in Agriculture, developing countries have also been pursuing a set of common objectives in many negotiating areas by submitting joints proposals, sponsored by alliance of developing countries with similar interests from different geographical regions.

In particular, in the area of Agriculture, several proposals were made by net food-importing developing countries, which were also supported by other developing countries. These proposals substantiated the need and ways to take into account of the possible negative effects of the agriculture reform process on net food-importing developing countries.

In the areas of TRIPs, TRIMs and services, developing countries have submitted a number of joint negotiating proposals, *inter alia,* on the structure of a multilateral framework for trade in services; multilateral framework of principles and rules for trade in services; sectoral annexes on temporary movement of labour and on telecommunications; draft proposals on TRIMs, TRIPs, etc.. In addition, a number of proposals were submitted by developing countries' economic groupings and special coalitions, such as ASEAN, CACM, SELA, PTA for Eastern and Southern African States and ACP countries. The least-developed countries have made joint proposals in every negotiating group, introducing their special concerns and needs.

(a) Tariffs

248.   Despite the relatively low level of average tariffs in developed countries, which has resulted from successive rounds of multilateral trade negotiations since the Second World War, in certain sectors tariffs remain high. The incidence of high tariffs on imports from developing countries in developed country markets is greater than that on imports from other developed countries as a result of the biais against developing countries in MFN liberalizations undertaken in the previous rounds of MTN.[73] This is so despite the existence of preferential schemes, as many high tariff items are excluded from the product coverage of preferential schemes such as the GSP.[74]

249.   Examination of the tariff schedules of major markets indicates that in recent years almost $100 billion worth of (1988/89) imports of non-agricultural products[75] into the EEC, the United States and Japan face high MFN tariffs, of which some $57 billion originate in developing countries. As table II-3 in the annex indicates, the developing countries' share in high tariff items (59 percent) is larger than what their share in total imports (33 percent) would indicate. A number of high tariff product groups are excluded from the product coverage of some GSP schemes or receive far smaller benefits than other tariff items.

---

[73] However, a number of developed countries undertook unilateral liberalization in the second half of the 1980s, such as Australia and Austria, and Japan.

[74] Annex table II-1 shows the number of tariff lines covered by GSP and LDC preferences for different MFN tariff ranges in each importing market. Annex table II-2 shows the value of imports from developing countries under different ranges of applied tariff rates.

[75] Including tropical agricultural products and natural resource based products, but excluding oil.

250.	The sectoral frequency of high tariffs is quite similar across developed country markets. Tariffs in the textile and clothing sector are generally high. A number of subsectors in the area of natural resource based and tropical products also face high tariffs.[76] With regard to the rest of the industrial sector, high tariff items appear to be frequent in a number of sectors of export interest of developing countries, including certain chemical products, glass and glassware, cutlery, household equipment of basic metals, bicycles, trunks and suitcases, footwear, toys, articles of precious materials and miscellaneous articles.

251.	Despite unilateral trade liberalization by many developing countries and their active participation in the Uruguay Round negotiations, tariff discrimination against them has in fact increased.	As in previous rounds, there are important exceptions from tariff offers on non-GSP products of particular export interest to the developing countries.	It should be noted that some developed countries also made tariff concessions on products of interest to developing countries contingent on reciprocity.	Finally, for many products of export interest to developing countries tariffs tend to escalate by processing stages.[77] The effective protection afforded to the processing industries through escalation of tariffs is therefore likely to be higher than what is indicated by nominal tariffs.	Products especially affected by such escalation of trade barriers are tropical beverages, spices, vegetable plaiting material, oilseeds and vegetable oils, tropical fruits and nuts, tobacco, rice, manioc, roots and tubers.

## (b)	Non-tariff measures

252.	As tariffs have been reduced substantially through several rounds of multilateral trade negotiations, the importance of non-tariff measures (NTMs) as instruments of protection has increased.[78] Some NTMs, such as quantitative restrictions, State import monopolies and discretionary licensing, are more formidable obstacles to trade than tariffs.	Annex table II-4 shows that at the end of the period 1981-1989, despite continued economic growth since 1983 and the ongoing Uruguay Round negotiations, only a few countries made significantly less use of NTMs.

253.	The application of NTMs is often not transparent, thus leading to uncertainty and unpredictability about market access.	A major problem with some types of NTMs is that they are not easy to identify or quantify.	Domestic policies and instititutional practices (e.g. internal taxes and services charges, the complexity of the distribution system) may sometimes by themselves constitute non-tariff obstacles to trade.	Finally, NTMs are more often applied on a selective basis, thus discriminating among suppliers.

254.	Imports into developed market-economy countries of all products less minerals originating in developing countries represented over $335 billion worth of trade in 1988.	Product-specific border non-tariff measures affected approximately 22 per cent of these imports, or not less than $75 billion of trade.[79]

255.	The most important single non-tariff measure affecting developing countries is the MultiFibre Arrangement (MFA) covering some $36 billion worth of trade.	The MFA (IV) which

---

76	See annex table II-1.

77	This is one of the outstanding problems which should deserve special attention in the present round of negotiations. The need for increased exports from developing countries of domestic processed products mainly exported at present in their primary form has often been stressed. In the case of tropical products, developing countries are in a position to engage themselves in the processing of their primary products up to a fairly high level of the processing chain. But these efforts would not be rewarded unless the importing countries reduce high tariffs affecting products at higher levels of processing which allow them to maintain high effective rates of protection for their processing activities.

78	In principle, all government interventions in production and trade, other than tariffs, but including private restrictive practices tolerated by governments, which may affect relative prices, market structures and international trade flows, could be considered as non-tariff measures. Such measures include, for instance, quantitative restrictions, customs and administrative entry procedures, government aids, government procurement, export subsidies, charges on imports, voluntary export restraints, countervailing and anti-dumping actions, border tax adjustments, State-trading, standards and regulations.

79	UNCTAD, *Problems of Protectionism and Structural Adjustment, Part I: Restrictions to Trade.*, TD/B/1282, 20 December 1990. NTMs include certain para-tariff measures, variable levies, countervailing and antidumping actions, quantitative restrictions, the surveillance of quantities and or prices of imports, automatic licensing and measures to control the price level.

came into force in 1986 was extended on 31 July 1991 for a further 17 months. The MFA represents a major derogation from the GATT rules in that it allows contracting parties to negotiate quantitative restraint arrangements on a discriminatory basis against developing countries.

256.   Non-automatic licensing and quotas (other than MFA quotas) affected some $26 billion of trade (all products except fuels), of which $14 billion corresponded to agricultural products. Countervailing and antidumping actions affected about $8 billion of trade, covering a wide range of products. Price control measures, including variable levies, affected about $4.5 billion of trade, covering principally agriculture. Some $8 billion worth of trade was covered by voluntary export restraints (VERs). In steel, for example, since the mid-1980s imports from developing countries have stagnated in absolute terms (and have actually declined in the United States), mainly owing to the imposition of voluntary export restraints and other measures. In other areas such as consumer electronics, automobiles and automobile equipment, leather manufactures and chemicals, VERs and other quantitative restrictions, as well as invocation of anti-dumping measures, have been prevalent.

257.   A disproportionate share of the NTMs applied in developed countries is directed against developing countries, resulting from the combined effect of the composition of trade and the selective application of NTMs.[80] Discriminatory application of NTMs against developing countries exists principally with regard to NTMs taken outside the GATT system and "grey area" measures, where the MFN principle is not observed. The clearest example is the the MFA. Because of their weaker bargaining position and weaker retaliatory powers, developing countries tend to be more easily persuaded to engage in VERs. NTMs, even those compatible with GATT, can also have a discriminatory character because of the differences in the degree of trade restrictiveness of the same measure for different trading partners. For instance, the tendency to allocate import quotas on the basis of historical trade flows affects more severely newcomers in a specific product area.

258.   A number of non-tariff measures have been eliminated since the the mid-1980s. In some cases Governments suspended national legislation under which quantitative import restrictions had been maintained.[81] A number of other non-tariff measures which were liberalized had previously been challenged under the GATT dispute settlement mechanism.[82] In some cases, safeguard actions under GATT Article XIX were allowed to lapse.[83] Other liberalization efforts were intended to support the reform process in the countries of Central and Eastern Europe, *inter alia*, dismantling specific non-tariff measures.

259.   Indeed, almost all NTMs due to expire at dates after the adoption of the Punta del Este Declaration have been renewed and new trade distorting measures have been introduced. Moreover, very few GATT-inconsistent trade measures have been rolled back. This, despite the fact that principally on the insistence of developing countries, a major objective of the Uruguay Round in the area of non-tariff measures has been to dismantle measures inconsistent with GATT (rollback) and to avoid the introduction of new ones (standstill) (see annex tables 6 and 7).

(c) Tropical products

260.   Changes in market access conditions for tropical products since UNCTAD VII reflect mainly developments in the Uruguay Round. At the Mid-Term Review of the Round in Montreal in December 1988, a set of specific results was achieved in regard to tropical products, with the objective of early implementation. Negotiated contributions were made by the EEC and 10 de-

---

[80] Annex table II-5 shows the incidence of the application of various types of NTMs to imports of selected product sectors, according to the origin of imports.

[81] For instance Australia lifted quantitative restrictions on sugar imports that had been justified under the Sugar Agreement Act and the Protocol of Provisional Application.

[82] For instance in Japan (market opening measures in the agricultural sector), Sweden (abolishment of quantitative restrictions on imports of apples and pears) and the United States (replacement of sugar quotas by a tariff quota system).

[83] For instance in Canada (the phasing out of quantitative restrictions on footwear was completed by November 1988), Australia (termination of safeguard actions, involving four wheel drive cars and certain textile products) and the United States (termination import quotas and additional duties on specialty steel, introduced in July 1983. However, specialty steels were included in VERs governing imports of iron and steel products, through 31 March 1992, under the "Steel trade liberalization program").

veloped market-economy countries and 11 developing countries. Autonomous contributions were also tabled in the negotiations by three socialist countries, one additional developed country and two other developing countries. The contributions by 10 developed market-economy countries and the EEC have for the most part been implemented in 1989, except those by Australia, implemented on 1 July 1988 or in stages from that date to 1 July 1992 and those by New Zealand, staged from 1 July 1988 to 1 July 1992. They involve mostly reduction of most favoured nation (MFN) and the binding of existing rates. In addition, generalized system of preferences (GSP) improvements were made by Australia, Austria, EEC, Finland, Japan, Norway, Sweden and Switzerland. Contributions regarding special treatment for the least developed countries were made by Austria, Japan and New Zealand. Contributions regarding liberalization of non-tariff measures were made only by the EEC and Japan. Australia undertook to remove the few quantitative restrictions on tropical products in 1995. Binding of the concessions was in general offered conditionally.

261.   In February 1990, the negotiating group on tropical products established detailed procedures and a timetable for the continuation of negotiations enabling participants to make further offers, including improvements of earlier proposals. By July 1990, about 45 participants had submitted offers on tropical products. Offers of tariff concessions (as at the end of July 1990) by major industrialized trading countries (including Australia, Austria, Canada, the EEC, Finland, Japan, New Zealand, Norway, Sweden, Switzerland and the United States) suggest the following direct trade effects: the improvement in market access corresponding to these offers would create additional trade (imports by the markets), in the products covered, amounting to about US$ 746 million or about 3 per cent of the 1986 import value of such products by those markets; only a third of the additional imports created (that is, US$ 245 million) would come from developing countries, representing only a 1.7 per cent rise in their exports to those markets of the products covered. The remainder of the additional trade would accrue to the industrialized countries themselves. On an aggregate regional basis, the African region is the only one among the developing regions that experiences a net loss (approximately US$ 118 million), about 3 per cent of its 1986 export value of covered products.

262.   These results are explained by several factors. For one thing, the offers are made for the most part on an MFN basis. Therefore, in so far as certain products are also produced by industrialized countries (for example, processed tropical products) liberalization in the tropical products sector will bring benefits not only to the developing countries. Moreover, to the extent that developing countries already enjoy preferential tariff treatment on such products, liberalization on an MFN basis implies an erosion of preference margins; hence trade losses can be expected. In fact, for least developed countries that enjoy better than GSP treatment in some markets, even liberalization on a GSP basis would not bring additional trade benefits for such countries. A similar situation would apply to ACP countries with respect to the EEC market.

263.   The willingness of developed countries to liberalize imports of tropical products has become a test for respect of commitments. Although the Punta del Este Declaration has recognized the importance of trade in this sector for a large number of developing countries, the progress of the negotiations aimed at achieving the "fullest liberalization" was impeded mainly by two factors: (i) the linkage between products in this sector and those in the agricultural sector, where there is an impasse which has further complicated the negotiations on tropical products, and (ii) the reciprocity being demanded by the developed countries.

(d) Natural resource-based products

264.   Market access conditions affecting trade in fisheries, forestry and mineral and metal products have experienced little change since UNCTAD VII. Progress has been slow in the Uruguay Round negotiations on natural resource-based products whose objective is "the fullest liberalization of trade in natural resource-based products, including in their processed and semi-processed forms" by reducing or eliminating tariff and non-tariff measures, including tariff escalation. Difficulties have arisen over attempts by some developed countries to link a reduction of tariff and non-tariff measures in this sector with issues covering access to supplies, particularly fishing rights, and to extend the product coverage beyond that already agreed for the Round - in particular, to include energy-related products.

265.   A simulation exercise has been carried out of the potential trade effects of MFN tariff re-

duction on fisheries, forestry and mineral and metal products in major markets (i.e. Canada, EEC, Japan, Sweden and United States), using the proposed tariff cutting approach outlined in the Chairman's 16 November 1990 text. The results indicate that world trade in natural resource-based products would increase by US$ 823 million (in terms of additional imports by the indicated markets) with US$614 million of imports originating in industrialized countries and only US$ 210 million in developing countries. Developing countries would experience their largest gain in fishery products, followed by forestry products (ex-tropical), and a net loss in mineral and metal products. African countries as a whole would experience a net trade loss in all three product categories, with their biggest loss occurring in fishery products. Erosion of preferential margins due to MFN liberalization is the principal explanation for the relative small gains of developing countries and the net loss of African countries.

(e) Agricultural trade

266.   Since the preparatory phase of the Uruguay Round, it has generally been considered that the success or failure of the Round will, to a large extent, depend on the ability of the negotiators to establish more effective multilateral disciplines over trade in agricultural products.

267.   The international market for agricultural products is affected by a variety of policy measures applied by Governments. These measures include internal support policies (subsidies in various forms to domestic producers) the effect of which is to raise domestic production higher than it would otherwise be, thus reducing domestic demand for imports or leading to higher export availability; border protection (tariffs, tariff escalation and non-tariff measures) to limit import access; and export subsidies, which distorts competition among exporting countries. While policies falling into one or more of these categories are applied by many Governments, those applied in the markets of the industrialized countries, because of the importance of these markets in international trade, have the greatest impact on the world market.

268.   An aggregate measure, in monetary terms, of all transfers to farmers affected through domestic support programmes and trade measures is the producer subsidy equivalent (PSE). Estimates of PSEs for major farm commodities (e.g. grains, meat, dairy products and sugar) by the OECD Secretariat indicate that transfers to farmers in OECD countries in 1987, at about US$ 177 billion, were the highest of the decade. In that year producers obtained about 50 per cent of their agricultural income from these transfers. Since then, there was a relative decline in transfers, to US$ 168 billion in 1988 and US$ 151 billion in 1989, followed however by an upturn in 1990 to US$ 175 billion.[84] The cost to consumers resulting from domestic prices being supported at levels higher than what would prevail in the absence of policy interventions (measured as a negative consumer subsidy equivalent - CSE) rose to US$ 133 billion. Moreover, because PSE and CSE estimates neither cover all agricultural products nor include all transfers due to agricultural policies, they understate overall transfers from taxpayers (net of budget receipts from tariffs) and consumers (through higher prices) which attained an estimated US$ 299 billion in 1990 - an increase of 12 per cent over the 1989 figure.

269.   Export subsidies have been a major source of disputes in agricultural trade in recent years because of their use to dispose of production in excess of domestic requirements on world markets. Because subsidized exports can lower world market prices and can be used to capture market share, they inflict income losses on non-subsidized exporters. However, they provide income transfers to importing countries of agricultural products benefiting from subsidies. The share of export subsidies in the 1986-1988 average levels of agricultural support (in terms of PSEs) in six OECD countries (including Australia, Canada, EEC, Japan, New Zealand and United States) ranged from 0.3 per cent of New Zealand to 43.7 per cent for the EEC.[85]

---

[84] In absolute terms, the EEC (US$ 81 billion), Japan (US$ 31 billion), and the United States (US$ 36 billion) accounted for the bulk of farm support in the OECD area in 1990. On a percentage basis Switzerland, Norway, Finland and Japan have the highest rates of assistance (over 65 per cent). New Zealand (5 per cent) and Australia (11 per cent) have the lowest rates. Estimates of PSEs for specific commodities, expressed as a proportion has been quite high for products such as sugar, cereals, and meat, which are of major trade interest to many countries. See, *OECD, Agricultural Policies, Markets and Trade: Monitoring and Outlook 1991,* (Paris, 1991).

[85] See, *OECD Economic Studies,* "Modelling the effects of agricultural policies", No.13, Winter 1989-90, table 2. p.137.

270. The Uruguay Round of multilateral trade negotiations has provided the framework since UNCTAD VII in which efforts are being made to achieve fundamental reform of world agricultural trade. When Ministers met at Punta del Este in 1986 to start the new Round they agreed, *inter alia*, that the negotiations in the field of agriculture should "aim to achieve greater liberalization of trade in agriculture and bring all measures affecting import access and export competition under strengthened and more operationally effective GATT rules and disciplines". A mid-term review of the negotiations, begun in December 1988, was completed in April 1989. In the area of agriculture, a "framework approach" was agreed, covering interrelated long- and short-term elements and arrangements on sanitary and phytosanitary regulations.

271. Regarding long-term reform, it was agreed that the objective is to establish a fair and market-oriented agricultural trading system and to provide for "substantial progressive reductions in agricultural support and protection" sustained over a period to be agreed upon, resulting in correcting and preventing restrictions and distortions in world agricultural markets. Concerning the short-term, during the remaining period of the Uruguay Round negotiations, it was agreed that current domestic and export support and protection levels in the agricultural sector are not to be exceeded. In particular, tariff and non-tariff barriers are not to be intensified and not to be extended to additional products, while support prices to producers are not to be raised.

272. The Mid-Term Agreement included important decisions concerning the interests of developing countries which formed a milestone in the negotiations on agriculture. The Agreement specifies in relation to long-term elements, that: (a) Special and differencial treatment to developing countries remained an integral element of the negotiations, particularly on the strengthened and more operationally effective GATT rules and disciplines; (b) Government measures on assistance, whether direct or indirect, to encourage agricultural and rural development were an integral part of the development programmes of developing countries; and (c) Ways should be developed to take into account the possible negative effects of the reform process on net food-importing developing countries." Also, in relation to the short-term elements, it was agreed that "developing countries are not expected to subscribe to the short-term commitments."

273. At the Brussels meeting, Ministers were unable to bridge the gap between the offers made by various participants on agriculture. There were widely differing views, particularly on: (a) the size and duration of the commitment to be entered into to reduce domestic agricultural support, border protection and export subsidies; (b) the modalities of reduction, including which subsidies and protective measures should be reduced; and (c) which products precisely should be covered. In the event, it was decided to suspend the formal negotiations to allow participants more time to reconsider and reconcile their positions in some key areas of the negotiations, including agriculture. At the same time, the Director-General of GATT, in his capacity as Chairman of the Trade Negotiations Committee (TNC) at Official level, was requested to pursue intensive consultations in the period from the close of the Ministerial meeting to early in the new year with a view to achieving agreements in all the areas.

274. On 26 February 1991, the TNC reconvened in Geneva and decided to restart the Uruguay Round negotiations. With respect to agriculture, participants agreed to conduct negotiations to achieve specific binding commitments on each of the following areas: domestic support; market access; export competition; to reach an agreement on sanitary and phytosanitary issues; and that technical work would begin immediately to facilitate these negotiations.

(f) Textiles and clothing

275. Since UNCTAD VII the policies of developed countries towards textiles and clothing imports have remained basically restrictive. Protectionist policies have affected established textile and clothing exporters among the developing countries and have imposed ceilings to export and production growth in newly emerging exporting countries. There has been, however, some softening of restrictions in favour of individual least developed countries; or more favourable treatment within certain regional preferential arrangements, such as those between the United States and the countries included in the Caribbean Basin Economic Recovery Act (CBERA) for assembly products, or the EEC agreements with ACP countries and a few Mediterranean countries.

276. The Uruguay Round has provided the framework over the past four years in which efforts

are being made to liberalize trade in textiles and clothing. At the completion of the Mid-term Review of the Round in 1989, participants agreed that modalities for the integration of this sector into the GATT should, *inter. alia*, cover the phasing out of restrictions under the Multifibre Arrangement and other restrictions on textiles and clothing not consistent with GATT rules and disciplines, the time span for such a process of integration, and the progressive character of this process which should commence following the conclusion of the negotiations. By the end of 1990, while there has been some reconciliation of positions, in particular with regard to the length of the transitional period and the technique for the phase-out of restrictions, there remained a divergence of views on transitional arrangements, including a transitional safeguard mechanism. Since the Uruguay Round was not completed as scheduled in December 1990, in July 1991 the MFA was extended for a further 17 months.

277.   After the negotiations had been deadlocked for some time as a result of opposition to proposals for a "global quota" or "tariff quota" system put forward by certain developed importing countries, the participants have finally agreed to negotiate a mechanism that would phase out the MFA and "phase in" GATT disciplines so as to integrate textiles trade into the General Agreement.

3. GSP and other preferential arrangements

278.   Preferential imports by OECD preference-giving countries in 1988 amounted to about US$ 60 billion - a fivefold increase from the US$ 12 billion recorded in 1976, the first year that all schemes were in operation (see annex table II-8). These imports have on average increased almost twice as fast as imports from all sources. This serves as a demonstration of the increased product coverage of the schemes, the enhancement of beneficiary export-supply capabilities and efforts to diversify exports towards non-traditional products. However, while the GSP has brought considerable trade benefits to developing countries during the decade of the 1980s, the evolution of the system has not been favourable in all respects. There have been tendencies in some major preference-giving countries to exclude countries from benefits on a unilateral basis. Limits to preferential treatment through various mechanisms have proliferated. Non-tariff measures outside the GSP have also limited effective access to preferential treatment. The rules of origin continue to be complex and different from scheme to scheme, discouraging the utilization of the system, particularly by least developed and other low-income countries. As a result, the proportion of dutiable imports which actually received preferential treatment has varied slightly during the years but has remained around 20 per cent.[86]

279.   The second comprehensive review of the GSP covering the second decade of its operation (1979-1989) has been carried out by the Special Committee on Preferences at its annual session in May 1990. The Committee reaffirmed its commitment to the GSP and stressed its importance as an instrument for the expansion of multilateral trade in the 1990s. At the same time, it recognized that the objectives of the GSP have not been fully realised and that to ensure that its full potential is achieved, there was a need for preference-giving countries to maintain, strengthen and improve their autonomous schemes and for developing countries to make complementary efforts to utilize as fully as possible the benefits from the potential trade advantages created by the GSP. Together with enhanced product coverage, the Committee recommended that preference-giving countries consider granting deeper tariff cuts aimed, where possible, at duty-free treatment under the GSP. Preference-giving countries were also urged to strive to reduce *a priori* limitations and restrictions on preferential imports as this imparted stability and predictability to the schemes. In the same vein, the Committee recommended that safeguard measures taken in the context of the GSP be based on objective criteria and transparent procedures. It also agreed that special consideration should be given to products of export interest to least developed countries, in particular by the provision of duty-free treatment.

280.   Regarding other preferential trading arrangements between developed and developing countries, mention should in particular be made of the Lomé Convention and the Caribbean Basin

---

[86] For more details see the *Fourteenth general report on the implementation of the GSP*, report by the UNCTAD secretariat (TD/B C.5/134 and Add.1). See also table II-8 in the annex to this chapter.

Box II-2

THE GSP IN ACTION

UNCTAD Conference resolution 21 (II) established the following objectives for the generalized system of preferences in favour of the developing countries: (a) to increase their export earnings; (b) to promote their industrialization; and (c) to accelerate their rates of economic growth. A comprehensive study programme completed in 1989 attempted to assess the extent to which the GSP has achieved all three of its objectives [a]

The study programme validated previous research finding positive GSP effects. The amount of post-Tokyo-Round annual exports attributable to the GSP was found to be probably in the range of US$ 1-4 billion, and this estimate did not include dynamic effects which accrued over longer time periods. While a few relatively competitive beneficiaries accounted for most of this expansion, another study had found that 19 beneficiaries had been able to increase their exports under the GSP by more than 10 per cent.

Of course, for products that had been consistently denied preferential treatment because of GSP limitations, there were no discernible positive effects. These products accounted for over half of those nominally covered by the GSP. Utilization rates (the ratio of imports to a ceiling or quota) were shown to be inaccurate indicators of GSP benefits, since they may depend on arbitrary adjustment of the GSP limits, origin rules, stringency of enforcement, and non-tariff measures. The trade effects of the limits were difficult to analyse because of an element of endogeneity in the schemes. Withdrawal of preferential treatment only occurred whenever import growth surpassed that of the limitations. Nevertheless, it could be inferred that imports denied preferential treatment were smaller than they otherwise would have been.

GSP limits on major beneficiaries had not spread the benefits of the GSP. This was a contention made frequently in support of limitations on preferential treatment. The study programme found that in some cases the withdrawal of preferences from beneficiaries increased the market shares of non-beneficiaries, in particular the advanced, industrialized countries. In other cases, domestic producers in the preference-giving countries appeared to benefit from the limits. Although the limits mainly affected major beneficiaries, it was noted that they also resulted in the withdrawal of preferential treatment from many small or least developed beneficiaries. Overall, the limits on imports from major beneficiaries did not enhance the market share of less competitive beneficiaries.

Despite estimated trade effects in the billions of dollars, the GSP-induced exports from beneficiary developing countries still accounted for only 1 or 2 per cent of total exports from developing countries. The latter are measured in hundreds of billions of dollars, yet in turn they accounted for only 10-30 per cent of total economic activity in most developing countries. Therefore, in the aggregate, the GSP could make only a very small contribution to overall industrialization and economic growth. This conclusion would differ, of course, for a country which was highly specialized in the export of GSP-covered products.

---

[a] See Craig R. MacPhee, "A synthesis of the GSP Study Programme", study by UNCTAD, UNCTAD/ITP/19 (English only).

Initiative (CBI). The fourth Lomé Convention was signed on 15 December 1989 between the European Economic Community and 69 developing countries of Africa, the Caribbean and the Pacific (ACP) for a period of ten years ending 1 March 2000. The new Convention provides improved market access conditions for ACP products to the EEC market, notably the access of agricultural products, the only area still subject to restrictions under the previous Lomé III trade arrangements.

281. Trade preferences granted to 28 Caribbean and Central American countries by the United States under its Caribbean Basin Economic Recovery Act (CBERA) of 1983, initially for a period of 12 years up to 1995, were made permanent by the United States Customs and Trade Act of 1990. This Act provides for more open access to the United States market for CBI designated countries, particularly in certain products previously exempt from the programme.

4. Security of market access

282. Trade rules under the multilateral trading system permit countries, in certain defined circumstances, to impose import restrictions or suspend tariff concessions to safeguard a domestic industry that is threatened by a surge of imports or to counter the dumping of foreign goods en-

tering the domestic market and to countervail subsidized foreign goods entering the domestic market. Experience (e.g. the results of panel investigations) has shown however that the desire of governments to have legal cover for their actions to restrict imports has, on a large number of occasions, led to the invocation of GATT provisions concerning safeguards, anti-dumping and countervailing action, although the situation fell far short of the requirements of GATT provisions.

(a) Safeguard actions

283.   In the Uruguay Round negotiations on safeguards, a draft agreement was included in the draft Final Act which aims at clarifying and reinforcing "the disciplines of the General Agreement, and specifically those of its Article XIX, to reestablish multilateral control over safeguards and eliminate measures that escape such control".[87] It contains many positive elements from the point view of the developing countries, which include (a) strong obligations on causality to ensure that the injury to domestic industry should definitely be attributed to increased imports, (b) improved provisions relating to the determination of injury, i.e. that more than just a few firms would have to be affected, (c) preference for tariffs over quantitative restrictions, (d) time limitations with provisions for phase-out, and most importantly, (e) a commitment to eliminate "grey area" measures (e.g. "voluntary export restraints") or to bring them into conformity with the proposed safeguards agreement. On the question of selectivity, where developing countries want to ensure that any safeguard action against imports would be on a non-discriminatory basis, discussions in Brussels would appear to suggest some prospects for a satisfactory outcome. In addtion, provisions to exempt least developed countries and developing country suppliers with less than one percent market share, or where the products is of crucial importance for export earnings, are still being considered.

(b) Anti-dumping and countervailing measures

284.   In recent years, antidumping and countervailing practices have become the most frequently invoked trade policy instruments after tariffs.[88] Australia, Canada, EEC and United States have been the most frequent users of anti-dumping and coutervailing measures in the 1980s.[89] The most affected sectors have been iron and steel, chemical and petrochemical products, and machinery. In iron and steel, the number of new cases has decreased significantly since the last surge in 1985,[90] while the number of investigations has held steady in chemicals and machinery. However, there was a noteworthy increase in the number of cases concerning electronics in 1988.

285.   Analysis shows that only in Canada have investigations led to imposition of duties in more than 50 per cent of the cases.[91] In Australia, more than half of the cases have resulted in negative findings of dumping (i.e. non-substantiation of the alleged dumping). The EEC has shown a high propensity to settle cases through price or volume undertakings,[92] and a large number of cases have been withdrawn in the United States. In these markets, on the whole, duties have been imposed relatively more often against developing country exporters than against other exporters. Almost 60 per cent of the investigations involving other developed market-economy countries were either

---

[87] GATT document, MTN.TNC W 35 Rev.1, draft agreement on Safeguards, preamble, p. 183.

[88] In 1980-1988 there were 1824 AD CVD actions. The number of outstanding cases in 1989-1990 remained practically constant (see UNCTAD ITP 24, "Selected Issues on Restrictions to Trade", pp. 18-20; and TD B 1282, "Problems of Protectionism and Structural Adjustment", p.6. See also GATT document C/171, p.8.

[89] Countervailing actions are much more frequent in the United States than in the other countries. A limited number of anti-dumping and countervailing cases have been initiated in Brazil, Chile (countervailing cases only), Finland, New Zealand, Republic of Korea and Sweden. There was a surge in anti-dumping proceedings in Mexico in1988 as the country liberalized imports and abolished a system of "official prices" for customs valuation purposes.

[90] The EEC and the United States have concluded voluntary export restraint agreements with most of their major suppliers of iron and steel products. In some cases, previously imposed anti-dumping measures were suspended as the suppliers agreed to limit their exports.

[91] See UNCTAD ITP 24 (12 March 1990).

[92] The exporter undertakes to raise his export prices at least to a minimum level.

withdrawn or resulted in negative findings. The corresponding rate for developing countries (including China) was only 46 per cent.

286.   Since UNCTAD VII the scope of anti-dumping actions has widened in the EEC and the United States. In 1988 the EEC Council of Ministers approved a new Regulation which modified and strengthened the Community's anti-dumping legislation.[93] It incorporated a Regulation adopted in 1987 which was designed to counter circumvention of anti-dumping duties on final products through the assembly of parts in the Community.[94] Other modifications were largely of a technical nature.[95]

287.   In the United States, the Omnibus Trade and Competitiveness Act of 1988 introduced new rules with regard to anti-dumping and countervailing duty laws, including the cumulation of imports from two or more countries when determining threat of material injury, provisions to prevent circumvention of duty orders through assembly or finishing operations in the United States or shipment via a third country, the possibility of producers of a raw agricultural product to be included in the domestic industry producing the processed product and authority for the United States Trade Representative to revoke the injury test in countervailing duty cases in certain circumstances.

288.   The number of newly initiated anti-dumping and countervailing cases has decreased from its peak levels observed in the mid-1980s. However, the number of cases involving developing countries has not decreased at the same speed. Consequently, the share of outstanding cases directed at developing countries increased from around 35 per cent in 1986 to more than 45 per cent in 1990 (see table II-9 in the annex). Although fewer cases have been added annually to the stock of outstanding antidumping and counteraviling duty cases, no significant progress was made in reducing this stock, with the exception of Australia.[96]

289.   The draft Final Act, presented to the Brussels Ministerial meeting of the TNC of the Uruguay Round, contained no common negotiating text on Anti-Dumping as a basis for further negotiations, nor could any text be prepared by the 13 November 1991. The draft Final Act did, however, include a text on a new Subsidies and Countervailing Measures Code, which required a number of drafting changes, but also called for major political decision. The outstanding issues related mainly to the level of disciplines on the use of domestic subsidies through establishing quantitative thresholds and time periods for developing countries, and more precise rules on the use of non-actionable subsidies. Moreover, the product coverage of the Agreement remained to be decided depending on results in other areas. The area of greatest concern for developing countries related to proposals for the expansion of the scope of prohibited and actionable subsidies to cover those used for promoting and enhancing investments necessary for socio-economic development, without sufficiently clear disciplines on the conditions of applications of countervailing measures.

(c) Transparent mechanisms

290.   The gains from protectionist action are often concentrated in specific segments of the economy or in certain interest groups. However, the cost of protection, which can be many times greater than those gains, are often dispersed and borne by the whole society. This well-known phenomenon in the political economy of protectionism calls for strengthening the institutions which, through scrutinizing the implications and disseminating this information, contribute to the understanding of the issues in the overall national context.

---

[93] Council Regulation (EEC) No. 2423 88 of 11 July 1988 on protection against dumped or subsidized imports from countries not members of the European Economic Community.

[94] Council Regulation (EEC) No. 1761 87 of 22 June 1987.

[95] A detailed analysis of the 1988 Regulation can be found in Jean-François Bellis, Edwin Vermulst and Paul Waer, "Further Changes in the EEC Anti-Dumping Regulation: A Codification of Controversial Methodologies", *Journal of World Trade, 1989*, Vol.23, No.2. The authors concluded that the changes were either neutral or they increased the probability of finding dumping.

[96] In recent years the number of outstanding cases has dropped dramatically in Australia, See Gary Banks, *Australia's Anti-dumping Experience*, Canberra, Centre for International Economics, 1990.

291.   At UNCTAD VII, member States agreed upon the importance of national review mechanisms in the fight against protectionism. As agreed, "Governments should consider, as part of their fight against protectionism, as appropriate, the establishment of transparent mechanisms at the national level to evaluate protectionist measures sought by firms/sectors, and the implications of such measures for the domestic economy as a whole and their effects on export interest of developing countries".[97]

292.   The need for greater transparency in domestic policies and the role of independent institutions to avert protectionism has been stressed in other forums as well, including GATT and OECD. One of the proposals was to analyse the costs and benefits of trade policy actions, existing and prospective, through a "protectionist balance sheet".[98] An OECD report analyses the experience of several countries in improving the transparency of public assistance.[99] OECD also issued a checklist for the assessment of trade policy measures that would contribute to the rationalization of national trade policy measures and encourage structural adjustment.[100]

293.   In many developed market-economy countries there are academic, private and public institutions which analyse broad aspects of domestic trade policies and have some influence in the decision-making process. In the public sphere, three relatively autonomous agencies can be cited as having some characteristics of a national mechanism. These are the International Trade Commission (ITC) in the United States, the Industries Assistance Commission (IAC) in Australia, and the Economic Development Commission (EDC) of New Zealand.

294.   One of the functions of ITC is to advise the President as to the probable effect on the domestic industry and consumers of modification of duties and other barriers to trade that may be considered for inclusion in any proposed trade agreement with foreign countries.[101] Furthermore, the Commission conducts studies, investigations and research projects on a broad range of topics relating to international trade, pursuant to the requests of the President or the legislative bodies and on its own motion.[102] Hence the mandate of ITC is broader than the questions of "injury" to particular import-competing industries.[103]

295.   In carrying out its role to facilitate public scrutiny of protectionism and to assist the Government in rationalizing trade policies, IAC in Australia, *inter alia*, publishes a detailed annual report on industrial assistance as well as on the Australian economy as whole. For any change in the level of assistance to a particualr industry, the Government is required to ask the advice of IAC, although it is not obliged to follow this advice.

296.   New Zealand's EDC was established for roughly similar purposes.[104] Though the functioning of the two institutions is very similar, the Government is not required to seek EDC's advice. On the other hand, EDC can initiate inquiries on its own.

297.   The experience of the working of such mechanisms in some countries can offer some guidelines for countries wishing to do likewise. Governments may also have to see how the existing national mechanism can be improved and strengthened in order to evaluate the implications of the

---

97   Final Act of UNCTAD VII (TD/350), paragraph 105(4).

98   See the *Leutwiler Report, "Trade Policies for a Better Future"*, GATT, 1985.

99   *Transparency for Positive Adjustment*, OECD, 1983. Other OECD reports which reflect the growing interest in the issue of domestic transparency are: *Competition and Trade Policies; Their Interaction, 1984, Costs and Benefits of Protection, International Trade and the Consumer* (forthcoming).

100 The checklist was prepared jointly by the OECD's Committee of Experts on Restrictive Business Practices and its Committee on Consumer Policy, in Consultation with its Trade Committee.

101 Section 131, Trade Act of 1974.

102 Section 322, tariff Act of 1930.

103 In the context of further broadening the mandate of ITC, a Senate Ammendement (No. 571) proposed that the Commission annually submit to the Congress "a report on the negative economic effects on the US of significant existing trade import restraint programmes of the US". Furthermore, according to this proposed ammendment, ITC is required to provide a supplementary report, within a given period, for each "new or significantly altered trade import restraint programme". The latter term was defined broadly to cover most NTMs, but excluded "any import restraint imposed to redress *unfair trade practices* pursuant to the trade laws of the US".

104 The need for an independent body such as EDC was formulated as follows: "There is a role for an independent body to act as a vehicle for increasing public information and scrutiny of economic adjustment policies. This body would aim to increase the accountability of the policy formation process and expose it to the scrutiny of groups or citizens outside the bureaucracy and the political system. The emphasis in its reporting would be highlighting the various economic issues, detailing opinions and trade-offs and, on the basis of these, making recommendations". *Report of the Steering Committee Established to Advise on the Proposed Industrial Development Board*, Wellington, 1986, page 15.

measures for the national economy as a whole and also to evaluate the effects of such measures on the export interests of developing countries. It may also be useful to work out the broad elements which could be taken into account while evaluating the implications mentioned above".[105] In this connection, Governments having national transparent mechanisms and those wishing to establish such mechanisms might wish to hold period meetings of relevant officials/experts for an exchange of information and experiences. The reports on these meetings could be made available to the Trade and Development Board.

5. Competition policy and restrictive business practices

298.   Protectionism involves diverse types of restrictions on trade, not only governmental tariff and non-tariff barriers to trade but also opaque barriers centered on restrictive business practices of enterprises, the two sometimes complementing each other. Restrictive business practices are actions taken by enterprises to limit competition and exclude outsiders/newcomers and thus to maintain or strengthen their position on a given market (national, regional or global), either individually in order to acquire or reinforce a "dominant position of market power", or in concert with other enterprises supplying (or purchasing) similar goods or services.

299.   Cartel-type collusion among firms usually involves price-fixing (monopolistic or monopsonistic, including collusive tendering), market-sharing and concerted action to bar market entry to outsiders. RBPs also include the imposition of restraints by dominant firms on smaller firms and operators in the supply and distribution chain, such as resale price maintenance agreements, prohibition to discount resale prices, tied selling, exclusivity of markets or customers, prohibition to export, refusal to deal and predatory pricing. Through the use of RBPs, enterprises can achieve "monopolization" or control of national, regional, or international markets, thus hampering or effectively eliminating access to markets for products of new entrants on the market, in particular developing countries. Cases of such practices which have had the effect of protecting specific markets against competitive imports have been found in all sectors, including raw materials, manufactures and services, including technology.[106]

300.   Concentration of market power through mergers, takeovers, joint-ventures and other acquisitions of control can also reinforce the market dominance of enterprises over specific markets, and have anti-competitive effects on foreign markets, including those of developing countries.[107]

301.   With the relative decline in governmental barriers to trade resulting from several GATT rounds, the role of enterprise-level trade distortions and anti-competitive practices has acquired greater importance in the international trading system. Moreover, the economic reforms being implemented in both developing and Eastern European countries all tend towards more reliance on the market mechanism and hence on the forces of competition. Structural adjustment programmes adopted in numerous developing countries all have in common the liberalization of prices, deregulation of previously regulated sectors of the economy and privatization of State enterprises including monopolies, and the opening of domestic markets to import competition. Central and Eastern European countries are also moving from a planned economy based on State-owned enterprises to a market-based economy. With the move to greater reliance on market mechanisms, both domestically and in international trade, it becomes essential, if markets are to function optimally in allocating resources and increasing welfare, that enterprise distortion of markets and anti-competitive practices be avoided. This implies the adoption of pro-competition legislation aimed at controlling RBPs at both the domestic and international level.

---

[105] Some norms that might be taken into account in the formation of national mechanisms are spelled out in "Case for evaluating protection in an economy-wide perspective", by S. Laird and G.P. Sampson, in *The World Economy*, Vol. 10, No. 2, June 1987.

[106] See, UNCTAD, Annual Report 1989 on Legislative and other Developments in developed and developing countries in the control of Restrictive Business Practices, (TD/B/RBP/61); 1985-88 (TD/B/RBP/51); and 1983-84 (TD/B/RBP/29), and specific studies such as: Collusive Tendering (TD/B/RBP/12/Rev.2) and Tied Purchasing (TD/B/RBP/Rev.2).

[107] See, UNCTAD study "Concentration of market power through mergers, take-overs and joint ventures and other acquisitions of control, and its effects on international markets, in particular the markets of developing countries", TD/B/RBP/80.

302.   At the domestic level, a conscious competition policy would enhance the development of private initiative by ensuring the access of new entrants to markets and thereby would ensure that private cartels and monopolies, protecting their interests through restrictive business practices, would thus be avoided. At the international level, while there are elaborate procedures for relief against governmental trade barriers, including a dispute settlement mechanism in GATT, relief procedures to counter the adverse effects of RBPs have never been applied. The consultation procedures provided for in the Set of Multilaterally Agreed Equitable Principles and Rules for the Control of Restrictive Business Practices[108] are not mandatory, nor has the Set been systematically and adequately applied in resolving barriers to trade resulting from the utilization of RBPs by enterprises. This has been a longstanding lacuna in the trading system which was recognized in the Final Act of UNCTAD VII, when the Conference agreed that "ongoing work in UNCTAD should continue and be strengthened, particularly with a view to ensuring transparency and to defining consultation procedures".[109]

303.   The Second United Nations Conference to Review all Aspects of the Set, which took place in November/December 1990,[110] adopted a resolution aimed at strengthening the implementation of the Set through, *inter alia*, (a) improving transparency by setting forth specific action concerning the collection, dissemination and exchange of information on RBPs; (b) defining consultation procedures (in this connection the UNCTAD secretariat was requested to prepare a checklist of possible steps which countries may wish to follow in preparation of a case involving RBPs); and (c) providing increased technical assistance to countries upon request, in order to help them adopt and effectively implement RBP control legislation.

304.   The United Nations Review Conference on Restrictive Business Practices, and UNCTAD's Intergovernmental Group of Experts on Restrictive Business Practices, both aim at ensuring application and implementation of the Set of Principles and Rules, which is the only body of rules on competition which meets with a consensus at the multilateral level. However, in its present form, the Set is a recommendation unanimously adopted by the General Assembly of the United Nations. Hence, a longer-term objective would be to develop, as an integral part of the international trading system, a comprehensive agreement on competition policy. Such an agreement should encompass all goods and services, including technology, investment and commodities.

C. MAJOR POLICY ISSUES FOR THE 1990s

305.   International trade relations are at a crossroad. On the one hand the rules and norms which helped shape the post-war growth in international trade are the subject of widespread erosion. At the same time, multilateral rules and disciplines are being evolved in several new areas, notably intellectual property, investments and services in the context of the Uruguay Round of multilateral trade negotiations. The reconciliation of these seemingly contradictory tendencies poses a major challenge to policy-makers in an international economic and trading environment that is evolving at a pace possibly faster than at any other period in history.

306.   The following sections address a number of selected issues of a systemic character warranting policy guidance and consideration by the Conference. These issues are likely to remain at the core of the national and international policy agenda over the foreseeable future, notwithstanding the outcome of one or the other set of trade negotiations in progress. These issues range from the implication of the emerging regional blocs and plurilateral trading arrangements to the questions of sustainable development, environment and integration of developing countries and those in Central and Eastern Europe in the international trading system. The policy questions that arise in this regard have also thrown into sharp relief the need to address institutional issues and reforms. The need for dealing with institutional dimensions of trade relations arises in part from the concern that present institutions and the rules and principles which underpin their activities do not reflect fully evolution in the international economy, which is now largely investment-,

---

[108] See TD/RBP/CONF/10/Rev.1.

[109] See TD/350, para.105(18).

[110] See the Report of the Conference, TD/RBP/CONF.3/9.

knowledge- and technology-driven. The Conference may therefore wish to address the question of rules and multilateral disciplines tailored to the nature of the emerging international economic transactions. In addressing these problems, Governments now face essentially two choices: seeking *ad hoc* solutions to the problems of the system, including piecemeal reform of the GATT/MTN system, or initiating fundamental reforms in trade relations parallel with those of the international monetary and financial systems.

1. Trade policy reform in developing countries

(a) Recent policy changes

307.   Beginning in the 1980s, a growing number of developing countries have adopted policies to integrate their economies more closely into international markets. These policy changes have often been accompanied by moves to give market forces a greater scope, the privatization of State enterprises, the adoption of more liberal regulations toward foreign direct investment, and liberalization of financial markets.

308.   In the trade policy area, the key features of recent policy changes have been towards liberalization, both unilaterally and within groups of countries (for the former, see tables II-3 and II-4; the latter issue is treated in the section of this report on economic groupings). An important change has been a substantial reduction in the use of non-tariff import restrictions, in particular the most distortive ones (restrictive licensing, quotas and prohibitions). Moreover, in several countries average tariff levels and the dispersion of tariff rates have also been reduced considerably. A large number of developing countries are participating in the tariff negotiations taking place in the framework of the Uruguay Round and have offered to bind their tariffs and reduce rates further. Five Latin American countries - Bolivia, Costa Rica, Chile, Mexico and Venezuela - have already bound their entire tariff schedules. These are the only GATT members to have done so.

309.   The break with the past has been most marked in Latin America, where tariff reductions and the elimination of NTMs represent a radical liberalization of trade policy. Several countries in other regions (e.g., Morocco and Republic of Korea) have also participated in the liberalizing trend.

Table II-3

VALUE OF EXPORTS OF MANUFACTURES FROM DEVELOPING COUNTRIES AND TERRITORIES, 1970, 1980 and 1988 [a]

(Million US dollars)

Country/Territory	1988 Value	Rank	1980 Value	Rank	1970 Value	Rank
Korea, Republic of	56 431.5	1	15 622.3	2	634.9	6
Taiwan, Province of China	55 486.2	2	17 428.6	1	1 082.3	2
Singapore	27 553.7	3	9 048.4	4	427.7	7
Hong Kong	26 596.6	4	13 079.3	3	1 949.3	1
China	21 994.9	5	8 680.0	5	1 019.0	4
Brazil	17 261.9	6	7 491.9	6	362.5	10
Mexico	10 392.9	7	1 839.2	11	391.3	9
Yugoslavia	9 849.6	8	6 533.0	7	1 001.5	5
Malaysia	9 196.9	9	2 426.7	9	110.4	14
India	8 604.5	10	4 404.3	8	1 040.2	3
Thailand	8 032.7	11	1 604.1	12	32.2	26
Turkey	7 491.9	12	782.0	16	52.6	21
Indonesia	5 622.9	13	500.6	21	12.2	31
Pakistan	2 960.5	14	1 247.2	13	397.6	8
Argentina	2 888.7	15	1 856.4	10	245.9	11
Philippines	2 274.2	16	1 213.2	14	79.2	16
Egypt	2 016.2	17	333.5	25	206.6	12
Morocco	1 807.1	18	565.1	18	47.2	22
Tunisia	1 617.5	19	797.8	15	34.9	25
Colombia	1 207.1	20	775.1	17	58.7	19
Ecuador	1 024.5	21	74.3	33	3.3	34
Bangladesh	988.0	22	500.8	20	170.0	13
Sri Lanka	689.7	23	193.5	28	4.7	32
Mauritius	623.6	24	115.0	32	1.2	35
Chile	620.9	25	416.8	23	53.3	20
Uruguay	548.4	26	401.7	24	46.5	23
Trinidad & Tobago	461.3	27	202.5	27	61.8	17
Peru	431.8	28	550.2	19	14.8	30
Côte d'Ivoire	427.1	29	149.3	30	28.0	28
Zimbabwe	416.7	30	470.2	22	59.0	18
Jordan	396.2	31	135.7	31	4.2	33
Costa Rica	343.7	32	292.1	26	43.1	24
Senegal	157.4	33	71.9	34	30.2	27
Kenya	126.3	34	159.4	29	25.0	29

Source: UNCTAD secretariat, based on data of the United Nations Statistical Office.

a Countries included are those whose manufactured exports were at least $100 million and whose share of manufactures in total exports exceeded 15 per cent in 1988.

310. At the same time, in a majority of developing countries real effective exchange rates have depreciated, as a result of either market forces or of large nominal devaluations by the authorities. This, in itself, has favoured a shift in the allocation of resources from the non-tradable to the tradable sectors of the economy. Large currency depreciations in real terms have left governments room to rationalize tariff structures and reduce effective rates of protection.

311. Several countries have also moved to strengthen their incentives for exporters in order to counter-act the anti-export bias of tariffs and remaining NTMs. Tariffs in developing countries continue to be generally higher than in developed countries, partly because developing countries rely on tariffs for government revenue to a much greater extend than developed countries. More-

Table II-4

EXPORT GROWTH PERFORMANCE INDICATORS IN SELECTED DEVELOPING COUNTRIES OR TERRITORIES, 1970-1980 and 1980-1988 [a]

(Percentages)

Country/territory [b]	Rate of growth of manufactured export volumes		Rate of growth of total export volumes		Rate of growth of GDP volumes		Rate of growth of manufactured value added		Rate of investment to GDP [c]		
	1980-88	1970-80	1980-88	1970-80	1980-88	1970-80	1980-88	1970-80	1970	1980	1988
Indonesia	30.3	20.8	2.8	6.9	3.8	7.3	8.4	13.1	14.4	25.4	28.5
Turkey	23.3	13.2	14.3	4.2	5.3	5.5	7.6	5.9	20.6	22.3	19.6
Mauritius	19.8	33.2	11.4	3.7	5.9	6.2	10.8	6.9	15.4	20.9	38.1
Mexico	19.1	6.3	5.4	12.6	0.4	6.0	0.2	6.8	22.2	28.0	17.4
Thailand	17.6	16.2	10.7	9.6	5.7	6.7	6.5	10.0	28.7	26.6	26.5
Malaysia	14.8	15.1	9.0	4.7	4.1	7.4	7.0	11.0	23.5	31.6	27.6
Sri Lanka	14.1	20.8	5.7	1.9	4.2	4.7	6.1	1.9	15.4	34.0	23.3
Korea, Republic of	13.7	23.4	13.7	21.1	9.7	8.7	12.7	15.7	25.2	32.8	33.1
Taiwan Province of China	13.1	16.1	12.6	14.5	-	9.4	-	12.3	26.2	32.6	-
China	12.5	8.3	11.2	8.3	9.8	5.0	16.3	7.0	26.3	32.2	37.6
Morocco	11.3	13.7	4.8	3.8	4.0	5.2	4.1	5.8	21.3	25.0	25.5
Hong Kong	11.2	10.5	11.6	10.3	5.8	8.8	-	10.6	25.8	36.0	27.1
Pakistan	10.1	-0.4	8.1	0.6	6.1	4.5	7.7	5.3	20.9	18.7	18.0
Tunisia	8.3	19.3	2.9	7.2	3.1	6.5	5.8	9.8	33.0	30.3	14.6
Chile	8.1	20.3	4.4	9.76	1.6	1.2	1.9	-0.8	21.0	21.6	16.9
Egypt	7.7	-10.4	6.0	1.5	5.3	6.5	5.5	-4.4	14.2	29.4	22.0
Singapore	7.3	18.2	7.0	4.2	6.8	7.8	4.7	9.3	43.3	48.1	35.3
Bangladesh	6.8	2.5	5.9	3.6	3.5	3.5	2.4	11.2	14.2	15.0	14.5
Brazil	6.0	18.8	5.9	8.1	2.9	7.5	4.2	8.6	20.9	23.6	17.4
Jordan	5.6	20.1	6.3	18.6	3.0	7.8	3.4	16.8	12.0	41.4	25.0
Zimbabwe	4.8	7.4	1.5	2.8	2.5	3.5	2.0	2.8	26.5	19.1	15.2
Senegal	4.8	-2.6	6.8	1.8	3.1	2.0	3.3	2.6	17.5	15.8	15.0
India	4.5	7.5	4.6	5.4	5.5	3.3	7.9	4.5	19.3	22.8	21.7
Costa Rica	4.5	10.6	2.9	5.0	2.3	5.3	2.3	7.9	19.0	27.9	25.8
Trinidad & Tobago	4.1	0.7	-6.2	-7.6	-05.8	4.9	-10.0	1.7	12.4	32.2	9.7
Philippines	3.0	25.6	0.4	5.8	-0.0	6.4	-0.3	6.7	23.6	30.7	16.9
Uruguay	2.0	14.9	2.0	6.3	-0.7	3.2	-0.5	1.8	10.1	17.5	9.4
Ecuador	1.4	22.5	5.5	11.8	1.9	8.9	0.6	10.0	24.0	27.5	16.7
Yugoslavia	0.5	7.2	0.9	5.2	0.5	5.8	1.3	7.7	38.0	40.3	38.3
Kenya	0.3	6.8	0.1	-1.9	3.0	5.4	2.9	5.6	20.3	19.1	17.9
Colombia	0.3	12.8	7.9	1.9	3.0	5.4	2.9	5.6	20.3	19.1	17.9
Guatemala	0.1	4.8	-2.0	5.5	-0.3	5.8	1.1	6.0	12.3	11.6	10.3
Côte d'Ivoire	-1.0	12.4	1.5	4.7	0.4	5.6	7.5	7.7	19.3	29.8	12.9
Argentina	-1.3	9.1	0.1	6.9	-0.3	2.3	-0.2	1.3	20.0	22.4	12.2
Peru	-2.4	35.3	-2.5	4.5	1.1	3.1	1.6	3.0	17.3	28.8	23.6

Source: UNCTAD secretariat, based on official international sources.

  a Countries included are those whose manufactured exports were at least $100 million and whose shares of manufactures in total exports exceeded 15 per cent in 1988.

  b Countries ranked according to the rate of growth of manufactured export volumes in 1980-1988.

  c Both GDP and investment are measured in real 1980 prices.

over, trade policy instruments have traditionally been used as an adjunct to industrialization policies. In contrast to the way developed countries use NTMs, such trade actions in developing countries tend to be broad in product coverage and are applied on a general, non-selective basis.[111]

312. The motivations for these policy changes have varied. The persistence of foreign-exchange constraints and the need to service external debt were determining factors in a large number of countries. Several countries in need of external financial assistance also came under pressure from the multilateral financial institutions to liberalize their economies, including their trade policies. A greater awareness of the benefits to be derived from export orientation and of the limits of import-substituting industrialization also played an important role.

313. The scope and pace of the reforms have varied significantly among countries. A few countries introduced drastic reforms and implemented them in a relatively short period of time. These reforms included the elimination of non-tariff barriers and, simultaneously, a sharp reduction in average tariff levels and in the dispersion of tariff rates. Some examples of this approach are Chile (1974-1979), Bolivia (1985), Guinea (1985) and Mexico (1985-1988). Recently, the introduction of drastic and rapid trade liberalization programmes has been a key feature of broad-based reforms in several Latin American economies (Argentina, Brazil, Peru, Venezuela).[112] Other countries eliminated or significantly reduced quantitative restrictions while only gradually reducing tariffs (e.g., Costa Rica, Côte d'Ivoire and Uruguay). In some countries, tariff rates were raised at the same time as non-tariff barriers were liberalized (e.g., Ghana, Nigeria and Turkey), suggesting that the intended policy was one of tariffication of NTMs. Still other countries introduced gradual programmes of trade liberalization intended mainly to rationalize the structure of incentives and to open the economy progressively to foreign trade. This group includes countries such as Bangladesh, Indonesia, Morocco, Pakistan and Senegal.

314. As noted above, policies toward domestic and foreign investment have also been liberalized in many developing countries. On the domestic front, reform has progressed significantly in the areas of investment licensing and local content regulations. The direction of reform as regards investment licensing has varied from total abolition to circumscribing licensing to specific sectors or fields of activity. Even in countries where investment licensing is still required, efforts have been made to streamline the administrative procedures for processing start-up, investment, import and other licenses. In this respect, the most common approach has been the establishment of "one-stop shops" to process all the licenses and approvals that are needed to make an investment or set up an enterprise.

315. There continue to be, however, significant differences among countries with respect to reforms of local content regulations and policies. In countries whose local content requirements tended to stifle investment, such restrictions have been largely abandoned. However, in more industrially advanced developing countries, local content programmes remain in force, although in recent years they have been administered more flexibly.

316. Other changes in investment policies over the 1980s focused on stimulating foreign direct investment (FDI) and, particularly, encouraging export-oriented investment by foreign companies. The liberalization of FDI rules and regulations has included permitting FDI in sectors hitherto reserved for nationals, the relaxation of equity ceilings for foreign investors, and the easing of restrictions regarding profit remittances and capital repatriation. A large number of countries created or strengthened existing export processing zones and other similar régimes aimed at attracting export-oriented foreign investors.

---

[111] See Sam Laird and Rene Vossenaar, "Why we should be worried about non-tariff measures", *Información Comercial Española* (Madrid), 1991 (forthcoming); and R. Erzan, H. Kuwahara, S. Marchese and R. Vossenaar, "The profile of protection in developing countries", *UNCTAD Review*, Vol. 1, No. 1, Geneva, 1989.

[112] In the cases of Argentina, Bolivia, Brazil and Peru, the trade liberalization programmes were introduced in a macroeconomic context of hyper-inflation, suggesting that they were partly used to lend credibility to the entire package of economic reform. See Dani Rodrik, "Trade policies and development: some new issues", *Discussion Paper Series* No. 447, Centre for Economic Policy Research, London, August 1990.

(b) Impact on economic performance

317.   An analysis of the relationship between policy régimes and growth performance during the 1970s and 1980s yields rather agnostic conclusions.[113]   As can be seen in tables II-3 and II-4, in the period since 1970 the four more industrialized economies of South East Asia have maintained consistently rapid rates of growth of total and manufactured exports, high investment rates, and fast overall economic growth.[114] Their policy régimes, however, have been quite disparate. Hong Hong and Singapore are small open economies with no natural resources, and both have consistently pursued liberal trade policies, although Singapore went through a phase of import-substituting industrialization in the 1960s. By contrast, both the Republic of Korea and Taiwan, Province of China have maintained significant inter-industry selectivity in their trade and industrialization strategies, they both initially relied on import substitution, and their superior export performance can no wise be ascribed to a free trade régime. Import policies have been gradually liberalized in both economies only since the early 1980s, after export-oriented industrialization had become well established.

318.   Especially rapid gains as exporters of manufactures were made during the 1970s and 1980s by a diverse group of countries which includes Indonesia, Turkey, Mauritius, Mexico, Thailand, Malaysia, Sri Lanka, and Morocco. With the exception of Mexico, none of these countries can be described as having embraced liberal trade policies.[115] In most of them, a comprehensive set of export promotion measures was superimposed on an existing import substitution régime. At the same time, the structure of protection was rationalized and the dispersion of effective rates of protection was significantly reduced. Several of these countries have made extensive use of export processing zones.

319.   Generally, there are two factors related to trade policy which largely explain the export and growth success of the four established exporters of manufactures of South East Asia and of the more recent newcomers to international markets for manufactures.[116] In the first place, they succeeded in establishing a domestic economic environment which enabled firms to compete in international markets. This involved the avoidance of currency overvaluation, unrestricted access to imported inputs at world market prices, access to imported capital goods and investment finance, and the provision to exporters of adequate investment and short-term trade finance at low interest rates.

320.   Secondly, these countries found ways of overcoming their lack of technical, managerial and marketing know-how by combining local productive capacity with foreign expertise. In some cases, this was achieved by recourse to fairly liberal policies towards foreign investors. In others, policies favoured either joint ventures or non-equity forms of association such as technology licensing or sub-contracting arrangements (by which local firms produced for international markets using specifications, models and even inputs provided by foreign firms).

321.   Of course, it needs to be emphasized that countries experiencing rapid economic growth and sustained export expansion and diversification have met other conditions which are unrelated to trade policy. There is ample evidence that a fundamental factor accounting for the long-term success of the established exporters of manufactures of South East Asia has been the combination of large investments in basic and technical education with the maintenance of an incentive system

---

113 For more details see, Manuel R. Agosin, "Trade policy reform and economic performance: A review of the issues and some preliminary evidence", *UNCTAD Discussion Paper* No.41, August 1991.

114 China, which has remained among the top 5 developing economies exporting manufactures and has also recorded rapid growth and high investment rates, is excluded from the analysis because its size makes it, evidently, a special case among developing economies.

115 In the case of Mexico, strong growth in manufactured export - which began in 1983, well before the adoption of the trade liberalization package - is explained mainly by the strong incentive to such exports given by the very sharp depreciation of the exchange rate following the eruption of the debt crisis. It should be noted that strong growth in manufactured export has not been accompanied by growth in the economy in generally and that, therefore, it cannot yet be considered an indicator of development "success" in the same way as in the South East Asian economies.

116 These arguments are made by Noland for the eight Pacific Basin economies. They are equally applicable to other successful exporters. See Marcus Noland, *Pacific Basin Developing Economies: Prospects for the Future* (Washington, D.C., Institute for International Economies, 1990). For the experience of the Republic of Korea, see Alice H. Amsden, *Asia's Next Giant - South Korea and Late Industrialization* (New York and Oxford, Oxford University Press, 1989); and Alice H. Amsden and Yoon-Doe Euh, "Republic of Korea's financial reforms: What are the lessons?", *UNCTAD Discussion Paper No. 30*, April 1990. The experience of Turkey is discussed in Ercan Uygur, "Trade Policies and Growth in Turkey, 1970-1990", *UNCTAD Trade Policy Series* No.4, 1991 (forthcoming).

that did not discriminate against exports. The development of human skills facilitated the transfer of labour from agriculture to export-oriented manufacturing.[117] In the Republic of Korea, the Government's ability to impose wage controls facilitated the export drive directly and indirectly: the competitiveness of firms was not periodically threatened by a restive labour force, and price and exchange rate stability were easier to maintain.

322.   The importance of human resource availability is highlighted by the experience of the lower-income, commodity-dependent developing countries which attempted to introduce trade and industrial policy reforms. In some cases, there were gaps between the reform commitments of governments and the reforms that countries were able to implement in practice, owing largely to domestic macroeconomic environment. In these countries, expansion of supply capabilities remains the major priority.

323.   In some cases, even where it was feasible to carry out reform programmes, they did not lead to sustained export and growth success. In lower-income, commodity-dependent countries, it is clearly not sufficient to change the structure of incentives, because supply responses to relative price changes tend to be weak. For example, in these countries, real devaluations have little or no impact on the real economy: since exports are not consumed domestically, the shift in consumption to non-traded goods which follows a devaluation has no impact on the availability of exports; and the greater incentives to produce importables which would normally result from devaluation are not translated into larger production because these economies' imports consist mostly of intermediate and capital goods which cannot be produced domestically. In these countries, structural change and adjustment require sustained efforts to build supply capabilities, rather than just "getting prices right".[118]

324.   As already noted, countries liberalizing their trade régimes drastically do not yet have a track record which would permit one to draw some conclusions from their experience. The one experience is Chile: its trade liberalization has established the basis for long-term export-oriented growth. However, in the transition from the import-substitution régime, policies could have ensured a more gradual programme of trade liberalization and could have made better use of the capabilities built during an earlier period of industrialization.[119]

(c) Issues for the 1990s

325.   Experiences with trade policy, both recently and in a longer time perspective, leave some lessons for the future. Countries that have introduced coherent and stable export promotion measures have undoubtedly fared better than those which have geared incentives exclusively toward the domestic market. Management of the exchange rate so as to avoid overvaluation and maintain roughly stable incentives for the production of tradables appears to have been more significant than import liberalization in those countries with the best outward-oriented industrialization records. In these countries import liberalization came later, after export success had been consolidated.

326.   So far there are no examples where import liberalization, by itself, has led to rapid growth. In fact, the mere withdrawal of protection without its replacement by supportive policies to reallocate resources or to improve productivity in industry is extremely costly. The economy responds very slowly and inefficiently to this kind of shock treatment. On the other hand, experience also shows that import-substituting policies can be carried to extremes which result only in the retardation of economic growth and which even defy rationality. Such policies can easily give rise to widespread rent-seeking and serve no long-term development goal. Therefore, a rationalization of the structure of incentives would appear to be a major goal for a number of countries.

---

[117] See the studies cited in Howard Pack, "Industrialization and trade", *Handbook of Development Economics,* Vol. I, ed. by Hollis B. Chenery and T.N. Srinivasan (Amsterdam, North Holland, 1988).

[118] A recent study finds econometric evidence that real devaluations are effective in improving the trade balances in manufactures exporters but not in primary commodity exporters. See Jaime de Melo and Riccardo Faini, "Adjustment, investment and the real exchange rate in developing countries", *Economic Policy* No.11, October 1990.

[119] Ricardo Ffrench-Davis, Patricio Leiva and Roberto Madrid, *Trade Liberalization in Chile: Experiences and Prospects,* Trade Policy Series No.1. UNCTAD, Geneva, 1991.

327.   This does not mean that import substitution should have no role in industrialization strategies. Protection of the domestic market may be unavoidable, especially in the early stages of industrialization. However, the experience of developing countries does teach that, if protection is chosen as a policy option, it should be highly selective, moderate, and decreasing over time. Only in this way can a government ensure that infant industries will "grow up" in a reasonable period of time. As far as possible, it is also desirable to compensate the anti-export bias of import substitution policies with roughly equivalent export incentives. Duty drawbacks for direct and indirect exporters[120] have proven to be useful in giving exporters access to imported inputs at world prices.

328.   The desirability of a selective trade policy must, of course, be weighed against a country's ability to implement it. This will depend partly on the availability of skilled manpower and on the ability of the public sector to work together towards common and coherent objectives with well-understood policy tools. Another important determinant will be the capacity of the government to steer the private sector towards socially useful goals and to avoid being captured by special interest groups.

329.   The basic lesson of successful industrializers is that an industrial policy is indispensable to sustained growth and that trade liberalization cannot be considered a substitute for such a policy. In this context, industrial policy should be understood in a broad sense as the measures that are needed to raise the rate of investment, to increase the absorption of foreign technologies and the capacity to innovate, and to upgrade the skills of the labour force.

330.   Another ingredient in the attainment of international competitiveness is reaching a consensus on income distribution which contributes to social peace and, at the same time, does not undermine an export-oriented growth strategy. The policies used to keep wages down in some of the countries of South East Asia are unlikely to prove acceptable in more democratic societies.

331.   The difficulties that the lower-income countries have in mobilizing domestic resources for investment in physical and human infrastructure are well-known and do not need repeating here. Suffice it to say that, if these countries are to make headway in this regard, they will need significant inflows of foreign resources in order to break the initial resource constraints to sustained growth.

332.   Trade policy reform alone is not enough to bring about structural adjustment. During the 1980s, some countries succeeded in increasing exports relative to GDP, in some cases spectacularly so. However, GDP growth did not always follow strong export growth. The experience of the 1980s shows that, in the absence of import growth, increasing exports can lead to falling output and living standards. The effects of the debt overhang and deteriorating terms of trade are today the major impediments that many developing countries face in translating growth in export volumes into larger imports. Domestic policy reform is, therefore, a necessary but insufficient condition for greater outward orientation.

2. Need for adjustment-oriented policies in developed countries

333.   The pace of structural change in the developed countries accelerated considerably in the 1980s. Breathtaking technological progress, fast-changing consumer tastes, shorter product life cycles in some sectors and market saturation in others and the growing internationalization of these economies combined to create pressures for structural adjustment. As regards the products of export interest to developing countries, adjustment pressures in developed countries have been strongest in agriculture, textiles, footwear, consumer electronics, shipbuilding and steel.

334.   Developed countries have in many cases attempted to cope with structural change by resorting to policies which are defensive and protectionist in nature, trying to resist change and reverse fundamental market forces. While such policies have not been successful in preventing structural change, they have certainly slowed it down and raised its costs. At the same time, they have penalized efficient producers in third countries, including those in developing economies,

---

[120] Indirect exporters are those producing inputs for exporters.

which have been denied free market access for their exports.

335.   Defensive support policies have not prevented downward adjustment in employment, nor have they helped the assisted industries to become more competitive, although strategic responses have enabled some firms within declining industries to compete and even to thrive. But such adjustments have generally depended on entrepreneurial ability, in particular the ability to move production "up-market" into more sophisticated products and carve out new market niches, rather than on the provision of government assistance.

336.   Reducing subsidies and protection which distort resource allocation is crucial for improving the flexibility of economies and for increasing international trade on a competitive basis. Faster progress in the reduction of subsidies and protection would help to accelerate the reallocation of resources in a dynamic perspective from the more stagnant or declining sectors to the more productive and growing sectors of the economy.

337.   However, a programme which relies solely on market forces to bring about structural adjustment can be costly and slow, and can meet with substantial political resistance. The challenge for governments is to devise adjustment assistance programmes which contribute to the transfer of resources out of sectors experiencing adjustment pressures and into sectors with greater long-term potential and with higher resource productivity. As experience has shown, in some cases the needed shift in resources can take place within the same industry, from more labour-intensive to more skill- and capital-intensive segments.

338.   Adjustment assistance can be aimed at workers or at firms. With regard to workers, the objective of such programmes should be to improve the flexibility of the labour force to adjust to changing patterns of demand. While several countries already have in place programmes of this nature, their size and scope are, in many cases, inadequate. Workers who are displaced by competition from imports need time to find new employment. Therefore, the extension of unemployment insurance benefits for time periods commensurate to the nature of the problem would be an appropriate policy response. The other components of adjustment assistance to workers displaced by import competition relate to expenditures on retraining and skill development, the provision of information needed to make decisions about change of employment and/or location, and the facilitation of geographical mobility through grants to defray costs of job search and relocation.

339.   In most developed market economies, the largest portion (1 to 3 per cent of their GDP) of public expenditure on adjustment assistance programmes geared to the labour force is allocated to income maintenance, essentially unemployment compensation and, in some countries, early retirement benefits. While income maintenance is without doubt necessary and socially desirable, improving the capability of labour markets to accomodate structural change also requires the provision of the other public services noted above. However, comparatively few resources have been allocated to labour market programmes with the economic objective of improving the flexibility of labour markets in matching the supply and demand for labour and in directing labour continuously and promptly to its most productive and rewarding use. Public expenditure on such "active" labour market programmes accounts in most developed market-economy countries for less than 1 per cent of their GDP.

340.   The challenge for labour market policies in the 1990s reaches well beyond finding jobs for those currently unemployed. Policies must help all workers to change jobs and activities whenever required to adjust to structural change. There is a clear need for developed countries to give a more prominent place to the economic and structural dimensions of labour market policies in developed countries. A greater focus on placement, retraining and mobility schemes can help to match to a greater extent skills in demand and skills on offer. Since the social benefits of such schemes outweigh the private costs, a sound case can be made for government subsidization.

341.   As regards firms experiencing adjustment pressure, it is possible to envisage special programmes for them as well. For example, for tax purposes, corporations entering new industries could be allowed to use their losses to offset future profits. Another alternative would be for the appropriate government agency to purchase the net operating loss carry-forwards of such firms at "face value" (the amount of such carry-forwards times the marginal corporate tax rate), on condition the beneficiary firm invest at least an equivalent amount in a new industry.[121] Such

---

[121] For a similar scheme, see Gary S. Hufbauer and Howard F. Rosen, "Trade Policy for Troubled Industries", *Policy Analyses in International Economics*, No. 15, Institute for International Economics, Washington, D.C. March 1986.

programmes could differentiate benefits according to firm size, with proportionately larger benefits made available to small and medium-size firms, which are less able to effect adjustment than larger and more diversified enterprises.

342.   Adjustment programmes aimed at enterprises could also incorporate an element of technological diffusion. In many cases, firms experiencing adjustment pressures have very imperfect information on the technologies that are available for reducing costs or increasing efficiency. This is particularly the case of smaller firms with inadequate technical personnel. Addressing the problem would require closer integration of technology and labour market policies and increased investment in human capital.

343.   The design of more effective structural adjustment policies in the developed countries would benefit significantly from evaluations of the achievements of their past and current policies in promoting adjustment to change. The annual reviews conducted by the Trade and Development Board on protectionism and structural adjustment could focus more sharply on the technical issues involved in such structural adjustment programmes. In view of the close inter relationships between protectionism and structural adjustment, the reviews of structural adjustment policies could take place concurrently with those on the transparent mechanisms for evaluating trade actions called for in section of this report. Given the technical nature of the subject matters, the Secretary-General of UNCTAD could convene a group of experts from capitals to assist him and the Board in preparing for a discussion of the issues and in making concrete recommendations for action.

3. Reform process in the countries of Central and Eastern Europe

344.   Systemic changes and economic reforms continue in Central and Eastern Europe, although their scope and pace differ from one country to the other. The legacy from the past is a major factor underlying the recent rapid deterioration in economic performances, exacerbated by the costs associated with the on-going systemic changes and by external developments. Past investment strategies often resulted in the allocation of fixed investment to less productive areas, favouring heavy industry at the expense of consumer goods and technology-intensive capital goods. Levels of productivity are accordingly low and productivity growth has been poor. Moreover, the assured market in the Soviet Union has in the past reduced considerably the necessity for Eastern European countries to modernize obsolete equipment and achieve improvements in production efficiency.

345.   The change-over from a planned to a market economy will create significant economic and social cost in the period of transition, although some countries - Czechoslovakia, Hungary, and Poland - are better prepared than others to cope with the challenge of systemic changes, particularly as they benefit from a national consensus on their political leadership and the main features of their reform programmes. The moves towards market-oriented systems will inevitably involve the closure of uncompetitive enterprises, the displacement of workers, and a disruption of many production activities. The success of efforts to limit these costs will be crucially determined by the speed of the learning process of economic agents who have to familiarize themselves with new market institutions, and overcome the inertia of past attitudes incompatible with market-oriented behaviour. Moreover, economic disarray at the national level has been compounded by the adverse impact of the collapse of the CMEA, the associated decline of trade among the countries in Eastern Europe, higher oil prices in the wake of the Gulf crisis, and reduced oil supplies from the Soviet Union.

346.   The reform agenda for a broad-based transition to a market economy is long and challenging. While reform needs and the appropriate mix of reforms will vary from country to country, there are a number of key components that would be needed to move these countries along the road to market economies. Major changes are needed in the macro-economic setting, new institutions must be built and fundamental structural change and adjustment in the productive base must be brought about:

(a) The transition to market economies needs to be supported by fiscal and monetary policies which promote and sustain a stable macroeconomic framework. A system of macroeconomic management and control through monetary and fiscal policies is, however, still largely non-existent in the Soviet Union and in some other East European economies.

(b) Tax systems need to be restructured and made more transparent, in conformity with the pattern of taxes in market-economy countries where value-added tax, company income tax and personal income tax are major revenue items. The creation of a modern business infrastructure also requires the early establishment of an effective legal system (property rights, banking regulations, competition law, labour legislation, etc.)

(c) An important component of the financial sector reforms is the transformation of the monobank system into a two-tier system consisting of a central bank with broad powers to execute monetary policy and a second tier of independent, profit-oriented commercial banks.

(d) Further challenging tasks are the privatization and the breaking up of state monopolies, the liberalization of price-setting mechanisms and the dismantling of subsidies. Enterprise autonomy over the recruitment and dismissal of workers requires, on the other hand, the establishment of a social safety net, including unemployment insurance programmes and offically supported retraining schemes.

(e) The development of financial markets is important to mobilize savings and help direct scarce capital to the most productive investments. And the development of equity markets can support the financing of new and expanding firms, and facilitate the privatization of public enterprises.

(f) Exchange rate systems based on currency convertibility allowing realistic market-determined exchange rates are essential to bring domestic prices into line with those on the world market. In the same vein, a progressive liberalization of foreign trade is indispensable to help integrating the national economies in the international trading system.

(g) Serious obstacles hampering foreign investment have to be removed. In particular the legal infrastructure of property rights is inadequate and often ambiguous, constraining the possibilities of foreigners to own or sell private property. The protection of intellectual property also needs strengthening. On the whole, significant foreign investment will only come on stream once reforms to establish market-oriented economies have taken shape and progressed sufficiently to instill confidence in investors that there will be no reversal in the drive towards economic liberalization.

347.   All these reforms are interrelated and mutually reinforcing and will have to be pursued more or less simultaneously. Postponing one set of reform measures is likely to obstruct the efficient deployment of others. However, even when reforms are pursued simultaneously on all major fronts, it will still take time to transform command economies into fully-fledged market-oriented systems. Accompanying social measures will, therefore, be important to alleviate the welfare cost of the transition process.

348.   The most daunting task may prove to be the broad-based modernization and restructuring of the agricultural, industrial and services sectors of the economies to establish or strengthen international competitiveness of output. All the economies in Eastern Europe lag significantly behind the developed market-economy countries in technologically advanced areas. In particular, industries with high intensity in raw material and energy consumption, notably the metallurgical and chemical sectors, face adjustment problems on a large scale. Moreover, the overhaul of the physical infrastructure, in particular transportation and telecommunication, will be necessary to provide effective support to the productive base and the export sector. The process of adjustment can prove to be protracted and its cost will undoubtedly be massive.

349.   The developing economies could gain new export opportunities in Eastern Europe as and when countries in the region become more market-oriented and open up to exports from developing countries through active trade policy measures. Increased exports to these markets could meet hitherto unsatisfied demand or replace trade among countries in Eastern Europe, reflecting a shift of these economies towards more competitive sources of supply. The developing countries could, in particular, benefit from strong pent-up demand for tropical products and a wide range of manufactured consumer goods. As foreign exchange shortages will still constrain the import capacity of economies in Eastern Europe for some time to come, these countries may give preference to

lower-priced products from developing economies. On the other hand, it can be expected that investment goods will dominate the imports of countries in Eastern Europe. These economies will procure most of the capital goods required for the modernization of their productive base in the developed market-economy countries, although a few developing country exporters of manufactures in the South-East Asia could be in a position to enter these new markets.

350.   The systemic and economic changes which are under way in Eastern Europe call for strong international support. Financial assistance has been provided or promised by governments and financial institutions such as the World Bank, the IMF, and the EBRD to a number of countries in Eastern Europe in support of their economic stabilization and adjustment efforts. And technical assistance has been made available in the context of the introduction of market mechanisms and the promotion of market-oriented attitudes, in particular through management and vocational training in industry, agriculture and trade. Such international support should continue and be further expanded.

351.   On the other hand, international aid can be effective only if the countries in Central and Eastern Europe accelerate the adoption and ensure the implementation of laws and regulations indispensable for the functioning of market mechanisms; create favourable conditions for foreign investment, including the unhindered repatriation of capital and profits; expedite improvements of their infrastructure indispensable for efficient domestic production and the attraction of foreign investors; liberalize progressively their trade and import policies; participate in existing international mechanisms aimed at avoiding market disruptions in third countries; and last, but not least, continue with the process of democratization. Some of the countries have already made considerable headway; others need to be more active and more consistent.

4. New issues on the trade negotiations agenda

352.   The globalization process referred to at the beginning of this chapter has been both a cause and a consequence of an expansion in the volume, and a diversification, of international transactions. Some of these transactions extended the traditional boundaries of international trade: for example, an increasing range of services became the subject of international exchange. In other cases, there was a transformation in the nature of trade: the globalization and regionalization processes both increased, for example, the proportion of manufactured components and parts in total international trade.

353.   At the same time, there was dramatic growth in newer forms of international exchange. Financial transactions multiplied and now vastly exceed, in financial terms, those in goods. Within this broad category, inter-country flows of foreign direct investment reached unprecedented magnitudes. In addition to capital, these foreign direct investment flows usually involved a transfer of technology, a form of international transaction that has grown further through such arrangements as licensing, franchising, management contracts and various forms of sub-contracting. More particularly, there has been an increasing number of joint ventures among firms from different countries specifically to undertake research and product development.

354.   Increasingly, commercial competitiveness depends on technological prowess, on the possession of various forms of knowledge and on access to information. This explains why the owners and creators of such assets attach great importance to preserving control over them, as well as why there is such keen competition from others to acquire them. Developing countries, in particular, are largely bereft of these newly-important assets, but recognize the crucial role they can play in development.

355.   Despite the potential international economic conflict that such a situation could imply, there has been no corresponding addition to, or broadening of the scope of, institutional arrangements and multilateral instruments to embrace the increasing variety of international transactions.

(a)   Investment

356.   Thus property issues in general and investment, intellectual property and services took on a new importance which was reflected in the inclusion in the Uruguay Round of the so-called "new issues" such as trade-related investment measures (TRIMs), trade-related aspects of intellectual property rights (TRIPs) and trade in services. Such initiatives are directed, to a large extent, at the strengthening of international rules dealing with property rights and linking them to market access commitments. This would appear to constitute a new approach in pursuit of certain longstanding objectives with respect to the rights and privileges of international property owners, which in the past have been pursued bilaterally or as a reaction to developing-country initiatives in United Nations bodies in the 1970s.

357.   Although there are agreements dealing with some aspects of international investment at bilateral and regional levels, strictly speaking there is no agreement that deals with the issue comprehensively. Investment issues have repeatedly arisen in international discussions, often as areas of contention. While the developed countries and transnational corporations describe the issues as matters of contractual reliability and security of acquired rights, developing countries perceive the issues in terms of their economic sovereignty and of their national development needs and priorities. Thus, proposals put forward in the Uruguay Round aimed at reducing the scope for Governments to regulate and to place terms upon foreign investment, met the determined opposition of developing and some developed countries that are of the view that the right to determine whether and to what extent, and upon what terms, they would permit foreign investment was necessary to ensure the maximum development impact of foreign investment and to counter or pre-empt anti-competitive practices of TNCs. The negotiations on TRIMs in the Uruguay Round have evolved into an area of major disagreement with little scope for convergence of views among the participants, and lack of a fundamental consensus on the negotiations on this issue. Some developed countries sought to establish a prohibition for investment measures *per se,* while developing and certain other developed countries considered that the Punta des Este mandate was solely to address the trade-restrictive effects of investment measures.

(i)   Trade-related investment measures (TRIMs)

358.   Most developing countries have liberalized their policies towards FDI, with incentives to attract FDI tending to replace limitations on its entry. At the same time, host Governments are endeavouring to ensure that the behaviour of TNCs conforms with national development objectives by imposing conditions on their operations. These so-called performance requirements take a variety of forms, with a minimum local equity requirement probably being the most common. Some have direct consequences for trade flows, for example when they take the form of minimum local content requirements (implying a maximum import content) or minimum export levels. Because they distort the normal pattern of trade, a number of countries have called for such measures to be included in trade negotiations. In particular, an important element in the launching of the Uruguay Round was the agreement to broaden the negotiations to include, *inter alia*, these so-called trade-related investment measures (TRIMs).

359.   In the course of these negotiations, it has been argued by some countries that subsidies to attract foreign direct investment should also be addressed, on the grounds that they all affect trade, either directly or indirectly. Subsidies take a variety of forms and are now widespread in both developed and developing countries. In many instances, they are an integral component of national trade policy (particularly in the context of efforts to develop Export Processing Zones), but in other cases they are a local government issue. For example, some of the largest subsidies to FDI have been those offered by individual states within the United States to Japanese companies considering establishing automobile manufacturing plants in the country; within the EEC, there was corresponding competition among countries for such plants. Despite the measures taken by developing countries to attract FDI, flows of FDI have been increasingly concentrated in developed countries. In the 1970s, one third of such flows went to developing countries while in the 1980s was only one fifth - with 10 countries receiving 75 per cent.[122] This decline has been the result of a number of internal and external factors, such as the total debt of developing countries exceeding

[122] See *World Investment Report 1991,* "The Triad in Foreign Direct Investment", UNCTC Document ST/CTC/118, July 1991.

one trillion U.S. dollars, large-scale "capital flight," increased investment flows among the developed countries, and recent economic transformation of the Central and East European countries.

360. Subsidies and performance requirements cause resources to be allocated in a way other than would be the case in their absence and, indeed, this is their objective. In a highly competitive world, such a distortion in the allocation of resources would lead to economic inefficiencies and would not be to the advantage of the country imposing the condition. In reality, world market conditions fall far short of this competitive ideal, particularly since firms that undertake foreign direct investment tend already to have a degree of market power. Other "imperfections" in markets increase the possibility that some form of government intervention may improve the situation: it no longer follows that performance requirements will necessarily be contrary to a country's interest. It may be possible, for example, for a country to acquire, in effect, some of the "profits" that might otherwise accrue either to the firm or to another country.

361. A form of infant industry argument might be used to justify requiring foreign affiliates to purchase inputs locally (as is frequently the case in the automobile industry in developing countries). Such a performance requirement may foster local producers of components, stimulate domestic investment and create jobs. However, the long-run efficacy of such an approach depends, as in the more traditional case, on whether the infant industry matures. If not, inputs may continue to be more expensive than if they were imported; this might reduce the firm's profits, but it would also impose a cost on the consumer and would reduce the international competitiveness of the parent industry.

362. Export requirements may also make a positive contribution to development: by requiring companies to export, they not only ensure that the firms are internationally competitive but also force them to seize part of the global market for a product. It can be shown analytically that, as with tariffs, an appropriate subsidy can have the same effect as a performance requirement but without some of the disadvantages. For developing countries, however, subsidies have the disadvantage that they have to be paid: revenue constraints make it easier to adopt the second best approach that requires no financial outlay on the part of the Government.

(ii) A more comprehensive approach to the issue of international investment

363. Thus, TRIMs and similar measures may in some cases be considered as falling under the rubrique of the exceptional measures that developing countries are allowed to take, in the context of GATT, to establish an industry. Moreover, exclusive concentration on restricting TRIMs as currently defined is likely to encourage countries to find other ways of achieving the same objective, thereby defeating the purpose of the exercise. This suggests that a more comprehensive approach to the problem is required.

364. As mentioned earlier, efforts to reach multilateral agreement on a set of principles to cover the new dimensions of international investment and related issues in a comprehensive manner (such as the Code of Conduct on Transnational Corporations and the Code of Conduct on the Transfer of Technology) have not been successful. A renewed effort needs to be made to achieve some of the objectives of these initiatives. These include programmes and policies to promote socio-economic development of the developing countries, such as: (a) ensuring the most efficient and fullest contribution of investments to the national economy; (b) enhancing and maximizing employment opportunities; (c) facilitating restructuring under socially acceptable conditions; (d) eliminating industrial, economic and social disadvantages of specific regions; (e) diversifying and expanding economic activities and export markets; (f) alleviating pressures on available foreign exchange and making the fullest and most efficient use of it in the context of the conditions of their external sectors; (g) ensuring the most effective use of natural resources and value-added contributions to the economy; (h) ensuring adequate supply of certain products for the needs of local markets; (i) enhancing the contribution of investments to building and upgrading domestic technological capability; (j) encouraging research and development programmes, and (k) promoting the transfer of technology.

365. It is also imperative for the international community to support developing countries' measures to offset trade restrictive and distorting effects of corporate practices and behaviour. These include measures to: (i) counter international market allocation by ensuring corresponding market power for local producers of manufactures who might otherwise be eliminated by unfair

foreign competition; (ii) avoid abusive pricing practices by corporate enterprises; (iii) protect local firms from predatory practices; (iv) ensure that certain products are available in the host country in sufficient quantities and at appropriate prices for the needs of local market; (v) counteract the corporate entities refusal to deal or unfair (cartel) pricing; (vi) limit the net outflow of foreign exchange; (vii) combat international market allocation arrangements within and among foreign firms, long-term exclusivity contracts or tied-selling arrangements; (viii) ensure a degree of control for local management; (ix) counter enterprise-to-enterprise market allocation or exclusivity contracts; (x) counter international market allocation by foreign enterprises, and restrictions on exports; and (xi) ensure access to international distribution channels.

366.   In the Uruguay Round, any agreement reached on TRIMs should clearly recognize the right of developing countries to establish conditions on foreign investors intended to promote development and enhance competition, so long as such measures do not cause injury to trading partners.

(b) Intellectual property rights

367.   The protection of intellectual property rights (IPRs) has been covered by multilateral instruments, now administered by WIPO, some of which (e.g. the Paris Convention) have been in force for over a century. Treatment of this issue has always been complicated by the fundamental contradiction between IPRs which create monopoly situations, and competition legislation which aims at preventing firms from attaining and abusing dominant positions of market power, as well as by the need of developing countries for greater access to technology. Developing countries have pursued the latter objective in the negotiations within UNCTAD of a Code of Conduct on Transfer of Technology and within the WIPO in efforts to revise the Paris Convention aimed at establishing a balance between the interests of the intellectual property holders, and the needs of developing countries with respect to access to technology and to the pursuit of social and development objectives.[123]

368.   In the Uruguay Round, the discussion on the trade-related aspects of intellectual property rights (TRIPs) occupies an important place, with initiatives to link intellectual property rights to trade rights and obligations under the GATT - in other words to incorporate intellectual property rights as a component of the international trading system.[124]

369.   Developing countries have recognized the need for disciplines to eliminate counterfeiting, which deprives legitimate producers of sales reputation and reduces incentives to maintain high quality standards, while it contributes nothing to national efforts aimed at building up industrial and technological capabilities. The establishment of substantive and uniform standards involving a higher level of protection for intellectual property rights has been questioned by developing countries because of the implications for their own technological development. In countries that have already attained a certain degree of industrial and technological development, intellectual property protection may well be an important tool in fostering innovation, to the extent that it ensures the exploitation of R & D results through the vehicle of exclusive rights. Developing countries, which barely account for some 3 per cent of world expenditure on research and development, have not viewed the relationship between protection and innovation from the same perspective.   Those few developing countries that have shown significant improvement in their innovative capacities have been criticized for maintaining particularly weak levels of intellectual property protection.

370.   The concern of developing countries is that they may be limited in the possibility of following an imitative path of technological development, based on reverse engineering, adaptation and the improvement of existing innovation, and that a TRIPs agreements may be biased in favour of monopolistically controlled innovation, and impede the broad-based diffusion through free-market competition. This does not imply opposition to intellectual property protection, simply that they should retain a degree of liberty to apply the type and extent of such protection in con-

---

123 Refer to the chapter on "Technology".

124 See VanGrasstek Communications, "Trade-Related Intellectual Property Rights: United States Trade Policy, Developing Countries and the Uruguay Round", UNCTAD study UNCTAD ITP/42, pp.79-128.

formity with their particular situation, and to take measures needed to mitigate its undesirable monopolistic effects. These concerns are likely to be heightened as an increasing number of developing countries are launching trade and domestic policy reforms which can enable them to emulate the path of technological accumulation that was followed by developed countries themselves.

371.   While improved property protection can enhance the process of technology transfer, such protection by itself will not offset the lack of trained personnel, of equipment and general infrastructure, and of proximity to major research centres, that are key factors in decisions to locate R & D facilities. On the other hand, stronger protection will naturally strengthen the bargaining position of proprietary rights holders which will be reflected in demands for higher royalty rates and in the imposition of restrictive clauses of various kinds. The impact of intellectual property protection on consumers is also a matter of concern. As a rule, the stronger and broader the exclusive rights granted, the higher the risk of exorbitant prices and of other abusive practices. For example, high prices charged for patented pharmaceuticals have often triggered corrective measures by governments, including the establishment of special compulsory licensing mechanisms.

372.   As shown in chapter III of this report, it is important to reach an agreement that would enable developing countries to devise intellectual property systems in conformity with both international undertakings and their own development objectives. It is also important for such an agreement to ensure no "cross-retaliation between trade in goods and IPRs".

(c) Trade in services

373.   Developing countries accepted the inclusion of trade in services in the Uruguay Round negotiations[125] on the basis that the Ministerial Declaration on the Round clearly established a legal separation between negotiations on trade in services and those on trade in goods. The negotiations on services have resulted in the Governments having to address a variety of issues such as labour movement, capital movement, electronic data flows, and cultural identity - issues with broad and varied implications and difficult to deal with in a trade-negotiating context. The draft multilateral framework on trade in services which is currently emerging defines access to markets and national treatment so as to include the presence of juridical persons (i.e. that "access" be interpreted to include "establishment") and provides that such access be limited to specific commitments at the sectoral and sub-sectoral level that could be negotiated in successive rounds (the "positive list" approach); the first negotiations on "initial commitments" have been taking place over 1991. A fundamental element of the developing-country position has been to maintain the right to impose conditions on foreign suppliers who seek "presence", and to introduce obligations on developed countries to assist in correcting the "asymmetry" between developed and developing countries in trade in services, so that the latter countries can be provided with the means to strengthen their domestic service sectors and gain effective access to world markets.

374.   A unique element of the negotiations on trade in services has been the evolving "trade off" between the movement of capital presence of legal persons ("commercial presence") and the movement of labour (presence of "natural" persons), both recognized as constituting "trade" in services for the purposes of the framework, with efforts to negotiate a text defining "trade" obligations with respect to the movement of persons. The application of the principles of universal coverage and of the unconditional most-favoured-nation treatment is complicated by the existence of international agreements and organizations dealing with trade in certain service sectors (e.g. air transport). How the framework would "cohabit" with the ICAO, the United Nations Code of Conduct for Liner Conferences, ITU, etc., has been a matter of preoccupation in the later stages of the negotiations. Despite initial views regarding "applying GATT to trade in services", all participants now admit that the multilateral framework for trade in services would have to constitute a separate legal instrument and could not be linked to the legal framework of GATT without special institutional provisions being made.

---

[125] For a more detailed discussion of trade in services in the framework of the Uruguay Round negotiations, see chapter IV, section A, sub-section 2.

375.   In the view of the developing countries, a multilateral framework for trade in services should be based upon the principles of unconditional most-favoured-nation treatment and universal coverage and under such framework any liberalization commitments by them would be made in the light of the progress made in the strengthening of their domestic service sectors and the means given to them for this end (e.g. transfer of technology and conditions imposed on foreign suppliers), and their being granted effective access to world markets, including through the movement of labour. The multilateral framework can make an important contribution to the trade and development of developing countries, if it effectively permits them to obtain credit for liberalizations in terms of effective reciprocal access for their services to developed country markets, access to technology and networks and distribution system.

376.   Negotiations on trade in services are proceeding on the basis of a draft text of a General Agreement for Trade in Services submitted at the Brussels meeting and on the assumption that they should be concluded by the end of 1991. They contain three major elements: the text of the multilateral framework, sectoral annexes, and schedules of commitments. Sectoral annexes in maritime, air, road and inland waterway transport, "basic" telecommunications and audio-visual services had been proposed to deal with difficulties faced by some countries in applying the unconditional MFN clause in these sectors. Proposals have been made for alternative means of dealing with this problem. By the end of October 1991, 40 countries had submitted preliminary offers, and negotiations on initial commitments following a request/offer procedure had been initiated.

377.   On trade in services, the multilateral framework agreement should assist in enhancing the international competitiveness of developing country service firms and in enabling them to gain effective access to world markets, and should permit them to receive credit for any liberalization in the form of reciprocal effective access to markets for their service exports, transfer of technology, etc..

5. The trend towards regional economic integration

378.   In the recent past, several developments in Europe and in the Americas have increased the likelihood that the structure of the international trading system will be altered very significantly in the near future. In Europe, the completion of the Single European Market (SEM), scheduled for January 1993, is proceeding on schedule. In addition, negotiations between EEC and EFTA on closer economic links are nearing completion, and three countries in Eastern Europe (Czechoslovakia, Hungary and Poland) are in the process of negotiating association agreements with EEC and free trade agreements with EFTA. In the Americas, the Canada-United States Free Trade Agreement is being implemented, and Mexico has started negotiations with the United States and Canada on the formation of a North American Free Trade Area. In June 1990 the United States launched the "Enterprise for the Americas Initiative", one of its objectives being the negotiation of free trade areas with groups of countries in Latin America and the Caribbean. At the same time, and apparently under the stimulus of the United States initiative, several Latin American countries have entered into bilateral or plurilateral negotiations among themselves or have decided to strengthen existing integration agreements.

379.   It is difficult to say what these recent moves portend for developing countries as a whole, for different groups of developing countries, or for the international trading system. Developing countries have a clear stake in the strengthening of the multilateral trading system. While this or that group of countries may obtain temporary gains from preferential access to one of the main markets, in the long run all countries would lose if the international trading system is split up into a few large economic blocs characterized by managed imports. In their more protectionist options, regional groupings would significantly affect incentives to locate productive facilities in different regions and countries. As such, they would lead to a heavy interference of political factors in the efficient allocation of worldwide investment.

380.   As regards the effects on the international trading system, formal integration groupings - while inherently discriminatory - could represent either building blocks towards a more open trading system or stumbling blocks in the way of its achievement. Everything will depend on the

policies of the groupings towards imports from non-participating countries.

381.   Developments in Asia could also be contributing to the regionalization of the international trading system, but the modalities of integration in that area are assuming a different character. While there have been some discussions toward the end of setting up a preferential trading arrangement in Asia, these are still at a preliminary stage, and the eventual shape of such an arrangement is still not clear. It is clear, however, that Japan will figure prominently in any emerging group in the region.[126]

382.   The more informal, investment-led grouping that some see as emerging in Asia presents its own distinct opportunities and problems. In so far as these trade links depend on market forces, any developing country adopting policies conducive to international competitiveness would have an opportunity to participate in the economic dynamism of that area. However, to the extent that trade among countries in the area is conditioned by informal intra-firm arrangements, international measures to safeguard competition would seem to be in order.

383.   Most developing countries are either already associated with one of the main trading groups or are actively seeking to become so. However, individual developing countries, or even groups of them, lack leverage, not only in negotiations for membership or association but also in subsequent discussions within the groupings. Trade groupings also create difficult policy choices and problems of market access for developing countries not associated with them. A system of international review of the *modus operandi* of such groupings and of their policies toward countries not associated with them could help protect the interests of both weaker members and non-participants. The Secretary-General of UNCTAD could convene a high-level group of experts from Governments to assist him and the Trade and Development Board in conducting such reviews.

(a) Developing countries and greater European integration

(i) Recent policy developments

384.   As noted above, the transformation of EEC into a true common market is on course. The SEM will involve a harmonization of policies among member States going well beyond border measures. These include the adoption of Community-wide technical standards, the opening up of national public procurement to companies from all member States, the harmonization of national competition policies, the opening up of national markets for services, and complete freedom of movement for labour and capital.[127] Negotiations between EEC and EFTA countries on the formation of a European Economic Area (EEA) are in their final stages.

(ii) Impact on developing countries

385.   As discussed in detailed in the *Trade and Development Report, 1991*, these developments suggest that an essentially integrated market covering most of Europe is emerging, with major consequences for the rest of the world. The trade of developing countries with Europe is bound to be affected, and groups of developing countries will be affected in different ways, depending not only on the composition of their exports to Europe but also on the position they are able to negotiate within Europe's scale of preferences.

386.   Much of the current interest in European integration focuses on the completion of the Single European Market (SEM). Even with unchanged policies towards non-participants, the SEM is expected to have both trade-creating and trade-diverting effects on developing countries.[128]

---

[126] For an analysis of trade between Japan and the developing countries of the Asia-Pacific region, see UNCTAD, *Trade and Development Report 1990*, pp.91-96.

[127] For the contents of the programme, see Paolo Cecchini et al., *The European Challenge 1992: The Benefits of a Single Market*, (Aldershot: Wildwood House, 1988).

[128] The meaning of the terms "trade creation" and "trade diversion" as used here (and in much of the recent writings on the SEM) differs from that given to them in the literature on customs unions. In the latter, trade creation is defined

The trade-creation effects arise from increases in income in the Community as a result of the SEM which will raise demand for imports from developing countries. On the other hand, the essence of the programme is to reduce costs within the Community by increasing competition and by reducing existing national barriers to trade such as border controls or eliminating differences in technical standards; the lower costs of producing in the Community would shift demand away from imports and towards EEC producers, causing trade diversion.

387. The net trade creation effects (trade creation minus trade diversion) on developing countries as a whole and by major region will be positive but small.[129] For developing countries as a whole, it is estimated that the SEM will induce an increase in exports to EEC of about US$ 10 billion, or 7 per cent of their exports in 1988 (see table II-5). The biggest gainers will be the oil exporters of West Asia and North Africa and the economies of South and South-East Asia, which are the Community's major developing-country suppliers of high-technology manufactures. The oil-exporting countries will benefit from higher incomes in the Community, since the income elasticity of demand for oil exceeds unity. While significant trade diversion is expected in the more complex manufactures (e.g., machinery and office equipment), the Asian economies will benefit from the fact that a significant share of their exports to EEC have high income elasticities of demand. The estimated net trade creation for the ACP and Latin American countries is thought to be much more modest, because their exports consist largely of income-inelastic primary commodities or manufactures.

388. While an increase of US$ 10 billion may appear large, it needs to be placed in perspective. During the period 1985-1989, developing country exports to EEC grew at an average annual rate of 8 per cent in volume. Therefore, the estimated overall export gain of 7 per cent for developing countries represents an average of about one year's export growth, and considerably less than the year of peak export growth during the past decade (10 per cent in 1988). The effective phasing-out of the MFA and/or other non-tariff barriers constraining the exports of developing countries would have considerably more powerful effects than the completion of the SEM.

389. The SEM may have other favourable, but less measurable, effects. The terms of trade of primary commodity exporters are likely to improve. This is because EEC demand for primary commodities will rise together with incomes and, other things being equal, primary commodity prices will be higher; at the same time, the prices of manufactures exported by EEC will decline. Moreover, the elimination of national quotas for textile and clothing imports (even if they are replaced by their equivalents at the Community level) would result in a greater utilization of MFA quotas by exporting countries which at present are being constrained by the application of national quotas. Excise taxes on tropical beverages will also be harmonized and reduced, to the benefit of developing countries.[130] These positive impacts, which have not been included in the estimates quoted above, are likely to be small in absolute value.

390. On the other hand, the trade diversion effects of the SEM could have also been underestimated, since the impact of economies of scale has not been taken into account. If there are important economies of scale to be reaped, their effects on the competitiveness of EEC firms could be considerable, and the displacement of supplies from third countries could be much larger than assumed here. Finally, the abolition of national trade restrictions would be detrimental to producers from ACP countries and overseas territories of EEC member States, who at present enjoy preferential access to specific EEC markets for commodities such as bananas, rum and sugar. The abolition of national quotas would probably be accompanied by a shift in demand to lower-cost suppliers among developing countries which now face national trade restraints.

391. Given the relatively small size of the positive net effects estimated on the assumption of

---

as the union-induced shift from consumption of domestic products to the consumption of imports from other members, and trade diversion is the union-induced shift in demand from outside the union to higher-cost products from within the union. Here the terms are used to reflect the positive ("trade creation") and negative ("trade diversion") impacts on the exports to EEC by non-EEC countries.

[129] The estimation procedure assumed that the SEM would cause EEC incomes to increase by 5 per cent, which is roughly the mid-point of the range estimated in a report prepared for the EEC Commission (4.3 per cent to 6.4 per cent). In addition, income elasticities of demand for imports from developing countries were calculated, and sectoral trade diversion effects as estimated by the Community were used. For the estimates of income growth resulting from the SEM, see Paolo Cecchini et al, p. 84; trade diversion effects were taken from Commission of the European Communities, "The Economy of 1992", *European Economy*, No.35, March 1988.

[130] For a discussion of these effects, see Michael Davenport with Sheila Page, *Europe: 1992 and the Developing Countries* (London: Overseas Development Institute, 1991).

Table II-5

ESTIMATED NET TRADE CREATION EFFECTS OF THE SINGLE EUROPEAN MARKET ON DEVELOPING COUNTRY EXPORTS BY REGION AND COMMODITY GROUP

(Millions of dollars)

Region	Primary Commodities	Fuels	Manufactures	Total	As percentage of 1988 exports to EEC
All developing countries	1,923	3,306	4,920	10,149	6.9
of which:					
ACP	491	443	85	1,019	5.2
Mediterranean *a*	225	694	754	1,673	6.4
South-East Asia *b*	266	..	2,587	2,853	6.8
Latin America *c*	894	261	404	1,559	5.4
West Asia *d*	24	1,346	177	1,547	9.1

Source: UNCTAD secretariat estimates, based on official international data.
  a Algeria, Cyprus, Egypt, Lebanon, Malta, Morocco, Syrian Arab Republic, Tunisia, Turkey, Yugoslavia.
  b Hong Kong, Indonesia, Malaysia, Philippines, Republic of Korea, Singapore, Taiwan Province of China, Thailand.
  c Excludes Caribbean countries and territories (which are included in ACP).
  d Bahrain, Islamic Republic of Iran, Iraq, Kuwait, Oman, Saudi Arabia.

unchanged policies, the evolution of trade policy toward non-EEC countries will be a fundamental determinant of the size, and even the direction, of the effects of the SEM on developing countries. In this respect, the handling of national quantitative restrictions after 1992 - whether they will simply be eliminated, or whether they will be replaced by Community measures, and how restrictive would be the latter - will be crucial. The optimal solution would be their elimination, but that outcome is far from certain, particularly in the current trading environment. In this connection, recent resort to Community-wide VERs in sectors undergoing structural adjustment, attempts to create new MFA-like arrangements such as recent proposals for steel, and the upsurge of anti-dumping actions are a cause for concern. The temptation to use VERs and anti-dumping action at the Community level to pass on to trading partners the costs of adjustment to the SEM should be strongly resisted.

392.   In services sectors, the access of developing country service firms to the EEC market could be affected by the concept of reciprocity, which raises the question as to whether European firms would have equivalent benefits (as opposed to national treatment) when they are in foreign countries. This issue is particularly relevant to the Second Banking Coordination Directive of the European Community, which will be effective in 1993. The Directive includes provisions which give banks in the EC countries freedom to offer a full range of financial services directly to customers in other member States without further authorization. At the same time, it also contains provisions which restrict market access in the case of countries which do not provide to EC banks "effective market access comparable to that granted by the Community" and "national treatment offering the same competitive opportunities as are available to domestic credit institutions". Similar concerns could be extended virtually to all tradeable services such as distribution, air transport, telecommunications and professional services. Details of these implications are discussed in the chapter on services.

(b) Liberalizing trade among countries in the Americas

393.   The United States has been prompted to strengthen its trading relationship with the rest of the Americas at least in part by changes in the trading environment elsewhere in the world. By the same token, many countries in Latin America feel that they may become marginalized in the world economy of the 1990s if they do not associate themselves with one of the world's three poles of economic activity. North America is a logical first choice. Avoidance of the trade sanctions that the United States is able to impose under the so-called "Super" and "Special" provisions in section 301 of its Omnibus Trade and Competitiveness Act of 1988 has also been an incentive to enter into trade agreements with the United States.

394.   Negotiations are already under way between the United States, Canada and Mexico on a free trade area which would comprise 360 million people with a GNP of US$ 6,000 billion - a market much larger than that of EEC. This new, unified market would have important consequences for the world trading system as a whole, but particularly for Latin American economies. In this context, the "Enterprise for the Americas Initiative" is particularly important. The Initiative has three pillars - trade, investment and debt - but the most wide-ranging proposals in the Initiative relate to trade, notably the proposal to establish a free trade area covering the whole western hemisphere. While the Initiative is not clear on how such an arrangement is to be achieved, the United States has indicated its willingness to enter into free trade agreements either with individual countries or with groups of countries that have trade liberalization agreements among themselves. The bilateral "framework agreements" that already existed with Bolivia and Mexico were regarded as initial steps towards such trade arrangements with the United States. Sixteen countries have since signed "framework agreements" and several have also expressed interest in initiating negotiations on bilateral trade agreements with the United States. This has given new impetus to integration in Latin America, as reflected in the various trade agreements that have been signed among the Latin American countries since its announcement.[131]

6. Sustainable development and the international trading system

395.   There appears to be a broad consensus that ultimately there should be no conflict between trade and sustainable development. However, there has been an increasing concern that in the short and medium run, measures adopted for environmental considerations may have adverse impacts on trade and impede economic growth, particularly in developing countries, and may thus come into conflict with the objectives of "sustainable development". It is increasingly recognized that policy actions, both at the national and international level, are required to ensure that the goal of sustainable development and the rules of the international trading system are mutually supportive.

(a) Environmental policies and trade

396.   Environmental policies can affect trade in a number of ways, including: (i) environmental protection measures introduced by Governments could reduce the competitiveness of a specific industry, leading to pressures for trade protection on the grounds that competition from imports from countries where environmental protection is lower is unfair;[132] (ii) environment, safety or

---

[131] In March 1991, Argentina, Brazil, Paraguay and Uruguay signed the Treaty of Asunción. This is a transitional agreement to liberalize trade, the objective being to lay the ground for the creation of a Southern Cone Common Market (MERCOSUR) starting in 1995. In May 1991, the Andean Group adopted the Acta de Caracas to accelerate the establishment of a free trade zone, which is to come into effect on 1 January 1992. Representatives of Colombia, Mexico and Venezuela have also discussed the mutual elimination of tariffs with a view to reaching zero tariffs on a wide range of products by July 1994, starting with the establishment of maximum levels to be applied from 1 July 1991. Chile also has initiated negotiations to liberalize trade with several countries in the region.

[132] Environmental protection measures introduced by the governments could increase production costs and affect the

health protection measures introduced by Governments could lead to trade restrictions or embargo on imports;[133] (iii) environmental protection programmes in the developed countries can have an impact on the total location of investment as it could lead to relocating environmentally-damaging (or "polluting") industries from developed countries to developing countres with lower environmental requirements.

397.   Although the right of countries to apply trade measures for "protection of human, animal or plant or health" and "conservation of exhaustiable natural resources" is recognized under the GATT (on the condition that these measures should be applied consistent with multilateral obligations, the drafters of the GATT obviously did not foresee the current preoccupation with environmental protection.   Later the GATT 1979 Agreement on Technical Barriers to Trade ("Standards Code")[134] was aimed at ensuring that technical regulations and standards - including environmental - do not act as unnecessary barriers to trade. Under these rules, some specific case law has been developed as a result of decisions taken under GATT's dispute settlement mechanism which offers some guidance to distinguish between genuine environmental measures and protectionist measures.[135]

398.   These GATT provisions and those of the Standards Code are appropriate for dealing with situations where a trade restrictive measure is imposed on a product in the home market (through their distribution, use or disposal) on the basis that the product itself is a threat to health, safety and the environment.

399.   However, the GATT rules are less able to deal with situations beyond the national territory, i.e. when the protection of the transnational or global environment is at issue and the domestic situation is only secondarily or indirectly affected. An example is the case of where a country imposes restrictions on imports (e.g. on tropical timber) to induce other countries to conserve their resources.

400.   GATT rules are also less clear when a Contracting Party imposes restrictions on a product which though not by itself environmentally hazardous nor itself in short supply, is produced through a process or production judged by that contracting party to be environmentally unacceptable.[136]

401.   Finally, it has been argued that since higher product or environmental protection standards result in increasing the cost of production, imports from sources (usually the developing countries) where the standards are not so stringent actually amount to a subsidy and constitute an "unfair" trade practice in the exporting country (e.g. the "pollution haven" argument). The absence of an international consensus on this issue threatens to lead its abuse, to modifications in domestic trade law and to presures to amend multilateral disciplines (e.g. GATT) which could open the door for a proliferation of trade harassment and restrictions. It is thus crucial that an international consensus, based on factual analysis, be established urgently, before trade laws and multilateral trade agreements are modified unilaterally, based on negotiating considerations, unilaterally devised criteria and economic power which ignores the trade and development aspects.

402.   While the GATT rules[137] need to be clarified and strengthened to deal better with trade-

---

competitive position of specific industries vis-a-vis their counterparts of other countries and as a result products from these countries, particularly that from the developing countries, have faced increased restraints (such as VRAs and OMAs, as well as antidumping and countervailing actions).

133 For example, the United States ban imports of a number of European wine bacause of detection of trade quantities of a pesticide call procymidone; the EC ban on imports of meat from cattls treated with hormones, and the recent United States ban on imports of tuna from Mexico, Venezuela and Vanuatu under the provisions of the United States Marine Mammal Protection Act and the Dolphin Protection Consumer Information Act.

134 At present, the Standards Code has thirty-eight members.

135 For example, the panel reports on Canada's measures affecting exports of unprocessed herring and salmon and on the United States' prohibition of imports of tuna and tuna products from Canada. In both cases, panel found that measures introduced did not comply with the provisions of the relevant Articles and were in disregard of GATT obligations. In a more recent case of the United States complaint against Thailand's restrictions on the imports of cigarettes, the panel acknowledged the possibility of the priority of human health over trade liberalization. For details see GATT Basic Instruments and Selected Documents 29th Supplement pp. 91-109, 35th Supplement pp. 98-115 and GATT document DS10 R of 5 October 1990.

136 For example, the recent United States ban on imports of tuna fish from Mexico, Venezuela and Vanuatu. The case was brought to GATT by Mexico and a GATT panel was established. The panel decided recently that the United States action violated the GATT rules.

137 GATT was not designed for addressing environmental problems as a general trade policy issue but merely as a

related aspects of environmental policies,[138] GATT should continue to act as a multilateral discipline that prevents national implementation of environmental policies from creating trade distortions.

403.   Trans-frontier and global environmental problems could be tackled through international conventions. A number of such conventions use trade measures to realize their objectives.[139] Many obervers believe that, in case of conflict, international environmental agreements should prevail over GATT rules, to prevent an outlet for free riders, provided that agreements are ratified by a large number of countries. To the extent that trade measures are found necessary to promote environmental objectives in these agreements, certain principles should be observed, such as: non-discrimination; rules governing the appropriate use of trade measures for environmental purposes; the principle that the measures be proportional to the legitimate objectives pursued; transparency; and adequate notification of national regulations which are not based on international standards. Effective dispute settlement procedures would also be required.

(b)   The impact of trade, trade practices and policies on environment

404.   While it is a priority concern of the developed countries to prevent a further degradation of the global environment, the developing countries are primarily concerned by the major economic and social problems they face in terms of poverty[140] and development. For the majority of developing countries the low level of their overall economic development, their weak economic structure, the small size of their domestic markets, their heavy dependence on the production and export of primary commodities, and their need for foreign exchange earnings, have meant that their ability and capacity to respond to the concerns for environment were impeded by a number of external constraints.

405.   Thus, the combined effects of low commodity prices, increasing import prices, high debt-service ratios, tariff escalation processed products and increased non-tariff measures on such sensitive products as textiles and food, have forced developing countries to expand their commodity production and to take an "export-at-any-cost" approach to avoid economic collapse. This has led to excessive use of natural resources and transfer of arable land to cash crops, and has considerably aggravated the poverty-resource degradation cycle in which a number of resource-dependent developing countries are trapped.   Meanwhile, low export prices for resources encourage resource consumption in importing countries, thereby hastening the depletion of non-renewable resources.

---

multilateral rule to prevent national implementation of environmental policies from creating trade distortions. The present GATT rules are too vague to deal with emerging trade and environment issues, such as lack of clarity with Article XX and the Standard Code on coverage of process, production, transnational and global-related measures. Anti-dumping and countervailing measures could also be abused for environmental purposes.

[138] Some attempts have been made recently to discuss issues such as the envionmental impact of trade policies in the GATT, including the items on the Uruguay Round agenda, i.e. woking party on domestically prohibited goods, recent debate in the GATT Council on trade and environment as proposed by the EFTA countries, negotiations of sanitary and phytosanitary measures in the Uruguay Round, negotiatons in relation to subsidies and countervailing measures in the Uruguay Round, and the newly established panel on the United States restrictions on imports of tuna fish from Mexico.

[139] Examples are the Montreal Protocol on Ozone Depleting Substances; the Basel Convention on the Transboundary Movement of Hazardous Waste; and the Washington Convention on International Trade in Species of Wild Flora and Fauna Threatened by Extinction (CITES). Discrimination in the application of such trade measures with regard to non-participants (to deal with the problem of free riders) can have impacts on international trade. For instance the Montreal Protocol on Substances that Deplete the Ozone Layer contains trade measures both on imports and exports by non participants. In the view of some trade experts such measures might, strictly speaking, not be in conformity with the GATT. Trade measures may not be the most appropriate policy instrument or even act as a hindrance to better resource management, as has been shown in the case of elephant products. An example is the ban on ivory trade, agreed under CITES in October 1989 and formally in effect since 1 January 1990 (the African elephant was transferred from an Appendix II listing to Appendix I, banning all trade in elephant products). While the elephant population had drastically decreased in Kenya, other African countries (e.g. Zimbabwe) had healthy elephant populations. In a number of African countries ivory trade provided resources for wildlife conservation projects and sustainable development of elephant populations. It also provided incentives to local communities to participate in the conservation of the elephant.

[140] In the case of developing countries, poverty is the principal factor of unsustainability. Poverty exercises pressure on the natural and ecological resource base and prevents an adequate response to environmental concerns. Informal Encounter on International Trade and the Environment. Oslo, Norway, 28 February - 1 March 1991.

406. On the other hand, the liberalization of international trade could have positive effects on the environment. Improved access of developing countries to developed countries' markets for their processed and manufactured products should allow for diversification of exports and thus diminish their excessive dependence on exports of a few primary commodities. Removal or reduction of protectionist measures in the agricultural sector would result in higher and more stable world market prices, thus creating better conditions for sustainable land management in the developing countries. At the same time, a good balance needs to be achieved between the protection of technological innovation and the wider diffusion of basic, environmentally sound technologies.

407. In the specific Uruguay Round context, there would appear to be at least four areas where the outcome could have an impact on the ability of governments, particularly those of developing countries, to implement policies consistent with sustainable development: (i) On *anti-dumping and countervailing rules*, the environment as an excuse can increase the already prominent abuse. Negotiations in these areas should aim at to prevent any further abuse of the rules; (ii) In the area of *agriculture*, in order to be consistent with sustainable development, a solution would have to ensure that the large number of small producers in developing countries were not faced with competition that would result in their being forced from the land, and should reduce the extent to which export subsidies in developed countries are undermining the reduction of traditional foodstuffs; (iii) With respect to *natural resource-based products*, any situation that provided for "access to resources" and restricted the extent to which developing countries could control (through quotas or taxes) the export of natural resources would encourage resource depletion; the elimination of tariff escalation, which also contributes to lower resource prices in developing countries, could be seen as consistent with sustainable development. (iv) *TRIMs* is the area where the thrust of negotiations would appear to contradict directly the evolving international consensus in favour of sustainable development, which obviously calls for improved (not weakened) mechanisms at the national and international levels to control the activities of TNCs. As for *TRIPs*, it is important for the future protection of environment, health and safety that any multilateral agreement reached should ensure that environment-related technologies will be developed and will be transferred to the countries that need them. The problem here relates not so much to stricter IPR protection *per se* as to the need to arrest the current trend under which more and more technologies are falling under private control. The environment-related technologies should be in the public domain and should remain freely shared by government and industry with those who may have a need for it, in order to ensure both developed-country enterprises and developing-country governments that some reasonable mechanism for assisting the transfer of environmentally desirable technology can be developed that balances all interests and concerns, including through the establishment of public networks.

(c) Multilateral approaches to interactions between environment and international trade

(i) Harmonization of standards and joint actions for protection of environment

408. One response to trade problems arising from differing national environmental standards has been to attempt to harmonize these standards internationally,[141] through agreements aimed at the direct harmonization of approaches to protection of environment through the negotiations of multilateral agreements.[142]

409. While harmonization of standards may be preferred from the trade point of view, from the point of view of sustainability it would be desirable that differences in environmental conditions be allowed to offset competition so that international specialization is efficient also from an envi-

---

[141] A recent example in this context is the efforts made in the Uruguay Round to harmonize the sanitary and phytosanitary standards.

[142] For example, the Montreal Protocol on Substances that Deplete the Ozone Layer, first negotiated in 1987 and extensively revised in June 1990. One of the earliest mutilateral environmental agreements is the Convention on International Trade in Endangered Species (CITES), first negotiated in 1973 and now including about 108 parties. Related agreements include the International Convention of the Regulation of Whaling, the United Nations Conference on the Law of the Sea (UNCLOS), the Convention for the Prohibition of Fishing with Long Driftnets in the South Pacific, and the Protocol on Specially Protected Areas and Wildlife (SPAW) to 1986 Cartegena Convention on cooperation in the wider Caribbean region.

ronmental point of view.[143] This is because the enforcement of stringent environmental regulations or product standards can restrict market access. Standards should neither be discriminatory nor a disguised barrier to trade, but rather transparent, subject to international monitoring and adequately notified to trading partners. Technical assistance must be provided to developing countries to enable them to meet standards in export markets.[144]

(ii) The role of UNCTAD

410.   Given its broad mandate, UNCTAD, as an organ of the General Assembly, would seem to constitute an appropriate forum to discuss issues such as the enviromental impact of trade and development policies as well as the implications of trade measures taken for environmental purposes.

411.   The role of UNCTAD in the area of trade development policies and the environment could be: (a) to identify measures taken on environmental grounds that may have a bearing on international trade, or which more generally impede the efforts of Governments to implement policies designed to achieve sustainable development; (b) to maintain a database on such measures, in accordance with Trade and Development Board decision 384 (XXXVII) of 12 October 1990, which requested the secretariat to adjust the UNCTAD Trade Control Measures Data Base to monitor environmental regulations for possible protectionism and to monitor non-tariff measures which have a bearing on the environment;[145] (c) to undertake research on the linkages between environmental policies and international trade, particularly through case studies, with a view to proposing policy recommendations. Basic questions are how trade liberalization can provide wider options for sustainable development in developing countries and how to prevent environmental policies and regulations from becoming unnecessary restrictions to trade; (d) to provide technical assistance to developing countries in overcoming the adverse effects of these measures; (e) to work towards a general consensus in this area which would be useful for governments, international organizations and private sectors in adopting a common approach to environmental problems; (f) to take action to deal with environmental degradation with a view to reducing poverty and improving the livelihood of the people in the developing countries while ensuring that environmental concerns should not be used to introduce a new form of conditionality in aid, development financing, and trade; (g) to encourage and enable developing countries to pursue sound management of their environment while recognizing their permanent sovereignty over the use and management of resources within their own territories, and the right to develop them in accordance with their needs and level of socio-economic development; (h) to make policy recommendations with a view to enabling the developing countries to improve their market access for resource-based products, to increase their export earnings, to reduce over exploitation and the export of their natural resources and raw materials, to overcome obstacles to sustainable development, and to cope with environmental degradation.

7. The trading system and institutional questions

412.   It is well-known that the planners of the post-war international economic system envisaged

---

[143] See: UNCED PREPCOM, "The International Economy and Environment and Development, Report of the Secretary-General of the Conference" (A/CONF.151/PC/47). Geneva, July, 1991.

[144] The GATT Agreement on Technical Barriers to Trade (TBT) recognizes that while it is desirable to base technical regulations on the basis of international standards, in practice this may not always be possible. The TBT Agreement, therefore, requires countries, when they adopt mandatory regulations which are not based on international standards, to notify them in draft form so that other countries can comment on them. The obligation to take into account comments reduces the possibility of the new regulations causing barriers to trade.

[145] A plan of action to carry forward UNCTAD's work on monitoring non-tariff measures which have a bearing on the environment, in particular by means of UNCTAD's Data Base on Trade Control Measures, is contained in Chapter II of the Report of the Secretary-General of UNCTAD, submitted to the Secreatry General of the UNCED Conference pursuant to General Assembly 45/210. See "Environment and International Trade" (A/CONF.151/PC/48), submitted to the PrepCom for UNCED at its third session.

that an international trade organization would be one of the major components of the system, the others being the organizations dealing with money and with finance (i.e. the World Bank and IMF). The international trade organization was to be endowed with a wide mandate, covering a wide range of subjects in the area of trade, employment and development. The statutes of the proposed international trade organization were embodied in the Havana Charter, drawn up at the United Nations Conference on Trade and Employment and annexed to its Final Act.

413.   Following the failure of the United States Senate to ratify the Charter, international trade was left to be regulated by the General Agreement on Tariffs and Trade, which came into force in January 1948, largely corresponding to the Commercial Policy Chapter (IV) of the Havana Charter. At the 1955 "Review" session, the GATT Contracting Parties drew up a draft Agreement on an Organization for Trade Cooperation (OTC), intended as a device to give the GATT a more permanent institutional status. However, again the United States did not take the necessary steps to implement the proposed agreement. Since that time, no further formal attempts have been made to convert GATT into a new trade organization, although proposals were made in the context of multilateral trade negotiations to improve its legal status through its "definitive" application (i.e. elimination of the Protocol of Provisional Application).[146]

414.   Since its inception, UNCTAD has been mandated to "review, in the light of experience, the effectiveness and further evolution of institutional arrangements with a view to recommending such changes and improvements as might be necessary"; and to "study all relevent subjects, including matters relating to the establishment of a comprehensive organization based on the entire membership of the United Nations system of organizations to deal with trade and with trade in relation to development".[147]

(a) Recent approaches

415.   Proposals have been advanced in the Uruguay Round context to the effect that the outcome of the negotiations should result in GATT being given a more solid institutional character through the establishment of a new international trade organization. For example, a formal proposal was made by the European Community to the Negotiating Group on the Functioning of the GATT System on 9 July 1990 advocating the "Establishment of a Multilateral Trade Organization" (MTO).[148] The draft Final Act presented to the Brussels Ministerial Meeting of the Trade Negotiations Committee in December 1990 foresaw at least two (or three) new legal instruments embodying (a) the results of the negotiations on trade in goods (including market access concessions, amendments and interpretations of GATT Articles, revision of the Tokyo Round Codes, new agreements on agriculture etc.), (b) the multilateral framework for trade in services, and (c) the agreement on TRIPs, to the extent that the developed countries would be unsuccessful in including the TRIPs agreement in (a). The fourth Annex to the draft Final Act provided for the initiation of work towards the establishment of a new institutional instrument to provide the administrative and institutional base for these legal instruments.

416.   Such proposals are not prompted exclusively by the need to incorporate the results in the new areas (services, and possibly TRIPs) into the multilateral framework of trade rights and obligations, but also by the need to deal with the legal and procedural problems involved in introduc-

---

146 The Tokyo Round (1973-79) resulted in a series of Codes on certain non-tariff barriers and product sectors which were not subscribed to by all Contracting Parties. This fragmentation of GATT is further exacerbated by the continued existence of the Multifibre Arrangement - a major derogation from GATT principles, governing trade in a sector of vital interest to a large number of developing countries.

147 United Nations General Assembly Resolution 1995 (XIX) of 30 December 1964 on the Establishment of the UNCTAD.

148 One of the objectives of the EEC proposal on MTO was to establish a legal basis for effective implementation of the Uruguay Round results. In particular, to adopt a unique dispute settlement system applicable to all separate multilateral trade agreements. GATT MTN.GNG NG14/W/42, 9 July 1990.

BOX II-3

HAVANA CHARTER FOR AN INTERNATIONAL TRADE ORGANIZATION

BASIC FACTS

Immediately after the conclusion of World War II, international action was initiated to devise an international trading system and to establish an International Trade Organization to manage it. In April 1946, the U.N. Economic and Social Council unanimously approved a resolution submitted by the United States convening a world conference on trade and employment. A Preparatory Committee was set up which met twice in 1946 and in 1947 before the convening of the Havana Conference later in that year. During the 1947 meeting of the preparatory Committee the General Agreement on Tariffs and Trade was negotiated.

After months of deliberations the Final Act of the Havana Conference was signed by 53 countries in March 1948. But the Charter for an ITO did not enter into effect as the United States failed to ratify it due to domestic opposition. The United States was the dominant economic power at that time, and other participants had made their acceptance conditional upon acceptance by that country.

The General Agreement on Tariffs and Trade came into force on 1 January 1948, while the Havana Conference was in session. Largely corresponding to the Commercial Policy Chapter (IV) of the Havana Charter it thus became the only part of the Charter to come into effect, albeit only through a Protocol of Provisional Application, (i.e. until the Havana Charter came into force), which permitted Contracting Parties to maintain existing trade legislation inconsistent with its provisions (i.e. the "grandfather clause").

Those Chapters of the Charter which did not enter into effect dealt with (a) Employment and Economic Activity (Chapter II), (b) Economic Development and Reconstrucion (Chapter III), Restrictive Business Practices (Chapter V), Intergovernmental Commodity Agreements (Chapter VI), as well as the establishment of the International Trade Organization (Chapter VII). Much of the history of the activities of international economic fora over the last forty years, particularly that of UNCTAD, has been directly influenced by the failure of the Havana Charter to come into force. These have related to the absence of common macroeconomic objectives, the absence of a development orientation, the lack of discipline on the activities of private enterprises, the bias against countries dependent on commodity exports and the lack of an effective international trade organization.

ABANDONED CHAPTERS OF THE HAVANA CHARTER

Chapter II at the Havana Charter on "Employment and Economic Activity" saw full employment not as merely a domestic objective but a matter of common responsibility (Article II). Members would be obliged to take action designed to achieve and maintain full and productive employment and large and steadily growing demand within their territories.

Chapter III on "Economic Development and Reconstruction", recognizes the importance of the industrial and general economic development of all countries, particularly of those in which resources are as yet relatively underdeveloped, and states that "the productive use of the world human and material resources is of concern to and will benefit all countries" (Article 8). It notes that development requires "adequate supplies of capital funds, materials, modern equipment and technology and technical and managerial skills" (Article 11.1) and calls for cooperation among members to stimulate and assist in the provision and exchange of these facilities.

Chapter V on "Restrictive Business Practices" contained definit ions of RBPs, envisaged consultation and investigation procedures among Members, as well as general obligations to avoid such practices. Special procedures were elaborated regarding RBPs in Services, such as transportation, telecommunications, insurance and the commercial services of banks.

Chapter VI on "Intergovernmental Commodity Agreements" recognized that production and trade in primary commodities may be affected by a tendency towards persistent disequilibrium between production and consumption, the accumulation of burdensome stocks and pronounced fluctuations in prices. The objective of price stabilization and the need for economic adjustment was stressed and reference was made to the protection of the natural resources of the world from "unnecessary exhaustion" and to the equitable distribution of primary commodities in short supply. Special attention was given to commodity control agreements, defined as involving (a) the regulation of production or the quantitative control of exports and imports, or (b) the regulation of prices.

Chapter VII of the Charter provided for the establishment of the International Trade Organization (ITO), and Chapter VIII for the settlement of differences within its auspices. The ITO was intended to be very active organization, concerned with virtually all issues in the areas of trade, employment, and development and, in general, the management of the world economy. The institutional aspects of the ITO coveres such subjects as:

- Membership;
- Functions;
- Bodies (Conference, Executive Board, Commissions, Director-General and Staff) and their rules of procedure;
- Relations with the United Nations and other international organizations;
- International legal status;
- Contributions.

ing amendments to GATT,[149] revising the Tokyo Round Codes, etc.[150] One idea is that of a "single protocol", i.e. that all the agreements emerging from the Uruguay Round would be incorporated into a single legal instrument which would thus contain not only any agreement reached with respect to TRIPs and Services, but also the various negotiated modifications in the Tokyo Round Codes and in the GATT articles themselves.[151]

417. Meanwhile, the idea of a new initiative towards strengthening institutional arrangements in the area of multilateral trade has also be en revived in the United Nations. The General Assembly, in its resolution 45/201 of 21 December 1990, has called for a report by the Secretary-General on institutional developments, taking into account all relevant proposals, related to the strengthening of international organizations in the area of multilateral trade. The UNCTAD secretariat has been entrusted with the preparation of this report, after soliciting the views of all governments and specialized agencies and other organizations and programmes of the United Nations system on this matter.

418. The raison d'être of UNCTAD was "to formulate principles and policies on international trade and related problems of economic development." With one major exception (i.e. the negotiation of the GSP which established the principle of preferential treatment for developing countries in conflict with the established MFN clause of GATT), negotiations within UNCTAD have not posed a direct challenge with the rules and principles of GATT. Rather, UNCTAD has tended to address the development aspects of issues where the multilateral disciplines envisaged in the immediate post-war period did not materialize as a result of the failure of the ITO (e.g. shipping, commodities, RBPs, transfer of technology), as well as specific areas of trade policy not contemplated in the immediate post-war era (i.e. trade with socialist countries, trade among developing countries). In some cases, such negotiations served to establish multilateral instruments (e.g. Code of Conduct for Liner Conferences, Set of Rules and Principles on RBPs, commodity agreements). Certain issues from the Havana Charter were taken up by other United Nations bodies, notably the consideration of investment issues by the United Nations Centre on Transnational Corporations.

419. A major factor which limits the ability of the Uruguay Round to address the full range of trade and development issues stems from the absence of a broad international consensus with respect to the issues involved. Some of the areas of note include (a) non-economic aspects of agricultural support (particularly for developing countries); (b) the dichotomy between more stringent and wider protection of intellectual property rights and developing countries' need for access to technology and for the development of an indigenous technological capacity; (c) the link between investment, trade, technology and development policies as well as the probable conflicts of interest between foreign investors and developing host countries; (d) the trade impact of practices of TNCs;

---

149 With the existing provisions of the GATT an amendment is very difficult to be made. Under Article XXX of the General Agreement, a) unanimous acceptance is required for amendments covering Parts I (Articles I and II) of the General Agreement and of Article XXIX (The relation of the General Agreement with the Havana Charter); and b) other amendments to the General Agreement shall become effective, in respect of those contracting parties which accept them, upon acceptance by 2/3 of the contracting parties and thereafter for each contracting party upon acceptance by it. Where substantive amendments are not involved, decisions can be taken by "joint action" under article XXV.

150 The results of the Tokyo Round were in the forms of: (i) The Geneva (1979) Protocol to The General Agreement On Tariffs And Trade. This procedure followed the precedent of previous rounds of MTNs which involved the results of the tariff negotiations being embodied in a protocol annexed to the General Agreement; (ii) MTN Agreements and Arrangements. The issue of unity and consistency of the GATT system was addressed through a decision of the CONTRACTING PARTIES of 28 November 1979 - Action By The CONTRACTING PARTIES on The Multilateral Trade Negotiations. This decision defines the relationship between the MTN Agreements and Arrangements (Codes and sectoral arrangements) on one hand and the CONTRACTING PARTIES on the other. Each of these Agreements/Arrangements were separately open for acceptance. This decision specifically notes that the existing rights and benefits under the GATT of Contracting Parties not parties to these Agreements and Arrangements, including those derived from Article I, would not be affected; and (iii) Other results. The remaining results took two forms. Firstly, Decisions, through the invocation of Article XXV were adopted on Safeguards, More Favourable Treatment, Reciprocity and Fuller Participation of Developing Countries, Safeguard Action for Development Purposes and Examination of Protective Measures Affecting Imports From Developing Countries. Secondly, a Declaration on Trade Measures Taken For Balance Of Payments Purposes and An Understanding Regarding Notification, Consultation, Dispute Settlement and Surveillance were adopted.

151 Some informal discussions have also taken place recently, in which some approaches have been suggested to deal with the international implementation of the results of the Uruguay Round, such as: (a) unlike the previous rounds of MTNs, especially the Tokyo Round, Contracting Parties would not have the option of following "à la carte" approach towards acceptance of the results of the negotiations. Rather, the objective is to ensure the acceptance "of all or most results of the negotiations by a maximum of (if not all) GATT Contracting Parties" (and also by participants which are not yet CP's)"; and (b) unlike the previous Tokyo round which resulted in MTN Agreements and Arrangements' acceptance by interested parties, thus giving rise to variations in levels of rights and obligations amongst Contracting Parties, the Uruguay Round should "avoid as much as possible the legal fragmentation of the Multilateral Trading System".

and (e) the role of services in the development process, in international competitiveness, and in the division of labour and value-added.

(b) The case for institutional reform

420. The recent institutional proposals should be welcomed as timely initiatives. However, they require the most careful examination in a broader context of international trade and trade-related matters. In other words, the need for strengthening and consolidating international trade organizations is more comprehensive than issues arising from the modalities of implementation of the Uruguay Round results, first of all in the new areas.

421. At least four main themes emerge in the various approaches toward strengthening international trade organizations; they are that it is necessary to (a) effectively address the issues now arising from the growing interdependence in the international trading system, including the globalization of markets and linkages between trade, technology, investment and services; (b) ensure universality of participation in decision-making and comprehensive subject coverage; (c) enable the developing countries to transform their economic structures and improve their levels of living so as to ensure accelerated and sustained world economic development; and (d) provide the administrative and institutional support for the implementation and enforcement of multilateral agreements.

422. In particular, the strengthening of international organizations in the area of multilateral trade should be seen as an inherent component of efforts to revitalize the central role of the United Nations through providing a stable economic basis for the maintenance of world peace and security, and for the effective pursuit of the objective of sustainable world development. UNCTAD's basic mandate instructs it to work toward the establishment of a comprehensive organization to deal with trade and with trade in relation to development.

423. Many of the basic ideas underlying the Havana Charter remain valid. Any new institutional arrangements in the field of international trade should be comprehensive in subject coverage, universal in membership, based on agreed objectives and norms of behaviour, responsive to the interests of all members, equitable in decision-making and organically linked to related institutional arrangements in the areas of money and finance.

424. To be successful, efforts to strengthen international organizations in the area of multilateral trade must be also adapted to the realities of the 1990s, which are the result of the rapid political, economic and technological changes of the preceding decade. There is now virtually universal acceptance of the merits of an open competitive international trading system. If such a trading system is to provide a stimulus to the development process, good management, the flow of financial resources and secure and non-discriminatory access to markets remain essential. However, while these prerequisites provide countries with an opportunity of penetrating world markets, they do not equip them with the means to compete. Indeed, the major challenge facing the international trading system in the 1990s could be that of ensuring that all countries are provided with the means of competing in an open trading system so as to improve their position in the international division of labour. This would require that international organizations address a wider range of issues, including access to technology and to information, capital and labour flows, competition law and the elimination of anti-competitive practices. In addition, there is a need to ensure that trade policies and development strategies conform to the global public interest in sustainable development.

425. Furthermore, it cannot be expected that all countries will be able to derive effective benefit from this more competitive system in the short or medium term. Many countries are burdened with handicaps of a geographical or historical nature, and will require the assistance of the international community as a whole, if they are to participate in the trading system. The United Nations has the responsibility of ensuring that international trade does not result in an exacerbation of disparities in standards of living, nor in the marginalization of countries in the trading system.

D. ENHANCING EFFICIENCY IN INTERNATIONAL TRADE

1. Introduction

426.   In any international trade transaction the exporter-importer tandem is only one link in a complex chain of players, which include, *inter alia*, their respective banks, insurance companies, customs, and various intermediaries. Modern "global trade" involves an intricate combination of transaction-networks, which include trade itself (circulation of goods and services), financial flows (payments, credit, insurance), information flows (market intelligence, various forms of hedging, managerial information), and procedures-related flows (paperwork and information transmissions for customs purposes, e.g.).

427.   International trade appears to rely increasingly on a number of information-intensive non-physical infrastructures, or "networks", which are often described by analysts by the phrase *infostructures*. A consequence of this is that the competitiveness of the various players involved in international trade is more and more directly linked to their ability to (1) acquire and master generic information technologies (i.e., basically, telecommunications and computer technologies), (2) build, operate and maintain the local technical equipment (commmunications lines and exchange systems, computer facilities), as well as local physical infrastructures (ports, airports, rail and road systems), and (3) access the above-mentioned four types of major networks (i.e. trade, finance, information and procedural networks).

428.   In many respects, such conditions seem to be currently fulfilled by a very limited number of global players in international trade. Most developing countries and economies in transition are actually operating under sub-optimal conditions when it comes to international trade. This lack of efficiency leads to substantial losses in competitiveness and resources, and hinders the capability of these countries to use international trade as an engine for growth. At the same time, it may dampen their interest for further integration in the present international trade system. In many instances, the same limitations also diminish the interest of potential foreign investors to move to countries where minimal infostructures are not available.

429.   This is paradoxical, since the last few decades have been marked by the so-called "information revolution", which has in fact vastly diminished the costs of information technologies, and information management and transmission generally. However, as is common in periods of rapid technological change, the transmission of advances in the field of information and information technologies has taken place in a rather uncoordinated, uneven and thus sub-optimal fashion.

430.   The time has come for a series of more coordinated and forward-looking strategies, which will accelerate and deepen the current trend towards greater efficiency and steady growth in the world economy. One of the major goals of such an effort would consist in the more rapid integration of developing countries and economies in transition into a durably dynamic international trade.

2. Trading in a globalizing world economy

431.   In the 1980s, largely due to advances in information technologies, international economic relations have been affected by a set of trends generally referred to as "globalization". Strategic alliances between transnational firms, and the pervading use of planetary information networks are spearheading a reshuffling of comparative advantages, in which continuous innovation and flexible organization become crucial sources of profitability. Therefore, the consideration of interdependence now requires that increased attention be given, in addition to trade and finance, to technology, as well as to the rationale and impact of the global strategies of private firms.

432.   The process of globalization has proved to be a contradictory one, whereby trends towards global integration (e.g. of financial markets) co-exist with trends towards regionalization[152] as well as with tendencies towards fragmentation, in particular through the establishment of incompatible and competing standards and procedures in sectors dominated by proprietary networks.

(a)   Globalization, technology and trade: opportunities and challenges

433.   The dramatic increase in the power cost ratio of international telecommunications, as well as significant breakthroughs in computer technology, have radically affected the respective abilities of various countries to utilize or build comparative advantages. While such trends undoubtedly carry unprecedented threats to the international competitiveness of developing countries, they also contain considerable potential for improving the overall efficiency of international trade, and enhance its input to the development process.

434.   By making "internationally tradeable" many products (especially services) which could not be traded before, information technologies have contributed to creating new markets. Some of these markets (in particular those related to financial services) have exhibited impressive growth rates, and yielded substantial profits for those who accepted the risk to compete in them. However, this has put at a disadvantage developing countries that do not possess the necessary infrastructures, or whose competitiveness in activities where they used to have a comparative advantage, has been eroded by competition shifting to a higher (i.e. generally more information-intensive) level.[153]

435.   Another challenge for governments in all types of economies is that a large part of the phenomena through which technological innovation has affected production and trade has been taking place within firms. In this respect, two trends are worth noticing, which, although largely confined to the large firms of industrialized countries, are bound to affect the constraints under which developing countries will trade in the near future, namely:

• advances in information technologies have dramatically changed the relative costs of production factors (including labour, capital and information), thus rendering economically feasible certain modes of organization which hardly existed a few decades ago. In particular, sophisticated networking technology has allowed the rapid expansion of a number of management techniques (such as "just-in-time delivery" or "zero-inventory"), which are now the common denominator among chains of enterprises (producers, exporters, importers, distributors): such chains exhibit a tendency to rapidly globalize, and to increase their market domination through the marginalization of those of their competitors who do not have access to such techniques (and their underlying technologies);

• a new situation has developed whereby large multinational firms weave international strategic alliances with their competitors. Such alliances allow them, through a delicate mix of competition and cooperation, to pool resources in critical areas such as R & D, marketing or distribution. On the other hand, strategic alliances contribute to heighten the barriers which new competitors have to face when attempting to penetrate the corresponding international markets.

436.   Although they can only have limited influence on such trends, the governments of developing countries can however significantly enhance the capability of their respective countries to "hook up" to the on-going revolution of international trade by granting adequate priority, in their development strategies, to the building and maintenance of infostructures. So far, however, the information revolution has materialized in such an uneven fashion that it is widening rather than narrowing the gap between developed and developing countries.[154]

---

[152] See chapter V, section C.5 of this report on 'The emergence of large economic spaces'.

[153] Such a phenomenon is evident in areas like air transport and tourism, where the emergence of global computerized reservation systems (CRSs) is radically affecting the structure of competition.

[154] Some recent analyses have even concluded that information technologies are providing advanced companies with new ways and means of decentralizing their activities worldwide without decentralizing in a proportionate fashion their power structures nor their value-adding processes. Developing countries are generally the first possible victims of such

437.   This is particularly noticeable in the area of international trade. In many respects, the advent of **global trade** is opening a competitiveness gap between the *haves* and the *have nots* of information technologies and their offspring. This is particularly true for services, but it is even spreading to more traditional areas of international trade, including commodities, semi-manufactures and manufactures. One major reason can be found in the increasingly higher efficiency of trade transactions in the North. There is, however, no reason why information technologies, through appropriate international action, cannot also allow developing countries to increase the efficiency of their trade practices.

(b) Competition and efficiency: practical dimensions

438.   The cost of procedures has been estimated at around 10 per cent of the total value of international trade. This is without taking into account indirect costs (see box II-4). On those bases, it can be estimated that a mere improvement of 25 per cent in the efficiency of such procedures would yield savings of roughly US$ 75 billion per annum.[155] This figure thus provides a reasonable target[156] to be reached by year 2000.

3. International competition in the 1990s: trends and needs

(a)   Rules of the game: current trends

439.   As networks multiply, so do the rules of the game: strategic alliances between users and providers of information equipment, for example, often dictate the norms and standards for the equipment to be used on the network. Similarly, the choice of one major software provider may largely influence the protocols and data compressing techniques which will be usable on a particular network. A consequence of this "fragmented rule-setting" process is that the degree of inter-connectivity between networks (which is both a condition for their profitability and for their accessibility) is becoming more and more limited.

440.   One of the reasons most often mentioned by users for this marked tendency away from "universal norms and standards" is that the pace of technological and managerial innovation is such that large bureaucracies cannot provide standards soon enough for the industry to use them. One clear result is that an increasing part of the world economy (and probably the most dynamic one) is rapidly moving to a universe of *de facto* (as opposed to *de jure*) standards.

441.   There is now a growing consensus that such a context can only lead to sub-optimal (or second best) situations. As far as international transactions are concerned, it is clear that the time has now come for far-reaching initiatives in the domains of network-inter-operability, norms and standards. If one waited much longer, this situation would soon cristallize, and, as dominant positions start to emerge, vested interests will make universal arrangements more difficult, and more costly.

---

selective by-passing'. See *'Technology and the Economy: the Key Relationship'*, OECD (TEP Report), Paris, June 1991 (Chapter *'Technology and Competitiveness'*).

[155] All figures are given in constant US$ of 1991.

[156] Recent experiences show that this may even be a rather conservative target. For example, as a result of harmonization and simplification procedures, as well as of intensive use of information technologies for commercial and administrative procedures, the procedures transactions ratio in the European Community has been reduced from a 7 to 10 per cent range in the 1960s to about 1.8 per cent in the last few years.

Box II-4

THE COST OF PROCEDURES IN INTERNATIONAL TRADE

A comprehensive analysis and assessment of the costs involved in document preparation and handling in connection with the movement of goods in international trade was jointly carried out in 1971 by the then National Committee on International Trade Documentation (NCITD, now the International Trade Facilitation Council) and the Department of Transportation (DOT) of the United States concluded that the total cost of paperwork and procedures could amount ot 10 to 15% of the value of the goods traded. This was recognized a conservative estimate by the experts participating in the work of the UN/ECE Working Party on Facilitation of International Trade Procedures (WP.4).

It should be noted that the U.S. study did not take into account *indirect* costs, which can be quite substantial although they are not easy to quantify, like those caused by delays in transport resulting from cumbersome procedures, delays in payment caused by errors in documentary credits, losses due to deterioration or pilferage while cargo is waiting for clearance or onward transportation, etc. Neither did it refer to lost opportunities, nor the strong disincentive for potential exporters caused by the complication of international trade procedures.

Since 1971, there has not been any study as detailed and comprehensive as the one carried out by NCITD/DOT; the range of 10 - 15% of the value of the goods traded is still generally accepted in trade facilitation circles as an order of magnitude for the direct and indirect costs of procedures, bearing in mind that in a number of individual countries and economic groupings, substantial improvements have been achieved as a result of measures taken to facilitate trade. As an example, in the seventies, the standardization of international trade documents on the basis of the "UN Layout Key" (promoted by the UN/ECE and UNCTAD/FALPRO) and the introduction of "one-run" systems for document preparation have been estimated to reduce by 75% the time required for completing a set of export documents. Further savings result from the harmonization of customs procedures, promoted by the Customs Co-operation Council, the economic integration being achieved in several sub-regions, etc.

Electronic Data Interchange (EDI) is introducing a new dimension in information transfer, with a direct impact on paperwork and procedures.

- A document transfer currently costing $ 50 can be reduced to $7. IBM claims to have already saved $ 60 million by using EDI (*Source: Eurotech Forum*, October 1989).

- In domestic trade in the USA, the average paper transaction costs $ 49 to process, as opposed to an average of $ 5.70 per EDI transaction (*Source: Journal of Commerce*, 13 December 1988).

- At present, Customs documentation adds 1.5 per cent to the cost of moving goods across Europe. By 1993 that will fall to 0.5 per cent and EDI will reduce the cost of an invoice from £2 ($ 3.20) to about 30 pence (*Source: Journal of Commerce*, 2 October 1985).

(b) The need for concerted action

(i) Accelerating growth, development and North/East/South integration

442.   Partly due to the unprecedented pace of technological innovation, partly due to the lack of responsiveness of standard setting organizations to the needs of the business community, considerable losses are now accumulating in the area of international trade. The tremendous potential generated by the information revolution remains largely untapped, and many of its uses remain sub-optimal for lack of coordination and because of multiple duplications of efforts.

443.   Gathering existing energies to foster a process of multilateral cooperation in these domains would considerably enhance the prospects for an acceleration of growth in international trade. In particular, it would provide significant additional possibilities to integrate developing countries and economies in transition into a stable and dynamic trading system. By contrast, if present trends continue unchecked, the result will be a further marginalization of developing countries, and a lower overall degree of fluidity, efficiency and dynamism in international trade.

444.   This is particularly important with regard to the growing use of EDI (Electronic Data Interchange),[157] i.e. the direct transfer of information between computers. EDI is currently revolutionizing business practices and management techniques in the public and private sectors of the

---

[157] See Box II-5.

more advanced countries. In addition to adequate telecommunications facilities and appropriate software, EDI requires universal standards in order to become truly global. So far, the efforts carried out for the development of such standards (most notably the EDIFACT standards in the framework of the United Nations Economic Commission for Europe (see Box II-5)) have concerned only developed countries, and a limited number of technically-advanced developing countries.

(ii) Main obstacles requiring international action

445. A prime objective of concerted action for the rationalization of world trade is the removal of a number of obstacles to trade efficiency. These obstacles are of five types: legal, technical, commercial, political and institutional.

Box II-5

A. TOWARDS PAPERLESS INTERNATIONAL TRADE: ELECTRONIC

DATA INTERCHANGE (EDI)

EDI is the replacement of paper-based exchange of information between trading partners by direct transmission of structured data between computers: Invoices, Customs entries, funds transfers, transport documents, etc. take the form of standardized electronic messages, automatically generated by one computer and transmitted to another. This combination of automatic data processing and tele-transmission speeds up the information flow and avoids the slow, costly and error-prone manual preparation and processing of documents as well as the necessity of re-capturing data in the information systems of the numerous users and public services involved in an international trade transaction.

EDI started in the United States in the seventies, first in the transport sector. It is estimated that 30.000 US companies will use it by the mid 1990s, essentially in the wholesale trade, manufacturing, retail trade and communication sectors. In Western Europe, EDI users will be 40,000 by 1994, covering various business activities (chemicals, electronics, motor manufacturing, retailing, banking, international trade) as well as Customs and other governmental and public services. In Singapore, EDI is extensively used for international trade procedures as well as for internal data exchange related to medical information, graphic information in the engineering, architectural and manufacturing sectors; electronic billing services and corporate payments; electronic inventory management for Just-in-Time procurement, Electronic Tendering.

B. ELECTRONIC DATA INTERCHANGE FOR ADMINISTRATION,

COMMERCE AND TRANSPORT (EDIFACT)

To be able to communicate, computers have to be fed with data in a sequence and format they have been programmed to process. Interchange partners have to agree beforehand on the format of these data, the codes used, the method of transmission, the respective responsibilities of each of them. When several partners come into play, such agreement should be based on recognized standards. So far as data formating and assembling is concerned, there is one universal, global standard: EDIFACT.

EDIFACT provides the syntax needed to structure the information, i.e. to construct in an organized configuration the information elements passing from one computer to another, in the same way as a language is the structuration of words into sentences used to convey a meaningful message to the interlocutor. EDIFACT also includes the standard data elements and codes used in specific official data interchange (e.g. with Customs). The EDIFACT syntax is an ISO International Standard. EDIFACT as a whole is supported and promoted by the EEC, the Customs Co-operation Council, all major international trade, transport and banking organizations and a number of industrial sectorial groupings.

EDIFACT is being developed in the framework of the UN/Economic Commission for Europe. The development of EDIFACT messages is based on user requirements, and such work has been decentralized to sub-regional EDIFACT Boards in Eastern and Central Europe, Western Europe, North America, Australia/New Zealand, and Japan/Singapore. Additional bodies have to be set up to cover the needs of other parts of the world, in particular for developing countries.

Legal questions

446.   They arise when traditional paper documents are replaced by alternative methods of transferring information, such as Electronic Data Interchange. Some of the problems concern Commercial Law (e. g.. the requirement that certain documents be in writting; the rules, concerning contract conclusion and the date and place of the contract; the reference to the conditions of an insurance or transport contract - what is called "small print" at the back of a paper document; the fundamental issue of negotiability, e.g. for Bills of Lading, or payment instruments, etc.), Evidence Law (the rules for a document to be admissible in court proceedings), Fiscal Law (the requirement that, for instance for income tax purpose, documents be kept a number of years), Administrative practices (e.g. the requirement for a signature, or for an "original" document; requirement for the legalization of certain documents e.g. by consular authorities; the requirement for some documents which must travel with the goods, e.g. TIR Carnets, etc.)

447.   Some of these problems could be resolved contractually by the trade partners, who would agree beforehand on the respective rights and duties of each party. However, in the perspective of a global network in which traders who do not know each other would enter into contractual re-

lationship, there is a need for a model universal "interchange agreement" to which partners would refer.

448. Multimodal transport will be more and more extensively used in the framework of a global trade. To facilitate its development, the legal responsibilities of multimodal transport operators and consignors have to be clearly defined. Pending the entry into force of the UNCTAD Convention on the subject (which so far has only five contracting parties) the UNCTAD/ICC Rules for Multimodal Transport Documents should be actively promoted. Other practical questions of a "legal" nature concern the development of codes which are needed to facilitate the interchange of trade information. This is mentioned below under "commercial practice".

Technical issues

449. Technical problems linked with trade-related information transfer basically concern the generalization of Electronic Data Interchange (EDI) in trade procedures. This involves :

- awareness raising, in particular in developing countries. Governments and trade operators should be made aware of the potential of this new technique for the facilitation of trade procedures, as well as of the conditions to be fulfilled for its introduction;

- spreading of technical know-how. As illustrated by the case of Singapore (where a central information system links all trade operators, including public authorites, thus permitting the smooth functioning of simplified formalities and procedures, without paper documents), the creation of a "community network" is a suitable solution for facilitating trade-related information transfer at the local or national level. A model system might have to be developed, to be introduced in requesting countries. Alternatively, ASYCUDA could be expanded to serve as a hub for such a community network;

- adequate telecommunication services. A global survey of existing technical possibilities should be made, and appropriate recommendations should be presented to the relevant national and international organizations for upgrading the existing technical infrastructure, as required;

- development of the required software. The software necessary for EDI in developed economies is currently available on a commercial basis. It might be appropriate to develop software packages adapted to the specific needs of developing countries and to make them available in the framework of technical co-operation projects;

- development of messages. Global EDI will use the EDIFACT messages developed in the framework of UN/ECE. It is necessary to ensure that specific needs of developing countries be taken into account in that exercise;

- network inter-operability. A growing number of commercial firms offer "Value Added Networks" for linking EDI users with their correspondents. Although there is a theoretical possibility to transmit data pertaining to a commercial transaction form one network to another, it is not yet possible to trail these data from beginning to end, an essential requisite for global EDI. The required international standards should be developed and agreed by all network operators. There is also a need for an agreement on a universal identification and addressing scheme, on an established "minimum service level", on reverse charges (with "one stop shop" for the users), on more sophisticated security techniques to ensure confidentiality, security of payments, etc.

Questions linked to commercial practices

450. Global information transfer requires full harmonization of "business practices" in a broad sense, with universally agreed definitions of the terms used and unique codes for representing the information whenever required. Regarding terminology, for instance, the same word may cover different concepts, depending on the practices in various sectors, or different regions of the world. Misinterpretations and misunderstandings may have serious adverse effects in international trade transactions and can be avoided by a world-wide agreement on a unique "Trade Information Dictionary" (TID).

451. Drawing from existing agreed sources, complemented as required, the TID, which would be centrally maintained by the UNCTAD secretariat and made available through distributed data bases, would contain agreed definitions (and codes, as required) for all terms and concepts used in trade in general, as well as a specification of standards to be used.

452. A comprehensive inventory of sectors where harmonization is still required has to be carried out, including:

- Terms and conditions of payment, for which there is no agreed international code;

- Description of goods: although the CCC Harmonized System provides an internationally agreed basis, national and regional extensions of the six digit codes prevent its utilization on a global basis;

- Detailed delivery terms: the universal INCOTERMS of the ICC cover general delivery conditions; an agreement is required at a more detailed level (e.g. the definition of "immediate" when immediate delivery is required in a purchase order).

- Standard bar coding: a number of systems are in operation, but there is no international standard;

- Unique consignment number: it should be possible to identify a given consignment from departure to arrival, with a unique number, assigned by sender, that would be used by all information systems along the transaction and transport chain (as is the case for air transport with the AWB number);

- Coded identification of the International Convention which applies to a given transport contract;

- Unique coded identification and address of organizations and companies (which exists only at the national level, or by service provider in electronic mail). An international directory, maintained by an agreed 'naming and addressing authority', would facilitate global information interchange).

Political aspects of transborder data flows

453. Access to databases and transfer of data from one country to another may be impeded by national legislation concerning data protection (for privacy, or the protection of national information services (data banks, etc.). A survey of the prevailing situation in this field should be conducted, to prepare for appropriate solutions, as required.

Institutional issues

454. Existing information networks with world-wide coverage are limited in their scope, e.g. the SITA network for air transport reservation systems, or the S.W.I.F.T. network for international funds transfers between banks; commercial value added networks co-exist and do not really interconnect; their geographical coverage is not global. There will thus be a need for a global trade network, with universal coverage, providing all services required for managing the transfer of trade-related data and disseminating all types of information required by trade operators to conduct their business.

455. Such a global trade network would require a substantial investment to create the required infrastructure and to operate it. The volume of information that would be handled, and the economies of scale which could be realized through using a global system remain to be assessed before one could determine whether the investment would pay for itself. A pre-feasibility study could be conducted to determine the desirable scope of the project and the conditions in which it could materialize.

(c) Possible institutional set-up

456.   The evolution of international trade practices and patterns calls for a systematic and universal approach to the issue of optimization of trade-related information flows. This is clearly a function to be fulfilled by UNCTAD, which has both the experience and the mandate to promote global norms and procedures in this area. UNCTAD VIII could launch an important initiative in this area, by calling for an international conference on trade efficiency.

457.   It will be crucial, however, that such a role be clearly defined and delimited, so as to prevent any redundancy with other international efforts. In particular, close collaboration should take place between UNCTAD and the United Nations regional commissions. As far as EDIFACT is concerned, a clear division of labour could emerge, whereby UN/ECE would promote the development of the specifications of messages, while UNCTAD would participate in formulating their content, and would be responsible for organizing and optimizing the related procedures, and making proposals for improvements.

458.   UNCTAD would participate actively in the promotion of EDIFACT standards by advising developing countries and economies in transition about the removal of legal and technical obstacles to the introduction of new technologies, and by providing adequate technical solutions, relying inter alia on its experience with ASYCUDA.

459.   Close co-ordination should also be maintained with other specialized United Nations organizations (such as UNCITRAL as regards trade law issues, or ITU/CCITT for the technical questions concerning telecommunications and networks), intergovernmental bodies like the Customs Cooperation Council, non-governmental organizations such as the International Chamber of Commerce, international transport organizations, etc. Without interfering with these bodies' mandates, UNCTAD could play a catalytic role by identifying the issues falling under these organizations competences that will need to be resolved in .establishing the infrastructures required for the implementation of the trade efficiency initiative.

460.   The resulting global infrastructures for international trade should be regarded as *global commons* for international competition. They should in particular allow all partners to take part on an equitable basis in international competition. At the same time, the capability offered to all trading partners to access such infrastructures should not be considered in any way as preempting or conditioning the individual choices which they will wish to make in terms of policies (including trade policies, as well as policies regarding foreign direct investment, or intellectual property).

E. CONCLUSIONS AND POLICY RECOMMENDATIONS

461.   Although the volume growth of world trade and output has decelerated over the past three years, it has nevertheless remained positive. The 1980s was a dynamic decade for world trade, the growth of which continued to outstrip that of world output. If the growth of world trade in the 1990s is to remain buoyant and if its benefits are to be more widely spread, a strengthening of the multilateral system is required, through measures covering: (i) further trade liberalization through the dismantling of barriers, particularly non-tariff barriers, in particular those facing the exports of developing countries goods and services; (ii) fuller integration of multilaterally agreed competition policies and RBP control in the multilateral trading system; (iii) special measures in favour of commodity-exporting countries; (iv) assistance to developing countries in building supply capabilities in manufacturing, and modern services; (v) the deepening of trade and economic reforms in developing countries, in particular innovative policies toward foreign investment and the development of a multilateral framework to govern foreign investment; (vi) improved market access to technology for developing countries; and (vii) fuller integration of the countries of Central and Eastern Europe in the multilateral trading system.

462.   The trade negotiating agenda for the 1990s will continue to expand in response to changes in patterns of production, composition of trade and further rise in the importance of technology and investments. UNCTAD should be called upon to contribute in each of those areas as well as in identifying emerging systematic barriers facing developing countries.

463. The export supply capabilities of the developing countries need to be expanded and diversified, and their international competitiveness requires further strengthening. In the case of many countries, economic policy reforms can help to improve the competitiveness of production and the attractiveness of the countries as locations for investment. Liberalization of industrial and trade policies should proceed in a judicious and gradual manner dovetailed to each country's specific economic conditions, and development objectives can play an important role in this regard. As a complement to reform, developing countries will require international support to increase investment in tradable goods and services, enhance their technological abilities and build economic and human infrastructure.

464. The globalization of corporate activity has resulted in far-reaching changes in the nature of competition - and barriers to entry - for developing countries. These barriers are qualitatively different from the traditional ones stemming from differences in comparative advantage, productivity and prices. The adoption of industrial policies designed to influence competitiveness and market shares has added a new dimension to the constraints developing countries face in participating in the globalization process. The Conference may wish to initiate consideration in UNCTAD of the implications of the globalization process, particularly as it bears on issues of competition.

465. The increasing trend towards regional economic co-operation and integration can stimulate the multilateral liberalization process but should be in conformity with international obligations and with the objective of maintaining and strengthening the multilateral trading system. Moves towards greater regional co-operation, particularly through free trade areas and customs unions, may prove useful as a stepping stone to promote further multilateral liberalization. The new regional trading arrangements, both in Europe and in the Americas, need to evolve in a liberal direction, bringing about improvements in market access conditions also for those countries which are not members of the regional arrangements. The Conference may wish to propose arrangements for regular reviews and monitoring of these arrangements so as to ensure that they function in a non-discriminatory manner.

466. Finally, the daunting economic problems which the countries in Central and Eastern Europe and the USSR face in the short and medium-term will have to be overcome if these economies are to contribute to the growth of world trade. The international community will have to meet the challenge of assisting in their full integration into the global trading system. In the long term, such integration can be expected to be beneficial for world economic growth and trade and open up new export opportunities for all trading partners.

1. Improving the dialogue on trade and structural adjustment issues

467. The Conference might call for action, such as the implementation of commitments to halt and reverse protectionism, including those in paragraph 105(I) of the Final Act of UNCTAD VII. The Conference might make specific recommendations with regard to further trade liberalization in the post-Uruguay Round environment including: substantial cuts in remaining tariffs, in particular in tariff peaks, and reduction in tariff escalation; substantial reduction in the use of remaining non-tariff protection and the conversion of such measures to tariff equivalents.

468. In order to facilite the transition to a tariff-only system, it may be necessary to implement in the interim a system of tariff quotas where the absolute value or volume of imports of the product is not restricted but there is an additional rate of duty on all imports above the specified quota level. The "in quota" tariff could be the rate which is seen as the objective "longer-term" MFN bound rate; elimination of remaining VERs and other grey area measures; tighter disciplines on the use of safeguards and anti-dumping actions; faster phase-out of the MFA.

469. The Conference might wish to urge Governments to establish transparent mechanisms as a follow-up to the recommendation of UNCTAD VII contained in paragraph 105(4) of the Final Act according to which Governments should consider as part of the fight against protectionism the establishment of transparent mechanisms at the national level to evaluate protectionist measures sought by firms/sectors and the implications of such measures for the domestic economy as a

whole and their effects on the export interests of developing countries. The Trade and Development Board may be requested to consider the matter further. The Conference may also wish to request the secretariat of UNCTAD to organize periodic meetings of government experts to exchange views and experiences on national mechanisms and to report to the Trade and Development Board thereon.

470. In order to enhance the effectiveness of the Board's annual review of protectionism and structural adjustment, there is a need to improve its technical content. This objective could be served by instituting the practice of convening high-level expert groups on specific issues. The experts would be officials in Governments dealing with issues under discussion and academics of international standing.

471. These expert groups would assist the Secretary-General of UNCTAD and the Board in addressing technical issues involved in the discussions relating to trade and structural adjustment. Their assistance could be sought by the Board in connection with issues to which the Board attaches importance. Three policy proposals made in this report lend themselves well to this more technical approach: a review of transparent mechanisms referred to above for evaluating industry requests for protection against imports, a review of the structural adjustment policies of developed countries, and the monitoring of the formation or strengthening of regional integration arrangements.

(a) Structural adjustment in developed countries

472. The Conference may reiterate the request for periodic evaluations by the Board of achievements of structural adjustment policies in developed countries in encouraging the private sector to reallocate labour and capital out of "sunset" sectors where developing countries have acquired or are acquiring comparative advantge into "sunrise" sectors which hold out the promise of higher incomes for their own labour force. In this respect, the annual reviews conducted by the Board of protectionism and structural adjustment could focus more sharply on the technical issues involved in such structural adjustment programmes. As noted above, given the technical nature of the issues involved, the Secretary-General of UNCTAD may seek the views of high-level experts on the subject to assist him and the Board with the elucidation of the issues and to make concrete recommendations for action.

(b) Trade policy reform in developing countries

473. Research and technical cooperation activities in UNCTAD should be intensified, to assist Governments of developing countries in evaluating trade policy options and in tailoring reforms to their country's characteristics, objectives and needs. The Conference should call upon the UNCTAD secretariat to increase such activities and promote the interchange of information and experiences amongst countries concerned. A call should also be made to both bilateral and multilateral donors to make additional resources available for this purpose.

(c) Support for structural adjustment in developing countries

474. Trade policy reform by itself is insufficient to bring about structural adjustment. In many developing countries experiencing severe foreign exchange scarcities, investments in tradeable goods and services (which tend to be import-intensive) cannot be made without a major increase in private and public external financial resources. The low-income, commodity-dependent countries also need assistance to build the supply capabilities which are indispensable if their economies are to respond to the stimuli of trade policy reform.

475. The Conference may wish to propose modalities to channel external public and private fi-

nancial resources - as well as innovative ways of co-financing between the public and private sectors - to building supply capabilities in tradeable goods and services, keeping in mind the special need of low-income, commodity-dependent countries for concessional financing.

(d) Regional economic groupings

476. In order to preserve the character of the multilateral trading system, the formation and strengthening of economic groupings should be accompanied by trade liberalization towards non-participants. A system of international review of the impact of emerging trade groupings, and of their policies towards those countries not associated with them, should help to protect the interests of the both the weaker members of the groupings and of non-participants. The Conference could request the Trade and Development Board, assisted by high level experts, to conduct such reviews.

477. Trade liberalization in developing countries will give strong impetus to South-South trade. There are, however, other barriers to such trade. These include the inadequacy of transport and telecommunications infrastructures, and of the institutions supporting such trade. Efforts to overcome them will require large financial resources. The Conference could call on bilateral donors and regional and multilateral financial institutions to increase their commitments in this area.

2. Uruguay Round and trade agenda for the 1990s

478. To achieve a balanced and substantial package of results in all areas of the negotiations in the Uruguay Round is of vital importance to all participants, particularly to developing countries. Despite differing nuances and emphases placed by developing countries on individual subjects and issues of interest to them, or the emergence of issue-based coalitions such as in agriculture, developing countries have, by and large, been pursuing a set of common objectives, such as:

(a) in *market access*, as a top priority, to seek substantial concessions with respect to tariffs and non-tariff measures in order to promote trade liberalization and to expand the opportunities for developing-country exports into world markets, while providing adequate compensation for the erosion of preferences under existing schemes;

(b) in *agriculture*, reformed GATT rules in this area should provide developing countries with improved and secure access to markets and recognize the developmental role of agriculture in the economies and societies of developing countries and mitigate negative impacts on net-food importing countries;

(c) in *textiles and clothing*, the negotiations should lead to an agreed programme for the phasing out of the MFA and for the reintegration of trade in textiles and clothing within the rules and principles of the General Agreement within a reasonable time frame;

(d) in *tropical products*, the trade in this area should be liberalized to the fullest possible extent on a non-reciprocal basis;

(e) with respect to *safeguards*, for developing countries, it is important that the Uruguay Round negotiations would conclude a comprehensive agreement on safeguards which imparts stability and predictability to international trade, and which excludes all possibility of discriminatory action in violation of the most-favoured-nation (MFN) principle, complemented by rules governing the application of anti-dumping and countervailing measures which would *eliminate* rather than *increase* the scope for the harassment of developing country exports, thus ensuring that such measures cease to provide a substitute for discriminatory safeguard action;

(f) the stability and predictability of international trade would also be reinforced by a refinement of the rules governing the applications of *anti-dumping and countervailing measures* so as to reduce the scope for harassment of developing-country exports;

(g) to provide special treatment for developing countries, the acceptance by all parties of tighter disciplines over their resort to trade policy measures on a mutual and equitable basis, taking into account the importance of flexibility (especially in relation to balance-of-payments problems in the context of development strategies) as well as levels of development;

(h) on *trade-related aspects of intellectual property rights (TRIPs)*, the final agreement should facilitate the access of developing countries to technology and their pursuit of public policy and social objectives;

(i) on *trade in services*, the multilateral framework agreement should assist in enhancing the international competitiveness of developing-country service firms and in enabling them to gain effective access to world markets;

(j) on *trade-related investment measures (TRIMs)*, any result reached in the Uruguay Round should clearly recognize the right of developing countries to establish conditions on foreign investors intended to promote development and enhance competition, so long as such measures do not cause injury to trading parnters; and

(k) a legal structure for the implementation of the results of the Uruguay Round should also be found to preclude both unilateral action and cross-sectoral retaliation between trade in goods and measures relating to intellectual property protection, investment and services, and to ensure that the scope for developing countries to effectively pursue their trade and economic interests is not undermined.

479.   As foreseen in Part I.G of the Punta del Este Declaration, the Group of Negotiations on Goods was called to conduct, before the formal completion of the negotiations, an evaluation of results in terms of the Objectives and General Principles Governing Negotiations as set out in the Declaration, with a view to ensuring the effective application of differential and more favourable treatment for developing countries. This evaluation should afford the possibility of introducing corrective measures to ensure that a balanced outcome is, in effect, reached. It would also seem important for such an evaluation to be conducted comprehensively within a sufficient time-frame to be able to influence the final outcome.

480.   UNCTAD VIII provides a good opportunity to make an important contribution to the evaluation of the outcome of the Uruguay Round. Further, the Conference might address the broad range of issues that will affect the ability of developing countries to participate effectively in the world trade in the 1990s so that trade can continue to provide the main impetus to economic and social development. The Conference may wish to draw up an agenda for action for the 1990s.

481.   Specifically, it could: (a) analyse and assess the outcome of the Uruguay Round, from the trade and development perspective, examining in particular the impact of the results of the Round on the access to markets for developing-country exports of goods and services, and upon their ability to develop a competitive capacity in international trade in such goods and services, as well as upon their possibilities for sustainable development; (b) identify the aspects not adequately addressed by the Uruguay Round and formulate suggestions for possible action thereon; (c) examine the main features of the post-Uruguay Round international trading system, with a view to identifying, in particular the main problems and opportunities confronting developing countries in international trade in goods and services in the 1990s; and (d) propose ways and means of effectively addressing these issues, including through policy measures at the national and international levels, joint action by member States, as well as the negotiation of contractual multilateral agreements. The Trade and Development Board should continue to follow closely developments in the Uruguay Round.

482.   The Conference may also reaffirm continued support for technical assistance with respect to the participation of developing countries in negotiations to improve their market access, defend and promote their trade interests in general, and recognize the need for expanded technical assistance to enable developing countries to construct the necessary institutional infrastructures to participate effectively in trade negotiations and in the conduct of their trade relations.

483.   The Conference might wish to make recommendations concerning ways and means to offset trade losses, particularly of the least developed among the developing countries, due to the erosion of preferential margins resulting from MFN concessions in the Uruguay Round, as well as on the transitional adverse effects of the reform process in developing countries.

484.   The Conference might wish to reaffirm the need to maintain, strengthen and improve the GSP and to recommend specific measures for this purpose, in particular by extending preferential treatment to all products of export interest to developing countries and by eliminating, or substantially reducing, all *a priori* limitations and non-tariff measures affecting these products. The Conference might wish to consider extending preferential treatment to developing countries in relation to transactions in areas other than goods.

3. Competition policies and restrictive business practices

485.   Corporate practices affecting market access and competition, as well as measures to discipline such practices, warrant policy consideration by the international community. More systematic implementation of the Multilaterally Agreed Equitable Set of Principles and Rules for the Control of Restrictive Business Practices should be recommended, taking into account the results of the Second Review Conference on the subject, and work should be initiated on the relationship between competition policy and trade policy.

486.   The Conference may wish to initiate a work programme aimed at fully integrating multilaterally agreed competition policies and restrictive business practices control in the international trading system.

487.   The Conference may also wish to take note of the positive results of the Second Review Conference on RBPs and support the implementation of its resolution. In this respect, it should (a) call upon countries which do not have effective RBP control legislation to take the necessary steps to adopt such laws; (b) call upon countries with experience in this area to provide expertise and technical assistance to countries requesting such assistance, and to consider favourably requests for information and consultations emanating from developing countries; (c) reiterate the Review Conference's call to financial organizations and donor countries for necessary supporting funds for technical assistance in this field; (d) seek to establish a consensus for multilateral negotiations in this areas aimed at harmonizing competition policies and mobilizing efforts to promote competition, and eliminate anti-competitive practices at the international level.

4. Trade, environment and sustainable development

488.   An international consensus needs to be established with respect to an appropriate balance between environmental protection and multilateral trade obligations. Any trade rules and disciplines regarding trade policy measures that can be taken, or should be taken, for environment-related reasons should provide predictable and transparent protection for the environment. UNCTAD bodies should monitor and analyse the linkages of trade, environment and sustainable development.

489.   The Conference might wish to request the Secretary-General of UNCTAD to undertake analytical work and studies on linkages between environmental and trade policies and to recommend policy actions that can be taken, at the national and international levels, to ensure that environmental and trade policies are mutually supportive, with a view to achieving sustainable development.

490.   The Conference might request UNCTAD to evolve a conceptual framework for establishing the link between the removal of trade barriers on goods and services (including access to technology) and the enhancement of sustainable development in developing countries.

491.   The Conference might request the Trade and Development Board to secure continued analysis and discussions, within UNCTAD, on the relationship between environmental policies, trade, and the international trading system, *inter alia,* through expert group meetings.

492. The Conference might wish to take note of progress made in the collection and analysis of factual information on environmental regulations and measures which may have an impact on trade, in accordance with Board resolutions 384 (XXXVII) and 383 (XXXVIII), as well as in the progress made in securing appropriate and efficient dissemination of that information.

493. The Conference might wish to recall Board resolution 383 (XXXVIII) requesting the Secretary-General of UNCTAD to arrange for technical assistance programmes in the field of trade and environment and to invite international development agencies, such as UNDP, and donor countries in a position to do so, to provide voluntary extra-budgetary resources to UNCTAD for this purpose.

5. Enhancing efficiency in international trade

494. Recent advances in information technologies have allowed a handful of enterprises and nations to take a quantum leap in the area of trade efficiency. In the absence of comprehensive guidelines, norms and standards, the broad majority of firms and nations involved in international trade will remain excluded from the resulting new sources of efficiency and competitiveness. Such a situation would result in (a) a further widening of the North-South competitiveness gaps, and (b) considerable loss in terms of efficiency and dynamism in international trade.

495. The member Governments of UNCTAD should call for the convening of an International Conference on Global Infrastructure for Trade and Trade Efficiency. This Conference should focus on the legal, technical, procedural and institutional aspects of setting up an International Network for Trade Efficiency and Development, and generate the international agreements thereof. UNCTAD VIII should provide for the necessary political impetus, and the resources, to allow the UNCTAD secretariat to start the background work required, and to establish the inter-governmental working groups that will make recommendations to the Conference.

496. There is an urgent need to set up truly universal electronic data interchange (EDI) in particular, and "networked markets" in general, so as to give developing countries access to new opportunities for trade facilitation and efficiency stemming from recent advances and the application of information technologies in this area.

497. Developed countries should foster transparency in trade-related information, especially through the granting of univeral access to existing information on markets and market opportunities in their respective economies. They should assist in spreading know-how in key areas, such as Electronic Data Interchange (EDI) and Trade Facilitation.

498. Developing countries should pursue their own efforts towards higher efficiency in trade-related fields, in particular through improving their trade procedures.

499. The institutional machinery of UNCTAD - and especially the Trade and Development Board - should grant adequate priority to the issue of trade efficiency in their future deliberations. This issue also needs to be raised in the Second Committee of the General Assembly of the United Nations, in order to obtain the convening of the International Conference on Infrastructures for Trade and Trade Efficiency. This should be done in close collaboration with institutions involved in trade facilitation, such as the United Nations Regional Commissions and the International Trade Centre.

500. Positive results have been registered from the joint efforts of the UNCTAD secretariat and recipient developing countries in the area of trade efficiency: the circulation of goods has been accelerated, while customs revenues have been increasing, in spite of tariff cuts. Policy decisions have been made on the basis of significantly improved and more recent trade statistics. Among the avenues for facilitation which need to be further evolved, the improvement of transit facilities is vital for the expansion and development of the foreign trade sector of the land-locked countries, and their transit neighbours should be assisted by the international community through financial and technical assistance for the improvement of their transit infrastructure. Additional efforts are now required to enhance the awareness of developing countries of the positive results they can expect from the Trade Efficiency Initiative, as well as to provide them with the necessary technical,

procedural, legal and institutional knowledge required to be part of "Efficient Global Trade". UNDP and the agencies of the United Nations system, as well as donor countries, are thus called upon to pursue their support of the work of UNCTAD in the area of trade efficiency, and in particular in organizing the International Conference on Global Infrastructures for Trade and Trade Efficiency.

6. Supporting reforms in Central and Eastern Europe

501. The far-reaching systemic changes taking place in Central and Eastern Europe and the USSR need to be supported by the international community. In the area of trade, market access conditions for these countries' exports have improved considerably since the process of reforms gathered momentum. However, much still needs to be accomplished. It is important that relaxation of NTMs in their favour be accomplished without a tightening of restrictions on developing countries. This is particularly important in sensitive sectors such as agriculture, textiles and clothing, footwear and steel. The best approach would be a relaxation of restrictions on an MFN basis. The interest of the world economy would be best served if the trade regimes that are emerging in the Central and Eastern European countries are kept open to imports from all potential trading partners on an MFN basis. UNCTAD should be called upon through its technical assistance programmes to support these countries in their reform process.

502. The Conference could propose policy measures designed to promote in a timely way the full integration of the USSR and other East European countries into the world economy and international trading system, as an integral part of the efforts for the creation of an equitable, healthy and secure world trading system.

7. Institutional issues

503. The inadequacy of existing mechanisms to deal with the wide range of issues involved and their various impacts in other areas and on different countries and population groups, would seem to call for a initiation of work towards major reform aimed at strengthening international organizations in the area of multilateral trade. In this context, the various initiatives already put forward in the context of both the Uruguay Round and the United Nations are to be welcomed. Further work in the United Nations system is needed on: (a) establishment of a mechanism for the international community to set its objectives with respect to international trade and development, within a rational framework designed to facilitate consideration of interrelated issues, including trade, investment, technology, information, financial instruments, labour migration, environmental protection, anti-competitive practices, access to networks and distribution channels, taking fully into account their impact on various countries and populations; (b) setting up of a forum for international consensus building, and a source of intellectual support with respect to these objectives, so as to provide a solid basis for decision-making which would ensure "universality" in the sense of maximum transparency and full participation of all countries and contribute to achieving greater coherence in global and economic policy-making, in particular by strengthening coordination among relevant international organizations; (c) construction of an effective mechanism for joint action, i.e. a mechanism in which these objectives and emerging consensus can be translated into concerted action by the member States through the acceptance of general principles, programmes of action tailored to particular situations and the negotiation of contractual multilateral agreements; (d) consolidation of an institutional and legal basis for administration of contractual multilateral agreements, including a possible revised institution based on the current GATT for contractual agreements on trade in goods; agreements which may arise from the Uruguay Round on trade in services and trade-related intellectual property rights; and future agreements which may be negotiated (e.g. competition law, environment, investment, TNCs, technology, etc.); (e) designing a framework for the implementation and surveillance of such principles, programmes and agreements and the reconciliation of different positions and affected in-

terests with respect to the above, and for regular monitoring of trade policies and practices of individual countries or groups of countries and their impact on the functioning of the trading system; (f) strengthening research capacity of the secretariat, ensuring the independence of its analysis and strengthening its right to initiative and its capability to provide technical support and expertise to smaller and more vulnerable countries, aimed at the building of capacities of these countries to enable them to take part effectively in the consensus-forming and negotiating process within any reformed institutional structure, which should ensure that all countries have the opportunity of focusing the attention of the international community on their particular problems; and (g) strengthening and streamlining co-ordination mechanisms for mutual support between programmes and agencies of the United Nations system, particularly to enhance the contribution of all relevant specialized agencies to the process of consensus-building, joint action and negotiation as well as strengthening of the role of United Nations regional economic and social commissions in this process, including possible joint action aimed at resolving trade, economic and social problems of individual countries or groups of countries, and supporting specific development programmes.

504.   The Conference provides an opportune forum to resume work within UNCTAD's mandate relating to the establishing of a comprehensive International Trade Organization. In pursuance of the general objective, recognized in General Assembly resolution 45/201, of strengthening international organizations in the area of multilateral trade, this would include consideration of all relevant proposals, *inter alia*, put forward in the Uruguay Round.

Annex table II-1

Frequency [a] of GSP and LDC preferential rates, by range of MFN tariffs, in major DMECs

(Number of tariff lines)

Product group and Importing market	MFN dutiable			0 < MFN duty ≤ 5%			5% < MFN duty ≤ 10%			10% < MFN duty ≤ 15%			MFN duty > 15%		
	total MFN	items under GSP	items under LDC	total MFN	items under GSP	items under LDC	total MFN	items under GSP	items under LDC	total MFN	items under GSP	items under LDC	total MFN	items under GSP	items under LDC
EEC															
All items	8011	5953	7537	2275	2048	2136	3689	3071	3582	1384	547	1315	663	287	504
Agriculture	405	291	384	92	77	83	116	84	107	59	40	58	138	90	136
Natural resource-based prods.	772	530	704	156	110	119	380	345	366	158	53	158	78	22	61
Tropical products	775	230	484	133	57	102	146	36	80	141	37	85	355	100	217
Textiles and clothing	1264	205	1257	56	23	50	514	99	513	680	83	680	14	-	14
Other	4795	4697	4708	1838	1781	1782	2533	2507	2516	346	334	334	78	75	76
Japan															
All items	7235	5874	1274	2544	2357	5	2756	2268	232	866	698	583	1069	551	454
Agriculture	387	243	56	113	104	3	95	77	11	35	17	11	144	45	31
Natural resource-based prods.	689	494	59	251	154	-	342	281	22	86	51	34	10	8	3
Tropical products	759	132	94	82	17	2	127	18	11	78	21	17	472	76	64
Textiles and clothing	1975	1648	922	53	53	-	1026	747	169	610	563	507	286	285	246
Other	3425	3357	143	2045	2029	-	1166	1145	19	57	46	14	157	137	110
United States															
All items	7462	4070	4070	3200	2439	2439	2640	1353	1353	719	167	167	903	111	111
Agriculture	331	201	201	155	112	112	103	66	66	27	10	10	46	13	13
Natural resource-based prods.	568	464	464	364	311	311	167	129	129	19	10	10	18	14	14
Tropical products	702	289	289	346	159	159	186	88	88	66	18	18	104	24	24
Textiles and clothing	1379	74	74	130	32	32	538	39	39	253	1	1	458	2	2
Other	4482	3042	3042	2205	1825	1825	1646	1031	1031	354	128	128	277	58	58

Source: UNCTAD Data Base on Trade Control Measures.

a Number of tariff items in the corresponding customs tariff schedule falling under each MFN tariff range.

Annex table II-2

Trade coverage of tariffs applied on imports *a* from developing countries by major DMECs

(Millions of $US)

Product group and Importing market	Dutiable *b*	Duty-free	0 < duty ≤ 5 %	5% < duty ≤ 10 %	10% < duty ≤ 15 %	Above 15 %
EEC						
All items	31522.5	74633.0	9638.5	9604.5	7923.3	4356.2
Agriculture	6188.0	10234.8	3317.0	1182.9	177.2	1510.9
Natural resource-based	2433.2	9480.7	770.0	825.9	347.5	489.7
Tropical products	3450.5	7600.7	1075.7	475.9	321.4	1577.4
Textiles	5732.1	12687.3	109.8	837.3	4784.8	0.1
Other	13718.9	34629.4	4365.9	6282.5	2292.4	778.0
Japan						
All items	21198.1	40545.9	8412.5	8738.0	1575.3	2472.3
Agriculture	2012.7	4685.7	343.3	159.5	525.2	984.7
Natural resource-based	5960.8	7675.3	4413.2	1436.8	73.6	37.2
Tropical products	3092.4	2431.9	351.4	1092.0	279.4	1369.6
Textiles	6304.1	1432.3	752.1	5507.9	44.1	0.1
Other	3828.2	24320.6	2552.6	541.8	653.6	80.7
United States						
All items	90144.3	46125.5	39315.2	28875.8	3975.3	17978.0
Agriculture	3612.3	6968.4	2247.3	1108.3	60.5	196.3
Natural resource-based	2331.1	7515.3	1215.2	834.5	278.6	2.8
Tropical products	2170.1	2549.2	886.8	363.4	261.4	658.6
Textiles	22895.2	494.9	625.1	6082.6	1175.3	15012.2
Other	59135.5	28597.7	34340.8	20487.1	2199.6	2108.1

Source: UNCTAD Data Base on Trade Control Measures.

a Imports in 1988 for the EEC and Japan and in 1989 for the United States.
b Imports dutiable under MFN and GSP or other preferential tariff.

Annex table II-3

Developing countries' exposure to high MFN rates of duty in major DMEC markets

Product groups and markets	Total imports [a]			Imports [a] subject to "high" MFN rates of duty							
				Situation pre-UR				Situation post-UR [b]			
	World ($bn) (1)	Developing countries ($bn) (2)	Share of devng. cntrs. (%) (3)	World ($bn) (4)	Developing countries ($bn) (5)	Share of devng. cntrs. (%) (6)	Ratio (7)=(6)/(3)	World ($bn) (8)	Developing countries ($bn) (9)	Share of devng. cntrs. (%) (10)	Ratio (11)=(10)/(3)
Total of three markets	851.8	282.8	33.2	98.6	57.8	58.6	1.76	49.1	30.5	62.0	1.87
Tropical products	46.6	33.7	72.4	7.3	5.1	70.4	0.97	4.2	3.2	76.1	1.05
NRBPs	103.5	35.4	34.2	6.4	3.9	60.9	1.78	6.0	3.7	61.3	1.79
Textiles	65.4	49.5	75.8	43.2	35.1	75.8	1.07	20.0	17.2	85.7	1.13
Other products	636.3	164.2	25.8	41.8	13.6	32.7	1.27	18.9	6.4	33.9	1.31
EEC	329.7	95.0	28.8	49.0	26.9	55.0	1.91	10.8	6.2	57.3	1.99
Tropical products	21.6	16.4	75.9	4.1	3.0	72.1	0.95	3.2	2.3	71.3	0.94
NRBPs	40.9	11.9	29.1	4.7	2.7	56.9	1.95	4.5	2.5	56.9	1.95
Textiles	26.6	18.4	69.2	17.6	13.7	77.7	1.12	0.1	...	14.8	0.21
Other products	240.5	48.3	20.1	48.3	22.5	33.6	1.67	3.1	1.4	43.6	2.17
Japan	138.5	56.2	40.6	12.8	9.3	72.7	1.79	5.8	4.4	75.4	1.87
Tropical products	9.5	6.7	70.4	2.7	1.8	66.4	0.94	1.0	0.9	90.7	1.29
NRBPs	32.7	13.6	41.7	1.3	0.9	70.1	1.68	1.2	0.9	72.5	1.74
Textiles	10.2	7.7	75.9	7.7	6.6	79.6	1.05	1.7	1.4	82.3	1.08
Other products	86.1	28.1	32.7	2.1	1.3	59.9	1.83	1.9	1.2	61.8	1.89
United States	383.6	131.6	34.3	36.9	21.6	58.6	1.71	32.6	19.9	61.1	1.78
Tropical products	15.4	10.6	68.7	0.4	0.3	79.2	1.15	0.4	0.3	76.8	1.12
NRBPs	29.9	9.8	79.5	0.4	0.3	77.4	2.35	0.3	0.3	79.5	2.35
Textiles	28.6	23.4	81.8	19.0	16.2	85.3	1.04	18.3	15.6	86.1	1.05
Other products	309.7	87.7	28.3	17.1	4.8	27.9	0.99	13.9	3.9	27.9	0.98

Source: : E. Duran, S. Marchese and R. Vossenaar, *Aranceles elevados en los grandes mercados: desventaja comercial para los países en desarrollo*, (forthcoming).

a Excluding agriculture.
b Offers as of end-1990.

Annex table II-4

TRADE COVERAGE RATIOS [a] OF SELECTED NTMS APPLIED BY SELECTED DEVELOPED MARKET-ECONOMY COUNTRIES [b] IN THE PERIOD 1981-1990

Index numbers (1981 = 100)

All sectors (SITC 0-9), all selected NTMs [c]

	1981	1982	1983	1984	1985	1986	1987	1988	1989	1990
Total	**100.0**	**102.1**	**103.4**	**83.5**	**85.5**	**88.0**	**91.7**	**90.0**	**95.7**	**95.1**
Austria	100.0	100.0	100.0	100.0	100.0	99.7	99.7	99.7	99.7	99.7
Canada	100.0	113.3	114.4	117.1	119.8	194.2	197.3	150.7	135.6	135.6
EC	100.0	104.7	109.9	111.0	114.5	114.2	116.8	114.9	113.9	113.4
Finland	100.0	101.9	101.8	101.8	101.6	101.6	101.7	101.7	101.7	101.7
Japan	100.0	100.0	100.1	100.1	100.1	97.9	97.9	98.1	98.2	98.0
New Zealand	100.0	100.0	100.1	100.1	72.0	70.8	64.7	47.9	32.4	25.1
Norway	100.0	101.0	100.3	96.0	95.7	95.4	95.4	95.3	95.3	88.1
Switzerland	100.0	100.5	100.5	101.3	101.3	101.3	101.3	101.3	101.3	101.3
United States	100.0	100.5	99.6	55.5	57.6	61.1	67.1	66.7	80.6	79.9

Non-fuel trade, core measures [c]

	1981	1982	1983	1984	1985	1986	1987	1988	1989	1990
Total	**100.0**	**101.6**	**101.7**	**104.1**	**103.8**	**103.3**	**104.7**	**105.3**	**104.6**	**103.0**
Austria	100.0	100.0	100.0	100.0	100.0	99.6	99.6	99.6	99.6	99.6
Canada	100.0	114.6	114.6	114.6	107.6	107.6	110.1	80.2	68.1	68.1
EC	100.0	106.2	114.2	111.7	110.0	108.9	108.4	108.6	108.5	109.0
Finland	100.0	100.0	106.0	106.0	106.0	105.5	105.5	105.5	105.5	105.5
Japan	100.0	100.0	100.1	100.1	100.1	97.2	97.2	96.8	96.7	96.7
New Zealand	100.0	100.0	100.0	100.1	69.2	66.0	39.8	39.8	25.8	19.6
Norway	100.0	101.0	100.3	99.1	98.9	98.6	98.6	98.4	98.4	90.9
Switzerland	100.0	100.1	100.3	100.8	100.8	100.8	100.8	100.8	100.8	100.8
United States	100.0	96.3	88.5	97.7	100.0	101.1	106.5	110.7	110.4	106.0

Source: S. Laird and R. Vossenaar, "Por que deberíamos preocuparnos por las medidas no arancelarias", *Información Comercial Espa + %ola* , No.698, October 1991.

[a] Ratios have been computed using 1988 trade weights (except for the EC and the United States, for which 1989 trade weights were used).

[b] Austria, Canada, EC (12), Finland, Japan, New Zealand, Norway, Switzerland and the United States.

[c] The group "all selected NTMs" includes certain para-tariff measures, surcharges, variable levies, anti-dumping and countervailing actions, quantitative restrictions (including prohibitions, quotas, non-automatic licensing, state monopolies, "voluntary" export restraints and restraints under MFA and similar textile arrangements), import surveillance, automatic licensing and price control measures. The group of "core" NTMs excludes from the group defined above, para-tariff measures, antidumping and countervailing actions, automatic licensing and import surveillance measures.

Annex table II-5

Import coverage ratios of selected non-tariff measures applied in 1990 by selected developed market-economy countries [a]

(Percentages)

Product groups and origin of imports	Imports (billions of $US)	Broad definition [b] of NTMs			Narrow definition [c] of NTMs				
		Total	Para-tar.	AD/CVD	Total	Quantit. Restraints	NAL/Q/P	VERs	Price actions
Developing Countries									
All items	487.0	20.1	1.7	1.8	16.3	15.6	3.6	9.8	1.7
All items, excluding fuels	362.4	23.2	1.5	2.5	19.2	18.3	4.8	13.1	2.2
Tropical products	41.6	8.4	1.7	0.7	5.9	5.5	3.5	1.6	2.1
Natural resource-based	42.5	18.1	0.9	0.3	16.5	15.6	15.0	0.0	0.9
Agriculture	27.6	34.2	12.8	1.0	25.7	21.1	19.5	0.4	16.8
Textiles	61.6	74.6	1.0	6.2	70.9	70.9	5.1	67.1	0.0
Other	191.1	9.2	0.2	2.3	5.0	4.1	0.6	2.8	1.2
Iron and steel	13.0	38.6	0.0	7.8	28.7	15.9	0.0	15.6	16.9
Motor vehicles	7.2	3.1	1.7	0.2	0.8	0.3	0.0	0.0	0.0
Consumer electronics	37.8	6.2	0.0	2.7	3.9	3.9	0.0	2.3	0.0
Other	133.0	7.4	0.1	1.8	3.2	3.2	0.8	1.9	0.0
USSR and Eastern Europe									
All items	44.9	29.4	1.2	1.1	23.5	20.2	7.9	6.5	5.8
All items, excluding fuels	29.2	26.3	1.0	1.7	21.4	17.2	5.4	10.1	8.9
Tropical products	1.4	3.9	0.2	0.0	3.5	3.1	1.7	0.1	0.6
Natural resource-based	7.4	11.0	0.0	0.4	8.0	6.8	4.9	0.0	1.2
Agriculture	3.8	48.7	7.5	0.0	45.3	28.2	26.8	3.6	32.3
Textiles	2.6	80.8	0.3	0.3	78.5	78.5	4.1	75.4	0.0
Other	14.5	19.8	0.0	3.1	12.8	9.4	0.5	5.9	8.8
Iron and steel	2.9	57.7	0.0	3.6	49.9	33.8	0.0	29.8	43.8
Motor vehicles	0.9	11.5	0.4	0.0	10.4	9.8	0.0	0.0	0.0
Consumer electronics	0.1	3.1	0.0	0.0	2.6	2.6	0.0	0.0	0.0
Other	10.7	10.4	0.0	3.2	3.1	2.9	0.7	0.0	0.2
DMECs									
All items	939.4	16.7	1.4	3.5	9.9	8.6	3.3	4.1	1.3
All items, excluding fuels	895.5	16.4	1.3	3.6	9.5	8.3	3.0	4.3	1.3
Tropical products	20.0	9.7	1.5	1.0	6.5	5.0	3.1	0.0	1.4
Natural resource-based	85.2	7.4	0.3	1.0	5.5	5.2	5.0	0.0	0.4
Agriculture	52.6	39.8	5.3	1.3	31.8	24.8	21.6	1.2	12.1
Textiles	29.1	17.8	0.6	0.3	9.4	9.4	5.3	0.9	0.0
Other	720.6	15.6	1.2	4.3	8.3	7.4	1.3	5.3	0.7
Iron and steel	36.0	42.3	0.0	3.2	31.4	27.8	0.5	27.1	13.3
Motor vehicles	127.4	45.5	6.3	12.2	22.4	19.2	0.0	18.7	0.0
Consumer electronics	65.5	15.7	0.2	11.4	5.3	5.2	0.0	3.6	0.0
Other	491.7	5.9	0.0	1.4	3.4	3.2	1.8	0.4	0.0
World									
All items	1476.8	18.2	1.5	2.9	12.4	11.3	3.6	6.0	1.5
All items, excluding fuels	1292.4	18.5	1.4	3.2	12.5	11.3	3.5	6.9	1.8
Tropical products	64.1	9.1	1.6	0.7	6.4	5.6	3.3	1.0	1.8
Natural resource-based	136.3	10.9	0.4	0.7	9.1	8.5	8.1	0.0	0.6
Agriculture	84.4	38.6	8.0	1.1	30.6	23.9	21.2	1.0	14.8
Textiles	93.4	57.0	0.8	4.2	51.8	51.8	5.1	46.6	0.0
Other	929.3	14.3	0.9	3.8	7.7	6.7	1.1	4.8	0.9
Iron and steel	52.2	42.0	0.0	4.3	31.6	25.0	0.3	24.2	15.8
Motor vehicles	136.1	42.9	6.0	11.4	21.1	18.0	0.0	17.5	0.0
Consumer electronics	103.6	12.2	0.1	8.2	4.8	4.7	0.0	3.1	0.0
Other	637.3	6.3	0.1	1.5	3.3	3.2	1.6	0.7	0.0

Source: UNCTAD Data Base on Trade Control Measures.

a Australia, Austria, Canada, EEC (12), Finland, Japan, New Zealand, Norway, Sweden, Switzerland and the United States. Ratios have been computed using 1988 trade weights except in the calculations regarding the Eurpean Economic Community and the United States for which statistics for 1989 were used.

b The "broad" group of NTMs includes certain para-tariff measures, surcharges, variable levies, anti-dumping and countervailing actions, quantitative restrictions, import surveillance, automatic licensing and price control measures.

c The "narrow" group of NTMs includes quantitative restrictions (including prohibitions (P), quotas (Q), non-automatic licensing (NAL), "voluntary" export restraints and restraints under MFA and similar textile arrangements and state monopolies), surcharges, variable charges, price surveillance, minimum pricing and "voluntary" export price restraints.

Annex table II-6

Selected border non-tariff measures implemented or renewed since the Punta del Este Declaration (September 1986)

Country	Date	Type of non-tariff measure	Affected countries/territories	Products covered	Operation of the measure
Australia	Jun/87	Tariff quota	World	Certain cheeses and curd	The quota system maintains existing duty rate ($A96 per tonne) as primary rate. The above quota rate is $A2100. Quotas have been allocated to foreign suppliers on the basis of 1985/1986 import volumes. Tariff quotas are to be phased out on 1 July 1992.
Austria	Mar/87	Import relief (quota)	World	Broken rice	Measure under GATT Art. XIX. This measure was terminated on 31 October 1991.
	Mar/90	Import relief (quota)	World	Certain types of prepared fowls	Measure under GATT Art. XIX. The quota was applicable until 31 December 1990.
	Sep/91	Import relief (quota)	World, excluding EEC and EFTA countries	Cement	Measure under GATT Art. XIX. The quota is applicable until 31 August 1992.
Canada	Jan/88	Bilateral restraint agreement	Former German Democratic Republic	Hosiery	For period 1 Jan 1988 - 31 Dec 1991
	Jan/88 and May/89	Quantitative restrictions	World	Certain dairy products and broiler hatching eggs and chicks.	Extension of products covered by supply management programmes for manufactured milk (Jan/88) and broiler hatching eggs and chicks (May/89) Canada has justified such import restrictions under GATT Article XI:2(c)(i).
EEC	Jan/87	VER	China	Manioc, and sweet potatoes.	Agreement to restrain exports during 1987-1989, following consultations held under Article 6 of the Trade and Co-operation agreement between the EEC and China
	Jan/87	VER	Thailand, Indonesia	Manioc	Extension of the agreements, until 31 Dec. 1990
	Feb/87	Community surveillance	World	Urea	Imposed following a surge of imports from some Eastern European Countries
	Apr/87	VER	Venezuela	Steel products	VER in return for suspension of antidumping duties. Not renewed in 1990.
	May/87	Community surveillance	Japan	Colour TVs, personal computers and craft tools	Following arrangement between the United States and Japan on trade in semi-conductors. Renewed for personal computers and electropneumatic drills, effective 31 May 1989.
	Nov/87	Suspension of imports	World	Certain frozen squid	Emergency measure under GATT Art. XIX, following increased imports at alleged abnormally low prices
	Dec/87	VER	Former German Democratic Republic	Sheep and goat meat	Similar to existing arrangements with other suppliers, under the Common Market Organization for sheep and goat meat. Without effect after the German unification.
	Dec/87	Extension of import surveillance	Egypt, Turkey and Malta	Certain textile imports	Voluntary export restraints in return for preferential tariff treatment

Source: UNCTAD secretariat, compiled from official published information.

Note: The list of actions is not exhaustive. In particular, it includes neither anti-dumping and countervailing duty measures nor bilateral actions under the MFA. The inclusion of non-tariff measures in this list does not prejudge the consistency of the measures with GATT.

Annex table II-6 (continued)

Country	Date	Type of non-tariff measure	Affected countries/territories	Products covered	Operation of the measure
EEC (cont'd)	Jan/88	VER (unilateral action by exporter)	Japan	Fork-lift trucks	Self restraint of exports for one year, extended for a subsequent year.
	Feb/88	Import surveillance	Southern hemisphere	Dessert apples	Measures under the Common Market Organization for fruit and vegetables. In Feb/88 surveillance licensing was introduced on basis of high export forecasts by main suppliers. In Apr/88 import quotas were established and imports from Chile were suspended In Jul/88 all imports were suspended until Aug/88.
	Apr/88	Import quotas			
	Jul/89	Minimum import prices	World	Processed cherries	Emergency action under GATT Art. XIX. The measure provides for a countervailing charge to be levied on imports from third countries which do not observe minimum import prices.
	Jan/89	Import surveillance	World	Steel	Extension, for 1989, of the import surveillance of certain steel products
	Apr/89	Renewal of VERs	Main suppliers (among others: Brazil and Republic of Korea)	Steel products	Imported steel products are controlled by basic import prices and VERs, negotiated with main suppliers on an annual basis. VER with the Republic of Korea was not renewed in 1990.
	Jul/90	VERs	Republic of Korea and Taiwan, Prov. of China	Footwear	The Republic of Korea and Taiwan, Province of China, undertook to limit footwear exports to the EC from 1 July 1990 until 31 Dec. 1992. National restrictions (quotas) applied by France and Italy were replaced by prior Community surveillance.
	Jul/91	Restrospective surveillance	World	Atlantic salmon	Commission regulation 1658/91
Denmark	Jan/87	Import quotas	Poland	Certain porcelain products	Temporary emergency measures for one year
France	Mar/88	VER Bilateral quota	Rep. of Korea Taiwan, Prov. of China	Footwear	Until 30 June 1990. See OJ L 54 of 1 March 1988.
Greece	Nov/87	Import ban	World	Almonds	Ban was lifted as from 29 April 1988.
Ireland	Mar/87	Import quotas	Countries in Eastern Europe and USSR	Urea	Emergency measure taken until December 1987
Italy	Dec/87	Bilateral quota	Taiwan Prov. of China	Slide fasteners	
	Mar/88	VER Bilateral quota	Rep. of Korea Taiwan Prov. of China	Footwear	Until 30 June 1990. See OJ L 54 of 1 March 1988.
Spain	Mar/87	Quotas	World	Certain steel products	Extension of safeguard measures under Art. XIX of GATT.
	Dec/87	Bilateral quota	Taiwan Prov. of China	Slide fasteners	
Portugal	May/88	Quotas	World	Refrigerators and freezers	Safeguard measures under GATT Art XIX.
UK	Jan/87	Import quotas	Countries in Eastern Europe and USSR	Urea	Emergency measure taken until December 1987

Annex table II-6 (continued)

Country	Date	Type of non-tariff measure	Affected countries/territories	Products covered	Operation of the measure
Finland	May/88	Import licensing	Romania	Certain steel products	Safeguard action (Romania's protocol of accession)
Japan	Feb/89	VER, autonomous action by exporter	Republic of Korea	Certain knitwear	Industry undertaking to limit growth of exports to one-percent annually and to monitor export prices
South Africa	Mar/88	Increased duties	World	Certain footwear	Emergency action under GATT Art. XIX. Temporary extension of suspension of GATT bindings.
	Aug/88	Import surcharges	World	Generic	Extension and modification of the rate of import surcharge introduced in 1985.
United States	Dec/86	Customs user fee	World	Generic	The "merchandise processing fee", enacted in the Omnibus Budget and Reconciliation Act, imposes an ad-valorem charge for the processing of commercial merchandise entering the United States. The "Customs and Trade Act of 1990" modified the structure of the fee as from 1 Oct. 1990, in order to bring it in conformity with GATT.
	Jan/87	Tax on imported petroleum	World	Petroleum and petroleum products	Increased tax on petroleum with a differential between 8.2 cents per barrel for domestic oil and 11.7 cents per barrel on imported petroleum products, provided in the "Superfund Reauthorization and Amendments Act of 1986". In Dec. 1989 the United States indicated that an amendment to the "Superfund" tax legislation was approved by the Congress to equalize the current tax between domestic and imported products.
	Jan/87	VERs	Japan and Taiwan, Prov. of China	Machine tools	VRAs for a five-year period under Section 232 of the Trade Expansion Act of 1962 (National Security).
		Import monitoring	Federal Republic of Germany and Switzerland		A surge of exports to the United States may trigger unilateral action under Section 232.
	Jan/87	Textiles agreement	El Salvador	Certain textiles	Quotas for certain textiles (until 31.12.89; new agreement until 31.12.92)
			Myanmar		Quotas for certain textiles (until 31.12.90)
	Apr/87	Textiles agreement	Panama	Certain apparel	Quotas for wool and mmf sweaters (until 31.3.90)
	Apr/87	Increased duties	Japan	Certain electronic goods (lap and desk-top computers, certain colour TV-receivers and certain hand power tools).	The increased tariff duties of 100 per cent (affecting some $300 million of imports) were partially removed in June and November 1987 as Japanese firms ceased alleged dumping in third country markets.
	Jul/87	Extension of import relief (quotas and increased tariffs)	World	Specialty steel	Import relief granted under section 201 of the Trade Act of 1974 through quotas and additional duties. The relief expired on 30 September 1989.
	Jul/87	VER (unilateral action by exporter)	Republic of Korea	Video-cassette recorders, microwave ovens, TV sets	Combination of floor price and volume restrictions (autolimitation to prevent unfair practices and excessive competition among exporters).

Annex table II-6 (continued)

Country	Date	Type of non-tariff measure	Affected countries/territories	Products covered	Operation of the measure
United States (cont'd)	Aug/87	Textiles agreement	USSR	Certain textiles	Quotas for certain textiles (agreement until 31 December 1992).
	Oct/87	Orderly Marketing Arrangement	China	Ammonium paratungstate and tungtic oxide	Following affirmative USITC decision on market disruption under Section 406 of the Trade Act of 1974
	Oct/87	VERs	Australia, New Zealand	Bovine meat	VERs negotiated for 1988 with a view of avoiding import quotas under the Meat Import Act of 1979
	Oct/87	VERs	China Trinidad and Tobago	Steel products	VERs negotiated under the Steel Import Programme (as those negotiated previously with other suppliers) to last until 30.9.89.
	Apr/87, 88,89,90	VER (unilateral action by exporter)	Japan	Automobiles	VER at the level of 2.3 million units was extended successively for fiscal years 1987, 1988, 1989 and 1990
	Jun/88	Import quotas	United Arab Emirates	Certain textile products	Quotas, the last of which is scheduled to expire on 26.11.90, have been imposed unilaterally pending negotiation of a bilateral agreement. A tentative agreement until 31.12.91 was concluded in Feb/89 but it was not signed as of May 1990.
	Oct/88	Increased duties	Brazil	Certain non-benzenoid drugs, paper products and consumer electronics	The measure (100 percent ad valorem duties) was imposed in retaliation for the alleged Brazil's failure to provide patent protection for U.S. pharmaceuticals and related products. It was lifted in June 1990.
	Jan/89	Quotas	Thailand	Certain textile products	Certain textile categories are subject to unilateral import restraint after the bilateral textile agreements expired at the end of 1988.
	Jan/89	Increased duties	EEC	Beef without bone, porc hams and shoulders, tomatoes, coffee extracts essences or concentrates, alcoholic beverages, fruit juices and pet food	Tariffs of 100 per cent ad-valorem imposed on $100 million worth of imports from the EEC in retaliation for the ban of imports of hormone-treated meat. Retaliatory duties on pork hams and shoulders and tomato sauce were removed in 1989.
	Sep/89	Global quota	39 countries	Sugar	Extension, through September 1990, of the system of allocation of quotas established in 1982. The quota system was superseded by tariff quotas, as from 1 October 1990, to comply with a GATT panel finding that the import quotas violated GATT rules.
	Sep/89	Extension of VERs	19 countries and the EEC	Steel products	A "Steel Trade Liberalization Programme" extended VERs for two and one-half years until 31 March 1992, with imports allowed to increase by one percentage point per year. The VERs will be phased-out after this period during which an international consensus for "fair and open" steel trade is to be negotiated.
	Mar/91	Ban of imports	Mexico, Venezuela and Vanuatu	Tuna and tuna products	The United States alleged that fleets harvesting yellowfin tuna in the Eastern Tropical Pacific with purse-seine nets violated a US law aimed at limiting dolphin kills.

Annex table II-7

Selected border non-tariff measures which were eliminated or reduced since the launching of the Uruguay Round MTNs (September 1986)

Country	Type of non-tariff measure	Affected countries/territories	Products covered	Date	Remarks on actions taken
Australia	Import licensing	World	Second-hand dredgers of more than 200 gross tons	Jan./87	Import licensing controls were removed
	Import prohibition	World	Certain medical devices	Mar./87	
	Tariff quotas	World	Motor vehicles	Apr./88	The mid-term review of the 1985 car industry plan showed that there was room for further efficiency in the local industry.
	Import ban	World	Sugar and sugar products	Jul./89	The ban, which was in effect since 1923 and justified under the Sugar Agreement Act and the Protocol of Provisional Application, was lifted and replaced by import duties.
	Marketing arrangements	World	Wheat	Jul./89	New wheat marketing deregulation arrangements were adopted. Reform of marketing arrangements aimed at aligning domestic prices with world prices for a number of other commodities was also undertaken.
	Quantitative restrictions	World	Used four-wheel drive cars	Jul./89	Repeal of GATT Art.XIX action
	Increased duties	World	Certain apparel items	Apr./88	Repeal of GATT Art.XIX action
	Subsidies	World	Certain fertilizers	Jul./88	Reduction of assistance to agricultural industries involving inter-alia the elimination of subsidies on nitrogenous and phosphatic fertilizers.
	Import restrictions	World	Second-hand ships	Dec./88	Restrictions were removed following relaxation in 1987.
	Subsidy system	World	Steel	Dec./88	A steel plan and subsidy system which provided bounty payments to users of Australian steel was terminated following a recommendation of the Steel Industry Authority advisory group.
	Import licensing	World	Used, second-hand and disposals of earth moving and excavating machines and equipment and four-wheel drive vehicles.	Jul./89	Import licensing controls were removed.
	Local content	World	Passenger motor vehicles	Jan./89	The 85 per cent local content requirement was modified so as to reduce assistance to local component manufacturers.
Austria	Import restrictions	World	Certain medicaments containing penicillins or other antibiotics.	Jan./91	Imports of these items were liberalized as from 1 January 1991.

Source: UNCTAD secretariat, compiled from official published information.

Note: The list of actions is not exhaustive. In particular, it includes neither anti-dumping and countervailing duty measures nor bilateral actions under the MFA. The inclusion of non-tariff measures in this list does not prejudge the consistency of the measures with GATT.

Annex table II-7 (continued)

Country	Type of non-tariff measure	Affected countries/territories	Products covered	Date	Remarks on actions taken
Canada	Quotas	World	Women's and girls' dress and casual footwear	Nov./88	Remaining safeguard measure on footwear, taken under the Export and Import Permits Act, which was totally phased-out in November 1988.
EEC	Pricing, listing and distribution	EEC	Alcoholic beverages	Jan./89	Removal of certain Provincial liquor board practices which discriminated against imported alcoholic beverages, following an agreement negotiated with the EEC on the implementation of a GATT Panel recommendation. The provisions of the agreement were implemented on a MFN basis.
	VER	Australia	Steel products	Jan./87	The voluntary export restraint agreements were not renewed since 1987.
	Quantitative restrictions (national)	Japan	Various industrial products	Jul./89 Feb./90	Certain national QRs on products originating in Japan were removed following an agreement between Japan and the EEC in March 1989.
	Quantitative restrictions (national)	Hungary, Poland	Various products	Nov./89	A number of specific quantitative restrictions on imports from these countries were removed.
	VER	10 countries	Steel products	1989	Reduction of the product coverage and relaxation of market access conditions, in particular increase of quotas for Bulgaria, Czechoslovakia, Hungary, Poland and Romania.
	VER	Rep. of Korea, Venezuela	Steel products	Jan./90	The voluntary export restraint agreements were not renewed since 1990.
	VER	Brazil	Manioc	Jan./90	The voluntary export restraint agreement remained in force until end 1989
	VER	Uruguay	Sheep and goat meat	Mar./88	
	Retrospective control	World	Footwear	Dec./87	Retrospective control introduced in 1979 to monitor the threat of injury to EEC producers resulting from pressure of imports from third countries. (Regulation (EEC) 4086/86)
	Quantitative restrictions (national)	World	Certain tropical products	Jul./89	Contribution to the results of the negotiations on tropical products at the Mid-term Review of the MTNs in December 1988.
France	Quantitative restrictions	Hong Kong	Toys, radios	Jan./87	Remaining QRs on imports into France of certain products from Hong Kong were lifted following a GATT dispute settlement panel recommendation.
	Quantitative restrictions	Japan	Various products	Feb./91	Elimination of quantitative restrictions on imports of umbrellas, certain ceramic, porcelain and pottery products, certain toys and certain electronic measuring instruments.

Annex table II-7 (continued)

Country	Type of non-tariff measure	Affected countries/territories	Products covered	Date	Remarks on actions taken
Germany	Non automatic licences	Eastern European countries	Various products	Dec./89 May./90 Oct./90	
Greece	Import deposits	World	Various products	Apr./87	Expiration of transitional period of accession(??)
	Import restrictions	World	Various products		Many of the residual national import restrictions maintained under EC Art.115 were terminated
	Quantitative restrictions	Eastern European countries	Various products	Jan./89 May./90	
U.K.	VER	Rep. of Korea	Stoneware		
	VER	Japan, Rep.of Korea, Singapore and Taiwan, Prov. of China.	Colour television viewers		
	Quantitative restraints	United States	Fats of bovine cattle, sheep or goat; fertilizers; bleached paper and paperboard	Sept/86	Products previously subject to quantitative restraints were placed under open general licence
Finland	Quantitative restrictions	World	Certain fresh fish items fresh fruit and vegetables fruit and vegetable preparations.	Jul./90	A number of quantitative restrictions on imports of agricultural products were abolished
Japan	Import quotas	World	Processed cheese	Apr./89	Market opening measures implemented following a recommendation of the GATT Council in February 1988.
			Sugar and sugar syrups excl. lactose	Apr./90	
			Fruit puree and paste: -non-citrus fruit	Oct./88	
			-citrus fruit	Apr./90	
			Fruit pulp: -apples, grapes, peaches	Oct./88	
			-citrus fruit	Apr./90	
			Pineapples, prepared or preserved	Apr./90	
			Non citrus fruit juices: -for infants	Oct./88	
			-fruit other than apples, grapes and pineapples	Apr./89	
			-apples, grapes and pineapples	Apr./90	
			Mixtures of fruit juices	Apr./90	
			Tomato juice, ketchup and sauce	Jul./89	
			Food preparations n.e.s. mainly of sugar	apr./90	
			Beef products	Apr./90	Import quota system eliminated by stages, on a product-by-product basis, as from October 1988.

Annex table II-7 (continued)

Country	Type of non-tariff measure	Affected countries/territories	Products covered	Date	Remarks on actions taken
Japan (cont'd)			Dairy products: -pasta -frozen yogurt, whipped cream, ice cream and concentr. protein products Some dried leguminous vegetables	Oct./88 Apr./90 Oct./88	
	Import quotas	World	Fresh and provisionally preserved oranges and tangerines; Beef	Apr./91 Apr./91	Market opening measures implemented on a MFN basis, following an agreement with the United States in settlement of a long-standing issue regarding agricultural imports.
	Import quotas	World	Purees and pastes of pineapples; Other pineapple products	Oct./88 Apr./90	Contribution to the results of the tropical products negotiations at the Mid-term review of the MTN in December 1988.
	Sugar excise tax and commodity taxes	World	Sugar and certain tropical products	Apr./89	The entry into force of the new Tax Law abolished the taxes on imports of some tropical products. Also in the context of the overal tax reform, commodity taxes on a wide range of "luxury" items were removed and replaced by a uniform 3% consumption tax.
	Liquor tax	World	Wine and alcoholic beverages	Apr./89	The amended Liquor Tax Law abolished the ad-valorem tax on certain alcoholic beverages as well as the "grading system" concerning whiskies, brandies etc. and reduced considerably the differences in tax-bearing between these and "shochu".
Norway	Bilateral quantitative restraints & licences		Products other than textiles	in 1987	Remaining restraints abolished
New Zealand	Licensing	World	Footwear	Jul./87	Import access levels were enlarged through licence tendering
	Licence requirements	World	Products not under industry plans	Jul./88	To be replaced by tariffs as the main form of protection.
			Products subject to industry plans	Until Jul./92	Licensing has been steadily removed to be replaced by tariffs as the form of protection

Annex table II-7 (continued)

Country	Type of non-tariff measure	Affected countries/territories	Products covered	Date	Remarks on actions taken
Sweden	Licensing	Portugal	All clothing items	Feb. 89	Same treatment as for other EC countries.
	Quotas	Taiwan, Prov. of China	Various clothing items	Aug., 88	The product coverage of quotas was reduced and the quota amounts were increased for the remaining products.
United States	Quotas and increased duties	World	Specialty steel	Sep., 89	Safeguard measure under Art. XIX of GATT. The import relief was granted under section 201 of the Trade Act of 1974, for a period of 4 years since July 1983 and extended until September 1989. However, specialty steel products were thereafter covered by the VERs which were extended until 31 March 1992, as called for in the Steel Trade Liberalization Programme.
	VER	Hungary, Poland	Steel	Dec./89	The import quotas under the bilateral agreements were substantially increased.
	Embargo	Nicaragua	All products	Mar.,90	The embargo and other economic measures applied to Nicaragua since May 1985 were lifted.
	Import quotas	World	Sugar	Oct.,90	The import quota system was replaced by tariff quotas. A GATT Panel report adopted in June 1989 foud the quota system in violation with Art. XI and recommended that the United States import policy either be brought into conformity with it or eliminated.

Annex table II-8

Imports of preference-giving countries from beneficiaries of their schemes, 1976-1989

(Millions of US dollars)

Year	Total imports	MFN dutiable imports	GSP imports		Percentage share		
			Covered	Preferential	(4)/(3)	(5)/(4)	(5)/(3)
(1)	(2)	(3)	(4)	(5)	(6)	(7)	(8)
1976 *a*	133 675.0	50 981.3	23 259.9	9 848.4	45.6	42.3	19.3
1976	136 496.5	52 016.7	23 812.7	10 401.2	45.8	42.7	20.0
1977	136 401.7	58 541.8	27 260.5	12 299.1	46.6	45.1	21.0
1978	145 084.0	67 254.6	33 312.0	15 023.6	49.5	45.1	22.3
1979	233 017.0	76 654.2	44 472.6	20 966.6	58.0	47.1	27.4
1980	248 716.1	116 806.9	57 483.7	25 825.9	49.2	44.9	22.1
1983	220 936.4	121 541.6	60 365.7	28 656.7	49.6	47.5	23.6
1984	232 733.7	147 177.9	69 820.5	33 472.5	47.4	47.9	22.7
1986 *a*	236 713.6	160 487.9	81 222.4	35 347.5	50.6	43.5	22.0
1987 *a*	293 809.7	194 314.2	115 279.4	47 168.1	59.3	40.9	24.3
1988 *a*	370 937.1	281 936.4	137 514.9	56 417.5	48.8	41.0	20.0

Source: Notifications from preference-giving countries and UNCTAD calculations.

a Less Australia and New Zealand. Preferential imports by these two countries are estimated at $3 billion in 1988.

Annex table II-9

Flows and stocks of anti-dumping and countervailing actions taken against imports from all sources and from developing countries

(Number of cases)

Country	Cases initiated from 1 July to 30 June — From all sources				From DCs				Cases revoked/terminated from 1 July to 30 June — From all sources				From DCs				Outstanding cases at the end of June — From all sources					From DCs				
	86-87	87-88	88-89	89-90	86-87	87-88	88-89	89-90	86-87	87-88	88-89	89-90	86-87	87-88	88-89	89-90	1986	1987	1988	1989	1990	1986	1987	1988	1989	1990
Anti-dumping actions																										
Australia	24	29	16	23	9	11	8	10	-	102	44	20	-	28	19	11	123	147	74	46	49	36	45	28	17	16
Brazil	-	1	1	-	-	1	1	-	-	-	-	-	-	-	-	-	-	-	-	2	2	-	-	-	1	1
Canada	22	21	14	15	6	9	4	8	-	31	26	42	-	6	8	6	146	168	158	146	119	41	47	50	46	48
EEC	30	41	38	38	18	26	24	26	25	56	36	38	8	7	12	13	208	213	198	200	200	53	63	82	94	107
Finland	4	5	2	-	-	-	-	-	-	1	3	1	-	-	-	-	1	5	9	8	7	-	-	-	-	-
Mexico	2	24	10	10	-	6	4	4	-	3	7	7	-	2	2	1	-	2	23	26	29	-	-	4	6	9
New Zealand	3	6	5	2	-	3	1	1	1	1	2	6	-	-	1	-	3	3	9	12	8	-	1	3	3	4
Republic of Korea	1	-	1	3	-	-	-	-	-	-	-	-	-	-	-	-	3	3	2	4	6	-	1	1	1	1
Sweden	-	-	2	4	-	-	-	-	-	-	-	6	-	-	-	-	2	2	2	4	2	-	-	-	-	-
United States	39	33	18	22	12	6	9	13	29	3	11	15	12	2	6	4	159	169	199	206	213	57	57	61	74	83
Total	125	170	107	117	45	61	51	62	55	197	129	135	20	45	48	35	642	712	675	653	635	188	213	229	242	269
Countervailing actions																										
Australia	4	-	2	7	2	-	-	3	1	7	3	5	1	1	-	3	9	12	5	4	6	1	2	1	1	1
Canada	2	-	1	2	-	-	1	2	-	-	3	-	-	-	-	-	6	8	8	9	11	-	1	1	2	4
EEC	-	1	2	-	-	1	2	-	-	-	2	-	-	-	2	-	3	3	4	4	4	3	3	4	4	4
New Zealand	-	4	-	-	-	-	-	-	-	-	3	1	-	-	-	-	-	-	4	1	-	-	-	-	-	-
United States	10	13	5	3	5	12	3	2	11	3	7	14	7	2	5	13	102	101	111	109	98	73	71	81	79	68
Total	16	18	10	12	7	13	6	7	12	10	15	20	8	3	7	16	120	124	132	127	119	78	77	87	86	77
All actions	141	188	117	129	52	74	57	69	67	207	144	155	28	48	55	51	762	836	807	780	754	266	290	316	328	346

Source: UNCTAD secretariat, on the basis of GATT reports to the Committee on Anti-dumping Practices and to the Committee on Subsidies and Countervailing Measures and of other official published information.

a New cases only (*i.e.*, excluding cases reviewed).
b Including duty orders, price undertakings and pending investigations.

Chapter III

THE TECHNOLOGICAL DIMENSION OF INTERNATIONAL TRADE AND DEVELOPMENT

INTRODUCTION

505.   Technology, after having been considered by economists as late as the 1950s to be a residual factor in explaining the growth of output, has come to be universally recognized as fundamental to economic growth and development. Since the impact of technological progress differs and its diffusion is unevenly distributed across countries, technology is also a determinant of the evolution of international economic relations. Not long after an idea has been appropriated by its inventor and has been transformed into a new or improved product or process, it also becomes the object of trade in goods and services and in technology itself, through direct foreign investment, capital goods exports, and licensing of patents and know-how, linked closely to both the direction and composition of international trade and to the process of economic development, the two corner-stones of UNCTAD. Over the past two decades, the subject of technology has come to form an integral component of the fundamental issues analyzed and negotiated in UNCTAD and an integral part of its technical co-operation activities.

506.   During this period, and particularly since the beginning of the 1980s, important developments have been taking place that have affected and will continue to affect profoundly international technological co-operation and technology flows, particularly to developing countries. For the latter, not being producers of technology, one of the main means for obtaining it is through trade. Thus, changes that affect technology transfers to developing countries have an impact on their development more generally.

507.   Technology flows to developing countries are influenced by macro-economic conditions, technological capabilities, as well as government policies. In recent years, such flows to most developing countries have declined. Government policy reforms aimed at revitalizing these flows have not met with success. A review of their evolution (section A) shows that technology flows to developing countries are concentrated in a small number of countries, mainly in Asia. This development raises two issues: the first relates to the financial constraints faced by many developing countries; the second, is the issue of absorptive capacity or, more generally, of "technological dynamism", i.e. the ability of countries to absorb and efficiently deploy new technologies, adapt them to local conditions, improve upon them and ultimately create new knowledge.

508.   The analysis of the experience of a number of countries (section B) reveals that technological dynamism is not the result of the minimalist government role prescribed by current orthodoxy. While the nature of interventions needed varies with stage of development and national objectives, and with the ability of governments to mount interventions, the need to intervene remains. This leads to very different implications concerning technology-related policies in developing countries.

509.   In a highly interdependent global economy, the prospects for the development of technological capabilities in developing countries are determined not only by domestic but increasingly by external forces, notably the emergence of new technologies, policy responses in developed market-economy countries induced by technology-related shifts in competitiveness and the evolution of international trade relations (section C).

510.   Finally, the special problems raised by the promotion of the use of environmentally sound technologies in developing countries and the growing concerns about the impact of technology or sustainable development required that this topic be treated separately (section D).

511.   The main findings of the analysis are summarized together with policy recommendations in the last, section E, of this chapter.

A. Technology flows

1.   Shifting positions in the origin and direction of technology flows

512.   While a few developed market-economy countries continue to dominate international technology markets, the most significant development in recent years has been a catching up with the United States by other countries as a source of innovative capacity and technology exports. During the two decades preceding the 1970s, the United States was the undisputed leader in the development and application of industrial technology. However, owing to a rapid increase in the innovative efforts of Japan and, to a lesser extent, a number of other developed countries, the gap between these countries and the United States diminished.

513.   The result has been an intensified rivalry in international markets and a growing multi-polarity in the supply of technology. Reflecting this multipolarity, but also other factors such as shifting exchange-rate differentials and the desire to protect market position, the United States has become the major net recipient of world foreign direct investment flows. Similarly, its relative position as capital goods exporter has undergone changes, in particular through increased compe-tition from Germany and Japan. Indeed, in 1985, the United States became a large net importer of capital goods. This deficit, however, does not apply equally to all capital goods. In certain branches such as aeronautics, telecommunications, office equipment and large construction ma-chinery the United States retains a commanding position in international markets. In others, such as machine tools, textiles and printing machinery, its market share has fallen sharply. It is in terms of technology payments, in the form of royalties and fees, that the United States still remains by far the most important technology supplier, especially to developing countries. However, such receipts are more a reflection of past than of present United States success in innovation.

514.   The most dynamic performer in overall technology exports since the 1970s among devel-oped market-economy countries has undoubtedly been Japan. Its strengthened competitive posi-tion is reflected by the fact that it is the only country among developed market-economy countries that has shown a trade surplus in the last decade and a half in all categories of manufactures, i.e. low, medium and high technology-intensive as measured by the ratio of R and D expenditures to production.[158] The availability of such large trade surpluses and external as well as internal pres-sures (rising costs and labour shortages) have induced a major outflow of foreign direct investment by Japanese firms.

515.   The technological leadership of Japan is particularly pronounced in several key areas that are likely to have a major impact on the future of the world economy (e.g. microelectronics, robotics and new materials). In others of more immediate concern to developing countries, such as chemicals and agro-food, its position is relatively weaker.

516.   The position of the Western European countries is more ambivalent. Germany has strengthened its position as a technology source in several of the relatively old industries (e.g. machine building and textiles), where it has maintained a sustained technological advantage through accumulated experience in machine design and manufacture. France has made important strides in telecommunications and telematics. Increased co-operation among the main European economies has recently led to a strengthening of their position in aeronautics. Switzerland and especially Sweden have kept their command of certain key technologies, such as metal-working, precision instruments and civil engineering. Their increased involvement in the more rapidly-

---

[158] For a discussion of the concept of R and D intensity and its limitations in interpreting the technology content of trade, see *Trade and Development Report, 1987*, (UNCTAD TDR7) (U.N. publication, Sales No. E.87.II.D.7), pp. 113-118.

growing developing countries, particularly in Asia, has been noteworthy. By and large, however, the Western European firms continued to develop their strongest technological links with the African countries and a wide array of the less-advanced developing countries.

517. Over the past decade, developing countries have increased their importance as exporters of capital goods and as foreign investors. Though still small in absolute terms, the growth of these outflows from developing countries outpaced the corresponding outflows from developed countries. However, only a very small number of developing countries, primarily the major exporters of manufactures in Asia, have been responsible for these outflows. Part of these flows was directed towards other developing countries, particularly in Asia, to take advantge of lower wage costs and other locational advantages, as well as growing regional markets. The most rapidly growing part of these flows, however, has been directed to developed market-economy countries, where it has been attracted by markets and by the accessibility of technology.

518. The countries of Central and Eastern Europe continue to play only a minor role in commercial technology flows to developing countries (their share in the total capital goods exports to developing countries remains around 8 per cent), although they are still an important source of technology flows for some developing countries.

519. As to technology flows into the developing countries (table III-1) there has been increasing divergence in recent years. On a regional basis, the share of Asia in the flows of capital goods to developing countries continued to climb, reaching 62 per cent in 1989. Flows of foreign direct investment to developing Asia surged even more rapidly, particularly during the second half of the 1980s, by which time this region had overtaken developing America as the major recipient of foreign direct investment among developing countries. The main beneficiaries, in recent years, have been Singapore and Hong Kong and, more recently, Malaysia and Thailand which, by the end of the decade, had joined the former two countries on the list of the ten largest host countries for such flows. Their rapid growth, concentration on manufacturing, export performance and relatively undervalued currencies, coupled with a skilled and low-cost workforce, have acted as a magnet for foreign direct investment and absorbed substantial capital goods imports. The analysis of their experience as recipients of technology flows could provide important insights in the design of policies for promoting such flows. In addition, intra-developing-country foreign direct investment has become increasingly more important in this region, as the exporters of manufactures, in order to safeguard competitiveness in foreign markets, have emerged as important investors in other developing countries. One implication of this trend may be the continuing growth of foreign investment inflows to these countries, even if flows from developed countries decline, or are directed to other regions.[159]

520. The diminished role of Latin American countries as technology importers is probably strongly related to the financial crisis of the region, but may also be due to the large stock of foreign direct investment already in the leading Latin American States prior to the present decade. This decline notwithstanding, Brazil, Mexico and Argentina are still among the largest receivers of foreign direct investment, absorbing, respectively, 12, 11 and 4 per cent of the average flows to developing countries in the period 1980-1989.

521. As regards Africa, which has been absorbing only a small share of commercial technology flows to developing countries, the onset of the debt crisis and the deterioration in commodity markets have further weakened the region's ability to import technology. Throughout the 1980s, imports of capital goods declined in nominal terms and foreign direct investment fluctuated between US$ 1 billion and US$ 2.5 billion.[160] Furthermore, foreign direct investment has been concentrated in a relatively small number of oil-exporting countries. Algeria, Cameroon, Egypt, Nigeria and Tunisia absorbed over 90 per cent of all capital inflows to the region during the first

---

[159] For the Thai case, see Linda Y.C. Lim and P.E. Fong, *Foreign Direct Investment and Industrialization in Malaysia, Singapore, Taiwan and Thailand* (OECD, Paris, 1991), p. 50.

[160] Foreign direct investment to Africa increased significantly in 1989. However, it would be premature to speak of a shift in the trend on the basis of only one year.

Table III-1

Technology-related flows between developed market-economy countries and developing countries and territories

(Billions of dollars)

Indicator	All developing countries [a]		By geographical region						By analytical group				China [c]	
			Developing America		Developing Africa		Developing Asia		Major exporters of manufactures [b]		Least developed countries [b]			
	Inflow	Outflow	Inflow	Outflow	Inflow	Outflow	Inflow	Outflow	Inflow	Outflow	Inflow	Outflow	Inflow	Outflow
I. Capital goods [d]														
1980	115	14	31	4	23	-	57	9	28	8	6	-	3	-
1981	130	16	36	4	26	1	65	10	28	9	6	-	3	-
1982	122	17	29	5	23	-	68	12	25	10	5	-	2	-
1983	106	21	20	5	18	-	65	15	24	13	4	-	3	-
1984	106	28	24	7	18	-	62	20	28	17	4	-	4	-
1985	101	28	25	8	17	-	57	19	28	18	4	-	10	-
1986	112	34	29	9	17	1	64	24	35	22	4	-	11	-
1987	126	45	32	10	16	1	74	32	46	31	5	1	9	1
1988	144	60	35	14	17	1	87	44	56	41	5	-	9	1
1989	155	67	36	16	18	2	96	48	62	44	5	1	9	1
II. Foreign direct investment [e]														
1980	9.9	1.1	6.2	0.4	0.3	0.1	3.3	0.6	5.9	0.5	0.3	-	0.1	0
1981	14.6	0.2	8.2	0.2	1.5	0.1	5.8	0.2	8.4	0.3	0.2	-	0.3	0
1982	13.0	1.1	6.2	0.4	1.4	0.1	4.9	0.6	4.9	0.9	0.2	-	0.4	-
1983	10.0	0.9	3.5	0.3	1.2	0.1	5.1	0.1	4.0	0.2	0.1	-	0.6	0.1
1984	10.6	0.6	3.2	0.1	1.4	0.1	5.8	0.4	4.3	0.2	0.1	-	1.3	0.6
1985	11.7	1.1	4.0	0.1	2.6	-	5.0	1.0	3.3	0.4	-	-	1.7	0.4
1986	12.3	1.7	3.5	0.7	1.7	-	7.0	1.0	5.3	0.5	0.2	-	1.9	0.6
1987	19.9	2.4	6.0	0.2	2.1	0.2	12.0	2.0	12.0	1.2	0.2	-	2.3	0.6
1988	25.3	5.9	8.1	0.3	2.1	0.1	14.9	5.5	12.9	0.8	0.1	-	3.2	0.8
1989	29.8	8.9	7.4	0.2	4.3	0.1	16.7	8.7	12.1	7.3	0.2	-	3.4	0.8
III. Technical co-operation grants [f]														
1980	7.3										1.5		0.1	
1981	7.4										1.6		0.1	
1982	7.4										1.6		0.1	
1983	7.7										1.6		0.1	
1984	7.7										1.6		0.1	
1985	8.2										1.8		0.1	
1986	9.7										2.1		0.2	
1987	11.6										2.4		0.3	
1988	12.9										2.6		0.3	
1989	12.7										2.7		0.3	

Source: UNCTAD secretariat computations based on data from: (i) United Nations, for capital goods imports; (ii) UNCTC, for foreign direct investment; and (iii) OECD, for technical co-operation grants.

a Total also includes developing countries and territories of Europe and Oceania, and is subject to rounding.

b Major exporters of manufactures: Brazil, Hong Kong, Mexico, Republic of Korea, Singapore, Taiwan Province of China and Yugoslavia. Least developed countries: See UNCTAD, *Handbook of international trade and development statistics, 1989*, United Nations Sales No. E/F.90.II.D.I, September 1990.

c Memo item.

d Includes SITC/Rev. 1, section 7, Machinery and Transport equipment *except* 7194 domestic appliances, non-electrical; 7241 television receivers; 7242 radio broadcast receivers; 7250 domestic equipment; 7321 passenger motor cars; 7326 chassis for passenger motor cars; 7329 motor cycles; and 7331 bicycles.

e Excluding The Bahamas, Bermuda and Cayman Islands.

f Grants that the donors have not allocated to individual countries are not included in the regional or analytical groups, but are included in the total for developing countries.

half of the 1980s. By 1989, Egypt and Nigeria accounted for 86 per cent of such flows to the region. Foreign investment flows to non-oil sub-Saharan countries, many of which are least developed countries, have remained below US$ 0.5 billion since 1981, despite the enactment of legislation favourable to such investment. Commercial technology flows to the least developed countries as a group have remained unchanged during the decade.[161]

522. Technical assistance figures appeared to respond to the relatively strong performance of Asian economies, as their share of the developing countries' aggregate went from 25 per cent in 1980 to 22 per cent in 1989.

2. Evolving nature and sources of technology flows to developing countries

523. In contrast to the shrinkage in the volume of technology transfer to developing countries in recent years, international technology markets have become more diversified and open through a widening of the forms of technology transfer more commonly applied and of the sources of supply. This has been a significant development for developing countries, as it has increased the range of options available to technology-receiving firms and allowed them to assume a greater involvement in the design, construction and operation of investment projects.

524. The most apparent change has been the trend towards non-equity or minority ownership forms of technology transfer, as compared to that through majority-owned affiliates. These forms include joint ventures, licensing and know-how agreements, machinery imports, management contracts, franchising, international subcontracting, leasing and countertrade arrangements involving technology transfer. This trend has been influenced by several factors. Firstly, the policy and legal measures adopted by host-country governments in the 1960s and early 1970s relating to foreign direct investment encouraged joint ventures and new forms of transfer of technology. Secondly, the relative importance of Japanese and Western European, as compared with United States-based, firms as suppliers of technology to developing countries has grown. The former have had a relatively greater propensity than the United States firms to share ownership with local partners and to supply technology to non-affiliated enterprises. Thirdly, it is likely that there has been a reaction by potential foreign investors to the uncertainty created by the economic slow-down in developed market-economy countries and to the high volatility of foreign exchange markets. A tendency to shift from long-term investment commitments to greater reliance on other mechanisms for exploiting technological advantage in developing countries, involving a shorter time perspective, was probably seen as a way of reducing financial exposure. Fourthly, there has been a rapid internationalization of a variety of services ranging from advertising and accounting to car rentals, hotels and fast foods. In these service activities, the common technology transfer arrangements involve management, marketing and technical assistance contracts and, in particular, franchising and licensing of trade marks, without any direct or only minor equity participation.

525. Finally, since the early 1970s, there has been an emergence of small and medium-sized enterprises from developed market-economy countries, as well as firms from developing countries, as technology suppliers in international markets with a more diversified approach to technology transfer than in the past. These two emerging sources merit special attention, given their future potential impact on developing countries.

---

[161] For a more comprehensive analysis of the evolution of technology flows to least developed countries, see UNCTAD "Transfer and development of technology in the least developed countries: an assessment of major policy issues", report by the UNCTAD secretariat in co-operation with L. Krieger Mytelka, Carleton University, Ottawa and LAREA/CEREM, Université de Paris. (UNCTAD ITP TEC 12), August 1990.

(a) Small and medium-sized enterprises (SMEs)

526.   Many SMEs of developed market-economy countries are increasingly involved in technology transactions and investments in developing countries. An UNCTAD study has shown that, in France, for example, the value of technology flows from SMEs to developing countries increased three to four-fold between 1976 and 1985.[162] The same trend has been observed in several other developed countries, particularly Germany and Italy. The Japanese SMEs accounted for about half of the total number of overseas investments made by that country's enterprises in the 1970s.[163]

527.   SMEs have characteristics which differentiate them from larger transnational corporations with respect to their motives and strategies for internationalization through technology transfer and with respect to their impact on the technological development of their recipient partners in developing countries. In fact, mounting evidence suggests that SMEs are, to some extent, complementary to transnational corporations (TNCs) in developing countries. They operate in different industries and in different contexts. In general, SMEs are situated in smaller-scale industries, particularly metal working and engineering industries, characterized by the relatively standardized technologies which make them suitable to the requirements of those sectors in developing countries. However, assistance is needed in identifying practical ways and means for effectively promoting increased transfer of technology flows from SMEs to developing countries.

528.   The growing role of SMEs is also apparent in technology transfer to countries of Eastern Europe. About half of all the 168 joint ventures that evolved during the 1980s between developed market-economy countries and Eastern European firms in response to these countries' new policies aimed at attracting foreign technology and open export markets have involved SMEs from Western Europe.[164]

(b) Developing countries' firms

529.   Another alternative source of technology transfer to developing countries - that from other developing countries - is still comparatively small in quantitative terms. The potential of technology co-operation among developing countries has not been fully exploited mainly due to the absence of information on possible sources of technology in these countries and to the lack of adequate guidelines and arrangements to carry out such co-operation. However, this form of co-operation appears to be growing. It is significant because it indicates that a considerable advance has taken place in these countries as sources of technology. Exports of turnkey plants and individual pieces of machinery and equipment of locally-owned firms in Argentina, Brazil, India, Mexico, the Republic of Korea, and Taiwan Province of China grew dramatically during the 1970s.[165] After a period of stagnation or decline during the first half of the 1980s, these exports resumed their buoyant growth from 1986 onwards. Foreign direct investment by developing country transnational corporations also expanded rapidly during the 1980s. Both exports of capital goods and foreign investment to the developed market-economy countries more than quadrupled during the decade.

530.   In the technology-related services sector, developing country transnationals have also been competing with their developed country counterparts, especially in construction and engineering design (CED) services. Thus, of the US$ 570 billion awarded during the period 1978-1983, about

---

162 See "Transfer of technology to developing countries by France's small and medium-sized enterprises (UNCTAD/TT/84), November 1986.

163 For further details concerning these countries, see UNCTAD publications reviewed in the UNCTAD report, "Trends in international transfer of technology to developing countries by small and medium-sized enterprises" TD/B/C.6/138. See also CEDREI (Centro de Estudios de Desarrollo y Relaciones Económicas Internacionales, Buenos Aires), "Technology transfer and international investments by small firms in developing countries", April 1986, Buenos Aires.

164 Tribune de Genève , 9 May 1988.

165 A review of the status of capital goods and industrial machinery manufacture and trade in selected developing countries is contained in D. Chudnovsky, M. Nagao, S. Jacobsson, Capital goods production in the Third World: an economic study of technology acquisition, London, Frances Pinter, 1982.

16 per cent was earned by developing-country and Chinese firms.[166] During that period, the Repubic of Korea was unquestionably the leader, having received more contracts than all of the remaining top developing-country firms combined; it was followed by Yugoslavia, Brazil and India.

531.   The 1980s were marked initially by a reversal in this trend for developing countries' firms, followed by a certain degree of recovery after 1987. This was in line with the decline in the world market for CED services which, as measured by the value of foreign contracts awarded to the top 250 international contractors, declined by almost 50 per cent between 1981 and 1987. This decline was brought about by several factors, including the sluggish performance of the world economy, the debt crisis, the drop in oil revenues arising from the fall in oil prices after 1983, and the fact that the large basic infrastructure in many oil-producing developing countries had been completed. In 1989, the value of the CED services market increased to US$ 112.5 billion, up from US$ 94 billion in 1988, but still remaining below the 1981 peak. Such recovery could be attributed to the increasing infrastructure needs of countries which have managed to improve their economic performance, such as China. There are two main features of the recent recovery. First, the share of the Republic of Korea continued to decline steadily in the period 1987 to 1989. Second, the share of other developing countries exporting CED services increased both in absolute and relative terms, accounting for 7.5 per cent of total CED services in 1989.[167]

532.   One important factor affecting competitiveness of firms in international markets is project financing. Here there is a distinct advantage for developed country firms, for the limited experience of firms from developing countries in making use of international financial markets for arranging low-cost financing for clients in other developing countries, together with the rise of labour costs of skilled and unskilled labour in exporting countries, has been a barrier to CED services exports to other developing countries. In contrast to the 1970s, when the bulk of developing country exports of CED services went to the capital-abundant oil-producing countries where projects were financed from internal funds, the 1980s exhibited a dramatic decline of that lucrative regional market which forced international firms to venture into new developing-country markets, many of which are in capital-deficient countries that require external financing.

533.   The above developments also call for increased technical assistance to developing countries to enable them to promote and use effectively alternate forms and sources of technology transfer in consonance with their development priorities.

3.   Financial constraints and technology flows

534.   In contrast to a minority of rapidly growing exporters of manufactures in Asia, the majority of developing countries have, by comparison, remained severely limited in their ability to acquire technology in the 1980s. The majority of developing countries produce only a limited range of capital goods which are required to sustain investment in plant and machinery, focusing mainly on the low-technology-intensive metal products industry. Moreover, the high degree of specialization in the capital goods sector makes it virtually impossible even for advanced countries to rely exclusively on domestically produced capital goods.[168]

535.   The quantitative evolution of productive capacity (see figure III-1) can be observed by an estimation of the net stock of invested capital. Although the assumptions needed to estimate this figure are imperfect, the marked differences across the geographical regions[169] highlight the long-term implications of capital accumulation. The recent declines in capital stocks for developing

---

[166] For analytical figures, see table 30 in *Trade and Development Report*, 1987.

[167] See, Y. Soubra, "International competitiveness and corporate strategies in the construction and engineering design services sector" in *Proceedings of the Conference on Coalition and Competition: Globalization of Professional Services*, 20-21 October 1990, Duke University, U.S.A., forthcoming.

[168] It has been suggested that the economically efficient limit to import substitution in the capital goods sector has probably been adjusted downward due to the economies of specialization. See C. Edquist and S. Jacobsson, *Flexible automation - The Global Diffusion of new Technology in the Engineering Industry* (Oxford, Basil Blackwell, 1988).

[169] Among the selected countries there are a few exceptions which do not conform with the geographical development paths.

America and Africa are understimates, because they do not take full account of the decline of asset values due to technological change. In this context, a decline of capital stock does not simply reflect a reduction of productive capacity,[170] it also implies that the ability to keep up with global technological advances has diminished. Since these advances have been taking place so rapidly, the shrinkage in capital stock will make it even harder for some countries to maintain or achieve international competitiveness in the 1990s.[171]

536. Compounding the problem is the cumulative effect of financial constraints in influencing developing countries' productive capacity and their ability to keep pace with global technological changes. This concern gains particular importance as it has proven difficult to replace imported goods with domestic ones.[172]

537. It should also be noted that it is at least arguable that "opening economies to foreign investment" will not by itself[173] cause foreign investment inflows to grow more rapidly and reduce these constraints. This is because foreign investment is influenced by country credit ratings which are themselves determined by the existing status of a country's balance of payments, reflecting inter alia the role of other financial flows. The evidence shows that the countries which have received the bulk of foreign direct investment have been the ones which also received other types of financial flows such as commercial lending and official assistance.[174] Moreover, least developed countries, including those in sub-Saharan Africa, that were among the first to enact legislation favourable to foreign investment in the 1970s and earlier, have been singularly unsuccessful in attracting this form of technology transfer.

---

[170] On the basis of the selected countries, developing African countries as a group experienced a shrinking in their productive capacity of over 15 per cent during the 1980s and developing America of about 10 per cent, while developing Asia increased total capital stocks by around 80 per cent.

[171] For empirical evidence in the textile and metal products industry and an analysis of the evolution of the productive capacity and the nature of export performance, see G. Kell and S. Marchese, "Developing countries' exports of textiles and metals: The question of the sustainability of recent growth", UNCTAD Review, forthcoming.

[172] For a discussion on factors that impede substitutability and empirical evidence for limited possibilities of substitution, see J. Hentschel, "Availability of intermediate and capital goods in import-restrained debtor countries", UNCTAD discussion paper No. 29 (April 1990).

[173] See "Mosbacher presses LDCs to open up to investment", U.S. Daily Bulletin, 1 June 1989, Geneva.

[174] Source - unpublished UNCTAD research work based on cross-country and time-series analysis of over 50 developing countries.

Figure III-1

TOTAL NET CAPITAL STOCK[a] OF 29 SELECTED DEVELOPING COUNTRIES[b] BY GEOGRAPHICAL REGION, IN BILLIONS US $ (1980)

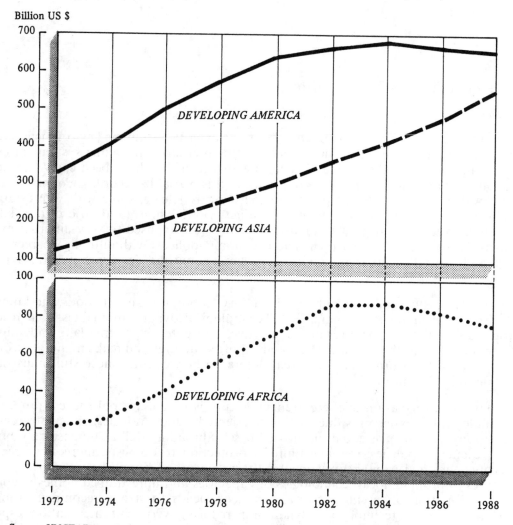

Source: UNCTAD secretariat computations based on data from UNSO and UNIDO.

a The net stock of capital was calculated on the basis of imported capital goods and domestic capital goods output. See note in table III-1 for a definition of imported capital goods. The domestically originated contribution to the capital stock was calculated by taking the output of industries (ISIC 381 to ISIC 385 minus exports). IMF exchange rates were applied to convert national currencies into US dollars and UNCTAD country-specific deflators for SITC 7 to arrive at real values. A straight-line method of depreciation was applied to calculate net stocks, based on the assumption of a useful economic life of 11 years. Since data for both trade statistics and industrial production were available for 1962 and onwards, an initial capital stock could be estimated for 1972.

b For a list of the 29 selected developing countries and territories, see table III-2 or III-3. These countries and territories represent 67 per cent of the total GDP (1987) and 72 per cent of the total population (1987) of the developing countries. The geographical representativeness in terms of population is 86 per cent for developing America, 40 per cent for developing Africa, and 81 per cent for developing Asia.

B. TECHNOLOGICAL DYNAMISM: CONTRASTING NATIONAL EXPERIENCES AMONG DEVELOPING COUNTRIES

1. The basis of technological dynamism

538.   The ability of countries to adjust to changes in the external economic environment and thus the extent to which they can share in the benefits of the international trading system varies considerably and is a reflection of the degree of success with which they have been carrying out their industrialization.   Many factors have contributed to this variable record.   Countries started (around the 1950s) from very different points on the industrial scale, some with well established manufacturing bases, others with rudimentary manufacturing facilities (and little of the skills, institutions and infrastructure that go with industry).   They were exposed to very different external economic environments and managed their macroeconomic policies with differing degrees of success.   Political and natural events were conducive to some countries' development efforts and not to others.

539.   Industrial success depends not only on the ability to buy the capital goods and know-how needed, but also on 'technological dynamism'.   Technological dynamism enables even resource-poor countries to invest their scarce resources effectively, to enter export markets and substitute efficiently for imports, diversify their industrial and export structures and make manufacturing lead to sustained structural transformation.   The real difference between the successful industrializers and others lies in this dynamism.

540.   The dominant explanation in the current literature is that industrial success (and, by implication, technological dynamism) is due to export-oriented trade strategies.   Such strategies are usually taken to involve not just equal incentives to sell abroad as well as domestically but also "neo-liberal"[175] economic policies: low and uniform protection to domestic industries, free flows of foreign technologies and capital, investment patterns governed by market incentives, the absence of measures to promote local technologies or capacities and unrestrained domestic competition.[176] This interpretation of recent industrial experience leads to strong recommendations for countries wishing to achieve technological dynamism: reduce government intervention, especially in trade; liberalize in respect of direct investment flows; promote competition, and so on (generally described as 'getting prices right').   The appropriate role for the Government is then to provide physical infrastructure and set the legal rules of the game.

541.   This section argues that while export orientation (in the sense of providing neutral incentives between foreign and domestic markets) is desirable, the experience of successful industrializers does not support the minimalist government role prescribed.   On the contrary, the most successful industrializers have been dynamic precisely because they intervened heavily in the process of building up technological capabilities.   Their interventions were both "functional" (to strengthen market forces without favouring particular activities) and "selective" (to promote particular activities or firms over others), though the extent and choice of interventions varied greatly.

542.   A country's technological dynamism in manufacturing has many elements.   These can be grouped under two headings: first, the capabilities of its individual manufacturing enterprises; and second, the interactions among individual manufacturers and between them and the supporting environment.   Firm-level capabilities consist of the skills, knowledge and institutional coherence which enable a manufacturer to do three things: first, to identify and engineer viable projects,

---

175 By "neo-liberal" in this report is meant the view that all markets operate efficiently without government intervention.

176 The "liberal" or neoclassical interpretation of the industrialization experience is represented by authors such as Balassa, Krueger, Harberger, Bhagwati and Lal.   A good review is given in J. Weiss, *Industry in Developing Countries*, (Croom Helm) London, 1988.

purchase the relevant technology and capital goods, and execute the investment efficiently (or 'investment capabilities'); second, to master the process and product technology, achieve efficient levels of quality, maintenance and operating procedures, adapt the technologies to local materials and customer needs, improve the technology over time and diversify and add to the technological base ('production capabilities'); and third, to establish efficient flows of knowledge and information with suppliers, customers, consultants and science and technology institutions ('linkage capabilities').[177]

543.   Some of these capabilities can be acquired by an enterprise "ready made" from the market. However, many of the skills needed to handle new technologies do not exist in developing countries and have to be acquired by the firm. This entails a conscious (and often prolonged and expensive) process of training, acquiring new information, experimentation and interaction with other agents. Thus, even gaining mastery of a given technology is a "learning process" in developing countries, requiring effort and expense at all levels of operation.[178] Different firms achieve different levels of efficiency depending on their learning investments, the skills available on labour markets and the support provided externally. Technological mastery shades into improvement and, as the firm matures, into innovation (with formal R and D becoming prominent), but technological dynamism in essence is a process of constant capability-building in every aspect of manufacturing activity.

544.   As with any investment, investment in capability acquisition is conditioned by incentives arising in the markets facing firms. Two aspects need mention here. First, the macroeconomic environment has strong effects. Stability, growth and a predictable policy structure are clearly conducive to investments in capability aquisition (just as they are to investments in physical capacity). A favourable growth setting also enables greater capability acquisition in a physical sense: enterprises have more opportunities and resources to repeat particular tasks and add to capacity. The 1980s have therefore been disruptive for technological development for a number of developing countries, apart from the broader stresses they generated (some of these points are taken up below).

545.   Second, competition, both domestic and international, provides a powerful stimulant to technological dynamism. However, it is a double-edged sword: the full force of external competition from mature enterprises can prevent new entrants from acquiring a base of capabilities and so retard capability development. This is the "infant industry" case for providing protection during the learning period. Since protection itself can reduce pressures to invest in capabilities, it has to be temporary (geared to the learning period of the relevant technology), transparent, selective (only a few activities protected at one time and protection not given to compensate for inefficiencies arising outside the firm, e.g. lack of education or infrastructure), and counter-balanced by incentives to achieve world standards of performance (for instance, by making exporting attractive even when protecting domestic sales). Protection that is excessive, prolonged and not supported by measures to reduce costs external to the protected activity can lead to permanent "infants" that never mature to competitiveness in world markets.[179]

546.   Even given optimal incentive structures, firm-level technological development does not occur in isolation. It entails intense and continuous interaction with the industrial environment, which provides the human and financial resources needed for internal capability development, determines the extent to which firms specialize and so increase their productive efficiency, and supplies such "public goods" as standards, testing, basic R and D and other forms of institutional

---

[177] The constituents of technological capability are further explored in C. Dahlman, B. Ross-Larson and L.E. Westphal, "Managing technological development", *World Development*, 1987, p.759-75; J. Katz (ed.), *Technology generation in Latin American manufacturing industries*, (Macmillan, London, 1987); S. Lall, *Learning to industrialize*, (Macmillan, London, 1987); and S. Teitel, "Technology creation in semi-industrial economies", *Journal of Development Economics*, 1984, p.39-61.

[178] A similar process occurs in enterprises in developed countries, with the important difference that most "routine" capabilities can be readily hired from the labour market and in-firm efforts can concentrate on mastering the more novel, innovative features of technologies. Despite the broad availability of routine capabilities and open, competitive markets, however, individual enterprises in advanced industrial countries also display persistent differences in productivity (i.e. in technological mastery). See R.R. Nelson, "Research on productivity growth and productivity differences: Dead ends and new departures", *Journal of Economic Literature*, 1981, No. 19, p. 1029-64.

[179] The case for selective protection is presented in H. Pack and L.E. Westphal, "Industrial strategy and technological change: Theory versus reality", *Journal of Development Economics*, 1986, p.87-128, and S. Lall "Explaining industrial success in the developing world", in V.N. Balasubramanyam and S. Lall (eds.), *Current issues in development economics*, (Macmillan, London, 1991) (forthcoming). The risks of infant industry over-protection are analysed in M. Bell, B. Ross-Larson and L.E. Westphal, "Assessing the performance of infant industries", *Journal of Development Economics*, 1984, 16, p.101-128.

support that enable firms to conduct in-house technical work effectively. Thus, national technological dynamism is more than the sum of individual enterprise capabilities: it is the synergy arising
from the interaction of enterprises, markets and institutions.

547.   National technological dynamism is thus subject to policy interventions at three points:[180]
first, in the *incentive structures* that induce enterprises to build up capabilities, requiring sound
macroeconomic management, including fiscal and credit policies, interest rates, etc. and the
provision of selective infant industry protection for activities with costly "learning" periods;
secondly, in the development of *capabilities* to respond to incentives, requiring interventions to
develop the skill base (education and training), to promote appropriate technology inflows, and to
induce domestic R and D activity; thirdly, in supporting a variety of *institutions* to facilitate the
functioning of markets, in particular the flow of information and skills and inter-industry linkages.
Moreover, it is the complex *interaction* of these three factors that determines technological
dynamism: simply providing incentives without building up capabilities or institutions (or vice
versa) may be ineffective, even counterproductive. This simplified framework for analysing the
process of industrial development yields useful insights into recent experience.[181] It also yields rich
policy implications, sometimes quite different from the prevalent "neo-liberal" orthodoxy.

2. Contrasting experiences of technological dynamism

548.   The relative industrial and technological performance of developing countries can be
gauged in many ways. Table III-2 presents several indicators of performance in 29 developing
countries and territories for the period 1970-1988. Some of the indicators are subdivided into two
periods (1970-1980 and 1980-1988) to show the impact of the debt crisis and terms-of-trade shocks
on some of the sample countries. These data need careful interpretation in order to arrive at a
meaningful picture of recent performance, partly because there is no unambiguous measure of
dynamism and partly because of the effects of the shocks of the 1980s.[182]

549.   In terms of the levels of industrialization, the four more advanced countries and territories
of East Asia (Hong Kong, Republic of Korea, Singapore, and Taiwan Province of China) have the
highest shares of manufacturing in GDP (27 to 43 per cent), followed by Turkey with a manufacturing share of also 27 per cent of GDP. The Asian four also recorded some of the highest growth
rates in manufacturing over the period 1970-1987 (from 8 to 14 per cent per annum), though some
of the second-tier newly industrializing countries -- Indonesia, Malaysia and Thailand -- as well
as Tunisia also fall in this range. The complexity of the manufacturing sector, as indicated by the
share and growth of capital goods production, is also the highest in East Asia, though Hong Kong
is distinctly below the others and falls between Argentina and Brazil. Capital employed per worker
has risen fastest in East Asia and showed fairly high values by 1988, although Argentina (with the
longest established industrial base), Brazil, Venezuela and Turkey also showed high levels. Productivity growth is consistently high for Taiwan Province of China and the Republic of Korea
(data for Hong Kong are only available for the 1980s and are high, while Singapore performed well
in the 1980s but poorly in the 1970s). The productivity performance of several other Asian countries (India, Malaysia, Pakistan, Philippines, Thailand, and Turkey) improved significantly in the
1980s, while Latin American and African countries had a relatively weak showing in both periods.
The incremental capital output ratio (ICOR) tended to rise in most countries in the 1980s as a
result of worsening capacity utilization (India being a major exception) and/or the rising complexity of manufacturing activities (as in the Republic of Korea and Singapore).

550.   Manufactured export performance, as measured by market shares, reveals the strong competitive position of the more advanced East Asian economies. All other Asian countries also

[180] See S. Lall, *Building industrial competitiveness in developing countries*, Paris, OECD Development Centre, 1990.

[181] It is important to note that historical and geoeconomic conditions also have an impact on national technological
dynamism, but upon those conditions governments do not have extensive influence.

[182] It may be argued that the extent of the shocks felt by particular countries themselves reflected, at least in part, past
industrial dynamism: countries with small or inefficient industrial structures fared worse in the deteriorating international environment.

Table III-2

Technological development and related economic performance

29 developing countries and territories by region	Manufacturing value added		MVA [a] in capital goods industry [b]			Capital stock per employee in manufacturing [c]			Productivity [d]		ICOR [e]		World market share in manufactured exports			External patenting [f] accumulated 1962-1987	
	Growth 1970-1987	as % of GDP 1987	Growth 1970-1980	Growth 1980-1987	as % of GDP 1987	Growth 1972-1980	Growth 1980-1988	Value 1988	Growth 1970-1980	Growth 1980-1987	1970-1979	1980-1988	% change 1970-1980	% change 1980-1988	% 1988	No. [g]	No. [h]
Côte d'Ivoire	3.3	9	1.3	2.0	2.1	2	-3	4	-0.4	1.3	3.3	17.2	-0.002	0.006	0.013	4	0.49
Egypt	6.2	11	-0.8	4.2	1.3	11	4	1	2.3	3.3	2.8	2.7	-0.045	0.060	0.076	35	0.84
Kenya	7.6	12	-4.3	-5.6	0.7	6	-1	1	2.1	1.3	5.6	6.2	-0.004	-0.003	0.005	23	1.37
Nigeria	5.2	4	21.0	-17.2	0.7	16	-3	2	0.0	-0.8	5.1	..	-0.013	-0.004	0.003	22	0.27
Tunisia	9.7	14	11.9	4.3	1.8	8	3	3	3.3	2.0	4.2	9.1	0.024	0.011	0.048	13	2.03
United Rep. of Tanzania	0.5	7	6.7	-12.0	0.4	3	-9	1	-3.7	-3.8	6.5	15.1	-0.002	-0.001	0.002	9	0.48
Zambia	1.6	20	5.7	1.7	3.0	..	..	5	-2.0	0.6	44.0	44.0	-0.076	-0.019	0.037	11	1.95
Argentina	0.5	24	-1.3	1.9	7.0	6	-1	30	3.1	2.5	9.0	7.1	0.017	-0.007	0.083	520	18.71
Brazil	5.7	25	1.8	-0.4	5.7	6	-1	13	1.0	1.3	3.2	..	0.250	0.134	0.486	478	3.94
Chile	1.0	21	-6.5	-2.8	1.5	0	-1	7	2.8	2.4	13.4	11.9	-0.021	-0.021	0.109	79	7.10
Colombia	4.6	22	2.3	-1.9	2.0	3	4	6	1.8	4.2	3.1	6.0	0.017	-0.007	0.029	110	4.26
Costa Rica	5.1	19	5.2	-3.1	1.2	..	..	..	0.5	1.9	3.8	11.9	0.004	-0.007	0.008	32	14.04
Ecuador	5.8	17	8.0	-1.1	1.4	8	2	4	1.9	0.1	..	..	0.003	-0.002	0.001	33	4.06
Guatemala	3.1	16	-0.1	-5.7	0.5	4	-6	1	3.6	2.3	3.3	..	-0.003	-0.017	0.003	45	6.51
Mexico	4.3	21	1.9	-3.2	2.9	3	0	7	0.1	2.9	3.5	23.1	-0.041	0.147	0.252	1301	18.75
Peru	3.0	21	6.5	-9.0	1.7	3	-2	5	3.4	2.9	6.9	..	-0.006	-0.035	0.037	67	3.87
Uruguay	1.5	22	0.4	-0.1	2.8	0	2	4	..	5.5	3.8	..	0.003	-0.002	0.016		
Venezuela	4.1	19	9.2	-0.3	2.2	4	3	11	-2.7	3.6	6.0	41.2	0.018	-0.007	0.027	220	14.64
Hong Kong	13.4	30	..	..	6.1	..	..	..	..	6.7	3.8	4.2	0.590	0.650	1.640	387	76.81
India	5.7	19	1.3	3.2	2.9	3	9	3	0.1	7.6	7.4	3.9	-0.071	0.015	0.237	301	0.44
Indonesia	11.8	17	22.0	7.4	1.1	18	4	2	7.4	-0.5	2.1	6.4	0.041	0.136	0.183	75	0.50
Malaysia	9.9	24	13.8	1.3	3.5	7	10	4	0.9	6.5	3.1	8.0	-0.002	0.070	0.232	74	5.38
Pakistan	6.9	17	2.6	-0.2	0.9	1	9	2	5.0	8.2	3.4	4.0	-0.055	0.024	0.080	15	0.17
Philippines	3.8	24	0.9	-10.8	0.8	-4	1	2	-2.6	5.6	3.5	54.6	0.077	0.031	0.133	132	2.73
Rep. of Korea	13.6	34	9.7	8.7	10.3	15	11	15	5.8	6.9	2.7	4.0	0.543	0.703	1.412	331	8.68
Singapore	8.1	27	8.7	1.9	16.9	11	8	18	1.7	6.5	4.8	8.5	0.362	0.331	0.813	76	31.48
Taiwan Prov. of China	11.2	43	..	..	10.3	..	..	..	11.9	7.7	3.9	4.1	0.497	1.080	1.630	1289	72.40
Thailand	8.4	22	6.1	0.6	3.0	3	8	4	3.4	8.1	3.6	4.7	0.067	0.124	0.236	19	0.41
Turkey	6.7	27	5.6	1.2	2.7	7	6	11	0.9	5.7	4.3	3.1	0.020	0.170	0.206	41	0.92

Source: UNCTAD secretariat computations based on data from UNSO, UNIDO, IMF, OECD, and United States Patent Office.
a Manufacturing value added.
b Capital goods industry defined as output of ISIC 381 to ISIC 385.
c For the computation of capital stock, see footnote a of figure 1. The values in 1988 are relative values only. They are estimated on the assumption that the share of capital goods in the manufacturing sector is proportional to the share of the manufacturing sector in total GDP.
d Value added per employee in the manufacturing sector.
e Incremental capital output ratio (ICOR) for the period i to j is defined as the ratio of gross fixed investment over the period i minus 1 to j minus 1 to output in period j minus 1 minus output in period i.
f External patents granted in the United States, accumulated 1962 to 1987.
g Number of patents granted 1962 to 1987.
h Cumulative number of patents 1962 to 1987 per million of population in 1980.

recorded increases in market shares in the 1980s, in contrast to most African and Latin American countries. Finally, table III-2 gives data on patents taken out internationally. This is a very crude indicator of technological dynamism, since the true economic "value" of patents is difficult to judge, propensities to patent may differ, and some national patents may in fact be taken out by resident foreigners. Nevertheless, the data (normalised by population) reinforce the impression of dynamism in the more advanced East Asian economies. Some Latin American countries (Argentina and Mexico) also have impressive patent records, testifying to latent capabilities that are not revealed in industrial growth or competitiveness (see below).

551. It is difficult, thus, to provide a complete explanation of recent industrial performance because of the influence of macroeconomic factors discussed in the preceding chapter. Nevertheless, it appears from many indicators that the more advanced countries of East Asia, and to a lesser extent the newly industrializing countries of Asia, manifest greater dynamism than other developing countries. It is this phenomenon that has formed the empirical basis of the current orthodoxy on industrialisation: viz, industrial success is based on neo-liberal incentive structures, as manifested in outward-oriented trade régimes.

552. This school argues that such régimes lead not only to better export performance (i.e. the exploitation of existing comparative advantage) but also to greater technological dynamism (the creation of new competitive advantages). In other words, providing a neutral structure of incentives encourages competitive industries to export. But it does more: it lowers ICORs by enforcing efficient specialization, leads to the realization of economies of scale (in capital-intensive industries), promotes faster and healthier accumulation of skills and technological capabilities, provides an additional (and largely free) channel of information to exporters, and, by easing foreign exchange constraints, permits steadier growth and greater availability of imported equipment, inputs and technologies.

553. These arguments clearly have a lot of validity. Incentives do matter, and specialization by comparative advantage does offer benefits. International competition and contacts with world markets do stimulate technological dynamism and a diversified export base does help steady long-term development. The record of industrialization supports a broad association between export orientation, export growth and industrial development, though the relationship may not hold for all periods or for the degree of export orientation (some "moderately inward-oriented" countries do better than some "moderately outward-oriented" ones).[183] The more advanced East Asian economies are the best performers and also the most outward-oriented régimes, and the newly industrializing economies appear set to follow them down the export-based growth path.[184]

554. The lessons that can be drawn from this are not, however, as simple and straightforward as current orthodoxy suggests. "Export-orientation" does not represent a uniform set of policies, nor does it necessarily carry the neo-liberal connotations noted earlier. There are two major sets of qualifications to this interpretation. The first concerns *incentive structures* in product markets, the second the role of *intervention on factor markets*. These are discussed in turn.

555. A neutral structure of incentives between domestic and export markets can coexist with neo-liberal trade régimes (low and uniform protection) or with highly variable protection for import-substituting activities. Export success may be based on instant entry into world markets, or it may derive from long periods of "learning" based on serving protected domestic markets (import substitution).

556. The more advanced East Asian economies display a wide range of export-oriented strategies. Hong Kong is the closest to the neo-liberal paradigm: free trade policies from the inception of industrialization. The Republic of Korea is at the other extreme: a high degree of selective intervention (to pick and promote 'winners', especially in heavy and high-technology activities) and high rates of protection sustained for long periods for new activities offset by export incentives, combined with low protection for mature industries.[185] Singapore had an initial period of import

183 See the World Bank's *World Development Report*, New York, Oxford University Press, 1987.

184 For a review of issues associated with policy orientation, exchange rates and trade policy reform, see M. R. Agosin, "Trade policy reform and economic performance: a review of issues and preliminary evidence from the 1980s", 1991, UNCTAD, Geneva, unpublished.

185 This form of export-orientation is analysed in detail for the case of the Republic of Korea by L.E. Westphal, "Industrial policy in an export-propelled economy: Lessons from South Korea's experience", *Journal of Economic Perspectives*, 4:3, 1990, pp.41-59.

substitution followed by liberal trade policies. Taiwan Province of China was closer to the Republic of Korea, with selective and often high rates of protection; however, it was less interventionist in promoting heavy industry.

557. Each of these economies is successful and competitive, yet the resulting industrial structures are vastly different. Hong Kong remains specialized in light consumer goods, with a high reliance on foreign technology and inputs; its industrial structure has little depth or innovative capability and is, therefore, vulnerable to rising costs. It has survived by rapidly shifting its manufacturing offshore, mainly to China, because it could not diversify into more complex activities at home. By contrast, the Republic of Korea has built up a diversified industrial base, with a range of efficient heavy and technology-intensive industries, a high degree of local integration and well-developed local design and innovation capabilities. The *chaebol* (diversified business groups) of the Republic of Korea are investing abroad mainly in sophisticated activities to serve local markets (mainly in developed market-economy countries), while upgrading domestic activity to cope with rising wages. Singapore has entered into much heavier industry than Hong Kong by intervening pervasively in the labour market, in the direction of investment flows and through ownership of enterprises, rather than via protection, but its product range is narrow and its technology is almost entirely provided from abroad by transnationals that, in general, dominate its manufacturing.[186] The industry of Taiwan, Province of China, has a diversified structure, but is smaller in scale and less capital-intensive than the Republic of Korea's: the former's strategy has been more incremental and less aimed at large leaps into heavy industry than the latter. Taiwan, Province of China, like Hong Kong, has moved low-tech small and medium-sized enterprises to China, instead of increasing the scale or capital intensity of enterprises at home. It is the Republic of Korea that has come closest to emulating the Japanese strategy, and it is indisputable that it was only its massive interventions, within an export-oriented framework, that made this possible.[187]

558. While export-orientation is compatible with interventions in incentive structures, the form of interventions differs significantly from interventions as practised in inward-oriented economies. The two key differences lie in *selectivity* and *offsetting safeguards*. The two larger East Asian NIEs did not give widespread, protracted, haphazard protection to all industrial activities started in their markets. They promoted a few new activities at any given time, letting mature activities operate effectively in a free trade régime; they geared protection to the "learning" period involved and forced firms to enter export markets as soon as possible to reap the competitive benefits of world exposure; and the overall incentive structure always favoured exports.[188] By contrast, most inward-oriented economies promoted industries by means of high, haphazard and widespread protection, giving net disincentives to exporting and sustaining activities regardless of their efficiency. It was not intervention (and protection) *per se* that was wrong, but the particular interventions utilized: the export-oriented interveners were truly selective, while the inward-oriented interveners were largely unselective and failed to offset the effects of protection. Moreover, in the field of macro-economic policy, an additional disincentive to exports was provided by large fluctuations in the real exchange rates. Since some of the countries which adopted inward-oriented development strategies were characterized by high inflation rates, the real exchange rate was often too high and thus prohibitive to exporters.[189]

559. Malaysia and Thailand have been following the example set forth mainly by the Republic of Korea. Both countries have moved from first to second-stage import substitution, lowering the incentives afforded to the consumer goods industries in order to force them into competition and maturity, while picking winners among the high-tech, high-value added industries. The main difference in their industrialization strategy is that their industrial structure is markedly characterized by the presence of offshore electronics assembly.

560. The second major qualification to the neo-liberal view on export orientation concerns the

---

[186] See L.B. Krause, "Hong Kong and Singapore: Twins or Kissing Cousins?", *Economic Development and Cultural Change*, 1988, 36:3, pp.45-66.

[187] See P.W. Kuznets, "An East Asian model of economic development: Japan, Taiwan and South Korea", *Economic Development and Cultural Change*, 1988, 36:3, p.11-13, and R. Wade, "The role of government in overcoming market failure: Taiwan, Republic of Korea and Japan", in H. Hughes (ed.), *Achieving Industrialization in East Asia* (Cambridge University Press, Cambridge, 1988).

[188] See Pack and Westphal (*op.cit.*) and Westphal (*op.cit.*) on the strategy of the Republic of Korea.

[189] On the subject of exchange rates and export performance, see chapter V, "Trade policy reform and export performance in developing countries in the 1990s" in UNCTAD, *Trade and Development Report, 1989* (United Nations publication, Sales No. E.89.II.D.14), New York, 1989.

role of *government interventions in factor markets*. These are portrayed as being minimal and non-selective. This interpretation is unwarranted. Each of the Governments of the more advanced Asian countries intervened in a sustained manner to develop the capabilities and institutions necessary for technological dynamism. Some of this intervention was non-selective (or functional); some was highly selective, aimed at promoting the growth of particular activities, particular capabilities, even particular enterprises.

561. This is illustrated in table III-3 for the sample countries with reference to the major components of national technological dynamism identified earlier: human capital or skills, imports of technology and domestic technological effort (institution-building cannot be measured so is ignored for the present). Table III-3 also shows the rate of investment in plant and equipment in manufacturing in the 1970s and 1980s. While such investment is governed to a large extent by macroeconomic and exogenous factors beyond the concerns of this report, it forms one of the necessary conditions for industrial growth[190] (the data shown are of particular interest because they are not calculated elsewhere).

562. The more advanced and the newly industrializing countries of Asia (Republic of Korea and Singapore), but also Indonesia, Malaysia, Turkey, India and Thailand, as well as Egypt and Tunisia, had among the highest increases (during the period 1972-1988) of equipment investment in manufacturing, having used it with different degrees of efficiency. What the data do not show is the role of government intervention in channelling those investments. With the exception of Hong Kong, each of the more advanced East Asian economies influenced resource allocation in industry. Singapore directed FDI inflows into more high-value-added, high-tech activities. Taiwan Province of China used tariffs to influence investment, as well as directly taking the public sector into heavy industry and providing various inducements (such as joint ventures and science parks) to attract private industry into areas of future competitiveness. The Republic of Korea intervened most heavily of all through its import-substitution programmes (accelerated in the 1970s in the "Heavy and Chemical Industries" drive), its allocation of credit via the State-controlled banking system, its promotion and subsidisation of selected private businesses into giant conglomerates (the *chaebol*) to lead its heavy industry drive, its close direction of activity and exports in the business sector, and some public sector industrial investments (its famous Pohang steel mill). The *chaebol* strategy was clearly not free competition in the traditional sense, since entry and growth were controlled by the Government (although the giants competed fiercely with one another).

563. The domestic production of capital goods has a special significance for technological dynamism because of the central role of machinery manufacture in generating and diffusing technology. However, the promotion of local equipment manufacture runs the risk of creating technological lags if designs and performance are not up to world standards. The correct balance between making and buying capital goods is thus important for long-term industrial dynamism and competitiveness. The most successful countries, such as the Republic of Korea, have promoted local equipment manufacture selectively, while importing large amounts of foreign equipment to retain export competitiveness. Some, like Argentina, Brazil or India, have pursued stringent import-substitution in capital goods, thus creating a broad domestic capability in design and manufacture but risking the competitiveness of user industries. Others, like most sub-Saharan African countries, have low domestic equipment manufacturing and rely largely on foreign capital goods. However, their low levels of skills and technological ability (see below) have reduced their ability to deploy their capital stocks efficiently. The ability to import of many Latin American and African countries has, as noted in section 1, suffered from recent economic shocks: this has probably led to a deterioration not just in the stock of productive capital but also in its modernity and quality.

---

[190] See C. Bradford, "NICs and the next-tier NICs as transitional economies", in Colin Bradford and W. Branson (eds.), *Trade and Structural Change in Pacific Asia* (University of Chicago Press, Chicago, 1987).

Table III-3

INVESTMENT IN TECHNOLOGY AND SKILLS

29 developing countries and territories by region	Total capital stock a (1980=100)		Technology inflows as % of GDI b			Human resources 1987 or closest available year				Research and development expenditure (latest available year)	
						Literacy rate %	Educational enrolment At 2nd level as % of age group	Per 100,000 population: Science and technology 3rd level f	Per 100,000 population: Vocational training 2nd level	Total as % of GNP	Of which the productive sector as % of GNP
	1972	1988	MCG c 1975-87	FDI d 1975-87	TC e 1975-87						
Côte d'Ivoire	43	73	26.2	3.6	4.0	43	18	27	249	0.3	
Egypt	26	184	62.0	14.6	6.4	44	69	167	1833	0.2	0.039
Kenya	56	103	30.2	2.1	7.3	59	21	22	25	0.8	..
Nigeria	22	74	18.2	3.4	0.3	42	29	24	98	0.3	..
Tunisia	28	133	28.4	5.6	3.0	51	40	126	1225	..	..
United Rep. of Tanzania	42	68	20.8	0.6	11.3	46	4	3		..	..
Zambia	78	87	42.3	7.1	8.2	76	17	18	38	0.5	..
Argentina	67	76	8.1	2.0	0.1	94	74	363	3834	0.4	0.179
Brazil	35	100	8.7	3.5	0.1	78	38	160	1092	0.4	0.268
Chile	96	88	21.5	3.8	0.9	91	70	538	1062	0.5	0.211
Colombia	56	119	20.4	9.5	0.9	85	56	387	1515	0.1	0.002
Costa Rica	49	92	20.9	6.9	3.4	93	41	312	981	0.3	0.000
Ecuador	29	101	26.3	2.8	4.6	80	56	636	2624	0.5	..
Guatemala	55	64	18.1	8.1	2.4	46	20	..	430	0.6	..
Mexico	61	111	21.0	3.5	0.1	90	53	453	1051	0.6	0.173
Peru	54	78	17.3	0.2	1.7	82	65	563	297	0.2	..
Uruguay	69	74	13.2	0.4	1.0	95	73	379	1359	0.2	..
Venezuela	38	96	22.6	0.6	0.1	85	54	558	304	0.3	..
Hong Kong	..	165	39.0	7.0	0.1	77	72	318	800	..	..
India	63	177	8.6	0.2	0.4	41	35	16	80	0.9	0.191
Indonesia	26	167	17.2	1.5	1.1	67	39	85	626	0.3	..
Malaysia	33	165	34.9	9.0	0.8	70	59	..	122	..	..
Pakistan	80	71	20.4	1.3	2.4	26	18	28	51	0.4	0.327
Philippines	62	239	29.3	1.5	1.1	83	64	770		0.1	0.023
Rep. of Korea	21	169	25.7	0.9	0.1	88	89	765	1970	2.3	1.543
Singapore	25	..	88.4	16.8	0.3	83	69	704	372	0.9	0.521
Taiwan Province of China	..	147	33.2	3.3	..	92	91	795	2082	1.1	0.738
Thailand	49	156	23.6	3.0	1.4	79	30	..	648	0.3	..
Turkey	44	..	25.0	0.8	0.5	74	46	222	1402	0.7	0.532

Source: UNCTAD secretariat computations based on data from UNIDO, UNSO, UNCTC, OECD and UNESCO.

a See note a of figure 1 for the calculation of capital stocks.
b Gross domestic investment.
c Capital goods imports.
d Foreign direct investment.
e Technical co-operation grants.
f Third-level students in natural science, mathematics and computer science, engineering, and transport and communications.

564. The accumulation of physical capital in manufacturing cannot be efficient if it is not accompanied by the creation of new skills, the import of new technologies and the launching of domestic technological effort. The skills needed for industrialization are diverse. At the lowest level, literacy helps the labour force to be productive and is an important determinant of labour productivity in very simple industries. Secondary education, and in particular vocational training, become increasingly important for shopfloor skills as industry grows more complex. Tertiary-level skills, especially in science and engineering fields, are needed for all industries, but they increase sharply in significance with growing industrial complexity.

565. The more advanced East Asian economies in general have invested intensively in recent years in creating the skill base needed for technological dynamism,[191] and this is a vital ingredient of their dynamism. However, three important points have to be noted here. First, some other developing countries have also invested heavily in human capital (particularly in Latin America, the Philippines, Egypt, and Turkey). Since it is the interaction of human resources with incentives, physical investment and technological effort that drives technological dynamism, the mere possession of skills is a necessary but not sufficient condition for success. Other countries with ample human resources may have suffered from inappropriate incentive structures, inadequate technological effort or institutional weaknesses. This point is borne out more strikingly by the record of Eastern Europe, where there has long existed an ample stock of human capital and technical skills. Yet distorted incentives, combined with institutional weaknesses and isolation from world technologies, have led to very poor industrial performance.

566. Secondly, there are important differences between the more advanced East Asian economies. The two larger ones have a broadly stronger skill base than the smaller economies. Hong Kong appears weak in high-level technical skills and Singapore in vocational training.[192] This difference reflects the drive of the two larger economies into technologically demanding activities, as well as high skill inputs into their mature industries. Some other countries (like Brazil and India) have even more complex heavy industrial structures but have developed lower skill bases: the result is probably lower efficiency. Thirdly, educational enrollment figures have to be corrected for variations in dropout rates, overseas education, quality of training and relevance of curriculum content to make them fully comparable. This is not always possible, but it is likely that such corrections would increase the observed lead of East Asia.[193] The data also exclude employee training by firms: here the Republic of Korea (with 5 per cent of sales of all larger firms required to be invested in training) is likely to lead the other sample countries.

567. The growth of human resources for industrialization has been an essential precondition for export success, and it has not been caused by neutral incentives. The "education market" has required heavy intervention to provide the level, quality and technical orientation of the resource base. This point is strengthened if in-firm worker training is taken into account: firms tend to underinvest in such training when there is a risk of leakage (workers moving to other firms) and government support is needed to ensure adequate investments. Human resource interventions have been partly functional, to create general skills, and partly selective, to create the particular skills needed by the activities being promoted by the Government. Education markets do not function efficiently, especially in developing countries,[194] but neo-liberal economists (while they may accept the need to boost education) tend to ignore the critical role of such intervention in the context of industrial policy and experience. While human resources may not be the binding constraint in the industrialization of some (mainly Latin American) countries, they do constitute major impediments to industrial development in others (mainly in sub-Saharan Africa).[195]

---

191 Even by the 1960s, the East Asian NIEs had among the best developed human resources in the developing world, though some Latin American countries (like Argentina, Uruguay, Chile and Venezuela) also had substantial bases.

192 It should be noted, however, that Singapore's vocational training figures may be misleading because it has a large programme for post-employment worker training, regarded as one of the world's best. However, such worker training is likely to provide more specialized skills than vocational training and may be less suited to the diverse industrial structures of larger countries.

193 See Lall, 1990, op.cit., pp.47-48. The East Asian NIEs have substantial numbers of tertiary students registered in foreign universities. For instance, Hong Kong has 24,700, Singapore 8,900 and the Republic of Korea 29,400 compared to Argentina 3,100, Brazil 6,700 and Mexico 8,200.

194 The debate over skill gaps in the United states and the United Kingdom suggest, moreover, that they do not always function perfectly in mature, open economies either. See, for instance, OECD, *Structural Adjustment and Economic Performance*, Paris, 1987; Office of Technology Assessment, *Making Things Better*, Washington, D.C., 1990.

195 On the role of education and skills in constraining African industrialization, see S. Lall, "Structural problems of African industry", in Frances Stewart, S. Lall and S. Wangwe (eds.), *Alternative Development Strategies for Africa*, (Macmillan, London, 1991) (forthcoming).

568.   Technological effort and imports are also essential ingredients of technological dynamism. To a large extent, they complement each other. Developing countries need to import a great deal of embodied and disembodied technology; they also need to do a lot themselves to absorb it and build upon it. Technology imports in the form of capital goods are the most accessible but require the greatest local capabilities and efforts to operate efficiently. Most complex technology transfers also need disembodied transfers of know-how, training, patents and the like; these are available via FDI, licensing or other forms of contractual arrangement. International technology markets can be fragmented and oligopolistic and may call for official intervention to strengthen the informational and negotiating position of developing country buyers. They are, however, fairly open to all developing countries, with two qualifications: first, the more advanced, export-oriented enterprises may find it difficult to buy state-of-the-art technology at arms' length because of the competitive threat they pose (the leading *chaebol* in the Republic of Korea now have to develop many of their own new products because of the reluctance of technological leaders to license them). Secondly, some new technologies are very expensive to create and are being held more tightly than were earlier technologies. There is also a growing propensity for leading innovators to form "strategic alliances" in developing new technologies. These tendencies raise the cost of entry to all newcomers, in developed or developing countries.[196]

569.   Different forms of technology imports have differing implications for technological development. FDI may be a very effective means of transferring rapidly the results of new innovations as they appear. It may not, however, be equally effective in transferring innovative capabilities: transnationals generally find it economical to centralize R and D in developed countries with an ample skill base and established linkages with a highly advanced science and technology infrastructure. Thus, the building up of local innovative capabilities may require the promotion of indigenous firms and selective restrictions on FDI inflows. Experience shows that countries with technological ambitions have indeed been selective in allowing FDI at critical junctures. The Republic of Korea is again a case in point. It has the lowest reliance on FDI of all the NIEs despite its advanced industrial structure, making up the gap with its own intense technological effort (see below) and the promotion of *chaebol*, which are large and diversified enough to bear the cost and risk of entry into high-tech activities. In fact, the Republic of Korea does not even figure among the ten largest host economies to FDI, these being Singapore, China, Brazil, Mexico, Hong Kong, Egypt, Thailand, Malaysia, Argentina and Colombia. In 1988 and 1989, FDI to these countries averaged 19.25 billion dollars per annum. Still, FDI to the Republic of Korea has grown consistently, both in absolute and in relative terms during the 1980s (US$ 102 million, or 0.15 per cent of GDP, in 1981, to US$ 758 million, or 0.41 per cent of GDP in 1989). Given the Republic of Korea's well-established capabilities in different areas, this increase in FDI results from a relaxation of the previous restrictions on foreign inflows helping to stimulate domestic competition and to compound gross investment.

570.   Heavy reliance on FDI does not stifle industrial growth; it may only reduce the indigenous technological content of industrialization. On the other hand, simply restricting FDI without providing the incentives or skills to develop local technologies can be very counterproductive, leading to inefficiency and obsolescence. If this is combined with restrictions on other forms of technology inflows and high inward-orientation, the costs can be compounded -- as happened in India in the 1970s.[197]

571.   The import of technology by successful industrializers like the Republic of Korea has been subject to considerable interventions by the Government. In turn-key projects, the Government has insisted that local engineers participate in all stages of design and engineering. In licensing, local firms were provided with information and assisted with bargaining. "Reverse engineering" was encouraged and intellectual property laws were liberally applied and weakly interpreted (as in Taiwan Province of China): this followed the earlier model of Japan,[198] and for some time has characterized the industrialization strategies of Thailand and Malaysia. Interventions with technology transfer were non-existent in Hong Kong and Singapore, though the latter (as noted) strongly guided the nature and sophistication of FDI inflows.

---

[196] D. Ernst and J. O'Connor, *Technology and global competition: The challenge ahead for newly industrializing economies*, Paris, OECD, 1989.

[197] Lall, *Learning to industrialize*.

[198] See Alice Amsden, *Asia's Next Giant: South Korea and Late Industrialization*, Oxford University Press, New York, 1989.

572. Formal R and D efforts are shown in the last two columns of table III-3. Total R and D figures include agricultural, defence, construction and other forms of effort, but it is not possible to obtain manufacturing R and D data on a comparable basis for all sample countries. The nearest approximation is R and D in the "productive sector" (which includes agriculture); this is also shown where available. The Republic of Korea leads the field by far, testifying to the needs and capabilities generated by past policies to diversify and deepen industry; the bulk of its R and D emanates from its *chaebol*, themselves the result of highly selective intervention. Taiwan Province of China comes next, followed by Turkey and Singapore. Brazil's R and D has dropped sharply since the early 1980s, presumably because of debt-induced problems, while Argentina, despite its human resources, spends little on productive sector research.

573. Although it cannot be established quantitatively, the successful industrializers have invested heavily in setting up industrial support institutions, especially to promote technological activity and export marketing in addition to what is carried out by enterprises. In contrast, in the majority of developing countries, very little R and D takes place in productive enterprises. Furthermore, the performance of publicly-funded R and D laboratories has fallen short of expectations. Even where innovation and research outputs have been high in relation to the allocation of human and financial resources, improved products and processes have often failed to bring about innovations by industry.

574. One reason behind such under-performance would appear to be that research has not adequately focussed on issues reflecting the needs of domestic manufacturers. A possible remedy lies in refocusing R and D activities by concentrating on selected technical areas in line with actual and future demand. Measures to this end might include increased emphasis on single-purpose instead of multipurpose research, higher priority for technical services as opposed to basic research and measures to enhance the demand orientation of R and D activities, such as the promotion of contractual research, fee-based incentive schemes and risk-sharing schemes.[199]

575. Recent industrial history shows that successful innovation requires very close interlinkages within the firm between research, production, marketing and management. A redistribution of responsibility for industrial research from public laboratories to productive enterprises will take time. The duration will vary from country to country depending on the re-directioning of financial resources for research and on the skill endowment of enterprises and on the possibility of drawing qualified industrial researchers from the public laboratories. Ideally, the initiative should come from the enterprises themselves, but it is the combination of export-oriented incentives and high levels of skill that has enabled the more advanced Asian economies to set up more effective institutions, exploit them better and make them useful to the private sector. Again, widespread and selective interventions were needed to set up the institutional support structure.

576. In synthesis, technological dynamism cannot be explained by partial theories that stress selected aspects of the incentives-capabilities-institutions nexus. In particular, the neo-liberal interpretation, relying heavily on "getting prices right" in a supposedly efficient market setting, has ignored the role of capabilities and institutions. It has also underemphasized the positive role of interventions, especially selective interventions, in providing correct incentives and developing the technological capacity to respond to those incentives.

577. While interventions are necessary for sustained industrial development, however, not all interventions are efficient or desirable. Development experience is replete with cases of uneconomic interventions. Excessive, haphazard protection has bred not technological dynamism but many "infant" industries that have never matured. The setting up of heavy industrial structures without providing an adequate skill or institutional basis has often led to inefficiency. Creating skills without proper incentives has wasted human resources. On the other hand, "getting prices right" without offering infant industry protection or institutional or skill back-up has sometimes led to industrial stagnation. The secret of success has been in combining incentives with adequate capabilities and institutions, each supported by a proper mix of selective and functional interventions. With the benefit of hindsight, one must also not overlook the influence of external factors which, on the whole, were less constraining on the policy options available during the 1970s. The implications for replicability of the East Asian experience are, therefore, manyfold. The ex-

---

[199] See "Research and development institutes in developing countries and their contribution to technological innovation", report by the UNCTAD secretariat (UNCTAD ITP/TEC/11) September 1990; also, "Utilization and commercialization of UN system-funded R and D results: case studies on the Indian experience", report by the UNCTAD secretariat in co-operation with R. Kumar (UNCTAD ITP/TEC/20).

ternal environment which includes intellectual property rights régimes affecting the supply-side of technology should continue to be of an "enabling" nature in the future. This makes rapid technology accumulation possible for the countries that are willing to adopt appropriate and effective domestic policies. Consequently, new proposals for stronger systems of intellectual property rights protection will affect the possibility of following a time-tested path of technological development based on reverse engineering, adaptation and the improvement of existing innovation, which is being promoted by the governments of developing countries to build up technological dynamism.

C. INTERNATIONAL ENVIRONMENT FOR TECHNOLOGY TRANSFER

578.   The past two decades have brought significant changes in the environment for the transfer of technology. Major advances have occurred in biotechnology, materials technology, microelectronics and other disciplines. An increasingly competitive global technological climate has induced changes in policies on the part of both firms and governments - a development that is likely to affect the transfer of technology to developing countries during this decade. Also likely to affect developing countries is the inclusion of technology-related trade issues in negotiations that have taken place in various fora, the creation of economic groupings and the transformation of Eastern Europe. The remainder of this chapter takes up the issues that are raised for developing countries by these developments.

1. Technologies, trade and technology transfer

579.   Of all the major/recent technological advances, those that appear to be the most far-reaching are in biotechnology, materials and microelectronics. Modern biotechnology has a large potential that is already being realized in pharmaceutical and medical applications and is just beginning to be exploited in agriculture.[200] The development of this industry in developed market-economy countries is said to be connected with judicial decisions that have granted intellectual property rights to innovators over genetically engineered 'forms of life'. The enormous costs of biotechnological R and D are leading to a growing concentration of activities in this field in the hands of large pharmaceutical and chemical companies. What these two developments mean in terms of the generation and diffusion of innovations in this field and of their transfer to developing countries is still not well understood. The need to amortize their investments in research has meant that biotechnological companies have been concentrating their efforts on applications tailored for the largest and most lucrative markets, primarily in developed market-economy countries. Although genetic engineering is beyond their reach, a fair number of developing countries may be in a position to obtain spin-offs from the above applications adapted to their own needs through the utilization of biotechnologies at the less sophisticated end of the spectrum, for example tissue culture and cloning. Access during the 1990s will depend on the domestic availability of skilled scientific and technical personel and on the ability to link up with external suppliers for the basic technology.

580.   With respect to *materials technologies*, previous UNCTAD reports have underscored their adverse impact on the consumption in developed market-economy countries of raw materials of export interest to developing countries.[201] There is little reason to believe that technological and other factors shaping the intensity of use of raw materials will diminish their force during the

---

[200] See "Agricultural biotechnology: preliminary assessment of potential impact on developing countries' trade", note by the UNCTAD secretariat (TD/B/C.6/154), for a more detailed discussion of these and related issues for agriculture.

[201] See "Impact of new and emerging technologies on trade and development: a review of the UNCTAD secretariat's research findings", report by the UNCTAD secretariat (TD/B/C.6/136) and "Impact of technological change on patterns of international trade", report by the UNCTAD secreariat (UNCTAD/ITP/TEC/3).

present decade.[202] Although economic growth, particularly in developing and Eastern European countries, could be sufficient to offset these trends and permit a modest expansion in materials demand, such expansion is highly unlikely to match the pace achieved during the 1950s and 1960s. Consequently, technology flows into mines and materials-based manufacturing will also be modest during this decade.

581.   Modern industry in the developed market-economy countries has been undergoing a fundamental structural, technological and organizational transformation. Its key features are growing product diversity, quantum leaps in productivity and increasing flexibility, stemming from the development and diffusion of a family of automation technologies. Some have argued that the spread of these technologies may cause developing countries to lose their attractiveness as low labour-cost locations for production and lead to an erosion of their global comparative advantage, leading to a shift of production location to the north. Thus far, however, trade figures do not reveal an adverse impact. From a share of about 5 per cent of world exports of manufactures in 1970, developing countries accounted for 9 per cent in 1980 and 15 per cent in 1987.[203] The behaviour of the transfer of technology also fails to reveal evidence of a shift in the location of production.   There must therefore be offsetting positive factors that explain the continued competitiveness of developing country exports. While no systematic empirical studies have been made to explore this issue, scattered evidence from a number of sources, including the UNCTAD secretariat's background research, provide indications that investment in computer-driven equipment by exporters of manufactures in the developing countries may be one of the reasons that they have been able to continue increasing their shares in international markets throughout the decade.[204] For the 1990s then, the available evidence suggests that the overall impact of computer technologies on competitiveness and technology transfer in the developing countries need not be adverse. There is a strong possibility, though, that the more technologically advanced developing countries will pull ahead of other developing countries whose education and skill levels are not adequate for the transformation. For some countries, this disadvantage would add to the other constraints that they already face in attracting foreign and domestic investment in new plant and equipment.

582.   A wholly different type of issue is raised by the impact of the new technologies in developed countries themselves. The slow structural adjustment of many of these countries suggests that the diffusion of technological innovations in their industries is not taking place fast enough. Costly protectionist policies have delayed the movement of resources in those countries out of declining industries in which comparative advantage has shifted to developing countries and into promising areas where the new technologies have the greatest potential impact.[205]

2. Firms' strategies and policy responses

583.   The increasingly competitive global technological climate has induced changes in policies on the part of both industry leaders and governments - a development that is likely to affect the transfer of technology to developing countries during this decade.

584.   As a consequence of the growing number of technologically proficient firms and of the ability of competitors to assimilate, reproduce and improve upon technology, the importance of protection of firms' technological assets has become more keenly felt. As has happened in the past, companies have relied on a variety of means to protect their technology from imitation by

---

[202] John E. Tilton, "The new view of minerals and economic growth", *The Economic Record*, vol. 65, no. 190 (September 1989).

[203] Secretariat estimates based on data of the United Nations Statistical Office.

[204] See "The diffusion of electronics technologies in the capital goods sector in some developing countries" - study prepared by Charles Edquist and Staffan Jacobsson in co-operation with the UNCTAD secretariat (UNCTAD/ITP/TEC/10); "Special report - computers at work", *Asian Business*, November 1987, pp. 74-76; A.Y.C. Nee and S.L. Long, "Microcomputer-aided material management in a furniture factory", *Computers in Industry*, vol. 10, no. 4 (1988); K.H. Poh, "NC applications - its present and future in Singapore's industries", *International Journal of Operations and Production Management*, vol. 4, no. 1 (1984).

[205] See "Structural adjustment issues in the world economy" - report by the UNCTAD secretariat (UNCTAD/ITP/25), 9 March 1990.

competitors, including intellectual property rights protection (patents, copyrights and trademarks), proprietary secrecy, lead time in introducing new products, learning curve advantages and access to complementary assets without which the technology cannot be exploited. While relying on all of these approaches, United States firms which felt most threatened by increasing global competition led the way in pressing for greater enforcement of intellectual property rights protection during the 1980s - a trend that has been followed in the EEC, Japan and other industrialized countries. Damages awarded to petitioners have risen and, in the United States, it has become easier since 1988 to bar imports of goods alleged to be infringing. The threat of trade retaliation and other inducements brought forth in bilateral negotiations has led a considerable number of developing countries to strengthen their standards of intellectual property protection. Indicative of the change in climate for those industries that depend on patents is the pattern of judgements on patent infringement cases in United States courts. Whereas two-thirds of such judgements had gone against the patent holder in the 1970s, the rulings in the 1980s were running 70 per cent in favour of the patent holder.[206] Moreover, the courts in many developed market-economy countries have increasingly applied doctrines which exempt restrictive practices in licensing agreements from the application of competition laws, where such practices result from market-dominating positions of firms conferred by intellectual property rights.

585.   Government measures have also aimed at extending or strengthening the scope and time coverage of intellectual property protection, particularly in respect of new technologies, such as informatics, telecommunications and biotechnology, in which it is argued that the possibility of legally protecting easily copied technologies was unclear and non-existent. In the case of biotechnology, a recent UNCTAD secretariat study[207] has shown that the drive to extend the scope of intellectual property rights protection through reform of industrial patent and/or plant breeders' rights legislation could affect unfavourably the diffusion and transfer and applications of innovation in this area which is of vital importance for developing countries as regards both production and trade.

586.   Paralleling the trends towards strengthening property rights protection, there have been the mergers, joint ventures and various types of strategic technological alliances that have characterized the behaviour of many firms manufacturing high-technology products in the developed market-economy countries. Whereas inter-firm collaboration is not a new phenomenon, international and domestic inter-firm agreements bearing to some degreee or another on technology represent a novel development of the 1980s. Until recently, the underlying purpose of inter-firm agreements was to overcome trade barriers or restrictions imposed by host governments. Though these factors are - and are likely to remain - of significance, new motivations are urging enterprises to engage in collaboration schemes. The underlying factors can be grouped under two related developments: the growing cost of R and D and the desire of firms to protect innovations from imitation. First, the growing science-intensity and interdisciplinary character of innovation - i.e. an innovation depends on simultaneous developments in several scientific disciplines - are pushing the costs of in-house R and D to levels that can be supported by only a few enterprises. Thus, mounting R and D expenditures have induced companies to establish formal and informal collaborative links with other companies - often in the same industry - in order to spread the large risk involved and permit the realization of complementarities and economies of scale in research. Moreover, in view of the acceleration of technological innovation and the shortening of product lead-times and life cycles, alliances can provide shortcuts for several firms racing to improve their production efficiency and quality control. Partners in such ventures are able to benefit from specialization and cross-fertilization while diminishing the cost of duplicative research efforts.[208] Finally, technology has also acted as an enabling factor for such collaboration. The convergence of technologies in what were formerly separate market sectors (i.e. close relations among technological applications in different sectors) have made collaboration more attractive. Similarly, the convergence of computer, communication and control technologies are opening vast possibilities for new forms of collaboration and for the growing internationalization of competition.

587.   The second, and perhaps more important, driving force behind inter-firm research and in-

---

[206] See J. Kerr, "Management's new cry: fight for your technology rights", *Electronic Business* (15 August 1988); and G.M. Hoffman in J.Osepchuk (ed.) "A written panel discussion on patent issues", *IEEE Technology and Society* (September 1988).

[207] See *Trade and development aspects and implications of new and emerging technologies: The case of biotechnology* (TD/B/C.6/154), March 1991.

[208] This is not an absolutely positive development. Duplicate efforts do not always lead to similar results. Therefore, they also create opportunities. See M. Porter, *The Competitive Advantage of Nations* (London, MacMillan, 1990).

novation linkages in the developed market-economy countries stems from the desire of firms to protect their innovations from imitation. Despite the campaign to strengthen intellectual property rights protection, empirical investigations have shown that in practice intellectual property rights alone do not offer adequate protection from imitation by competitors, and managerial personnel themselves have given relatively little weight to the importance of patents and copyright alone in protecting against imitators. This is in line with the stagnation in the number of internationally registered and approved patents in recent years[209] and the relatively slower growth of technology licensing compared with other technology transfer activities.[210] Experience has shown, particularly in the cases of United Kingdom and United States companies, that the ability to generate innovations is not sufficient to guarantee the greatest share of returns from their exploitation, and that complementary assets such as well-developed manufacturing, marketing, after-sales service or other capabilities are often more critical. Competitors better endowed with such assets may have an edge in getting the most profit from the originating firm's innovation. Thus, an important rationale for the observed tendency towards co-operative innovation is the perceived need to bring together R and D capabilities with other types of assets that are missing in order to protect returns from new technology and maximize the gain from its exploitation. Similar complementarities are at the heart of growing collaboration by enterprises with government agencies, universities and research institutes.

588. Among the sectors of high R and D intensity, the trend towards collaborative innovation has been particularly evident in biotechnology. The emergence of strategic alliances in the development of biotechnology exemplifies the interaction of the factors mentioned above. High R and D and the inter-disciplinary, as well as multisectoral nature of biotechnological applications, has forged inter-firm collaboration in the development of biotechnology applications, while the closeness between basic and applied research in genetic engineering has been behind the public/private-sector collaboration. As regards biotechnology R and D for agricultural applications, these developments, combined with the strengthening of intellectual property protection of living material, are leading to a privatization of knowledge previously unknown in this area.

589. Increased inter-firm collaboration has also been supported by changes in policies towards competition. The application of laws on mergers, on R and D collaboration among enterprises and on restrictive practices in licensing agreements, have been liberalized. The National Co-operative Research Act of 1984, which gave preferential antitrust treatment to such ventures in the United States, and Regulation 418/85 under Article 85, Section 3 of the EEC Treaty, which gives a so-called "block exemption" from anti-monopoly regulations for both the conduct of R and D and the joint exploitation of the results, fall into this category.[211] In addition, government measures have sought to support actively innovation efforts. Measures have included most notably government sponsorship of applied research; the granting of fiscal or other incentives for R and D; grants and soft loans for the establishment of new industries; and public procurement policies.[212] Other governmental measures adopted in these countries have aimed at promoting the technological edge of domestic enterprises by restructuring the legal framework governing competition among them.

590. One fear that has been expressed is that the developments described in this section will raise the cost and hinder the access of developing countries to imported technology in the coming years. Tighter intellectual property rights protection and growing secrecy would be expected to permit technology suppliers to seek higher economic rents on their innovations. Interviews carried out on behalf of the UNCTAD secretariat do suggest that royalty rates on patents, know-how and other forms of intellectual property may be on the rise. Thus, developing countries can be expected to experience higher licencing payments in patent-intensive industries during the 1990s.

591. Secondly, the easing of competition rules for innovative collaboration among firms does reduce constraints against cartels and monopolistic practices. Even if such collaboration did not lead to an increase in anticompetitive practices, it is to be expected that there will be a greater tendency to transfer technology within the collaborative group than to the outside. Since devel-

---

[209] Data on patents of foreign origin supplied by the United States Patent Office.

[210] Graham Vickery, "A survey of international technology licensing", *STI Review*, OECD, Paris, No. 4 (December 1988).

[211] Referred to in Carl Shapiro and Robert Willig, "On the antitrust treatment of production joint ventures", *Journal of Economic Perspectives*, vol. 4, No. 3 (Summer 1990).

[212] See "Technology-related policies and legislation on a changing economic and technological environment" (TD B C.6/146).

oping countries lack the research capabilities and other assets to take part in these collaboration schemes, their access to technology could be adversely affected as such arrangements grow in importance. Equality of access to basic research may be compromised as a result of growing linkages between private enterprises and public-sector research laboratories. Attempts to restrict access of foreign researchers to strategic areas of basic research, such as superconductivity, or growing secrecy of research carried out in public institutions but financed by private enterprises are indicative of this trend. This is an extension of "technological restrictionism" that is being witnessed in trade in the form of restrictions on exports of products or processes which are considered of strategic importance.

592.   Thirdly, there are technology-related factors which may also tend to limit the scope for latecomers and new entrants in such collaboration. Further, there may be greater incidence of anti-competitive practices. The currently emerging system of adoption of norms and standards, especially in the new industries, can be such a source of "anti-competitive" practices followed by oligopolistic firms. As any technology develops and matures, such norms and standards are set *de facto* by dominant suppliers, or *de jure* by national and international organizations, or by a combination of the two. Software and telecommunication networks are two areas where norms and standards may create barriers to entrance of developing countries and other countries not participating in the creation of such networks. Once created, it is not obvious how telecommunication networks can be modified. The growing role of such networks in trade transactions and other services of importance to developing countries requires that the norms being established take into account the specific requirements of developing countries. There is a need for dissemination of information on, and for an analysis of, the implications of these networks for more effective decision-making by developing countries.

3. Technology and trade negotiations

593.   Technology-related policies have led, or have the potential of leading, to conflicts entailing an erosion of the multilateral trading system embodied in GATT. These conflicts have occurred, or may occur, just as much among developed countries as between developed and developing countries, but the bargaining power of developing countries is, of course, weaker. Furthermore, since developing countries do not produce technology, trade is one means of obtaining it. It is in this context that developing countries seek more liberal and secure conditions of access for their exports into markets of developed countries. It also explains their concern over any move that would bring into question the principle of differential and more favourable treatment of developing countries. Apart from the overriding question of market access, several issues being discussed have a particular bearing on technology transfer and technological development prospects of developing countries.

594.   Most directly relevant to technology is the campaign aimed at the establishment of uniform and strengthened international standards of protection of intellectual property rights.[213] The economic rationale for increased protection is the expectation that the growth and productivity-generating effects from encouraging global investment in R and D will more than offset the slower diffusion of the resulting innovation - a slower diffusion that arises on account of the increased cost of the technology to users. Proponents of the reforms have sought to tilt towards holders of innovations the balance which has heretofore existed between promoting innovations and securing their adequate diffusion. Their call for uniform protection across all countries and technologies tends to discriminate against users of technology in both developed and developing countries. However, a developed country may be able to recoup losses to its technology users in one activity by reaping high returns in other activities in which its firms have a technological edge. Few developing countries are in a comparable position. Hence, they will be net losers as a result of having to pay the higher costs of technology in industries subject to protection, especially since the ben-

---

[213] A more complete discussion of these issues is contained in A. Yusuf, "Developing countries and trade-related aspects of intellectual property rights", *Uruguay round papers on selected issues* (UNCTAD ITP/10), United Nations, New York, 1989, and T. Ganiatsos, "Technology and trade: the developing country perspective" - paper presented to the Symposium on Technology and Trade Policy at the 1990 American Association for the Advancement of Science Annual Meeting, New Orleans, February 1990.

efits from technology generation will not accrue until the more distant future when their firms have achieved the capacity to produce patentable innovations. A more flexible approach would allow individual countries to fix the level of protection according to the technological capability of their industries under the principle of national treatment (see box III-1). This would avoid discrimination against net users of technology, most of which are developing countries.

Box III - 1

POLICY OPTIONS RELATED TO INTELLECTUAL PROPERTY PROTECTION

With respect to the TRIPSs negotiations, several basic principles need to be put in evidence. The most fundamental is that, if the developing countries cannot ignore the developed countries' need to repress counterfeiting in their own markets (as well as those of third countries), the developed countries cannot ignore the need of the developing countries to tie the provision of intellectual property protection in their markets to domestic development needs. Such an approach is consistent with that taken at the Paris Diplomatic Conference in 1971, which saved the international copyright conventions, and it is consistent with the principle of non-reciprocity embodied in the GATT via paragraph 5 of the Enabling Clause adopted in 1979.

To the extent that a standard-setting exercise ignores the legitimate needs of the developing countries for differential and more favourable treatment, and overrides the element of consensus that has hitherto characterized the formation of international intellectual property norms, it may well cause disruption to a system that has survived over a century owing to its flexibility and capacity of adaptation to the needs of countries at different levels of development. By the same token, efforts to reach a good faith compromise in which "adequate and effective protection" is correlated with economic status and capabilities could end by reinforcing the commitment of the developing countries to the principles underlying the Intellectual Property Conventions, just as occurred after differential and more favourable treatment was introduced into the Berne Convention and the Universal Copyright Convention (UCC) in 1971.

It may be assumed that all countries need public interest exceptions to the basic norms governing patents and other modalities of intellectual property protection, just as all countries impose immunities and exceptions on copyrightable works in addition to broad fair use exceptions. In this regard, rather than constituting an endless list of specific exceptions, it might facilitate matters if a basic principle were formulated that tied general norms ensuring "adequate and effective" (but not maximum) levels of protection to language that explicitly recognized the developing countries' special needs and requirements. For example, article 14, paragraph 5, of the Subsidies Code requires a developing country to "endeavour to enter into a commitment to reduce or eleminate export subsidies when the use of such export subsidies is inconsistent with its competitive and development needs".

If the TRIPs negotiations are successfully concluded, developing countries will face the need to devise intellectual property systems in response to international requirements, on the one hand, and to pursue their own technological development goals, on the other. The task is difficult, because most of these countries have not yet reached levels of technological development that would permit them to extract the full benefits obtainable from these systems in the immediate future. However, greater benefits may be expected as their economies grow and the scientific and technological infrastructure develops.

The reinforcement and expansion of intellectual property protection in developing countries is not likely to create, of itself, more favourable conditions for technological development. Nor will it necessarily foster FDI and the transfer of technology. Legal protection is to be viewed as just one component of a larger framework conducive to innovation; the general macroeconomic environment, the investment rate, the availability of qualified personnel are far more decisive factors. In this connexion, a major shortcoming of the present negotiations is their narrow focus on the static aspect of intellectual property rights. The dynamic aspects, and particularly those related to technology transfer and diffusion, are virtually absent from the current debate. A new framework should not deny the developing countries the possibility of following the "catching-up" practices successfully followed by the present-day developed countries in their own technological development.

Source: See *Trade and Development Report*, 1991, part III, chapter III.

---

595.   Though greater intellectual property protection may be a necessary condition for the transfer of technology, developing countries argued that it is not a sufficient condition, emphasizing that, in practice, most patents registered in developing countries have remained unexploited (in the sense that they have not led to the creation of domestic production capacity). Thus, the indiscriminate strengthening of intellectual property protection would be unlikely to promote increased diffusion and transfer of technology to most developing countries during the decade, particularly in view of the macroeconomic constraints discussed earlier in this chapter. Instead, the effect would be to elevate the cost of imported products covered by intellectual property protection.

596.   The liberalization of world trade in services can in principle benefit all countries, including developing countries. It has the potential to accelerate the technological development of developing countries in the years ahead by stimulating efficiency in key sectors, improving access to imported technological inputs and providing support to exports. The extent to which this actually happens will be determined by whether the liberalization of services trade through negotiated exchange of concessions adequately takes into account the fundamental asymmetries between developed and developing countries in the existing capabilities of their services sectors, particularly those core sectors such as construction and engineering design services, telecommunications, transport and professional and business services in which the technological dimension is most crucial. Trade liberalization, compelling developing countries to adhere rigidly to principles of national treatment, market access and right of establishment would prevent them from taking measures to build up the technological dynamism of their local services firms. Thus, the recognition that their participation in world services trade is to be provided for through a strengthening of their domestic services sectors and that the negotiated access to their markets under schedules of concessions is to proceed with due respect for national policy objectives and levels of development has been viewed as a positive sign. What this might imply in individual sectors and countries will vary with the level of existing capabilities. As an illustration, qualified application of national treatment in construction and engineering design services could involve measures to prompt foreign companies to make maximum use of locally manufactured equipment and local engineers and technicians and to train local personnel.[214] As suggested by the discussion in section B, the contribution of such measures to technological dynamism and competitiveness will also be influenced by how effectively they are administered.

597.   The drive to circumscribe the use of investment measures - that is, the attachment by Governments of certain conditions to their approval of investments - raises points similar to those discussed above. One position maintains that disciplines should be established across-the-board, in particular on local content and export requirements, on the grounds that such measures distort international trade. A more extreme version of this position would restrict even those investment measures such as joint venture requirements which have no obvious trade-distorting effect on the grounds that they limit the international flow of investment. The alternative view would give scope to developing countries to employ such measures where they deem them necessary in order to ensure the maximum impact of foreign direct investment on development, especially technological development, and to counter any anti-competitive restrictive business practices that might be engaged in by foreign investors. Failure to accord this flexibility for developing countries would be likely to affect those few of them that have been and will continue to be the most successful in attracting foreign investment.

598.   Although possible international accords on the three types of technology-related reforms do not pose a grave risk of seriously limiting access to and raising the cost of technology inflows when such reforms are considered individually (except for intellectual property rights), the picture changes when their combined effect on developing countries is considered. Taken together, the uniform imposition of stricter standards of intellectual property rights enforcement, restriction of performance requirements on investment and (possibly) opening up of developing countries' services sectors before they are on a competitive footing could affect developing countries' technological and economic development prospects by limiting significantly the policy options at their disposal for promoting the development of their industrial and services sectors. In particular, in the case of intellectual property rights and investment performance requirements, the bargaining power of developing country Governments in negotiating foreign investment and technology licensing agreements would be much smaller. By contrast, all countries, and particularly developing countries, could benefit from greater harmonization of the norms and standards for, as well as conditions of access to, trade-related information networks. Currently, the majority are privately owned and managed. As such, they tend to differ in design and operation modes, hardware and software, as well as in the conditions governing access to them. These differences could act as systemic barriers to the entrance of latecomers, particularly developing countries. The establishment of international guidelines in this area could enhance the developing countries' opportunities for accelerated integration in the international trading system.

---

[214] See Y. Soubra, "Construction and engineering design services: issues relevant to multilateral negotiations on trade in services", *Trade in services: sectoral issues* (UNCTAD ITP/26), New York, 1989.

D. TECHNOLOGY AND SUSTAINABLE DEVELOPMENT

599. A major challenge for the world community in the 1990s and beyond is how to elaborate and implement a strategy for sustainable development. Technology occupies a strategic place in the determination of such a strategy. If total world output doubles, trebles or quadruples with the application of the technologies that currently prevail in energy production, transportation, manufacturing, agriculture and other sectors, future generations can experience a sharp deterioration in climate, health and productivity. Technology is both the source of assaults on the ecosystem and the potential solution to the apparent conflict between increased material prosperity for all and improvement in environmental quality.

600. Today, the climate for innovation seems uniquely rich, with some technological revolutions in progress and others just emerging. If environmental goals are integrated in these innovations, the transition to a sustainable future will be faster, cost less and have longer-lasting effects. The prospects for advances in such areas as renewable sources of energy, mass transit, new materials, recycling information technologies and biotechnology offer an unmatched technical potential for environmental improvement which needs to be exploited. Up to now, most environmental technologies have been developed in response to the appearance of environmental problems and had to be retrofitted to existing systems. It need hardly be argued that prevention of environmental degradation, where feasible, is usually more effective and less expensive. Therefore, the challenge will be, not only to encourage these innovations, but also to ensure that environmental considerations are incorporated at an early stage of their development.

601. At the same time, substantial improvements in reducing the emission of pollutants, wasteful consumption of resources and disruption of natural habitats could be made with existing technologies. Examples in agriculture, energy use and materials consumption abound in the literature.[215] If environment-friendly technologies are not being applied, developed and transferred on a large enough scale to slow down environmental degradation, it is not because they do not or could not exist but because the costs and benefits of many production decisions affecting the environment do not accrue to or are not perceived by those who make the decisions. To remedy this situation, experts have identified a variety of policy options to make these costs and benefits explicit and stimulate enterprises and other economic agents to deploy clean, natural resource-conserving technologies. Lack of information, financial constraints, or out-of-date public policy also contribute.

602. The increasingly global character of contemporary environmental problems means that both developed and developing country governments have an interest in establishing the necessary framework for promoting these technologies. However, if the imperative for action is not only to carry conviction for the rest of the world, but also to ensure an equitable utilization of existing resources by all citizens of the world community, it is for the developed market-economy countries to lead and point the way by demonstrating that it is possible to apply modern knowledge to the continued improvement of their living standards without clinging to the outmoded lifestyles associated with the use of the destructive production and consumption technologies that are currently dominant. Furthermore, these countries, by possessing the technological capabilities and the financial means, are in a position, and have the main responsibility, to put the world on a path of sustainable technological development.

603. Promotion of the use of environmentally sound technology in developing countries raises several issues. First, the conditions for the successful transfer, application and development of such technology in developing countries are much the same as those for technology generally. The greater a country's existing knowledge and skill base the greater the ability of its enterprises to select, make efficient use of and adapt and modify imported technology, including the hardware component of more environmentally benign technologies. Environmental concerns strengthen the case for promoting the development of human resources, and more generally, the technological

---

215 G. Heaton, R. Repetto and R. Sobin, *Transforming technology: An agenda for environmentally sustainable growth in the 21st century*, World Resources Institute, April 1991.

dynamism of developing countries. Acceleration of the present low rate of investment relative to the existing capital stock in many developing countries, particularly in developing Africa and Asia, is a must if new, ecologically sound technologies are to be diffused more rapidly.

604.   Second, environmental concerns do not enjoy the same priority in developing as in developed countries; and the focus of these concerns also differs. Beset by the immediately pressing needs of young rapidly growing populations, by financial instability and socio-political turbulence, the planners and leaders of developing countries are likely to have a relatively short time perspective that understandably limits their attention to those environmental problems having immediate consequences for the health or livelihood of their citizens. Their priority requirement is for resources to finance investment in technologies for environmentally sound domestic development.

605.   Third, and related to the preceding points, the resource requirements of developing countries will have to be highly concessional in order to support the added cost of importing environmentally sound technology and of developing the capacity to assess and take decisions on the environmental impact of technology. In particular, the additionality of concessional financing, such as that provided by the recently-created Global Environment Facility, is crucial if developing countries are to divert resources to attacking the more universal problems of ozone layer depletion, global warming, loss of biodiversity and pollution of international waters. Special attention may be given to financing schemes and incentives (tax-credits, tax-exemptions, etc.) for environmentally sound technologies on the grounds that the rise in demand created from such use will provide incentives for the further development of such technologies. But the fragility and vulnerability of developing countries' economies and ecological systems to these problems, irrespective of how remote they may be from more pressing concerns, would make it irresponsible to expect only the industrialized world to deal with them. Assistance from the developed countries can only yield results if there is a will to seek out solutions within developing countries.

606.   Fourth, as mentioned, although clean technologies are available and generally part of the public domain, information about them is not universally accessible. Very often, such technologies are also more efficient and, therefore, not necessarily more costly. More effective arrangements (including the possibility of international register) for the dissemination of information on existing environmentally sound technologies and on the environmental risk of technologies currently on the international market, including information about comparative costs, productivity, etc., are needed in order to guide decision-making in developing countries, as well as other countries. The inclusion of data on "environmental performance" in the information that producers are required to disclose, as is already the case in many countries with energy consumption, nutritional value, unit price, etc. would also enhance transparency in this area.

607.   Fifth, it is difficult to asses the extent, if any, to which the availability of environmentally sound technologies in developing countries is or will be impeded by intellectual property rights protection. Where the process or product know-how is patented, adequate protection is essential if the cooperation of the patent-holder must be sought in order to be able to make effective use of the technology. However, given the growing community of interest that exists in protecting the global environment, it is important to work out principles, such as compulsory licensing, that would apply to such technologies in the future in order to assure that their price provides an incentive to both those who generate them and those who use them.

608.   Sixth, the specificity of environmental conditions in individual developing countries combined with their weak R and D capacities, reinforces the need to channel greater R and D to their technological problems. However, the tendency towards growing involvement of the private sector in R and D (particularly in areas of importance to developing countries, as is the case with agricultural biotechnology) may have the opposite effect, in addition to giving rise to problems of access. The returns from R and D of relevance to developing countries are often too small to justify such investment for large corporations, and the smaller enterprises cannot afford them. Government incentives to private enterprises and new mechanisms for a meaningful involvement of developing countries in the research networks being formed in the developed countries could be envisaged in addressing the problem of inadequate R and D on developing countries' environmental concerns.

609.   Finally, it needs to be reiterated that rapid technological change remains the key force in reconciling economic development with a livable environment. To achieve this objective requires a genuine partnership between developing and developed countries. Building up such a partnership calls for a better understanding of the problems involved. On the one hand, there is still consid-

erable uncertainty about the contribution of the different sources to environmental degradation, the overall size of the different impacts and their future implications for the global environment.[216] On the other hand, one cannot predict future technological advances. Further analytical work, complemented by technical assistance, will contribute considerably to reducing some of these uncertainties and thus improve development options of the developing countries. UNCTAD can and should intensify its work in this vital area.

E. CONCLUSIONS AND POLICY RECOMMENDATIONS

610.   A mixture of success and failure characterizes the technological development experience of developing countries in Africa, Asia and America. Recent history shows that progress in these countries will continue to be determined by a combination of domestic and external forces. Under the influence of structural adjustment programmes, economic policies have been liberalized so as to increase the role of the price mechanism in allocating resources more efficiently. At the same time, efforts by developing countries to attract foreign direct investment and transfer of technology have intensified. But one cannot avoid reiterating the fact that, without decisive steps by the international community to relieve the pervasive effects of excessive debt, the absence of external bank lending and weak commodity prices, risk-averse domestic and foreign enterprises will continue to hold back their spending on the introduction of new products and processes in the industries of these countries, and foreign direct investment and transfer of technology will remain stagnant. Even if the international community produces a workable package of measures to deal with the external financial and other dimensions of the slack economic performance of most developing countries, the cumulative effects from the past of reduced investment in technology are likely to affect future economic growth and therefore dampen the prospects for an acceleration of the inflow of technology in the near future.

611.   The trade impact of global technological advances varies between raw materials and manufactures. Their depressing effect on raw materials demand makes it doubtful that the expected improved growth of raw materials exports from developing countries during the 1990s will regain the pace set in the 1970s. On the other hand, such advances (primarily in computer technologies) have not had and are unlikely to have during this decade the negative impact on manufactured exports of developing countries predicted by some experts. There is a strong possibility that the cost of, and constraints on access to, technology in some sectors for developing countries will increase as a result of both a tendency towards technological alliances with growing cartelization effects and recent trends towards more restrictive intellectual property rights enforcement on the one hand, and relaxation of competition legislation in developed market-economy countries on the other. This may be offset by other forces that are diversifying the sources and driving down the cost of technology. These factors make all the more neccesary national and international measures to promote competition policies and to control restrictive business practices in both product and technology markets.

612.   The growing complexity of the emerging pattern of relationships in international technology trade reinforces the need for elaborating a framework of rules on technology transfer. The failure to adopt such a framework for inter-enterprise and intergovernmental co-operation on the transfer of technology might result in an unbalanced situation to the particular disadvantage of less technologically advanced countries, which might then be required to improve the terms of protection of foreign technologies without a concomitant improvement in the terms of transfer of such technologies.

613.   A framework of rules and procedures would greatly enhance the stability and predictability needed for the free flow of technology among nations, thus benefiting not only technology recipi-

---

[216] For example, carbon-dioxide emissions from deforestation and land use are very uncertain: estimates of net global emissions have ranged between 0 and 2.6 billion tonnes of carbon annually, with recent detailed analysis suggesting 1.0 ± 0.6. Similarly, while it seems certain that increasing concentration of CO2 will be raising the temperature of the earth's surface, the consequences of such an increase are difficult to predict, because they depend on a multitude of factors not easily quantifiable. See Michael Grubb *The Greenhouse Effect: Negotiating Targets*, The Royal Institute of International Affairs, London, 1989.

ents, but also technology suppliers. The efforts undertaken since the 1970s to formulate an international code of conduct on the transfer of technology constitute an attempt at establishing such a framework. However, in order to achieve such an objective, the negotiations on the draft code of conduct would need to take into account the relative shifts in concerns in the area of technology and of technology policies that have occurred since the inception of the negotiations. The nature and contents of the draft code of conduct reflected certain concerns and policy approaches at that time which have since then undergone important changes. At the same time, other needs and concerns have emerged in recent years. These include the pressures for a stronger protection of intellectual property rights, the growing collaboration among enterprises and between enterprises and governments to promote technological innovation, the need to take advantage of opportunities for participation in strategic alliances in the field of technology, the increasing emphasis in the policies of developing countries on attracting foreign investments and promoting technology transfer, the relaxation of controls on restrictive practices in developed market-economy countries, the specific protection régimes and licensing practices relating to new technologies, the increasing concerns about the effects of technology upon the environment, health or safety, the shift in developing countries' technology policies towards advisory services and assistance to local enterprises (rather than the screening of technology transfer contracts) and the emerging opportunities for developing countries' participation in technological co-operative schemes and in joint ventures on research and development.

614.   A global framework of rules and principles on the transfer of technology will have to reflect all these needs and concerns and, at the same time, provide for the normative flexibility and institutional follow-up necessary for the accommodation of further changes in a continuously shifting technological environment. The recent informal consultations on the code of conduct (April 1991) revealed that differences in conceptual approaches, which had in the past made it difficult to agree on the finalization of the negotiations, may have been narrowed down as a result of recent policy developments, both at the domestic and the international levels. Consideration, therefore, may be given to resuming such negotiations on the basis of a fresh approach susceptible to resulting in the formulation of universally acceptable basic rules and principles on technological co-operation and transfer.

615.   Turning to the realm of international trade policy, there is no doubt that progressive trade liberalization and elaboration of disciplines governing trade relations have strong implications for the technological development prospects of developing countries in the 1990s. A positive outcome that takes adequate account of their developmental, trade and technological needs would, by reversing the present tide of protectionism and managed trade, secure greater market access for their exports and, at the same time, have a dynamic impact on their access to technology and on industrial and technological development. The interplay between exports and access to technology points to the fact that participation in trade is an instrument for improving mastery of technology and that, at the same time, the ability to export is not possible without the acquisition of technology. The dynamics of trade and industrialization have a bearing on the development dimension of a number of technology-related trade reforms that have been under consideration in various fora. Of particular relevance is the need to provide for flexibility in favour of developing countries in any future régime on intellectual property rights in view of their special developmental and technological needs. While the possible dilution of some investment measures, such as export and local content requirements, might help to eliminate trade distortions, its impact on access to technology and on the strategies for strengthening of local capacities can be adverse for the developing countries in negotiating terms and conditions.

616.   Quite apart from the preceding issues, the resolution of other international trade policy issues, such as market access for exports, dumping and countervailing measures and safeguards, will have a strong indirect influence on transfer and development of technology in the years ahead. The boost to exports arising from elimination of the panoply of restrictions and trade harassments that have proliferated in recent years could increase the volume of resources available for investment in new technology in developing countries and expose a greater number of their manufacturing enterprises to the necessity of adapting their processes and products to the rigours of competition. For this to happen, they will need the freedom (following the principle of differential and more favourable treatment) to intervene selectively with timebound measures that promote the technological dynamism of their infant industries without being forced to make reciprocal concessions to their developed country partners.

617.   The pervading effect of trade-related, worldwide information networks, many of which are privately owned, will certainly be increasingly felt by developing countries. The present landscape

of such networks is one of fragmented standards and limited access. If left to market forces alone, this situation could lead to further marginalization of developing countries and economies in transition. There is, therefore, need for internationally accepted rules and guidelines that could cover not only norms and standards, but also the conditions governing the access of outsiders (both firms and governments) to such networks. The Conference could take the lead in launching an international initiative in this area.

618.   Governments of the most successful industrializers have all involved themselves actively in support of industrialization. However, one of the arguments of this report has been that not all interventions are efficient and desirable for fostering dynamism. The policies and supportive measures of the poor performers have often been indiscriminate, which suggests that the future pattern of interventions be changed so as to pay closer attention to market signals. As markets and capabilities develop, the need for interventions declines and the feasibility and mix of policy options changes.

619.   In so far as developing country Governments are expected to play a role in guiding the technological transformation of their economies, a re-direction of structural adjustment programmes is called for in order to restore spending on basic infrastructure, training, R and D, information systems, standardization and quality control and other activities that form a part of the framework of incentives to enterprises to invest in new technologies. Related to this is the need for greater caution than at present to ensure that reforms to improve efficiency, such as liberalization of imports and the "rehabilitation" and restructuring of the enterprise sector, are consistent with the longer-term development objective of stimulating technological dynamism and international competitiveness. As an increasing number of developing countries, at different levels of development, are liberalizing their economies and adopting "export-oriented" strategies, there is a need to deepen understanding of the role of policy intervention in building technological dynamism in this new context.

620.   From an action-oriented perspective, the major changes taking place also create fresh opportunities for technological co-operation. Developing countries' continued efforts to promote their technological development in the changing international context require the enhancement of their capacity to deal with the rapid changes in technology, and its impact on international trade and competitiveness, in order to accelerate their technological transformation and expand their exports. Such enhancement will, in general, have to include strengthening their institutional and human-resource base to take advantage of the opportunities arising from the new technologies, and accordingly, adopting policies and measures to stimulate the transfer of technology on equitable terms and conditions and in consonance with their development priorities. Towards this end, it will be essential to strengthen developing countries' technological capacities through targeted national action and international co-operation, as well as the provision of technical assistance support.

621.   The stagnation of technology flows to developing America and Africa and individual countries in Asia suggests the need to explore possible initiatives for revitalizing these flows and stimulating technological co-operation. The Committee on Transfer of Technology, at its eighth session, made several recommendations in this area. The Conference may want to reiterate and strengthen these recommendations. In this context, further action in developed countries might be envisaged for encouraging technology transfer to developing countries, for example tax incentives (e.g. greater possibilities for offsetting losses on investments in developing countries against home-country tax liabilities), investment guarantees and concessional credit for technology transfer (including liberalized credit guarantees on machinery exports). Secondly, consideration could be given to possible measures for encouraging non-commercial forms of enterprise-to-enterprise co-operation in training of engineers, technicians and R and D personnel, either on-the-job or on an exchange basis. The formation of economic groupings among industrialized countries may give an impulse to nearly dormant efforts for increased co-operation among developing countries and their enterprises. The time may be ripe to give renewed consideration to such schemes, especially those involving foreign direct investment, joint R and D and scientific and technical co-operation with other economic groupings.

622.   Increased technological co-operation will depend heavily on the provision of technical assistance to developing countries. There will be a need to: assist developing countries in identifying policy options for the transfer and development of technology, and strengthening institutional, legislative and administrative frameworks, including the capacity to evaluate, select and negotiate technology transfer arrangements; provide technical support in the field of economic and techno-

logical co-operation among developing countries, including schemes involving foreign investment and joint R and D; provide technical assistance concerning the technology dimension of trade in services, e.g. in consulting and engineering design services; assist the least developed and island developing countries undertaking technological and structural change (including qualitative assessments of progress achieved); and to provide technical assistance in identifying the linkages between technology, trade, environment and sustainable development and, by extension, the policies and measures to ensure favourable access to and transfer, adaptation and generation of environmentally sound technology for the developing countries.

623.   Providing technical assistance support for all these actions calls for renewed efforts by all concerned, particularly Governments, enterprises such as equipment manufacturers and consulting and engineering design firms, and universities and R and D institutes.   Priority attention will have to be paid to human resource development programmes aimed at improving the skilled personnel profile at the various levels required for handling technology matters, and to systematically exploring possibilities and modalities for technological co-operation, including co-operation between enterprises from developed and developing countries. UNCTAD could play an important role in continuing and strengthening the provision of technical assistance to developing countries in the areas above.

624.   The role of technology in resolving the apparent conflict between higher standards of living for all and the improvement of environmental quality is primordial. Although the main responsibility for developing and promoting environmentally sounder technologies rests with the developed countries, the increasingly global character of contemporary environmental problems means that both developed and developing-country governments have an interest in ensuring the promotion of such technologies. For developing countries, the promotion of the use of environmentally sound technology presents many of the same problems as technologies more generally, plus additional ones. This would imply concerted action by the international community and the governments of both the developed and developing countries for the acceleration of the transfer and development of environmentally sound technologies to the latter. In this context, consideration could be given to mechanisms for additional concessional financing, not only for attacking the more universal environmental problems, but also for reducing the dependence of their economies on resource exploitation. Special attention should be given to financing schemes and incentives (tax-credits tax-exemptions, etc.) for users in developing countries adopting environmentally sound technologies on the grounds that the consequent rise in the demand for such technologies will provide incentives for their further development by activating "demand-pull" factors for a further spurt in innovation. Secondly, in order to increase the information universally available on environmentally sound technologies, consideration might be given to the creation of an international register in UNCTAD that would include information on environmental risks, comparative costs, productivity, etc. Thirdly, it is important to work out principles which would ensure that the price of environmentally sound technologies provides an incentive to producers of such technologies and is equitable to users. Lastly, further action in developed countries might be envisaged for encouraging technology transfer to developing countries and for promoting increased R and D collaboration on these countries' specific technological problems.

Annex table III-1

R AND D INTENSITY CATEGORY, MARKET SHARES AND GROWTH RATES OF DEVELOPING COUNTRIES' EXPORTS OF MANUFACTURES TO DEVELOPED MARKET-ECONOMY COUNTRIES

R and D intensity category/ Product group	Market share (%)					Value ($ billion)	Growth rate (%)			
	1970	1975	1980	1985	1989	1989	1970-75	1975-80	1980-85	1985-89
High R and D	*2.49*	*6.09*	*9.04*	*12.20*	*14.73*	*347.3*	*43.8*	*30.6*	*12.0*	*23.9*
Aerospace	1.42	2.76	3.05	3.54	2.81	46.4	30.5	28.5	5.5	11.7
Office machines and computers	1.33	6.69	3.84	8.76	22.21	59.4	67.9	7.3	34.9	54.8
Electronic components	10.34	20.97	28.66	28.79	28.30	40.8	42.2	31.5	8.7	19.6
Telecommunication equipment	4.85	10.77	18.94	21.53	19.33	32.6	44.6	33.4	10.9	16.2
Drugs and medicine	6.89	8.18	6.86	4.60	3.61	8.2	24.1	9.8	-4.8	9.8
Scientific instruments	1.32	5.41	9.88	8.85	11.19	38.9	59.5	34.9	.8	19.1
Electrical machinery	1.91	5.16	8.50	15.40	16.48	38.5	46.4	30.5	17.0	21.6
Non-electrical machinery	1.63	3.36	5.78	15.47	14.42	38.3	37.9	28.2	30.1	14.6
Chemicals	.39	.52	3.75	4.20	5.24	44.4	31.3	85.5	3.6	22.8
Medium R and D	*4.34*	*4.44*	*6.27*	*8.33*	*10.12*	*783.8*	*19.8*	*27.3*	*9.2*	*22.1*
Motor vehicles	.22	.59	.92	2.07	3.56	224.8	45.7	29.0	26.1	30.5
Other chemicals	4.37	3.83	4.29	6.15	6.24	150.3	16.9	21.7	9.8	14.8
Other manufacturing industries'	16.47	14.38	15.32	24.47	25.85	88.4	15.3	30.1	6.5	22.7
Other non-electrical machinery	.66	1.27	2.31	5.84	6.29	177.9	35.0	30.7	22.8	19.7
Rubber, plastics	6.07	5.94	8.12	13.06	13.31	38.2	22.5	26.2	12.3	22.2
Non-ferrous metals	30.21	33.70	41.35	31.36	33.77	10.1	10.8	24.3	-13.9	23.2
Other electrical machinery	5.40	9.93	15.85	18.67	25.23	70.4	35.8	27.9	10.5	23.9
Other scientific instruments	0.72	2.19	4.74	7.03	6.94	23.9	46.3	40.7	12.3	26.0

Annex table III-1 (concluded)

R AND D INTENSITY CATEGORY, MARKET SHARES AND GROWTH RATES OF DEVELOPING COUNTRIES' EXPORTS OF MANUFACTURES TO DEVELOPED MARKET-ECONOMY COUNTRIES

R and D intensity category/ Product group	Market share (%)					Value ($ billion)	Growth rate (%)			
	1970	1975	1980	1985	1989	1989	1970-75	1975-80	1980-85	1985-89
Low R and D	*14.97*	*17.49*	*20.05*	*24.41*	*23.70*	*675.3*	*23.3*	*19.7*	*4.0*	*12.7*
Stone, clay, glass	2.78	3.57	5.47	11.36	12.14	32.9	23.4	29.8	15.4	20.1
Food, drink, tobacco	25.17	24.93	20.32	20.47	17.48	132.8	18.0	8.3	-1.0	9.0
Shipbuilding	3.96	3.57	12.15	21.23	36.15	11.8	20.5	30.4	4.0	53.1
Petroleum refineries	29.77	29.34	34.52	37.25	38.21	61.5	31.4	26.0	24.6	-3.7
Ferrous metals	2.86	3.44	5.96	10.55	13.23	71.0	20.9	25.7	9.7	17.5
Fabricated metal products	2.46	3.97	7.62	13.16	14.58	51.0	31.0	33.9	11.3	20.2
Paper and printing	.93	1.50	3.00	3.88	4.43	76.0	29.2	33.1	6.4	22.5
Wood, cork, furniture	14.90	14.96	16.87	20.16	21.73	54.5	17.0	24.3	1.8	21.7
Textiles, clothing, footwear, leather	18.94	25.64	30.30	38.00	39.72	183.8	33.9	21.8	6.7	17.6

Source: UNCTAD secretariat calculations based on United Nations Statistical Office trade data (Comtrade).

Note: The classification to R and D intensity categories is based on the methodology described in *Selected science and technology indicators: recent results, 1979-1986* (Paris: OECD, September 1986) and OECD "Commerce des produits de haute technologie: première contribution à l'analyse statistique des échanges de produits de haute technologie" (DSTI/IND/84.60), Paris, 31 January 1985.

Chapter IV

SERVICES

INTRODUCTION

625.   At the sixth session of the Conference, UNCTAD was assigned the task of studying the role of services in the development process, and in paragraph 105 (19) of the Final Act of UNCTAD VII, the Conference requested UNCTAD to "continue its useful work in the field of services" under its existing mandate, as contained in Conference resolution 159(VI) and Board decision 309(XXX). In the context of overall development objectives, the Secretary-General of UNCTAD was requested: (i) to analyse the implications of the issues raised in the context of trade in services; (ii) to explore appropriate problematics for trade in services, keeping in view the technological changes in the field of services. UNCTAD has explored a variety of aspects of services and trade in services and their role in the development process which has been submitted in reports to the Board or circulated as special publications.[217] The following sections recall briefly some of the findings of these documents: Section A analyses the importance of services in international trade the emerging trends in the services sector; Section B examines the situation of developing countries in the context of the specific characteristics, problems and policy considerations of selected services sectors; Section C summarizes the problems faced by developing countries in strengthening their services sectors and considers possible solutions for them at the national and international levels and outlines areas for future work by UNCTAD.

A. INTERNATIONAL TRADE IN SERVICES AND ITS IMPACT ON DEVELOPMENT

626.   The importance of the services sector in economic growth began to be recognized in the late 1970s. This renewed interest derived from the fact that employment in services had rapidly increased in the developed market-economy countries, largely compensating for the decline in employment in the agriculture and manufacturing sectors.[218] The rise of services in advanced societies was seen by many theorists as a function of rise in income, but it was further argued that productivity in services had a tendency to rise more slowly than in goods, thus leading to a disproportionately fast growth in employment as well as higher costs and prices in comparison to manufacturing. At the same time, note was taken of several new features of services production and trade which enable the sector to overcome the tendency towards increasing costs, particularly the externalization of services inputs into the production process, the use of new managerial approaches, major economies of scale through centralization of functions, and the delivery of services in dispersed outlets. Similarly, authors have noted the role of widespread application of information technologies in services production and transaction, as well as the importance of services for the competitiveness of manufacturing and agricultural sectors.[219]

---

217 For example, Part II of *Trade and Development Report* 1988, (TDR 8), *Trade in Services: Sectoral Issues* (UNCTAD/ITP/26, 1990), *Services in Asia and the Pacific* Volumes I and II (UNCTAD/ITP/51, 1990), and *Mexico: Una Economia de Servicios (UNCTAD/ITP/58, 1991)*.

218 See UNCTAD, *Services in the World Economy* (United Nations Publications, UNCTAD/TDR/8/Offprint, 1989), pp. 139-40.

219 *Ibid*, pp. 141-44.

627.   Special attention is now being given to the factors contributing to a competitive position in world trade in services. Even though natural attributes such as tourist sites and geographical proximity to certain markets can influence competitiveness in certain services, the dynamic changes in production methods and consumption patterns in many of the faster-developing services sectors have pointed to other factors as more crucial in determining competitiveness. Many of these factors are the result of level and pattern of prior development, and are related to resources invested in R & D and education, the state of technological and industrial development, and the state of regulation. The existence of a large domestic market facilitating economies of scale and specialization as well as the accumulation of specific know-how, and the state of domestic regulation are also significant factors in determining competitiveness in many services sectors. As discussed below, a strong services sector, particularly "knowledge-based" services, is an essential component of international competitiveness in manufactures and processed agricultural products. In their absence, it is difficult to imagine how a country would develop its industry and promote the growth of its exports of goods and services.

1. The new international services economy

(a) The services revolution

628.   One of the major changes that led to what has been characterized by many writers as the "services revolution" is the key importance of producer services - i.e. services that are used as inputs into the production process - to international and economic growth. This is largely due to microeconomic factors, notably the tendency toward increasing externalization of services by manufacturing firms, which have enabled the producer services sector to attain greater efficiency through specialization, in addition to allowing substantial operating and research cost reductions for manufacturing firms. The externalization of services inputs, for example, allows firms to meet peaks in demand without undertaking any permanent expansion of staff or any investment in new capital equipment; it also means that they can obtain services from the most efficient providers and are not locked to in-house providers. Information technology has been crucial in this, as the increase in the use and capacity of computers stimulates the externalization process by facilitating the operation of small, specialized service firms. Knowledge-intensive services have become crucial for competitiveness and efficiency in production and trade of both goods and services.[220]

629.   Producer-service inputs are required at various stages in the production process: at the "upstream" stage prior to the production process (e.g. feasibility studies, market research, product design), "onstream production" of goods (e.g. quality control, equipment leasing), "onstream parallel" for the operation of firms (e.g. accounting, personnel management, legal), and "downstream" (e.g. marketing advertising, transportation, distribution). Feedback links between services at these various stages have become a key to competitiveness, as they ensure product acceptability, increased sales, reduced inventory costs, and rapid delivery. To ensure such feedback, firms are increasingly resorting to vertical integration in order to control supply and distribution channels. As noted below, such integrated systems have been enhanced by the use of new technologies. The producer-service sector performs the role of converting technological advances into productive capacity and international competitiveness.

630.   Advanced computer and telecommunications technologies have become crucial determinants of efficiency and competitiveness in a variety of services such as banking, insurance, business services, software services, air transport and tourism. The combination of computer-related technologies and telecommunications has given rise to a number of new services which can be described as 'telematic' services, which play an increasingly greater role in the organization, regulation and delivery of services, expanding the possibility of service transactions beyond the

---

220 Several studies on services -e.g. those by FAST, EEC, United States OTA and the Softnomics Centre in Japan - have stressed the strategic role fo the sector, especially of knowledge-intensive services. See, for a discussion, *Services in the World Economy, op. cit.*, pp. 173- 84.

traditional requirement of simultaneous presence of service provider and consumer. It provides a major mode of delivery in several traditional as well as new services, increasing the tradability of services and modifying the relationship between goods and services by increasing the service content of goods, and providing new service export opportunities.

631.   As a result of this information-intensive transformation, telecommunications infrastructures, traditionally regarded primarily in the light of their public-utility functions, have assumed crucial importance for facilitating trade and for the competitiveness of firms in all sectors, providing a single distribution system for several services, as well as for services essential for trade in goods. The lack of adequate telecommunications infrastructures means exclusion from an increasingly larger number of markets, and the uneven distribution of such infrastructures and systems can impede the contribution of increased services trade to the development process. Human capital, in the form of telematically skilled labour force, has become another important factor determining competitiveness of countries. Knowledge-intensive services can function as a mechanism for organizing human capital in such a way as to adapt technological advances to commercial needs and other national objectives.[221]

(b) The emerging structure of the international services sector

632.   In recent years, the world service markets have increasingly come to be characterized by vertical integration and networking, i.e. the setting-up of systematic linkages among activities within the enterprise, between associated firms and with suppliers and customers. Through networking various service providers coordinate their activities in order to attain economies of scale and scope, to create value added, and to compete against the networks of competitors. While facilitating greater efficiency in the provision of services and often allowing small and remote providers to benefit from electronic distribution networks, networking reduces the incidence of arms-length relations and can also result in greater barriers to entry. Access to information networks involves much more than just "plugging in" but is closely linked to access to and transfer of technology. The competitive position of developing-country firms would be greatly enhanced by the development of public networks (or example public R & D networks along the lines of ESPRIT in Europe) at the world level.[222]

633.   The above-mentioned trends have contributed to the emergence in many services sectors of large transnational firms, often possessing a very large share of the international market. Foreign direct investment (FDI) in services as a ratio of the total world stock of foreign direct investment has increased dramatically over the past two decades - from 25 per cent in 1970 to 50-60 per cent now.[223] A major part is in financial and trade-related services, and foreign affiliates in these sectors appear to be much larger than those in other services sectors. There has been a world-wide expansion of transnational banking networks in the 1970s, and financial corporations have also tended to establish financial affiliates, a process which has been at the heart of the emerging globalization of the world economy. Services FDI in developing countries has been different from that in developed countries, concentrating on construction, tourism, basic financial, services and "trading", i.e. the acquisition of distribution channels. Distribution, rather than material production, has become the "commanding element" in the value-added chains.[224]

634.   In developing countries, affiliates of TNCs can become dominant entities in specific service industries and in segments of service markets, condemning local suppliers to the less lucrative segments of the market. Sustaining such dominance is made possible by the financial strength of TNCs, economies of scale, and the use of superior management, networking and marketing techniques. Anti-competitive policies and restrictive business practices of the TNCs have been detected

---

[221] See *Services in the World Economy, op. cit.*, pp. 174-75. See also UNCTAD, *Technology, Trade Policy and the Uruguay Round* (United Nations Publication, UNCTAD/ITP/23, 1990), pp. 254-60.

[222] See Albert Bressand, "Access to Networks and Services Trade", in UNCTAD, *Trade in Services: Sectoral Issues* (United Nations Publication, UNCTAD ITP/26), pp. 237-42 *op. cit.*; Bressand and Nicolaides, "Networks at the Heart of the Service Economy" in *Strategic Trends in Services*, edited by the same authors, New York, Harper and Row, 1989.

[223] See the *World Investment Report*, 1991, UNCTC document ST/CTC/118 July 1991.

[224] See Bressand in *Trade in Services: Sectoral Issues, op. cit.*

in a variety of service sectors, many of which adversely affect developing countries, but they are often extremely difficult to prosecute under their national competition laws.[225] In addition, the increasing use of networking strategies, aimed at establishing closer links to suppliers "upstream" and customers "downstream", while not constituting RBPs *per se*, tend to create barriers to entry for developing country firms, a phenomenon often described as "systemic barriers". The expansion of TNCs in manufacturing and services has also led to a dramatic rise in intra-corporate service transactions - i.e. the production and consumption of services within corporate structures.

635.   Traditionally, the Government has assumed the major, if not the exclusive responsibility in providing basic infrastructural services, including those that might be termed the "social infrastructure" for economic activities. With the growing complexity of the services sector, the role of the Government is changing from a provider of basic services, to that of a regulator, aimed at ensuring the availability of competitive services on an equitable basis.

636.   The services sector has been subject to extensive regulation in most countries, but relatively more so in developed countries, reflecting the complexity of the economy. Restrictions on international trade in services are frequently associated with the principle of "use national" which is similar to the principle of "buy national" in goods - as, for example, in shipping and civil aviation. In insurance, domestic firms are often provided with a monopoly access to the domestic market as there are restrictions on insurance policies that can be taken out overseas. There are also government restrictions on trade in labour services which are embodied in immigration policies or consular practices that restrict even the temporary movement of labour across national boundaries. Restrictions on international investment in services, on the other hand, seek to regulate either the entry of foreign firms or the operations of already established foreign firms, in much the same way as regulations on foreign investment in the sphere of goods. However, State intervention in the services sector, particularly in public utilities, is often premised on coinsiderations of social welfare without differentiating between national and foreign firms.

(c) Trends in services trade[226]

637.   In 1989, world exports of services are estimated to have amounted to US$ 608.5 billion, the bulk of this - i.e. US$ 485.4 billion (80 per cent) - being accounted for by developed countries. World imports of services are estimated to account for US$ 614.5 billion, of which US$ 483.4 billion (80 per cent) was traded by developed countries. For developing countries, travel was the highest item in their exports of services, accounting about 18 per cent of the world total. The exports of "other services" and transportation" from developing countries constitued about 13 per cent and 14 per cent, respectively, of the world total. Although international trade in services is dominated by developed countries some developing countries experienced a significantly high growth of trade in services during the second half of the 1980s.[227]

638.   In 1989, France, the United Kingdom and the United States were the 3 largest exporters of services, and the 13 largest exporters were developed countries. Developing countries which were included among the 20 largest exporters of services were Mexico, the Republic of Korea and Singapore. The Federal Republic of Germany, Japan and the United States were the 3 major importers of services, and the largest 14 importers were developed countries. Mexico the Republic

---

[225] See P. Brusick, M. Gibbs, M. Mashayekhi, "Anti-Competitive Practices in the Services Sector, Uruguay Round" *Further Papers on Selected Issues* (UNCTAD ITP/42, 1990).

[226] Analysis of trade in services is hindered by the unreliability of services statistics due to (a)different methods of classification and reporting used by different countries, (b) lack of disaggregation, and (c) the inability to identify sources and destinations of service transactions with precision. See Maria Dunavolgli: "Statistics on Service Trade in Asia", in *Services in Asia and the Pacific* Vol. II, UNCTAD ITP/51, Vol. II., Geneva 1991. Furthermore, a high percentage of the international service transactions take place within or among TNCs, and thus usually goes unrecorded. Payments of royalties and fees linked to the sale of intellectual property also pose problems since these are sometimes considered as a return on property and in other instances as trade in services. Moreover, unrequited transfers and labour remittances often represent exports of services. The only international comparable overall figures on trade in services are derived from the balance of payments figures of the IMF. For many reasons, however, these appear to understate international service flows especially if the definition of trade in services, emerging in the context of the Uruguay Round is adopted.

[227] In identifying the major exporters and importers of services among developing countries data for 1988 were used due to the lack of the necessary data. Hong Kong is excluded from the observation as the territory does not report its balance-of-payment statistics to the IMF.

of Korea, Singapore and Yugoslavia, were among the 20 largest importers. Among developing countries, Mexico, the Republic of Korea and Singapore, were the top 3 exporters of services in 1988, and the 3 largest importers were the Republic of Korea, Saudi Arabia and Yugoslavia. The 20 largest exporters and importers of services are indicated in the Statistical Annex.

639.   Some developing countries experienced a remarkable growth in trade in services during the period between 1984 and 1988. For example, Ecuador increased its exports of "shipping" services by the annual growth rate of 24 per cent, and exports continued to rise in 1989. Brazil, Côte d'Ivoire, Morocco and the Republic of Korea, increased their imports of "shipping" services, recording a 10 per cent to 17 per cent annual growth rate. Bahrain and Malta expanded their exports of "other transport" services at the annual growth rates of 50 per cent and 25 per cent, respectively. Chile, Ethiopia and Mauritius, increased their exports of passenger services with the annual growth rates of 40 per cent for Mauritius and 20 per cent for Chile and Ethiopia, while Pakistan and Senegal increased their imports of "passenger" services with the annual growth rate of 20 per cent. Colombia, Cyprus and Egypt expanded their exports of "travel" by 20 per cent to 28 per cent annual growth rate, while the Bahamas, Brazil, Côte d'Ivoire, Pakistan, Peru, and Thailand significantly increased their imports under the "travel" item. Colombia, Jordan, Argentina, Morocco and Dominican Republic increased the exports of "other services" rapidly recording the annual growth rate of 13 per cent to 20 per cent, while Chile, Côte d'Ivoire, Peru, Thailand and Venezuela increased their imports of "other services" by the annual growth rate of 15 per cent to 20 per cent.

640.   Services exports were a major source of foreign-exchange earnings for a number a island countries, particularly for many Caribbean countries. The service exports in these countries represented from 45 per cent to 90 per cent of their total exports in 1988, and they were equivalent to 20 per cent to 50 per cent of the gross domestic product. Service imports in these countries accounted 20 per cent to 30 per cent of their total imports. For these island countries the item "travel" was by far the most important source of their foreign-exchange earnings. The contribution of services exports to foreign-exchange earnings also appeared highly important for other developing countries such as Egypt, Jordan, Nepal, Tunisia, and Yemen, accounting 40 per cent to 90 per cent of their total exports in 1988. Available figures for these countries indicated that the ratios of service exports over gross domestic product were relatively high in Jordan and Tunisia accounting 18 per cent to 24 per cent. In Egypt and Jordan their exports of services were diversified while the other countries indicated the concentration of export on particular services, i.e., "travel" and "other services" in Nepal, "travel" in Tunisia, and "other services" in Yemen.

641.   However, for a large number of developing countries, services are a deficit item in the balance of payments. Though services contribute substantially to output as well as to employment in many developing countries, they are unable to satisfy the demand for specialized knowledge emanating from other sectors. In fact, the growth of employment and output in services in these countries is largely attributable to the supply of low-productivity services arising from rapid urbanization and lack of alternative employment opportunities in the agricultural and industrial sectors, rather than from demand on the part of producers or final consumers. This growth does not represent a proportionate level of skill formation and is not integrated with manufacturing or with other sectors.

642.   Although international transactions on labour services are usually separated from services[228] in the balance-of-payments accounts, as noted above, in some instances the frontier between labour remittances and "other services" is rather arbitrary. There is, however, another category of developing countries which run surpluses in services primarily derived from the outward movement of persons in the form of temporary movement of labour, as well as the inward movement - as tourists, and from the movement of goods - e.g. canals, maritime and airport facilities. This form of participation in the international division of labour makes countries paticularly vulnerable to events of a political nature over which they have no control, and to the vagaries of the economies or immigration policies of the countries that are hosts to their nationals. Such countries are giving priority to policies designed to channel the acquired skills of returning migrants into new service exports (as well as to obtaining concessions with respect to this "mode" of service supply in the Uruguay Round). Relevant data indicated that the developing countries of which revenues from labour services exceeded one quarter of the total exports of merchandise and services in 1988 include: Lesotho, Egypt, Sudan, Mali, Pakistan and Bangladesh. The coun-

---

[228] They are included in "Labour Income" or "unrequited Transfer" in the IMF Balance-of-Payments Statistics. There are a number of countries which report the transactions to "Other Services".

tries of which external revenues from labour services exceeded the total revenues from their service trade include: Bangladesh, Bolivia, Burundi, Cape Verde, Egypt, El Salvador, Guatemala, Honduras Morocco, Nicaragua. Pakistan, Sri Lanka, and Yemen.

2. International policy developments and issues since UNCTAD VII

(a) The Uruguay Round negotiations

643. The current focus of the Uruguay Round negotiations is on the liberalization of regulations which impede trade in services on the basis of offers and requests on a sectoral or sub-sectoral basis, within a framework of unconditional most-favoured-nation treatment and universal coverage.[229] Commitments to liberalization are taking place with respect to four modes of delivery or supply of the service: the movement of capital, in the form of commercial presence; the temporary movement of labour; the movement of consumers; and "cross border" supply which is being defined as that where no "persons" (natural or juridical) cross the frontiers - in practice mainly services supplied through telecommunications concessions. The result will be to bring within in the scope of a framework multilateral rights and obligations aspects of investment immigration, communications, monetary, policy etc. The developing countries' ability to derive meaningful benefit from such access is impeded by the weakness of their service sectors enterprises, which, faced with the dominant market power and technological advantages of developed-country TNCs, lack the capacity to deliver their services to foreign markets. With the exception of those relating to labour movements, the liberalization of regulations cannot generally be expected to lead to an increase in the share of developing-country suppliers in world services markets. However, there are some highly regulated sectors, notably air transport, where the provision of more liberal access, including on a preferential non-reciprocal basis, to developing-country suppliers could have a positive effect.

(b) Regional groupings

644. The position of developing-country service suppiers in the world market and their access to markets are influenced by the treatment of trade in services in regional arrangements, notably by the consolidation of the single European market, and the inclusion of services within the Canada/United States Free Trade Agreement (and presumably their inclusion in future free trade arrangements negotiated by the United States). Given that no multilateral framework of bound access commitments exists for trade in services comparable to that in GATT, the potential for trade diversion by regional arrangements would seem to be much greater than for trade in goods. The regulatory structure for services being evolved in the European Economic Community has strongly influenced positions in the Uruguay Round[230] and in addition, has provoked a flood of foreign direct investment in the EEC services sector.[231] Some of the most significant market access issues in the 1992 context relate to air transport, computer reservation systems, financial services and maritime transport. Another crucial set of issues for developing countries relates to an eventual common EEC policy for the temporary movement of labour.

645. The Canada/United States FTA primarily involves an exchange of national treatment between the two countries with respect to most services, with, however, very notable exceptions (e.g. transportation). It extends to the movement of labour in the form of specific provisions on the temporary entry of "business persons". While the initial impact of this FTA on trade in services of developing countries may be relatively minor, it establishes a mechanism for intensified prefer-

---

229 See discussion in chapter II on international trade.
230 See R. Grey "1992, Services and the Uruguay Round" in *Trade in Services: Sectoral issues op.cit.*).
231 See World Investment Report 1991, *op. cit.*

ential terms of market access. The Uruguay Round framework should provide a means of pre-empting discriminatory measures which could have an adverse effect on developing-country services exports[232] to Canada and the United States.

(c) Services and sustainable development

646. Environmental degradation in the developing countries arises in part from the inadequacy of essential services such as transportation and public utilities. Differences in standards of environmental protection may result in developing countries becoming the location of the more polluting components of the production chain with the more lucrative and "environment friendly" "upstream" and "downstream" services being located in the developed countries. Regulations imposed to protect the environment can also result in barriers to developing country trade in services, notably air tranport, where developing countries will be required to make large investments in new aircraft to meet more strict noise pollution standards in developed countries. The expansion of tourism exports has, in many developing countries entailed considerable damage to the environment, and their efforts to protect their environment while expanding tourism earnings seem to warrant the support of the international community.

647. Furthermore, the science of "environmental management" is rapidly evolving into a producer service in its own right, and the development of such indigenous services in developing countries seems not only to be essential for their own sustainable development but also to present potential export opportunities.

(d) Services and the international division of labour

648. The division of labour between developed and developing countries has traditionally taken the form of industry versus primary production, or that of mature industries versus labour-intensive industries. However, this division of labour is now being influenced by competitiveness in services. The developed countries have managed to create, control and retain within their borders those services which constitute not only the highest value-added segments of the value-added chain, but also those most strategic in character with respect to innovation (e.g. R & D, strategic planning, design, engineering, etc.) and to market control (e.g. marketing, distribution). This has enlarged the gulf between developed and developing countries, both in terms of their competitiveness in international trade and their ability to derive value added from such trade. The strengthening of the services sectors in developing countries and the increasing participation of developing countries in international trade in services would seem vital to the success of any initiatives to improve the position of developing countries in the international division of labour.

649. In situations where free trade in services has been largely attained, it has been found that a concentration of services firms in large metropolitan areas, near the headquarters of large firms, has occured, so as to take advantage of economies of scale and specialization, as well as of proximity to centres of decision-making.[233] Thus, the peripheral regions remain the most disadvantaged, where the lack of development of an industrial base or the lack of integration in the structure of the industry has hindered the spontaneous development of producer services. Such regions are characterized by branch plants dependent on external inputs and decision-making, small-sized local firms aimed at local markets, and fragmentation in industrial structure. They are caught in a vicious circle, whereby the limited regional demand does not stimulate local supply and the absence of external services further limits industrial growth, and the resultant overall stagnation worsens unemployment.

---

232 Peter Burn and Peter Clark "Canada-United States FTA and its Impact on Developing Countries" (UNCTAD ITP/42 op. cit.)

233 H. Howells, "Technological innovation, industrial organization and location services in the European Community. Regional development prospects and the role of information services", FAST occasional paper 142, Commission of the European Communities, Brussels, April 1987.

650.   These tendencies within industrialized countries have caused concern to developing countries. They fear that their peripheral position in the international chain of value added will be exacerbated by liberalization of trade in services. They believe this process would leave them with the least value-added and the least competitive activities, in the primary and the secondary sectors, and oblige them to import an increasing amount of services from the central regions, merely to remain competitive in international trade; they would thus remain 'captive suppliers' of given products and inputs. However, while it is true that the application of producer services has resulted in a continued reduction of the labour content in the productive process, and international competitiveness can no longer be based exclusively on low-cost labour, it is also true that low cost labour can provide the developing countries with opportunities for exports of skilled and semi-skilled services where they have a comparative advantage.

B. SECTOR-SPECIFIC CONSIDERATIONS

651.   The following paragraphs summarily address the major issues facing the increased participation of developing countries in trade in selected individual services sectors.[234]

1. Financial services, including insurance

(a) Banking services

652.   International trade in banking services takes place by means of both cross-border transactions and the provision of such services through a commercial presence in the importing country. In practice the latter form of trade cannot be separated from foreign direct investment. With the enhanced telecommunication and computer links that now exist, a large number of capital and expertise-intensive activities can be undertaken without significant personal contact between the consumer and the provider, assuming capital movements are not controlled. However, several banking services still require a high degree of personal contact. For these services, the establishment of local production facilities, especially through foreign direct investment, is the principal means of extending sales to foreign markets.

(i)   Recent trends in liberalization and regulatory convergence

653.   Liberalization of international trade in banking services is strongly influenced by the on-going internationalization of financial services in the OECD countries and the broader movement towards more open markets and regulatory convergence. While the internationalization of banking in the OECD area would not have begun in the absence of government measures making it possible, internationalization in turn has generated pressures on policies in the regulatory field. Differences in national regulations can be a source of competitive advantages and disadvantages to banks in international markets, thus constituting a force for increased regulatory convergence.

654.   At the national level the resulting trend has been generally in the direction of a reduction of controls over banks. But there is also recognition that deregulation needs to be accompanied by steps ensuring that banks are subject to stronger and more uniform regimes of prudential

---

[234] There are a number of important sectors not discussed, including (a) processing (maquiladoras); (b) retailing and distribution; (c) printing and publishing. These are examined in certain national contexts in UNCTAD publications, such as Mexico, Una Economía de Servicios, *op. cit.*, and Services en la República Dominicana, *op. cit.* In addition, maritime transport has been treated as a separate issue.

supervision.[235] Measures in pursuit of this objective at an international level have entailed an extension of co-operation among countries' regulators. Notable manifestations of the process are various initiatives under the auspices of the Basle Committee on Banking Regulations and Supervisory Practices concerning such subjects as the distribution of supervisory responsibilities for international banks between authorities in parent and host countries, and the international convergence of measurement and minimum levels for banks' capital. This combined movement towards greater liberalization and regulatory convergence presupposes a certain degree of homogeneity among the economies of the countries in question. One should thus not anticipate an analogous process in the case of banking relations between OECD countries, on the one hand, and developing ones or the countries of Central and Eastern Europe, on the other. Here account must be taken of the much more disparate levels of both financial and overall economic development.

(ii)   Structure of markets

655.   Most developed countries have systems of nation-wide banking (the United States being the most notable exception). The European Economic Community (EEC) is moving towards cross-border provision of international banking services in the unified market of its twelve member countries. Of particular importance in this context is the Second Banking Coordination Directive. This Directive specifies the conditions under which a credit institution authorized in one member State (including credit institutions owned or controlled in non-member States) may offer a full range of financial services directly to customers in other member States without further authorization (the "single passport"). The banking régime in the EEC, which has been described as one of the most open banking markets in the world, contrasts with that of the other major financial powers. In the United States there is a sharp division under the Glass-Steagall Act between banking and dealing in securities, and banks may be authorized and regulated by individual states. A new proposal of the Treasury would reform banking regulations to allow universal banking in the United States. In Japan, the banking and securities markets have traditionally been separated and access to the market has been based on reciprocity. The Government, however, is considering relaxation of the separation of commercial and investment banking.[236]

656.   Reciprocity considerations shaped the debate leading to the formulation of the Second Banking Coordination Directive (which will come into effect in 1993). These reflected concern that foreign banks should not be given access to the "single passport" if their home countries did not provide equivalent treatment to EEC banks. Although the original, more stringent reciprocity proposals have been somewhat diluted, the Directive contains provisions for restricting market access in the case of countries which do not provide to EEC banks "effective market access comparable to that granted by the Community" and "national treatment offering the same competitive opportunities as are available to domestic credit institutions". Moreover, in such cases the EEC may initiate bilateral negotiations designed to redress the situation faced by its banks. These provisions of the Directive are applicable to developing countries.[237]

(iii)   Benefits and costs of a more liberal regime

657.   Liberalization of international trade in banking services generally entails both costs and benefits. The divergent positions of different groups of countries participating in the negotiations at the Uruguay Round have concerned the respective weights to be given to these costs and benefits, and the nature of the measures required if liberalization is to lead to favourable balance between them.[238] In arguments supporting liberalization the emphasis is on the way in which barriers to trade in banking services restrict the choices of economic agents, thereby raising their costs and

---

235 Accentuated by the recent BCCI scandal.

236 See the Japan Research Institute "Service in the Japanese Economy", in *Services in Asia and the Pacific* UNCTAD ITP 51 Vol. II.

237 See R. de C. Grey: 1992, Financial Services, and the Uruguay Round, UNCTAD Discussion Paper, 1991.

238 See Andrew J. Cornford "The Multilateral Negotiations on Banking Services" UNCTAD discussion paper, April 1991 and by the same author "Notes on Multilateral Framework on Trade in Banking Services" in Uruguay Round: *Further Papers on Selected Issues*, UNCTAD ITP 42, *op. cit.*

otherwise reducing their opportunities to increase their incomes. Thus, for example, it is pointed out that restrictions on the establishment of foreign banks lead via lower levels of competition to reduced innovativeness and microeconomic efficiency in a country's financial sector. Similarly, operating restrictions can lead, via the increased costs imposed on the banks affected, to higher interest rates and other charges to borrowers and to lower levels of lending. The dangers of liberalization, on the other hand, stem from potential loss of autonomy and flexibility in macroeconomic and development policies, and from harmful forms of competition. Key areas of economic policy which may be affected by liberalization include exchange control, monetary policy and the allocation of credit. Moreover, liberalization is capable of sharply reducing or eliminating the scope for providing infant-industry support to national financial institutions and thus harming the development of indigenous banking systems. While developing countries have not denied the potential benefits from a measure of liberalization, they have emphasized the need to maintain control over the process, so that its costs are minimized and policy autonomy is not threatened.

(iv) Policy considerations

658.   Technology and financial strength are perhaps the most important problems faced by developing countries in attaining competitiveness in the financial services sector. The use of telematic technologies in effecting long-distance transactions and of electronic equipment in the delivery of a large number of banking services to the customer is of crucial importance in this sector. Furthermore, in most developing countries there is a great need for increasing the range of financial instruments available in the market, as well as for extending the banking network and its services to larger sections of the population. There is also an urgent need for transfer of skills and of banking techniques, and a controlled liberalization of international trade in financial services may assist in this.

659.   Developing countries, however, need to ensure that during financial liberalization cognizance is taken of the importance of autonomy in monetary and credit policies, prudential considerations, the governability of foreign banks and national development objectives. Financial services play a pivotal role in economic development. Liberalization must not adversely affect national financial institutions and the overall general well-being of the economy.

660.   Thus, commitments under an agreed framework for trade in services need to be compatible with the flexibility required by governments and monetary authorities in developing countries for the pursuit of autonomous monetary policies and other measures influencing the pace and direction of lending. For this reason governments may decide to limit the entry of foreign banks to certain banking sub-markets or to grant market access only subject to operating restrictions. Particular importance under the heading of monetary policy attaches to exchange control. Liberalization of several categories of international banking transaction, especially those which would be classified as cross-border trade, is linked in many ways to the incidence of a country's exchange-control regime. There are now indications of more general acceptance at the Uruguay Round negotiations that the provisions of the framework should not take precedence over the rights and obligations of member countries of the IMF under its Articles of Agreement concerning the use of exchange controls and exchange restrictions.

661.   Regimes of prudential regulation in developing countries are frequently rudimentary. Thus, commitments under a services framework should not impede the elaboration and strengthening of these regimes. Authorities in developing countries tend to feel concern as to the governability of foreign banks. Sources of this concern include the possible use by foreign banks of their international networks to evade taxes and regulations regarding levels of foreign-exchange exposure, maturity mismatching, etc. Difficulties in this area have recently been experienced by regulatory authorities in OECD countries, and a services framework should accommodate regulatory responses to the problem of foreign banks' governability.

662.   In the provision of many services, indigenous banks in developing countries are characterized by competitive weaknesses in relation to their counterparts from OECD countries. The latter benefit from advantages deriving from their international networks and relationships with other banks as well as from their longer involvement in banking business generally. In view of the resulting differences in levels of efficiency and expertise, measures furnishing protection and support to indigenous institutions are a frequent feature of policies towards the banking sector in developing countries.

663.   For the purposes of a framework for trade in services it is important to make a clear distinction between "market access", which covers the right of entry to particular banking sub-markets, and "national treatment", which concerns the treatment received from the authorities by a supplier of banking services after the granting of such access. Control over market access is the policy instrument perhaps most crucial to enabling governments in developing countries to choose the banking regimes which they believe to be most appropriate to their particular circumstances and needs. Banking consists of several sub-markets, and the access granted to foreign banks generally applies only to certain of them. Control over such access makes it possible for governments to pursue policy objectives in the areas mentioned above. Moreover, even in cases where access to certain sub-markets has been granted to foreign banks, infant-industry policies aimed at redressing the competitive weaknesses of indigenous banks may require certain deviations from national treatment.

664.   Progressive liberalization of banking services in developing countries must go hand in hand with the strengthening of indigenous banking systems. Thus, such liberalization should generally be a gradual process in which admission of foreign banks and relaxation of controls on banking transactions are used as instruments for stimulating greater efficiency among domestic institutions, while avoiding destructive competition, and for achieving transfers of technology and skills.

(b) Insurance

665.   International operations connected with insurance and having an impact on the balance of payments of countries are common. A distinction should be made, however, between primary (direct) insurance activities and reinsurance activities. The first category of international operations results from the inability of a national market to offer adequate risk coverage. The second category covers reinsurance operations which, by their very nature, are international. Reinsurance is a mechanism for the distribution and sharing of risks, and provides a protection to a primary insurer by transferring part or all of the risk to another. It can be described as trade on a secondary market of insurance contracts issued by a primary insurer, i.e. trade in insurance services.

(i) Trends in the market

666.   With the ever-increasing number, size and complexity of risks insured and the emergence of risks of an international character, the trend of internationalization has been enhanced in the insurance sector. The role of reinsurance has grown steadily. Reinsurance has been traditionally much less regulated, both in domestic and international markets, than direct insurance.   This greater freedom has permitted reinsurance groups to play a more active role in trade in insurance services. The major international brokers play a very important role in trade in insurance services. The ability of the major brokers to assist multinationals, industrial and commercial groups derives from the fact that they have built up networks of offices throughout the world which can provide risk-management advice, local insurance market knowledge and assistance in the settlement of claims. They have played an increasing role in assisting multinationals to put together their global insurance programmes and have also played a major role in the complex reinsurance networks that have been set up.   There has been a growing tendency for large corporations to set up their own insurance companies, so-called captive insurance companies, through which they can channel part of their corporate insurance needs. These companies, generally located in offshore centres, are however not allowed to participate in the local business. Assuming liberalization of trade in insurance services, many firms will need only one insurer instead of going to each country and buying local policies for each location.

Table IV-1

Concentration of the world reinsurance market in 1986

Number of companies	Share of world market *a* (percentage)	Countries of origin
4	30.3	Fed. Rep. of Germany (1), Switzerland (1), United States (2)
8	40.7	Fed. Rep. of Germany (1), Switzerland (1), United States (4), United Kingdom (1), Sweden (1)
16	53.6	Fed. Rep. of Germany (5), Switzerland (1), United States (5), United Kingdom (1), Sweden (1), Japan (3)
32	70.6	Fed. Rep. of Germany (6), Switzerland (2), United States (11), United Kingdom (1), Sweden (1), Japan (7), France (3), Italy (1).

Source: Calculated from company data published in *ReActions*, March 1988.
a Share in world's top 100 reinsurers.

Table IV-2

Insurance density in selected countries

(Gross premiums written as a percentage of GNP)

	12 DMECs				12 developing countries		
Country	1987	1985	1983	Country	1987	1985	1983
Fed. Rep. of Germany	6.40	5.90	5.83	Brazil	0.86	0.85	0.90
France	5.06	4.50	4.08	Chile	2.20	2.16	1.75
Italy	2.35	2.49	2.25	Colombia	1.53	1.47	1.34
Japan	8.69	6.94	5.90	Egypt	1.05	1.00	0.93
Netherlands	6.29	5.60	5.57	India	1.29	1.22	1.22
Norway	5.08	4.38	4.20	Indonesia	0.92	0.76	0.73
Portugal	2.69	2.73	2.85	Mexico	1.02	1.01	0.90
Spain	3.31	1.89	1.79	Morocco	1.88	1.84	1.90
Sweden	4.49	4.72	3.94	Peru	1.08	1.29	1.52
Switzerland	8.02	7.07	6.56	Philippines	1.78	1.40	1.86
United Kingdom	8.35	7.11	6.35	Rep. of Korea	8.85	6.92	5.28
United States	9.07	7.52	6.90	Singapore	2.78	2.40	2.52

Source: Sigma, Swiss Reinsurance Company (May 1983, April 1985, May 1987 and March 1989).

(ii) Regulation

667. There is today general agreement that supervision of financial services including insurance is a fundamental requirement for the sound development of these activities. It would not be realistic to expect a general agreement on the methods or extent of State intervention but the overall goal falls into two basic motives: (a) the protection of the consumer's interests and the soundness of the institutions (micro-economic supervision); and (b) the recognition of the role of financial services in the process of economic growth (macro-economic supervision). Laws and directives

exist in almost all countries. The few exceptions which do exist do not invalidate the rule that when the volume of transactions reaches a certain level, legislation must be enacted to provide for some degree of supervision of the activities. Moreover, the spectacular growth of the financial services industry during the past half century may be said to be closely connected with the existence and efficacy of the legislation and supervision to which the State has made it subject.

668.   Regulations vary from country to country because of differing national goals in protecting the consumer, relating investment controls to national objectives and countries seeking to protect their domestic industries. In a world where cross-border financial transactions are expected to grow rapidly, the disparities in regulatory regimes may become difficult to maintain. It is clear that the regulatory authorities of a single open economy concerned with the micro-prudential protection have a much more difficult task than would their counterparts in a closed economy. Similarly, macro-prudential oversight of the financial system in a single national economy becomes increasingly problematic as the economy becomes more open.[239] The competition between regulatory systems will necessarily be accompanied by distortion in competition. The principle of mutual recognition of each other's national regulations would be a step in the right direction. However recognition frequently engenders anxiety that quality standards may be lowered. Consequently, minimal harmonization is an expression of mistrust on the part of the "high standard countries" vis-à-vis the requirements made by other individual national legislation. In this vision, regulation with respect to the licensing, capital and reserve requirements, management qualities and the like, function as inquiring instruments about the minimal quality of the financial intermediaries.[240] In the insurance sector the principle of mutual recognition is far from been accepted although it would certainly be a desirable objective for international transactions such as reinsurance activities.[241]

669.   Since the developing countries are moving progressively towards a more detailed supervision of the operation of financial intermediaries, administrative services responsible for this supervision are becoming better equipped to cope with their complex tasks. Where the supervisory services are for one reason or another unable to carry out the tasks for which they were set up, the resulting distortions are likely to render the law inoperative and the purposes of the legislation are then frustrated. Many inefficiencies are less a function of ownership than of government regulation and market structure. Adequate regulation of an industry requires so much information that outright ownership is sometimes likely to be more efficient. In some cases, information costs are considerably high for State regulation and establishing effective regulation of the privatized firms may prove more demanding of the State's administrative capabilities than operating a State-monopolistic institution. On the other hand, if the supervisory personnel is highly qualified, both personally and professionally, it can usefully fill gaps in the legislation and become, especially in developing countries, one of the main instruments available to the State for promoting the rational development of financial intermediaries. Co-operation among regulators of different countries should not be viewed only as an exchange of information but more attention should be paid to the exchange of experience and human resources development. The need for education is even greater than the present situation would indicate.

(iii) Policy considerations

670.   The importance of the insurance sector for trade and development was formally acknowledged at the first session of the Conference, which stated that "a sound national insurance and reinsurance market is an essential characteristic of economic growth". Since then, insurance laws and regulations have been enacted to establish stricter supervision and control. As the governments of many developing countries believed that the financial system they had inherited could not be made to serve the country's development needs adequately, they have in the past 30 years directed considerable efforts to change the structure of the financial system and controlled its operations to channel savings to such investments which were considered a priority in their development programmes. To achieve better performance of the insurance markets, nationals established domestic insurance enterprises to limit the operations of foreign companies.

---

[239] Bryant, op.cit.

[240] Regulation is seen as possessing an aspect of public good. Holcombe, A.G. and Holcombe, L.P. "The Market for Regulation", Journal of Institutional and Theoretical Economics, vol. 142, 1986, pp. 684-696.

[241] UNCTAD, Reinsurance Security, Geneva, TD B C.3 221, 1987.

671.   As recognized in the Uruguay Round negotiations on trade in services, progressive liberalization needs to be pursued in this sector through rules, modalities and procedures with due respect to national policy objectives and taking into account the level of development of individual signatories. Certain developing countries are offering to liberalize components of their insurance sectors in this context. Many countries consider that the existence of strong national companies is an essential component of their economic and even political independence. Any special efforts which have been made to develop a local market should be taken into account. This argument is certainly not confined to the markets of developing countries. Policies to mobilize national and international production resources in accordance with national objectives will have to reflect the existing structure and particular character of national markets. In some countries, it will be noted that the rigidity of existing structures is largely due to the application of protective policies that may result in a lack of drive in the protected sector. In other countries, market structures are so designed as to give the market the necessary strength. To the extent that the development of the insurance sector reflects a country's economic growth, it may be forecast that such markets are, or in the short term will be, in a position to benefit from an international liberalization of insurance services. In many developing countries, for historical reasons or owing to a lack of adequate administrative and legislative measures, insurance markets are characterized by the existence of too large a number of small domestic companies with low retention limits. The conditions for healthy competition between companies from these countries and companies from developed countries do not exist. In general, developing countries show a low insurance density which can be expected to increase rapidly with economic growth, making many developing countries extremely attractive potential markets for insurance, a fact that should be taken into account in negotiations of specific commitments in this sector.[242]

2. Telecommunications

(a)   The dual role of telecommunications

672.   Telecommunications has a dual function as a service sector: it is a service in itself, and it is a "mode of delivery" or distribution channel for the flow of information essential for the cross-border provision of other services. Traditionally, the telecommunications sector has been regarded as a public service with vital implications for national security , and the provision of basic services - e.g. voice telephony, telegraphy and telex - has been viewed in a public-utility rather than in a trade context, with government monopolies being the rule rather than the exception. Although privatization of many such monopolies, and the opening of the sector to private enterprise more generally, has recently been taking place in many countries, for developing countries, the public-utility function remains paramount, and is dominated by the pressing need to improve infrastructures.[243] Consequently, adopting a "cost-based" approach in the pricing of telephone calls is often not prevalent in developing countries, for whom the principal aim is the provision of services to a wider range of the population. For example, the cross-subsidization of local calls and infrastructure development by long-distance calls is a normal practice.

---

[242] See for example, Un Hoe Park "Trade in Insurance in Korea" in Services in Asia and the Pacific Vol. I., *op. cit.*

[243] "Developing countries, which account for 70 per cent of the world population and 20 per cent of the world GDP use 7 per cent of the world's telephones. There are more telephones in Tokyo than in the whole of Africa".

673.   Whether viewed as a public utility or not, the telecommunications sector is subject in all countries to a wide range of national regulations, aiming *inter alia* to ensure the provision of universal telecommunications services and the security of telecommunications networks, to maintain the provision of certain telecommunication services within regulated public or private monopoly structures, to organize the international provision of services, to ensure respect for privacy of citizens, and to protect users as well as national sovereignty and security. Increased international trade in telecommunications may therefore require greater coherence between national regulatory structures, although it will need to be recognized that governments may wish to retain certain goals which may differ country to country.

(b)   International frameworks

674.   At the international level, the provision of telecommunications services between two or more administrations has been undertaken within the framework of the International Telecommunications Convention (ITC), its Regulations, and the recommendations of the International Telegraph and Telephone Consultative Committee (CCITT) of the International Telecommunications Union (ITU). The World Administrative Telegraph and Telephone Conference (WATTC) agreed on a new set of International Telecommunications Regulations in 1988 in order to cater for the new situation in the field of telecommunications services. The new Regulations place emphasis on national sovereignty and the right of ITU members to grant or withhold authorization for telecommunications services and to service providers within their territories, and allows for special arrangements to be made between member States.

675.   CCITT recommendations, although non-binding, play a significant role in providing the modalities for the provision of international telecommunications services, and have traditionally been aimed at constraining competition. They concern aspects such as tariffication, communication on private leased circuits, leased line interconnection, etc. Restrictions also pertain to the formation of networks using leased circuits, in particular to ensure that they carry traffic directly related to the customer's activities and are not used for traffic normally carried over the public network or for connecting the public switched networks of two countries.

676.   International telecommunications has been radically transformed by satellite communications. INTELSAT communications satellite system, owned by a consortium of over 100 countries, operates as a non-profit cooperative, providing developing countries with satellite access capabilities at rates set according to an averaging formula which provides cost savings and immediate reliable communication with the entire world. There has been concern that the establishment of private international telecommunications satellite systems may cause substantial traffic diversion and economic harm to Intelsat, leading to revenue shortfalls and price increases for developing countries which would pay considerably higher rates if prices were based on actual volumes on the route concerned.[244]

677.   The Uruguay Round negotiations on trade in services addressed both the concerns of telecommunications users which sought provisions to ensure their access to telecommunications services, including the "right to plug in " to national telecommunications networks, and those of telecommunications services suppliers which sought the right to provide their services to customers in foreign markets. The negotiations were also complicated by the fact that most countries wished to draw a distiction between "basic" telecommunication services, where government ownership would remain the rule and "enhanced" or "value-added" services where liberalization could be negotiated. Developing countries sought adequate recognition of their special objectives and needs in the sector, and the importance of drawing a distinction between "access to" domestic telecommunications networks as a "mode of delivery" for other services, and "access for" providers of telecommunications services to foreign markets. In the negotiations of specific commitments at a sectoral level access to telecommunication services may be used in order to obtain conditions from users. Access for enhanced telecommunications services may depend on the conditions offered by the provider of the service and on the reciprocal access for other services. Many of the offers of intial commitments included various "enhanced" or "value-added" services.

---

[244] Other satellite systems include: INMARSAT, INTER SPUTNIK, EUTELSAT and ARABSAT.

678.   The European Economic Community's 1992 Programme is aiming at the liberalization of telecommunications services within the EEC although the possibility of retaining monopolies for certain "reserved" (i.e. basic services) is at least temporarily admitted. The Canada United States FTA covers "telecommunications network-based enhanced services and computer services" but again basic service are excepted. Improved access for enhanced services have been pursued in bilateral negotiations, in particuler by the United States with Japan.[245]

---

[245] See R. Pipe *op.cit.*

Box IV-1

TRANSBORDER DATA FLOWS: BRAZILIAN POLICY OBJECTIVES

Transborder data flows that are internal to corporate systems have also been considered to have significant development effects by some countries. One such issue relates to the siting of information systems and the related decision-making process. All too often, both are located in the headquarters of the transnational corporations. The Brazilian policy with respect to transborder data flows was essentially devised to deal with a situation in which affiliates of transnational corporations in Brazil were conducting all their more sophisticated operations abroad (e.g. data bank operations, data processing). IBM, for example, was operating two data channels and six voice networks that had the effect of centralizing decision-making in its main headquarters to such an extent that, according to the Brazilian Government, it prevented its subsidiairies including those in Brazil, from developing even a minimum level of indigenous technology [a]. Pursuant to this findings, in 1978 the Brazilian Government instituted a policy of controlling transborder data flows.

The Brazilian policy on transborder data flows originated, therefore, from the perception that in the absence of conscious decisions by the authorities, the potential benefits of greater tradeability of data services could be frustrated by the strategies of transnational corporations strategies, transborder data flow links were not only used to move data internationally but also to centralize information resources such as man agerial and engineering skills, computer and technological capacities, database management systems, and specialized software.

The policy decision of the Brazilian Government was based on the view that, given prevailing patterns of global distribution and administration of information resources and skills, developing countries risked being relegated to the less sophisticated periphery of corporate structures, just as more peripheral regions have emerged within developed countries themselves. The objective was to ensure that data processing and data structuring activities were, to the greatest extent possible, carried out in Brazil. For example, data base access was to be allowed only if a copy of the data base was retained in Brazil, while data processing done outside Brazil through computer-communication systems would not be permitted. The intention was to modify the "architecture" of corporate transnational computer communication systems to ensure the accomplishment of the above objectives [b]. The possession of human and electronic means of structur ing data was seen as an essential element in the creation of "knowledge-intensive" services.

---

a See E. Fregni, "El reto informático y sus implicaciones para América Latina" (Buenos Aires, Papeles del SELA 9, Ediciones de la Flor, 1987), and UNCTC, *Transborder Data Flows and Brazil* (United Nations publication, Sales No. E.83.II.A.3).

b The idea of imposing regulations to increase national "information wealth" is not new. In ancient times, ships passing by Alexandria were required to provide copies of all manuscripts on board for the famous library of that city (from Luciano Cantora, *La Véritable Histoire de la Bibliothèque d'Alexandrie*, Paris, de Jorquière), quoted in *L'Hebdo*, Lausanne (Switzerland), 17 March 1988.

(c) Policy considerations

679. The major problem faced by developing countries in the sector concerns infrastructures. With their scarce resources for infrastructural upgrading, developing countries face a dilemma in terms of policy priorities: while increased trade in telecommunications services would require advanced infrastructures in urban areas in order to facilitate the functioning of TNCs and large domestic firms, social development objectives would give priority to the extension of telecommunications networks to rural areas. As a result, developing countries face a difficult choice between the public-utility function and the trade-supportive function of telecommunications in infrastructural investment. The problem is aggravated by the shortage of foreign exchange that many developing countries need in order to import the necessary equipment. A strategy followed by some countries has been to encourage TNCs to invest in telecommunications infrastructure (money, equipment, and expertise) as condition for obtaining access to developing-country mar-

kets. The "build, operate, and transfer" (BOT) policies applied by certain developing countries involves the building and operation of relevant telecommunications infrastructures by the foreign company, followed by their transfer after a specified period of time, to the host-country authorities.

680.	There is also a need for concerted international effort for the development of telecommunications infrastructures in developing countries. The ITU programmes providing technical assistance for telecommunications development, the Centre for Telecommunications Development (CTD) and the newly created Telecommunications Development Bureau (TDB) could be designated as recipients of funds or in-kind support for telecommunications services development, support by multilateral donor organizations and lending agencies, as well as by those transnational corporations benefitting from access concessions in developing countries. In pursuing this objective a balance will have to be struck between the provision of efficient telecommunications services to producers and exporters and the satisfaction of the public service role of the sector in enabling all members of society to have access to basic telecommunications services.

681.	In addition to the expansion and enhancement of infrastructures, transfer of technology and skill formation remain imperatives for a developing-country strategy in the sector. Here too, a strategy combining market access with carefully formulated conditions for foreign entities might be useful. Policies that aim at using domestic financial and human resources to generate a national capacity to produce, collect, process and use information efficiently and competitively are essential for increasing the efficiency and competitiveness of various sectors. Regional and subregional corporations may also assist in tackling infrastructural and technological problems.

682.	Advanced corporate telecommunications capabilities pose a dilemma for developing countries. On the one hand, new business activities can result in local employment, training technology imports and financial benefits. On the other, granting special concessions to selected TNCs would necessitate giving the same treatment to national enterprises, which would require a reallocation of resources to serve their sophisticated business demands.

683.	To ensure global end-to-end compatibility and interoperability of telecommunications services, many developing countries consider a single, universal standard for public services and inter-connection of value-added and leased lines to be necessary, because a multiplicity of private, proprietary, equipment standards could entail costly redesign of public facilities.

684.	The modernization of the telecommunications infrastrucures in developing countries gives rise to a new set of policy considerations relating to transborder data flows, particularly as regards competition between the import of data services and efforts to develop a domestic data services capacity. Trade-offs also are likely to arise between the desire to take advantage of transborder data flows to support exports of goods and services as well as to attract foreign direct investment, and the desire to promote the growth of indigenous knowledge-intensive services. In these cases, access to the public domestic telecommunications system would obviously be one tool in negotiations with foreign entities in pursuit of these policy objectives.

3. Construction and engineering design (CED)

(a) Definition

685.	Engineering design services[246] could generally be defined as the essential intellectual activities needed to optimize investment in all its forms, in its choices, in the technical process of its realization and in its management.[247] The designs and specifications that these services produce should in principle be the least-cost and highest-productivity solutions which are consistent with

---

[246] See Y. Soubra, "Construction and Engineering Design Services: Issues Relevant to Multilateral Negotiations on Trade in Services", in *Trade in Services: Sectoral Issues*, UNCTAD ITP/26, Geneva, 1990.

[247] J. Roberts, "Engineering Consultancy, Industrialization and Development" in *Journal of Development Studies*, vol. 9, no. 1, pp. 39-42. October 1972

the economic and social constraints of individual markets. Engineering design services generally determine the technology dimension of an investment project through the techno-economic specifications they produce for its civil construction part, the materials to be used and the machinery and equipment to be purchased. Many of these services are multidisciplinary in nature and technology-intensive, and some of them are relatively more skill- and/or knowledge-intensive than others. Construction services are those require for the physical construction of investment projects, be they of an infrastructural, industrial or agricultural type. They bring together labour, materials and equipment in order to translate the techno-economic specifications produced by the engineering design services into concrete physical entities (e.g. industrial plants, infrastructure projects). While construction services require general and specialized engineering and managerial skills, they also make use of abundant unskilled and semi-skilled labour.

(b) Trends in trade

(i) Engineering design services

686. In engineering design services, the global market for the top 200 international firms, measured by their foreign billings, amounted in 1988 to US$ 7.4 billion compared to US$ 4.16 billion in 1988. About 70 per cent of the international market is presently found in the developing countries, compared to about 85 per cent in the early 1980s. Asia is the largest single market ($2,000 million) in 1989 followed by Europe (US$ 1,770 million), North America (US$ 1,433 million), Africa (US$ 938 million), the Middle East (US$ 803 million) and Latin America (US$ 444 million). In 1988, 10 of the 20 most attractive markets in the world were Asian countries, among them: Australia, Bangladesh, China, Indonesia, India, Malaysia, the Philippines, Singapore, and Thailand. With the exception of the Latin American and African markets, which declined respectively by 26 and 13 per cent in 1988 compared to 1987, the markets in other regions witnessed an increase that more than offset the decline experienced in these two regions. Moreover, much of the business in Africa and Latin America is aid-related, as a substantial proportion of Japan's official development assistance in 1988 was mainly directed to countries in these two regions.[248]

687. As to the supply of such design services, it continues to be dominated by firms from the industrialized countries, which control over 90 per cent of the market. Among developing countries, the Republic of Korea has a share of around 1.5 per cent. Firms from a few other developing countries have also been present in the international market, but their individual shares remain very small: out of the top 200 international design firms in 1988, only 14 came from developing countries.

(ii) Construction services

688. As measured by the value of foreign contracts awarded to the top 250 international contractors, the international construction market amounted to US$ 112.5 billion in 1989. Europe was the largest export market with a volume of international business going up by 31 per cent in 1989 to 25.4 billion dollars followed by Asia (US$24.5 billion). In 1988, as much as 45 per cent of the European market was controlled by American firms and about 10 per cent by French and Italian firms respectively. Japanese companies took the lion's (27 per cent) share of the Asian market, American firms (22.7 per cent) and the Republic of Korea (2 per cent). In the Middle East, construction contracts awarded to the top 250 international contractors continued to pick up in 1989 - after falling every year since 1984, they rose to about US$ 17.4 billion in 1988 and US$ 17.8 billion in 1989. Similarly, construction contracts awarded to those firms in Africa increased in 1989 by 40 per cent to US$ 14.3 billion and in the United States and Latin America by 43 per cent and 2 per cent to US$ 13 billion and US$ 7.5 billion, respectively.

689. The emergence of developing-country exporters have contributed to fuelling competition over the last ten years in the international construction market. Among the developing countries, the Republic of Korea has continued to be present in the international market, but its share has

---

[248] *Engineering News Record*, vol. 223, no. 6, 10 August 1989.

Table IV-3

MARKET SHARE OF INTERNATIONAL DESIGN, 1983-1988
(as measured by foreign billings of the
top 200 international design firms)

(Millions of dollars, and per cent share in brackets)

Country	1983	1984	1985	1986	1987	1988
United States	1,204 (31)	1,037 (30)	1,165 (32)	918 (26)	1,042 (26)	1,039 (25)
France	361 (9)	234 (7)	239 (7)	306 (9)	260 (6)	133 (3)
Germany, Fed. Rep. of	253 (7)	249 (7)	230 (6)	282 (8)	356 (9)	302 (7)
United Kingdom	592 (15)	454 (13)	463 (13)	481 (14)	451 (11)	440 (10)
Canada	269 (7)	287 (8)	266 (7)	204 (6)	518 (13)	672 (16)
Japan	127 (3)	166 (5)	226 (6)	221 (6)	259 (6)	257 (6)
Netherlands	203 (5)	228 (7)	219 (6)	259 (7)	358 (9)	424 (10)
Other countries	841 (22)	809 (23)	832 (23)	869 (25)	774 (19)	933 (22)
Total	3,850 (100)	3,464 (100)	3,640 (100)	3,540 (100)	4,017 (100)	4,200 (100)

Source: Engineering News Record, various issues, McGraw-Hill Inc.

declined since 1983, to about 2 per cent in 1988. Firms from other developing countries and territories have gained access to the international market but their individual shares are very small; they come from Argentina, Brazil, China, Hong Kong, India, Mexico, Singapore, and Yugoslavia.

(c) Construction and engineering design (CED) services and development

690. The CED services industry plays a critical role in the domestic economies of many countries, be they developed or developing. This sector accounts for about 10 per cent of GDP in industrialized countries and provides employment for a fairly sizeable segment of the labour force.[249] The importance of CED services for development stems from their direct contribution to the design and implementation of investment projects and from the interlinkages they produce between different parts of the economy, in particular between productive units, capital goods manufacturers, research and development and the financial sector. Building up local capabilities in construction and engineering design services and promoting their utilization in the development process could become an additional source of foreign-exchange earnings with favourable effects on balance of payments. Furthermore, the role of construction projects in employment generation in developing countries makes it a crucial element in development strategies.

---

[249] The World Bank, *The Construction Industry: issues and strategies for developing countries*, Washington D.C., 1984, pages 3 and 11.

Box IV-2

THE WORLD'S 20 LEADING CONSTRUCTION COMPANIES
BY TOTAL CONTRACTS, 1988

(Millions of dollars)

Rank	Firm	Total Contracts	Foreign Contracts
1	Shimizu Construction Co.Ltd (Japan)	12,840.0	500.0
2	Fluor Corporation (United States)	12,169.4	1,819.1
3	Kajima Corp. (Japan)	11,790.7	493.8
4	Bechtel Group Inc. (United States)	10,877.0	5,034.5
5	Taisei Corp. (Japan)	10,667.1	313.2
6	Takenaka Corp. (Japan)	9,971.4	648.4
7	M.W.Kellogg Co. (United States)	9,303.9	4,621.4
8	Ohbeyashi Corp. (Japan)	8,905.4	641.5
9	Bouygues (France)	8,100.0	1,780.0
10	Kumagai Gumi Co.Ltd. (Japan)	7,797.7	780.0
11	Mitsubishi Heavy Industries Ltd.(Japan)	6,280.0	2,270.0
12	Parsons Corp. (United States)	6,177.6	3,075.0
13	SGE Group (France)	5,802.0	1,836.0
14	Philipp Holzman AG (F.R. of Germany)	5,652.6	2,622.9
15	Lummus Crest, Inc. (United States)	5,430.0	4,200.0
16	Davy Corp.Plc (United Kingdom)	4,819.1	3,892.3
17	DUMEZ (France)	4,329.9	2,587.7
18	Hazama-Gumi Ltd (Japan)	4,199.1	472.5
19	SAE-Societe Auxiliare d'Enterprises(France)	3,926.0	1,523.0
20	George Wimpey Plc (United Kingdom)	3,803.5	724.0

Source: "Directory of the World's Largest Service Companies", Series I - December 1990; and Moody's investors Service; United Nations Centre on Transnational Corporations

---

691.   The experience of those few developing countries which have succeeded shows that to penetrate the international market, the availability of professionally qualified and skilled personnel, together with low labour cost, particularly when compared to the corresponding cost in industrialized countries, are important factors. So too are efforts deployed for promoting local technological development and the use of imported technology, particularly the indigenous accumulation of know-how through learning-by-doing and selective use of foreign inputs. Finally, some kind of specialization in specific CED services and sectors helped those few countries to develop an export capability. While the Republic of Korea specialized mainly in infrastructure-related services, Brazil built up specific competence in mining and petroleum-related CED services, and India in steel and metalwork.[250] Very often the success of firms from developing countries in entering the international market was very much dependent on their ability to move skilled and unskilled labour to the construction site from their country of origin and/or other third low-wage countries.

(d) Policy considerations

692.   Technological factors such as computer-aided design and drafting and the development and application of automated construction methods and new construction materials, are becoming particularly important in this sector as well, pointing to the need for appropriate stipulations concerning training and diffusion of technology as part of market-access commitments.

693.   In all success stories, government policy to promote exports of these services was a main factor contributing to the development of an export capability. In the Republic of Korea, for example, the Overseas Construction Act of 1975, together with tax incentives, accelerated depreci-

---

[250] S. Lall, "Exports of technology by newly industrializing countries: an overview" in *World Development*, vol. 12, no. 5 6, May June 1984.

ation allowance for equipment used in overseas construction and banking credits have all helped this country to increase its participation in international trade in those services. Other countries like Brazil, India, Argentina and Mexico have also adopted policies to promote the development of an export capability in those services, including the use of different tax incentive schemes.

694.   The cross-border movement of labour at various skill levels is essential for the delivery of construction services from developing countries to international markets. In the absence of appropriate provisions for such mobility in the proposed multilateral framework for trade in services, developing countries may not be able to take advantage of their lower labour costs. Multilateral action in this area would need to ensure that visa and work permit regulations do not act as barriers to increased trade in services in this sector. Such restrictions may also adversely affect the increased participation of a wider group of developing countries in trade in construction services, as many of the higher labour cost developing countries have shown a tendency to subcontract the lower value-added end of their construction projects to other developing countries with lower labour costs.

695.   The experience of some developing countries have shown that joint ventures with the developing-country firm in a lead position may serve to facilitate both the temporary mobility of labour across borders and adequate technology transfer conditions. Specialization in some submarkets of construction may also serve to increase the competitiveness of developing-country firms.

4. Air Transport

(a) State of the sector

696.   It is estimated that the operating revenues of international airlines may account for as much as 15 per cent of international trade in services. Indeed, in the past decade, total passenger air transportation has grown at the same average rate as receipts from tourism, while air freight has grown at rate four times faster than the production of manufactured goods. International unscheduled and charter flights are dominated by the airlines of developed countries. This is less the case of scheduled international operations, but the only developing countries among the top 20 in terms of international scheduled traffic are Singapore, Republic of Korea, Thailand, Brazil, India and Indonesia.[251]

697.   In terms of regional shares in international scheduled air transport, Europe accounted for around 36 per cent of the total in 1988, followed by the Asia-Pacific region (29 per cent) and North America (22 per cent). The share of Latin America and the Caribbean was almost 6 per cent, that of countries in the Middle East 5 per cent, and that of African countries 3.4 per cent. It was expected that an average annual growth rate of 7 to 9 per cent would be maintained by the sector in the coming decade. Ongoing regulatory and structural changes in some key regions, aggravated by the effects of the Gulf war, have recently placed civil aviation in a temporary but grave crisis. Analogous recessions have happened (generally with a ten-year cycle) in the past without reversing the general long-term trend.

---

[251] In 1988, the ranking of States in international scheduled air traffic (in terms of passenger, feight and mail carried by their airlines) was as follows: (1) United States, (2) United Kingdom, (3) Japan, (4) Federal Republic of Germany, (5) France, (6) Netherlands, (7) Singapore, (8) Australia, (9) Canada, (10) Republic of Korea, (11) Italy, (12) Switzerland, (13) Thailand, (14) Spain, (15) USSR, (16) Brazil, (17) SAS countries (Denmark, Norway, Sweden), (18) India, (19) Indonesia, and (20) Israel. See ICAO Circular, 222-AT/90, p. 61, 1990.

Table IV-4

THE WORLD'S 20 LARGEST AIRLINE COMPANIES BY REVENUES: 1988

Rank	Firm	Revenues
1	UAL Corp	9.014.6
2	AMR Corp	8.824.3
3	Texas Air [a]	8.572.9
4	Japan Airlines [b]	7,776.6
5	Delta Airlines	6.915.4
6	Lufthansa	6,739.9
7	British Airways [b]	6,690.4
8	Air France	5,953.7
9	NWA Corp	5,650.4
10	All Nippon Airways [b]	4,427.4
11	SAS	4,412.0
12	TWA	4,361.1
13	Hanjin Group	3,731.9
14	Pan Am	3,569.0
15	Alitalia	3,258.1
16	USAir [c]	2,980.4
17	Swissair	2,927.8
18	Iberia	2,874.2
19	KLM [b]	2,823.2
20	Air Canada	2,777.8

Source: "Directory of the World's largest Service Companies", Series I - December 1990, Moody's investors
Service, United Nations Centre on Transnational Corporations
a Data for 1988 include the 1988 data of Eastern Airlines and Continental Airlines.
b Fiscal years ending 31 March respectively.
c USAir and Piedmont merged on 5 August 1989.

(b)   Regulatory system

698.   International trade in civil aviation is regulated through a number of international bilateral agreements or air service agreements (ASAs), which deal with aspects of air transport such as fares (price), capacity and frequency of service, access to passengers and freight, ancillary services, taxation, licensing and similar matters, as well as aviation security arrangements. The ASAs involve the granting of a set of quasi-exclusive operational rights under agreed terms (including rigid prices), and this gives even to the weakest airline some minimum rent, to support its international operations. However, it has been argued that in practice the bilateral regulatory regime has slowed the entry of new airlines into the international market as new suppliers have to resort to diverting traffic from other destinations in order to build up market share. Moreover, given the "rent" derived from the bilateral regime, lack of established access to markets can have a negative impact on the financial strength of new developing-country airlines.

(c)   Market tendencies and problems faced by developing-country airlines

699.   A number of changes related to technology as well as market structure have become crucial factors influencing competition in the international air transportation market.

700.   The profitability of air transportation seems to be derived less from the revenues from transportation services *per se* than from a number of other services and downstream economic activities. Computerized reservation systems (CRSs), in particular, have assumed a major role as a source of profits and as a catalyst in the forming of strategic alliances. CRSs enable long-distance and quasi-instantaneous marketing of services and place non-member airlines at a

---

Box IV-3

"THE FREEDOMS OF THE AIR"

The five "freedoms of the air" which are negotiated in bilateral air service agreements (ASAs) are the following:

(i) the privilege to fly, and carry traffic, non-stop over the grantor State;

(ii) the privilege to fly, and carry traffic, over the territory of the grantor State and to land for non-traffic purposes;

(iii) the privilege to fly into the territory of the grantor State and there put down traffic destined for the flag State of the carrier;

(iv) the privilege to fly into the territory of the grantor State and there pick up traffic destined for the flag State of the carrier; and

(v) the privilege to fly into the territory of the grantor State for the purpose of picking up, or putting down, traffic destined for, or coming from, third States.

In the context of the Open Skies Policy within the European Community, these "freedoms" will become generalized rights for all Community airlines. In addition, EC airlines will have the right to pick up passengers in the second member State and transfer them to a member State via their own, and of "cabotage" within the member States (i.e. sixth and seventh freedoms).

---

serious disadvantage in their ability to be present in markets competitively. The operation of CRSs normally involves some inherent biases, including bias in the display of flight information in favour of the owner-airlines, distortion of information on competing airlines, and demands on the loyalty of travel agencies. In the European Economic Community, regulations[252] on CRSs have been passed in order to restrict airlines in using CRSs to gain an unfair advantage over their competitors or to discriminate against EEC carriers. A notable aspect of the EEC regulations is their reciprocal character in that the airlines operating the CRS are obliged to practice fair competition only with respect to those entities which also abide by this principle. It would seem evident that a proliferation of such approaches will eventually necessitate the negotation of multlateral principles or rules to define acceptable competitive practices.[253]

701.   Internationally, airlines are forming strategic alliances to strengthen their position in world markets through sharing of CRS ownership or, at least, CRS operational access. There is concern that such alliances will lead to the emergence of transnational mega-carriers, analogous to TNCs in other industries, which create captive markets principally through the control over global CRSs and major congested airports. As the mega-carriers usually do not externalize their "in house" producer services, they are also able to cross-subsidize their customers for targeted discount plans, thus capturing an additional share of the market.

702.   Increased air traffic has also brought to the fore issues related to environment. The problem of noise levels has received considerable attention in international forums. Standards on noise levels have placed developing-country airlines at a particular disadvantage, as they often do not have the financial resources to replace their aircraft, and the standards may function as barriers to entry into certain markets. In contrast, there has been so far little multilateral action on the depletion of the ozone layer by supersonic air transport (SST). It has been pointed out that a fleet of 500 SSTs would start reducing global ozone levels at a rate of 20 per cent per year within ten years, and that the largest reduction in the ozone levels would be in tropical latitudes above developing countries. This adds another serious threat to the sustainable development of these countries.

---

[252] Council Regulation (EEC) 2299/89; see discussion in R. Grey, "1992", Services and the Uruguay Round Negotiations, in UNCTAD, ITP/26 *op. cit.*

[253] Network informations systems, as Alvin Toffler pointed out, "are increasingly seen as strategic weapons, helping companies protect established markets and attack new ones". Alvin Toffler, "*Powershift*", November 1990, p. 108. See also Albert Bressand, "Access to Networks and Service Trade: Uruguay Round and Beyond", in *Trade in Services: Sectoral Issues* (United Nations Publication, UNCTAD/ITP/26), pp. 215-47.

703.   The above-mentioned factors are among those exerting pressure towards a more competitive environment and eventual creation of an international aviation market. The achievements of a common air transport liberalization policy in the European Community and the changes in the United States air transportation policies may lead to changes in the regulatory systems at the national and international levels in other parts of the world. The outcome of recent bilateral negotiations between the United Kingdom and the United States involving, *inter alia*, unprecedented concessions on airline ownership and a grant of fifth and seventh freedom rights appear to signal a major move in the direction of further liberalization. The question arises, however, whether this will facilitate entry into these markets for developing-country airlines in the coming years. It is feared that the unified European market may result in a further reduction in the relative bargaining power of developing country airlines and that bilateral exchanges of concessions between the United States and the EEC may further restrict their access to these markets.

(d) Policy considerations

704.   In the air transport sector, the national policy priorities of developing countries will include the upgrading of technological capacity and human capital as well as addressing the problem of financial strength. Regional co-operation may enable developing countries to tackle some of these issues more effectively as, for example, through the pooling of resources for airport infrastructures as well as for the training facilities for pilots. Co-operation is particularly crucial in strategic alliances. Some airlines in South East Asia have formed their own computerized reservation systems, and alliances on a regional or subregional basis among developing-country airlines could strengthen their profitability and negotiating strength.[254] Until externalization and fair access to the major competitive factors of the mega-carriers' alliances is achieved multilaterally, the majority of developing-country airlines will have no clear possibility of increasing their share in the international market through increased liberalization and therefore will have very little stimulus to move away from the established bilateral framework. Externalization of ancillary services starting with CRSs and free auctioning of all ground facilities and services offered in the international airports may be major elements in the possible multilateral policy efforts.

705.   The policy priorities of some developing countries, at the international level, would continue to include improved access to international markets, especially to the third, fourth and fifth freedom rights; as well as some peripheral cabotage rights in developed country markets, where increasing congestion of airports and air space as well as asymmetries in market power, make it very difficult to negotiate improved access conditions within the existing framework. To some extent, such objectives may be pursued under the current system of ASAs. However, the market access of many potentially competitive developing country airlines is hindered by the asymmetry in the negotiating strengths as between developing and developed countries, and the former's weak financial position. The application of differential and more favourable treatment for developing-country airlines, through the granting of third, fourth and fifth freedom rights (and even cabotage) on a non-reciprocal basis, would provide a stimulus to developing country airlines and facilitate their financial viability.

706.   The Uruguay Round negotiations on trade in services have taken into account the existence and rules of functioning of the ICAO/IATA regime, but the multilateral framework should provide a set of rules and principles that would favour non-reciprocal market access as well as financial and technological assistance for developing-country airlines. The need for assistance to meet environmental standards could be taken up in the general context of action in favour of sustainable development.

---

254 See Findlay and Forsyth, *op. cit.*

5. Professional services

(a) Definitional aspects

707.   The business and professional services sector encompasses a wide range of different professions, most of them being highly specialized and knowledge-intensive such as legal services, accounting and taxation services, real estate services, mining and oil-field services, management consulting, advertising, market research and opinion polling, and computer-related services (including hardware-related consulting, installation, data processing, software development). International trade in professional services involves cross-border trade, commercial presence, and the international movement of persons. Even though independent practitioners are becoming increasingly common, international trade in the sector is done primarily by firms enjoying some form of commercial presence.

(b) Professional business services

708.   Of particular interest in this sector are professional business services. These are purchased primarily by other producers (i.e. by firms, not individuals) for the purpose of being consumed in further rounds of production; are mostly involved with delivering expertise, necessitating a major input from skilled or highly skilled professional, technical, and managerial personnel; comprise a mix of activities, some of which are restricted to licensed or accredited professionals, and others that are opened to all; and can be delivered either by firms, ranging from very large to very small, or by self-employed professionals.[255] Since the 1950s, world-wide employment and output have expanded at rates markedly higher in these services than employment and output in the world economy as a whole, with the growth accelerating further in 1980s.

709.   Although some developing countries are strengthening their domestic and international capabilities in such business services as data processing, software, project management, advertising, and consultancy,[256] the internationalization of professional business service firms has resulted in the formation of large transnational firms. This is particularly apparent in computer services, accounting and advertising. In contrast, in sectors such as legal services, such concentration is not evident.

(c) Barriers to trade in professional services sector

710.   Barriers to liberalization of professional services are extremely numerous,[257] and thus major

---

255 Thierry Noyelle, "Business Services and the Uruguay Round Negotiations on Trade in Services", Trade in services: Sectoral Issues (United Nations Publication, UNCTAD ITP 26), pp.309-63, op.cit.

256 Sieh Lee Mei Ling, "Professional Business Services in ASEAN and the Uruguay Round Trade Negotiations", Serices in Asia and Pacific: Selected Papers, Volume one (United Nations Publication, UNCTAD ITP 51), pp.35-74, op.cit.

257 They include cases of non-accreditation, non-recognition of foreign qualifications, denial of access to examinations for completion of qualifications, non-recognition of non-citizens or non-residents, requirements of joint venture or prohibition against joint venture, local establishment requirements, foreign exchange controls affecting the repatriation of

Box IV-4

ILLUSTRATIVE LIST OF
ACCREDITED AND NON-ACCREDITED PROFESSIONAL SERVICES

This indicative list of accredited and non-accredited professional services has been used as a reference in the discussions in the Working Group on Professional Services in the Uruguay Round.

A. ACTIVITIES GENERALLY CONSIDERED TO BE ACCREDITED PROFESSIONAL SERVICES

- Legal professions (lawyers, solicitors, etc.)
- Legal advice/consultancy
- Accountancy services (accounting, auditing, taxation advice, insolvency)
- Architectural services
- Construction and engineering services
- Quantity surveyors
- Health services (e.g. medical and veterinary practitioners, nurses, pharmacists, dentists, opticians)
- Linguistic services (e.g. interpreters)
- Others (e.g. estate agents, patent agents, actuaries, notaries, stockbrokers, teachers, psychologists, tourist guides, criminologists, journalists)

B. ACTIVITIES GENERALLY CONSIDERED NOT TO REQUIRE ACCREDITATION AND OFTEN REFERRED TO AS BUSINESS SERVICES

Marketing services

- Advertising, direct marketing and sales promotion
- Market research and public opinion polling
- Public relations
- Fairs and exhibitions, other marketing services

Consultancy services

- Management and administrative services
- Computer related services and software development
- Recruitment consultancy
- Training and education services/consultancy
- Other specialisations (e.g. mining/geology, agriculture and fisheries)

Operational services

- Provision of personnel (e.g. secretarial, temporary labour)
- Contract cleaning services
- Waste disposal and processing
- Security services
- Translation services
- Other operational services

Other technical services

- Maintenance and repair of equipment
- Quality control and inspection
- Testing and certification
- Design
- Photographic services, commercial art
- Other technical services

Other business services

problems face developing countries in exporting their business services. Building competitiveness necessitates increasing size in order to create economies of scale, but the limited size of the domestic market is often a constraint on local firms. Generating expertise is also crucial in competitiveness and this necessitates obtaining access to complex assignments (access to foreign markets) and access to advanced business service technology. Developing expertise also requires improved and expanded educational infrastructures. An improved legal framework at the national level for intellectual property protection is often required in many countries.[258]

(d) Access to information networks and distribution channels

711.   The networking used by firms in the modern professional services sector creates a two-tier market, i.e. a few large firms supplying multinationals and large local firms supported by their access to intra and intercorporate information networks and a large number of small firms supplying small and medium-sized local enterprises. If developing-country exports of these services are to increase, they would need to have access to networks and distribution channels for the delivery of services.

(e) Financial strength

712.   The provision of many professional services sold in packages by large transnational companies requires extensive financial inputs in some cases, thus making difficult the participation of developing countries in many international projects. In software and computer services, several developed-country firms are heavily subsidized by various government projects. Additionally, the high cost of establishing a foreign presence in developed countries constitutes another financial problem in this sector for a developing country firm.

(f) Domestic regulations

713.   The prevalence of complex and not always transparent regulations and bureaucratic procedures and of differences in the qualification and certification systems impede growth in professional services sector trade. Transparency, both as regards what countries require and how these requirements are to be met, needs special attention. Transparency is also relevant in cases of regulations imposed by private professional associations. The mutual recognition of professional qualifications and harmonization agreements is, therefore, of utmost importance.

714.   Conditions for temporary mobility of labour, such as visa and work permit requirements, can also restrict the ability of countries to trade both accredited and non-accredited services. Software and computer services are a case in point, particularly as the use of subcontracting and personnel dispatching, also called "body-shopping", is an important means of delivery of software services. Work permit restrictions have entailed major losses in potential business for India's software firms, and have impeded the development of computer services from other developing

---

earnings by firms, counter-trade payments, restriction of staff that could be employed, mandatory use of local consultants, discriminatory regulation of fees and expenses, discriminatory purchasing arrangements, entry restrictions such as visa restrictions, prohibition of using firm's name, denial of access to transborder data flows or telecommunication services, the use of subsidies or other forms of official support being granted to domestic suppliers (such as mixed credits, general financial assistance, direct exports or operating subsidies), and anti-competitive practices of TNCs (for example cartel- type agreements to fix prices and preserve markets and global client relationships). Philippe Brusick, Murray Gibbs and Mina Mashayekhi, " Anti- Competitive Practices in the Services Sector", Uruguay Round: Further Papers on Selected Issues (United Nations Publication, UNCTAD ITP 42) pp. 129-51, op. cit.

[258] See Borja, et. al., "Servicios de Software y Computación" Mexico, Una Economia de Servicios, op. cit.

countries.[259] These restrictions further impede the development of expertise which can only be attained by participating in the most sophisticated and dynamic markets.[260] Unless adequate means for the temporary mobility of labour can be effectively achieved within the multilateral framework for trade in services being negotiated, this would continue to frustrate the possibilities of developing countries benefiting from trade liberalization in these services.

Table IV-5

The ten largest advertising groups, 1987

(million US dollars)

	World-wide billings	World-wide gross income	Country

1. Saatchi & Saatchi Plc
   Saatchi, Saatchi Advertising World-wide
   Baker Spielvogel Bates World-wide
	11 360	1 680	UK/US

2. Dentsu Inc	6780	885	Japan

3. Interpublic Group of Cos
   McCann Erikson World-wide
   Lintas World-wide
	6 620	993	US

4. Omnicom Group
   BBDO World-wide
   DDB Needham World-wide
	6 270	896	US

5. Young & Rubicam	6 290	940	US
6. WPP Group Plc J. Walter Thompson	5 950	893	UK/US
7. Ogilvy Ogilvy & Mather, World-wide	5 040	723	US

8. Foote Cone/Publicis International
   Foote Cone & Bielding
   Publicis International
	3 390	509	US/France

9. Hakuhodo International	2 900	383	Japan
10. Eurocom	2 760	420	France
TOTAL	57 360	8 322	

Source: Advertising Age, March 1988.

Note: Indents indicate principal agency networks that belong to the group.

---

[259] Saurabh Srivastava, "Computer Software and Data processing", in *Services and Development Potential: The Indian Context* (United Nations Publication, UNCTAD ITP/22), p.191

[260] Borja in Mexico, *Una Economía de Servicios, op. cit.*

(g) Policy considerations

715. That the developing countries need effective access to world markets for professional services has been demonstrated above.

716. In addition, however, there is need for more active support to international initiatives to promote the mutual recognition of qualifications; in particular, a professional services body could be established to deal with the thorny issue of mutual recognition and harmonization of professional qualifications and standards to achieve a world wide system of mutual recognition and a world wide system of minimum standards. Such a body would also be responsible for establishing international criteria for scope of practice and disciplinary procedures and co-ordinating the activities of governmental bodies and non-governmental professional associations regulating professions. A professional services body could also give particular attention to the need to expand the participation of developing country professionals, and professional and business service firms in world trade in such services, including the recognition of qualifications on a preferential non-reciprocal basis.

717. Developing countries are demonstrating a clear advantage in providing certain business or office services on an "offshore" basis providing them telematically. The possibilites for taking advantage of this greater tradeability of such services requires greater study including as to appropriate strategies for increasing the technological level and value added of such operations while reducing vulnerabilty.

Table IV-6

The 20 largest management consulting firms, 1987

Firm	Country	World-wide revenues [a] (Million dollars)	United States revenues [a] (Million dollars)	Number of professionals worldwide [a][c]
1. Arthur Andersen	US	838	522	9600
2. Marsh & McLennan	US	530	393	6400
3. McKinsey	US	510	255	1600
4. Towers Perrin	US	465	380	3085
5. Peat Marwick	US	438	253	4700
6. Booz Allen	US	412	345	2100
7. Coopers & Lybrand	US	381	199	4700
8. Ernst & Whinney	US	374	230	3255
9. Price Waterhouse	US	345	160	4300
10. Saatchi & Saatchi	UK	267	176	1500
11. Touche Ross	US	248	157	2100
12. Wyatt	US	237	207	1600
13. Arthur D. Little	US	218	151	1500
14. Deloitte Haskins	US	209	91	2300
15. Arthur Young	US	204	133	2400
16. Bain	US	200	140	800
17. PA Managment Consult.	UK	175 [b]	n.a.	n.a.
18. Alexander Proudfoot	US	170	60	1100
19. Hewitt Associates	US	161	152	1400
20. American Management Systems	US	145	145	1600
TOTAL		6 527	4 149	

Source: Consulting News, The Economist.
  a Management advisory service revenues only.
  b 1986 revenues.
  c As defined by company - does not include support staff.

Table IV-7

The largest accounting firms, 1989

Firm	Country	World-wide revenues (Million dollars)	United States revenues (Million dollars)	World-wide employees
1. Ernst & Whinney Arthur Young	US	4 462	-	68 300
2. KPMG	US	4 300	1 639	68 000
3. DRT International	US	3 500	-	-
4. Arthur Andersen & Co.	US	3 382	1 710	51 414
5. Coopers & Lybrand	US	2 800	-	51 000
6. Price Waterhouse	US	2 458	960	40 770

Source: Directory of the World's Largest Service Companies, Series I, December 1990, Moody's Investors Service, UNCTC.

Table IV-8

The 15 largest computer service firms, 1986

Firm	Country	1986 (Million dollars)
1. TRW Incorporated	US	1 450.0
2. ADP Incorporated	US	1 298.1
3. General Motors Corporation - EDS	US	1 125.9
4. Computer Sciences Corporation	US	977.7
5. McDonnell Douglas	US	803.2
6. Control Data Corporation	US	752.0
7. Martin Marietta	US	659.4
8. Nippon Telegraph & Telephone	Japan	577.6
9. General Electric Company	US	550.0
10. Arthur Andersen	US	546.0
11. Cap Gemini Sogeti	France	419.9
12. NCR Corporation	Japan	350.0
13. Boeing Company	US	300.0
14. IBM	US	300.0
15. Nomura Computer Systems Company	Japan	263.5
TOTAL		9 396.0

Source: Datamation.

Table IV-9

The 15 largest computer software firms, 1986

Firms	Country	1986 (Million dollars)
1. IBM	US	5 514.0
2. Unisys Corporation	US	861.0
3. Digital Equipment Corporation	US	560.0
4. NEC Corporation	Japan	507.1
5. Fujitsu Limited	Japan	389.2
6. Siemens AG	Fed. Rep. of Germany	387.1
7. Hewlett-Packard Company	US	375.0
8. Hitachi Limited	Japan	331.0
9. Nixdorf Computer AG	Fed. Rep. of Germany	299.5
10. Lotus Development Corporation	US	283.0
11. Microsoft Corporation	US	260.2
12. Compagnie General d'Electricité	France	238.1
13. Computer Associates International	US	226.5
14. Olivetti SPA	Italy	225.3
15. Wang Laboratories Incorporated	US	200.0
TOTAL		10 657.0

Source: Datamation.

6. Labour mobility

718.   The international movement of labour, currently under discussion in the Uruguay Round negotiations, refers to the temporary relocation of service providers and excludes permanent migration. Such movement of persons constitutes a "mode of delivery" for other services.

(a) Magnitude and direction

719.   International transactions on labour services are recorded in the IMF balance-of-payments statistics.[261]

720.   Many developing countries rely heavily on the cross-border movement of persons for their services exports. For developing countries that have a comparative advantage in labour-intensive activities and lack alternative means for delivering services, labour remittances from the cross-border movements of people are an important source of foreign exchange. Regional mobility of labour appears to contribute substantially to economic welfare, although it seems far from adequate to accommodate available labour force in labour sending countries in the developing regions. In Africa, for countries such as Lesotho, Egypt, Sudan and Mali, labour exports accounted for 30 to 80 per cent of total exports in 1988.[262] The Asia and Pacific region is overwhelmingly dominated by net-sending countries, with eight Asian countries recording a net of migrant outflow of more than 100,000 during 1985-1990. The reliance on revenues from migrant workers was notably high in Pakistan and Bangladesh (representing 35 per cent and 47 per cent respectively of their total export earnings in 1988), while India and Sri Lanka also registered substantial external revenues from the exports of labour services. The share of labour service exports in the total exports of Latin American countries has been lower than for African and Asian countries, amounting to 1 to 7 per cent in 1988, while in the Caribbean countries it has been higher. In the Middle East, external income from migrant workers in the same region had tremendous importance for many countries, exceeding the revenues from the total export of merchandise and services.

---

[261] In national income accounts, the provision of a service is considered to involve trade in services only if the stay abroad is less than three months and if the service provider is paid by a foreign firm. If the provider stays longer than three months and/or is paid by a local enterprise (either domestic or foreign-owned), the services provided are not considered to be imports but contributions to GDP as if they had been made by a resident of the country. The balance-of-payments accounting practices of countries to record international transactions on labour services are not uniform. The majority of countries classify it either under "labour income" or under "workers remittances", while some countries record it under "other services". Labour income consists of wages, salaries, and other compensation that persons earn in an economy other than the one in which they reside by working for a resident of that economy in the period of less than one year. Workers remittances cover unrequited transfers by migrants who have come to an economy and who stay, or are expected to stay, for a year or more. The criterion used in the balance-of-payments accounting practice is to consider all stays abroad of one year or more as *de facto* immigration (change of residency), and consequently, the item "workers remittances" is classified under the category of "unrequited transfers", i.e. one transactor provides an economic value to another transactor but does not receive a *quid pro quo* on which economic value is placed. However, this is simply a convention, and in practice, it is hard to draw a clear distinction. The item "migrant transfers" is also relevant in discussing international transactions on trade in services. It signifies the new worth of the migrants including household, personal, and movable capital goods as well as the migrants' interests in local enterprises and any nonfinancial intangible assets.

[262] For detailed information see Chapter 3: "Organized and clandistine migration", in *International Migration in Africa: Legal and administrative aspects* (Sergio Ricca, ILO, 1989). See also "The Reorganization of Mine Labour Recruitment in Southern Africa: Evidence from Botswana" by John Taylor, in *International Review,* Vol.24, No.90.

Box IV-5

**Countries dependent on export of labour services in 1988,
and percentage of their total exports**

Country	Percentage
Lesotho	75
Egypt	50
Bangladesh	47
Sudan	37
Pakistan	35
Mali	29
Yugoslavia	25
Morocco	24
Portugal	24
Sri lanka	19
India	16
Greece	15
Tunisia	13
Philippines	12

Source: : Calculated based on the IMF Balance-of-Payment Statistics.

---

721.   Most West European countries had a system of recruiting guest-workers to fuel the post-war boom; in recent years, however, they have restrained the entrance of migrant workers, particularly those from non-EEC countries.[263] The IMF Balance-of-Payments Statistics indicated that Switzerland and Germany had the highest proportion of payment on labour services to total imports of goods and services while in terms of value the United States was the largest importer of labour services.

(b) Labour mobility and development

722.   The developed countries have been reluctant to liberalize those service sectors where comparative advantage in production depends on labour costs rather than on capital and technology. Since the 1970s the trend in national immigration and related administrative policies in the OECD countries has been the imposition of new restrictions on the cross-border movement of labour. Exceptions to this policy relate to the movement of highly-skilled personnel and certain professions which are needed in the host country, and thus serve to exacerbate the reverse transfer of technology.

(c) Barriers to trade in labour services

723.   For a variety of reasons - public order, security, public health, protection of local employment - all countries have national laws and measures that restrict the cross-border movement of labour. They stipulate conditions for entry into their territory and specify regulations covering such matters as issue of entry permits, visas, residence and temporary work permits. They also set conditions relating to the right of approved foreigners to pursue a particular profession or activity mainly intended for the protection of the employment of local labour. Other conditions include

---

[263] See Charles Castles, "The Guest-Worker in Western Europe: An Obituary", in *International Migration Review: Temporary Worker Programs: Mechanisms, Conditions, Consequences*, Vol. 20, Winter 1986, Centre for Migration Studies, p. 761.

lack of guarantees that remuneration received can be remitted to the country of origin, difficulties in dismissing local staff, inadequate access to national education and health services, and discrimination on the basis of nationality, race, sex or religion. Quotas may be used to restrict the number of individuals admitted to a professional association even if the candidates satisfy all other requirements, or particular types of work may be reserved for local nationals. Financial guarantees - in the form of a deposit or the requirement to establish in the host country - may be demanded of the foreign national to protect consumers and ensure credibility, but may also discriminate against developing-country suppliers.

(d) International frameworks

724.   The International Labour Organisation (ILO) has adopted a number of conventions and recommendations regarding treatment of migrant workers. ILO Conventions concerning Migration for Employment (1949), and Migrant Workers (Supplementary provisions 1975) which set out in general terms conditions and rules for specified types of labour migrants have been ratified so far by only 15 member countries. Both conventions exclude from the definition of migrant worker certain categories of foreign workers, including artists and members of the liberal professions who have entered the country on a short-term basis. The latter convention also excludes employees of organizations or undertakings operating within the territory of a country who have been admitted temporarily to that country at the request of their employer to undertake specific duties or assignments, for a limited and defined period of time, and who are required to leave that country on the completion of such duties or assignments. Both conventions specify, among other rights, equality of treatment with nationals in regard to certain specified labour rights.

(e) International action and policy considerations

725.   The Uruguay Round of negotiations on trade in services agreed the inclusion of an annex recognizing that commitments with respect to temporary movement of labour can be included in the process of progressive liberalization and the subject of specific commitments at the sectoral and sub-sectoral level. There is also agreement that the framework on services would not apply to individual "job seekers", nor would it apply to measures regarding citizenship, residence or employment on a permanent basis. The negotiations have addressed the possiblity of establishing an illustrative list of natural persons performing particular services covering broad categories of sectors and skill levels, which could serve as a guide for negotiations on market access commitments on the temporary movement of natural persons providing services. It is recognized that once a commitment with respect to the temporary movement of particular categories of natural persons supplying a specific service has been negotiated in accordance with market access provisions of the framework, such categories of persons should be free to move in order to provide the service. It has also been pointed out that once such a commitment has been undertaken it should not be frustrated through the application of laws and regulations relating to the movement of natural persons, in particular the requirement of an economic needs test.

726.   Developing countries have argued that, since the exports of developing-country services are primarily accomplished through the "mode of delivery" of persons crossing international frontiers, any multilateral regime which liberalized capital movement while continuing to restrict labour movement would, in effect, promote only the exports of developed countries, and thus aggravate existing asymmetries. This applies not only to unskilled labour - a crucial element in the competitive advantage of developing countries in services such as construction - but also to those sectors where a combination of relatively high skills at relatively low costs provides firms from developing countries with a clear comparative advantage (what might be called an advantage in "low-cost high tech"). The temporary movement of persons from developing countries can further facilitate their entry into trade in higher technology services (such as software services, where the ability to have direct contact with clients is an important mode of transfer of soft technology) and support their exports of manufactures through after-sales services. Acceptance of the principle that the temporary movement of labour to supply services constitutes a "trade", not an "immigration" issue and the consolidation of this principle through the negotiation in specific sectoral concessions in the

Uruguay Round would constitute a major step forward for those developing countries where the skills of their people are significant resources. It could also open the way to more structured and mutually advantagous mechanisms for responding to pressures for labour movement.

727.   Of course, the countries which export labour services are dependent on the vagaries of the economies that are hosts to their nationals and on their employment and immigration policies. Recent events have demonstrated the vulnerability of such countries, some of which have been faced with the need to re-absorb a large number of such migrants and to generate new sources of foreign exchange. The challenge facing these countries is to channel the acquired skills of returning migrants into new service exports (or goods) which could help compensate for lower labour remittances. The support of the international community could help in this endeavour.

7.   Tourism services

(a)   Definition and importance

728.   As a result of the development in air transportation, higher personal incomes and longer paid holidays, there has been a remarkable increase in tourism trade in recent years. For many developing countries, tourism provides the main source of foreign-exchange earnings and employment. Furthermore, the linkage between tourism and other sectors of the economy - such as construction, transportation, telecommunications and professional services - has increased the importance of the tourism sector for development strategies. The provision of tourism services may involve the cross-border movement of incorporated goods (e.g. food and beverage, souvenirs), of information (airline and hotel reservation), of labour (management personnel, journalists), and of capital (e.g. equity involvements, management contracts). In the negotiations on trade in tourism in the Uruguay Round, the liberalization of such trade has been seen as involving primarily (a) the movement of consumers (i.e. tourists); (b) the movement of enterprises seeking to provide touristic services in the world market.[264] Developing countries have, however, seen the issue as that of not only attracting more tourists, but of gaining a greater share of the value added generated by tourists travelling to other countries, including that obtained in the home countries of the tourists.

(b)   Trends in the international tourism market

729.   The tourism services sector has undergone a number of significant changes in recent years in relation to market structure and to the factors that determine competitiveness in the sector. Firstly, the internationalization of the sector has been followed by a tendency towards greater vertical integration in various segments in the industry as a means of controlling the quality and availability of services - especially among airlines,[265] hotel chains, travel agencies and tour operators. Secondly, computerized reservation systems (CRS) and other strategies of networking have become crucial factors in attaining and maintaining competitive positions in the sector. Thirdly, the emergence of strategic alliances between providers of various tourism-related services have given rise to absolute advantages, eroding the competitiveness of smaller firms and of developing countries.

---

[264] In the balance-of-payments accounts, the International Monetary Fund (IMF) includes travel as a services item, and this entry is usually taken as a measure of trade in tourism services. Some analyses tend to include passenger services also in measuring tourism, and WTO includes international transport in a simplified model for the elaboration of balance for tourism. The list of tourism-related services used by the Group of Negotiations on Services (GNS) in the Uruguay Round does not provide any definition, though its coverage encompasses almost all activities related to international trade in tourism.

[265] See also the section on air transport.

(i) Demand for tourism

730.   Measured in terms of travel receipts alone, tourism trade accounts for approximately 5 per cent of total world trade and 16 per cent of international trade in services.[266]

731.   Western Europe and North America dominate the market for tourism exports, accounting for 76 per cent of total receipts and 73.9 per cent of passenger services receipts. In both relative and absolute terms, developed countries are both the biggest spenders as well as the biggest receivers of travel income. Mexico is the only developing country that figures among the leading exporters of tourism services. On the other hand, almost all the countries for which tourism accounts for more than 50 per cent of private services exports, are developing countries.

(ii) Supply of tourism services

732.   The supply of tourism services shows a high degree of market concentration and domination by transnational corporations (TNCs), most of which originate in developed countries. This seems to parallel the concentration of tourist arrivals and travel receipts in developed countries. The three major segments of the supply of tourism-related services, accounting for the great bulk of international tourism transactions, are (a) airlines, (b) hotels and restaurant chains, and (c) tour operators and travel agents.

733.   Airlines, the most important means for the delivery of tourism services, have been dealt with earlier in this chapter.[267]

734.   International hotels and restaurants are also major players in this field, providing tourists with the type and quality of services that they are accustomed to at home. In many cases, the chains have been associated with airlines, tapping passenger pools. The chains are highly concentrated, with 25 of them controlling 80 per cent of the associated hotels; of the 10 largest chains, eight are from the United States.

735.   In developing countries, 74.2 per cent of transnational hotels operate under management contracts and 24.9 per cent under leasing arrangements. Some developing countries (e.g. Mexico and South-East Asian countries) have large domestic hotel chains, and some operate as transnational hotel chains in other developing countries.[268] Computerized reservation systems are among the most important advantages offered by hotel chains in their franchising arrangements, their networks arranging for air transport, hotel reservations, car rental and even restaurant reservations.[269]

736.   Although transnational chains have a major share of the world market in tourism, a large number of small and medium-sized hotels are managed in the form of family enterprises in both developed and developing countries, varying in terms of standards of quality. In order to face competition from transnational hotel chains, many of these hotels have been associated in voluntary chains, especially in Europe, the United States, France and in some developing countries. Such consortiums, or co-operatives enable hotels to derive economies of scale in the acquisition of the necessary goods and services, promotion campaigns, access to information and reservation systems, and to obtain better bargaining positions vis-à-vis tour operators, travel agencies, and the public sector.[270]

737.   The restaurant sector has experienced a lesser degree of internationalization in comparison to hotel chains. Two segments of the sector that present very high growth trends are: (a) catering of flights undertaken by subsidiaries of airlines or by independent chains, and (b) fast food and

---

[266] It is important to note that travel receipts do not reflect income accruing to international tour operators (airlines, tour operators, hotel chains, and travel agencies), and the global market for tourism flows far exceeds the indications provided by the IMF balance-of-payments statistics.

[267] See section of air transport, elsewhere in this chapter.

[268] UNCTC, *Foreign Direct Investment and Transnational Corporations in Services* (United Nations Publication, Sales No. E.89.II.A.1), 1989.

[269] For a discussion of networks, see Bressand, *op.cit.* See also the section on civil aviation in the annex to this chapter.

[270] Carner Françoise, "America Latina y el Caribe : El comercio de servicios en turismo y los negociaciones de la Ronda Uruguay", CEPAL Document No. LC R.937, reproduced in UNCTAD/CEPAL/SELA/UNDP study, "Sectores de servicios en America Latina", UNCTAD ITP forthcoming, 1991.

Box IV-6

THE 20 LARGEST HOTEL COMPANIES BY NUMBER OF ROOMS: 1988

(Millions of dollars)

Rank	Firm	Home Country	Number of rooms
1	Holiday Corporation	USA	360,958
2	Best Western International, Inc	USA	255,217
3	The Sheraton Corporation	USA	135,000
4	Ramada Inc.	USA	130,932
5	Marriott Corporation	USA	118,000
6	Quality Inns International, Inc	USA	112,810
7	Days Inns Of America	USA	104,625
8	Hilton Hotels Corp	USA	95,862
9	Trusthouse Forte Plc	UK	89,546
10	Accor	France	80,034
11	Logis et Auberges	France	77,985
12	Prime Motor Inns Inc	USA	66,245
13	Club Mediterranee	France	61,860
14	Balkantourist	Bulgaria	56,250
15	Motel 6 LP	USA	51,572
16	Hyatt Hotels Corp USA	USA	50,797
17	Radisson Hotel Corp	USA	46,600
18	Ladbroke Hotels Plc	UK	45,630
19	Bass Plc	UK	45,099
20	Intercontinental/saison	Japan	38,921

Source: "Directory of the World's Largest Service Companies" Moody's investors service, United Nations Centre on Transnational Corporations, December 1990.

---

self-service chains, most of which are based in the United States. Though catering of airlines operate in many developing countries due to lower costs, in most cases they are subsidiaries of big hotel chains. In 1986, two thirds of the establishments operated by the ten biggest firms were under franchising contracts and one third were the property of chains.

738. Both tour operators and travel agents - which are the most important intermediaries between the suppliers and the final consumers of tourism services - are concentrated mainly in the high per capita income countries, while developing-country firms in this sector mainly service the smaller domestic market or assist operators from developed countries. The domination of the travel market by tour-operators from the generating country can be attributed to factors such as (a) knowledge of tastes and needs of their customers, (b) economies of scale in servicing various markets, and (c) connections with airlines and hotel chains in the same countries. Unlike hotel chains, the internationalization of tour operators does often not require establishment in the foreign country; they are usually associated with other TNCs, mainly hotel chains and airlines. Salient features of their operation include their substantial bargaining capacity and their use of pricing in order to attract tourism to particular destinations.

(c) Policy considerations

739. The key to future success in international tourism lies in the ability to identify clusters of wants and to provide service modalities that will meet them. In general, developing countries do not have the technological and managerial capacities to respond quickly to market changes, posing a challenge to developing-country firms in gaining competitiveness in the sector. Inadequate technological and transport infrastructures pose a further problem for developing countries, as they constrain the efficient delivery of many tourism-related services and can preclude the use of

advanced electronic networks.

(i) National policies

740. Developing countries therefore need to adopt clearly focused policies at the national level that would integrate strategies in the sector with overall development objectives. Such policies may include: (a) strengthening of strategies for the development and monitoring of the sector, with a view to obtaining better retention of value added, upgrading of skills in the sector, and the growth of surpluses in tourism trade; (b) the improvement of infrastructures crucial for the efficient delivery of tourism services; (c) participation in information networks and distribution channels; (d) strengthening and diversification of supply innovations through collaboration agreements between firms in various segments in the tourism market; (e) focused policies for the development of specific segments in the market, coupled with policies aimed at minimizing the adverse impact of the development of tourism on the ecological and cultural environment; and (f) implementation of training programmes for personnel in accordance with the needs in supply and demand.

741. While the above-mentioned policies focus on the development of the domestic sector, a second set of policies may need to be formulated in order to enable developing-country tourist firms to obtain a higher and more profitable access to foreign markets. This may include: (a) targeted development of profitable segments in the sector, especially those with potential for the retention of higher value-added, employment opportunities and foreign-currency earnings; (b) improvement of the organizational structure at the enterprise level, supplemented by incentives and promotional mechanisms, especially to national investors; (c) obtaining access to networks as a means for enlarging access to the marketing chain, as well as the establishment of domestic reservation networks and marketing chains in connection with existing networks in developed and other developing countries; (d) setting up of appropriate structures for international negotiations with trading partners, as well as for the upgrading of the negotiating capability of the private sector; and (e) development of co-operation schemes with other countries so as to attract higher levels of demand. A third set of national policies would need to address the question of unreliability and insufficiency of data in the tourism sector, which have been pointed out as a major problem for developing-country policy-making in this sector. Policies for improving the measurement of tourism activities are a prerequisite for a clearer determination of the impact of the sector on the economy as a whole, to formulate appropriate and well-integrated development strategies, and for enhancing the negotiating capability of the countries.

(ii) Policies at the international level

742. In order to improve the participation of developing countries in the international trade in tourism, appropriate international policies also need to be devised. In this regard, four lines of action deserve special mention: (a) harmonization of efforts, through relevant international organizations (e.g. WTO, UNSO and IMF) to improve the collection and processing of data related to international transactions in tourism; (b) support of the international community for the efforts of developing countries to obtain improved access to the market (e.g. the establishment of reservation networks in developing countries and their connection with existing networks in developed countries), as well as international co-operation to make adequate financial and technical resources available for enhancing the competitiveness of segments of the tourism sector in developing countries; (c) subregional, regional and interregional co-operation aimed at increasing intraregional tourist flows (in this regard, special efforts would need to be made by the international community to eliminate the barriers facing developing-country inflows of tourism such as the restrictive business practices of major tourism companies, and the operation of computerized reservation systems. Preferential action could be undertaken by developed market-economy countries to promote tourism to developing countries through the provision of fiscal advantages, duty free allowances, etc.); (d) in the Uruguay Round negotiations on trade in services, attempts would need to be made to ensure the increased participation of developing countries in international trade in this sector, through providing better access for developing-country firms to developed country markets and by attaching transfer of technology and access to networks as conditions for developed-country firms benefiting from access commitments in developing countries; and (e) technical and financial assistance to developing countries for dealing with the negative environmental aspects of tourism.

8. Audiovisual services

(a) Definition and scope

743.   There is no single commonly accepted definition of "audiovisual services".[271] The following analysis focuses mainly on cimena and video films, television programmes, and to some extent on the economic significance of audiovisual services-related equipment.

(b) Industry and trade

744.   Even though detailed factual descriptions are difficult because of the paucity of reliable data, available information clearly shows the dominance of the United States in the sector, accounting for half the overall world industry, followed by the European Economic Community with a quarter of the industry. International flows of film and television programming take the form mainly of "one-way" traffic from a small number of exporting countries to the rest of the world. Most countries import the majority of the films viewed by their populations, and the United States is by far the largest supplier of imported films and television programmes, with Western Europe and Japan far behind. The trade flow consists mainly of programmes of a recreational nature, e.g. entertainment programmes, feature films, sports programmes, etc.

745.   In the case of trade in equipment related to audiovisual services, the OECD study[272] found that the household equipment market (i.e. video recorders, television receivers, cable systems, etc.) had a significant importance in the trade, accounting for some $20 billion, and this is expected to grow (particularly for video players and tapes). The link between trade in audiovisual services and in the related equipment has become increasingly prominent in recent years.[273] The likelihood of a mega-conversion to high-definition TV is particularly relevant in this context.

746.   Observations on the audiovisual services industries by region highlights some specific characteristics of different geographical areas. Three Asian countries and territories - India, Japan and Hong Kong - figure among the nine major world film exporters.[274] In Latin America, the mass-media industries are becoming more complex, more diversified and more transnational - especially in countries with the largest private media conglomerates such as Mexico and Brazil. On average, half the programmes broadcast in the region are imported,[275] and more than half the imported programmes come from the United States. Among the Arab countries, the exchange of

---

[271] An OECD study on the sector observed that audiovisual services are a component of a communications and information sector, and that these services are animated sequences of pictures that maybe accompanied by sound material. OECD, *International Trade in Services: Audiovisual Works* (Paris, OECD, 1986), pp. 8 and 10. It defined the services further: (a) they are recorded or are transmitted; (b) they are for use by one or more individuals or corporate bodies for private, semi-commercial or commercial purposes, the customer's purpose being professional or private; and (c) they have a cultural, educational, scientific, advertising, or entertainment content. A study prepared by UNESCO referred to the term "media", and defined it as a sector which includes the press, publishing, recording industry, television, radio and cinema. UNESCO, *World Communications Report, 1989* (United Nations Publication, Sales No.). UNESCO regularly attempts to measure the international flows of film and television programmes.

[272] *Ibid..*, pp.10-11.

[273] By the end of 1986, it was estimated that video will have achieved 120 million units - a figure which has been reached within the last decade, half of these sales having taken place in the last two years. See Manuel Alvarado, ed., *Video World-Wide* (UNESCO, 1988), p. 3.

[274] See Malati Tambay Vaidya, "Trade in Media Services: Asia and the Pacific Region", in UNCTAD, *Services in Asia and the Pacific: Selected Papers*, Vol. 1 (United Nations Publication, UNCTAD ITP/51), p. 293.

[275] *Ibid.*, p. 26.

films is quite pronounced, accounting approximately for a third of the imported programmes.[276] The high penetration rate of VCRs in the region is mainly due to: (i) the high per capita income; (ii) the large number of expatriate workers; and (iii) limited television programming. In Africa, it is estimated that over 55 per cent of the annual TV broadcast hours are filled by imported programmes.[277]

(c) Technological changes

747. Technological progress in the areas of information and telecommunications has had a great impact on contemporary media services, especially on the distribution of media products.[278] The major developments include the use of satellite, cable television and fibre-optics grids. The term "satellite television" is now mostly used in order to refer to DBS (direct broadcasting by satellite), which involves the reception by consumers, on their own special receiver dish, of a low-powered signal from a dedicated satellite in geostationary orbit. One of the features of satellite television is its disregard for national borders. The importance of satellite distribution of television programming has increased dramatically during the last two decades, the programming volume of INTELSAT increasing ten-fold during this period. Cable television generally refers to a cable-based carrier that delivers multiple programmes from a cable station operator simultaneously to subscriber households. Cable system appears to suffer from a number of drawbacks such as: (i) limited choice of programming; (ii) lack of portability; (iii) obligation to use the operator's equipment only. However, cables made of optical fibre that carry digital signals in the form of light pulses can prove to be the most important developing communication technology for the carriage of voice, data and video. The opportunity to link satellite and cable technology for the provision of satellite-delivered programmings in Europe has attracted a number of entrants into the market, the largest being Sky Channel. The impact that these entrants have had on the regulated European television industry has been profound.[279]

(d) Regulatory issues

748. Trade in cinema film was the only service-related subject which was addressed in the original 35 articles of the GATT.[280] At the time of the drafting of the national treatment obligations under the Havana Charter, it was recognized that the application of these provisions to film screening could cause difficulties from the point of view of cultural protection. Countries felt that tariffs were not an effective way of protecting a domestic cinematographic film industry, and resorted to quotas on screen time, which has been reflected in Article IV of GATT. The Article specifically allows the establishment and maintenance of film screen quotas to guarantee that a minimum percentage of total screen time is alloted to the exhibition of films of national origin.

749. A directive adopted by the Council of the European Communities[281] which was implemented in October 1991, stipulates that all television channels within the member countries should transmit at least 50 per cent European works, "where practicable". The United States attempted to challenge the directive in GATT in 1989, but no action was taken in this case.

750. There have been national regulatory changes which may affect the structure of the audiovisual services sector in the major audiovisual services exporters. For example, in the United

---

276 "International Flow of Television Programmes", op. cit., p. 53.

277 "International Flow of Television Programmes", op. cit., p. 47.

278 See Susan Christopherson and Stephen Ball, "Media Services: Considerations Relevant to Multilateral Trade Negotiations", in *Trade in Services: Sectoral Issues* (United Nations Publication, UNCTAD/ITP/26), p. 272.

279 *Ibid.*, p. 54. See also Christopherson and Ball, *op. cit.*

280 For more detailed information on this subject, refer GATT Document "Matters relating to trade in audiovisual services", MTN.GNG/AUD/W/31, p. 2.

281 See, for a discussion of the directive, John Howkins and Michael Foster, *Television in 1992: A Guide to Europe's New TV, Film and Video Business* (Cooper and Lybrand, 1989), pp. 57-89 and 121-24. For the text of the directive, see *Ibid.*, Appendix II.

Box IV-7

EMERGING PATTERNS OF OWNERSHIP, DISTRIBUTION AND PRODUCTION [a]

The dominant trends in media industries today, are (1) an increasing concentration of programming finance and distribution in a small number of transnational firms; (2) the integration of production and distribution, albeit in a different form than is typicall associated with classical "vertical integration" (where a firm both produces and distributes a product); and (3) cross-industry investment, especially in film and television production, in order to have maximum domination over their end markets. Media experts predict that four or five programme distributors will dominate the international market for broadcasting entertainment products within the next five years.

Currently the firms that finance and distribute the majority of entertainment products are located in the United States. They include the seven "majors" (Columbia (recently purchased by SONY), 20th Century-Fox, MGM/UA, Paramount Pictures, Universal Pictures, Warner Brothers, and Walt Disney Studios), descendants of the film protection studios, and the powerful private broadcasting networks (ABC, owned by the media conglomerate Capital Cities; NBC, owned by General Electric; and CBS.

There is a general trend of the horizontal consolidation of ownership of media production. Firms originally present in one subsector are now expanding into the other media sectors, e.g. from publishing to television. This process is assisted by the growing commonality of management and technical skills, especially with respect to computer technologies. An examination of the world's top "Media Giants", including Bertelsman (Federal Republic of Germany), Capital Cities/ABC (United States), Thompson (Canada), Time/Warner (United States) and Hachette (France) demonstrates this phenomenon.

---

a From Christopherson and Ball, *op. cit.*

States, such changes include: (i) a federal decision not to enforce the anti-trust provision that has prevented production and distribution firms to merge, and (ii) the possible abrogation of the "consent decrees" that prohibit television networks from producing their own programming, to be resolved in 1990.[282]

(e) *Impacts of technological and regulatory changes to world trade in the sector*

751. Technological progress, in conjunction with regulatory changes, has resulted in an increasing concentration of programming, finance and distribution in a small number of transnational firms; the integration of production and distribution; and cross-industry investment, especially in film and television production and distribution companies and publishing.[283] Possible consequences of these trends may include: (i) the failure of many of the new enterprises; (ii) the take over of weaker enterprises; (iii) the survival of enterprises only at the expense of cost-cutting and consequent poor-quality programming; and (iv) instability in domestic broadcasting.

(f) *Audiovisual services and development*

752. Audiovisual services are distinct from the other sectors discussed in this paper, because of their significance in relation to cultural and national identity which, in their turn, are increasingly being seen as essential to development. Films and television programmes can function as effective

---

282 See Christopherson and Ball, *op. cit.*, p. 289.

283 See Christopherson and Ball, *op. cit.*, pp. 284-88, for a discussion of the emerging patterns in ownership, distribution and production.

means for training and education, as well as for disseminating information and cultural values among the population. By provoking an enhanced sense of cultural and national identity, the audiovisual sector can make a major contribution to the development effort; it can also enhance the national prestige and have complementary effects on the exports of goods, services and technology. Therefore, in considering ways to strengthen the audiovisual services sector, conventional factors of competitiveness such as efficiency and marketability may not prove adequate.

753.   Studies on audiovisual services have shown that the present unidirectionality in the international traffic in this sector is largely due to economic factors rather than to regulatory barriers. They attribute the success of the United States exports of audiovisual services to: (i) the sheer size of the domestic market where production cost can be recuperated; (ii) the control of distribution channels by production firms (classical vertical integration), and (iii) the use of trade-restrictive business practices in order to maintain market domination. A new trend which would have a considerable impact on the international market is increasing cross-industry/country investment in film and television production and distribution companies. Presumably, the notion of origin of an entertainment product will be less significant in the context of world trade than how firm ownership patterns influence the nature, availability, diversity and cost of programming.[284]

754.   Trade in audiovisual services differs from that of many other services in that, unlike in tourism, construction or professional services where employment occurs and value is added at the final destination of the service, films and television programmes are finished products which are merely distributed at their final destination. The distancing of production and distribution in these industries virtually eliminates possibilities for technology transfer or highly skilled employment at the point of distribution. Thus, by contrast with some services in which developing countries could compete on the basis of a comparative labour-cost advantage, the production of media products is organized in such a way that almost all the labour inputs and certainly all the skilled labour inputs occur in centralized locations far removed from the distribution point. Secondly, all the costs in making the product are incurred in turning out the first copy of the film or television programme. Additional copies can be reproduced very inexpensively. So, profitability in this sector depends on timing and strategic control of the release of the film or programme, a process that has become more complicated as the number of different types of potential distribution outlets has multiplied world-wide. This constraint on potential profit intensifies the need to control distribution very tightly through, for example, ownership of distribution networks.

(g)   Audiovisual services in the Uruguay Round

755.   Negotiations in this area in the Uruguay Round are influenced by four main considerations: (a) the extremely dominant position of the United States in trade in cinema and television programmes, and the dependence of the United States film and television industry on export markets; (b) the widespread practice of most countries to restrict presentation of imported programmes for motives relating to the preservation of cultural values; (c) technical advances such as satellite TV broadcasting, high-definition television and expanded cable TV networks, particularly in Europe; and (d) "Europe 1992" and the "Television without Frontiers" initiative, which should result in broadcasting preferences in favour of EEC material in all EEC member States.

756.   The discussions in the Uruguay Round have focused on the issue of preservation of cultural values. The United States has strongly opposed any exception that would permit the restriction of trade in audio-visual services for cultural reasons, whether as a general exception in the overall framework or in any sectoral annotation. Most other countries recognized that the cultural issue was of crucial importance in this sector and would have to be taken into account in negotiating any liberalization commitments in trade in audio-visual services, but they had different views on how to deal with the issue in the multilateral framework. Some were in favour of drawing up a particular sectoral annotation which would provide for a liberalization in this sector while recognizing the legitimacy of policy instruments aimed at preserving cultural values. The EEC subsequently submitted a specific proposal in this respect.

757.   Some other countries recognized the legitimacy of cultural conservation, but considered

---

[284] See Christopherson and Ball, op. cit., p. 287.

that this could be covered by reservations in the schedules and not require a separate sectoral annotation. Certain other countries, including Canada, considered that cultural aspects extended beyond the audio-visual sector and should be through a general cultural exception to the framework itself. It should be borne in mind that Canada was successful in excluding "cultural industries" a much wider concept, from the Canada-United States Free Trade Agreements.[285] On the other hand, the dominant export cartel, the Motion Picture Association of America has been filing complaints against a variety of countries for alleged demand of market access for theatrical motion pictures, television programmes and the home video market[286] (under section 301 of the Trade Act of 1974 as amended) to encourage unilateral retaliatory action by the United States.

(h) Policy considerations

758.   Given the asymmetries in the market structure and in technological capability discussed above, and in the light of the uncertainty on the impact of technological advancement in the area of audiovisual services, developing countries may need to protect their national audiovisual industry in order to strengthen their domestic sector so as to enable it to face competition from foreign suppliers in the future, as well as to enter into agreements with countries in the same region or those with similar languages or cultural affinities. In the Uruguay Round negotiations on trade in services, the importance of such a right was recognized by the majority of the participants. It therefore seems necessary to preserve this right. The development of satellite television has already made the conventional concept of "national borders" meaningless. Financial and technical co-operation at the international level in the production of audiovisual products may help in reducing the risks and in increasing international market share. Production firms in developing countries could explore such co-operation with neighbouring countries and with developed countries in the production of cinema films and television programmes. Efforts might be made to create common "audiovisual spaces" based on common cultural affinities as has been decided in Europe and is being developed in Latin America and among Arab countries. Developed countries could assist by providing incentives to private channels or reserving time on public channels to show developing country films and other productors.

C. CONCLUSIONS AND POLICY RECOMMENDATIONS

759.   In paragraph 105 (19) of the Final Act of UNCTAD VII, the Conference requested UNCTAD to "continue its useful work in the field of services" under its existing mandate, as contained in Conference resolution 159(VI) and Board decision 309(XXX). Pursuant to this, UNCTAD has examined the general aspects of the changing role of the services sector in the world economy and its specific impact on the development process and on efforts of developing countries to improve their position in the international division of labour; it has also focused on trade in specific services sectors and the postion of developing countries in such trade. The former aspect was dealt with in considerable detail in the Trade and Development Report 1988, while this present study has given relatively more attention to sectoral issues.

760.   In addition, UNCTAD has been carrying out its technical assistance programme at the national level (see Box IV-9) which has enabled the secretariat to gain more specific, empirical experience and thus to enhance its expertise and its capacity to execute such national projects, as well as to attain more completely its original objective - i.e. to obtain a better understanding of the role of services in the development process.

---

[285] Peter Burn, "Professional Services and the Uruguay Round: Lessons from the Canada-United States Free Trade Agreement", in UNCTAD, *Trade in Services: Sectoral Issues* (United Nations Publication, UNCTAD ITP/26), pp.365-405, *op. cit.*

[286] See Christopherson and Ball, *op. cit.*

1. Common elements in increasing services trade

761. The preceding sections of this chapter have addressed the specific problems and opportunities facing developing countries in increasing their participation in world trade in specific services sectors. What is evident from this sectoral analysis is the remarkable extent to which these sectors, which until recently were considered to comprise largely unrelated activities falling into the residual category of "services", and governed by separate regulatory frameworks at both national and international levels, are in fact closely related in that a there seems to be a common set of factors which determine international competiveness in world trade in all traded services to varying extents. Action to address these factors effectively should form the main components of programmes of action at the national and international levels aimed at strengthening the services sectors in developing countries and enabling them to increase their share of world trade in services.

(a) *A modern telecommunications infrastructure*

762. It is not possible to imagine the development of a efficient and competitive services sector in the absence of a modern telecommunications and telematic infrastructure, which will contribute to increasing the overall efficiency of the domestic economy through the generalized reduction of transaction costs and permit the transborder data flows and the information networks which provide the mechanisms for intergration in the world economy to function. The financial services and air transport serctors have been the vanguards in this respect but all services have become dependent on telecommunications for their effective delivery, and increased tradability has opened up new export possobilities. The extremely uneven distribution of the systems and infrastructure necessary to increase the productivity of services and to transport services to export markets is a major impediment to increasing the contribution of services to the development process.

(b) *Access to technology and training facilities*

763. Advanced technology - especially information-related technology - is becoming increasingly crucial for competitiveness in a number of services, both traditional services such as insurance and shipping as well as "new services" such as computer-related services. The increased participation of developing countries in international trade in these services depends on their ability to meet the challenge of updating their technological base and providing adequate telecommunications infrastructures to enable the delivery of services. Technological change has necessitated investment in heavy capital equipment in some traditional services such as shipping, where containerization of cargo and transshipment have adversely affected developing-country participation in shipping trade. In a number of business service sectors in developing countries, the introduction of new technologies - mainly by affiliates of transnational corporations - has aggravated the segmentation of the domestic market into a dual structure, where large firms cater to large corporations and transnational clients, while smaller firms are directed at small domestic clients. Marketability of a large number of service products also depends on advanced technology, availability of skills, and better telematic infrastructures for transmission.

764. In most of these services, human skill formation also remains a vital determinant of competitiveness. Appropriate education facilities, especially higher education, directed at the specific needs of technological transformation need to be developed in a large number of developing countries, but on-the-job training remains to the most effective method. In some sections, for example certain professional services, this can be part of normal business operations, while in others (e.g. audiovisual) imports of services may impact little or no transfer of technology. Furthermore, as has been noted above, technological advances in engineering design, for example,

many tend to reduce the automatic transfer of technology inherent in services imports. However, a major form of human resources development in several services sectors is the on-the-job training of employees,[287] and the operations of transnational corporations can be used in order to facilitate transfer of technology, especially of soft technology, in many sectors. Thus in a number of services sectors, developing-country governments would need to take appropriate policy measures such as tying tax incentives or market access to appropriate company-training programmes. In the absence of such stipulations, the actvities of TNCs may not lead to any substantial change in the host country's technological or skill capacity.

(c) Market entry and transnational corporations

765.   Industrial concentration and the growing importance of TNCs constitute a major source of trade distortions and barriers to entry, which make it difficult for new entrants, especially from developing countries, to break into existing markets. Although the action space of TNCs is international, their objectives may not coincide with that of the nation States, and may reflect only the interests of central commanding bodies internal to the corporate structure. Although technological advance stimulates the creation of a multiplicity of small firms, this tendency is increasingly undermined by the need for massive capital requirements and complex interdisciplinary work in R & D as well by need for established organizational and marketing structures to exploit products commercially. Moreover, the rapid pace of technological change requires quick capital amortization; hence the need to block the emergence of new entrants through sheer scale and to acquire potential competitors, so as to prolong product life cycles and reap the corresponding returns for as long as possible.[288]

766.   The structure of TNCs and the internalized flow of goods, services and information across the corporate structure may have further negative effects on the capacity of host countries to follow their development objectives, as the specialized resources are kept captive within corporate boundaries in order to internalize benefits and to limit opportunities for market entry for others. The maintenance of client relationships on a global basis (with advertising or accounting firms) can preclude access for developing-country suppliers even in their own countries.[289] In the case of intracorporate service flows, the exclusive proprietary use of such resources has greater negative effects than for other intermediate inputs, as they do not constitute an externality to the host economy. Not only do these service transfers correspond to increased imports for the host country, but they also compete with and/or prevent the local supply by diverting a substantial part of services demand from the local market.

767.   Anti-competitive or trade-restrictive practices of TNCs can be a serious threat to the development of host countries.[290] Intra-firm arrangements that convert possible competition to co-operation, adverse effects on balance of payments, and price discrimination are among the problems posed by TNC activities. Transnational banking networks have demonstrated their capacity to evade taxes, to facilitate capital flights, and to conceal their operations from regulatory authorities. Their access to external sources of funding can be used in order to evade the impact of host-country monetary policies that aim to restrain monetary expansion. All this points to the need for adequate policy measures to ensure that the operation of TNCs are consonant with the development interests of the host country. Some developing countries have seen joint ventures as a way of ensuring such consonance. Other countries have stipulated explicit measures ensuring transfer of technology, location of important operations and decision-making functions in the host country, and the local sourcing of inputs combined with fiscal and other measures to promote the externalization of services production.

---

[287] With a boom in tourism and with the emergence of free zones in the Dominican Republic, the country came to face a deficit of about 375,000 technicians, most of whom were in key services such as managers, accountants, and engineers. In certain cases, this shortcoming has been overcome with a programme under the modality of "on-the-job training", notably in the tourism sector.

[288] See Flavia Martinelli in *Services in Asia and the Pacific*, Vol. II, UNCTAD ITP 51, Vol. II.

[289] Seih Mei Ling, *op. cit.*

[290] See Philip Brusick, Murray Gibbs and Mina Mashayekhi, "Anti-competitive Practices in the Service Sector", in *Uruguay Round: Further Papers on Selected Issues* (United Nations Publication, UNCTAD ITP 42), pp. 129-56, *op. cit.*

768.   In the Uruguay Round developing countries have been striving to include within the multilateral framework provisions to deal with anti-competitive practices in the services sector. Such practices have been identified in various services sectors, including insurance banking, transportation and travel telecommunications, etc. The difficulty of developing countries in effectively controlling such practices which affect their interests and the possibilities of abuse of unilateral actions would call for the negotiation of tighter multilateral commitments to promote competition policy and control restrictive business practices in services sector.

(d)   Participation in information networks and access to distribution channels

769.   Difficulties in obtaining access to, and effective participation in, information networks and distribution channels present developing-country firms with further problems in effectively participating in international services trade (as well as trade in goods) and from gaining in real terms from possible liberalization thereof, particularly in the light of the increasing use of telematic technologies, especially in air transport, banking, business services and computer-related services. The efforts by the European Economic Community to deal with biases involved in the operation of computerized reservation systems (CRS) used in air transport, such as display bias in favour of host carriers, manipulation of flight information, discriminatory booking charges and requirements of subscriber loyalty, illustrate one particular aspect of the difficulty of defining the frontier between networking strategies and anti-competitive practices and RBPs.[291] Economies of networking in air traffic have created problems in relation to the tourism sector as well. Vertical integration of several subsectors involved in the provision of tourism services may strengthen the dominance of transnational firms in these sectors and aggravating the problems of market entry for developing-country firms.

770.   The problem of access to distribution channels has become more acute in a situation where distribution has become internationalized, arms-length relations, which in theory separated trade and distribution, can no longer be considered the norm, and control can become more important than efficiency in penetrating foreign markets. However, for an increasing number of services, the distribution channel has become the information network.[292] Control of the distribution channels is vital in assuring profitability in exports of certain services, notably audivisual services, and dominance of distribution systems by TNCs - e.g. in computer software - can restrict the market entry of developing country firms.[293]

771.   In financial and business services too, networking seems to determine competitiveness. The introduction of new financial instruments, the use of advanced technologies and networking with foreign firms have created a two-tier structure in many developing-country service markets. Without greater participation in networks and access to distribution channels, it will be impossible for developing-country exports in these services to expand, especially in sectors where small firms have to compete on disadvantageous terms with big distributors and cartels. There is a need for a better understanding of networking strategies to enable developing countries to draw up regulations to ensure that their firms are able to increase their share of the value added created by intercorporate and transcorporate networks. There is also a need for more public networks (along the lines of ESPRIT in Europe) to facilitate access to technology.

(e)   Financial assistance

772.   Under the three above-discussed headings, some of the difficulties faced by developing-country firms in competing with large transnational firms of major financial strength, especially in areas where the technological change has made heavy capital investment a prerequisite for being competitive, have been noted already. Financial weakness of small firms in many sectors effec-

---

[291] *Ibid.*, pp. 142-44.

[292] It should be noted that "distribution" was one of the three major topics which the United States included in its bilateral "Strategic Impediments to Trade Initiative" discussions with Japan. See Bressand "Access to Networks" *op. cit.*

[293] See T. Noyelle "Computer Software and Computer Services", in UNCTAD/ITP/51, *op. cit.*

tively means exclusion from certain networks and certain markets. Furthermore, the smallness of domestic market in many sectors has prevented developing-country firms from acquiring the economies of scale essential for penetrating world markets. The impact of currency differentials further aggravates the difficulty in attaining competitiveness.

773. Financial assistance is required for developing-country firms to acquire the means to update their capital, diversify their services and acquire a presence in foreign markets, including distribution system. A larger problem relates to the enormous financial resources required for the updating of basic infrastructures in developing countries to enable domestic firms to participate more effectively in world trade, including telecommunications facilities, airport and port infrastructures, purchase of new aircaft and ships, better inland transport facilities, computerization, and adequate higher education facilities, as well as to ensure environmental protection in the provision of services such as air transport, tourism etc. These goals should receive the support of multilateral donors and lending agencies.

(f) Access to markets

774. In the Uruguay Round developing countries are pursuing the liberalization of regulations which impede their actual or potential exports of services. One of their main concerns is to liberalize restrictions impeding the temporary movement of personnel as described below. In certain cases, such as air transport, regulation effectively hinders developing-country access to markets, and concessions with respect to commercial presence can also benefit developing country firms. However, in general the impediments to developing country's increased participation in international trade in services would seem to be the non-regulatory barriers discussed above.

775. In this context it is worth noting that the fourth Lome Convention included detailed provisions for the development of the service sector in the ACP countries, including services supportive of the development process, including those supporting foreign trade, producer services and those supporting regional integration, tourism and transport, communications and informatics. However, it is also forseen that substantive provisions with respect to trade in services could be inserted into the Convention in light of the results of the Uruguay Round.

(g) Movement of personnel

776. In many service sectors, the movement of personnel across national frontiers is essential to the effective export of a service. For developing countries, this "mode of delivery" may be the only one available to export a variety of services. Restrictions prevalent in developed countries concerning the temporary movement of personnel, including visa and work permit restrictions, thus have a particularly adverse impact on developing-country exports of services. Not only semi-skilled labour (e.g. construction) but also high-technology services such as software services, trade and the transfer of soft technology often involve cross-border mobility of service providers. Such restrictions also adversely affect training and after-sales service. The recognition of professional qualifications may also function in certain markets as a barrier to exports from developing countries.

777. Many developing countries are net labour exporters, and remittances by overseas workers form a major source of income to some of them. Increasing restrictions on cross-border mobility of personnel have prevented these countries from benefiting from such exports. The multilateral framework on trade in services will need to contain important concessions on labour mobility if it is to ensure the greater participation of developing countries in international service trade.

2. Service-sector development strategies

(a) National policies

778.   Developing-country governments thus need to pursue the objectives of strengthened service sectors and increased participation for their firms in international trade in services, and the ability of their firms to participate in world trade in general. Such strategies seem to involve three essential components: (a) establishing an improved policy framework at the national level; (b) strengthening their negotiating postion in dealing with foreign govermnemts and corporations; and (c) pursuing improved multilateral co-operation to support these policies. Such approaches would have to be pursued at both the general and the sectoral levels.

779.   Many developing countries are faced with the challenge of rethinking their development policies in the services sector to take into account the linkages between sectors. The role of governments in many service sectors is increasingly moving from that of owners to that of regulators, and this may require considerable reorientation of policies. A number of measures implemented by governments in a different trade environment may impede the growth of developing-country service firms. Import duties and quantitative restrictions on goods and equipment essential for the efficient production and delivery of services may disadvantage domestic firms in building up competitiveness and sizeable economies of scale. A high degree of market concentration by State-owned enterprises in certain sectors (e.g. banking) might lead to a deterioration of efficiency in these sectors. A further problem concerns the prevalence of complex and not always transparent regulations and bureaucratic procedures. A greater harmonization of various organs of the government and a simplification of bureaucratic procedures may facilitate the growth of services. Unless the domestic service sectors are trained to face competition, liberalization of international trade may badly hurt services firms in many developing countries. Policies that combine encouragement to competition and adequate regulatory considerations are called for in several sectors.

780.   In national policies in the services sector, the creation of more and higher-quality knowledge-intensive employment opportunities will remain a high priority for many developing countries. Policies directed towards the growth of producer services would merit particular emphasis, taking into account the reliance of growth in manufacturing on producer services. The development of indigenous producer services will also need to be appropriately integrated with the process of adopting and applying advanced technologies in various sectors of production.

781.   Such strategies will depend upon policies aimed at human resources development - another major priority in the national policies in services. This will involve improved education facilities as well as the provision of adequate on-the-job training, including by TNCs. Developing countries may find it useful to identify priority areas by studying the supply aspects of the services sector and demand arising from the competitive needs of other sectors.

782.   The upgrading of information and telecommunications infrastructures is an extremely important priority for developing countries. This, in combination with human-resources development, constitutes the "information wealth" of a country, facilitating the development of new knowledge-intensive services. Improved telecommunications infrastructures are necessary for enhanced service activity in several other sectors as well as for the integration of marginal sections of the population. The provision of improved health care and legal services will also be important from this perspective.

783.   Appropriate government policies would need to be formulated for the creation of entities to provide necessary services that are domestically unavailable, but for which the development of a domestic capacity is seen as essential for strategic and other reasons mentioned above. The creation of services centres with appropriate infrastructures and incentives may increase the efficiency and cost-effectiveness of service production. It may also correct asymmetries in the geographical deployment of services production within the country, as the lack of access to services by individuals can only impede their welfare and erode their contribution to economic growth. Such entities may also serve to attract investment in services sectors. Government procurement policies can be used to stimulate domestic services production, especially small and medium-sized firms. Regulations to ensure internationally acceptable standards and quality are also necessary for ensuring the upgrading of services.

784.   The increased tradability of services provides the means for supplying services from distant geographical locations and thus, in theory, should enable developing countries to participate more effectively in the world market for services. Account should be taken of the fact that TNCs are

important (if not the predominant) actors in international markets for modern services. Pools of highly-skilled labour supported by state-of-the-art telecommunications infrastructures can attract knowledge-intensive services industries. An astute policy mix of human capital and infrastructural development and a well designed regulatory framework for services TNCs could constitute central elements in a services development and trade policy.

785.   The special characteristics of services would need to be taken into account in pursuing improved access to markets. Physical or regulatory barriers pertaining to any of the modes of delivery of services can adversely affect services transactions. Visa and work permit restrictions seem to impede the delivery of certain services by developing-country service providers in international markets, and efforts to remove such barriers would need to be pursued in bilateral, regional and multilateral forums. Information-related services allow greater transportability, and some developing countries have found a niche in such markets.[294] Relying on the pool of skilled personnel, many developing countries may be able to "leap frog" in new services, if adequate telematic infrastrucres can be developed.

786.   The formulation of export strategies on services (see Box IV-8) required greater information with respect to demand, to technological developments and the experience of other countries. Appropriate export-promotion measures such as tax incentives, relaxation of foreign-exchange regulations, duty-free import of essential equipment, and so on, seem to have enhanced the export performance of services in certain developing countries. In addition to these, there is a need for greater dissemination of information on international standards in quality, as well as for wider access to market intelligence on the specific characteristics of various foreign markets, and on other significant aspects of export.

787.   In relation to imports, the policies of developing countries are influenced to a large extent by policy considerations pertaining to the perceived strategic importance of certain services, balance-of-payments considerations, restrictive business practices, etc. In addition to these, factors such as geographical location of decision-making, the creation of knowledge-intensive jobs, and the contribution to productivity and innovation in other sectors may need to be taken into account. Policy measures are needed that combine market access in certain sub-markets of services sectors in order to enhance competition in compliance with specific conditions to be accepted by the foreign supplier benefiting from access. Developing-country policies may seek to ensure that such operations contribute to development objectives, such as (a) transfer of technology, (b) contribution to infrastructure, (c) higher-skilled employment opportunities, (d) access to and participation in information networks, (e) location of information resources and important decision-making in the host country, (f) access to downstream services for distribution, market intelligence, etc., and (h) the use of local producer services. Furthermore, adequate prudential regulations may need to be formulated in order to cope with the anti-competitive effects of corporate practices in certain sectors.

788.   What is striking in this context is that the attainment of the ability to compete (i.e. primarily through the transfer of technolgy and financial resources) as well as the opportunity to compete (participation in networks and access to distribution channels, access for temporary movement of persons) would reflect to a large extent the negotiating ability of developing-country Governments, in negotiations with foreign governments and enterprises. It would thus seem advisable that national strategies in developing countries contain, as an inherent component, consideration of measures to strengthen the bargaining position and the negotiating capacity in negotiations relating to services. However, the majority of smaller and more vulnerable countries will find it difficult to mobilize effective bargaing power and will remain dependent upon the establishment of effectrive mehanisms for international cooperation.

[294] See *Services in the World Economy, op. cit.*,Chapter V.

Box IV-8

SERVICE EXPORT STRATEGIES [a]

Many developing countries recognize the need for the formulation of specific strategies to increase their foreign exchange earnings from the service sector. The development of export markets for services not only contributes to balance-of-payments equilibrium but provides a stimulus for improving employment opportunities and strengthening the domestic service sector in general. Service export strategies could also be seen as methods of strengthening domestic service firms and upgrading the knowlegde base of the population rather than simply as a source of foreign exchange.

The specific characteristics of services should be taken into account in the formulation of a strategy for the preparation of foreign service markets. One is that market penetration can be achieved using different modes of delivery or combinations of these modes; Physical or regulatory barriers affecting such modes of delivery will have an effect on the ability to penetrate foreign markets. Given the high human capital content of services, the key to many service export strategies is to offer relatively high skills at relatively low prices. The problem is the "delivery" of such services to customers. In many cases visa regulations particularly hamper the export of services that have a high labour content (e.g. construction or professional services) in which certain developing country firms have demonstrated their competitive ability.

Foreign exchange earnings from labour-intensive services can best be achieved, as noted above, by taking advantage of the greater transportability of goods and persons wherever possible. The information "mode" is where the most impressive advances in transportability have occured, and some developing countries are finding niches in the market for information or data services, especially in relatively labour-intensive segments, while others are exploring ways of using transborder information flows as a means of penetrating foreign markets for services.

Another characteristic is the link between services and trade in goods. The export of certain goods can lead to the export of services and vice versa. It would appear that this services-following-goods scenario is most effective in the case of high technology goods where specialized follow-up training and maintenance are required and can often only be provided by the producer of the goods for technical and/or contractual reasons. Developing countries' policies could aim at incorporating the maximum amount of domestically produced services in the goods before export and avoid the situation in which continually increasing service imports are required to export the same volume of goods. If this approach is to yield benefits, domestic production of services must be competitive.

Some developing countries have been able to develop goods-following-services strategies, linking their export of consultancy engineering services to subsequent exports of capital goods. In this area, however, the financing package is crucial. The more competitive developing country service suppliers are often placed at a disadvantage vis-á-vis developed country competitors who are able to offer a comprehensive services-goods-financing package.

Service export strengths are often found "locked-in" within the manufacturing, agroindustry and extractive sectors, and can become exportable if externalized. Given the growing demand for producer services, strategies based on externalizing the services content in other sectors and organizing them so as to penetrate export markets to a greater extent conssitute an approach that shows much promise. Whole "packages" of services can be provided from a specific goegraphical locality (i.e. a "service centre") by (a) ensuring the maximum transportability of the factors mentioned above through facilities for the movement of people (airports), goods (seaports), information (teleports) and capital (appropriate regulations), and (b) establishing the necessary services infrastructure (communications, education and finance), all of which can be concentrated in the locality concerned.

Competitive positions can be built on strategies that take into account the particular advantages of the country in terms of knowledge and experience that have developed for historical, geographical and cultural reasons. Often the factors contributing to such advantages may not have been recognized in the past. In this context, the development of a producer service sector linked to the manufacturing or agro-industry sectors can in itself provide an export capacity in services. In countries where these other sectors are not on a scale to permit this approach, advantages can be built upon in other more traditional services (e.g. transportation, tourism), modern information and telecommunication services or on special skills and cultural and geographical factors.

---

a From TDR/8/Part II/Offprint

(b) International cooperation

789.   Regional and subregional co-operation can facilitate the growth of trade in services. Services have already been included in various regional integration programmes among developing countries in the Caribbean including in West Africa, in Central America, and in ASEAN. Existing specializations and complementarities as well as cultural commonalities can be utilized here in order to enhance trade and competitiveness in services. Exports to outside the region can be promoted through joint corporate mechanisms, and joint approaches and common regulatory mechanisms may help in enhancing the bargaining power of member countries in such groups. Pooling of resources through regional co-operation in order to buy into information networks and distribution channels as well as for infrastructural updating can be a solution to the problems posed by the financial weakness of individual countries.

790.   A significant area for action in order to increase the participation of developing countries in international services trade is indeed the attempt to formulate a multilateral framework for trade in services in the context of the Uruguay Round of multilateral trade negotiations. However, in order to fulfil the objective of contributing to the development of developing countries, such a framework should include operationally effective provisions to ensure greater access for developing-country services exporters to developed-country markets. As the export potential of many developing countries depends on the liberalization of cross-border mobility of services providers, the framework would need to recognize the need for changes in the national regimes of developed countries to make possible such mobility. The framework would also need to ensure the prohibition of measures and practices that impede access to information networks and distribution channels as well as the elimination of measures that impede or limit free choice in the acquisition of access to technologies. The multilateral framework emerging from the Uruguay Round could provide a major stimulus to developing-country trade in services to the extent that it would allow them to gain credit for commitments to liberlaization in the form of effective access to world markets for their services exports and other benefits mentioned above.

791.   The developing countries have insisted in the negotiations of a multilateral framework on services that obligations be imposed on all parties to take all possible measures to prevent the use of unfair trade practices by services firms, including through the establishment of international standards and disciplines for the control of adverse effects of anti-competitive private sector behaviour, as well as an appropriate multilateral mechanism for the enforcement of such standards and disciplines. They have supported a multilateral framework on trade in services under which market access and national treatment will be accorded through specific concessions based on a "positive list" approach, and which would be based on the unconditional MFN principle and universal coverage. Provisions to the effect that foreign services providers in developing countries should accept conditions with respect to transfer of technology, training, and access to their information networks and distribution channels are seen as appropriate conditions for market access. The competitiveness of developing-country firms could be enhanced by the establishment of public information and R & D networks at the world level. The framework should formally recognize the pressing need for positive action on the part of developed countries to ensure effective market access for developing-country firms to their markets, including on a preferential basis where relevant. Concessions offered by developing countries will have to be made a function of the specific benefits contained in the offers of developed-country participants. Developing countries should be vigilant to ensure that the rules and procedures of the framework itself, as well as the concessions offered as initial commitments, are such as to ensure the maximization of their negotiating leverage in the future Rounds that will be conducted within the framework.

792.   However, access to markets provided as initial commitments in the Uruguay Round framework may provide limited benefits to developing countries in that, owing to the various other impediments mentioned above, developing countries may not be able to take advantage of market access opportunities. An intense programme of international cooperation would be required to strengthen the services sectors in developing countries to enable them to develop new competitive abilities in both services and goods.

(c)   *An action programme for UNCTAD*

793.   The preceding paragraphs have addressed the question of how to strengthen the services sectors of developing countries as a means to accelerate their development, to facilitate the adjustment process and to increase their participation in world trade in services. They have identified the impediments faced by developing countries in attaining this objective and suggest means of overcoming them. The following paragraphs suggest an UNCTAD role which would constitute an important initiative aimed at addressing and removing all such impediments.

794.   These impediments fall broadly into three categories. First, there are other countries' regulations which may act as barriers to developing-country exports of services. The Uruguay Round negotiations are currently involved in the negotiation of "initial commitments" under which specific commitments will be agreed to provide market access and national treatment for a list of sectors and subsectors, and with respect to four modes of delivery, i.e. cross-border movement, movement of consumers, commercial presence, movement of personnel. It would appear that, in general, liberalization with respect to cross-border movement and commercial presence may provide only limited benefit for developing-country enterprises which do not possess means comparable to TNCs to deliver their services so as to penetrate and compete in foreign markets. One notable example is air transport, where inadequate market access (reflecting their weaker negotiating postion) would appear to have penalized developing country airlines. On the other hand, the liberalization of the movement of personnel, accompanied by the recognition of professional qualifications, could provide substantial benefit to a significant number of developing countries.

795.   The negotiations currently under way are seen as the first of a series of "rounds" of negotiations aimed at increasing the level of liberalization commitments on services within the context of the multilateral framework, and could provide meaningful benefit to developing countries if concessions are made with respect to sectors and barriers of interest to developing countries. UNCTAD, drawing upon its experience to date, could help to identify sectors and subsectors of services of export interest to developing countries and barriers to such trade, as well as sectors where developing countries could derive substantial benefit from preferential market access.

796.   A second set of impediments to the achievement of the objectives of strengthened services sectors in developing countries, and their greater participation in world trade in services, relates to the practices of private enterprises. In the Uruguay Round negotiations, the draft multilateral framework envisages an article intended to oblige signatories to collaborate to deal with anti-competitive practices of what are termed "private operators". Traditionally the developed countries have taken the view that restrictive business practices (RBPs) should be eliminated through the effective enforcement of national competition legislation, and it is still not clear to what extent binding multilateral commitments will be incorporated in the multilateral framework. In any case, the established role of UNCTAD with respect to the identification of RBPs would appear particularly necessary in services, given the fact that the introduction of information technologies have somewhat blurred the frontiers between RBPs and legitimate networking strategies.

797.   It has been recognized that, in order to increase their participation in world trade in services, developing countries require improved access to information networks and distribution channels, as these again fall into the realm of the private sector and thus it may be difficult to obtain much more than a general exhortation in the multilateral framework. Access to and participation in networks require national strategies aimed at increasing the value added from such participation. This would require a better understanding of the functioning of networks which would have to be obtained through contacts with the private sector, while the implementation of a networking strategy would require an appropriate regulatory framework. UNCTAD could undertake studies on this issue and provide mechanisms for propagating information to developing countries in collaboration with the private sector.

798.   The third, and perhaps most important, barrier is that presented by the inherent weaknesses and lack of competitiveness of developing-country services sectors. As has been indicated above, a key element in strengthening developing country services is the effective transfer of technology, particularly from TNCs. Developing countries are placing high expectations on the conditions to be imposed on foreign suppliers benefiting from access commitments negotiated in the Uruguay Round, but a coherent across-the-board policy would seem to be called for as part of general services policies which take account of the relationships between the services and the manufacturing and agricultural sectors as well as those among services sectors. Such policies are emerging in the

context of studies organized by UNCTAD at the national level, leading to strategies aimed at increasing the support of the services sector to the competitiveness of other sectors, expanding the services sector's contribution to the balance of payments and making full use of the services sector role in upgrading and expanding employment opportunities.

799.   International co-operation is an essential component of such strategies, including regional and subregional cooperation among developing countries in the various areas described above and financial and technical assistance to developing countries. In addition to a continuation and intensification of its technical assistance programme, UNCTAD could assist developing countries by monitoring closely developments in the various services sectors with respect to trade flows, trade liberalization, identification of barriers and opportunities, possibilities for international co-operation, technological developments, etc.   In this respect, specific mechanisms, including a committee on services, could be established in UNCTAD, under the auspices of the Trade and Development Board,   which could assume the responsibility for (i) drawing up an action programme for the strengthening of the services sectors in developing countries and increasing developing-country participation in world trade in services; (ii) providing as appropriate studies, data and background information to facilitate the implementation of the action programme; and (iii) monitoring the implementation of the action programme;

800.   There would also be a need to build upon the existing technical assistance activities to establish a comprehensive programme of technical cooperation with developing countries in the area of services; such a programme would be aimed at supporting the national study exercises to ensure that the recent developments and trends in trade in services were taken into account and to provide a mechanism for cooperation among developing countries, and with developed countries, in the formulation and execution of service-oriented development strategies. It could also be directed to assisting developing countries to participate effectively in the future rounds of negotiations under the multilateral framework established in the Uruguay Round. UNDP is being approached to allocate sufficient resources for this purpose during the Fifth Programming Cycle.

Box IV-9

TECHNICAL ASSISTANCE ON SERVICES

Conference resolution 159(VI) instructed the UNCTAD secretariat to study the role of services in the development process. Subsequently, Trade and Development Board decision 309 (XXX) established a work progamme which specified that the UNCTAD secretariat, among other things, should assume the task of "assisiting, upon request and within available resources, Member States in their analysis of the role of services in their economies". In the Final Act of UNCTAD VII, UNCTAD was requested to continue its pro grammes of technical assistance to developing countries in the field of services, and the UNDP was invited to consider favourably the requests for the provision of adequate financial resources for this purpose.

UNCTAD has received requests from 40 developing countries, and has managed to obtain the reources to respond positively most of them, at least by sending a technical mission to assist in the conception and organization of a national study, and in the preparation of preliminary "profiles" of the services sector in the country concerned. This has been possible largely through UNDP support, particularly in the context of existing technical assistance projects. In certain cases developed countries have collaborated with UNCTAD in carrying out its mandate.

Full fledged, comprehensive studies have only been possible when national UNDP IPFs have been used. This was the case, for example, in Mexico, where the initiation of work under such a project as far back as 1987 is demed to have greatly assisted that country to assume a leading role in the UruguayRound negotiations on services and in the current negotiations aimed at a Free Trade Area for goods and services with Canada and the United States. Similar studies have been or are being conducted in various developing countries in all regions.

It can be observed that developing countries seeking assistance in this respect are guided by several different preoccupations, which lead them to give varying emphasis to such factors as (a) the contribution of the services sector to the productivity, efficiency, and international competitiveness of the manufacturing, agricultural and of other services sectors, as an element in the adjustment process, (b)the contribution of the services sector to balance of the external sector of the economy, and to actual and potential foreign exchange earnings, (c) the contibution of the services sector to more, and higher quality employment opportunities, and in increasing the knowledge-intensity of human capital, (d) the role of an efficient services sector in attracting foreign direct investment, (e) effective particiaption in multilateral, regional and bilateral negotiations on services.

Annex Table IV-I

THE TOP 20 EXPORTERS OF SERVICES IN 1989

Rank	ALL SERVICES	Value ($ billion)	Share (% of world total)	SHIPPING	Value ($ billion)	Share (% of world total)
1	United States	90.5	15.4	Japan	9.4	11.8
2	France	61.7	10.5	France	7.0	8.8
3	United Kingdom	45.6	7.8	Italy	6.8	8.5
4	Germany, Fed.Rep.of	39.0	6.6	Norway	6.2	7.7
5	Japan	37.1	6.3	United States	5.8	7.3
6	Italy	33.7	5.7	Germany, Fed.Rep.of	5.3	6.6
7	Spain	24.8	4.2	United Kingdom	4.6	5.8
8	Netherlands	23.9	4.1	Netherlands	4.6	5.7
9	Belgium/Luxembourg	22.1	3.8	Belgium/Luxembourg	4.0	5.0
10	Austria	18.0	3.1	Sweden	2.6	3.2
11	Switzerland	14.1	2.4	Denmark	2.5	3.1
12	Canada	13.8	2.4	Korea, Rep.of	2.2	2.7
13	Sweden	11.1	1.9	Czechoslovakia	1.6	2.0
14	Singapore	11.0	1.9	Spain	1.6	2.0
15	Norway	10.4	1.8	China	1.4	1.7
16	Denmark	9.8	1.7	Singapore	1.4	1.7
17	Mexico	9.4	1.6	Poland	1.4	1.7
18	Korea, Rep.of	9.3	1.6	Austria	1.2	1.5
19	Australia	7.9	1.3	Brazil	0.9	1.1
20	Turkey	5.7	1.0	New Zealand	0.9	1.1
	Top 20 countries	498.9	85.1	Top 20 countries	71.4	8.9
	World total	608.5	100.0	World total	80.3	100.0

Rank	TRAVEL	Value ($ billion)	Share (% of world total)	PASSENGER SERVICES	Value ($ billion)	Share (% of world total)
1	United States	34.4	18.1	United States	10.1	27.3
2	France	16.2	8.5	United Kingdom	4.5	12.2
3	Spain	16.2	8.5	Germany, Fed.Rep.of	3.9	10.6
4	Italy	11.9	6.3	Spain	1.7	4.6
5	United Kingdom	11.3	5.9	Japan	1.5	4.0
6	Austria	10.7	5.6	Italy	1.4	3.8
7	Germany, Fed.Rep.of	8.6	4.5	Switzerland	1.4	3.8
8	Canada	6.1	3.2	Netherlands	1.4	3.7
9	Switzerland	5.7	3.0	Australia	1.1	3.1
10	Mexico	4.8	2.5	Korea, Rep.of	0.8	2.2
11	Thailand	3.8	2.0	Belgium/Luxembourg	0.8	2.1
12	Korea, Rep.of	3.3	1.7	Sweden	0.8	2.1
13	Australia	3.2	1.7	Finland	0.5	1.3
14	Japan	3.1	1.7	Egypt	0.5	1.3
15	Belgium-Luxembourg	3.1	1.6	Thailand	0.5	1.3
16	Netherlands	3.0	1.6	Yugoslavia	0.5	1.3
17	Singapore	2.9	1.5	Norway	0.5	1.3
18	Portugal	2.7	1.4	Malaysia	0.4	1.1
19	Turkey	2.6	1.3	China	0.4	1.0
20	Sweden	2.5	1.3	Mexico	0.3	0.9
	Top 20 countries	156.1	81.9	Top 20 countries	33.0	89.0
	World total	191.0	100.0	World total	37.0	100.0

(For source see end of table.)

(.../. continued)

Annex table IV-I (continued)

THE TOP 20 EXPORTERS OF SERVICES IN 1989 (continued)

Rank	OTHER TRANSPORTATION	Value ($ billion)	Share (% of world total)	"OTHER" SERVICES	Value ($ billion)	Share (% of world total)
1	United States	14.6	20.8	France	26.7	12.7
2	France	11.8	16.9	United States	25.6	12.2
3	Japan	7.2	10.3	United Kingdom	21.4	10.2
4	Netherlands	5.7	8.1	Germany, Fed.Rep.of	17.5	8.3
5	United Kingdom	3.8	5.4	Japan	15.8	7.5
6	Germany, Fed.Rep.of	3.6	5.2	Belgium/Luxembourg	12.8	6.1
7	Singapore	2.4	3.5	Italy	12.7	6.1
8	Egypt	2.4	3.4	Netherlands	9.3	4.4
9	Spain	2.0	2.8	Canada	6.7	3.2
10	Belgium/Luxembourg	1.5	2.2	Switzerland	6.6	3.1
11	Australia	1.4	2.0	Austria	6.0	2.8
12	Denmark	1.2	1.7	Sweden	4.4	2.1
13	Sweden	0.8	1.2	Singapore	4.2	2.0
14	Yugoslavia	0.8	1.2	Mexico	3.9	1.9
15	Italy	0.8	1.1	Denmark	3.7	1.8
16	Norway	0.6	0.8	Spain	3.3	1.6
17	Finland	0.5	0.8	Greece	2.6	1.2
18	Korea, Rep. of	0.5	0.7	Korea, Rep. of	2.4	1.2
19	Panama	0.5	0.7	Turkey	2.2	1.0
20	Ireland	0.5	0.7	Philippines	2.0	0.9
	Top 20 countries	62.6	89.5	Top 20 countries	189.8	90.3
	World total	69.9	100.0	World total	213.7	100.0

Source: IMF, *Balance of Payments Statistics,* and UNCTAD secretariat Data Base.

Chapter V

COMMODITIES

A. COMMODITIES AND ECONOMIC DEVELOPMENT

1. Commodities in world trade

801. The importance of commodities in world trade decreased considerably during the 1980s, their share falling from 41 to 26 per cent. As can be seen from chart V-1, the share of fuels declined the most, from 23 per cent in 1979/81 to 10 per cent in 1987/89, but the shares of the three other commodity groups also declined. Overall, the value of commodity trade fell from an annual average of US$ 779 billion in the period 1979/81 to US$ 739 billion in 1987/89 (in SDRs, from 624 billion to 573 billion).[295] This decline was mainly due to a fall in prices: UNCTAD's commodity price index for this period shows a decline of 15 per cent in dollar terms, and 18 per cent in SDRs.

802. In terms of world market shares (see chart V-2), developing countries became less important as commodity exporters, mainly because of their declining role in fuel exports.

803. The reverse was the situation for developed market-economy countries. Developing countries' share of world commodity imports did not change significantly, both including and excluding fuels. However, their total commodity imports increased as a percentage of their total commodity exports from 37 to 56 per cent over the period. Developed market-economy countries took an increasing share of non-fuel commodity imports, while that of countries of Eastern Europe declined.

804. Developing countries' commodity export earnings fell dramatically from an annual average of US$ 405 billion during the period 1979/81 to US$ 271 billion in 1987/89 (325 billion to 208 billion in SDRs). West Asia accounted for most of this drop: its export earnings, mainly from fuels, fell from US$ 182 billion to US$ 79 billion (or 145 billion to 60 billion SDRs). Africa's commodity export earnings contracted by 40 per cent, while that of South and South-East Asia grew slightly as a result of a strong growth in new and traditional commodity exports.

805. Export earnings have been highly volatile at the country level and shortfalls in non-fuel commodity export earnings intensified during the second half of the 1980s, as illustrated in chart V-3, for the six commodities that account for the major part of these shortfalls. Virtually all developing countries experienced such shortfalls, which are estimated at an annual average of 4 billion SDRs for the commodity sector as a whole. In more than one third of the countries these shortfalls were of a recurrent nature. The size of shortfalls for fuels was even more dramatic, averaging 42 billion SDRs a year.[296]

806. As can be seen from chart V-3, shortfalls in export earnings of developing countries often tend to coincide with an increase in world export volumes. Thus, shortfalls reflect depressed world market prices rather than a temporary self-reversing problem at the individual country level. On the other hand, shortfalls in export earnings can reflect diversification of individual country exports in response to market conditions.

---

[295] Expressing trade in SDRs compensates partly for the fall in value of the $US in relation to other currencies.
[296] UNCTAD secretariat calculations based on four-year arithmetic average formula.

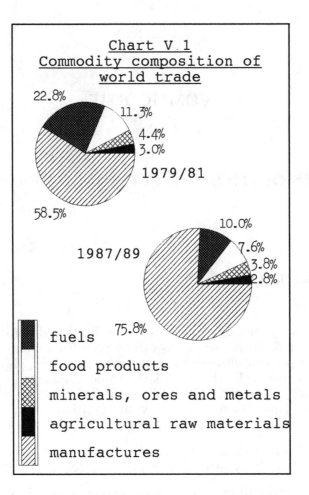

Chart V.1
Commodity composition of world trade

22.8%   11.3%
4.4%
3.0%

1979/81

58.5%

1987/89   10.0%
7.6%
3.8%
2.8%

75.8%

■ fuels
□ food products
⬚ minerals, ores and metals
■ agricultural raw materials
▨ manufactures

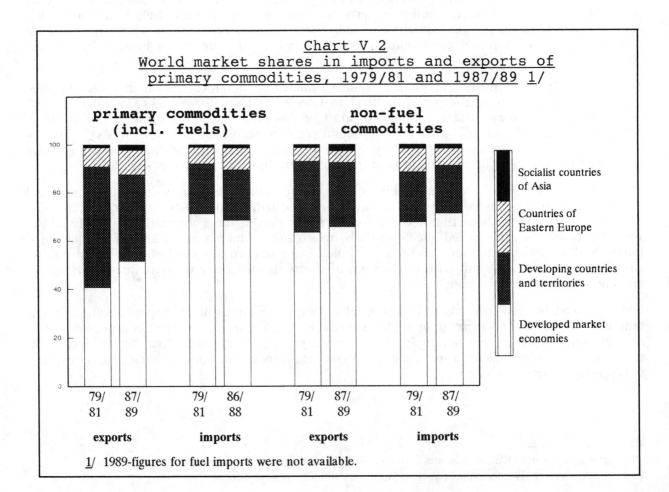

Chart V.2
World market shares in imports and exports of primary commodities, 1979/81 and 1987/89 1/

primary commodities (incl. fuels)   **non-fuel commodities**

Socialist countries of Asia

Countries of Eastern Europe

Developing countries and territories

Developed market economies

| 79/81 | 87/89 | 79/81 | 86/88 | 79/81 | 87/89 | 79/81 | 87/89 |

exports   imports   exports   imports

1/ 1989-figures for fuel imports were not available.

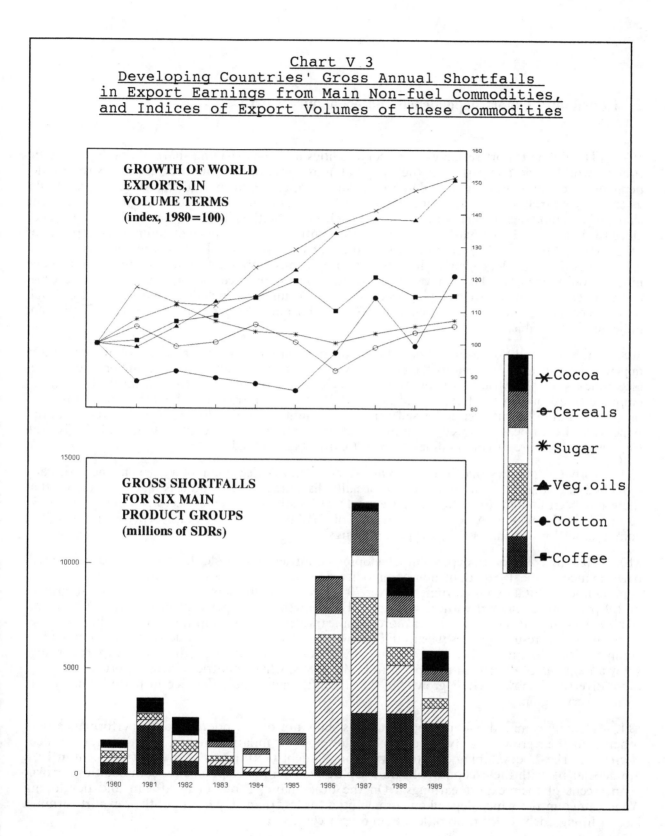

Chart V 3
Developing Countries' Gross Annual Shortfalls in Export Earnings from Main Non-fuel Commodities, and Indices of Export Volumes of these Commodities

GROWTH OF WORLD EXPORTS, IN VOLUME TERMS (index, 1980=100)

GROSS SHORTFALLS FOR SIX MAIN PRODUCT GROUPS (millions of SDRs)

Cocoa
Cereals
Sugar
Veg.oils
Cotton
Coffee

2. Commodity export dependence and economic growth

807. The falling export revenues from commodities and the declining share of developing countries in world trade contrast with the fact that most developing countries are still strongly dependent on commodities for their domestic production, employment and export earnings. While, as can be seen from table V-1, South and South-East Asian countries experienced a decrease of the share of commodities in their total exports which brought their level of commodity dependence close to that of developed market economies, the continuing importance of commodity exports for other Asian, African and developing American countries is striking. Table V-1 under-estimates the extent of commodity dependence, since exports of precious stones and gold have not been included in commodity exports. These have grown strongly in importance for many countries, and especially affect the figures for developing Oceania. For instance, by including gold exports for developing Oceania, commodity dependence in 1987/89 fell to only 83 per cent, vis-à-vis the 76 per cent indicated in the table.

808. In South and South-East Asia, most countries shared in the decrease in overall commodity dependence, but in other regions the decrease was confined to only a limited number of countries (see annex V-1). In Africa, five countries registered a decrease by over 10 per cent in the share of commodity exports in total export earnings, while in 40 countries, the share did not change significantly, and in four it even increased. In the 31 countries of developing America, ten (6 Latin-American, 4 Carribean) showed a significant diversification out of commodities, while in five (all Carribean) the share of commodities in export earnings increased.

809. Table V-2 shows that in developing America and Africa commodity dependence basically remained unchanged; a situation that is especially discouraging if account is taken of the fact that there has been limited diversification of exports within the commodity sector. Twenty out of 31 countries in developing America, and 39 out of 47 African countries are dependent on only 2 commodities for over half of their export earnings.

810. Heavily commodity-dependent developing countries as a whole show a much poorer growth performance in the 1980s than non-commodity dependent countries. Countries with a share of commodities in total export earnings of over 70 per cent had an (unweighted) average GDP growth of 1.9 per cent, compared with an average GDP growth of 3.2 per cent in countries where this share is less than 70 per cent. Even more significant, this relationship holds true within every region. A similar result emerges when GDP growth is related to extent of dependence on individual commodities. Countries where one or two commodities make up over half of total export earnings show an annual GDP growth of 2 per cent in the 1980s, while countries where export earnings are more diversified show a GDP growth of 3 per cent; again, this difference in performance exists within every region.

811. Heavily commodity-dependent countries show not only a poorer growth performance than others, but their growth in investment is also lower, their inflation higher, and their foreign debt is greater. The 25 developing countries with foreign debt/GNP ratios of over 100 per cent in 1988 are dependent, with the exception of Lao People's Democratic Republic, on commodities for over 70 per cent of their export earnings. On the other hand, 2 out of 3 African and developing American countries which depend on commodities for less than 70 per cent of their export earnings have a foreign debt/GNP ratio of less than 50 per cent.

812. Heavily commodity-dependent countries also experience relatively larger shortfalls in their export earnings. As shown in Table V-3, for the group of countries where non-fuel commodity export account for more than 70 per cent of total non-fuel export earnings, cumulative commodity sector shortfalls in the 1980s represented the equivalent of 7 months of total exports earnings - much higher than for other groups. In fact, their situation is even worse than appears from the table. In one fifth of them, commodity-sector shortfalls in the 1980s represented more than 2 years' export earnings.

813. Why have commodity-dependent countries performed so dismally? Several reasons can be mentioned. To begin with, as will be discussed in section B.2 below, for the past ten years inter-

Table V-1

Commodity dependence by region, 1979-1981 and 1987-1989

A. The role of commodity exports

| | | OECD | Countries of Eastern Europe | Asia & Pacific | | | Developing America | Africa | |
				West Asia	South & SE Asia	Developing Oceania		North Africa	Sub-Saharan Africa
share of primary commodities in total export earnings (%)	1979-1981	25.6	38.0	96.0	47.7	90.6	79.1	96.8	94.8
	1987-1989	19.1	36.4	84.2	21.5	76.0	67.3	85.9	91.6
share of non-fuel primary commodities in non-fuel export earnings (%)	1979-1981	20.4	10.4	38.3	29.1	90.3	68.1	74.1	87.3
	1987-1989	15.9	14.9	32.2	15.5	75.7	57.5	48.6	85.4

B. The role of commodity imports a/

| | | OECD | Countries of Eastern Europe | Asia & Pacific | | | Developing America | Africa | |
				West Asia	South & SE Asia	Developing Oceania		North-Africa	Sub-Saharan Africa
share of primary commodity imports in total imports (%)	1979-1981	50.4	40.8	27.2	41.3	46.8	27.7	35.4	30.4
	1986-1988	28.9	36.8	27.8	28.1	33.4	24.0	32.0	34.6
share of non-fuel primary commodities in non-fuel imports (%)	1979-1981	27.1	31.8	18.9	24.3	25.5	14.5	30.7	18.6
	1986-1988	21.2	22.7	21.3	19.1	23.1	14.7	29.6	25.2

Source: UNCTAD secretariat calculations, based on UNCTAD Commodity Yearbook 1991 and other sources.
a/ 1989-figures for fuel imports were not available.

national commodities prices have fallen in relation to those of manufactures. Commodity producers have generally been unable to translate increases in productivity into increases in factor payments (wages, land rent, capital income); instead, the productivity gains have tended to be absorbed by lower commodity prices. This limits the potential of the commodity sector to act as an engine for development.

814.   The negative effect of declining commodity prices on the growth of commodity-dependent countries is compounded by the fact that in these countries the commodity sector tends to account for a high proportion of total GDP. Analysis shows that for the 31 countries which depend on up to three non-fuel commodities for more than 75 per cent of their export earnings, such commodity exports constituted on average about 20 per cent of their GDP. In the case of fuel dependent exporters, the share in GDP was even higher. In contrast, where the three main commodities accounted for less than 50 per cent of total export earnings, the share in GDP of total commodity exports was under 9 per cent.

Table V-2

Extent of commodity dependence by region, 1979-1981 and 1987-1989

A. Share of commodities in total export earnings

		1979-1981			1987-1989		
		< 50%	50-70%	> 70%	< 50%	50-70%	> 70%
		(number of countries)			(number of countries)		
OECD-countries		17	1	3	17	2	2
Countries of Eastern Europe		5	1	-	5	1	-
Asia & Pacific	West Asia	-	1	9	1	1	8
	South & SE Asia	2	4	10	7	5	4
	Developing Oceania	1	-	8	-	1	8
Developing America		1	8	22	4	6	21
Africa	North-Africa	-	1	5	1	1	4
	Sub-Saharan Africa	-	3	38	1	-	40

B. Share of the two main commodities in total export earnings

		1979-1981			1987-1989		
		< 50%	50-70%	> 70%	< 50%	50-70%	> 70%
		(number of countries)			(number of countries)		
OECD-countries		19	1	1	20	-	1
Countries of Eastern Europe		5	1	-	5	1	-
Asia & Pacific	West Asia	1	-	9	1	1	8
	South & SE Asia	9	3	4	10	4	2
	Developing Oceania	2	1	6	2	5	2
Developing America		13	11	7	11	14	6
Africa	North-Africa	1	2	3	3	1	2
	Sub-Saharan Africa	4	15	22	5	12	24

Source: Annex V.I, and UNCTAD Commodity Yearbook 1991

Table V-3

**Commodity sector shortfalls for countries
grouped by dependence on non-fuel commodity export earnings**

Country category Dependence on non-fuel commodities in export earnings a/	number of countries	Total commodity sector shortfalls b/ (billions of SDRs)	Percentage of total developing country commodity sector shortfalls	Percentage of total developing country export earnings (1987-1989)	Commodity sector shortfalls in terms of months of export earnings c/
> 70%	66	21.0	51	17	7
50-70%	10	7.3	18	10	4
< 50%	18	12.2	30	73	1
Total	94	40.5	100	100	2

a/   Total non-fuel commodity export earnings divided by total non-fuel export earnings.
b/   Shortfall of commodity sector export earnings relative to four-year moving average of these earnings.
c/   Total commodity sector shortfalls for every category, divided by its monthly average total export earnings in the period 1987-1989.

815.   More generally, the same constraints that generally keep countries in a commodity dependent position - lack of human resource development, of infrastructure and of access to investment flows - also hinder overall economic development. An analysis of individual country experience shows that those which were heavily dependent in the late 1960s on up to three commodities for their export earnings have had a poorer record in diversifying than other countries. They were less able to introduce new exports or expand the role of minor exports, and when new commodity exports became important it often was at the expense of formerly important ones. Their manufacturing exports hardly grew and, indeed, in many countries fell from their already low levels.

816.   Furthermore, the commodity sector in many cases continues to show a lack of linkages with the rest of the economy. This is clearest in the case of minerals, notably in Africa. The share of wages in value added is generally low, and a considerable part of the revenues go to transnational corporations. Production is heavily based on imported intermediary goods and often expatriate expertise. The same situation also holds true for a number of other commodities. In a number of countries in Africa and Oceania a major part of the gross foreign exchange earnings of fishery activities is used to pay foreign factor costs.

817.   A point to be noted in connection with commodity dependence is that heavily dependent countries, while particularly vulnerable to developments on world markets, generally have only limited influence on such markets since most are minor suppliers. As can be seen from Table V-4, for developing countries where up to 3 commodities constitute more than half of total exports, in 50 per cent of the country-commodity cases where a product accounts for an important part of export earnings, the world market share of the country is less than 1 per cent. For example, in the case of fisheries, 10 developing countries depend on this product for more than 20 per cent of their total export earnings, but none has a share in the world market of more than 1 per cent. In contrast, for developed countries in 75 per cent of the cases where a commodity accounts for more than 5 per cent of their export earnings, market shares were over 5 per cent.

Table V-4

Commodity dependence and world market shares, 1988

Country-commodity cases where exports of an individual commodity represent more than 5 per cent of total export earnings of a country								
Country category	Total number of country-commodity cases	Country shares in world exports for individual commodities						
		< 1%	1-2%	2-5%	5-10%	10-20%	20-50%	> 50%
Developing countries dependent on up to 3 commodities for over 50% of export earnings (76)	225	112	29	39	19	14	11	1
Other developing countries (24)	41	3	7	12	2	9	6	2
Developed countries (27)	16	0	1	3	5	4	2	1

Source: UNCTAD secretariat calculations.

This table includes the 54 commodities which accounted in 1988 for over 0.01 per cent of world market trade and which accounted for at least 5 per cent of export earnings of one or more countries.
Figures in brackets indicate the number of countries covered by each category.

818. In a number of developing countries manufactured exports have surpassed or attained the level of commodity exports and have become the most dynamic sector in their economies. Nevertheless, for the majority of developing countries, commodities will have to continue to form the engine of growth, in particular for those which have little opportunity to diversify out of commodities. Where diversification is possible, this will often have to be based on inputs from the commodity sector, notably in the cases of processing and in the production of commodity-related services. It is highly unlikely that new activities will totally replace those in the commodity sector; rather, diversification out of commodities is likely to go hand in hand with diversification within the commodity sector and improved competitiveness and productivity for traditional export commodities. Indeed, experience shows that countries which have had most success in their traditional commodity exports have often also been the ones that have had the most success in reducing their commodity dependence.

819. Countries have a common interest in commodities. They provide the inputs on which the other sectors are built. Moreover, countries rarely simply export commodities, they also import them - both in Africa and South and South-East Asia non-fuel commodity imports now exceed non-fuel commodity exports. Petroleum-exporting countries are generally food-importers; 31 out of 35 countries where fuel exports account for more than 20 per cent of total exports find themselves in this situation. Conversely, food-exporting countries are generally petroleum importers; there are only very few exceptions to this pattern. For international action in the sphere of commodities to be viable, account must be taken of the cross-linkages of interests resulting from this dual position of countries, as importers and exporters of commodities.

B. Developments in commodity markets

1. Evolution of world supply and demand during the 1980s

820.   Generally speaking, world supply and demand for commodities grew steadily in the 1980s. However, for many products the growth in supply was faster than that of demand. The following discusses the evolution in the situation for the main agricultural as well as mineral and metal commodities.

(a) Agricultural commodities

821.   In respect of **basic foods,** the world market for wheat was generally characterized between 1980 and 1990 by a situation of oversupply (see annex V-II). Wheat stocks reached a peak of 165 million tonnes in 1986 and were still 139 million tonnes in 1990/91. Wheat production grew steadily except in 1987 and 1988. It fell dramatically in 1988 as a result of drought in the United States. Production is currently at a peak of 595 million tonnes, vis-à-vis a peak in consumption of 576 million tonnes. The main producing countries of wheat have remained the USSR, China, the EEC and the United States, which together account for more than 60 per cent of total production. It is forecast that world supply of wheat should fall by 6.8 per cent in 1991 to 555 million tonnes. Consumption should also fall but only by 1.6 per cent, which means that demand should exceed supply by 12 million tonnes in 1991, generating a small decline in stocks.

822.   **Rice** production grew steadily over the 1980s, rising from 400 million tonnes in 1980 to an estimated 518 million tonnes in 1990 (see annex V-II). Supply and demand were generally in balance with stocks fluctuating between 46 and 56 million tonnes, except in 1986 when global rice stocks closed at a record level of 58.8 million tonnes. China and India are the main producers of rice, accounting for more than half of world production, and virtually the totality is domestically consumed. It is expected that 1991 consumption requirements should easily be met, with global stocks forecast to rise to 57 million tonnes.

823.   The world catch of **fish** grew significantly during the 1980s, rising from 72 million tonnes in 1980 to a level near 100 million tonnes in 1989 (see annex V-II). The rapid increase in the world catch would seem to be related to the extension of national territorial waters to the 200 mile-limit, which may have permitted a better exploitation of marine resources, and to the use of factory ships. In addition, the share of aquaculture in total production of fish products has risen substantially.

824.   During the 1980s, the supply of **bovine meat** generally exceeded demand, and frozen meat stocks accounted for approximately 1 per cent of consumption throughout the decade (see annex V-II). The EEC intervention stocks remained the largest and the most influential part of the market. Production grew steadily but slowly over the past ten years, rising from 44.5 million tonnes in 1980 to an estimated 52.8 million tonnes in 1990. The main producing countries have remained the United States, the European Economic Community, Argentina and Australia. On the demand side, consumption increased at a lower rate than production to reach, in 1990, an estimated level of 50.8 million tonnes. Since the late 1980s, beef consumption has been stagnating. While bovine meat production is expected to slightly increase or to remain at least stable over the next decade, forecasts for consumption are more pessimistic.

825.   Regarding **dairy products,** world milk production decreased slightly over the past decade, as milk deliveries fell from an average of 483 million tonnes in 1981-83 to 473.8 metric tonnes in 1989. An increase of 1.3 per cent was however recorded in 1989, due to high outputs in USSR and India. A situation of oversupply prevailed for butter, cheese and skimmed milk powder throughout the decade, combined with wide fluctuations in intervention stocks of butter and skimmed milk. Reduced milk supplies and larger exports of dairy products had a significant impact on stocks of

butter and skimmed milk in the late 1980s. World butter production grew slowly in the past decade, from 7.3 to 7.6 million tonnes. For cheese, production rose from 11.9 million tonnes in 1981-1983 to 14.25 tonnes in 1989, exceeding demand by 3.9 million tonnes in 1989.

826. During the 1980s, *sugar* production generally exceeded consumption, with the exception of a three year deficit period which started in 1986/87 (see annex V-II). As a result, stocks grew significantly until then. The market situation stabilized in 1989 and 1990, but in 1991 stocks are forecast to rise by 3.7 million tonnes with world output at a peak of 113 million tonnes. While the main producers of sugar remained the EEC, India, the USSR, Cuba and Brazil, developing countries increased their share of world sugar output from 55 to 57 per cent between 1980 and 1990. Developing countries also took an increased share of world consumption. It was 65 per cent in 1989.

Chart V.4: PRODUCTION, CONSUMPTION, STOCKS AND PRICE OF COFFEE

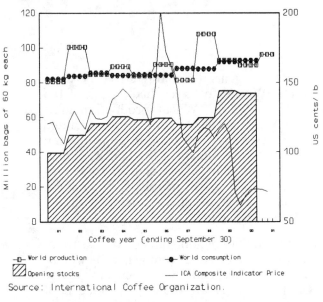

Source: International Coffee Organization.

Chart V.5: PRODUCTION, CONSUMPTION, STOCKS AND PRICE OF COCOA

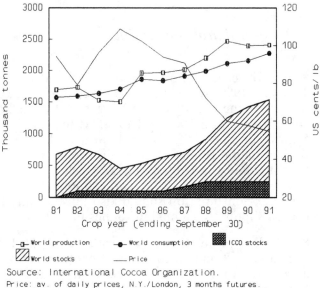

Source: International Cocoa Organization.
Price: av. of daily prices, N.Y./London, 3 months futures.

Chart V.6: PRODUCTION, CONSUMPTION, STOCKS AND PRICE OF COTTON

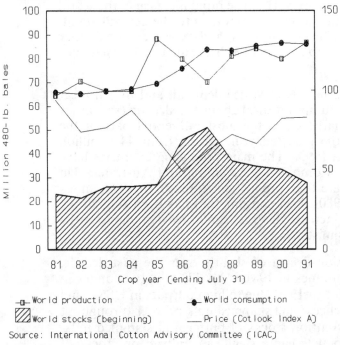

Source: International Cotton Advisory Committee (ICAC)

Chart V.7: PRODUCTION, CONSUMPTION, STOCKS AND PRICE OF JUTE, KENAF AND ALLIED FIBRES

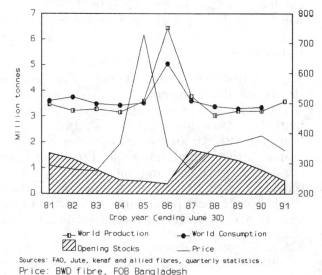

Sources: FAO, Jute, kenaf and allied fibres, quarterly statistics.
Price: BWD fibre, FOB Bangladesh

827.   World supply and demand of **bananas** grew strongly during the past decade, with production rising by 8 million tonnes to 45 million tonnes (see annex V-II).   Countries in Latin America and Asia accounted for 80 per cent during the period as a result of a substantial increase in production in China.

828.   Concerning tropical beverages, during most of the 1980s, the **coffee** market was generally characterized by an excess of supply over demand, as indicated in chart V-4, and by a steady accumulation of large stocks in both exporting and importing countries, in particular increasing in the latter following the suspension of export quotas under the International Coffee Agreement (1983) in July 1989.   This situation of oversupply was occasionally reversed as a result of poor harvests in some major producing countries, particularly in 1986/87.   In 1987/88, however, world coffee production reached a peak of 108 million bags and exceeded demand by some 20 million bags, leading to a record increase of 16 million bags in 1988/89 opening stocks.   World output of coffee increased by 6.9 per cent in 1990/91 to an estimated 96.2 million bags.

829.   Demand patterns for coffee changed during the 1980s, as the arabica group, particularly the "other mild", became increasingly favoured by world consumers.   Total consumption of coffee continued nonetheless to grow in the past decade, increasing by 1 per cent in 1989/1990 to 92.8 million bags.   It is expected that the world production of coffee should increase significantly to a forecast 99.9 million bags in 1991/92, as most Central American producers are expecting larger crops and a record output is anticipated in Colombia.

830.   As can be seen from chart V-5, during most of the 1980s, **cocoa** production persistently exceeded consumption, with world stocks mounting to well over half of consumption.   World output of cocoa beans peaked in 1988/89 at 2.46 million tonnes.   Consumption of cocoa grew strongly and steadily during the whole period with world grindings of cocoa beans attaining a peak of 2.27 million tonnes in 1990/91.

831.   World **tea** output grew steadily during the 1980s, rising from 1.87 to 2.5 million tonnes.   It exceeded consumption persistently throughout the decade, with the exception of 1990 (see annex V-II).   Production increased strongly in China, reaching one quarter of world production, and in Kenya, where it doubled.   Productivity gains were a dominant factor in output increases for most producing countries.   It is forecast that supply and demand should be in close balance by 1995, particularly for black tea.

832.   With respect to **vegetable oils and oilseeds,** production of palm oil more than doubled in the 1980s, from 5.1 to 11.2 million tonnes.   While consumption also grew strongly, stocks, nevertheless, increased to 1.2 million tonnes in 1990 as reflected in the chart in annex V-II.   A further expansion of 6 per cent to 11.9 million tonnes is expected in 1990.   Soybean oil production and consumption grew much less strongly, production attaining 16 million tonnes in 1990.   Although consumption growth was at a faster rate than production (see annex V-II), stocks were still at a high level in relation to consumption.   World supply of groundnut oil rose by 40 per cent to reach 3.7 million tonnes in 1990, keeping pace with a strong growth in consumption.   Coconut oil production and consumption remained in balance for most of the decade, with stocks growing at the end of that period.

833.   Regarding **agricultural raw materials,** as can be seen from chart V-6, world supply of cotton strongly fluctuated during the decade, while demand generally increased at a steady rate.   This led to wide variations in stock levels.   Cotton production peaked in 1984 with 88.4 million bales (480 lb each), and was only 86.7 million bales in 1991.   China, the United States, the USSR and India accounted for two thirds of world production in 1991.   On the demand side, world consumption of cotton decreased by 0.5 per cent in 1991 to reach 86.2 million bales, after 7 years of consecutive growth interrupted only in 1988.   World stocks represented at least 30 per cent of consumption.   It is forecast that the world cotton production should rise to an all time peak of 93.7 million bales in 1993, compared with a forecast of 91.5 million bales for 1992.   World consumption is expected to increase at a slower rate and to reach 87.8 million bales in 1992 and 90.3 million bales in 1993.   Stocks will increase accordingly.

834.   During the 1980s, world production of **tropical non-coniferous logs** increased by one fifth, rising from 131.6 million cubic meters in 1980 to 158.8 million in 1989.   South-East Asia remained the leading producing region with its production increasing by 29 per cent.   Large production increases of 31 per cent in Indonesia and 47 per cent in Malaysia brought the share of these two countries, taken together, to half of world production.   While production in Latin America rose

by 16 per cent, that in Africa declined slightly. Although figures on consumption are not available, data on imports give some insights. Japan's share of imports of tropical timber remained at a little less than one third in the 1980s. Shares of the next largest importers, China with 10 per cent and the Republic of Korea with 6 per cent were also unchanged. The share of the EEC's 12 member States of 14 per cent of imports in 1989, represented a slight decline from 1980. Developed countries imports have declined slightly since 1980 and now are a little over half of total imports.

835. The *natural rubber* market was characterized in the 1980s by a steady growth in production and consumption, while world stocks remained between 1.7 and 1.8 million tonnes throughout most of the decade (see annex V-II). Malaysia, Indonesia and Thailand continued to account for 75 per cent of world production. World consumption of natural rubber reached a peak of 5.3 million tonnes in 1990, exceeding production by approximately 180 thousand tonnes. It is forecast that growth in natural rubber production should accelerate in 1991 with an output rise of 1.6 per cent to 5.2 million tonnes. Demand, despite a decline of 0.9 per cent, should still exceed supply by approximately 50 thousand tonnes.

836. As can be seen from chart V-7, *jute* production, except for almost doubling in 1985 to 6.4 million tonnes, remained in the vicinity of 3 to 3.6 million tonnes level in the 1980s. India, Bangladesh and China account for 90 per cent of world output. World jute consumption slowly declined during the 1980s, except for its sharp peak in 1985. During this period, world stocks of jute were characterized by wide variations and followed the changes in the world supply/demand pattern.

837. World production of *sisal and henequen*, by far the largest sub-group of hard fibres, declined steadily during the 1980s, from 5.7 million tonnes in 1980 to 4.5 million tonnes in 1990 (see annex V-II). The main producers of sisal are Brazil, Kenya and United Republic of Tanzania, while henequen is grown mainly in Mexico. Although accurate figures on consumption of sisal and henequen are not available, they appear to have suffered severe market losses over the years in their traditional end-use of baling twine for agricultural purposes. Coir and abaca, the two other sub-groups of hard fibres, also suffered from weak markets.

838. *Tobacco,* which is the most widely grown non-food crop, is produced in over 100 countries, of which 78 are developing countries. During the 1980s, tobacco production grew strongly but at a lower rate than in the 1970s. Its growth was very irregular as can be seen from the chart in annex V-II. The share of developing countries grew from 62 per cent in 1980 to 74 per cent in 1990. Consumption steadily rose but tended to stagnate in developed countries. In 1990, world consumption of tobacco rose on the previous year by 2.1 per cent to reach an estimated level of 6.1 million of tonnes. It is forecast that consumption will continue to grow until the year 2000 at the rate of 1.9 per cent annually. Demand is expected to shrink in developed countries but to increase in developing regions.

(b) Minerals and metals

839. In the 1980s, the *aluminium* market was characterized by a sluggish growth in both supply and demand compared with earlier periods. While consumption exceeded production for a good part of the 1980s, both were roughly in balance in the last years of that decade (see annex V-II). World stocks contracted after 1984 and were at the end of the period at roughly their 1980 level. Production of aluminium reached a level of 18.2 million tonnes in 1990. The major restructuring process, which began in the 1970s, resulted in a significant shift in the geographical distribution of production. Japan's output of aluminium contracted from one million tonnes at the beginning of the decade to only 35,000 tonnes at its end. On the other hand, Australia increased its production almost fourfold and Brazil more than more than tripled its output during the period. Overall, developing countries doubled their share in world production from 11 to 20 per cent. On the demand side, consumption of aluminium grew strongly in developing countries, an increase of more than 70 per cent between 1980 and 1990. This contrasts with the slow growth in consumption in developed market-economy countries.

840. As can be seen in chart V-8, supply and demand of *copper* grew slowly in the 1980s. World production increased steadily to a peak of 11.03 million tonnes in 1990. Copper consumption generally followed the same pattern after a sharp fall in 1982 and grew slightly faster than pro-

duction after 1986, due to demand increases in the OECD and in industrializing developing countries of Asia. World stocks of copper reached a peak of 1.54 million tons in 1983 and then decreased to lower levels at the end of the decade.

841.   Between 1980 and 1983, production and consumption of *iron ore* contracted severely but steadily increased thereafter. For most of the period, however, production and consumption were in balance. The revival after 1983 was due to the expansion of economic activity in developed market-economy countries - and its positive impact on steel consuming sectors - and to increased competitiveness of primary iron vis-à-vis ferrous scrap in steel making. Iron ore production grew more strongly in developing countries than in other regions, with an increase during the last five years of 23 per cent. This was reflected in the steady growth in production in Brazil.

842.   The growth of the *lead* market was considerably weaker in the 1980s than in the 1970s, partly due to increasing environmental and health concerns which affected lead consumption in many of its end-use. As can be seen from the chart in annex V-II, a situation of slight oversupply prevailed for most of the decade. Refined lead production peaked in 1990 at 5.74 million tonnes and consumption at 5.86 million tonnes. A growing proportion of refined lead metal consists of recycled materials. While lead consumption seems to have stagnated in OECD countries, it has grown by 50 per cent in developing countries with a more than doubling of consumption in Asia.

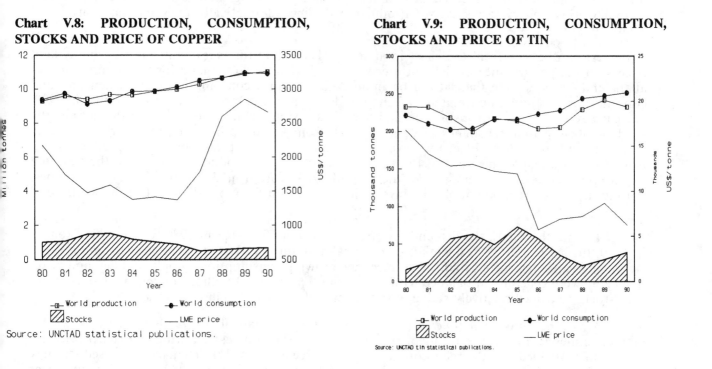

Chart V.8: PRODUCTION, CONSUMPTION, STOCKS AND PRICE OF COPPER

Source: UNCTAD statistical publications.

Chart V.9: PRODUCTION, CONSUMPTION, STOCKS AND PRICE OF TIN

Source: UNCTAD tin statistical publications.

843.   With some 95 per cent of its production consumed in the steel industry - the rest being mainly used in non-ferrous metallurgy, dry cell batteries and production of fungicides - *manganese ore* is heavily dependant on the steel industry. However, while steel output grew relatively strongly after 1983, world production of manganese tended to stagnate and in 1990 was 9 per cent below its level of 1980 (see annex V-II). This was mainly because of a drastic reduction in the quantities of manganese ore consumed to produce one tonne of steel in blast furnaces (from 1.5 kg in 1980 to 0.5 in 1990 in Western Europe), and of a relative increase in the direct use of high-grade ore in the converters. Production decreased dramatically in South Africa and stagnated in USSR. For those countries exporting high-grade ore, notably Gabon and Australia, production increased as a result of buoyant demand.

844.   As can be seen from the chart in the annex, the *nickel market* was characterized for most of the 1980s by an excess of demand over supply in contrast with an oversupply situation in the 1970s. Led by demand from the stainless industry, world consumption of nickel grew has grown steadily since 1982, with the exception of 1985, to a level of 878 thousand tonnes in 1990. World production generally followed the growth in consumption to reach 866.5 thousand tonnes in 1990, with stocks decreasing in the second half of the decade to 87.1 thousand tonnes in 1990. USSR

became the world's largest producer and developing countries slightly increased their share of world production. The shares of Canada and Australia both declined.

845. During the 1980s, *phosphate* production persistently exceeded consumption as a result of the dramatic fall in the use of phosphate fertilizers in the major markets (United States, Western Europe and China). Despite strong fluctuations, world production grew during the decade to 164 million tonnes in 1990 (see annex V-II). Efforts to restructure and rationalize the world phosphate industry, combined with a small increase in demand, led to a reduction of stock levels after 1987. While production stagnated in the United States, the world's largest producer, production in the USSR increased strongly to account now for roughly a quarter of world output. While production tended to stagnate in Morocco, the world's third major producer, it increased strongly in other developing countries.

846. As can be seen from chart V-9, in the beginning of the 1980s, *tin* production exceeded consumption as a result of which stocks increased dramatically to a peak of 72.7 thousand tonnes in 1985. Although production has been lower than consumption since then, stocks have remained relatively high and increased at the end of the 1980s to 38.9 thousand tonnes in 1990. World production peaked in 1989 but declined in 1990 to 231.9 thousand tonnes. A major restructuring of the world tin industry occurred during the decade, particularly following the collapse of the International Tin Agreement in October 1985. This involved the closure of a number of high cost mines. Brazil and China emerged as significant producers during the decade to become first and second world supplier respectively. Production declined dramatically in Malaysia, Bolivia and Thailand.

847. As can be seen from the chart in annex V-II, demand for *tungsten* has not generally kept pace with the performance of the world economy. Actual world demand for tungsten was lower at the end of the decade than at the beginning. Total world consumption of tungsten ores and concentrates fell from an estimated 49.3 thousand tonnes in 1980 to 42.8 thousand tonnes in 1990, particularly as a result of substitution and materials saving technologies. During the decade, the total number of tungsten mines in operation fell from 59 to 10 in developed market-economy countries and from 69 to 30 in the developing countries, while total world mine production fell from 50.1 thousand tonnes to 43.8 thousand tonnes. Despite production cutbacks, the tungsten market remained largely oversupplied, the level of stocks rose from 3.9 from 6.3 thousand tonnes. During the decade, China doubled its production to account for more than half of the world total output.

848. During the 1980s, the demand for *zinc* rose steadily from 6.3 in 1980 to 7.3 million tonnes in 1990, fuelled mainly by residential, commercial and automotive construction (see annex V-II). As mining capacities were expanded to meet the growing consumption, supply and demand of refined zinc were generally in balance with production reaching 7.3 million tonnes in 1990. As a result, stocks remained relatively stable in the vicinity of 0.5 to 0.9 million tonnes.

849. World demand for *petroleum* fell quickly in the first half of the 1980s to a low of 2781.1 million tonnes in 1983, as a result of oil substitution programmes following the sharp price increases in 1979/1980 and the recession in 1982/1983 (see annex V-II). Demand increased strongly in the second half of the decade and peaked at 3091 million tonnes in 1989, fueled by low prices and stronger world growth. On the supply side, production fell even more strongly than demand in the first half of the decade to a low of 2781.1 million tonnes in 1983, but increased rapidly in the second half of the 1980s, exceeding demand since 1986. World output of petroleum peaked at 3,142 million tonnes in 1989. Production increased substantially in non-traditional exporting countries, while demand grew significantly in developing countries.

2. Price movements during the 1980s and into the 1990s

850. As a result of the evolution of world supply and demand and of stocks as just described, commodity prices have generally been on a declining trend. At the turn of the 1990s, prices for coffee, cocoa, maize, silver, tin and tungsten were lower than at any time during the 1980s. Conversely, nominal prices of bananas, copper, groundnut oil, hides and skins, iron ore, jute, linseed

oil, manganese ore, nickel, pepper, tobacco, tropical timber and zinc reached high levels. In real terms, that is when deflated by the unit value index of manufactured goods exported by developed countries, the prices of all commodities declined except for bananas, manganese ore, nickel, tropical timber and zinc.

851. Table V-5 shows that the price index of principal non-fuel commodities exported by developing countries fell by a staggering 32 per cent in real terms between 1979/81 and 1988/90. In the case of *basic foods,* real prices fell 38 per cent. Real prices of *tropical beverages* plummeted by fully 52 per cent, the highest drop of any non-fuel commodity group. This reflects the sharp downward trend in prices of coffee and cocoa during most of the period. Coffee reached a 16 year low and cocoa an 18 year low in 1991. This situation is having catastrophic consequences for many countries in Africa and Latin America which rely on cocoa and coffee for the bulk of their export earnings.

852. The real price index for *vegetable oils and oilseeds* in 1988/90 was 54 per cent of its level a decade before. The only vegetable oil that showed any marked price improvement at the turn of the 1990s was groundnut oil. The sharp declines for palm and coconut oils contrast with the relative stability in nominal prices for sunflower and soybean oils.

Table V-5

**Changes in nominal and real commodity prices
between 1979-81 and 1988-90**

(Percentages)

	Nominal prices	Real prices [a]
All non-fuel commodities	-11	-32
Basic foods	-19	-38
Tropical beverages	-37	-52
Vegetable oils and oilseeds	-30	-46
Agricultural raw materials	+ 5	-20
Minerals and metals	+ 21	-7
Crude petroleum	-46	-60

a Based on a price in current US $ divided by the United Nations index of export unit values of manufactured goods.

853. Whilst agricultural raw materials performed better than other agricultural commodity groups, their real prices nevertheless fell by 30 per cent. The nominal price of tobacco remained more stable than those for other products throughout the decade while prices of tropical timber increased strongly. Jute prices were also at a relatively high nominal level at the beginning of the 1990s. At the other end of the spectrum, natural rubber prices were close to the very low levels experienced in the mid-1980s.

854. Overall, prices of minerals and metals fared best during the 1980s registering an increase of 21 per cent in nominal prices, which, however, translates into a decline of 7 per cent in real prices. While nominal prices of copper, iron ore, manganese ore, nickel, lead and zinc were at relatively high levels at the end of the decade compared with its middle year, silver, tin and tungsten prices fell to their lowest levels since the early 1970s. Since the late 1970s, the aluminium industry has gone through three major price cycles with peaks occurring in 1980, 1983 and 1988, and lows in 1982 and 1985. Since mid-1988, prices have again been moving downwards and may reach a low in 1991.

855. The real price of *crude petroleum* collapsed by about three-fifths during the decade. Prices in nominal terms declined steadily from 1979 to 1985. Following a sharp drop in 1986, they improved in 1987 to roughly their current level of about $US 18 a barrel. Monthly petroleum prices have been particularly volatile during the past six years. This contrasts with the reduced instability in prices for most other commodities during the 1980s.

Table V.6

Instability in monthly market prices for selected primary commodities

(percentage variation around a trend)

Commodity	Weight a/ 1983-1985 per cent	Instability index b/ 1971-80 percentage variation	1981-90
Coffee	11.42	23.7	16.8
Cocoa	2.73	26.4	15.5
Tea	1.77	12.4	17.9
Sugar	7.12	56.9	41.0
Soybean meal	1.86	21.6	14.1
Rice	1.78	32.7	20.0
Bananas	1.47	10.4	14.3
Maize	1.35	19.9	14.2
Wheat	1.06	25.2	11.9
Beef	0.86	16.8	6.1
Fishmeal	0.58	26.1	17.2
Pepper	0.45	20.4	43.8
Palm oil	2.31	20.9	22.6
Soybeans	1.22	18.7	12.5
Soybean oil	0.80	24.0	18.8
Coconut oil	0.67	33.1	32.2
Sunflower oil	0.44	23.2	18.6
Palm kernel oil	0.30	34.3	29.2
Groundnuts	0.15	18.4	11.6
Groundnut oil	0.14	20.2	27.3
Copra	0.12	35.7	30.3
Palm kernels	0.03	30.6	29.3
Rubber	2.96	15.5	13.8
Cotton (medium)	2.52	14.3	13.6
Tobacco	2.25	2.7	6.0
Tropical sawnwood	1.93	14.3	14.7
Tropical logs	1.79	15.2	11.6
Plywood	1.49	19.0	12.1
Hides and skins	0.45	22.5	10.8
Wool	0.25	23.8	18.5
Jute	0.14	11.7	26.1
Linseed oil	0.08	43.6	23.4
Sisal	0.06	36.7	5.3
Copper	4.45	20.6	18.3
Aluminium	3.22	15.0	20.2
Iron ore	2.94	8.6	5.4
Tin	1.38	9.9	14.6
Phosphate rock	0.96	47.4	12.7
Nickel	0.91	3.6	31.6
Zinc	0.31	32.5	19.7
Lead	0.25	20.0	21.5
Manganese ore	0.19	15.9	26.8
Tungsten	0.05	23.0	14.3

Source: UNCTAD data base.

a/ Derived from values of developing country exports.

b/ The measure of instability is $1/n[(/Y - Y_t/)/Y_t]$ where Y is the observed magnitude of the variable; Y_t is the magnitude estimated by fitting an exponential trend to the observed value and N is the number of observations. The vertical bar indicates the absolute value (i.e. disregarding signs). Accordingly, instability is measured as the percentage deviation of the variables concerned from their exponential trend levels for a given period.

856.   In what amounts to but cold comfort for commodity-exporting countries, as can be seen from Table V-6, the instability of commodity prices in the 1980s decreased vis-à-vis the 1970s. On average, price volatility, when expressed in dollar terms, was some 35 per cent lower. It dropped by almost 50 per cent for food items, although it increased in the cases of bananas, pepper and tea. It also increased, however, for palm oil, groundnut oil, tropical sawnwood as well as for jute and tobacco. Amongst the minerals and metals, price instability increased significantly in the cases of aluminium, tin, manganese ore and nickel - ninefold in the latter case - and slightly in the case of lead. It dropped dramatically for phosphate rock. However, for certain minerals and metals the comparison may be somewhat misleading. In the case of aluminium and nickel, the prices for the 1970s are based on contract prices while in the 1980s, the prices are based on those of the London Metal Exchange for cash sales, for which prices tend to be more volatile.

3.   Changes in the composition and direction of developing-country trade in commodities

857.   The marked variations in prices as between commodities have been an important factor behind the changes observed in the structure of developing countries' commodity exports and imports. Mineral fuels, which accounted at the beginning of the 1980s for three quarters of all primary commodity exports of developing countries, represented slightly over half by 1987-1989 following a sharp fall in their relative prices.

858.   As can also be seen from chart V-10, the share of tropical beverages in the non-fuel commodity export structure contracted and the share of basic foods increased, but relative price variations were not the sole factor. On the import side the main change was the increased importance of minerals and metals and the decline in the share of food imports, the latter in particular reflecting lower relative prices for basic foods.

Chart V-10

**DEVELOPING COUNTRY NON-FUEL COMMODITY EXPORT AND
IMPORT STRUCTURE, BY COMMODITY GROUPS, 1979-81 AND 1987-89**

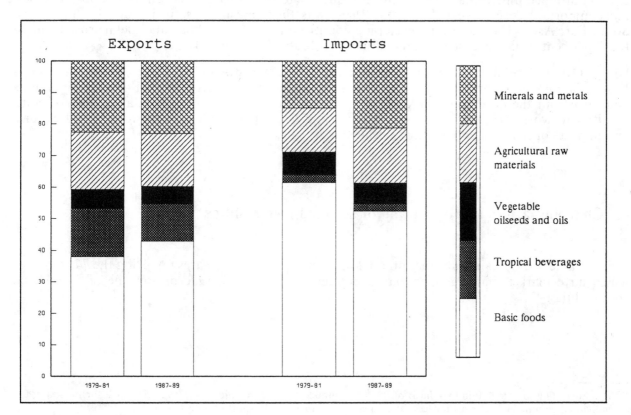

859.   Changes in the structure and pattern of developing countries' commodity trade in the 1980s reflected "successes" and "failures" for individual countries which affected both exports and imports. Among the main changes were: (a) some countries increased production and exports and captured greater export market shares; (b) some producers in response to lower world prices reduced exports and lost market shares as they processed domestically more of their production; (c) some, including the major exporters of manufactures increased their imports of raw materials and food as a result of rapid industrialization; (d) in line with their changing incomes, the food imports of major petroleum exporters - which had increased in the 1970s, declined as a proportion of world imports in the 1980s; and (e) some countries became net food importers as a result of growth in production falling short of rapid population growth. These developments are reflected in the changed regional composition of developing-country exports and imports, details for which are provided in annex V-III.

860.   The most important development in basic foods was the fast growth in exports from South and South-East Asia. Their share in developing countries' exports increased from 30 per cent in 1979-1981 to 39 per cent in 1987-1989. To a large extent this rapid rise was accounted for by fishery exports -- which were at the same time the most dynamic component of world trade in basic food items. The only other region which registered a modest export share growth was West Asia. Overall, the share of developing countries in world exports slightly declined, reflecting the increase in the production and exports of foodstuffs by industrialised countries.

861.   The share of South and South-East Asia in developing countries' exports of tropical beverages also increased significantly from less than 14 per cent to almost 20 per cent. At the same time developing countries' share in world trade of processed tropical beverages decreased in favour of the OECD countries and in particular Western Europe. With respect to vegetable oilseeds and oils, all regions other than Africa and Oceania increased their market shares.

862.   The main feature of developing-country exports of agricultural raw materials during the 1980s was the significant decline of their share in world exports from 31 to 25 per cent. Their proportion in world imports increased by 2.4 percentage points, in particular as a result of increased demand in newly industrializing countries of South and South-East Asia which resulted in a more than 10 percentage point increase in their share of developing countries' imports.

863.   Developing countries lost importance in the world as exports of minerals and metals. The decline was particularly pronounced for Africa, where the value of exports in nominal US dollars was lower at the end than at the beginning of the 1980s. Africa's share in developing countries' exports dropped 6 percentage points, from a quarter to less than a fifth. On the import side, the most important development during the 1980s was the rapid increase in imports by South and South-East Asia. Their share in developing country imports of minerals and metals rose from 44 to 62 per cent, while their share in world imports doubled, reaching 11 per cent.

864.   Overall, the most important feature during the 1980s was the fact that South and South-East Asia grew in importance as a destination for commodity exports from all developing regions and also from the developed market-economy countries. Its importance as a supplier of commodities to world markets also grew. Africa's and developing America's share in world exports and imports of non-fuel commodities declined markedly.

4. Changing actors in world trade of selected commodities

865.   Table V-7 contains information on 241 country-commodity cases involving the 74 countries which have market shares greater than 5 per cent in the world trade of any one of 54 selected commodities.[297]

---

[297] It is interesting to note that in two thirds of the total number of cases in which these countries have such a share, the individual commodity accounts for less than 5 per cent of their total export earnings.

Table V-7

CASES WHERE A COUNTRY'S EXPORTS OF AN INDIVIDUAL COMMODITY ACCOUNT FOR MORE THAN 5 PER CENT OF THE WORLD MARKET IN THAT COMMODITY, 1988

Country category	Total number of cases	Country shares in world exports for individual commodities			
		5-10%	10-20%	20-50%	> 50%
Developing countries dependent on up to 3 commodities for over 50% of export earnings (35)	61	27	17	16	1
Other developing countries (19)	67	28	20	15	4
Developed countries (20)	113	62	31	16	4

Source: UNCTAD secretariat calculations.

This table includes the 54 commodities which accounted in 1988 individually for over 0.01 per cent of world trade and which accounted for at least 5 per cent of export earnings of one or more countries.
Figures in brackets indicate the number of countries falling into each category.

866.   It emerges from the table that developed countries are almost as important as exporters in individual commodity markets as the developing countries. However, during the 1980s a number of developed countries became less important in the export of a particular commodity, a phenomenon that could also be observed among developing countries. New important exporters, other than Australia, were developing countries. In terms of importers, changes in market shares were nowhere as great and involved a small number of countries. These developments have had and will have important repercussions for international commodity policies.

(a) Exports

867.   The following describes the developments for each of the commodities in which important changes took place in the 1980s in terms of export shares. The commodities are examined in order of their importance in world trade.

Mineral fuels

868.   The world market export structure for mineral fuels changed radically during the last decade. The USSR, which in 1979/81 was responsible for 8 per cent of world exports, increased its share to 17 per cent in 1987/89 to become the world's largest exporter. Saudi Arabia occupied the second place, with its share decreasing from 23 to 8 per cent. The three important developed market exporters, Canada, Norway and the United Kingdom, all increased their shares, the United Kingdom becoming the third largest world exporter. Virtually all developing country exporters lost market shares.

Fish

869. The countries of the South and South-East Asian region as a whole increased their share in the rapidly growing world market from 20 per cent in 1979/81 to 25 per cent in 1987/89, particularly because of a strong growth in Thailand's exports of high value products such a shrimps and canned tuna, of which it has become the world's main supplier. Exports from Taiwan, Province of China, grew strongly, to make it the second most important developing supplier of fish after the Republic of Korea, which retained its number one position. The world market shares of all major developed country exporters (EEC, Canada, United States and Norway) declined.

Bauxite/alumina/aluminium

870. The world markets for bauxite (worth some US$ 1 billion in 1989), alumina (US$ 5 billion) and aluminium (US$ 16 billion) saw significant changes in the 1980s. The size of the world market for bauxite has been declining, with most countries shifting to the export of the processed products - alumina and especially aluminium. Guinea was the only country which reduced its alumina exports and increased its exports of bauxite - consequently increasing its share in the world bauxite market from 30 to 44 per cent, and reducing its share in alumina exports from 4 to 3 per cent. Jamaica is still the second largest exporter of bauxite, although its share declined from 17 to 12 per cent; this decline, however, does not reflect a concentration on higher value-added products, as its exports of alumina also declined, with its world market share falling from 17 to 9 per cent. Australia has gone up the processing chain in its exports: its world market share for bauxite fell (from 10 to 7 per cent), it consolidated its position as the main exporter of alumina (with its share increasing from 37 to 40 per cent), and it has become the world's third largest exporter of aluminium (its share increased from 1 to 11 per cent). The EEC is still the world's largest exporter of aluminium, despite an erosion of its share from 28 to 16 per cent (mainly reflecting the fact that its exports have not kept up with the explosive growth of the world market), followed by Canada (with a market share which remained around 15 per cent). Brazil is a major new entrant in the world market for aluminium: while it exported virtually nothing at the beginning of the period, in the late 1980s it supplied 6 per cent of world exports.

Vegetable oils and oilseeds

871. In the 1980s, the principal development was a strong decline in the share of the United States, from 43 to 28 per cent of the world vegetable oils and oilseeds market. There was a parallel increase in the share of the EEC from 14 to 25 per cent. Malaysia, which accounts for more than two thirds of world exports of palm oil, reinforced its leading position among the developing-country exporters, increasing its world market share in vegetable oils from 8 to 10 per cent. Indonesia also increased its market share, and is likely to become a major supplier of palm oil in the 1990s. Brazil's exports of soyabeans increased rapidly, its share growing from 5 to 13 per cent. In contrast, that of Argentina fell dramatically, but its exports of soyabean oil grew from 2 per cent to 19 per cent of the world market.

Wheat and wheat flour

872. While in 1979-1981 wheat and wheat flour exports of the United States were three quarters larger than those of the EEC countries (39 per cent of the world market compared with 22 per cent), by the end of the period the EEC countries had become larger exporters than the United States (a world market share of 32 per cent compared with 30 per cent for the United States). If trade among the EEC countries is excluded, the share of the EEC in world exports almost doubled, increasing from 8 to 15 per cent. Canada, Australia and Argentina remained the third, fourth and fifth largest exporters, with small changes in their shares.

Cotton and cotton yarn

873. The cotton market changed significantly during the 1980s. Pakistan more than doubled its share, from 5 to 11 per cent, and China increased its share even more, from 1 to 9 per cent,

changing from an important net importer to a main exporter. The United States kept its position as the world's leading exporter, but its share was eroded from 25 per cent to 16 per cent. The EEC became the second largest exporter, going from 10 to 13 per cent of the world market. Traditional suppliers like the USSR and Egypt retained stable though declining market shares, while Turkey's share contracted because of a rapidly expanding local textile industry. Australia became an important exporter of cotton during the 1980s.

Sugar

874. Cuba and the EEC increased their sugar market shares in the 1980s, respectively from 33 per cent to 38 per cent and from 18 per cent to 24 per cent. The shares of other exporters fluctuated. Only about one quarter of total sugar production is traded internationally. Therefore, changes in domestic consumption patterns and decisions to use even a small proportion of sugar cane or beet for other purposes can have a strong impact on the residual market. In this context, the importance of Brazil as an exporter varies to a large extent as a function of its use of sugar as fuel: in 1989/80, twice as much of Brazil's sugarcane crop was used for ethanol production than for refined sugar, with the result that the country's world market share declined from 7 to 3 per cent. Mauritius became the world's fourth largest exporter in 1987/89, with a market share of 5 per cent, up from 2 per cent in the early 1980s. The shares of Australia and the Philippines both declined considerably.

Coffee

875. The picture of world market trade in coffee was influenced by a shift in demand from robusta to mild arabica coffees. As a result, Colombia became the most important exporter in value terms. Viet Nam entered the market as an important small supplier.

Iron ore

876. Brazil reinforced its position as the world major exporter, increasing its share from 21 per cent to 25 per cent. Two other major exporters, Australia (from 17 to 18 per cent) and the USSR (from 12 to 15 per cent) also increased their market shares, while that of Canada fell sharply, from 16 to 10 per cent.

Nickel

877. The world market in nickel has seen important changes in the 1980s. Canada lost its leading role as an exporter of unwrought nickel (which accounts for around two thirds of total world trade in nickel), with its share declining from 29 to 7 per cent; for nickel intermediate products (one quarter of world trade) it overtook Australia as the main exporter, with its share increasing from one quarter to one third of total exports (while Australia's share declined from one third to one sixth). The USSR is now the world's largest exporter for unwrought nickel, with a market share that increased from 11 to 20 per cent. The Dominican Republic and Norway both increased their market shares, respectively from 5 to 11 per cent and from 9 to 14 per cent.

Natural rubber

878. Because rubber plantations and smallholders diversified into palm oil, Malaysia's share declined in the rubber market from 49 per cent to 38 per cent. Thailand took up most of this difference, with a share of 22 per cent in 1987/89, the rest being taken up by countries in Africa and Viet Nam.

Tropical timber

879. Malaysia and Indonesia have further enlarged their world market share in exports of tropical timber, from 65 per cent in 1980 to 76 per cent in 1989. A noticeable trend in these and other producing countries is the shift in composition of their exports to more processed products.

Rice

880. Thailand increased its share of world rice exports from 20 per cent in 1979/81 to 33 per cent in 1987/89. The EEC also expanded its share considerably, from 10 per cent to 17 per cent. The share of Viet Nam increased dramatically, making it the fourth largest supplier in 1989. Most other major exporters were confronted with a decline in their shares, particularly the United States, for which it fell from 25 to 19 per cent. Big falls were also experienced in the shares of China and Myanmar.

Cocoa

881. Côte d'Ivoire overtook Ghana in 1980 as the most important exporter of cocoa beans, a position which it consolidated during the 1980s. Both Malaysia and Indonesia increased their exports at a rapid rate, in the case of Malaysia to become the third largest exporter with a market share of 9 per cent, compared to 3 per cent in 1979/81. Indonesia in 1989/89 supplied 3 per cent of world exports, up from 0.4 per cent in the early 1980s, and this rapid export growth is expected to continue. Brazil's market share for cocoa beans fell from 12 to 7 per cent. For cocoa products, developing countries lost their majority share (56 per cent in 1979/81 falling to 47 per cent in 1987/89), mainly due to a decline in the shares of Ecuador from 9 to 2 per cent and Brazil from 22 to 15 per cent. In the case of Brazil, the export of cocoa products is more important than that of cocoa beans.

Tea

882. The main change in the world market was the rapid growth in China's exports; its share increased from 11 per cent in 1979/81 to 18 per cent in 1987/89. Kenya also continued to increase its importance in the world market during the 1980s, with its share growing from 9 to 11 per cent. The traditional main producers, India and Sri Lanka, both lost market shares.

Bananas

883. There was a considerable increase in Colombia's share of world trade in bananas, from 9 per cent in 1979/81 to 12 per cent in 1987/89. Costa Rica lost its number one position to occupy the third place with a decline in its share from 17 to 13 per cent. Ecuador steadily increased its exports to become the world's largest exporter in 1989.

Tin

884. In respect of tin ore and metal exports the major change during the 1980s was the rapid increase in the shares of Brazil and China from less than 5 per cent of the world market at the beginning of the decade to roughly a quarter in 1990. As a result, the major exporters - Malaysia, Thailand, Indonesia and Bolivia - all lost market shares.

(b) Imports

885.   Only in the cases of sugar and tea, and to some extent in a number of the metals and minerals markets, were there major changes in world import structures. On the world sugar market, there was a clear shift in imports from developed to developing countries, with the latter now accounting for two thirds of free market imports. At a country level, imports were highly erratic, reflecting changes in domestic supplies. China, India, Mexico, Nigeria and Pakistan have become important importers in certain years. The Republic of Korea emerged as a significant importer, with its share rising from about 2 to almost 5 per cent. The most radical change was that in the role of the United States as an importer: its share in world imports fell from 12 to 7 per cent.

886.   The importance of developing countries and of the USSR as tea importers increased strongly during the 1980s, while that of the EEC, United States and Japan declined. The USSR is now the largest single importer. Egypt has emerged as a major importer, increasing its market share from 3 per cent in 1979/81 to 9 per cent in 1987/89.

887.   Several South-East Asian countries and territories have emerged as important importers of a number of metals and raw materials. For example, the Republic of Korea was, in 1989, the world's second largest importer of hides and skins, the third largest importer of iron ore (with its market share increasing from 2 to 5 per cent), and an important importer of copper, nickel, tin and manganese; for all of these products, its market shares were small at the beginning of the 1980s. Taiwan Province of China, also became an important importer of hides and skins and copper, as well as of other metals. In the case of cotton and cotton yarn, most South-East Asian countries increased their imports.

888.   In food products other than sugar and tea, the principal importers have remained the same: the USSR for cereals, Japan for fisheries products and vegetable oils, Italy for live animals and meat. In the case of coffee, the EEC increased its share to 45 per cent of the world market, while that of the United States declined from 27 to 22 per cent during the period 1979/81 to 1987/89. For certain products (coarse grains, wheat, bovine meat and sugar), the role of Africa as an importer increased, while China emerged as an important importer of rice and vegetable oils.

C. Factors affecting commodity markets

1. Factors affecting demand

889.   In the 1980s sluggish economic growth was the main constraint on growth of commodity demand as only China and South and South-East Asia had rates of growth of GDP in this period which were roughly the same or higher than those of the 1970s. Nevertheless, demand for several commodities such as natural rubber, tea, cocoa, vegetable oils and aluminium outpaced general economic growth.

890.   In the OECD countries, there was a significant decline in the shares of agriculture, industry (including energy production and mining) and manufacturing in GDP in favour of services. The share of construction also declined. In contrast, in developing countries, manufacturing and, until the late 1980s, construction consolidated their shares at the expense of agriculture. The relative importance of these two relatively raw material intensive sectors was instrumental in the growth of raw material demand in the South.

891.   As far as food is concerned the pace of demand expansion slowed down in developed and developing countries alike in the 1980s; the reasons for this are very different, however. In OECD countries, income growth has ceased to be a main determinant of food demand. In these countries population growth, the demographic structure of societies, changes in habits and lifestyle are the

critical variables which determine the dynamics and structure of food consumption. Food demand in OECD countries has become more selective in terms of quality and dietary features. Moreover there is a trend towards an increasing popularity of snack and fast food items which is in particular encouraging consumption of fruits and vegetables as well as chocolate. In developing countries, in contrast, rapid growth of population has not fully been translated into increased demand because of constraints in the income of the poor and limited availability of foreign exchange for food imports.

(a) Demand for industrial raw materials[298]

892. In analysing the relationship between economic growth and structural change it is useful to examine changes in the rate of use of raw materials per unit of GDP, i.e. intensity of material use. A declining utilization of materials per unit of GDP can, however, be offset by a rapidly growing GDP. A sustained high rate of economic growth is normally accompanied by a high rate of investment, which in turn entails a more intensive use of raw materials as the importance of construction and capital goods branches within the economy rise.

893. Table V-8 shows the interplay between the use of raw materials per unit of GDP and the dynamics of economic growth. As far as OECD countries are concerned the rate of use of materials per unit of GDP declined for both agricultural raw materials and minerals and metals during the last two decades. In the 1980s, however, while the pace of decline accelerated for minerals and metals in general, it slowed down markedly for agricultural raw materials. Four minerals and metals saw their demand decline in the 1980s (manganese ore, phosphate rock, tin and tungsten); by contrast agricultural raw materials demand improved in the 1980s, notably demand for cotton.

894. In the case of developing countries, raw material demand in the 1980s was only little changed from the 1970s. Its rate of growth declined considerably as overall economic growth slowed down, but compared to the developed countries, there was relatively little impact stemming from the change in the consumption of raw materials per unit of GDP. There was a sharp difference between changes in consumption per unit of GDP as regards ferrous and non-ferrous metals and minerals. Although the rate of increase in non-ferrous minerals and metals consumption per unit of GDP remained unchanged, falling intensity of steel use brought to a halt the strong growth in overall minerals' and metals' usage per unit of GDP which was experienced in the 1970s.

895. The full impact of structural change in the economy on the utilization of raw materials per unit of output and on commodity demand also depends on the intra-industry shifts in output, in particular among manufacturing branches with different raw material intensities.[299] The aggregate share of relatively more raw material intensive branches in total manufacturing output has been higher during the 1980s in developing countries than in OECD countries. In both groups of countries, there was, however, a decline in this share: in the case of OECD countries from 46 per cent in 1980/81 to 44 per cent in 1988/89; in developing countries from 54 to 52 per cent.

896. In the OECD countries the decline in the share of manufacturing as a whole was coupled with a parallel decline in the relative importance of raw material intensive manufacturing branches. Thus, both inter- and intra-industry shifts have exerted a depressive impact on the use of raw materials per unit of GDP. In the developing countries, however, a slight decline in the relative importance of raw material intensive manufacturing branches was accompanied by a distinct expansion of the share of manufacturing in GDP. Thus in the South it is the increasing importance of industry in GDP rather than a shift towards more raw material intensive branches within industry which increases raw material demand.

897. The amount of raw material used per unit of output and the composition of these raw materials reflect the manner and efficiency of converting materials into final goods. The choice

---

[298] In this section raw materials are confined to agricultural raw materials and minerals and metals. Raw materials used in food processing and food based raw materials such as vegetable oils and sugar used in industrial production are not included in this category.

[299] Branches with more than 60 per cent contribution by intermediate inputs to unit value in OECD countries are regarded here as raw material intensive. They are food products, beverages, textiles, wearing apparel, leather and fur products, wood and cork products, paper, industrial chemicals, iron and steel, non-ferrous metals and transport equipment.

Table V-8

Changes in the consumption of raw materials per unit of GDP

(annual averages in per cent)

	1970/71-1980/81	1980/81-1988/89
OECD countries		
Agricultural raw materials	-1.7	-0.6
Cotton	-2.3	1.6
Natural rubber	-1.7	0.1
Wood	-1.6	-0.5
Minerals and metals	-1.9	-2.2
Steel	-2.3	-2.7
Non-ferrous metals and minerals	-0.6	-0.8
Aluminium	0.5	0.2
Copper	-1.4	-1.5
Growth of GDP	3.0	2.7
Developing countries		
Agricultural raw materials	-1.9	-0.2
Cotton	-2.3	3.1
Natural rubber	1.5	5.1
Wood	-1.9	-0.5
Minerals and metals	3.6	-0.2
Steel	3.5	-1.2
Non-ferrous metals and minerals	4.0	3.9
Aluminium	3.8	4.0
Copper	3.3	3.4
Growth of GDP	5.2	2.5

Source: UNCTAD secretariat calculations.

of raw materials and the amounts used per unit of output are affected by the state of technology and by social and economic conditions such as consumer preferences, (for example size of cars, local construction habits and the country's absorptive capacity for technological advances).

898.   There is competition among agricultural raw materials and among metals and minerals as well between these and synthetics. The decline in the utilization of agricultural raw materials per unit of GDP took place to a large extent before the 1980s and was caused by competition from synthetic substitutes. This slowed down in the 1980s. On the other hand, in the case of minerals and metals, substitution seems to have accelerated both among them and with plastics and composites. Changing technological requirements seem to be the dominant factor affecting material substitution which is only stimulated indirectly over the long run by price variations.[300]

899.   In the developed countries the amount of metals and minerals used per unit of output has declined considerably irrespective of substitution and as a consequence of the interplay between improvements in manufacturing efficiency (continuous production and control systems) and refinements in product design and processing technologies. Also there has been an increase in re-

---

[300] Deadman, D. and R.K. Turner, "Resource conservation, sustainability and technical change" in Turner, K. (ed), Sustainable Environmental Management, p. 87.

Table V-9

THE IMPORTANCE OF RECYCLING IN DEVELOPED COUNTRIES

	1970	1980	1988
Use of scrap and waste as percentage of consumption [a]			
Lead	45	52	53
Copper	56	52	55
Zinc	22	21	20
Aluminium	22	25	27
Use of scrap and waste as percentage of production			
Steel [b]		45	48
Waste paper/paperboard [c]	23	29	34

Source: UNCTAD secretariat calculations based on Metallgesellschaft, *Metallstatistik;* FAO, *Yearbook of Forest Products*, various issues; and UNCTAD and EEC databases.
 a For OECD countries
 b For Austria, Belgium, Czechoslovakia, Finland, France, FRG, Hungary, Italy, Japan, Luxembourg, Netherlands, Portugal, Spain, Sweden, USSR, United Kingdom, United States, and Yugoslavia. These countries account for more than two thirds of world crude steel production in the period under review.
 d For North America, EEC, Nordic countries and Japan.

cycling, stimulated particularly by pressures of environmental groups, leading to a reduction in the demand for primary materials. As table V-9 shows, recycling of materials (scrap and waste) has gathered importance for many raw materials. Copper and zinc are the two important exceptions; in the case of copper recycling for some time now has been at a very high level. In the case of steel, only slightly more than 50 per cent of steel production involves virgin material. The remainder is produced from recycled scrap, most of it being used in electric arc furnaces in both mini-mills and integrated steel works.[301] Recycling is much less important among special alloys and other high-technology metals than among conventional raw materials.

900.   In the case of most developing countries reductions in material requirements in some branches of manufacturing, owing to miniaturization, economies in input use and substitution in some industrial branches are likely to be offset by increasing material requirements in other branches, for example durable goods manufacturing, production of intermediate goods such as galvanized steel, and copper and zinc containing products as well as in infrastructure.[302]

(b)   Demand for foodstuffs

901.   In OECD countries, the rate of population growth, which is one of the main determinants of the change in total demand for food, is low. In addition per capita consumption of food items declined marginally in the 1980s as can be seen from table V-10.

301 For more information see, R. R. Miller, "The changing economics of steel, Finance and Development", Washington D.C., June 1991, pp.38-40.

302 ECLAC, "The potentialities of present technological capabilities in the Latin American commodity sector", LC/L.505, Santiago 1989, pp.43-48.

Table V-10

CHANGES IN PER CAPITA FOOD CONSUMPTION

(annual averages in per cent)

Developed market economies	1980/81-1988
Food	-0.1
Coffee	1.0
Cocoa	4.7
Meat	0.6
Vegetable oils/oilseed	0.6
Cereals	-3.7
Sugar	-0.9
Bananas	2.6
Growth of population	0.9
Growth of GDP	2.7
Developing countries	
Food	0.2
Sugar	1.0
Meat	-0.7
Vegetable oils/oilseeds	2.1
Cereals	0.3
Growth of population	3.0
Growth of GDP	2.5
China	
Food	9.7
Tea	5.5
Vegetable oils/oilseeds	4.5
Bananas	191.5
Meat	6.3
Cereals	1.6
Sugar	10.0
Growth of population	1.3
Growth of GDP	9.5
Countries of central and eastern Europe, USSR	
Food	1.0
Coffee	3.7
Cocoa	-1.7
Meat	1.8
Cereals	0.1
Sugar	-0.4
Bananas	-5.0
Growth of population	0.9

902. The impact on food consumption of factors such as dietary habits, lifestyles, and immigration are becoming particularly important in these countries. These factors influence food consumption in terms of volume, composition and quality. In OECD countries, and in the countries of Central and Eastern Europe as well as in the USSR, a significant aging of population has been taking place. Regarding food demand, the most obvious consequence of an aging population structure is the tendency towards a lower per capita food consumption.

903. Cocoa provides a good example of different factors with opposing impacts on demand. While the aging of the population would tend to depress cocoa demand other factors play a positive role. In fact the per capita consumption of cocoa went up strongly in the 1980s as the consumption of cocoa-containing snacks increased with changing lifestyles. Fruits also enjoy increasing popularity as snack items. Recent studies indicate that between 70 and 80 per cent of

the population in Western Europe consume fruit as a snack in addition to fruit eaten during main meals.[303] In the same period, health concerns and the changing tastes of the public led to a decline in the demand for some products such as meat and to an increase in that for substitutes such as fish.

BOX V-1

SUGAR AND GOVERNMENT INTERVENTION

Government intervention in sugar markets has a long history. In fact, it was the British blockade of continental Europe during the Napoleonic wars which led to sugar beet production. Since then, sugar beet production has been afforded high levels of protection.

During the 1980s, sugar substitutes have made major inroads in the sweeteners market, particularly in certain developed countries. In 1990, high fructose corn syrup (HFCS) accounted for 6.2 per cent of world sweetener consumption, and low-caloric sweeteners for 5.8 per cent.

Until now, the growth of HFCS consumption has mainly been restricted to two countries, the United States and Japan. Here, industrial users, particularly soft drink manufacturers, have substituted sugar with HFCS.

HFCS developed behind a shield of high domestic prices for beet and cane sugar which were well above world market prices. The accompanying chart describes the situation in the United States. HFCS currently accounts for 31 per cent of the United States sweetener consumption, compared with 14 per cent in 1980.

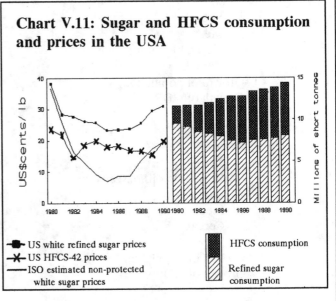

Chart V.11: Sugar and HFCS consumption and prices in the USA

US white refined sugar prices
US HFCS-42 prices
ISO estimated non-protected white sugar prices
HFCS consumption
Refined sugar consumption

Most developed countries have not managed to adjust their domestic sugar policies to the changing economic environment. Thus they have placed the burden of adjustment on the traditional cane sugar exporters.

---

904. The structure of the food demand also depends on agricultural and trade policies which affect relative prices. An example in this regard is sugar in the United States, where the high domestic price of sugar and the use of quotas to control the volume and price of imports made substitutes such as high fructose corn syrup price competitive.

905. In developing countries as a whole, per capita food consumption grew continuously but at a decelerating rate over the last two decades. After growing by 1.2 per cent in the 1970s, it dipped to a very low rate of 0.2 in the 1980s. Food demand growth in developing countries is particularly affected by changes in the income of the poor[304] and in the rate of population growth. It is also affected by the availability of foreign exchange for food imports. For example, in 1990 although the current price of wheat reached its lowest level for almost twenty years, certain heavily indebted developing countries had to reduce their wheat imports due to foreign exchange shortages. In contrast, some middle-income countries without similar pressures, particularly in Asia, increased

[303] *International Fruit World,* Vol. 48, No. 1/1990.

such imports and were more able to benefit from the low price levels.[305]

906. China's per capita food consumption levels doubled in the 1980s. Demand growth remained brisk for staple food and recorded phenomenal rates of growth for bananas.

907. In general, demand for basic food in countries of Central and Eastern Europe grew strongly. Relative per capita consumption levels for cereals and sugar, expressed as ratios to those prevailing in OECD countries, grew despite their already high levels at the beginning of the 1980s. On the other hand, for tropical products such as cocoa and bananas, already low levels of per capita consumption at the beginning of the 1980s decreased further to 36 and 5 per cent of the levels reached in OECD countries.

---

[304] For more information see: Mellor, J.W., "Food Price Policy and Income Distribution in Low-Income Countries," *Economic Development and Cultural Change*, No.13, 1978.

[305] OECD, *Politiques, marchés et échanges agricoles: Suivi et perspectives, 1991*, Paris 1991, p. 101.

Table V-11

Development of Yields for Selected Crops: Regions and Selected Countries
(1979-81 and 1987-89)
(kg per ha)

	1979-81 (1)	1987-89 (2)	percentage change 2/1
Cocoa Beans			
Developing Countries	357	438	22.7
Africa			
Cameroon	276	279	1.1
Côte d'Ivoire	507	709	39.8
Ghana	223	287	28.7
Nigeria	241	224	-7.0
Asia			
Indonesia	552	1240	224.6
Malaysia	1058	994	-6.0
Developing America			
Brazil	689	546	-20.7
Ecuador	308	245	-20.5
Coffee, green			
Developing countries	525	527	3.8
Africa			
Côte d'Ivoire	287	206	-28.2
Uganda	500	773	54.6
Asia			
Indonesia	602	583	-3.2
Developing America			
Brazil	589	573	-2.7
Colombia	692	720	4.0
Mexico	507	505	-0.4
Guatemala	667	744	11.5
Seed Cotton			
OECD countries	1572	2008	27.7
Australia	3233	3732	15.4
United States	1493	1911	28.0
Developing countries	799	1056	32.2
Africa			
Egypt	2646	2100	-20.6
Sudan	837	1459	74.3
Tanzania (United Rep.)	377	585	55.2
Zimbabwe	1620	1125	30.6
Asia			
China	1613	2371	47.0
India	495	573	15.8
Pakistan	1027	1693	64.8
Turkey	1967	2274	15.6

Table V-11 (continued)

DEVELOPMENT OF YIELDS FOR SELECTED CROPS: REGIONS AND SELECTED COUNTRIES

	1979-81 (1)	1987-89 (2)	percentage change 2/1
Developing America			
Argentina	904	1364	50.9
Brazil	465	904	94.4
Mexico	2718	3038	11.8
Paraguay	1010	1127	11.6
USSR	3057	2451	-19.8
Rice, paddy			
OECD countries	5466	6120	12.0
Japan	5581	6081	9.0
United States	5167	6284	21.6
Developing countries	2135	2625	23.0
Africa			
Egypt	5707	5909	3.5
Madagascar	1738	1893	8.9
Asia			
China	4244	5409	27.5
India	1858	2444	31.5
Myanmar	2689	2884	7.2
Bangladesh	1952	2426	24.3
Developing America			
Brazil	1436	1943	35.3
Colombia	4278	4422	3.4
USSR	4014	4072	0.3
Maize			
OECD countries	5760	6016	4.4
Canada	5672	6267	10.5
France	5458	7018	28.6
United States	6474	6630	2.4
Developing countries	1553	1704	9.7
Africa			
Egypt	3947	5257	33.2
Kenya	1360	1857	36.5
Tanzania (United Rep.)	1306	1417	8.5
Asia			
China	3038	3862	27.1
India	1100	1258	14.4
Indonesia	1458	2015	38.2
Thailand	2197	2384	8.5
Developing America			
Argentina	3159	3256	3.1
Brazil	1684	1975	17.3
Mexico	1718	1671	-2.7
USSR	2989	3466	16.0

2. Factors affecting supply

908. Several factors account for the rapid increase in supplies of commodities discussed in section B. They comprise technological developments as well as national policies at the macro and sectoral levels.

(a) Effects of technology

909. Technology has revolutionized the mining industry. As a result of technological developments metals can now be profitably extracted from lower grade ore and formerly inaccessible areas can be exploited. New computer software that turns three-dimensional seismic data into topographic models which can be examined from all angles was at the basis for the startling discovery of a more than one billion-barrel oil field in an already well-explored area near New Orleans in May 1991. New exploration technologies are also leading to a dramatic decline in exploration costs.[306]

910. Technology has also permitted qualitative improvements. The great challenge of the iron ore industry, for example, was to find out the most cost-effective ways of complying not only with the quantity but mainly with the increasingly strict quality requirements of steel consumers. The wide adoption of improved beneficiation techniques and concentration processes permitted a remarkable increase in Fe content of large deposits of low grade ores. Furthermore, improved techniques made it possible to reduce the content of impurities such as metalloides, alkaline oxides and other elements detrimental to the quality of the iron and steel products.

911. Technology and improved management methods have enabled both an expansion of the supply of agricultural produce and improved its quality. These comprise, on the one hand, introduction of high yielding and more disease-resistant varieties and, on the other, expanded use of inputs such as fertilizers and pesticides and improvements in farm management methods, all of which have increased yields. Studies in Europe indicate, for example, that grain yield increased through the introduction of new varieties by 35 to 50 per cent, through the use of fertilizers by 30 to 35 per cent and through the employment of pesticides and growth retardants by 25 to 30 per cent.[307]

912. Although crop yields will always be influenced by soil condiitons and climate there has been a general improvement in yields in developing countries. These improvements have varied among countries and regions. Table V-11 provides some examples of these changes and points to two findings concerning crops produced by both developed and developing countries, such as cotton, rice and maize. On the one hand increases in yields have been higher in the South than in the North; on the other, yield levels in developing countries continued to remain considerably lower than those in developed countries.

913. The wide use of high-yielding varieties has played a prominent role in expanding the supply of agricultural produce in developing as well as developed countries. The dominant proportion of cocoa plantings in the last 10 years, for example, has been of high-yielding hybrid varieties. Hybrids can potentially yield between 1,500 to 2,000 kg/ha but are very sensitive to management, maintenance and technical inputs (they require high applications of fertilizer, insecticides and

---

306 *Business Week,* 10 June 1991.

307 ECE, Committee on Agricultural Problems, "Technical and economic factors influencing the productivity of grain crops and the stability of grain yields", ECE/AGRI/104, New York 1989, p.12.

308 Malaysia increased the area under cocoa cultivation by 650 per cent in the 1980s. Most of the trees have not reached peak yield levels yet; cocoa yield therefore stagnated. Yields can, however, be expected to pick up strongly in the years to come.

309 For more information see: "Prospects for the world cocoa market until the year 2005", UNCTAD/COM/5.

herbicides). Hybrids reach their peak yield after 5-7 years. The pace of cocoa plantings has been far from uniform. Cocoa yields in South-East Asia almost trippled in the 1980s, as compared to a 30 per cent average increase in Africa. Cocoa output in Indonesia and Malaysia will continue to expand in coming years, since a large area of trees have yet to reach full yielding capacity.[308] One third of Malaysia's trees, for instance, are less than five years old, and over 80 per cent are under 10 years of age, while in Cameroon only 6 per cent of the tree population is younger than five years but 32 per cent of trees are over 40 years of age. The share of hybrids in the stock of trees in Ghana is some 15 per cent and in Nigeria slightly over one third.[309]

914. The increasing use of ancillary inputs in agriculture is another factor which is boosting yields. In spite of this increase, which as seen in table V-12, is a general phenomenon in developing countries, the level of input use there remains well below that in OECD countries with that in developing America the highest among developing regions.[310]

915. Divergences in the amount of inputs used do not by themselves explain the difference in yields. Firstly, more effective fertilizers, herbicides and pesticides already allow a sizeable reduction of the doses and the frequency of their application. Improvements in the quality of these inputs have also increased their effectiveness. Secondly, new disease or insect resistants varieties or hybrids require fewer inputs per hectare. Finally, there is the qualitative evolution of mechanization in agriculture. For example, the replacement in OECD countries of old models by multipurpose tractors can increase effectiveness without changing the number of tractors utilized.

(b) Effects of national policies

916. Commodity supply has proved to be very responsive to national policies at the macro and sectoral levels. While the former tends to influence commodity supply across the board (by, for example the liberalization of imports which reduces the cost or eases procurement of inputs), the latter encourages or discourages the supply of particular products. As far as developed countries are concerned, their sectoral policies, in particular for agriculture, solid fuels and steel, are major determinants of production levels.

917. While agricultural policies of developed countries reflect their perceived national interests, the effects of such policies spill over onto the world economy. According to OECD estimates, the cost of agricultural support programmes in all member countries, was $US299 billion in 1990, a figure which is more than twice the amount of aggregate export earnings from all non-fuel commodities of developing countries. The maintenance or guaranteeing of high domestic prices has encouraged overproduction of a wide range of commodities in OECD countries, and surpluses to domestic requirements have to be exported and subsidies used for their sale. With the exception of dairy products, such export supplies compete with exports from developing countries (e.g. cereals, sugar, vegetable oils and oilseeds, cotton and meat). As a result of the domestic policies pursued, imports of sugar by the United States have decreased significantly and the EEC has become a major net exporter of sugar. As can be seen from table V-13, the EEC in the 1980s markedly increased its share of world grain exports other than rice and of bovine meat. The United States and Canada almost tripled their shares of world bovine meat exports in the 1980s. On the other hand, while developing countries managed to consolidate their share in export markets for grains they distinctly lost ground in the world market for bovine meat. Developing America lost significant shares in respect of both products.

918. In contrast to developed countries, developing countries in general do not have such agricultural policies. Clearly their ability to subsidize production is limited and high levels of poverty require cheap, not dearer, food. Governments of developing countries have intervened more in the form of exhortation to farmers to increase production and in providing support services. Under their structural adjustment programmes, many have relied upon devaluations of their currencies and liberalization of imported inputs to spur commodity production and exports.

919. One would have expected that countries whose domestic currencies have depreciated the

---

[310] The data in table V-12, in particular figures on herbicides, should be regarded as orders of magnitude. For a good number of countries records are incomplete or inconsistent.

Table V-12

SOME INDICATORS FOR THE EVOLUTION OF INPUT USE IN CROP PRODUCTION [a]

Consumption of fertilizers (kg per ha of arable land and permanent crops)	Average 1972-77	Average 1983-88
OECD countries	109.9	114.0
Developing countries	22.3	41.0
Africa	6.6	10.1
Asia (South/South-East)	24.9	53.3
Developing America	31.3	44.0
Consumption of herbicides (kg per 1000 ha arable land)	Average 1969-71	Average 1986-88
OECD countries	481	440
Developing countries	33	127
Africa	9	16
Asia (South/South-East)	29	86
Developing America	120	300
Agricultural Tractors (Unit per 1000 ha arable land and permanent crops)	Average 1972-77	Average 1983-88
OECD countries	31.4	40.3
Developing countries	2.4	5.2
Africa	1.2	1.6
Asia (South/South-East)	1.2	3.8
Developing America	4.7	7.7

Source: FAO, Production Yearbook, various issues, FAO, Fertilizer Yearbook, various issues.

Table V-13

SHARE OF COUNTRIES/COUNTRY GROUPS IN WORLD EXPORTS OF GRAIN AND MEAT

(in percentages based on export volume)

	Average 1979-81		Average 1987-89	
	Grains[a]	Meat[b]	Grains	Meat
European Community countries	15.6	45.1	24.6	51.2
North America	64.5	3.2	55.3	8.4
Australia	7.2	18.9	8.6	14.2
Developing countries	7.9	17.5	8.9	13.7
Africa	(0.1)	(1.7)	(0.4)	(1.2)
Asia	(2.0)	(0.9)	(4.5)	(3.2)
America	(5.8)	(14.9)	(4.0)	(9.3)

Source: FAO, Trade Yearbook, various issues.
a/ Wheat and meslin, barley, maize, rye, oats
b/ Fresh bovine meat

most would have had the greatest increase in commodity exports. Available data reveal that there is no strong correlation between exchange rate changes alone and commodity export growth, rather the general picture is one of soaring commodity export volumes, independent of devaluation. Concerning the relationship between import liberalization and commodity export behaviour, results are again mixed. An increase in the ratio of commodity exports to GDP was experienced both by countries having introduced significant import liberalization programmes as well as by those with restrictive import policies.

920.   As pointed out above, sectoral policies have been the exception rather than the rule in developing countries during the last decade. The need to preserve employment, to earn foreign exchange and to avoid heavy closure and reopening costs has, on occasions, been a powerful influence for governments to maintain operating levels in the mining industry during periods of low prices through direct or indirect protection. The granting of low interest loans, the subsidizing of temporary losses or the provision of tax exemptions are cases in point.

921.   In most of the highly indebted developing countries there has been a shift of resources into the production of exportable commodities,as measured by an increase in the ratio of non-fuel commodity exports to GDP. This has been particularly significant for countries experiencing high debt service obligations. In almost all countries the growth in exports has been achieved at the expense of investment or at the cost of the availability of goods for domestic consumption.

3. Other factors

922.   Beyond the volume of demand and supply and of stocks held of a commodity entering the world market, price formation is affected by the structure of the market on both the demand and the supply sides, notably the number of market participants, and by the methods and practices of trading. The transparency of the market and in this context the ability of participants to gather, access and use relevant data are important factors for ensuring the effectiveness of marketing decisions. Commodity markets have rarely, if ever, met the conditions for perfect competition. The number and economic power of buyers and sellers, while varying among commodities, frequently portray oligopolistic and/or oligopsonistic characteristics while trade pratices have mainly been developed to reflect the interests of commodity users and traders.

923.   While information on ownership and changes in world industry and market structures for individual commodities is not systematically available at present, there are indications that during the 1980s there has been a shrinking number of major participants in many commodity markets, leading to their having increasing power to influence prices through their decisions on stocking and actions affecting demand. Information on demand is still basically available only to these major players and often trade houses-cum-processors, which are important actors in price formation with an interest in its results, are the major sources of publicly available information.[311]

924.   The actual number of firms directly involved in commodity transactions may have increased due to new entrants. However concomitantly the economic power of large firms, usually operating in more than one market and often worldwide, has increased through mergers and takeovers and installation of processing capacities in new locations. This is especially evident in the food sector. In the tea market, the already small number of main firms decreased[312]and the market power of these firms has increased significantly, including in developing country markets such as Pakistan and India. In the cocoa industry, the top five chocolate manufacturers now use almost 40 per cent of world annual cocoa bean production and cocoa marketing and intermediate processing have become increasingly concentrated in the hands of a few firms.[313] Similar changes have taken place

---

[311] For example Gill & Duffus for cocoa, and Metallgesellschaft for minerals.

[312] For example Unilever acquired both Brooke Bond and Lipton.

[313] In this area Nestlé took over Rowntree Mackintosh (United Kingdom) (a major chocolate multinational), Buitoni-Perugina (Italy), Allen Life Savers (Australia), Savoy (Venezuela) and Curtis Brands (US - RJR Nabisco); Philip Morris (United States) acquired Jacob-Suchard (Switzerland) which in turn had bought E. J. Brach (United States), Côte d'Or (Belgium), Leonard Monheim (Germany), Dulac SpA (Italy), Bensdorp (Austria) and a major share of Palvides (Greece), and ED & F Man (United Kingdom), one of the world's largest cocoa-coffee-and-sugar traders. Jacob-Suchard had also opened new subsidiaries in Japan, Australia, Republic of Korea and Hong Kong.

in the coffee industry. The sugar and the grains industries have also experienced acquisitions and major expansions by the principal firms.[314] In the agro-food sector several major firms either merged or bought out other firms.[315] A recent assessment concludes that "Bit by bit, the smaller players are disappearing, and the battle is on as large industrial manufacturers vie for position in an increasingly globalized international food sector".[316]

925.   In the minerals and metals area, there seems to have been a consolidation of market power through expansion. The earlier trend of horizontal diversification into mining by the major petroleum companies seems to have been reversed, with several selling back their acquisitions in the metals area to established mining and metal firms.

926.   The second feature of the increasing market power of large, mainly transnational, firms which purchase commodities is the significant involvement of these firms with a widening number of related commodities.[317] A third feature is the increasing cross-border nature of the takeovers and mergers occurring among firms. In order to get a foothold in expanding or new markets or within areas forming trading blocs (e.g. EEC-92), large firms are not only setting up subsidiaries or branches, but are acquiring firms already well-established in foreign markets with distribution networks and brand names.

927.   A fourth feature on the demand side is the move to increase vertical integration into final products. An important consideration in this regard is the market power exercised by ownership of brand names commanding consumer loyalty. In the minerals area another consideration is to ensure market outlets for production in a period of slower economic growth.[318] Developing country companies have also made efforts to secure their markets by vertical integration.[319] There have also been moves to increase integration into primary production by a number of major processing firms.[320]

928.   On the supply side of practically all commodity markets there has been a significant increase in the number of producers, not only in terms of the number of countries producing commodities for export but also in terms of the number of sellers. The increase in the actual number of sellers is particularly a result of the liberalization of export marketing in many countries, including those undertaking structural adjustment programmes under which centralized exporting through government agencies such as marketing boards has been abolished. The implication of such liberalization is not just an increased competition amongst sellers nationally but also their comparatively small size and inexperience in international marketing and marketing practices (contract terms, transport arrangements, etc.) which gives added bargaining power to the purchasers.

929.   For a few commodities, such as rubber, there has been a noticeable movement towards increased links between individual producers and processors whereby production quality and quantity is geared specifically to the input needs of a particular processing firm. This trend is also

---

Cadbury-Schweppes bought Chocolat Poulaire S.A. (France). Hersheys Corporation (United States) bought Cadbury-Schweppes (United States) confectionery operations and expanded operations in the Far East (Japan, Republic of Korea and the Philippines). Also the processing activities of S & W Beresford (United Kingdom) and W. R. Grace (United States) were merged and ED & F Man purchased the cocoa processing and marketing activities of Gill and Duffus. See UNCTAD/COM/5 op cit, especially paras. 303-311.

314 Tate & Lyle is now not only Europe's largest sugar refiner but also the largest in the United States where it bought out Amstar. In the grains area, Ferruzzi expanded through acquisitions (e.g. Lesieur, France) and new activities; Cargill bought Maple Leaf Mills (Canada).

315 For example Philip Morris bought Kraft (United States), Grand Metropolitan/(United Kingdom) acquired Pillsbury (United States) and Congra merged with Holly Farms.

316 Philippe Chalmin and Jean-Louis Gombeaud, International Commodity Markets Handbook (New York: Woodhead-Faulkner, 1989), p. 394.

317 This is illustrated by Pechiney's move into metal packaging through its purchase of American National Can.

318 For example, most major firms in the cocoa area, Nestlé, Jacob-Suchard, Cadbury-Schweppes, Hersheys, Mars, are also active in other food and beverage areas. One of the major tobacco companies, Philip Morris, has diversified into foods. In minerals, Rio Tinto Zinc and its affiliates are important in practically all minerals and metals, including zinc, copper, iron ore and uranium.

319 For instance, Indonesian and Thai tuna fish companies acquired respectively Van Camp Seafood (United States), controlling 20 per cent of the United States canned tuna market, and Bumble Bee Co.(United States), the world's second largest producer and marketer of canned tuna; Comilog (Gabon) acquired ferro-manganese interests in several European countries to improve its market access; and both the Chilean and Zambian state copper companies have set up joint ventures with European copper users for the production of copper rod.

320 This phenomenon can be illustrated by the setting-up of plantations by Hersheys in cocoa and Cargill in oranges.

noticeable in cocoa.[321] Increased links between producers and distributors have also developed for fruits and vegetables such as bananas, oranges, pineapples and tomatoes, and for flowers and decorative plants.

930.   The above developments have had important repercussions for the functioning of markets as an increasing amount of trade is taking place directly between buyers and sellers on a continuing basis without intermediaries. This has called into question the representativeness of price formation in international commodity markets as the percentage of trade of a commodity passing through trade houses and terminal markets has declined, particularly for several major agricultural products. The result has been the development of new types of risk management instruments (especially over-the-counter instruments such as swaps, floors, collars and caps) more suited to these marketing arrangements, a declining role for the trade houses, which were the traditional intermediaries in many commodity markets, and increasing importance of financial institutions in trade.

931.   Futures (and option) exchanges traditionally have had the role of providing a short-term hedging medium for trade participants, mainly trade houses. Increasing use is being made of prices on futures markets as reference prices in medium and long-term contracts, executable orders, and over-the-counter tailor-made instruments including swaps, for a widening range of both mineral and agricultural commodities. The volume of contracts traded on futures markets overall grew rapidly in the 1980s as a result of changes in exchange regulations especially affecting options and as an offshoot of the astronomical growth of trading in financial futures instruments. As a result, commodity futures markets have become an integral part of the international financial system and this has led to a questioning of whether futures prices for individual commodities adequately reflect physical market fundamentals.

932.   The reasons for this questioning are several. Firstly, the robustness of a futures market and its price discovery function vary directly with the degree of active involvement of physical trade participants (producers, traders and users) for hedging purposes. During the 1980s there was a sharp decline in the number of trading houses as a result of mergers and closures and a drop in the membership on commodity futures exchanges of trade houses or trading arms of major producers or users, who traditionally were the active participants on these markets. As a result, several futures markets which are dominated by physical trade users rather than speculators (rubber, cocoa, coffee, sugar, soyabeans, aluminium, nickel, zinc, among others) have at times become thin in terms of physical trade-related trading. For example on London FOX, the volume of raw sugar contracts has been steadily declining for years and dropped 68 per cent between April 1990 and April 1991, cocoa futures volumes halved over the last year and coffee is the only market left with solid volumes. For some other commodities, such as rubber and tin, as direct trade increased, physical trade-related activity on futures markets has declined and now has become of marginal importance. This has increased the possibility for individual actors to have a major influence on futures prices.   Practically all commodity futures markets (including those for cocoa, coffee, aluminium, tin, copper, palmoil, soyabeans, corn, zinc, nickel) have had problems of attempted squeezes, large "backwardations" and illegal trading practices during the 1980s.

933.   While the use of commodity futures for hedging related to physical trade has declined, there has been increased use of these futures contracts by investment funds and an increase in the membership on exchanges of financial intermediaries such as security houses and banks trading on behalf of clients (private and trade related) or to protect loans to clients. This has had two effects. The change in membership has reduced the influence on futures price movement of physical transactions and increased the role of short-term price speculation. Short-term movements in prices over hours and up to about 3 days increasingly reflect money-making out of instability (in either direction) and shifts in investment finance among markets for short-term profits; large investment funds tend to exacerbate the direction of price movements as their positions on markets are usually similar.

934.   Most investment funds require very liquid markets as they deal in large positions relative to individual speculators. On the markets on which they operate, there have been large increases in limits on daily permitted price movements to accomodate them. The commodity markets concerned are mainly metal and energy futures in New York and agricultural futures in Chicago but funds have also operated on soft commodity markets in New York and some metals in London. A futures fund manager of a large financial house recently summed up the change in commodity

---

[321] Both Hersheys and Mars have recently set up long-term contractual links with smallholders in Malaysia and Indonesia.

future markets' role as follows: "London FOX is run by an old guard that worries more about the needs of producers and manufacturers than those of the investment community. The exchange has got to understand its contracts have a wider audience than just the physical trade".[322] The result of this change is that hedgers using commodity markets need increased sophistication to interpret price movements and to plan their strategies. It has also meant that options based on commodity futures have become increasingly relevant as a hedging tool, since exposure to unpredictable margin calls in future trading are replaced by a known financial outlay when options are used.

935.   Despite concerted efforts by the exchanges and developed-country governments to encourage developing-country exporters to increase their use of futures and options as a means of "locking in prices for their commodity exports", there has been limited growth in such activity. The reasons for this include insufficient knowledge of the complexities of exchanges; problems of access to foreign exchange for hedging purposes; the need for constant contact with markets; and the use of standard contracts which do not necessarily correspond to the quality of the commodity exported. Other constraints are the speculative nature of future markets and difficulties and high cost in using them for small producers and small export transactions. Many exporters, while desiring to lock in a floor price for their contracts, also want to participate in possible price rises, and so are reluctant to use futures which do not allow for this. As a response to this situation several trade houses, in an effort to generate business, are writing over-the-counter options with floor prices and shared participation in price increases for exporters and covering themselves through futures - this is especially true for cocoa and coffee.

936.   A new development over the past few years, which is mainly a result of the debt situation in most developing countries and the dramatic drop in private investment in them, especially from financial intermediaries and banks, is the growing role of private financial institutions in commodity markets. To help reduce risks associated with old or new loans, they are becoming increasingly involved in trade deals with the writing of over-the-counter instruments such as swaps for which they use futures to offset their risks. Part of the motivation for the increased length of futures contracts adopted by many exchanges is to accomodate the swap market's need for hedging.

937.   There have been many initiatives during the 1980s to start new futures contracts - for different qualities of commodities already having futures or for new commodities. Many of these[323] have not attracted enough interest from the physical trade participants to be viable, while others have gradually gained in acceptance.[324] In other cases, competing contracts between exchanges[325] reduced liquidity and have led to discussions on merging or eliminating one of the contracts. Exchanges and contracts in developing countries, beyond those that are in reality terminal or forward markets, have not done well, mainly because of regulatory and liquidity problems. Without a solid base of support from the physical trade, futures markets risk becoming anomalies or a purely speculative investment tool, unlinked to physical market price behaviour.

D. Issues for the 1990s

938.   All the factors addressed in the previous section will continue to affect commodity markets in the present decade. Some of them will grow in intensity as a result of developments in the latter part of the 1980s, the effects of which will be felt more directly in the 1990s. Five developments in particular will affect the direction of commodity trade as well as its size and composition. These are: the changes taking place in countries of Central and Eastern Europe and the USSR; the formation and enlargement of regional common markets among developed countries; the increase in the potential for growth in South-South trade; demographic changes in traditional export markets and their impact on commodity production and trade; and the increasing concern about

---

[322] Quoted in the report "London FOX catches breath before chase", Futures, July 1991.

[323] For example MATIF for cocoa butter and white sugar; London Fox for rubber, rice and tea and COMEX for diamonds.

[324] For example LME for aluminium and the New York Cotton Exchange for orange juice.

[325] One example is the white sugar contracts on the MATIF and London FOX.

environmental issues and their impact on commodity production and trade.

1. The changes taking place in countries of Central and Eastern Europe and the USSR

939. Political and economic changes under way in these countries are having effects on commodity trade between them as well as on their commodity trade with the rest of the world. Recent developments paint a rather pessimistic picture of a sharp decline in imports, at least in the short term. Owing to a severe contraction in industrial activity and a severe shortage of foreign exchange, particularly in the case of the USSR, merchandise imports fell dramatically in the first quarter of 1991 vis-à-vis the first quarter of 1990. Those from developing countries are estimated to have plunged by about one half. These trends seem likely to continue during the transition period, despite the low current per capita consumption levels, especially for tropical fruits and beverages which in 1989 were 15 per cent of the level in OECD countries for coffee, 47 per cent for cocoa[326] and 6 per cent for bananas. On the other hand, because of the falling domestic demand, there has been an increase in exports, especially of minerals and metals from the USSR, which has tended to depress further metal prices.

940. The changes taking place are having important repercussions for certain developing countries which formed part of the CMEA (Cuba, Mongolia and Viet Nam) and which sold a high share of their commodity exports on eastern European markets in the 1980s. An illustration of the effects is given by the sharp fall in Cuba's exports of sugar which slipped precipitously from 3.7 million tonnes during the period November 1988/April 1989 to 2.1 million tonnes during the equivalent period in 1990/1991.

941. In the medium to long term, the resumption of economic growth in the countries of Central and Eastern Europe and the USSR combined with trade liberalization and currency convertibility should lead to a growth in trade with the rest of the world which could well exceed the growth in their economies. In the best position to benefit would be those commodities with relatively high income elasticities of demand in the region, such as tropical products. For agricultural raw materials, the relatively low consumption levels for certain commodities indicate a potential for substantial increases in demand in the longer term. For example, per capita consumption of natural rubber is only about one third of that in OECD countries, mainly because of low car ownership rates. In the case of cotton, the expected reduction in USSR exports to countries of Central and Eastern Europe may open up opportunities for increased supplies of cotton from developing countries, especially if the Central and Eastern European countries gain a competitive edge in textile manufacturing and import barriers to western Europe are removed. By contrast, these countries, with the exception of the USSR, are basically self-sufficient in temperate zone foodstuffs of grains, meat, and vegetable oils, and they may increase their production and exports during the 1990s. Sugar beet production is also growing and imports of cane sugar are therefore likely to decrease further. Moreover, although the USSR is at present a significant importer of grains, meat and sugar, it has a great potential to increase production of these products.

942. As regards fuels, countries of Central and Eastern Europe are heavily dependent on USSR deliveries of gas and crude oil. These must now be paid for in hard currency at world market prices. The decline in USSR crude oil production has forced these countries to diversify their suppliers. Higher fuel costs are likely to stimulate more efficient use of energy with energy-wasteful and economically non-viable plants closing down or their production significantly reduced. Many of these plants inefficiently consume considerable amounts of minerals and metals and their closure would reduce demand for these commodities. Further, a predicted shift in manufacturing from heavy industry to consumer goods may result in lower consumption of some minerals and metals. This is already taking place as is illustrated by developments in the steel industry. According to the International Iron and Steel Institute, steel production fell sharply in January-May 1991

---

[326] For example, the representative for the USSR, at the meeting of the Executive Committee of the International Cocoa Organisation (held on 17 - 18 June 1991), stated that "the hard-currency problems of his country meant that priorities for the purchase of various goods, including cocoa, had had to be established and that cocoa could not be very high on that list in the USSR's present circumstances".

compared to the same period in 1990, with the fall ranging from 6.3 per cent in Czechoslovakia, and to more than 17 per cent in Hungary.

943.   Finally, it is important to recall that long-standing trading links exist among countries of Central and Eastern Europe. Especially the existing relatively efficient transport system for bulk products will favour the USSR as a competitive supplier of raw materials.

2. Regional trading arrangements among developed countries

944.   There is a danger that increased emphasis on regional trading arrangements during the 1990s could accentuate access problems for commodities from non-member countries. The establishment of a single market in the European Economic Community by 1 January 1993 will, in stimulating intra-trade, particularly affect commodities including their processed forms. The enlargement of the Community as a result of Germany's re-unification is likely to increase even further its agricultural production, although both the magnitude and timing of this increase will depend essentially on how, and when, the centrally planned structure of eastern Germany's agriculture is reorganized, and on the resolution of questions of property and ownership. It should also be noted that new investments in the processing of commodities, both agriculture and mineral, in this region are coming from neighbouring countries, an indication of the strengthening trade and industrial links within Western Europe.

945.   The launching in June 1990 of the negotiations between the European Community and the EFTA countries on the creation of a European Economic Area, and the offer of association agreements by the European Community to countries of Eastern Europe are indications of the growing integration of trade and economic relations generally in Europe. This development is further underlined by the negotiations taking place for free trade agreements between EFTA countries and Czechoslovakia, Hungary and Poland. In all the above negotiations a central and very sensitive issue is trade in agricultural products, the resolution of which may well entail displacement of imported supplies from third countries. To the extent that increased integration within Europe takes into account the Community's close trading links with Africa under the Lomé, Maghreb and other arrangements, trade patterns of Africa's developing countries could well become even more oriented towards Europe.

946.   The Free Trade Agreement between the United States and Canada has potentially important repercussions for international trade in agricultural, timber and fishery poducts. Its possible enlargement to encompass Mexico could have even greater repercussions for commodity trade, in particular for tropical products and sugar. The launching of the Enterprise of the Americas Initiative may attenuate the effects of this development, but in turn it could well marginalize other developing countries in respect of trade prospects.

3. The increase in the potential for South-South trade

947.   The emergence and strengthening of regional and subregional groupings in developing countries can be seen as a complement to their economic relationships with other economic partners. There are moves in all three developing regions towards the strengthening of trading links, including the creation of the Latin American Southern Cone Common Market (Mercosur), the strengthening of the Andean Pact, the creation of an African Economic Community, and the strengthening of ASEAN and CARICOM. A number of bilateral trade agreements have also been negotiated, notably in Latin America. These developments should increase South-South regional commodity trade during the 1990s. Moreover, the following factors point to the potential for a substantial increase in interregional commodity trade.

948.   The projected high rate of population growth in developing countries will increase demand for food. A large part of the population of most developing countries is in its peak reproductive years. Given the fact that a number of developing countries have little potential for adding to their cropland area, their cropland in per capita terms will decline and, as a consequence, so will their food self-sufficiency ratios. In consequence, at least a part of the new demand will need to be filled by food imports. This creates a potential for greatly enhanced South-South trade in food products. Some of this potential may fail to be realised, however, owing to the lack of purchasing power in the importing countries and competition from export suppliers in developed countries with their subsidized excess production and food aid.

949.   Interregional South-South trade is also likely to be stimulated by the progress of industrialization in Asia which will continue to increase import demand for industrial raw materials. This will open up export opportunities for other developing countries, especially in terms of long-term contractual supply arrangements for minerals and metals such as iron ore and copper.

950.   Expansion in South-South commodity trade will, however, be heavily dependent on whether developing countries manage to offer competitive terms. It will also be dependent upon improved transport and communications and reductions in delivery uncertainties which currently act as a barrier inhibiting South-South trade flows.

4.   Demographic changes in traditional import markets and their impact on commodity production and trade

951.   Low and even stagnant population growth and an ageing population structure will continue to be the typical features in developed countries. This will certainly affect their demand for commodities in the 1990s.

952.   The declining share in a country's population of persons 15 years and under will affect food consumption. This share, for example, declined from 28 per cent in 1970 to 21 per cent in 1990 in the United States and from 25 per cent to 20 per cent in Europe in the same period. Per capita food consumption will inevitably decrease with the decline in this share. Coffee consumption, on the other hand, could well increase given the correlation between coffee consumption and age of population between 20 to 60 years. These developments will go hand in hand with a more pronounced impact of dietary consciousness which will probably favour increased consumption of fruit and vegetables.

953.   The increase in the share of persons between 20 and 40 years of age during the 1990s will also have a favourable impact on the demand for consumer durables and housing; as a result, demand for mineral and metals is likely to increase.

954.   The combination of even higher standards of living as a result of low birth rates in devel-

oped countries and the possibility of even lower standards of living in developing countries with fast growing populations will inevitably increase pressures for migration from South to North during the 1990s. One reaction may be the relocation of industries to the South, which in turn could stimulate processed commodity trade with the North.

5. Increasing concern about environmental issues and its impact on commodity production and trade

955. As the 1990s began, global concern was expressed about ozone depletion, climatic change, and extinction of unique genetic and other natural resources. Dealing with these concerns nationally and internationally will certainly have an impact on commodity production, processing and trade. The production and processing of commodities are key elements in both the pollution and the preservation of the environment. While the processing of commodities is an important polluter of the environment, reduction of pollution levels also concerns commodities. Reafforestation programmes or the incorporation of specific commodities, such as minerals of platinum, manganese and palladium, in anti-pollution devices are examples in this regard. Greater concern about the environment also affects the demand for natural biodegradable products and organically produced products.

956. Possible changes may take place in agriculture as a consequence of restrictions in developed countries on chemical fertilizer and pesticide use, which could lead to reduced yields. In the case of developing countries where the use of agricultural inputs is much less intensive than in the developed countries, fertilizer and pesticide use has recently been reduced as a consequence of low world prices for export products. Increased use of higher-yielding varieties and the development of plants with higher resistance to pests and diseases may, on the other hand, more than offset these developments. The hope is that biotechnology will increasingly exploit the use of the genetic potential inherent in plants and contribute to finding more environmentally friendly biological - as opposed to chemical - methods of fighting pests and enhancing yields.

957. Markets for recycled materials will probably gain in importance during the 1990s. For instance, rubber chipped from discarded tyres is already being used for industrial fuel and as an additive in road-paving materials; the aluminium can industry is recycling as much as 75 per cent of the aluminium it consumes and the plastics industry is beginning to recycle as well. These tendencies will increasingly affect fuel and non-fuel commodity demand.

958. As regulations regarding pollution become more stringent in terms of both levels and the disposal of wastes, new production techniques and the closing down of certain heavily polluting industries could result. This will favour new plants and could well open up new trade opportunities for industries in both the North and the South; in the latter case, increased exports by the South to the North might depend not only upon their being competitive but also upon their meeting pollution controls similar to those in the North.

959. Concerns about tropical forests will have effects on the demand for, and supply of, tropical timber. Demand will also be influenced by the possible exploitation of timber resources in other areas, such as Siberia. Concerns about the depletion of natural resources will also affect fisheries supplies, and energy conservation measures will continue to figure prominently in the 1990s.

E. Issues in international commodity policy

1. UNCTAD VII and international commodity policy

960.   The Final Act of UNCTAD VII recognized that international co-operation between producers and consumers was needed and should be strengthened in order to achieve lasting solutions to deal effectively with the short-, medium-, and long-term problems in the commodities area. To this end, it reaffirmed the validity of Conference resolution 93 (IV) and called for the implementation of, *inter alia,* certain agreed policies and measures.[327]

961.   In the above context, the Conference agreed that, where appropriate and feasible, producer-consumer consultations and co-operation should be enhanced, strengthened or established and that the operation and the functioning of existing commodity agreements should be improved. It also requested the Secretary-General of UNCTAD to convene or resume, in accordance with the results of comprehensive consultations with producers and consumers, *ad hoc* review meetings and/or preparatory meetings on individual commodities which are not covered by international commodity agreements/arrangements and which are included in the indicative list of resolution 93 (IV). The Conference underlined that disposal of non-commercial stocks should not disrupt commodity markets and should be done in consultations with producers, and where appropriate, commodity organizations. It was urged that once the conditions for entry into force of the Agreement establishing the Common Fund for Commodities were met, efforts should be made as soon as possible by the parties to ensure that the Common Fund was made operational.[328]

962.   Concerning other policies and measures in the area of commodities, the Conference agreed on the need for adequate financial resources to implement diversification programmes, including processing, marketing and distribution activities. Such medium-term and long-term financing should be complemented with technical assistance for the implementation of these programmes as well as for feasibility studies and infrastructural developments. The Conference also agreed that financial and technical support should be extended towards improving the competitiveness of natural products with respect to synthetics and substitutes. It noted that the Uruguay Round was an important opportunity to strengthen the multilateral trading system, to halt and reverse protectionism, to remove distortions to trade and thus to make, inter alia, a significant contribution to improve access to markets for commodities.[329]

2. Developments since UNCTAD VII

963.   Following UNCTAD VII, there were a number of important developments in respect of the implementation of the decisions of the Conference. To begin with, the long-awaited entry into force of the Agreement establishing the Common Fund for Commodities took place in June 1989. The first annual meeting of the Governing Council of the Common Fund was convened by the Secretary-General of UNCTAD in July 1989. At that meeting the Governing Council decided on the location of the Headquarters of the Fund in Amsterdam, appointed the Managing Director,

---

[327] See the Final Act of UNCTAD VII, para. 73.

[328] Ibid, paras. 75, 76, 77, 79 and 97.

[329] Ibid, paras. 83, 84, 86 and 95.

elected the Executive Directors, and approved the rules of procedure of the Governing Council and the Executive Board, as well as interim financial rules. Subsequently, the Fund has held a further meeting of the Governing Council, six meetings of the Executive Board and two meetings of the Consultative Committee which provides advice on the operations of the Second Account. It is expected that the Fund will begin to make grants/loans under the Second Account in the near future.

964.   In the field of international commodity agreements, the International Natural Rubber Agreement, which was negotiated under UNCTAD auspices in 1987, entered into force on 29 December 1988. At the present time, this is the only international commodity agreement with price stabilization measures in force. In 1989, the International Agreement on Jute and Jute Products was renegotiated and entered into force on 12 April 1991. The International Cocoa Agreement was extended for a period of two years from 1 October 1990, but the main economic provisions of that Agreement were not renewed. Similarly, the International Coffee Agreement was extended for a period of two years from the same date with its economic provisions suspended for the duration of the extension period. The International Sugar Agreement, the International Wheat Agreement, the International Agreement on Olive Oil and the International Tropical Timber Agreement were extended till 31 December 1992, 30 June 1993, 31 December 1993 and 31 March 1994 respectively.

965.   In May 1990, a meeting was convened by the Secretary-General of UNCTAD pursuant to paragraph 19(b) of the terms of reference of the International Nickel Study Group negotiated under UNCTAD auspices in 1985, at which the 12 States that had notified their acceptance of those terms of reference took a decision to put the terms of reference into effect among themselves. The inaugural meeting of the International Nickel Study Group was subsequently convened in June of that year. In addition, terms of reference for the establishment of international study groups on copper and tin were negotiated under UNCTAD auspices in February and April 1989 respectively. The provisional and definitive entry into force conditions for the terms of reference of the copper study group are respectively at least 60 per cent and 80 per cent of trade in copper. To date, acceptances only account for 29.01 per cent of such trade. In the case of tin, the entry into force requirement is at least 70 per cent of trade in tin and to date the acceptances account for 28.13 per cent of such trade. In view of this situation, it has not been possible to establish either of the two study groups.

966.   The Trade and Development Board, in decision 328 (XXXVII), decided that "UNCTAD work on iron ore should be maintained and that regular intergovernmental meetings of experts should be convened, with the participation of industry advisers, to exchange views on the iron ore situation and to review and enhance iron ore statistics". Moreover, as a result of the comprehensive consultations on individual commodities held pursuant to the request mentioned earlier in the Final Act of UNCTAD VII, an *ad hoc* review meeting on bauxite was convened in May 1991 and a second meeting has been requested as soon as possible after UNCTAD VIII which will, inter alia, discuss and examine the need and the level of support for a producer-consumer forum on bauxite/alumina/aluminium. The process of comprehensive consultations on individual commodities between producers and consumers did not lead to any other ad hoc review or preparatory meetings. Taking this into account, in its agreed conclusion 26 (XIV) the Committee on Commodities decided that "the process of consultations should only proceed where progress in such consultations has concretely demonstrated the appropriateness and feasibility of their continuation".[330]

967.   Two other commodity bodies exist within the GATT as a result of the Tokyo Round, namely the International Meat Council on bovine meat and the International Dairy Products Council on certain milk powders and milk fats including butter and certain cheeses. In addition, the Food and Agriculture Organization (FAO) convenes intergovernmental groups and meetings for a number of agricultural commodities namely, bananas, citrus fruit, grains, jute, hard fibres, kenaf and allied fibres, oilseeds, oils and fats, rice, tea, wine and vine products as well as for fisheries and forestry. Concerning minerals and metals, UNCTAD has its Committee on Tungsten and there is the International Lead and Zinc Study Group, which was established under the auspices of the United Nations. Outside of the United Nations framework autonomous commodity bodies on rubber and cotton have been established.

---

[330] See the Agreed Conclusion 26 (XIV) of the Committee on Commodities at its fourteenth session, November 1990, para. 10.

3. Present situation on producer/consumer co-operation

968. The inability of the international community to develop and implement an agreed and coherent international commodity policy is evident in two features of the current situation regarding commodities. The first is the wide divergencies in positions adopted by countries in the negotiations in the Uruguay Round concerning agriculture, tropical products and natural resource-based products, which, even if reconciled, will not result in complete trade liberalization in such products; rather the extent and forms of government intervention may change. In consequence, the basic issues of oversupply, stock overhangs, market access restrictions, consumption taxes and subsidies confronting most commodities will still remain. The second feature is the weakening of the content of producer-consumer and producer co-operation. With commodity prices being depressed, the desire for price stabilization measures in the context of commodity agreements has waned. Consumers are, in view of the abundance of supply, not particularly concerned about security of supplies and producers are more concerned about competing for market shares than in maintaining depressed price levels. In addition, in respect of various commodity agreements, important producers and/or consumers are not members. For example, Indonesia, Malaysia and the United States are not members of the International Cocoa Agreement and countries of Central and Eastern Europe and the USSR are not members of the International Coffee Agreement. Moreover, many commodity organizations have faced financial difficulties as a result of delays in payment of membership dues and certain countries have withdrawn from commodity arrangements as a result of financial constraints.

969. Arrangements for negotiating new commodity agreements on cocoa and sugar are currently underway and it is likely that arrangements will be made in the near future for negotiating new agreements on coffee, tropical timber, natural rubber and wheat. Clearly, such renegotiation processes would be greatly facilitated if there were an agreed and coherent international commodity policy which tackled the range of issues confronting the commodities in question.

970. The basic rationale for any type of commodity body is to improve the conditions of supply and demand. The first step in this regard is the exchange of information between producers and consumers on current and future prospects for the commodity. To the extent that information on either supply or demand is not available for one reason or another, including claims of confidentiality, the diagnoses of problems to be confronted and of remedial actions that should be taken will be deficient. For example, if complete information on stocks or re-exports is withheld then inevitably the supply/demand equation will be faulty. Recognition of this problem lies behind the frequent exhortation of the international community for improved market transparency.

4. Optimizing the contribution of the commodity sector to development, including through diversification

971. Given the role of the commodity sector in the domestic economies of most developing countries, the efficient management of a country's commodity dependency is vital, not least to enable the country to cope with external shocks. Thus national governments have developed or must develop and implement comprehensive commodity policies within the context of an appropriate macroeconomic framework. Such policies should include adequate provision of incentives to encourage private enterprise, development and maintenance of specific infrastructure, provision of support services and training, support for commodity research arrangements and the mobilization of domestic and international financial resources.

972. Efforts are also needed to strengthen linkages between the commodity sector and the rest of the domestic economy, in order to optimize the sector's contribution to overall economic development. Diversification in the commodity sector is a crucial component of these efforts, and

in turn has the effect of stimulating structural changes in the economy as a whole. This is especially relevant in small-holder agriculture, in agro-processing with local supply of equipment and other inputs and in the area of repair and maintenance. Also increased local participation in domestic, regional and overseas marketing stimulates the service sector in areas such as transport, communications, insurance and finance.

973. Thus, in addition to measures to improve the competitiveness of traditional commodity exports, national commodity policies need to incorporate specific actions to encourage horizontal and vertical commodity diversification. Decisions on diversification are necessarily country-specific and must be adapted to the long-term dynamic comparative advantages offered by a country's natural resource base, human resources and economic structure. While macro-economic adjustments are a necessary condition, they are not sufficient for diversification to occur; specific supportive interventions by governments are also needed. The existing export sectors, to the extent that they are viable, need to be strengthened and further developed; diversification should be aimed at stimulating additional activities, and not substituting traditional ones. Moreover, experience has shown that while most new export activities started from a domestic market base, protecting domestic sectors against outside competition is not a sustainable option in the long run.

974. A delineation of the respective roles of the government and the private sector should assist in optimizing the contribution of the commodity sector to development. Broadly speaking, the government's role should concentrate on creating an enabling environment allowing the private sector (both domestic and foreign) to achieve a degree of competitiveness domestically and on world markets. In some cases, however, direct government participation in commodity production and marketing may be necessary or desirable. An ongoing dialogue between the government and the private sector should be maintained.

975. In the Final Act of UNCTAD VII, new orientations were given to the work which was entrusted to the Working Party on Diversification, Processing, Marketing and Distribution, including Transportation, of the Committee on Commodities. In its consideration of constraints to diversification, it recognized that the extent of infrastructural development (ie. transport system, port facilities, storage, electricity, irrigation and communication systems) has an impact on diversification efforts, and its insufficiency has hindered such efforts.[331] The World Bank and bilateral aid agencies, which have been the main sources of external finance for infrastructure in the form of long-term, low-interest loans or grants, should strengthen their efforts in this field. Equally, the lack of appropriately skilled labour affects the capacity of developing countries to take advantage of existing or potential opportunities for diversification, processing, marketing and distribution and hence actions by the international community to provide the required technical assistance are imperative. However, often the problem is not so much insufficient assistance, as lack of co-ordination, which often makes it difficult to identify the most appropriate sources for assistance.

976. It has been recognized by the international community that while the diversification in a country should reflect its domestic factors and conditions, its viability is not necessarily ensured unless certain external conditions are also met. Despite commitments by governments to reduce trade barriers and set up preferential schemes to facilitate access to developed countries' markets for developing countries, obstacles remain in the form of tariff and non-tariff barriers to the exports of developing country commodities in primary and processed form. Restrictive business practices have similar negative effects as governmental barriers to trade. As stated in a recent General Assembly resolution, the international community has urged all the parties involved "to work for a balanced outcome to the multilateral trade negotiations within the Uruguay Round so as to ensure that their successful conclusion brings about further expansion and liberalization of trade in commodities, taking into account the special and differential treatment for developing countries, as well as all other principles contained in the Ministerial Declaration on the Uruguay Round".[332]

977. The availability of adequate information is a basic requirement for undertaking commodity sector development. The international community has recognized that existing commodity information is often incomplete for making investment, production and marketing decisions, and that there was a need for increased international co-operation to improve information flows through greater participation of governments and industry of both developing and developed countries in

---

[331] The report of the Working Party and its agreed conclusions are contained in TD/B/C.1/314.
[332] General Assembly resolution 45/200, "Commodities", para. 9.

producer-consumer forums as a means of exchanging information on investments, prospects and markets for individual commodities as well as for exchanging views. The Working Party also invited bilateral donors and UNDP and other competent United Nation organizations to continue providing financial support for improvements in information flows, for the co-ordination of information systems and for assistance to developing countries through training and development of analytical tools for better use of existing information. It requested the UNCTAD secretariat, within its existing resources and in light of the co-ordinating role of the Committee on Commodities, to provide technical assistance to developing countries to assist them in collecting, processing, disseminating and making full use of information; to analyse and disseminate, in collaboration with other competent organizations, publicly available information on industry and market structures for individual commodities; to draw up an inventory of the criteria for the evaluation of diversification projects; and to continue to develop a micro-computer-based commodity information and analysis system (MICAS) already started by the UNCTAD secretariat.

978.   The development of adequate export marketing policies is an essential part of any export-oriented diversification programme. Exporting commodities involves utilizing and interacting with international marketing systems and practices. These systems and practices vary among commodities and according to the stage of processing of a commodity, as well as among markets. While the private sector is often the agent handling exports, government policy considerably influences the systems and practices which are used. The combination of macro policy reform, deregulation and privatization, with poor prospects for traditional commodity exports and the efforts to diversify the export base has heightened the need for reviewing and formulating new export marketing policies and strategies. However, most governments require assistance in this task supplemented by exchanges of experience with particular marketing policies and strategies and the building-up of informational materials and training.

5. Commodity finance

979.   In the Final Act of UNCTAD VII, governments agreed on the need for adequate financial resources to implement diversification programmes, including processing, marketing and distribution activities, and called for an adequate expansion of official bilateral and multilateral resources, as well as private resources, including private investment, to finance appropriate diversification projects and programmes, possibly through special facilities for this purpose. The Working Party recognized that national diversification efforts of developing countries can only yield results over a period of time and require significant investment resources, including medium and long-term finance provided from multilateral and private sources. It also recognized that a chronic shortage of domestic financial resources coupled with a decline of foreign private capital flows and the latter's concentration on a few countries and sectors, as well as the relatively small proportion of official development finance directed to commodity-related export diversification activities, placed many - especially commodity-dependent low-income - developing countries at a disadvantage in their efforts to diversify commodity production and exports.

980.   Finance is needed not only for investment in productive and infrastructure facilities, but for all costs from the initial step of identifying a project right through to the production stage. Thus pre-investment financial assistance is needed to formulate diversification programmes and projects, notably for those that may aim to attract foreign investors. The World Bank and the regional development banks have been the main sources of international finance for commodity-related projects in developing countries. The World Bank's financial assistance has been directed mainly to food commodities and traditional export crops while there has been virtually no project lending in the area of minerals. The Working Party agreed that existing multilateral financial institutions should be encouraged to give appropriate emphasis to diversification in their overall financial programmes and to co-ordinate their efforts.

981.   In terms of assistance to mobilize private investment, the IFC and regional development banks have been the main sources of finance from international institutions to the private sector in developing countries. In 1989 the Inter-American Investment Corporation was established by the IADB and the Asian Finance and Investment Corporation by the Asian Development Bank. Both these corporations operate on the same lines as private investment banks. The African De-

velopment Bank has recently set aside $US 200 million for the development of its private sector lending arm. In addition, these regional banks have increased lending to the private sector through national development finance institutions.

982.   It has been recognized by the international community that international financial assistance is crucial to help developing countries cushion the impact of shortfalls in their commodity export earnings on their social and economic development. As indicated in Chapter I, shortfalls in commodity exports earnings can no longer be considered as a temporary and self-reversing balance-of-payments problem at the individual country level.   The problem which highly commodity-dependent countries must face is how to cope with contracting export earnings. Traditional compensatory finance cannot address or solve this problem and this has been reflected in the pattern of drawings from the IMF.   Between 1980 and 1989 total drawings by developing countries from the IMF compensatory financing facilities amounted to 10.5 billion SDRs.   The main beneficiaries have been the principal large commodity exporters, with Argentina and Brazil accounting for 27 per cent of total drawings.   The least developed countries in the same period received 7.5 per cent.   Since 1983, the number of drawings has shrunk dramatically, from over 20 to less than 10 a year.   For example, in 1990 there were only two drawings (Papua New Guinea and Côte d'Ivoire).   As a result repayments have exceeded new drawings in several years.   In response to disturbances in the oil market in 1990/91, an oil import facility was temporarily added to the compensatory element, operating in a similar way to the cereals import facility.   In the first half of 1991, nine middle income countries used the compensatory element of the IMF-CCFF mainly for export earnings shortfalls and oil import excesses.   Five countries from Eastern and Central Europe accounted for half of the total 2 billion SDR drawings.

983.   The STABEX scheme of the ACP-EEC Lomé Convention is not a compensatory financing facility in the IMF sense.   It provides funds for use in individual agricultural sectors suffering export earnings losses.   Where appropriate, funds provided can be used for diversification to other agricultural activities or for the processing of agricultural products.   Its resources were 925 million ECUs (815 million SDRs) for the five year period 1986-1990 and were increased under Lomé IV to 1.5 billion ECU (1.4 billion SDRs) for the period 1991-1995.   Total transfers in STABEX for the period 1980-1989 amounted to 1.8 billion SDRs, and STABEX ran out of money in three consecutive years in the mid-1980s.   For shortfalls experienced in 1989, 19 countries received 31 transfers involving a total amount of 181 million SDR's.   Under Lomé IV, all STABEX transfers will be in the form of grants.   Total eligible shortfalls for 1990 amounted to approximately 1.2 billion ECU (1.1 billion SDR's) of which 86 per cent were accounted for by cocoa and coffee.   The monies available amounted 386 million ECU, or 32 per cent of shortfalls.   After efforts to find extra funds (100 million ECU from SYSMIN left over from Lomé II and III), the gap remains in the order of 60 per cent of shortfalls.

984.   The EEC scheme STABEX-LDC-ACA (for least developed countries not signatories to the Lomé Convention) was established in 1987.   Under this system transfers must be used in the sector in which the loss of export earnings occurred, where circumstances which caused the loss might be alleviated or, if that is not the case, in other appropriate sectors for the purposes of diversification.   Between 1987 and 1991 four countries received 19 transfers for a total amount of 33 million ECUs.   All the transfers to date have been used in the sector suffering the shortfall.

985.   The SYSMIN scheme of the Lomé Conventions provides financial assistance in the form of low interest loans to countries experiencing difficulties in their mining sectors.   The main aims of SYSMIN are to safeguard the mining production and export sectors by actions to alleviate adverse effects on their economies caused by decline in their production or exports.   In addition, for States heavily dependent on exports of one mining product, it is designed to help diversify and broaden the bases of their economic growth, notably by helping them complete development projects and programmes under way where these are seriously jeopardized owing to substantial falls in export earnings from that product.   Under the Third Lomé Convention the amount of funds earmarked for SYSMIN totalled 342.8 million SDRs of which 119.6 million were committed to 7 countries for research and development, rehabilitation of equipment and infrastructural development.   Under Lomé IV 480 million ECUs (450 million SDRs) have been allocated to SYSMIN for the 1991-1995 period.

986.   Switzerland established its own compensatory programme in 1988 to compensate for shortfalls in selected commodities exported by least developed countries to Switzerland, with an initial allocation of 40 million Swiss francs (19.8 million SDRs). In September 1990, this amount was increased to 90 million Swiss Francs (49 million SDRs) for a 4 year period starting in 1991.

Since November 1990, agreements were reached between Switzerland and four least developed countries, three in Africa for an amount totalling 23 million Swiss francs.

987.   It is clear that funding for developing countries experiencing commodity export earnings shortfalls has been inadequate. The Intergovernmental Group of Experts on Compensatory Financing concluded that there was generally a significant difference between estimates of the size of total commodity export earnings shortfalls experienced by developing countries and the finance made available under existing compensatory financing facilities. In addition it agreed that compensatory financing could be commodity-related, and that it could also contribute to rehabilitation and diversification in the area of commodities.[333]

6.   Sustainability of development

988.   Degradation of the environment in developing countries is frequently the result of under-development and especially poverty, whereas in developed countries it is the result of their past development as reflected in their production and consumption patterns. Moreover, environmental problems frequently transcend national boundaries and therefore international co-operation is particularly necessary for finding solutions to them.

989.   Perceptions of the environment question changed significantly during the 1980s, broadening from its original concern about industrial pollution to the management and use of all natural resources. This is reflected in the context of UNCTAD in the Trade and Development Board decision 384 (XXXVII), and in the decision of the Committee on Commodities at its fourteenth session in 1990 calling for an examination of "the environmental effects of the intensity of resource utilization and the competitiveness and demand for environmentally-friendly products".

990.   International co-operation in dealing with environmental problems has already resulted in several international agreements on issues which have a direct bearing on natural resource use and trade. Among these are the Convention on International Trade in Endangered Species (CITES), the Montreal Protocol on Substances that Deplete the Ozone Layer and the Basel Convention on Transboundary Movements of Hazardous Wastes.

991.   In terms of specific commodities, recognition of the link between the environment issue and commodity production and use led to the incorporation of provisions on the environment in the International Tropical Timber Agreement, 1983 and the International Jute Agreement, 1989. Other commodity organizations, in particular some of the FAO Intergovernmental Groups, are also addressing the environment issues. The International Council on Metals and the Environment, a non-governmental mining industry organization, has as one of its objectives the working out of a set of environmental guidelines to which mining companies should adhere.

992.   The crux of the environment question is the scale on which natural resources are being consumed and the enormous quantities of waste products that are being produced. These have led to the following problems:

- degradation and toxification of the soil and water systems that sustain life;

- pollution of the air and damage to the earth's protective ozone shield affecting the global climate; and

- loss of unique plant and animal species.

993.   An important factor behind environmental degradation is that costs and prices of commodities often do not fully reflect their social cost (including that of environmental degradation). In certain cases, natural resources such as water and air are treated as virtually costless. As a result, incorrect price signals are given to producers and consumers. This leads to significant cost

---

[333] See TD/B/1216-TD/B/AC.43/11 Report of the Intergovernmental Group of Experts on the Compensatory Financing of Export Earnings Shortfalls, Conclusions and recommendations, Annex II, para. 2 and Annex III para. 6.

distortions, over-exploitation and mismanagement of resources.

994.   Such distortions and, therefore, sustainability of development is crucially affected, in all its facets, by governmental policies. Government decisions affect the rate and extent of utilization of all non-renewable and renewable resources, whether it be through the issuance of mining permits, fishing and logging concessions, or the provision of subsidies to stimulate agricultural production. In addition, trade policies affect the utilization of such resources not only domestically but also internationally, and especially through the effects of such policies on other countries' domestic and trade policies. In this context countries have used regulations relating to the environment to prevent imports, and threats of trade sanctions have been made.

F. International policy action

1. Producer-consumer co-operation

995.   Producer-consumer co-operation can cover several areas which are directly or indirectly relevant to achieving stable and more predictable conditions in commodity trade. It can take place in the context of regular or *ad hoc* meetings on individual commodities.

(a) Operational areas for producer-consumer co-operation

996.   An improved producer-consumer dialogue must take account of the structural changes affecting world commodity markets and the increasing competition in these markets between new and established producers and between new and traditional products, as well as past short-comings in producer-consumer co-operation to regulate international commodity markets. Efforts to achieve and maintain a better balance between supply and demand must continue to be the major component of producer-consumer co-operation. The actions to be taken must tackle the problems at their roots. They will need to include research and development to reduce costs of production and to identify new end-uses, market promotion to increase demand and improvements in the processing, storage, transportation and handling, quality control, grading, packaging and marketing of the commodities. An exhaustive listing of the areas for producer-consumer co-operation is not possible and clearly varies from commodity to commodity. In addition to environmental issues, on which suggestions are made later in this chapter, the following deserve particular attention:

> (i)   Supply management and rationalization
> (ii) Improvement in market transparency
> (iii) Research and development
> (iv) Promotion of local processing
> (v)   Market promotion
> (vi) Improvement in, and rational use of, marketing systems and practices.

(i) Supply management and rationalization

997.   When situations arise where the existence of a large stock overhang depresses prices for a particular commodity and threatens to trigger excessive market and price instability in the long-term, a joint effort by producers and consumers is called for in order to restore normalcy to the market concerned. This is particularly required when a major change occurs in the policy of consuming countries with regard to their government-held non-commercial stockpiles that involves

plans for a massive disposal of stocks of a particular commodity. It is also required in the situation of the liquidation of a "buffer" stock established under an international commodity agreement. Producer-consumer consultations which lead to harmonized actions for reducing stock overhangs is in the common interest of both parties.

998.   Supply management policies that are co-ordinated at the international level, either within the framework of a formal ICA when it is feasible and desirable, or through informal consultations and arrangements, would be useful in preventing the build-up of unreasonable stock levels. In the light of past experience, such policies should focus on actions at the investment and at the production and export stages. In this connection, a thorough examination is required of the medium to long-term impact of international buffer stocks, particularly in cases where they are the only or primary instrument for supply regulation.

999.   Such consultations and concerted actions can only be fruitful and effective if they involve the active participation of all the economic actors concerned, including industries in both producing and consuming countries, and the actual as well as potential producers and consumers. They also require the collaboration of international or regional financing institutions involved in investments in the commodity sector in question.

(ii)   Improvements in market transparency

1000.   Improving market transparency is an essential requirement for ensuring the maintaining an appropriate balance between supply and demand for particular commodities and for ensuring that the market performs efficiently and effectively.

1001.   Improved transparency requires the establishment of efficient systems for the regular collection and dissemination of comprehensive, reliable and up-to-date information, relating to the current situation and short-term prospects for production, consumption, trade and stocks as well as to new investments and the closing down of productive capacities, and to developments in market and industry structures. It is such information which enables participants in the market to plan the rational allocation of their resources, thus preventing the occurrence of major imbalances and the less than optimal allocation of scarce investment resources. In this context, full advantage should be taken of new technologies in data processing and communications. Financial and technical assistance to developing countries should be expanded in this regard, including for the development and use of the UNCTAD micro-computer based commodity information and analysis system (MICAS) referred to above.

(iii)   Research and development

1002.   Producer-consumer co-operation is vital in the area of research and development given the costs involved. It would allow producing countries to take advantage of the wealth of research results and experience available in consuming countries, and to make use of the facilities of the various research institutes or centers located in these countries. It would facilitate co-ordination among the existing research institutions. It would enable producing countries to appropriately orient their research undertakings so as to better adapt the quality and specification of their products to the evolving tastes and technical requirements of consumers, and to find new end-uses with good market prospects for their commodities. Finally, it would facilitate the design of international research and development programmes and projects that can command the support of both producers and consumers with a view to securing the necessary financing for them, whether from bilateral or multilateral sources.

(iv)   Promotion of local processing

1003.   Processing of commodities before export often requires blending with qualities that are not produced locally or the use of complementary materials which need to be imported. The unfavourable conditions under which developing countries often have to purchase the technology and other materials required, as well as the obstacles to market access in consuming countries, particularly the escalation of tariff and other barriers with the degree of processing, sometimes nullify the advantages of local availability of the commodity concerned and of low labour costs. Joint-ventures in exporting or importing countries may offer good prospects for overcoming these obstacles, particularly as a way of opening up new markets.

(v) Market promotion

1004.   Actions designed to open up new markets and expand consumption of commodities, including in semi-processed and processed forms, whether for traditional or new uses, are always a more desirable means to achieve a better market equilibrium than production cutbacks or withholding stocks. Strengthened co-operation between producing countries, which are interested in expanding their export outlets, and consuming countries, where most of the promotion outlays are incurred, can significantly enhance the effectiveness of market promotion campaigns, and would facilitate the design of joint projects in this area that could attract financing from bilateral and multilateral sources.

(vi) Improvement in, and rational use of, marketing systems and practices

1005.   An improved producer-consumer dialogue aimed at reviewing marketing systems being used for a commodity, including risk management instruments, would assist in the better functioning of commodity markets. Such a review should also cover problems in regulatory systems affecting physical and futures trading and changes in marketing structures in terms of major actors involved. Co-operation should encompass training activities in the marketing areas, especially for developing country exporters and importers, and exchanges of experience on the use of various practices, such as options, swaps and countertrade.

(b) Institutional frameworks for producer-consumer co-operation

1006.   The 26 commodities for which the producer-consumer bodies exist as described in chapter V represent around two fifths of world commodity exports. Producer-consumer consultations should be intensified, and the necessary assistance provided, for the setting-up of similar bodies for other commodities, particularly those of export interest to developing countries. The following have been designated as "international commodity bodies" (ICBs) by the Common Fund for Commodities, and are therefore qualified to sponsor projects for possible financing under the Second Account of the Common Fund: the International Cocoa Organization; the International Cotton Advisory Committee; the International Jute Organization; the International Lead and Zinc Study Group; the International Olive Oil Council; the International Natural Rubber Organization; the International Rubber Study Group; the International Sugar Organization; the International Tropical Timber Organization; the International Coffee Organization; the International Wheat Council; the UNCTAD Committee on Tungsten; the FAO Intergovernmental Group on Bananas, Citrus Fruit, Hard fibres, Meat, Oils and Oilseeds and Fats, Rice, Tea; and its Intergovernmental Sub-Committee on Fish Trade and the Intergovernmental Sub-Group on Hides and Skins.

2. Producer co-operation

1007.   Producer co-operation has a fundamental role to play, whether as a catalyst for launching co-operation with consumers, or as complementary to and an effective tool for strengthening producer-consumer co-operation when the latter exists, or finally as a substitute to the latter when it does not exist.

1008.   Producer co-operation can be instrumental in achieving a better balance between supply and demand in the short to long term by simultaneously acting on both parameters. On the supply side, action aimed at immediate improvements includes essentially supply management and rationalization measures, through such schemes as indicative voluntary production and export quotas. These measures are particularly called for in situations where there are excessive stocks overhanging the market which depress prices to unremunerative levels. Supply management would allow an orderly return to normal stock levels. In the case of mining, it would also permit the safeguarding of productive capacity needed to ensure continuity and security of supplies to consumers. Not to control supply in such circumstances is likely to lead to massive mine closures and capacity reductions which, once the stock overhangs are eliminated, would result in severe shortages and in an acceleration of price and market instability. On the demand side, intensified co-operation among producers is called for in order to undertake generic advertising and market promotion campaigns aimed at providing immediate relief by expanding the markets for their export commodities.

1009. For the long term, producers should co-operate in order to improve the structural characteristics and promote the development of their commodity markets. Such co-operation would need to cover:

(i) Research and development activities aimed at lowering the costs of production and improving the quality of their commodity in order to enhance its competitiveness vis-à-vis synthetics and substitutes; finding new end-uses for their commodity; and promoting local processing before exports. Such R & D efforts should include the breeding of new varieties with higher yields and quality and with improved disease and pest resistance; biotechnological engineering; agronomic management; improved processing techniques including through the use of small-scale equipment, and dissemination of R & D results.

(ii) Enhanced market transparency through the building of efficient systems of gathering and transmission of comprehensive, reliable and up-to-date information that would allow producers to evaluate market opportunities objectively and efficiently.

(iii) Improvement of marketing techniques including greater use of commodity exchanges and futures trading.

(iv) Joint procurement of imported inputs used for the production, local processing or marketing of commodities (fertilizers, pesticides, equipment, packing and packaging and complementary materials, etc.).

(v) Harmonization of production policies and marketing strategies. In order to avoid large market imbalances and a waste of scarce financial resources, regular and systematic exchange of information and consultations among all producers are required with a view to harmonizing their investment, production and marketing plans.

1010. On all the developmental activities referred to above, the Second Account of the Common Fund for Commodities, which is soon to begin its financing operations, is expected to play an important role in the mobilization of financial support for their implementation. This calls for an intensification of joint efforts among producers for the elaboration of a collective long-term strategy for their commodity and for the identification, within the framework of this strategy, of programmes and projects on developmental measures which could be sponsored by the competent international commodity bodies (ICBs) designated by the Common Fund.

1011. Producers associations are the usual institutional framework for co-operation among commodity producers. Practically all producers associations were established during the 1960s and the first half of the 1970s. Only one new association, for tin (1983), has been established after 1975. Their membership, while primarily composed of developing countries, is generally open to the participation of all concerned producers. For example, Australia is a member of the International Bauxite Association (IBA) and the Association of Tin Producing Countries (ATPC). Some of the existing associations are international in character (namely: cocoa, pepper, natural rubber, tea, bauxite, copper, tin and tungsten) while the others are regional (namely, bananas, coconuts, coffee, groundnuts oilseeds, sugar and tropical timber).

1012. The 14 commodities, to which the existing producers associations referred to above relate, represent around 17 per cent of world commodity exports. The actual membership of these associations accounts globally, however, for less than half of world exports of the commodities concerned.

1013. The issues dealt with by producer bodies widened considerably during the 1980s. In addition to exchanges of statistical and other information there was increasing consideration given to research and development related to production problems and the development of new end uses, to the position of producers in industry and market structures and to ways of increasing the participation of producers in international marketing systems and practices. For example, UPEB and GEPLACEA sponsored research programmes and projects on disease control, use of by-products and new commodity uses; GEPLACEA also involved international agencies such as UNIDO in its work. The IBA started a dialogue with TNCs and helped increase exchanges of experience among its members on relations with TNCs. GEPLACEA arranged several workshops on sugar marketing, including with the CSCE futures market in New York, and issued an international marketing handbook. CIPEC had meetings to discuss the implications of changes in copper futures contracts for its members and interacted with the LME. The Association of Natural Rubber Producing Countries developed a planting/replanting model for use in planning production decisions. The Cocoa Producers Alliance in Africa embarked upon a detailed discussion of its members' production policies. The Association of Tin Producing Countries set production and export targets for its members and observers. The Asian and Pacific Coconut Community was active in market research and promotion and the International Pepper Community developed its market survey and statistical work.

1014. Producer co-operation has an important role to play in the present circumstances of persistently depressed commodity markets and the collapse of practically all ICAs with economic provisions. As stated above, effective co-operation among producers is often a prerequisite for producer-consumer co-operation. Intensified international support is therefore required for the strengthening of existing producers associations and for the establihment of new ones for other commodities, particularly those of export interest to developing countries. More specifically, in this regard, a special facility should be established for the provision of the technical assistance and other backstopping needed for the identification and elaboration of multi-country or national projects on developmental measures and for their screening by competent ICBs for submission to the Common Fund.

3. International institutions

1015. Bilateral, multilateral and international agencies are providing a wide variety of technical and financial assistance in the commodity area. However, the lack of an agreed international commodity policy means that this assistance often reflects, at the bilateral and multilateral levels, the mandates and perceptions of donors and, at the international level, the mandates, interests and perceptions of the various secretariats. The usefulness of such assistance could be greatly enhanced by a more coherent, co-ordinated approach guided by a clearer statement of international policy objectives.

(a) Improving the supply/demand situation

1016. International agencies need to support measures to improve the supply/demand situation. The agencies concerned will need to take fully into account the outcome of intergovernmental discussions and analyses on the market prospects for individual commodities and related decisions in their consideration of financial assistance to countries for specific commodities. This is especially necessary when evaluating support for investment in rehabilitation, expansion or new production. This does not mean that support to make production more efficient and cost competitive should be withheld. Rather detailed and realistic evaluation is needed of the implications of adding further supplies, whether they be from small or large producers. Such an evaluation will clearly require close inter-agency co-operation and interaction between financial agencies and producer and producer/consumer fora.

1017. International agencies need also to increase their support in the form of technical and financial assistance programmes and projects for improving and diversifying commodity sectors in developing countries by making them more competitive, less vulnerable to natural disasters and more in harmony with environmental requirements of sustainable development. The potential of the Common Fund for Commodities should be fully developed and as agreed by the Working Party on Diversification, Processing, Marketing and Distribution "further voluntary contributions to the Second Account of the Common Fund for Commodities could assist in diversification efforts".[334]

1018.　International agencies have been over the years strong advocates of improvements in market access conditions for primary and processed commodity exports of developing countries and have made efforts to stimulate such improvements through research illustrating benefits, publishing detailed information on barriers and their effects, monitoring changes in protectionism and suggesting avenues for barrier reduction. These efforts have covered the whole range of tariff and non-tariff barriers, including restrictive business practices and export restrictions in investment contracts. These efforts should continue. Serious consideration needs to be given to the anomaly that when developing countries succeed in exporting new products in the commodity area (new primary commodities or more processed forms of traditional exports), new barriers arise. Adequate recourse procedures must be developed.

1019.　Another area where international institutions should continue to help with the balancing of supply and demand is in facilitating, through technical assistance, the realization of demand potential for specific commodities. This assistance takes the form of market surveys, buyers and sellers meetings, provision and distribution of information on products available including new end uses, and on market specifications, producers/consumers workshops in emerging markets and generic promotion campaigns. The International Trade Center UNCTAD/GATT is the main centre for provision of this type of assistance and its work in these areas should be strengthened. UNCTAD has conducted two workshops focussing on expanding coffee and cocoa trade directly between producing countries and countries in Central and Eastern Europe.

1020.　In the area of optimizing the contribution of the commodity sector to development, international organizations are uniquely placed to collect and disseminate worldwide in a cost-efficient and neutral manner, information on a number of aspects relevant to decisions on investment, production, marketing and consumption. Increased co-operation among the agencies is needed in the development and co-ordination of information systems which are readily accessible and easy to use. There is also a need for further development of analytical tools for the efficient utilization of information, particularly in regard to individual commodity industry and market structures (actors, ownership, investments and plans). To help fill this gap, UNCTAD will be undertaking a series of commodity studies during the next few years. In parallel, it is continuing to develop its micro-computer based commodity information and analysis system (MICAS).

(b)　Assistance in formulation and implementation of commodity policy

1021.　One of the main areas where there is a need for increased assistance is in the formulation and implementation of commodity policy in developing countries, especially low-income commodity-dependent ones. This assistance should take the form of exchanges of experience among policy makers, workshops and the provision of training materials. The formulation of a commodity sector policy within the general macro-economic framework of a country is an area where governments can learn from each other's experiences. The institutional and regulatory structures used in countries which have succeeded in developing and diversifying their commodity sectors can serve as examples, and exchanges of experience on problems and obstacles encountered can be of benefit to both parties. International agencies should help this process by providing the fora for such exchanges and by providing analyses and informational material and ensuring contacts between governments. Training workshops and exchanges of experience in areas such as traditional products, diversification within the commodity sector including for domestic consumption and diversification outside of commodities would be useful. These should also include regional or subregional workshops so that co-ordination of efforts and joint-ventures between countries are fostered.

---

[334] Agreed Conclusions adopted by the Working Party on Diversification, Processing, Marketing and Distribution, including Transportation, at its third session and endorsed by the Committee on Commodities at its fourteenth session (TD/B/C.1/314, Annex, para. 16(c)).

1022. As most commodity development programmes and projects have an export component or are export-oriented, training in respect of commodity export policies is essential. This is of increased importance now when national marketing systems are being liberalized. In order to participate effectively in the international market and to take part effectively in international commodity discussions and negotiations, governments need to understand the various marketing systems and practices employed, their advantages and disadvantages. More attention needs to be devoted to this area by international agencies in their training and assistance to government officials for devising their export policies.

(c) Financial assistance

1023. The discussion and analysis in the preceding chapter has made it clear that, although most developing countries will continue for many years to be heavily dependent on their export sectors for vital export revenues and development linkages, the environment within which they will be struggling to develop these sectors will not be hospitable. For this reason, it is crucial that they be able to develop viable projects in the commodities area, projects which will attract investment from within and without the countries concerned. To do so, they will need help. The will need assistance on resource assessments; on pre-investment activities such as prefeasibility and feasibility studies; on definition of government actions in terms of infrastructure or support services; and on measures to find investors, both local and foreign, and to promote projects.

1024. Since low-income commodity dependent countries are likely to continue to be at a disadvantage in terms of access to private finance, international agencies will have to continue to be the main source of investment and other financial flows. Concerted action by international agencies in the provision of adequate finance would seem to be the best way of stimulating a more focused effort by governments on development, including diversification, of the commodity sector. The earmarking of finance to stimulate diversification in highly commodity dependent countries suggested with increased frequency in the last few years[335] should be given high priority by these institutions. In particular, the creation of a diversification fund or funds would provide an essential focal point for diversification efforts and would galvanize the provision of the technical assistance that is required.[336] Such a fund or funds would obviously have to give priority in their assistance to countries which are highly commodity-dependent (for example, where 1 or 2 commodities account for at least 40 per cent of its total export earnings). There would also need to be a regular review of the implementation of the diversification programmes of recipients and, where appropriate, further assistance from aid co-ordinating mechanisms such as World Bank Consultative Groups, OECD, DAC country aid meetings and UNDP round tables could be sought. The funds themselves could be set up under existing financial institutions, such as the World Bank or regional development banks, or by groups of donors, in much the same way as special facilities have been created for meeting other designated purposes.

1025. The existing finance facilities for export earnings shortfalls will need to continue to play an important role. As recently stated: "Since the prospects for success for most of the least developed countries that depend on commodity exports are very poor, schemes to stabilise their incomes continue to offer a useful means of softening the impact of adjustment for those among them with limited potential to diversify their production. But these schemes have to be properly integrated with structural adjustment programmes, both to reduce substantially the risk of awarding a premium to uncompetitive structures and to ease the transition to other production lines with better export potential or with unsatisfied demand on local or regional markets such as food, ag-

---

335 See, for example, document A/45/591, Africa's common position on the report to the Secretary-General of his Expert Group on Africa's Commodity Problems and A/46/41, Report of the Secretary-General, *Final Review and Appraisal of the Implementation of the United Nations Programme of Action for African Recovery and Development*, 1986-1990, Annex, paras. 79-82.

336 Ideally, grants should be provided for resource and market assessments and for prefeasibility and feasibility studies, particularly for small- and medium-scale projects. For the development of information networks and of support services (extension, quality control, design and packaging) as well as for specific training in production, management and marketing, requests for such assistance should be handled by the appropriate multilateral and bilateral sources. In addition, diversification funds should provide concessional and non-concessional loans to venture capital companies, national development finance institutions and private enterprise for investment in diversification projects.

ricultural inputs or building materials."[337]

1026.   In complement to various financing schemes in the commodity area, international agencies can provide a direct stimulus to private investment flows for commodity sector development and diversification through their policy reviews and lending programmes, which send signals to the foreign private sector and significantly influence the latter's willingness to consider investing. Prefeasibility and feasibility studies financed by international agencies which have identified viable projects need to be followed systematically by concerted efforts to find finance for such projects, including in particular the provision of investment finance to the local private sectors in developing countries directly or through national development financing institutions.

1027.   Financial support for the development of the local enabling environment (specific infrastructure and support services) is also an important determinant for private investment. This can be done in several ways including through the creation of private entities to provide risk capital for small farmers for developing or expanding agro-processing facilities and to provide technology and marketing expertise for improving quality and competitiveness.[338]

1028.   It is important that institutions, both international and bilateral, work in a co-ordinated manner in this area, not to send conflicting signals. This can probably best be done through consultations and co-operative initiatives within an agreed international commodity policy framework.

(d) Assistance in ensuring the sustainability of economic development

1029.   As underdevelopment and poverty are the principal causes of environmental degradation in developing countries, development assistance and measures to eradicate poverty can make an important contribution to ensuring the sustainability of development. The need for providing resources, additional to those for development assistance, to resolve environmental problems in developing countries has been recognized on many occasions by the international community.

1030.   Developed countries carry the burdern of creating most of the major environmental problems and hence must use their financial and technical resources to solve them. However, measures must be implemented by all countries for the protection of the environment and the effective management of natural resources. These measures will involve additional expenditures in, and the foregoing of revenues from, commodity production, processing and trade by both enterprises and governments. These costs incurred at the various stages in the production, processing and marketing chain will need to be properly reflected in the prices of all final products be they natural or synthetic. Principles and guidelines should be established by the international community to do this. Many States presently tax specific commodities for revenue purposes. Such taxes discourage consumption of the products in question and hence indirectly affect resource utilization, irrespective of whether such action is optimal, or even desirable, in terms of sustainable development.

1031.   It is clearly a difficult task to identify, assess and correctly reflect all the environmental and natural resource costs in the prices of products and there is a very real danger of unwarranted discrimination occurring as between products and among suppliers unless the international community establishes precise principles and guidelines for this purpose. Assistance must be given to developing countries to ensure that they fully participate in the evolution of these principles and guidelines and in their subsequent implementation.

1032.   In the negotiation and renegotiation of commodity agreements specific attention must be paid to the impact of the commodity in question on the environment and its contribution to sustainable development. States must ensure that market conditions for individual commodities allow a proper reflection of their impact and contribution in their prices.

---

[337] Bernhard Fischer, "From Commodity Dependence to Development", *The OECD Observer*, April/May 1991.

[338] One example in this area is Bolivian Export Foundation, co-financed by the World Bank and the Government of the Netherlands, which will operate as a private entity to boost production and export of non-traditional agricultural commodities.

1033.   International commodity policy must address the issue of promoting the sustainable production and usage of natural products as well as the commercial exploitation and usage of waste, particularly when these are found to be environmentally advantageous. In this context international cooperation is called for to identify such products and their environmental advantages, and to propose policies and measures for promoting their utilization and trade.

Annex V-I

COMMODITY DEPENDENCE:
SHARE OF PRIMARY PRODUCTS IN DEVELOPING COUNTRIES' TOTAL EXPORTS

COUNTRIES	AVERAGE 1987-1989			AVERAGE 1979-1981			MAIN COMMODITIES as % OF TOTAL EXPORTS	
	ALL COMM.	FUEL	NON-FUEL	ALL COMM.	FUEL	NON-FUEL	1987-1989	1979-1981
AFRICA								
ALGERIA	96.9	95.8	1.1	99.9	98.7	1.5	fuel 96%	fuel 99%, alcoholic beverages 1%
ANGOLA	99.8	95.6	4.2	99.0	78.7	20.8	fuel 96%, diamonds 3%, coffee 1%	fuel 79%, coffee 9%, diamonds 9%
BENIN	99.0	9.8	89.2	84.6	2.2	82.4	cotton 63%, oilseeds 13%, fuel 10%	cocoa 26%, palm kernels 24%, cotton 19%
BOTSWANA	99.0	0.0	99.0	87.6	0.0	87.6	diamonds 79%, copper/nickel 11%, meat 4%	diamonds 51%, copper/nickel 21%, meat 14%
BURKINA FASO	95.5	0.0	95.5	86.4	0.3	86.1	cotton 45%, gold 35%, live animals 4%	cotton 39%, live animals 30%, oilseeds 22%
BURUNDI	93.5	0.0	93.5	99.4	0.5	98.9	coffee 79%, tea 5%, cotton 2%	coffee 91%, silver ore 3%, tea 3%
CAMEROON REP.	92.0	14.2	77.8	96.1	33.7	62.4	coffee 20%, cocoa 19%, fuel 14%	fuel 34%, coffee 22%, cocoa 21%
CAPE VERDE	91.0	0.0	91.0	97.0	0.3	96.7	fishery 65%, bananas 22%	fishery 42%, bananas 20%, vegetables 13%
CENTR.AFR.REP.	96.0	0.0	96.0	99.0	0.0	99.0	diamonds 49%, coffee 18%, wood 13%	wood 39%, coffee 26%, diamonds 12%
CHAD	97.8	0.0	97.8	99.0	0.0	99.0	cotton 45%, live animals 21%, gum arabic 18%	live animals 62%, cotton 37 %
COMOROS	85.3	4.7	80.6	68.0	0.0	68.0	spices 81%, fuel 5%	spices 64%, copra 4%
CONGO	98.3	80.5	17.8	97.7	88.3	9.4	fuel 81%, wood 11%, diamonds 4%	fuel 88%, wood 7%
COTE D'IVOIRE	84.2	11.0	73.2	89.0	4.6	84.4	cocoa 26%, coffee 13%, wood 8%	coffee 31%, cocoa 25%, wood 16%
EGYPT	82.5	34.1	48.4	87.9	59.2	28.7	fuel 34%, cotton 32%, aluminium 8%	fuel 59%, cotton 22%, aluminium 3%
EQ. GUINEA	99.0	0.0	99.0	99.7	0.0	99.7	wood 57%, cocoa 38%, coffee 4%	cocoa 83%, wood 14%, coffee 3%
ETHIOPIA	91.3	3.8	87.5	99.0	6.6	92.4	coffee 60%, hides 15%, fuel 4%	coffee 64%, hides 14%
GABON	99.0	70.0	29.0	98.4	80.0	18.4	fuel 70%, wood 10%, manganese 9%	fuel 80%, wood 7%, manganese 6%
GAMBIA	99.0	0.0	99.0	99.0	0.0	99.0	groundnuts 71%, fishery 17%	groundnuts 80%, fishery 8%
GHANA	99.0	2.9	96.1	98.7	3.6	95.1	cocoa 46%, aluminium 22%, gold 12%	cocoa 60%, aluminium 19%, gold 10%
GUINEA	99.0	0.0	99.0	99.6	0.0	99.6	aluminium 82%, diamonds 10%, coffee 2%	aluminium 88%, live animals 2%, coffee 2%
GUINEA-BISSAU	99.0	0.0	99.0	94.5	0.0	94.5	nuts 52%, fish 14%, cotton 10%	oilseeds 50%, fishery 32%, cotton 7%
KENYA	85.9	13.3	72.6	84.5	27.5	57.0	coffee 24%, tea 23%, fuel 13%	fuel 28%, coffee 23%, tea 14%
LIBERIA	99.1	0.1	99.0	99.7	0.4	99.3	iron/steel 43%, rubber 21%, diamonds 17%	iron/steel 56%, rubber 17%, wood 14%
LIBYA ARAB JM	97.7	97.4	0.3	99.7	99.7	0.0	fuel 97%	fuel 100%
MADAGASCAR	88.6	2.2	86.4	96.9	6.1	90.8	coffee 26%, spices 26%, fishery 13%	coffee 46%, spices 22%, fishery 6%
MALAWI	94.3	0.1	94.2	90.4	0.1	90.3	tobacco 63%, tea 12%, sugar 10%	tobacco 46%, sugar 17%, tea 14%
MALI	94.0	0.0	94.0	97.1	0.1	97.0	cotton 44%, live animals 32%, gold 15%	live animals 55%, cotton 36%, groundnuts 3%
MAURITANIA	99.0	0.6	98.4	99.8	3.2	96.6	fishery 48%, iron ore 42%, live animals 8%	iron ore 71%, live animals 18%, fishery 8%
MAURITIUS	40.2	0.0	40.2	69.7	0.0	69.7	sugar 35%, fishery 1%	sugar 63%, tea 2%
MOROCCO	51.6	2.4	49.2	70.6	4.4	66.2	phosphates 12%, fishery 12%, fruits 7%	phosphates 31%, fruits 12%, fishery 6%
MOZAMBIQUE	99.0	3.1	95.9	91.8	4.4	87.4	fishery 40%, nuts 27%, sugar 5 %	iron/steel 26%, oilseeds 20%, fishery 12%
NIGER	99.0	1.2	97.8	99.0	0.7	98.3	uranium 75%, live animals 10%	uranium 83%, live animals 9%
NIGERIA	99.7	95.3	4.4	98.1	95.2	2.9	fuel 95%, cocoa 3%	fuel 95%, cocoa 2%
RWANDA	99.4	0.0	99.4	99.0	2.3	96.7	coffee 76%, tea 15%, hides 4%	coffee 69%, tea 12%, tungsten 6%
SAO TOME PRN	99.0	0.0	99.0	99.5	0.0	99.5	cocoa 93%, copra 5%	cocoa 93 %, copra 6%
SENEGAL	90.0	16.6	73.4	89.6	24.2	65.4	fishery 47%, fuel 17%, groundnuts 11%	fuel 24%, fishery 20%, groundnuts 15%
SEYCHELLES	90.7	53.5	37.2	96.2	73.1	23.1	fuel 54%, fishery 34%, copra 2%	fuel 73%, copra 14%, fishery 5%
SIERRA LEONE	91.8	0.3	91.5	98.6	0.4	98.6	diamonds 37%, bauxite 22%, rutile 16%	diamonds 47%, coffee 14%, cocoa 12%
SOMALIA	99.4	0.4	99.0	99.6	2.0	97.6	live animals 54%, bananas 24%, fishery 8%	live animals 82%, bananas 9%, hides 4%
SUDAN	96.0	0.2	95.8	99.0	2.5	96.5	cotton 33%, gum hashab 14%, sesame 10%	cotton 40%, cereals 11%
TOGO	89.6	1.3	88.5	98.6	15.0	83.6	phosphates 48%, cotton 17%, coffee 11%	phosphates 45%, fuel 15%, cocoa 13%
TUNISIA	34.0	19.8	14.2	65.5	52.0	13.5	fuel 20%, fishery 4%, fruits 2%	fuel 52%, phosphates 2%, fruits 2%
UGANDA	99.2	0.0	99.2	98.5	1.3	97.4	coffee 97%, tea 1%, cotton 1%	coffee 98%, cotton 1%
UNTD. REP. TANZ	90.0	0.7	89.3	85.2	2.6	82.6	coffee 32%, cotton 19%, nuts 6%	coffee 28%, cotton 11%, spices 10%
ZAIRE	99.0	13.0	86.0	96.1	14.5	81.6	copper 55%, diamonds 13%, fuel 13%	copper 50%, fuel 15%, cobalt 11%
ZAMBIA	95.2	0.1	95.1	99.5	0.7	98.8	copper 88%, cobalt 4%	copper 88%, cobalt 5%, zinc 2%
ZIMBABWE	81.4	1.4	80.0	66.5	1.3	65.2	gold 21%, tobacco 20%, iron/steel 14%	tobacco 15%, iron/steel 8%, cotton 7%

Annex V-I (continued)

COMMODITY DEPENDENCE:
SHARE OF PRIMARY PRODUCTS IN DEVELOPING COUNTRIES' TOTAL EXPORTS

COUNTRIES	AVERAGE 1987-1989			AVERAGE 1979-1981			MAIN COMMODITIES (% OF TOTAL EXPORTS)	
	ALL COMM.	FUEL	NON-FUEL	ALL COMM.	FUEL	NON-FUEL	1987-1989	1979-1981
WEST ASIA								
BAHRAIN	89.9	79.4	10.5	97.3	93.5	3.8	fuel 79%, aluminium 10%	fuel 94%, aluminium 3%
IRAN	96.7	92.2	4.5	97.0	93.6	3.4	fuel 92%, nuts 2%	fuel 94%
IRAQ	99.0	97.5	1.5	99.5	99.1	0.4	fuel 98%	fuel 99%
JORDAN	47.8	0.1	47.7	59.3	0.0	59.3	phosphates 26%, cotton 1%, fruits 1%s	phosphates 24%, fruits 8%, vegetables 6%
KUWAIT	83.7	82.4	1.3	89.4	88.5	0.9	fuel 90%	fuel 89%
OMAN	99.8	95.8	4.0	96.2	95.0	1.2	fuel 96%, fishery 1%, copper 1%	fuel 95%
QATAR	89.8	89.6	0.2	96.7	94.0	2.7	fuel 90%	fuel 94%, iron/steel 3%
SAUDI ARABIA	94.3	91.9	2.4	99.3	99.1	0.2	fuel 92%, wheat 1%	fuel 99%
SYRIAN ARAB REP.	54.7	38.8	15.9	92.3	76.4	15.9	fuel 39%, cotton 5%, sheeps & goats 4%	fuel 77%, cotton 9%, phosphates 2%
UNTD. ARAB EM	82.6	79.0	3.6	97.3	95.9	1.4	fuel 79%, aluminium 2%	fuel 96%
SOUTH & SE. ASIA								
AFGHANISTAN	91.0	42.3	48.7	80.6	31.7	48.9	fuel 42%, raisins 22%, hides 10%	fuel 32%, fruits 28%, hides 9%
BANGLADESH	57.0	1.3	55.7	83.1	0.0	83.1	jute 27%, fishery 12%, leather 11%	jute 70%, leather 10%, tea 6%
BRUNEI	82.3	81.8	0.5	98.7	98.6	0.1	fuel 82%	fuel 99%
INDIA	48.3	3.2	45.1	56.5	0.4	56.1	gemstones 19%, tea 4%, iron/steel 4%	gemstones 12%, tea 6%, leather 6%
INDONESIA	72.5	42.8	29.7	89.6	67.5	22.1	fuel 43%, wood 14% rubber 6%	fuel 68%, wood 7%, rubber 5%
KOREA REP.	6.7	1.2	5.5	17.6	0.5	17.1	fishery 3%	iron/steel 9% fishery 4%
LAO P.DEM.REP.	57.3	0.0	57.3	55.8	0.0	55.8	wood 45%, coffee 9%	wood 33%, coffee 19%, tin 6%
MALAYSIA	58.6	19.0	39.6	80.7	23.3	57.4	fuel 17%, wood 13%, rubber 8%	fuel 23%, rubber 17%, wood 16%
MALDIVES	67.4	0.0	67.4	73.7	0.4	73.3	fishery 67%	fishery 73%
MYANMAR	98.0	1.3	96.7	92.3	6.0	86.2	wood 47%, rice 18%, fishery 10%	rice 40%, wood 24%, vegetables 6%
NEPAL	47.5	0.0	47.5	70.1	0.0	70.1	vegetables 18%, roots 13%, wood 7%	jute 18%, cereals 14%, wood 11%
PAKISTAN	45.8	0.6	45.2	64.4	6.7	57.7	cotton 31%, cereals 7%, leather 6%	cotton 21%, cereals 18%, fuel 7%
PHILIPPINES	36.9	1.8	35.1	61.4	0.4	61.0	coconut oil 6%, fishery 5%, fruits 5%	copra 15%, copper 9%, sugar 9%
SINGAPORE	24.6	14.8	9.8	41.4	28.8	12.6	fuel 15%, wood 1%	fuel 29%, wood 3%
SRI LANKA	52.9	6.0	46.9	83.7	14.8	68.9	tea 26%, rubber 7%, fuel 6%	tea 35%, rubber 15%, fuel 15%
THAILAND	43.9	0.6	43.3	71.2	0.0	71.2	fishery 10%, cereals 10%, roots 5%	cereals 21%, vegetables 11%, rubber 10%
OCEANIA								
FIJI	86.5	7.7	78.8	86.3	15.7	70.6	sugar 41%, gold 17%, fuel 8%	sugar 54%, fuel 16%, fishery 6%
KIRIBATI	84.9	8.0	76.9	42.9	0.0	42.9	copra 52%, fishery 21%, fuel 8%	phosphates 23%, copra 17%
NAURU	68.5	0.0	68.5	73.4	0.0	73.4	phosphates 65%	phosphates 73%
NIUE	99.0	0.0	99.0	81.6	0.0	81.6	fruits 52%, vegetables 17%	fruits 58%, copra 13%, vegetables 6%
PAPUA NEW GUINEA	98.1	0.1	98.0	92.9	0.1	92.8	copper 34%, gold 31%, coffee 10%	copper 29%, coffee 17%, cocoa 7%
SAMOA	96.1	0.0	96.1	95.3	0.0	95.3	coconut oil 32%, taro 19%, fruits 13%	copra 52%, cocoa 22%, vegetables 10%
SOLOMON ISLS	93.6	0.0	93.6	95.0	0.0	95.0	fishery 43%, wood 25%, copra 9%	fishery 36%, wood 24%, copra 20%
TONGA	71.5	0.0	71.5	93.2	0.0	93.2	spices 15%, fishery 14%, coconut oil 11%	copra 64%, fruits 9%, vegetables 8%
VANUATU	74.9	0.0	74.9	80.9	0.0	80.9	copra 38%, meat 10%, wood 10%	copra 38%, fishery 32%, meat 4%

Annex V-I (continued)

COMMODITY DEPENDENCE:
SHARE OF PRIMARY PRODUCTS IN DEVELOPING COUNTRIES' TOTAL EXPORTS

COUNTRIES	AVERAGE 1987-1989			AVERAGE 1979-1981			MAIN COMMODITIES (% OF TOTAL EXPORTS)	
	ALL COMM.	FUEL	NON-FUEL	ALL COMM.	FUEL	NON-FUEL	1987-1989	1979-1981
LATIN-AMERICA								
ARGENTINA	63.9	1.0	62.9	77.3	3.8	73.5	oilseeds 14%, cereals 11%, meat 3%	cereals 24%, meat 13%, soyabeans 8%
BELIZE	69.2	0.0	69.2	60.1	1.0	59.1	sugar 31%, fruits 25%, fishery 4%	sugar 36%, fruits 9%, fishery 5%
BOLIVIA	93.0	34.9	58.1	99.0	24.1	74.9	fuel 35%, zinc 13%, tin 12%	tin 37%, fuel 24%, silver 9%
BRAZIL	47.3	3.6	43.7	59.8	3.0	56.8	iron ore 6%, coffee 6%, soyabeans 4%	iron & steel 12%, coffee 12%, animal feed 9%
CHILE	92.5	0.1	92.4	91.1	1.5	89.6	copper 47%, fishery 11%, fruits 9 %	copper 46%, fishery 7%, iron ore 4 %
COLOMBIA	81.4	30.3	51.1	78.9	2.8	76.1	coffee 30%, fuel 30%, fruits 5%	coffee 57%, fruits 3%, cotton 3%
COSTA RICA	74.9	2.6	72.3	69.7	0.1	69.6	coffee 25%, fruits 25%, meat 4%	coffee 27%, fruits 22%, meat 8%
ECUADOR	96.6	45.6	51.0	91.8	57.6	34.1	fuel 46%, fish 21%, bananas 14%	fuel 58%, cocoa 9%, bananas 8%,
EL SALVADOR	61.3	1.1	60.2	76.4	1.7	74.7	coffee 51%, fruits 3%, sugar 2%	coffee 58%, cotton 8%
GUATEMALA	78.0	1.4	76.6	72.6	0.0	72.6	coffee 35%, fruits 9%, sugar 7%	coffee 30%, cotton 12%, sugar 5%
GUYANA	94.3	0.0	94.3	99.9	0.1	99.8	aluminium 33%, sugar 33%, fishery 7%	aluminium 48%, sugar 31%, rice 10%
HONDURAS	82.8	0.2	82.6	90.2	0.1	90.1	fruits 43%, coffee 23%, fishery 5%	bananas 27%, coffee 25%, meat 7%
MEXICO	55.8	35.6	20.2	87.4	64.8	22.6	fuel 36%, coffee 2%, fishery 2%	fuel 65%, coffee 3%, fishery 3%
NICARAGUA	92.5	1.2	91.3	94.7	1.6	93.1	coffee 39%, cotton 16%, fruits 6%	coffee 32%, cotton 19%, meat 12%
PANAMA EX. ZN.	82.4	0.3	82.1	88.4	22.0	68.4	fishery 32%, fruits 30%, coffee 5%	fuel 22%, bananas 20%, sugar 15%
PARAGUAY	76.1	0.0	76.1	95.1	0.4	94.7	soyabeans 29%, cotton 27%, meat 6%	cotton 36%, soyabeans 19%, wood 18%
PERU	74.6	12.1	62.5	69.8	16.6	53.2	copper 22%, fishery 13%, fuel 12%	fuel 17%, copper 15%, fishery 8%
SURINAME	99.0	0.0	99.0	90.8	0.0	90.8	aluminium 84%, rice 10%, bananas 3%	aluminium 79%, rice 8%, fishery 3 %
URUGUAY	48.5	0.1	48.4	58.9	0.0	58.9	meat 11%, wool 9%, cereals 8%	meat 18%, wool 10%, cereals 9%
VENEZUELA	93.0	82.5	10.5	91.2	87.1	4.1	fuel 83%, aluminium 6%, iron/steel 3%	fuel 87%, iron/steel 2%
CARRIBEAN								
BARBADOS	43.2	16.8	26.4	28.7	0.1	28.6	fuel 17%, sugar 16%	sugar 19%
CUBA	96.9	10.0	86.9	96.7	2.8	93.9	sugar 71%, fuel 10, nickel 5%	sugar 81%, nickel 5%
DOMINICA	69.3	0.0	69.3	57.2	0.0	57.2	bananas 65%, copra 1%	bananas 44%, coconut oil 3%
DOMINICAN REP.	93.6	0.0	93.6	74.2	0.0	74.2	nickel 20%, sugar 17%, coffee 9%	sugar 33%, iron & steel 11%, nickel 11%
GRENADA	84.0	0.0	84.0	91.2	0.0	91.2	spices 50%, fruits 20%, cocoa 12%	cocoa 42%, spices 23%, fruits 22%
HAITI	25.1	0.0	25.1	51.7	0.0	51.7	coffee 17%, fruits 2%, cocoa 2%	coffee 31%, aluminium 11%, hard fibres 5%
JAMAICA	77.5	1.9	75.6	93.4	2.8	90.6	aluminium 52%, sugar 9%, fruits 3%	aluminium 73%, sugar 6%
ST. KITTS NEVIS	55.9	5.7	50.2	91.2	31.9	59.3	sugar 40%, fuel 6%, margarine 4%	sugar 55%, fuel 32%
ST.LUCIA	99.0	0.0	99.0	54.0	0.0	54.0	bananas 83%, coconut oil 4%	bananas 32%, coconut oil 7%
ST.VINCENT	99.9	0.9	99.0	84.9	0.5	84.4	bananas 49%, vegetables 32%, cereals 12%	bananas 43%, vegetables 15%, cereals 12%
TRINIDAD TOBAGO	70.4	64.2	6.2	94.2	91.9	2.3	fuel 64%, sugar 2%	fuel 92%, sugar 1%

Source: UNCTAD secretariat estimates

Annex V-II

WORLD PRODUCTION, CONSUMPTION, STOCKS AND PRICES
FOR SELECTED COMMODITIES

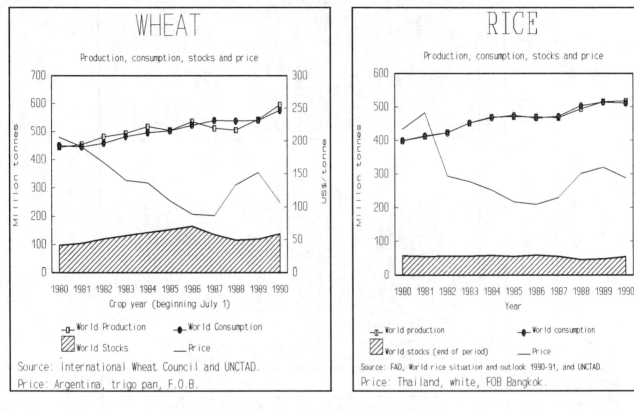

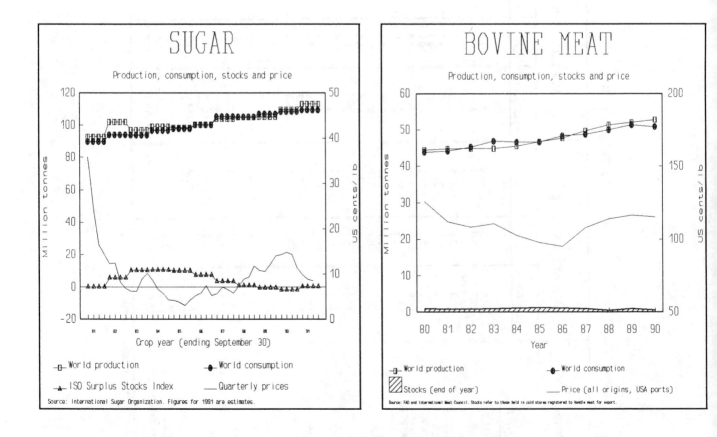

Annex V-II (continued)

WORLD PRODUCTION, CONSUMPTION, STOCKS AND PRICES
FOR SELECTED COMMODITIES

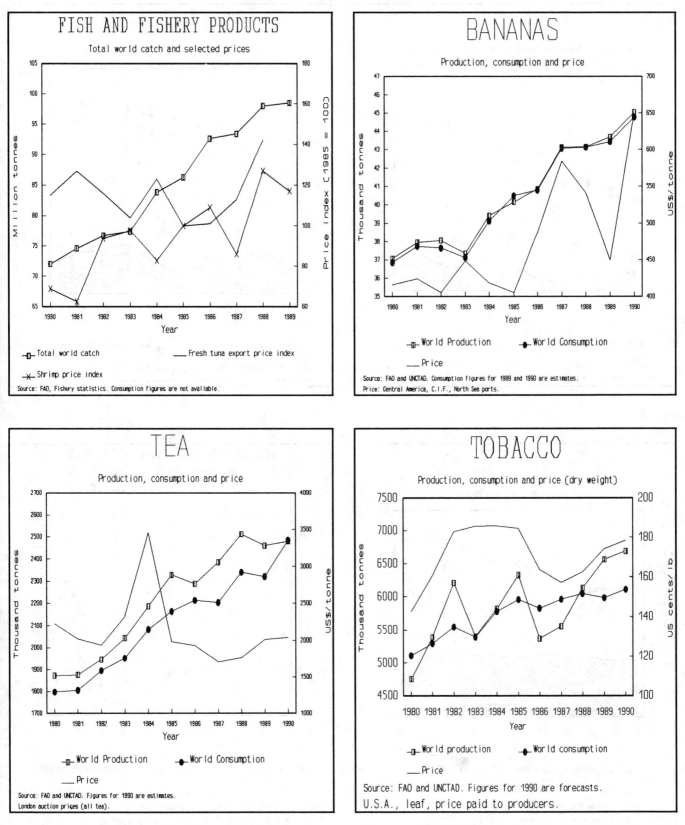

FISH AND FISHERY PRODUCTS
Total world catch and selected prices

—□— Total world catch   —— Fresh tuna export price index

—✕— Shrimp price index

Source: FAO, Fishery statistics. Consumption figures are not available.

BANANAS
Production, consumption and price

—□— World Production   —●— World Consumption

—— Price

Source: FAO and UNCTAD. Consumption figures for 1989 and 1990 are estimates.
Price: Central America, C.I.F., North Sea ports.

TEA
Production, consumption and price

—□— World Production   —●— World Consumption

—— Price

Source: FAO and UNCTAD. Figures for 1990 are estimates.
London auction prices (all tea).

TOBACCO
Production, consumption and price (dry weight)

—□— World production   —●— World consumption

—— Price

Source: FAO and UNCTAD. Figures for 1990 are forecasts.
U.S.A., leaf, price paid to producers.

Annex V-II (continued)

WORLD PRODUCTION, CONSUMPTION, STOCKS AND PRICES
FOR SELECTED COMMODITIES

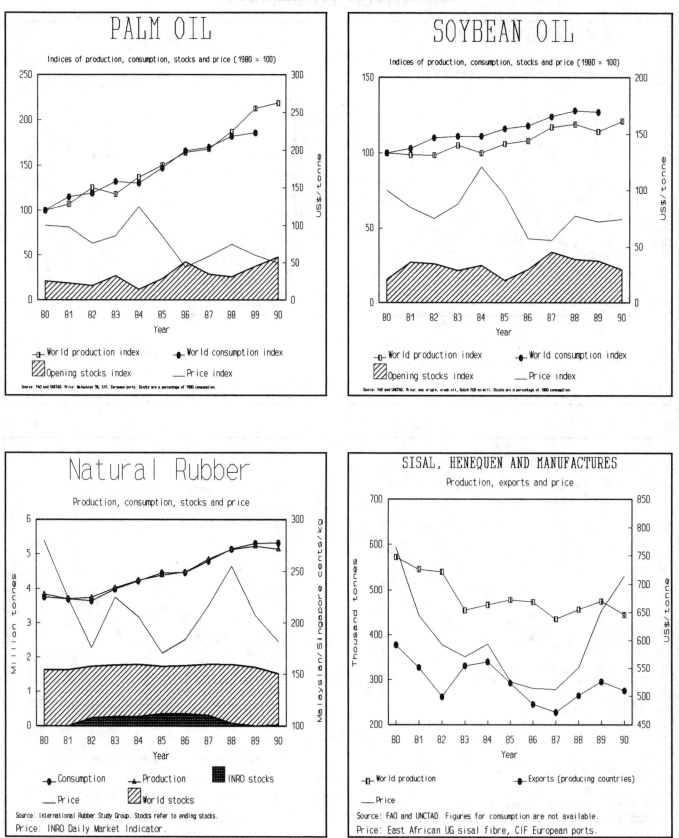

PALM OIL
Indices of production, consumption, stocks and price (1980 = 100)

- World production index
- World consumption index
- Opening stocks index
- Price index

Source: FAO and UNCTAD. Price: Malaysian 5%, CIF, European ports. Stocks are a percentage of 1980 consumption.

SOYBEAN OIL
Indices of production, consumption, stocks and price (1980 = 100)

- World production index
- World consumption index
- Opening stocks index
- Price index

Source: FAO and UNCTAD. Price: any origin, crude oil, Dutch FOB ex-mill. Stocks are a percentage of 1980 consumption.

Natural Rubber
Production, consumption, stocks and price

- Consumption
- Production
- INRO stocks
- Price
- World stocks

Source: International Rubber Study Group. Stocks refer to ending stocks.
Price: INRO Daily Market Indicator.

SISAL, HENEQUEN AND MANUFACTURES
Production, exports and price

- World production
- Exports (producing countries)
- Price

Source: FAO and UNCTAD. Figures for consumption are not available.
Price: East African UG sisal fibre, CIF European ports.

Annex V-II (continued)

WORLD PRODUCTION, CONSUMPTION, STOCKS AND PRICES
FOR SELECTED COMMODITIES

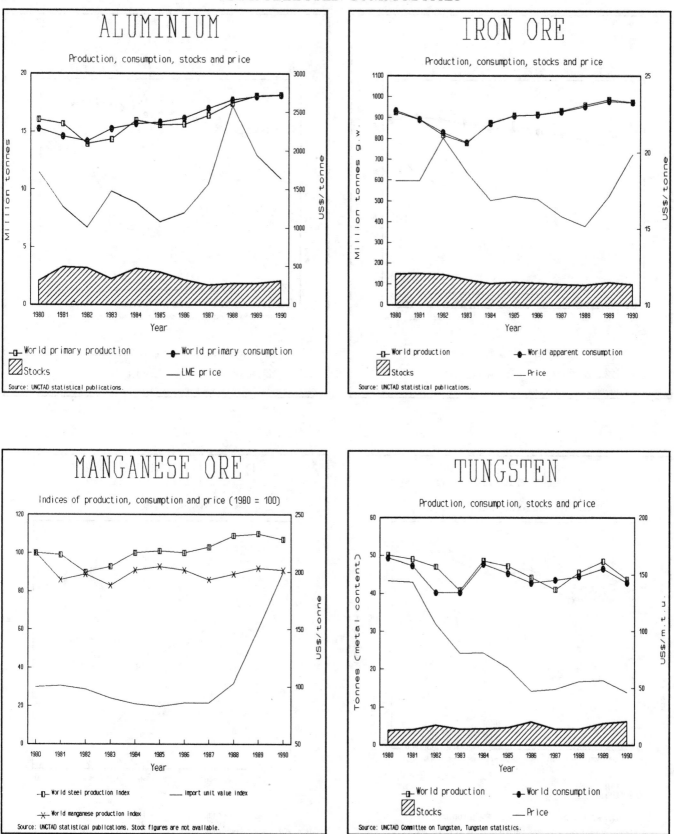

Annex V-II (continued)

WORLD PRODUCTION, CONSUMPTION, STOCKS AND PRICES
FOR SELECTED COMMODITIES

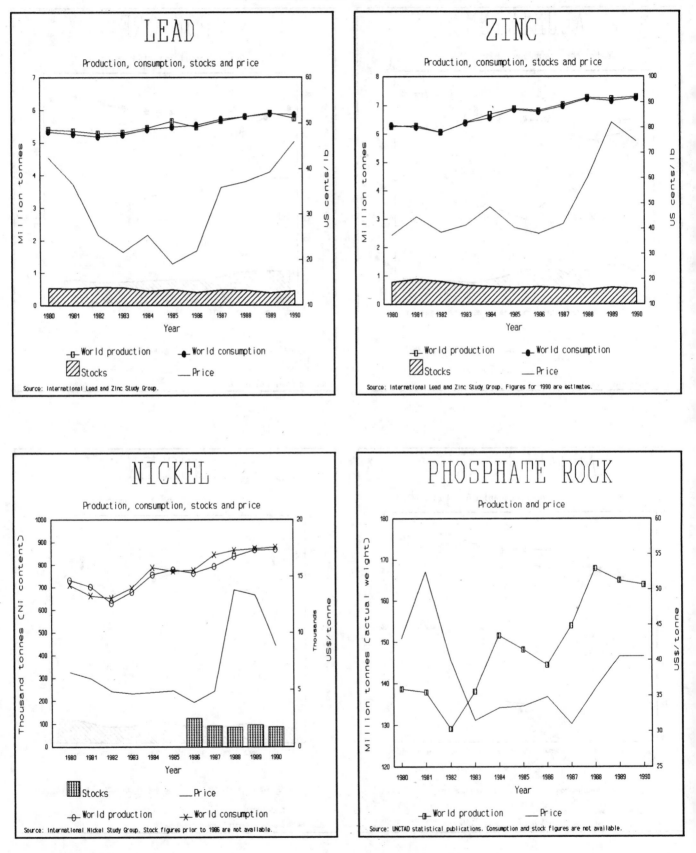

Annex V-II (continued)

WORLD PRODUCTION, CONSUMPTION, STOCKS AND PRICES
FOR SELECTED COMMODITIES

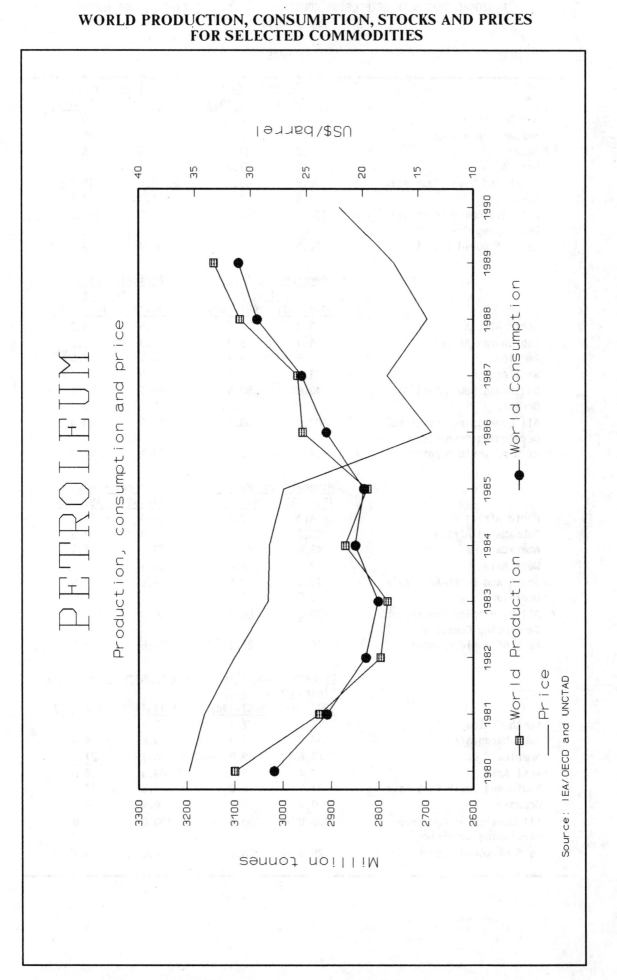

Source: IEA/OECD and UNCTAD

Annex V-III

REGIONAL SHARES IN DEVELOPING COUNTRIES' COMMODITY EXPORTS AND IMPORTS
(by groups)a/

EXPORTS

	Basic Foods		Tropical Beverages	
	1979-1981	1987-1989	1979-1981	1987-1989
North Africa	3.0	2.7	-	0.1
Subsaharan Africa	6.3	5.4	32.9	30.7
America	45.2	42.6	51.6	48.4
West Asia	6.6	7.7	0.3	0.2
South and South East Asia	30.3	39.1	13.7	19.1
Oceania	0.8	0.5	1.5	1.5
All Developing Countriesb/	100.0	100.0	100.0	100.0
Developing Countries				
as % of world exports	22.9	22.7	84.9	79.3

	Vegetable oilseeds and oils		Agricultural raw materials	
	1979-1981	1987-1989	1979-1981	1987-1989
North Africa	3.4	2.6	4.5	3.2
Subsaharan Africa	6.1	3.4	12.8	12.5
America	37.9	39.4	18.7	18.5
West Asia	1.5	2.1	5.6	4.7
South and South-East Asia	48.0	50.6	55.1	57.1
Oceania	2.6	1.7	0.5	0.8
All Developing Countriesb/	100.0	100.0	100.0	100.0
Developing Countries				
as % of world exports	34.9	35.8	30.7	24.6

	Minerals and Metals		Mineral fuels	
	1979-1981	1987-1989	1979-1981	1987-1989
North Africa	4.9	3.4	11.1	11.8
Subsaharan Africa	20.3	15.8	8.1	14.5
America	43.4	46.2	13.1	17.1
West Asia	3.3	6.6	58.7	48.1
South and South-East Asia	21.3	20.0	8.9	14.5
Oceania	3.9	4.3	-	-
All Developing Countriesb/	100.0	100.0	100.0	100.0
Developing Countries				
as % of world exports	28.1	26.3	70.6	52.9

	Primary commodities (excluding fuels)		All primary commodities	
	1979-1981	1987-1989	1979-1981	1987-1989
North Africa	3.3	2.7	9.1	7.7
Subsaharan Africa	14.7	11.8	9.8	9.9
America	42.6	39.9	20.7	27.3
West Asia	4.4	5.7	44.9	29.0
South and South-East Asia	31.3	36.0	14.6	24.2
Oceania	1.7	1.6	0.4	0.7
All Developing Countriesb/	100.0	100.0	100.0	100.0
Developing Countries				
as % of world exports	29.4	26.7	52.0	36.7

Annex V-III (continued)

REGIONAL SHARES IN DEVELOPING COUNTRIES' COMMODITY EXPORTS AND IMPORTS
(by groups)a/

IMPORTS

	Basic Foods		Tropical Beverages	
	1979–1981	1987–1989	1979–1981	1987–1989
North Africa	12.2	10.4	23.6	27.4
Subsaharan Africa	12.6	10.0	5.3	4.2
America	22.9	17.6	18.0	9.1
West Asia	24.6	24.1	21.9	23.1
South and South East Asia	24.9	34.9	18.9	27.0
Oceania	1.3	1.3	0.6	0.5
All Developing Countriesb/	100.0	100.0	100.0	100.0
Developing Countries as % of world imports	26.6	21.0	10.0	11.7

	Vegetable oilseeds and oils		Agricultural raw materials	
	1979–1981	1987–1989	1979–1981	1987–1989
North Africa	11.8	11.5	9.1	8.2
Subsaharan Africa	7.2	5.2	2.7	2.1
America	20.6	19.1	15.5	11.7
West Asia	14.1	14.4	10.3	8.1
South and South-East Asia	43.2	48.0	54.8	65.5
Oceania	0.2	0.2	0.2	0.2
All Developing Countriesb/	100.0	100.0	100.0	100.0
Developing Countries as % of world imports	29.4	32.4	16.2	18.6

	Minerals and Metals		Mineral fuels	
	1979–1981	1987–19899	1979–1981	1987–1989
North Africa	5.2	5.1	2.8	2.6
Subsaharan Africa	5.4	3.0	5.2	6.3
America	20.6	16.0	34.7	27.5
West Asia	12.6	10.8	10.6	11.8
South and South-East Asia	43.9	61.5	41.2	45.1
Oceania	0.2	0.1	0.7	0.9
All Developing Countriesb/	100.0	100.0	100.0	100.0
Developing Countries as % of world imports	13.2	17.7	18.0	20.9

	Primary commodities (excluding fuels)		All primary commodities	
	1979–1981	1987–1989	1979–1981	1987–1989
North Africa	11.0	9.3	6.9	6.7
Subsaharan Africa	9.6	6.7	7.4	6.5
America	22.1	16.2	28.3	20.5
West Asia	20.0	17.8	15.4	15.5
South and South-East Asia	33.0	46.5	37.4	46.0
Oceania	0.9	0.8	0.9	0.8
All Developing Countriesb/	100.0	100.0	100.0	100.0
Developing Countries as % of world exports	20.8	19.9	19.4	20.3

Source: UNCTAD secretariat.

a/ Basic foods: SITC 0+1+4-(071,072,074,121,22 and 42)
 Tropical beverages: SITC 071+072+074; Vegetable oilseeds and oils: SITC 22 and 42
 Agricultural raw materials: SITC 121+2-(22,27,28,233,244,266,267)
 Minerals and Metals: SITC 27+28+68+522.56; Mineral fuels: SITC 3
b/ Including Malta and Yugoslavia.

STATISTICAL ANNEX

GROWTH OF REAL GDP OF DEVELOPING COUNTRIES, 1970-1990

(Annual average percentage change or change over previous year)

Country group or region	1970-1975	1975-1980	1980-1985	1986	1987	1988	1989	1990*
Total	6.0	4.9	2.1	3.3	3.3	4.1	3.1	2.8
By major category								
Major petroleum exporters	7.1	3.7	0.5	-0.3	-0.7	3.5	2.3	2.6
Other developing countries	5.5	5.6	2.8	4.9	5.0	4.4	3.5	2.9
of which								
Major exporters of manufactures	8.6	7.4	2.7	5.1	5.6	3.5	3.5	1.6
Remaining countries	3.6	4.4	2.9	4.7	4.5	5.1	3.4	3.9
By income group								
High income	6.9	3.9	1.1	0.6	2.5	4.0	2.1	2.1
Middle income	6.8	5.8	1.9	4.0	3.3	3.2	3.1	2.8
Low income	2.4	3.5	4.3	4.8	4.3	7.6	4.5	3.8
By region								
Latin America	6.4	5.4	0.2	3.6	3.1	1.2	1.0	0.6
North Africa	2.1	7.3	2.5	1.0	0.0	1.1	3.0	1.1
Other Africa	4.4	2.8	-0.6	2.9	-0.6	3.5	3.8	3.3
West Asia	8.7	2.5	1.5	-1.7	0.0	3.0	1.9	1.4
South and South-East Asia	5.2	6.4	5.5	6.5	7.1	8.8	5.7	6.0
Memo items								
Least developed countries	1.9	3.5	1.9	4.6	3.0	3.6	3.4	2.2
Heavily indebted countries	6.6	5.3	-0.1	3.6	2.2	1.7	1.5	0.6
Developed market-economy countries	3.1	3.5	2.5	2.9	3.4	4.4	3.2	2.3

Source: UNCTAD secretariat calculations, based on official national and international sources.
*Preliminary estimates.

Annex table 2

GROWTH OF REAL GDP PER CAPITA OF DEVELOPING COUNTRIES

(Annual average percentage change or change over previous year)

Country group or region	1970-1975	1975-1980	1980-1985	1986	1987	1988	1989	1990*
Total	3.5	2.5	-0.4	0.8	0.8	1.7	0.7	0.5
By major category								
Major petroleum exporters	4.0	0.8	-2.3	-3.1	-3.3	0.8	-0.3	0.0
Other developing countries	3.0	3.3	0.4	2.4	2.6	2.0	1.1	0.6
of which:								
Major exporters of manufactures	6.0	5.1	0.7	3.2	3.7	1.6	1.8	0.0
Remaining countries	1.2	2.0	0.5	2.2	2.0	2.7	1.0	1.6
By income group								
High income	3.7	0.7	-2.1	-2.1	-0.1	1.3	-0.4	-0.4
Middle income	4.1	3.3	-0.5	1.7	1.0	0.9	0.9	0.6
Low income	0.0	1.2	1.7	2.2	1.7	5.0	1.9	1.4
By region								
Latin America	3.8	3.0	-2.0	1.4	0.9	-0.9	-1.1	-1.4
North Africa	-0.4	4.5	-0.4	-1.8	-2.7	-1.5	0.4	-1.4
Other Africa	1.5	-0.3	-3.6	-0.5	-3.9	0.3	0.6	0.2
West Asia	5.4	-0.5	-1.8	-4.5	-2.7	0.2	-0.9	-1.1
South and South-East Asia	2.7	4.2	3.2	4.1	4.9	6.5	3.4	3.8
Memo items								
Least developed countries	-0.8	0.9	-0.5	1.8	0.3	0.9	0.5	-0.6
Heavily indebted countries	3.9	2.7	-2.5	1.1	-0.2	-0.6	-0.8	-1.6
Developed market-economy countries	2.2	2.7	1.9	2.3	2.8	3.8	2.6	1.7

Source: UNCTAD secretariat calculations, based on official national and international sources.
*Preliminary estimates.

Annex table 3

GDP [a] by kind of economic activity and by major economic grouping, 1970-1989
(percentage of GDP)

Economic grouping	Year	Total	Agri-culture	Industry		Constru-ction	Services
				Total	Manufac-turing		
Developed market economy countries	1960	100.0	6.3	36.4	31.0	5.6	51.5
	1965	100.0	5.5	35.7	31.0	6.3	52.4
	1970	100.0	3.9	31.6	27.7	6.2	58.3
	1975	100.0	4.1	29.9	25.4	6.5	59.5
	1980	100.0	3.2	29.9	24.2	6.5	60.4
	1985	100.0	2.7	28.5	22.6	5.4	63.4
	1988	100.0	2.3	27.6	22.8	6.0	64.1
Developing countries and territories	1960	100.0	31.6	20.9	15.6	4.7	42.8
	1965	100.0	28.4	23.3	16.9	4.8	43.5
	1970	100.0	22.4	24.2	17.8	5.3	48.1
	1975	100.0	17.8	30.9	17.7	6.0	45.3
	1980	100.0	14.7	32.8	18.0	6.7	45.9
	1985	100.0	15.7	29.0	18.4	6.1	49.2
	1988	100.0	15.4	27.4	20.1	5.7	51.6
of which:							
Major petroleum exporters	1960	..	..	..	..	..	..
	1965	100.0	22.1	27.6	13.0	4.2	46.1
	1970	100.0	18.5	30.7	10.6	5.5	45.3
	1975	100.0	11.1	46.7	8.2	6.8	35.3
	1980	100.0	10.3	46.2	8.1	8.1	35.3
	1985	100.0	14.3	31.4	9.9	7.9	46.4
	1988	100.0	18.5	23.2	10.3	6.6	51.7
Other developing countries and territories	1960	100.0	32.9	20.2	16.9	4.7	42.2
	1965	100.0	30.4	21.9	18.2	5.0	42.7
	1970	100.0	23.3	22.8	19.4	5.2	48.7
	1975	100.0	20.4	24.7	21.4	5.6	49.2
	1980	100.0	16.6	26.8	22.3	6.1	50.5
	1985	100.0	16.4	27.8	22.4	5.3	50.5
	1988	100.0	14.1	29.1	24.3	5.3	51.5
of which:							
Major exporters of manufactures	1960	100.0	19.5	26.2	23.7	6.2	48.1
	1965	100.0	16.5	28.7	25.5	6.0	48.8
	1970	100.0	12.6	27.2	24.3	5.6	54.7
	1975	100.0	11.8	28.3	25.5	6.3	53.6
	1980	100.0	9.3	30.1	26.9	6.9	53.6
	1985	100.0	9.2	31.2	26.7	5.8	53.8
	1988	100.0	5.8	34.0	30.1	6.1	54.1
Least developed countries	1960	100.0	60.4	6.9	5.4	3.1	29.6
	1965	100.0	55.3	8.4	6.3	4.1	32.3
	1970	100.0	47.2	9.8	7.6	3.1	39.9
	1975	100.0	44.2	10.5	8.1	4.2	41.1
	1980	100.0	41.1	11.3	8.4	4.7	42.9
	1985	100.0	41.2	11.4	8.1	4.4	43.0
	1988	100.0	40.2	11.4	7.3	4.1	44.3
Remaining countries	1960	100.0	36.7	19.2	15.4	4.3	39.8
	1965	100.0	33.8	20.7	16.5	4.8	40.7
	1970	100.0	26.9	22.9	14.9	5.1	45.1
	1975	100.0	20.6	32.1	14.0	5.8	41.5
	1980	100.0	17.0	33.9	14.1	6.6	42.5
	1985	100.0	18.6	28.0	14.7	6.3	47.1
	1988	100.0	20.3	24.0	15.1	5.5	50.3

Source: UNCTAD *Handbook of International Trade and Development Statistics, 1990.*

Note: Percentages by kind of economic activity may not add to 100 because imports duties are in many cases not included in the reported industrial groups.

[a] At current prices.

Annex table 4

Net official development assistance from DAC member countries to developing countries and multilateral agencies as a percentage of GNP [a], 1989-1990
(1980-1990)

ODA ratio / country	1980	1985	1986	1987	1988	1989	1990
Countries which reach or exceeded the 0.7 percent target in 1990							
Norway	0.82	1.00	1.16	1.08	1.12	1.04	1.16
Netherlands	1.02	0.91	1.00	0.97	0.96	0.92	0.93
Denmark	0.72	0.79	0.86	0.85	0.87	0.92	0.92
Sweden	0.71	0.81	0.79	0.85	0.82	0.92	0.86
France [b]	0.64	0.78	0.70	0.73	0.71	0.76	0.78
Countries with ODA ratios above the DAC average in 1990							
Finland	0.20	0.38	0.44	0.48	0.57	0.61	0.61
Belgium	0.49	0.54	0.47	0.46	0.38	0.46	0.45
Canada	0.43	0.49	0.48	0.46	0.49	0.43	0.43
Germany	0.41	0.44	0.41	0.38	0.38	0.40	0.39
Countries with ODA ratios below the DAC average in 1990							
Australia	0.48	0.47	0.46	0.33	0.45	0.37	0.33
Italy	0.17	0.26	0.39	0.33	0.37	0.41	0.31
Switzerland	0.24	0.31	0.30	0.30	0.31	0.29	0.31
Japan	0.32	0.26	0.26	0.28	0.30	0.28	0.28
United Kingdom	0.35	0.33	0.31	0.27	0.31	0.31	0.27
New Zealand	0.33	0.25	0.30	0.26	0.27	0.22	0.22
Austria	0.22	0.37	0.21	0.17	0.22	0.18	0.18
United States	0.24	0.19	0.18	0.18	0.18	0.13	0.18
Ireland [c]	..	0.24	0.28	0.19	0.20	0.16	0.16
Total DAC member countries	0.36	0.31	0.33	0.33	0.34	0.32	0.34

Source: UNCTAD secretariat calculations based on OECD, *Development Co-operation*, various issues.

Note: [a] Ratios expressed as percentage of GNP, at market prices.
[b] Excluding French aid to Overseas departments and territories.
[c] Ireland joined the DAC in November 1985.

Annex table 5

SHARE OF WORLD EXPORTS BY REGION AND ECONOMIC GROUPING

(per cent)

Region	1955	1960	1965	1970	1975	1980	1985	1987	1988	1989	1990
World	100.0	100.0	100.0	100.0	100.0	100.0	100.0	100.0	100.0	100.0	100.0
Developed market-economy countries	64.1	65.9	67.9	70.9	65.6	62.6	66.0	69.6	70.2	70.3	71.5
United States	16.4	15.8	14.5	13.7	12.3	11.0	11.4	10.2	11.4	12.0	11.5
EEC	31.1	33.2	35.1	36.7	35.1	34.1	33.2	38.0	37.3	37.2	39.4
Japan	2.1	3.1	4.5	6.1	6.4	6.5	9.1	9.2	9.4	9.1	8.4
Countries of Eastern Europe	8.5	10.1	10.5	9.8	8.9	7.7	8.7	8.2	7.5	6.4	5.0
China	1.5	2.0	1.4	0.7	0.9	0.9	1.4	1.6	1.7	1.7	1.8
Developing countries	25.8	21.9	20.1	18.4	24.5	28.7	23.7	20.4	20.5	21.5	21.6
By major category:											
Major petroleum exporters	7.3	6.8	6.5	6.3	13.8	16.4	8.9	5.5	4.7	5.3	6.1
Other developing	18.6	15.1	13.6	12.1	10.7	12.3	14.8	14.9	15.8	16.2	15.5
of which:											
Major exporters of manufactures	4.4	3.6	3.5	3.8	4.3	6.1	8.9	9.5	10.3	10.5	9.9
Remaining countries	14.2	11.5	10.2	8.3	6.4	6.2	5.9	5.4	5.5	5.7	5.6
By region:											
Latin America	9.8	7.7	6.8	5.5	5.2	5.5	5.5	4.0	4.0	4.1	3.9
Africa	4.7	4.2	4.1	4.1	4.1	4.7	3.2	2.2	1.8	1.8	1.9
West Asia	3.5	3.4	3.4	3.4	9.4	10.6	5.1	3.5	3.1	3.5	4.0
South and South-East Asia	7.4	6.1	5.1	4.8	5.2	7.2	9.3	10.2	11.0	11.5	11.2
By income group:											
High income	7.9	7.4	6.9	7.1	13.8	16.3	10.9	9.5	9.3	10.0	10.4
Middle income	12.7	10.3	9.6	8.4	9.1	11.0	11.5	9.8	10.1	10.3	10.0
Low income	5.2	4.3	3.6	2.8	1.6	1.3	1.2	1.2	1.1	1.2	1.1
Memo items:											
Least developed countries	1.7	1.5	1.3	1.0	0.5	0.5	0.4	0.4	0.3	0.3	0.3
Heavily indebted countries	8.9	7.4	6.9	5.8	5.5	6.5	6.2	4.5	4.5	4.6	4.6

Source: UNCTAD secretariat calculations, based on data from UNSO, IMF and national sources.

Annex table 6

SHARE OF WORLD IMPORTS BY REGION AND ECONOMIC GROUPING

(per cent)

Region	1955	1960	1965	1970	1975	1980	1985	1987	1988	1989	1990
World	100.0	100.0	100.0	100.0	100.0	100.0	100.0	100.0	100.0	100.0	100.0
Developed market-economy countries	65.7	64.9	68.6	71.6	67.0	68.3	68.7	71.7	71.1	71.5	72.4
United States	11.7	11.1	10.8	12.2	11.5	12.5	17.9	16.6	15.7	15.7	14.5
EEC	34.2	34.1	37.1	37.8	35.8	37.2	32.7	37.0	36.7	36.9	39.6
Japan	2.5	3.3	4.1	5.8	6.4	6.8	6.4	5.8	6.4	6.7	6.6
Countries of Eastern Europe	7.7	10.2	10.5	9.7	10.2	7.7	8.3	7.7	7.2	6.4	5.5
China	1.8	1.9	1.1	0.7	0.9	0.9	2.1	1.7	1.9	1.9	1.5
Developing countries	24.9	22.6	19.5	17.9	21.6	22.9	20.5	18.5	19.4	19.9	20.3
By major category:											
Major petroleum exporters	4.7	4.8	3.9	3.5	6.3	7.0	5.6	3.9	3.8	3.6	3.5
Other developing	20.2	17.9	15.7	14.4	15.3	15.9	14.9	14.6	15.6	16.3	16.8
of which:											
Major exporters of manufactures	5.2	4.8	3.9	5.2	6.2	7.3	7.3	7.7	8.8	9.3	9.5
Remaining countries	15.0	13.1	11.7	9.3	9.1	8.5	7.6	6.9	6.8	7.0	7.3
By region:											
Latin America	8.9	7.2	5.9	5.5	6.2	5.9	4.0	3.4	3.3	3.2	3.2
Africa	5.3	4.9	4.1	3.4	4.3	3.6	2.7	2.2	2.1	2.0	2.1
West Asia	2.5	2.5	2.3	2.0	4.0	4.9	4.5	3.1	3.0	2.9	2.9
South and South-East Asia	7.4	7.2	6.4	5.8	6.1	7.4	8.6	9.1	10.4	11.1	11.4
By income group:											
High income	5.9	5.4	4.9	5.0	7.4	9.0	8.3	7.8	8.6	8.5	8.4
Middle income	13.9	12.1	10.1	9.9	11.8	11.7	11.0	8.8	9.0	9.6	10.2
Low income	5.1	5.1	4.5	3.0	2.4	2.2	2.2	1.8	1.8	1.7	1.7
Memo items:											
Least developed countries	1.7	1.6	1.6	1.2	0.9	0.9	0.8	0.7	0.7	0.6	0.6
Heavily indebted countries	8.5	7.1	5.8	5.7	6.6	6.5	4.1	3.5	3.5	3.5	3.7

Source: UNCTAD secretariat calculations, based on data from UNSO, IMF and national sources.

Annex table 7

TERMS OF TRADE INDICES OF DEVELOPING COUNTRIES
(1970-1990)
(1980 = 100)

Country or region	1970-1975	1975-1980	1980-1985	1985	1986	1987	1988	1989	1990
Total	50	78	101	96	71	75	71	74	75
By major category:									
Major petroleum exporters	34	68	107	101	53	61	49	56	65
Other developing countries	106	105	94	91	87	85	88	86	82
of which:									
Major exporters of manufactures	127	112	98	97	94	92	92	89	88
Remaining countries	100	102	92	87	83	82	86	85	79
By income group:									
High income	35	69	108	103	52	60	49	56	65
Middle income	73	89	97	92	80	80	80	80	78
Low income	105	108	94	93	94	88	93	90	83
By region:									
Latin America	77	93	95	91	77	76	74	75	74
North Africa	40	70	104	99	56	63	54	61	69
Other Africa	58	80	96	92	72	71	65	66	67
West Asia	31	67	110	104	52	61	49	57	66
South and South-East Asia	84	93	98	94	86	88	90	87	83
Memo items:									
Least developed countries	103	108	95	97	92	82	85	83	78
Heavily indebted countries	71	88	97	93	78	77	75	76	75
Developed market-economy countries	118	107	100	101	110	111	113	112	111

Source: UNCTAD secretariat estimates.

Annex table 8

IMPORT PENETRATION RATIOS OF SELECTED DEVELOPED MARKET-ECONOMY COUNTRIES, 1982-1988
(Percentages)

Sector	EEC			United States and Canada			Japan			Total		
	1982-1983	1984-1985	1987-1988	1982-1983	1984-1985	1987-1988	1982-1983	1984-1985	1987-1988	1982-1983	1984-1985	1987-1988
MANUFACTURES												
Apparent consumption ($ bill.)	1625.6	1560.5	2633.6	2202.4	2581.4	2977.2	872.7	978.5	1799.2	4689.7	5103.4	7386.5
Trade as % of consumption:												
External imports	10.5	11.7	11.7	7.4	9.4	11.3	5.0	5.2	5.2	4.4	4.8	5.3
by region:												
Developing countries	2.6	2.9	2.9	2.6	3.3	4.1	1.6	1.6	1.8	2.4	2.9	3.1
of which:												
Major petroleum exporters	0.5	0.6	0.3	0.3	0.4	0.3	0.4	0.4	0.4	0.4	0.4	0.3
Major exporters of manufactures	1.1	1.2	1.5	1.7	2.3	3.1	0.8	0.9	1.1	1.3	1.7	2.0
Remaining countries	1.0	1.1	1.1	0.6	0.6	0.7	0.3	0.3	0.3	0.7	0.7	0.7
Socialist countries	1.1	1.1	0.9	0.2	0.2	0.3	0.3	0.3	0.3	0.5	0.5	0.5
DMECs	6.7	7.4	7.7	4.5	5.8	6.8	3.1	3.1	3.0	1.3	1.3	1.6
Unallocated	0.3	0.3	0.3	0.2	0.2	0.2	0.1	0.1	0.1	0.2	0.2	0.2
External exports	15.1	16.4	14.1	6.2	5.2	6.3	16.1	17.4	13.5	7.7	6.9	6.5
TEXTILES												
Apparent consumption ($ bill.)	60.8	59.1	10.1	68.2	76.9	91.9	33.3	35.3	62.4	16.2	17.1	25.5
Trade as % of consumption:												
External imports	10.0	10.7	11.0	5.2	7.0	7.8	4.6	5.4	5.6	4.9	5.7	6.3
by region:												
Developing countries	4.2	4.6	4.9	2.2	2.9	3.6	2.1	2.3	2.3	2.9	3.4	3.8
of which:												
Major petroleum exporters	0.3	0.3	0.5	0.1	0.1	0.1	0.1	0.1	0.1	0.1	0.2	0.3
Major exporters of manufactures	1.3	1.5	1.5	1.3	1.7	2.1	1.4	1.5	1.3	1.3	1.6	1.7
Remaining countries	2.6	2.9	2.9	0.8	1.1	1.3	0.6	0.8	0.8	1.5	1.6	1.8
Socialist countries	1.2	1.3	1.3	0.5	0.7	0.9	1.0	1.5	1.5	0.9	1.1	1.2
DMECs	4.5	4.7	4.8	2.5	3.4	3.4	1.6	1.6	1.9	1.1	1.2	1.3
Unallocated	0.2	0.2	0.2	0.1	0.1	0.0	0.2	0.2	0.1	0.1	0.1	0.1
External exports	12.2	14.8	12.6	2.4	2.7	3.2	15.7	14.6	8.9	7.7	7.2	6.3
CLOTHING												
Apparent consumption ($ bill.)	52.7	50.1	90.8	73.0	81.9	98.2	15.6	16.7	35.8	14.1	14.8	22.4
Trade as % of consumption:												
External imports	20.7	22.8	26.3	22.3	30.4	36.8	14.6	16.0	21.1	18.3	22.8	26.9
by region:												
Developing countries	14.3	16.1	19.1	17.2	23.1	27.9	8.2	9.2	13.0	15.1	19.2	22.1
of which:												
Major petroleum exporters	0.1	0.2	0.3	0.1	0.3	0.5	0.0	0.0	0.0	0.1	0.2	0.4
Major exporters of manufactures	8.8	9.4	10.1	14.3	18.6	20.8	7.5	8.5	12.3	11.5	14.4	15.2
Remaining countries	5.3	6.5	8.7	2.8	4.1	6.6	0.6	0.6	0.8	3.5	4.6	6.5
Socialist countries	2.6	3.0	3.6	1.5	1.9	3.5	2.0	2.7	3.5	1.9	2.4	3.6
DMECs	3.5	3.5	3.3	3.6	5.4	5.3	4.4	4.0	4.4	1.1	1.1	1.2
Unallocated	0.1	0.1	0.1	0.1	0.0	0.0	0.0	0.0	0.0	0.1	0.1	0.1
External exports	16.5	21.2	18.1	2.0	1.6	2.3	6.5	7.0	2.9	5.5	5.7	5.9

Sources: UNCTAD, *Handbook of International Trade Statistics*, 1989 and 1990.

Annex table 9

**Direction of Commodity Exports of Developing Countries
averages 1966-1970, 1975-1979 and 1987-1989**

(Percentages)

Destination Origin	Developed market economy countries			Developing countries			Others		
	1966-1970	1975-1979	1987-1989	1966-1970	1975-1979	1987-1989	1966-1970	1975-1979	1987-1989
All developing countries									
Total primary, excl. fuels	75.4	67.7	62.8	14.7	19.8	24.9	9.9	12.5	12.3
Food products	73.2	65.9	62.7	16.9	20.1	23.3	9.9	14.0	14.0
Agricultural raw materials	65.2	60.9	55.2	19.1	26.9	32.6	15.7	12.2	12.2
Minerals and ores	89.8	80.4	69.2	5.7	12.0	22.8	4.5	7.6	8.0
Latin America									
Total primary, excl. fuels	81.1	68.4	66.6	10.0	14.7	17.3	8.9	16.9	16.1
Food products	78.0	65.9	64.3	10.4	14.1	15.1	11.6	20.0	20.6
Agricultural raw materials	74.0	64.4	58.3	18.5	25.8	31.4	7.5	9.8	10.3
Minerals and ores	91.7	79.9	75.6	5.1	13.0	18.6	3.2	7.1	5.8
Africa									
Total primary, excl. fuels	80.4	79.0	74.9	9.9	10.3	16.5	9.7	10.7	8.6
Food products	79.0	79.1	76.6	12.8	12.2	16.0	8.2	8.7	7.4
Agricultural raw materials	65.1	70.6	65.2	13.4	9.8	22.2	21.5	19.6	12.6
Minerals and ores	91.9	83.8	77.7	3.2	6.7	13.8	4.9	9.5	8.5
West Asia									
Total primary, excl. fuels	53.4	50.2	45.8	25.7	31.4	44.0	20.9	18.4	10.2
Food products	50.7	48.1	43.8	33.4	38.4	48.9	15.9	13.5	7.3
Agricultural raw materials	52.6	53.8	43.1	16.3	18.0	29.2	31.1	28.2	27.7
Minerals and ores	69.8	51.3	51.6	16.3	30.1	38.0	13.9	18.6	10.4
South and South-East Asia									
Total primary, excl. fuels	64.4	61.0	55.9	25.7	31.6	34.1	9.9	7.4	10.0
Food products	60.0	58.5	57.9	32.9	34.7	32.7	7.1	6.8	9.4
Agricultural raw materials	61.9	57.7	52.2	22.7	33.3	36.0	15.4	9.0	11.8
Minerals and ores	84.3	79.4	55.4	11.1	15.0	36.3	4.6	5.6	8.3

Source: UNCTAD *Handbook of International Trade and Development Statistics,* based on data from United Nations Statistical office.

Annex table 10

SELECTED ECONOMIC AND SOCIAL INDICATORS OF DEVELOPING COUNTRIES AND TERRITORIES (LATEST YEAR AVAILABLE)

Indicator / Country or territory	Population annual average growth rate (1970-1988) Per cent (1970-1988) [1]	Consumption of energy per capita kilogrammes of coal equivalent Kilogrammes 1989 [2]	% of arable land & land under permanent crops % 1987 [3]	Consumption of fertilizer per ha of agricultural area, permanent crops KG/HA 1988 [4]	Infant mortality rate per 1000 live births Number 1985-1990 [5]	Life expectancy at birth Years 1985-1990 [6]	Daily calorie per capita Number 1988 [7]	Percentage of total population with access to safe water 1987 [8]	Education rate — Illitracy In per cent 1990 [9]	Education rate — Primary 1988 [10]	Women — Maternal mortality per 100,000 live births Number 1980 [11]	Women — Education female primar per 100 males Number 1988 [12]
Afghanistan	0.8	226	12.4	6.4	162.4	43.5	2179	21	70.6		640	50 #n
Algeria	3.1	934	3.2	22.5	60.8	64.9	2726	71	42.6	89	129	80
Angola	3.0	89	2.8	2.6	127.0	46.5	1725	35	58.3 #q			
Antigua and Barbuda	1.4	1591	18.2					95				
Argentina	1.5	1938	13.1	4.7	29.0	71.4	3118	36	4.7	109 #n	85	
Bahamas	1.8	2523	0.8	50.0	22.3	71.9		59		111		
Bahrain	4.4	15614	2.9	200.0				100	22.6			
Bangladesh	2.4	73	68.4	86.2	107.5	52.9	1925	41	64.7	62	600	77
Barbados	0.3	1614	76.7	93.9	10.0	74.9		100	0.7 #a	110		
Belize	1.9	505	2.4	80.0				75	8.8 #a	50		
Benin	2.7	49	16.3	3.4	101.0	48.5	2145	35	76.6			51
Bhutan	1.9	19	2.2	0.8	118.2	50.0	2477	15				59
Bolivia	2.7	378	3.1	2.1	93.0	55.9	2086	47	22.5	83	480	87
Botswana	3.8	532	2.3	0.7	58.0	61.0	2269	57	26.4	97	300	107
Brazil	2.3	798	9.2	47.5	57.0	66.3	2709	96	18.9	84	150	
Brunei Darussalam	3.8	13883	1.3	57.1				90	22.2 #i			
Burkina Faso	2.4	28	11.5	4.3	126.5	49.2	2061	67	81.8	27	600	59
Burundi	2.2	18	51.9	1.9	102.7	51.0	2253	38	50.0	46		75
Cambodia	0.7	27	17.3	1.6 #k	115.7	50.9	2171	3	64.8			
Cameroon	2.9	252	15.0	5.0	86.0	53.0	2161	26	45.9	80	303	85
Cape Verde	1.5	103	9.4	2.5 #f	56.7	63.0		69	33.5 #q	108		
Central African Rep.	2.5	46	3.2	0.3	122.0	47.5	1980	16	62.3	49	600	62
Chad	2.2	17	2.5	2.1	122.0	47.5	1852	26	70.2	64	700	40
Chile	1.6	1205	7.5	74.3	19.0	72.0	2584	89	6.6	90	55	96
Colombia	2.2	818	5.1	98.2	42.0	65.9	2561	93	13.3	73	130	100
Comoros	3.6	47	43.9		71.7	54.0		58	52.1 #h	80·		95
Congo	3.0	355	2.0	4.2	65.0	50.5	2512	21	43.4			94
Costa Rica	2.8	497	10.3	191.1	17.0	75.2	2782	91	7.2			70 #n
Cote d'Ivoire	4.0	176	11.4	11.3	87.5	54.5	2365	19	46.2	85		
Cuba	1.1	1532	29.9	179.9	13.0	74.9	3088		6.0	105		
Cyprus	0.6	2524	17.0	137.4	9.9	76.5			6.0 #h	99		
Dem.People's Rep.of Korea	2.0		19.9	338.1	20.7	70.7	3113	100				
Djibouti	4.7	384			111.9	49.0		45				
Dominica	1.1	343	22.7	176.5				77	5.9 #a			162
Dominican Republic	2.5	395	30.5	51.5	57.0	67.6	2357	63	16.7	73	56	
East Timor	0.9	49	5.4		149.5	45.0						
Ecuador	2.9	661	9.6	26.8	57.0	66.6	2338	58	14.2	114 #n	220	96
Egypt	2.3	749	2.6	400.1	71.0	63.1	3213	73	51.6	72	500	75
El Salvador	1.9	224	35.4	111.3	48.0	66.4	2415	39	27.0	108	74	102
Equatorial Guinea	0.8	148	8.2	0.4 #f	117.0	48.5		47	49.8			
Ethiopia	2.6	24	12.7	4.7	142.8	43.0	1658	19	37.6 #k	26	2000	64
Fiji	2.0	482	13.1	105.0	23.6	71.5		83	14.5 #m	129		

Annex table 10 (continued)

SELECTED ECONOMIC AND SOCIAL INDICATORS OF DEVELOPING COUNTRIES AND TERRITORIES (LATEST YEAR AVAILABLE)

Country or territory	Population annual average growth rate (1970-1988)	Consumption of energy per capita kilogrammes of coal equivalent	% of arable land & land under permanent crops	Consumption of fertilizer per ha of agricultural area, permanent crops	Infant mortality rate per 1000 live births	Life expectancy at birth	Daily calorie per capita	Percentage of total population with access to safe water	Illitracy	Education rate Primary	Maternal mortality per 100,000 live births	Education female primar per 100 males
	Per cent	Kilogrammes	%	KG / HA	Number	Years	Number		In per cent	In per cent	Number	Number
	1	2	3	4	5	6	7	8	9	10	11	12
	(1970-1988)	1989	1987	1988	1985-1990	1985-1990	1988	1987	1990	1988	1980	1988
French Guiana	2.6	1749	0.1	152.3	:	:	:	:	17.0 #j	:	:	:
French Polynesia	2.3	1518	20.5	12.0	:	:	:	:	:	:	:	:
Gabon	4.4	1249	1.8	2.1	94.0	53.5	2396	92	39.3	:	124	98
Gambia	3.2	105	17.0	20.0	132.0	45.0	:	45	72.8	75	:	:
Ghana	2.8	108	12.5	4.4	81.1	56.0	2209	57	39.7	:	1070	80
Grenada	1.2	312	38.2	355.5	:	:	:	85	2.2 #a	:	:	:
Guadeloupe	0.3	1804	24.9	:	11.0	74.3	:	:	10.0 #j	:	:	:
Guam	1.7	5820	21.8	:	:	:	:	:	3.6 #h	:	:	:
Guatemala	2.9	197	17.2	68.6	48.0	64.8	2352	61	44.9	77 #n	110	82
Guinea	1.9	88	6.4	0.9	136.2	44.2	2042	32	76.0	23	:	45
Guinea-Bissau	3.2	74	11.9	1.6 #k	121.6	47.0	:	21	63.5	60	:	:
Guyana	0.6	393	2.5	28.9	25.3	71.0	:	61	3.6	90	340	:
Haiti	1.8	52	32.8	2.4	106.0	56.6	1911	41	47.0	44	82	100
Honduras	3.4	179	16.0	21.1	57.0	65.8	2164	50	26.9	91	:	92
Hong kong	2.1	2000	8.1	:	6.7	77.0	2899	98	11.9 #m	105 #n	4	64 #n
India	2.2	307	56.8	65.2	87.9	60.4	2104	57	51.8	100	500	93
Indonesia	2.2	274	11.7	112.8	74.0	58.5	2670	46	23.0	96	800	80
Iran (Islamic Rep.of)	3.4	1538	9.1	69.5	53.0	67.2	3100	78	46.0	84	:	79
Iraq	3.6	1057	12.5	45.1	56.1	66.2	2962	87	40.3	97	:	97
Jamaica	1.4	853	24.8	108.8	16.0	75.0	2572	72	1.6	:	100	94
Jordan	2.8	1005	4.7	72.6	36.0	68.0	2907	93	19.9	:	:	94
Kenya	3.8	105	4.3	51.4	64.0	61.0	1973	30	31.0	94 #n	510	95 #n
Kuwait	5.4	8283	0.2	193.8	16.0	73.9	3132	100	27.0	79	18	78
Lao People's Dem.Rep.	2.1	39	3.9	0.3	97.0	51.0	2637	21	16.1 #m	70	:	:
Lebanon	0.5	1441	29.4	75.1	34.0	68.5	3046	92	19.9	91	:	125
Lesotho	2.6	:	10.5	14.1	89.0	58.4	2307	48	26.4 #m	:	:	:
Liberia	3.2	154	3.9	9.1	79.0	56.5	2270	20	60.5	:	173	:
Libyan Arab Jamahiriya	4.3	4005	1.2	41.0	68.3	63.3	3384	97	36.2	:	80	:
Madagascar	2.9	38	5.3	3.5	110.0	55.5	2101	32	19.8	66	300	95
Malawi	3.4	40	25.3	21.5	138.3	49.0	2009	56	58.8 #m	55	250	80
Malaysia	2.5	1379	13.3	105.6	20.4	70.8	2686	51	21.5	:	59	95
Maldives	3.1	200	10.0	:	:	:	:	95	8.7 #m	:	:	:
Mali	2.6	25	1.7	6.4	159.0	46.0	2181	12	68.0	18	:	59
Malta	0.4	2050	40.6	41.8	9.1	73.8	:	:	15.9 #m	:	:	:
Martinique	0.2	1733	18.9	1018.3	11.0	75.3	:	:	7.2 #j	:	:	:
Mauritania	2.5	716	0.2	16.1	116.6	48.0	2528	95	66.0	:	119	70
Mauritius	1.4	438	57.8	265.6	19.6	70.2	2679	71	17.2 #m	95	99	88
Mexico	2.7	1689	12.9	71.1	41.0	70.4	3135	27	12.7	99	92	94
Morocco	2.5	368	19.0	37.0	68.3	63.3	2820	13	50.5	55	327	63
Mozambique	2.6	33	3.9	0.5	130.1	48.5	1632	30	67.1	45	479	78
Myanmar	2.2	62	15.3	10.6	59.1	62.5	2572	:	19.4	:	140	:
Namibia	2.8	:	0.8	:	97.0	58.7	1889	:	:	:	:	:

Annex table 10 (continued)

SELECTED ECONOMIC AND SOCIAL INDICATORS OF DEVELOPING COUNTRIES AND TERRITORIES (LATEST YEAR AVAILABLE)

Country or territory	Population annual average growth rate (1970-1988) — Per cent	Consumption of energy per capita kilogrammes of coal equivalent — Kilogrammes	% of arable land & land under permanent crops — %	Consumption of fertilizer per ha of agricultural area, permanent crops — KG / HA	Infant mortality rate per 1000 live births — Number	Life expectancy at birth — Years	Daily calorie per capita — Number	Percentage of total population with access to safe water	Illiteracy — In per cent	Education rate Primary	Women: Maternal mortality per 100,000 live births — Number	Women: Education female primar per 100 males — Number
(column)	1	2	3	4	5	6	7	8	9	10	11	12
(year)	(1970-1988)	1989	1987	1988	1985-1990	1985-1990	1988	1987	1990	1988	1980	1988
Nepal	2.6	24	17.1	24.0	118.2	53.5	2078	36	74.4	64	850	...
Netherlands Antilles	1.3	6621	8.3	60.0	...	...	...	...	6.2 #i	...	...	...
New Caledonia	2.6	4287	1.1	56.8	...	...	...	...	8.7 #d	...	...	...
Nicaragua	3.2	280	10.7	...	50.0	66.2	2361	54	13.0 #h	76	270	107
Niger	3.2	60	2.8	0.4	124.1	46.5	2340	34	71.6	...	420	56
Nigeria	3.3	192	34.4	10.0	96.0	52.5	2039	33	49.3	82	1500	79 #n
Oman	4.3	3426	0.2	84.6	84.2	58.4	...	14	...	...	...	87
Pakistan	3.2	267	26.9	83.2	98.4	59.0	2200	45	65.2	90	600	49
Panama	2.3	621	7.6	67.0	21.0	72.8	2468	84	11.9	...	90	92
Papua New Guinea	2.4	294	0.9	36.1	52.9	56.0	2236	34	48.0	...	1000	79
Paraguay	3.1	219	5.5	3.7	39.0	67.3	2816	26	9.9	90	469	93
Peru	2.7	488	2.9	57.8	76.0	64.6	2269	61	18.1	...	310	93 #n
Philippines	2.6	295	26.6	63.3	39.8	65.0	2255	66	10.3	98	80	97
Puerto Rico	1.3	2778	14.4	120.0	13.0	75.8	...	...	10.9 #h	94	...	...
Qatar	6.4	24088	0.4	...	25.9	70.8	...	95	24.3 #n	121	34	94
Rep.of Korea	1.5	2196	21.7	399.9	21.0	70.6	2878	78	3.7	100	...	...
Réunion	1.5	839	22.0	243.3	12.0	72.1	...	...	21.4 #j	...	210	...
Rwanda	3.4	29	44.9	0.5	111.9	50.5	1786	64	49.8	64	...	97
Saint Helena	3.0	132	6.5	221.4	...	...	...	...	2.7 #o	...	...	...
Saint Kitts & Nevis	1.4	627	38.9	94.4	...	...	...	100	2.4 #a	...	...	...
Saint Lucia	1.5	583	29.5	211.1	...	...	...	70	18.3 #a	...	...	...
St.Vincent & Grenadines	1.2	370	50.0	0.3 #f	...	...	...	75	4.4 #a	...	...	...
Samoa	0.9	351	43.1	...	...	...	...	83	2.2 #b	...	...	...
Sao Tome & Principe	2.6	144	38.5	...	...	...	...	82	42.6 #i	...	...	...
Saudi Arabia	4.7	6347	0.5	462.5	58.1	65.9	2832	97	37.6	56	52	80
Senegal	2.9	195	27.1	5.0	117.6	47.8	1989	54	61.7	50	530	69
Seychelles	2.6	739	22.2	66.3 #k	...	...	...	100	42.3 #b	...	...	...
Sierra Leone	2.2	76	25.1	0.1	142.8	43.0	1806	42	79.3	...	450	...
Singapore	1.4	4981	4.9	2800.0	8.0	73.8	2892	100	13.9 #m	...	11	...
Solomon Islands	3.6	244	2.0	...	...	...	...	82	...	100	...	89 #n
Somalia	3.7	58	1.5	2.1	121.7	47.0	1736	35	75.9	20 #n	1100	52 #n
Sri Lanka	1.6	110	29.1	111.3	28.1	71.6	2319	41	11.6	100	90	93
Sudan	3.1	62	5.3	6.6	99.1	51.8	1996	21	72.9	...	607	68 #n
Suriname	0.5	1260	0.4	95.6	25.9	70.5	...	68	5.1	133	...	...
Swaziland	3.2	313	9.5	45.7	107.0	58.0	...	50	32.1 #m	109	...	...
Syrian Arab Rep.	3.5	957	30.6	52.4	39.4	67.2	3168	75	35.5	99	280	87
Thailand	2.3	638	39.2	38.6	32.3	67.1	2287	66	7.0	...	270	...
Togo	2.8	69	26.3	6.9	85.3	55.0	2133	71	56.7	73	476	63
Tonga	2.0	300	66.7	3.0 #k	...	...	...	95	0.4 #d	...	...	...
Trinidad & Tobago	1.4	5654	23.4	17.9	18.0	71.4	2960	96	3.9 #m	88	81	98
Tunisia	2.4	714	30.1	21.0	47.3	67.4	2964	64	34.7	85	1000	82
Turkey	2.4	958	34.3	58.2	62.2	66.2	3080	83	19.3	84	300	89

Annex table 10 (concluded)

SELECTED ECONOMIC AND SOCIAL INDICATORS OF DEVELOPING COUNTRIES AND TERRITORIES (LATEST YEAR AVAILABLE)

Country or territory	Population annual average growth rate (1970-1988) Per cent (1970-1988)	Consumption of energy per capita kilogrammes of coal equivalent Kilogrammes 1989	% of arable land & land under permanent crops % 1987	Consumption of fertilizer per ha of agricultural area, permanent crops KG/HA 1988	Infant mortality rate per 1000 live births Number 1985-1990	Life expectancy at birth Years 1985-1990	Daily calorie per capita Number 1988	Percentage of total population with access to safe water 1987	Education rate Illitracy In per cent 1990	Education rate Primary 1988	Women Maternal mortality per 100,000 live births Number 1980	Women Education female primar per 100 males 1988
Indicator column	1	2	3	4	5	6	7	8	9	10	11	12
Uganda	3.3	27	33.6	0.1 #f	93.8	53.0	2103	20	51.7	53	207	82
United Arab Emirates	11.1	19864	0.2	253.8	22.3	71.9	3552	93	46.5 #c	93	::	94
United Rep. of Tanzania	3.6	36	5.9	7.8	96.6	55.0	2151	56	53.7 #f	50	370	99
Uruguay	0.5	783	8.3	50.6	25.0	71.6	2770	80	3.8	77	56	95
Vanuatu	3.4	199	11.9					100	47.1 #g	::	::	::
Venezuela	3.2	2822	4.4	177.9	33.0	70.3	2547	89	11.9	89	65	96
Viet Nam	2.3	108	19.9	80.7	53.8	63.7	2233	46	12.4	:	110	::
Yemen	2.8	361 #p	2.8	14.6	106.5	53.4	2322	31	61.5	:	::	29
Yugoslavia	0.8	2441	30.4	130.8	20.7	73.1	3505		7.3	:	27	93 #n
Zaire	3.0	64	3.0	0.4	90.0	54.5	2034	34	28.2	:	800	78
Zambia	3.6	197	7.0	16.2	71.7	55.4	2026	59	27.2	:	110	90
Zimbabwe	3.1	694	7.2	54.2	64.3	60.8	2232	52	33.1	100	150	95

Selected economic and social indicators of developing countries : populaton, energy per capita, agriculture, health, education, and women in development(latest year available).

Sources:

(Column 1) Population annual average growth rate 1970-1988. United Nations,IESA. Computer tape.

(Column 2) Consumption of commercial energy. Kilogramme of coal equivalent per capita in 1989. Handbook of International Trade and Development Statistics, UNCTAD, 1990.

(Column 3) Percentage of arable land and land under permanent crops in 1987. FAO, Production Yearbook 1988, computer tape.

(Column 4) Consumption of fertilizer per hectare of agricultural area in arable land and permanent crops in 1988. FAO, Fertilizer Yearbook 1989.

(Column 5) Infant mortality rate per 1,000 live births. Deaths of under one year old in 1985. United Nations,IESA. Computer tape.

(Column 6) Life expectancy at birth in 1985-1990. United Nations,IESA. Computer tape.

(Column 7) Daily calorie supply per capita in 1988. World Development Report 1991: The World Bank, 1991.

(Column 8) Percentage of population with access to safe water, 1988. World Development Report 1991: The World Bank, 1991.

(Column 9) Percentage of illiterates in 1990. UNESCO, Statistical Yearbook, and computer tape.

(Column 10) Enrolment ratios: Primary pupils enrolled including pupils of all possible ages as a percentage of the school-age population aged 5-19 in 1988.

(Column 11) Maternal mortality per 100,000 live births in 1980. World Development Report 1989: The World Bank, 1989.

(Column 12) Primary education of females per 100 males in 1988. World Development Report 1991: The World Bank, 1991.

Note:

#a 1970	#b 1971	#c 1975	#d 1976	#e 1977	#f 1978
#g 1979	#h 1980	#i 1981	#j 1982	#k 1983	#l 1984
#m 1985	#n 1986	#o 1987	#p 1988	#q 1989